Theophilus Adam Wylie

Indiana University

Its History from 1820, when Founded, to 1890

Theophilus Adam Wylie

Indiana University
Its History from 1820, when Founded, to 1890

ISBN/EAN: 9783337062200

Printed in Europe, USA, Canada, Australia, Japan

Cover: Foto ©ninafisch / pixelio.de

More available books at **www.hansebooks.com**

ITS HISTORY FROM 1820, WHEN FOUNDED, TO 1890,

WITH

Biographical Sketches of Its Presidents, Professor and Graduates, and a List of Its Students from 1820 to 1887.

BY
THEOPHILUS A. WYLIE,
Professor Emeritus of Physics.

INDIANAPOLIS:
WM. B. BURFORD, LITHOGRAPHER, PRINTER AND BINDER.
1890

PREFACE.

This Historical Catalogue was prepared under the auspices of the Board of Trustees of the University. The work has taken much longer time than was expected at its beginning. The loss of so many records and papers of the University by the fire of 1884, has prevented more of detail in some parts of the history. Fortunately one large volume of records from 1840 to 1859 was not in the Library at the time of the fire. No doubt many errors and defects will be noticed in the work of the compiler. It is a very difficult if not impossible work, where so much research has to be made, and where so many persons are concerned, to avoid mistakes of different kinds. Many, very many, letters of inquiry have been sent during the progress of the work, to most of which replies have been received. The addresses of some of the graduates have not been found, and from a few whose addresses were found, no reply could be obtained.

The compiler would take this occasion to acknowledge his obligations to Col. R. S. Robertson and Judge D. D. Banta for the chapters they have written, and for suggestions made. In addition to these he has received valuable assistance from graduates and students, and particularly the editors of the Indiana Student.

Through some accident the list of names of the Board of Trustees, which should have been in or near the beginning of the work, is placed at the end.

CONTENTS.

	PAGE.
The University as Fostered and Developed by Legislation, by R. S. Robertson....................................	5–37
The Indiana Seminary, by D. D. Banta.....................	38–46
The History of the University from 1828 to 1890.........	47–90
Sketches of the Presidents of the University.............	91–102
Sketches of the Professors............................103–165	
Sketches of the Graduates of the Collegiate Department..166–309	
Sketches of the Graduates of the Law Department.....310–364	
List of Non-Graduate Students of the Law Department 365–370	
Supplement to Collegiate Department 371–377	
The first College Catalogue... 378–379	
List of Students of the Collegiate and Preparatory Departments, Non-Graduates of Indiana University 380–463	
Members of the Board of Trustees and officers of the Board, preceded by a sketch of Dr. David H. Maxwell, its first president............................464–472	

THE INDIANA UNIVERSITY AS FOSTERED AND DEVELOPED BY LEGISLATION.

BY ROBERT S. ROBERTSON.

The history of legislation upon the subject of education, especially in its higher grades, in the territory now comprising the State of Indiana, discloses that the founders of the new Republics west of the Alleghenies were deeply impressed with the sense of the advantages to be derived from a liberal and thorough system of education by the States which were destined to "increase and multiply" towards the setting sun, and that their descendants and successors have fairly carried out their plans, and have built well upon the foundations which were laid broad and deep at the beginning of our civic existence. In the preparation of this sketch it has been thought best to give the language of the constitutional and legislative enactments, out of which have grown the structure known as the Indiana University, especially where important declarations or changes of system have been made, rather than to attempt to give the substance of the laws.

The legal history of the University has thus been traced through the laws organizing and governing the northwest territory, Indiana territory, and the State of Indiana, exhibiting the legislation of a century of marvelous progress in creating and fostering an institution which is justly the pride and boast of the State, and is recognized as one of its greatest bulwarks.

In the early planting of the educational germ in America, and its development through trials and vicissitudes to its present proportions, we owe nearly everything we have received to the Puritan of New England, for long before the more southern colonies had abandoned the ideas nourished by an aristocratic monarchy the New England colonies took advanced ground upon the question of free schools, and in 1647 the Plymouth colonists, by a public act, declared that, "the Lord assisting their endeavors," they would provide for "the education of the people" by establishing schools to teach reading and writing, and "grammar schools to fit youth for the University."

In contrast with this, we find the British Governor of Virginia in 1670 replying to queries addressed to him by the home government, using this remarkable language: "I thank God there are no free schools or printing, for learning has brought disobedience and heresy and sects into the world, and printing has divulged them." It is worthy of note that the great domain ceded by Virginia to the United States was endowed with the great boon of free education by New England pioneers, and enjoyed the benefits flowing from the gift nearly a century before Virginia herself overcame her prejudices and accepted the American idea of education for all, from the highest to the lowest of the people.

It would be gratifying if it could be said that the law-making power of the United States, in providing so liberally as it has done for the cause of education in the Northwest Territory, had been actuated solely by a desire to diffuse the benefits of learning and knowledge among the people. But the fact is otherwise, and a study of the early legislation upon this subject, and of its causes and motives, discloses that a mercenary desire on the part of the Government to sell its lands, and on the part of speculators to obtain good prices for the vast tracts they were negotiating to secure, entered largely into the causes which influenced, and finally brought about, the beneficent grants of public lands which became the foundation of our great system of free schools and free education.

Fortunately for the future of the great Territory which was the subject of negotiation and Congressional discussion, there were found, among both speculators and statesmen, men of broad and enlightened views and liberal minds who exerted a controlling influence in shaping the legislation, among whom stood prominently Col. Timothy Pickering and Manasseh Cutler, whose wise counsels and pertinacity of purpose had much to do with bringing about the final enactments which provided so liberally for establishing and maintaining not only a system of common schools for primary education, but the grander and far-reaching university system, in which the higher grades of learning should be open and free to all.

To them, and the noble men who followed the pathway marked out by them, we owe a debt of gratitude which has never been fully paid.

CONGRESSIONAL LEGISLATION.

THE ORDINANCES OF 1785 AND 1787.

While Congress was hesitating in regard to the disposition of the lands ceded by the States to the General Government, Rufus Putnam and others of the New England soldiers formed the idea of a State, to be located between Lake Erie and the Ohio, which should be settled by the army veterans and their families.

In April, 1783, Col. Timothy Pickering outlined a plan which Putnam and his associates submitted to Congress, with a petition for leave to found the colony. After providing for the distribution of lands to the soldiers in payment of their services, the plan was proposed that "all the surplus lands should be the property of the State, and disposed of for the public good, as for laying out roads, building bridges, erecting public buildings, *establishing schools and academies*, defraying the expenses of the Government, and other public uses." In a letter to Washington urging him to assist in furthering its objects, dated June 16, 1783, Putnam suggested the division of the lands into townships six miles square, with reservations for schools and the ministry.

The original ordinance presented by Jefferson in 1784 for the organization of the Territory, contained no provision for the school reservations, for on the 8th of March, 1785, Col. Pickering, writing to Rufus King, a member of the committee which had it in charge, objected to it because there was "no provision made for the ministers of the gospel, nor even for schools or academies," and said, "the latter, at least, might have been brought into view." On the 12th or 14th of April, 1785, the committee reported a new ordinance, in which the following clause was inserted: "There shall be reserved the central section of every township for the maintenance of public schools, and the section immediately adjoining for the support of religion."

Mr. Grayson, a member of the committee, in a letter to Washington, dated April 15, says: "The idea of a township with the temptation of a support for religion and education holds forth an inducement for neighborhoods of the same religious sentiments to confederate for the purpose of purchasing and settling together. On the 23d of April the clause relating to religion was stricken out, and on the 20th of May the ordinance, with many amendments, was adopted. The clause relating to education finally stood as follows: "There shall be reserved from sale the lot No. 16 of every township for the maintenance of public schools within the said township."

It will be seen not only that mercenary motives, the offering of inducements to purchase, entered largely into the scheme, but also that we owe the great endowment of western schools, not to Jefferson, as has been claimed, but to Col. Pickering.

This ordinance was a temporary expedient, and did not meet the expectation or demands of the soldiers, and the Ohio Company was formed in 1786, which, in March, 1787, elected as directors, Samuel Holden Parsons, Manasseh Cutler and Rufus Putnam, who in May presented a memorial to Congress, which was at once referred to a special committee. This committee in two days reported a bill, but differing materially from the plan proposed by the Ohio Company.

Two days later, July 13, 1787, it passed, and became the famous Ordinance for the Government of the Northwest Territory. The third article declared that "Religion, morality and knowledge being necessary to good government and the happiness of mankind, schools and the means of education shall be forever encouraged."

During this time the proposals of the Ohio Company to purchase lands were being considered by Congress, and finally the committee recommended the sale on the terms demanded by the company, i. e., one lot in each township for common schools, one lot for the support of the ministry, and four townships for the establishment of a university.

This recommendation Congress thought too liberal, and framed an ordinance reserving only lot No. 16 for schools, as provided in the ordinance of 1785. This did not suit Dr. Cutler, who submitted another proposal as containing the only conditions on which the company would purchase. Needing the money offered, Congress unwillingly accepted the terms, and on the 23d of July passed the ordinance, providing that lot No. 16 be given perpetually to the maintenance of schools, and lot 29 to the purposes of religion, and two townships near the center for the support of a literary institution, to be applied to the intended object by the Legislature of the State. Under this was the Ohio Company's purchase completed, and in the same year John Cleves Symmes purchased a large tract in the Territory with similar reservations for schools and the ministry, and one township for a seminary of learning.

Following upon this, the act of Congress of March 26, 1804 (U. S. Statutes at Large, 2277), entitled "an act making provision for the disposal of the public lands in the Indiana Territory, and for other purposes," established three land districts, viz: Detroit, Kaskaskia and Vincennes.

The fifth section enacts that certain lands "shall, with the exception of the section numbered sixteen, which shall be reserved in each township for the support of schools within the same; also of an entire township in each of the three described tracts of country or districts, to be located by the Secretary of the Treasury, for the use of a seminary of learning, * * be offered for sale," etc.

On the 10th of October, 1806, Albert Gallatin, Secretary of the Treasury, located township No. 2 south, range 11 east, now in Gibson County, Indiana, for the use of a seminary of learning, as required by said act.

On the 19th of April, 1816, Congress, by the act to provide for the admission of Indiana as a State of the Union, provided "that one entire township, which shall be designated by the President of the United States, in addition to the one heretofore reserved for that purpose, shall be reserved for the use of a Seminary of learning, and vested in the Legislature of said State, to be appropriated solely to the use of such Seminary by the said Legislature. (3 U. S. Statutes, 289.)

When the Convention met at Corydon to frame a Constitution for the State of Indiana, on motion of Mr. Johnson, a committee consisting of Jonathan Lindley, Benjamin Parke, and James Noble was appointed on the 19th day of June, 1816, to select such township for designation by the President. On the same day, the committee addressed a note to the Register and Receiver of the Land Office at Vincennes, both of whom were present at the Convention, John Badollet, the Register, being a member and serving upon the Committee on Education, requesting that township numbered eight, range one west, be recommended to the President for reservation. On the following day, June 20, the Register and Receiver complied with this request of the committee, and the location thus made was approved by President Madison on the 10th day of July, 1816.

The county in which the location was made was, when organized, christened with the name of President Monroe, and the township thus chosen was christened with the name of Commodore Perry.

THE NORTHWEST TERRITORY.

The first law-making power of the Northwest Territory created by the Ordinance of 1787, consisting of the Governor and Judges appointed by the President, seems to have enacted no laws upon the subject of free education, but when the people became entitled to representation in the Territorial Legislature we find them hastening to carry out the declaration of the Ordinance in regard to encouraging good government and the happiness of mankind by establishing and fostering a system of education, in which the higher branches of learning were to form a conspicuous part.

The first enactment to this end was passed during the first session of the first Territorial Legislature of the Northwest Territory. It was entitled, "An act establishing an university in the town of Athens," and was approved January 9, 1802. (Laws N. W. Ter. 1802, p. 161.) Its preamble recites: " Whereas, institutions for the liberal education of youth are essential to the progress of arts and sciences, important to morality, virtue and religion, friendly to the peace, order and prosperity of society, and honorable to the Government that encourages and patronizes them; and, whereas, the Congress of the United States did make a grant of two townships of land within the purchase made by the Ohio Company of Associates, for the encouragement and support of an university therein; and, whereas, the interference of the Legislature is rendered necessary to point out and direct the mode in which the same shall be brought into operation, that the benefit of the grant may be applied to the purposes designed, therefore," etc. It was to be known by the name and style of the "American Western University for the instruction of youth in all the various branches of the liberal arts and sciences, for the promotion of good education, virtue, religion and morality, and for conferring all the degrees and literary honors granted in similar institutions." Rufus Putnam, Joseph Gilman, Return Jonathan Meigs, Jr., Rev. Daniel Story, Griffin Greene, Robert Oliver, Ebenezer Sproat, Dudley Woodbridge and Isaac Pierce, with the President of the University for the time being, were created a body politic, with succession, as the President and Trustees of the American Western University.

INDIANA TERRITORY.

When Ohio became a State, and Indiana Territory was created, the same liberal policy was followed, and "An act to incorporate an university in the Indiana Territory" was passed, and approved by the Governor, William Henry Harrison, November 9, 1806. (Laws 1806, p. 6; revision 1807, p. 407.)

The preamble is as follows: "*Whereas*, The independence, happiness and energy of every republic depends (under the influence of the destinies of Heaven)- upon the wisdom, virtue, talents and energy of its citizens and rulers; *and whereas*, science, literature and the liberal arts contribute in an eminent degree to improve those qualities and acquirements; *and whereas*, learning has ever been found the ablest advocate of genuine liberty, the best supporter of national religion, and the source of the only imperishable glory which nations can acquire; *and forasmuch*, as literature and philosophy furnish the most useful and pleasing occupations, improving and varying the enjoyments of prosperity, affording relief under the pressure of misfortune and hope and consolation in the hour of death; and considering that, in a commonwealth where the humblest citizen may be elected to the highest public offices, and where the Heaven-born prerogative of the right to elect and reject is retained and secured to the citizens, the knowledge which is requisite for a magistrate and elector, should be widely diffused;

"SECTION 1. *Be it therefore enacted by the Legislative Council and House of Representatives,* That an University be and is hereby instituted and incorporated within this Territory, to be called and known by the name or style of 'The Vincennes University;' that William Henry Harrison, John Gibson, Thomas T. Davis, Henry Vanderburgh, Waller Taylor, Benjamin Parke, Peter Jones, James Johnson, John Badollet, John Rice Jones, George Wallace, William Bullitt, Elias McNamee, Henry Hurst, General W. Johnston, Francis Vigo, Jacob Kuykendoll, Samuel McKee, Nathanial Ewing, George Leach, Luke Decker, Samuel Gwathmey, and John Johnson, are hereby declared to be Trustees of the said University," with power to elect to fill vacancies, and to make by-laws, ordinances and regulations for its government not inconsistent with the charter or laws of the Territory, or of the United States.

By the terms of Section 6, the Trustees were, "as speedily as may be," to establish an University within the borough of Vincennes, and to appoint, to preside over and govern it, a President, and not exceeding four professors, "for the instruction of youth in the Latin, French and English languages, Mathematics, Natural Philosophy, Logic, Rhetoric, and the Law of Nature and of Nations." The Faculty was empowered to grant, with the consent of the Trustees, degrees in the liberal arts and sciences to such students of the University who, by their proficiency in learning, should be considered entitled to them, and to grant diplomas to authenticate and perpetuate the memory of graduations.

It was made the duty of the Trustees to establish a library, and from time to time elect a Professor of Divinity, of Law, and of Physic, whenever they might deem it necessary for the good of the institution, but no particular tenets of religion were to be taught. Then follows:

"*And whereas,* The establishment of an institution of this kind in the neighborhood of the aborigines of this country may tend to the gradual civilization of the rising generation, and if properly conducted be of essential service to themselves, and contribute greatly to the cause of humanity and brotherly love, which all men ought to bear to each other of whatever color, and tend also to preserve that friendship and harmony which ought to exist between the Government and the Indians," the Trustees were enjoined "to use their utmost endeavors to induce the said aborigines to send their children to said University for education, who, when sent, shall be maintained, clothed and educated at the expense of said institution."

It was further provided, that when the funds would permit, all students were to be educated gratis in all or any of the branches of education they might require.

Curious as it may seem at this day, the funds for the support of the institution, for procuring a library and philosophical and experimental apparatus, were to be raised by a lottery, " to be conducted by five discreet persons," to be chosen by the Board of Trustees. The sum authorized to be raised by this means was not to exceed twenty thousand dollars.

This University, at Vincennes, was destined in later days to come in conflict with the Indiana University in such a manner as to seriously threaten its stability, but fortunately the danger was averted.

THE STATE OF INDIANA.

The Constitution adopted at Corydon, June 91, 1816, upon which the territory became a State of the Union, declared with no uncertain sound in favor of advanced education, as well as common schools. Sections 1 and 2 of Article 9 read as follows (*Rev. Laws* 1824, *p.* 48):

"SECTION 1. Knowledge and learning, generally diffused through a community, being essential to the preservation of a free government, and spreading the opportunities and advantages of education through the various parts of the country being highly conducive to this end, it shall be the duty of the General Assembly to provide, by law, for the improvement of such lands as are, or hereafter may be, granted by the United States to this State for the use of schools, and to apply any funds which may be raised from such lands, or from any other quarter, to the accomplishment of the grand object for which they are, or may be intended, but no lands granted for the use of schools or seminaries of learning shall be sold by authority of this State prior to the year eighteen hundred and twenty, and the moneys which may be raised out of the sale of any such lands, or otherwise obtained for the purposes aforesaid, shall be and remain a fund for the exclusive purpose of promoting the interest of literature and the sciences, and for the support of seminaries and public schools. The General Assembly shall, from time to time, pass such laws as shall be calculated to encourage intellectual, scientific and agricultural improvement by allowing rewards and immunities for the promotion and improvement of arts, sciences, commerce, manufactures and natural history, and to countenance and encourage the principles of humanity, industry and morality.

"Sec. 2. It shall be the duty of the General Assembly, as soon as circumstances will permit, to provide by law for a general system of education, ascending in a regular gradation from township schools to a State university, wherein tuition shall be gratis, and equally open to all."

This was the voice of a people environed by all the dangers, and inured to all the toil and vicissitudes of a life in the wilderness, just emerging from the territorial form of government to enter the sisterhood of great, co-equal States in the Union, and who knew by hard experience the necessity of education to the welfare of the State; and it contrasts favorably with the declaration of the Constitutional Convention of 1851. (Rev. Laws 1852, 1, p. 62), which is as follows: "Art. 8, sec. 1. Knowledge and learning, generally diffused throughout a community, being essential to the preservation of a free government, it shall be the duty of the General Assembly to encourage, by all suitable means, moral, intellectual, scientific and agricultural improvement, and to provide by law for a general and uniform system of common schools, wherein tuition shall be without charge, and equally open to all."

The committee appointed by the Constitutional Convention of 1816, on the subject of "Education, and the universal diffusion of useful knowledge," to which we owe so much, deserves to have their names recorded. It was composed of John Scott of Clark, John Badollet and William Polke of Knox, Dann Lynn of Posey, and John Boone of Harrison.

THE STATE SEMINARY.

As soon as the four years prescribed by the Constitution of 1816 had expired, the Legislature of the young State made haste to comply with its requirements, and a "State Seminary" was founded, which, through the "Indiana College," ultimately became the "Indiana University."

An "act to establish a State Seminary, and for other purposes," was passed and approved January 20, 1820. (Laws 1820, p. 82). This was the beginning of the State University, so that its history dates from this period. By the terms of this act, Charles Dewey, Jonathan Lindley, David H. Maxwell, John M. Jenkins, Jonathan Nichols and William Lowe were constituted the Board of Trustees of the State Seminary, as a body corporate and politic. They were to meet at Bloomington, in the county of Monroe, on the first Monday of June following, or as soon thereafter as convenient, and after taking the oath of office, were to repair to the township of land granted by Congress to the State for the use of a seminary of learning, and to select an eligible and convenient site for the State Seminary. They were empowered to appoint an agent to lay off lots and sell them, not exceeding one section, or 640 acres in quantity. As soon as the Trustees deemed it expedient, they were to erect a suitable building for the seminary, and a suitable and commodious house for the professor, on the site they might select, and within ten days after the meeting of the next General Assembly were to lay before it a true and perfect statement of their proceedings, with a plat of the lots and lands laid off and sold, the proceeds of the sales, and a plan of the buildings erected or proposed to be erected.

Before entering upon their duties, the Trustees and their agent were required to give bond, with security, for the performance of their duties, and to the Governor was given the right to fill all vacancies occurring in the Board.

This act did not mention the Gibson County lands, but on the 22d day of January, 1820, a joint resolution was adopted by the Legislature, appointing Jesse Emerson a superintendent to rent said lands, and account to the State for the proceeds.

The next Legislature, by an act approved January 9, 1821, authorized the Trustees of the Seminary to loan any moneys in their possession belonging to the Seminary, on mortgage security.

At the same session, on the 9th day of January, a "joint resolution" was passed (Laws 1821, p. 139), as follows:

"WHEREAS, The General Assembly of the State of Indiana are deeply impressed with the importance of knowledge and learning being diffused through the rising generation of the State of Indiana; therefore,

"*Be it enacted by the General Assembly of the State of Indiana*, That John Badollet and David Hart, of Knox County, William W. Martin, of Washington County, James Welsh of Switzerland County, and Daniel I. Carswell, of Franklin County, Thomas C. Searle, of Jefferson County, and John Todd, of Clark County, be and they hereby are appointed a committee to draft and report to the next General Assembly of this State a bill providing for a general system of education, ascending in a regular gradation from township schools to a State University, where tuition shall be gratis and equally open to all, and particularly to guard against any distinction existing in any of said institutions between the rich and the poor.

"*Resolved*, That the said committee shall receive such compensation for their said services herein as shall be allowed by the next General Assembly.

"*Resolved*, That the Governor is hereby requested to notify the gentlemen appointed by the above resolution of their appointment, and he is also hereby requested to give the committee any information on the above subject in his possession."

The labors of the committee thus appointed, after having passed under the revision of Judge Parke and the General Assembly, were incorporated in the first general school law of the State, which appears in the Revised Statutes of 1824, page 379, under the title of "An Act Incorporating Congressional Townships, and Providing for Public Schools therein."

As this act failed to carry out that part of the resolution requiring that the bill should provide for "a general system of education *ascending in a regular gradation from township schools to a State University*," it has no place in this sketch.

On the 22d of January, 1822, an act was passed providing for the sale of the Seminary township in Gibson County, and requiring the money to be paid into the State Treasury, "that it may be made a productive fund for the benefit of the *State Seminary*." The seventh section of this act recites the fact that the Trustees of the *Vincennes University* had sold portions of such lands and had negligently permitted the corporation to die without having executed deeds to certain purchasers, and the Commissioners appointed were authorized to hear the claims and decide as seemed to them just and right, and to execute deeds to such purchasers.

By the act approved February 10, 1825 (Laws 1825, p. 97), it appears that John W. Lee was the agent for the Monroe County lands (doubtless appointed by the Board of Trustees), and he was required to rent all improved lots by letting them to the highest bidder at a "public vendue," to be held on the first Monday of March, biennially, the successful bidder to give bond with security for the payment of his rent on or before the first of December of each year, to keep the premises in good repair, and to prevent unnecessary waste; and the rent was to be not less than 62½ cents an acre.

The Trustees were authorized to receive all moneys arising in any way from the Seminary lands and from the State interest on all the Seminary funds in the treasury.

The next Legislature, by an act approved January 21, 1826 (Laws 1826, p. 82), appointed Daniel Rawlings, Edward Bowland, and William Marshall additional trustees for the State Seminary in Monroe County, upon their qualifying, to continue in office for one year and until others were appointed and qualified according to law.

By an act approved January, 25, 1827 (Laws 1827, p. 93), James Smith of Gibson, and James Borland of Monroe County, were appointed Commissioners, with power to sell the reserved Seminary lands in those townships; but three sections, one on the east, one on the south, and one on the west most contiguous to the section on which the Seminary buildings were situated, were reserved from the sale.

The Treasurer of State was required to keep an account current with the State Seminary of the moneyed transactions under this act, and to pay quarter yearly to the Trustees any interest that may have accrued.

Under these acts about 17,000 acres of the Gibson County lands were sold, and the proceeds paid into the State Treasury, to be accredited to the Seminary, College and University Funds, and out of this grew the subsequent important litigation between the State and the Trustees of the Vincennes University, hereafter to be noticed.

The same Legislature passed " an act appointing a Board of Visitors to the State Seminary, at Bloomington, and for advancing the interests of said institution." The act approved January 26, 1827 (Laws 1827, p. 99), is as follows:

"SECTION 1. *Be it enacted by the General Assembly of the State of Indiana,* That the Governor and Lieutenant Governor for the time being, the Judges of the Supreme Court of this State, the Judge of the District Court of the United States for the District of Indiana, the District Attorney of said District, Moses Tabbs, John E. Hubbs, Samuel Hall, Samuel Gwathmey, Jeremiah Rowland, Reuben W. Nelson, Jeremiah Sullivan, Samuel Merrill, John Test, William B. Laughlin, William McClure, William S. Cornett, Beaumont Parks, Henry Way, Jeremiah Cash, Samuel Scott and George H. Dunn, be and they hereby are appointed a Board of Visitors to the State Seminary at Bloomington, to continue as such for three years from the date of this act, and until successors are appointed, who, or any five of whom are authorized and requested to act as visitors aforesaid in the manner hereinafter specified.

"SEC. 2. The Board of Visitors aforesaid are hereby authorized semi-annually, on the Thursdays preceding the session of the Supreme Court at Indianapolis, to assemble in the town of Bloomington, and proceed to visit and inspect the Seminary aforesaid; whenever any five of the above-named visitors shall convene in pursuance of this act, they shall appoint from their number a President and Secretary of said Board: the President so appointed shall, as soon as convenient, notify the President or some one of the Trustees of said Seminary of their attendance at said place and readiness to proceed in visiting and inspecting the said Seminary; whose duty it shall be forthwith to call a meeting of said Trustees, who are hereby required to attend at the place of meeting of said Board of Visitors, with the records of the corporation, and also to give such verbal explanation of the past proceedings of such Trustees as may be called for, or which the said Trustees may deem necessary or proper. It shall further be the duty of said Trustees, at the same time, to exhibit in writing to said visitors a detailed report of the finances of the Seminary; the number of teachers and students belonging to said Seminary; the various branches of science and literature taught; the course of tuition and discipline adopted; the by-laws and regulations enacted, as well for the teachers as the students, and the progress made by the students, noting particularly in said report the names of those students who have distinguished themselves in any or all of the branches of education, and also those who have been exemplary for good conduct.

"SEC. 3. After the examination of the records aforesaid, together with the report of said Trustees, which shall be retained and preserved by the said visitors, it shall be the duty of the said Trustees to conduct the said visitors to the hall or building in which the students are assembled for the purpose of personally inspecting their studies and progress, during which inspection it shall be the duty of the principal and assistant teachers to call on the several students for such exhibition of their scholarship as may be in their power to give; and to invite the said Board of Visitors, individually or collectively, to propound any question to the students, or to suggest any course of examination they may think proper; and at the close of said examination, the visitors aforesaid, by their President or some member of the Board, shall deliver such address to the students as to them shall seem proper.

"SEC. 4. The said Board of Visitors are hereby authorized to recommend the repeal of any by-laws, rules or regulations adopted by the Trustees of the State Seminary which to them may seem inexpedient, improper, or contrary to the interests of the institution.

"SEC. 5. It shall be the duty of the visitors to make an annual report of their proceedings to the General Assembly, which shall be addressed to the Speaker of the House of Representatives, and which shall contain the report of the Trustees in the second section provided for, their own acts and opinions, and also any recommendations they may think proper to make of such measures within the competency of the Legislature as may tend to sustain, foster and improve the Seminary aforesaid."

THE INDIANA COLLEGE.

By the act approved January 24, 1828 (Laws 1828, p. 115), a college was established at Bloomington, under the name and style of "The Indiana College," for the education of youth in the "*American*, learned and foreign languages, the useful arts, sciences and literature."

A Board of Trustees consisting of fifteen persons, residents of the State, was appointed, consisting of Edward Borland, Samuel Dodds, Leroy Mayfield, Jonathan Nichols, James Blair, David H. Maxwell, William Bannister and William Lowe, of the county of Monroe; George H. Dunn, of Dearborn; Christopher Harrison, of Washington; Seth M. Leavenworth, of Crawford; John Law, of Knox; Williamson Dunn, of Montgomery; Ovid Butler, of Shelby, and Bethuel F. Morris, of Marion. They were empowered to fill vacancies in their own body, and after the first meeting, on the first Monday of May, 1828, were to determine the time of their future meetings and make all regulations for the government of the College and their own body as they deemed expedient, and to choose the officers and faculty. They also had the right to remove any officers of the corporation or College at discretion, and could remove members of their own Board for misconduct, breach of the by-laws or gross immorality. No President, professor or officer of the College could be a Trustee. No instructor could be required to profess any particular religious opinions, and no student was to be denied admission, or refused any privileges, honors or degrees, on account of religious opinions, and no sectarian principles were to be taught or inculcated.

All the moneys arising from the sale of the Seminary townships in Monroe and Gibson counties were to remain forever as a permanent fund for the use of the College, and all the property of the State Seminary was vested in the Board of Trustees of the Indiana College, to be used for the best interests and prosperity of the institution.

Benjamin Parke of Washington County, James Scott of Clark, Jesse L. Holman of Dearborn, Isaac Blackford of Knox, and George Bush of Marion were appointed a Board of Visitors to annually visit the college, examine its property, real and personal, inspect the course of instruction and the proceedings and by-laws of the Board of Trustees, and to recommend such alterations as they might deem necessary; to inquire into the financial condition of the college, and report the result to the Governor, who was to lay it before the General Assembly. This Board was. to continue until the Legislature appointed others in its stead.

By a joint resolution, approved January 28, 1830, Rev. Robert Roberts was appointed one of the Board of Visitors to fill a vacancy occasioned by the resignation of Hon. Benjamin Parke; and by a joint resolution, approved February 2, 1833, Allen Wiley of Switzerland County, and Calvin Ruter of Marion

SEMINARY. THE INDIANA COLLEGE, 1836. LABORATORY, 1840.

THE FIRST COLLEGE BUILDINGS.

were appointed Visitors to fill vacancies caused by the refusal of Robert R. Roberts and James Armstrong* to serve.

The act establishing Indiana College was amended by an act approved February 1, 1834. Under its provisions each county in the State became entitled to send a student, whose tuition was to be gratis, and who was to be selected by the Boards doing county business in the respective counties, preference being given to those least able to pay for tuition. Each student so selected was to have free tuition for two years, with all the privileges of those who paid for their tuition, and at the end of two years their places were to be filled by the County Board in the same manner as the first were selected.

Between the time of establishing the Indiana College and the year 1840, a number of special acts providing for the sale of lands, and the loaning and other disposition of the funds were passed, but they are deemed of too little importance in the legal history of the college to be worthy of insertion here.

THE INDIANA UNIVERSITY.

We have now reached a point of import to the institution, for the "Indiana College" was converted into "The Indiana University" by "an act to establish a university in the State of Indiana," approved February 15, 1838 (Local Laws, 1838, p. 294), and a new era in its history was entered upon. The act is as follows:

"SECTION 1. *Be it enacted by the General Assembly of the State of Indiana*, That there shall be, and hereby is created and established a University adjacent to the town of Bloomington, in the county of Monroe, for the education of youth in the American, learned and foreign languages, the useful arts, sciences (including law and medicine) and literature, to be known by the name and style of the Indiana University, and to be governed and directed as hereinafter directed.

"SEC. 2. There shall be a Board of Trustees appointed, consisting of twenty-one persons, residents of the State, who shall be, and hereby are constituted a body corporate and politic by the name of 'The Trustees of the Indiana University,' and in their corporate name and capacity may sue and be sued, plead and be impleaded in any court of record, and by that name shall have perpetual succession.

---

*The writer was unable to find the resolution appointing Armstrong as one of the Board.
3—HISTORY.

"SEC. 3. The said Trustees shall fill all vacancies which may occur in their own body, elect a President of the Board, Secretary, Treasurer and such other officers as may be necessary for the good order and government of said corporation, and shall be competent in law and in equity to take to themselves and their successors in their said corporate name any estate, real, personal or mixed, by the gift, grant, bargain, sale, conveyance, will, devise, or bequest of any person or persons whomsoever, and the same estate, whether real, personal or mixed, to grant, bargain, sell, convey, demise, let, place out at interest, or otherwise dispose of for the use of said University, in such manner as to them shall seem most beneficial to the institution, and to receive the rents, issues, profits, income and interest thereon, and apply the same to the proper use and support of the said University, and generally in their said corporate name, shall have full power to do and transact all and every the business touching or concerning the premises, or which shall be incidentally necessary thereto, as fully and effectually as any natural person, body politic or corporate, may or can do in the management of their own concerns, and to hold, enjoy, exercise and use the rights, powers and privileges incident to bodies politic and corporate in law and equity.

"SEC. 4. The said Trustees shall cause to be made for their use one common seal, with such devices and incriptions thereon as they shall think proper, under and by which all deeds, diplomas and certificates and acts of the said corporation shall pass and be authenticated.

"SEC. 5. The said Trustees, or any ten of them, shall meet at Bloomington, in the county of Monroe, on the last Monday of September next in the year, and after severally taking an oath or affirmation faithfully and impartially to discharge the duties by this act enjoined, shall proceed to organize a Board by electing one of their own members President, and the Board when so formed shall appoint a Secretary and Treasurer, who shall severally, before entering upon the duties of their respective offices, take an oath or affirmation faithfully and impartially to perform the duties appertaining to their respective offices, and the Treasurer shall give bond with three or more securities, to be approved by said Trustees, in the sum of twenty thousand dollars, payable to the State of Indiana, and conditioned for the faithful discharge of the duties of his office of Treasurer of the said corporation, and which bond, executed and approved as aforesaid, shall be deposited in the office of the Treasurer of State.

"SEC. 6. The said Board of Trustees, when organized in manner aforesaid, shall forever thereafter determine the time of their future meetings, the manner of notifying the same, and act on their own adjournments as to them shall seem most expedient, and shall from time to time, as occasion may require, make and ordain reasonable rules, ordinances and by-laws, with reasonable penalties, for the good government of the University, and the regulation of their own body, not repugnant to the laws and Constitution of this State.

"SEC. 7. The said Board of Trustees shall, from time to time, as the interest of the institution may require, elect a President of said University, and such professors, tutors, instructors and other officers of the same as they may judge necessary for the interests thereof, and shall determine the duties, salaries, emoluments, responsibilities, and tenures of their several offices, and designate the course of instruction in said University.

"SEC. 8. The said Board of Trustees shall have full power to remove any one of their own body for misconduct, breach of the by-laws, or gross immorality, and may at any time they may deem it necessary for the good of the institution, remove any of the officers of said University or corporation, and appoint others in their stead.

"SEC. 9. The President, professors and tutors shall be styled the faculty of said University, which faculty shall have the power of enforcing the rules and regulations adopted by the said Trustees for the government of the students, by rewarding or censuring them, and finally by suspending such as, after the necessary admonition, shall continue refractory, until a determination of a quorum of Trustees can be had thereon; and of granting or conferring by and with the consent and approbation of the Board of Trustees, such degrees in the liberal arts and sciences, including those of law and medicine, as are usually granted or conferred in other Universities in America, to the students of the University, or to others, who, by their proficiency in learning, or by other meritorious distinction, may be entitled to the same, and to grant unto such graduates diplomas or certificates, under their common seal, and signed by the Faculty to authenticate and perpetuate the memory of such graduation.

"SEC. 10. No President, professor or other officer of the University shall, while acting in that capacity, be a Trustee, nor shall any President, professor, tutor, instructor, or other officer of the University, ever be required by the Trustees to profess any particular religious opinions, and no student shall be denied admission, or refused any of the privileges, honors or degrees of the University on account of the religious opinions he may entertain; nor shall any sectarian tenets or principles be taught, instructed or inculcated at said University, by any President, professor, tutor, or instructor thereof: *Provided, however,* That if at any meeting of the Board of Trustees of the University, there should be one wanting to make a quorum, then, and in that case, the President of the Faculty of said University shall, for the time being, be considered as a member of said Board, and have power to act as such, but so soon as a quorum of said Board shall be present, then the President shall no longer sit as a member of said Board.

"SEC. 11. His Excellency, David Wallace, Governor of the State of Indiana (who shall be *ex officio* Vice President of the Board, and his successor in office forever), William Hendricks, of the county of Jefferson; Seth M. Leavenworth, of the county of Crawford; David G. Mitchell, of the county of Harrison; John M. Farrington, of the county of Vigo; John Law, of the county of Knox; Rev. Allen Wiley, of the county of Montgomery; Nathaniel West and Isaac Blackford, of the county of Marion, Jesse L. Holman, of the county of Dearborn; Jonathan Nichols, Paris C. Dunning, James Blair, Chester G. Ballard, Joshua O. Howe, Leroy Mayfield, and William Turner, of the county of Monroe; Robert Dale Owen, of the county of Posey; Richard W. Thompson, of the county of Lawrence; Samuel K. Hoshour, of the county of Wayne; George W. Ewing, of the county of Cass, and Hiram A. Hunter, of the county of Gibson, shall be and are hereby appointed Trustees of said University, agreeably to the provisions of this act, and shall hold their first meeting as hereinbefore directed: and should any ten of them (who shall at all times be necessary to constitute a quorum for the transaction of business: *Provided, however,* That deficiency of one may be supplied in the manner heretofore prescribed in the tenth section of this act), fail to meet on the said last Monday of September next, the Governor of this State is hereby authorized and required to appoint some subsequent day for the meeting of said Trustees, giving to each of them twenty days' notice in writing, and said Trustees, or a quorum of them, when convened, in pursuance of such notice, shall proceed to organize the Board in manner hereinbefore directed; and the President of the University shall be empowered to call occasional meetings of the Trustees in such manner as the Board of Trustees may by their by-laws direct.

"SEC. 12. That all moneys which have heretofore, or which may hereafter arise from the sales of the Seminary townships of land in the counties of Monroe and Gibson shall be and forever remain a permanent fund for the support of said University; and the interest arising from the amount of said sales, together with the amount of the sales of the three reserved sections in the Seminary township situated in the county of Monroe, the residue of the unsold sections aforesaid, and all the buildings which have been erected adjacent to the town of Bloomington, in the said county of Monroe, and which are now used by and belong to the Indiana College, together with all the estate, either real, personal or of any description whatever, belonging to, or in any wise connected with, the Indiana College, as the property of the State, and all gifts, grants and donations which have been, or hereafter may be, made, previous to the taking effect of this act, for the support of the Indiana College, shall be and hereby are forever vested in the aforesaid Trustees, and their successors, to be controlled, regulated and appropriated by them in such manner as they shall deem most conducive to the best interest and prosperity of the institution: *Provided*, That the said Trustees shall conform to the will of any donor or donors in the application of any estate which may be given, devised or bequeathed for any particular object connected with the institution, and that the real estate hereby vested in the said Trustees, and their successors, shall be by them held forever for the use of said University, and shall not be sold or converted by them to any other use whatever.

"SEC. 13. That it shall be the duty of the Secretary of said corporation to keep a full, true and faithful record of all the proceedings of said Board of Trustees, in a suitable book, to be procured by them for that purpose, and make such copies and transcripts of the orders and proceedings of the said Board of Trustees as may from time to time be required, and the same duly certify, under the seal of the corporation; and for his services he shall receive such compensation as said Trustees may from time to time allow, to be paid out of any funds in the treasury of said corporation, not otherwise appropriated.

"Sec. 14. That it shall be the duty of the Treasurer of said corporation to keep a full, true and perfect account of all moneys by him received by virtue of his said office, in suitable books, to be for that purpose provided, and pay such money out from time to time as may be required by and upon the order of said Board of Trustees, duly certified by the Secretary, and keep a similar account of all such disbursements, and furnish said Board of Trustees, whenever they may require the same, a full, true and complete statement of such receipts and disbursements, and exhibit to them, for their inspection, his original books of entry, and also exhibit his books for inspection and examination of the Board of Visitors of said University, which may, at any time hereafter, be appointed by the General Assembly of this State; and shall, moreover, annually transmit to the Governor of this State, by him to be laid before the General Assembly thereof, a true and complete statement of the annual receipts and expenditures of said corporation; and should said corporation ever be dissolved, by legislative enactment, or otherwise, it shall, in such case, be the duty of said Treasurer to pay over and deliver to the Treasurer of State, for the use of this State, all moneys and and funds in his hands derived from the State belonging to said corporation at the time of such dissolution; and should any Treasurer of said corporation at any time be guilty of any defalcation in the discharge of the duties of his said office, the said Trustees shall have the right of an action therefor against said Treasurer and his sureties upon his official bond, in the name of the State of Indiana, for the use of said Trustees, and of prosecuting the same to final judgment and recovery, or in case of the dissolution of said corporation, such action shall be sustained for the use the State.

"Sec. 15. That the power and authority of the present Trustees of the Indiana College, over and concerning the said Institution, the funds, estate, property, rights and demands thereof, shall forever cease and determine, from and after the organization of the Board of Trustees of the Indiana University, named in this act; and all the funds, estate, property, rights, demands, privileges and immunities, of what kind or nature soever, belonging or in any wise pertaining to said Indiana College, shall be, and the same are hereby, invested in the Trustees of the Indiana University appointed by this act, and their successors in office, for the uses and purposes only of said University, and the said Trustees and their successors in office shall have, hold, possess, and exercise all the powers and authority over the said Institution and the estate and concerns thereof in the manner hereinbefore prescribed.

"SEC. 16. That the Constitution of said University, herein and hereby declared and established, shall be subject to be changed, altered or amended by the Legislature of the State. All laws or parts of laws coming within the purview of this act are hereby repealed.

"This act to take effect and be in force from and after its passage."

Apparently the operations of this law were unsatisfactory, for by the "act to provide for the better regulation of the Indiana University," approved February 15, 1841 (Laws 1841, p. 110), the number of the Board of Trustees was reduced to nine, a majority of whom was to form a quorum, and Miles C. Eggleston of Jefferson, William T. S. Cornet of Ripley, Robert Dale Owen of Posey, Nathaniel West of Marion, John Law of Knox, David H. Maxwell of Monroe, Elisha M. Huntington of Vigo, Lot Bloomfield of Wayne and James Scott of Clark, were named as such Trustees. They were empowered to fill vacancies in the Board, and to determine the times of holding their semi-annual meetings after the first, which was to commence on the 3d Monday of July in that year. No two of the Trustees were to be from the same county.

The civil courts were deprived of jurisdiction to punish students for trivial breaches of the peace which might be committed within the college campus, and the students were exempted from militia duty and road taxes.

Any Trustee failing to attend two consecutive regular meetings, without presenting satisfactory excuse in writing, forfeited his seat as a member of the Board, and the compensation of the

Trustees was fixed at the same per diem and mileage as that allowed by law to members of the General Assembly, to be paid out of the University funds.

By an act, approved January 17, 1842 (Laws 1842, p. 143), each county of the State was authorized to send to the University one additional student free from payment of tuition fees.

A "Joint Resolution," approved January 27, 1842 (Laws 1842, p. 174), recites that—

"WHEREAS, It is made the duty of the General Assembly of the State of Indiana, by the second section of the 9th article of the Constitution of the aforesaid State, so soon as circumstances will permit, to provide by law for a general system of education, ascending in a regular gradation from township schools to a State University, wherein tuition shall be gratis and open to all; therefore,

"*Be it resolved by the General Assembly of the State of Indiana,* That the Trustees of the Indiana University be, and hereby are required, at the next regular meeting of said Board, to examine into the resources of said University, and make full and complete report of the same to the next Legislature, together with the amount of salaries paid to professors, and all other expenses of said institution; and also whether, in their opinion, the resources of said University are sufficient to enable the Legislature to pass a law making tuition gratis, in compliance with the Constitution of the State above referred to."

In all probability the report made in compliance with this act showed that it was impossible, without further and additional resources, for the Legislature never passed any law to carry out that provision of the Constitution, and when it was finally done, it was by the act of the Trustees, and not of the Legislature.

In 1845 the Board of Trustees of the Vincennes University made claim to the title in the Gibson County Seminary lands, and to proceeds of the sales made by the State, which had been transferred to the Indiana University, and a suit was brought to test the question of title. There being no law by which the State could be sued, this suit was abandoned, and application made to the Legislature for leave to test the question by a civil action. In response to this demand, "an act to authorize the Trustees of the Vincennes University to bring suit against the State of Indiana, and for other purposes," was passed, and approved January 17, 1846. (Local laws 1846, p. 233.) It authorized the filing of a bill in chancery, in the nature of an action of disseizin in the Marion Circuit Court, giving that Court full jurisdiction of the matter, and of the parties to the suit.

The Governor, upon whom process was required to be served, was required to employ counsel to defend. It was further provided that, if the suit was determined in favor of the Vincennes University, upon its Board of Trustees relinquishing to the State the lands sold, the State should set apart to its Board of Trustees the fund arising from the sales, and the bringing of the suit was to be deemed an election by said Board of Trustees to look to the State for compensation of their claim. Nothing in the act was to be construed to prevent the State from contesting the corporate existence of the Trustees of the Vincennes University.

The action was brought, and resulted in a decree by the Marion Circuit Court in favor of the complainants, and requiring the State to pay to them the sum of $30,099.66 as the proceeds of the sales of the land.

In this suit Samuel Judah appeared as attorney for the claimants and O. H. Smith and G. G. Dunn for the State and the interests of the University.

From this decree the State appealed to the Supreme Court of the State, which rendered its decision at the November term, 1850, reversing the decree of the Court below, and holding that the act of the Territorial Legislature of 1806, granting the lands to the Vincennes University was nugatory, because no such power was vested in it by the act of Congress, and that they were not then in existence as a corporation, having allowed their corporation to lapse (*State* v. *Trustees, etc.*, 2 *Ind. Rep.*, 293).

The Trustees of the Vincennes University, not satisfied with this decision, sued out a writ of error from the Supreme Court of the United States, which, at the December term, 1852, reversed the decision of the Supreme Court of the State, holding that when the Territorial Legislature of 1806 incorporated a "Board of Trustees of the Vincennes University," the grant of a township in the Vincennes district by the Congress of 1804, and which was located by the Secretary of the Treasury in 1806, attached to this Board, although for the two preceding years there had been no grantee in existence, and holding further, that if the Board of Trustees, by a failure to elect when vacancies occurred, or through any other means became reduced to a less number than was authorized to act by the charter, the corporation was not thereby dissolved, but its franchises only suspended until restored by legislative action. The Chief Justice Taney and Justices Catron and Daniel dissented from majority opinion of the Court. (*The Trustees* v. *State*, 14 *How.*, *U. S. Rep.*, 265). Mr. Judah and Mr. Dunham appeared for the Trustees in this proceeding and O. H. Smith for the State. As a sequel to this litigation, it may be interesting to note that the Trustees of the Vincennes University afterwards brought suit against Mr. Judah to compel him to hand over a large amount of the bonds of the State delivered to him in payment of this claim under the act approved February 13, 1855. He answered that they had, by resolution duly entered upon their records, contracted to pay him one-fourth of what they should recover in the suit for their services, and that he had retained $16,625, that being one-fourth of the sum paid by the State in liquidation of the claim. The Trustees replied that at that date he was Secretary of the Board and falsely entered the resolution upon their record, which was denied by him. The judgment of the Knox County Circuit Court was adverse to Mr. Judah, and he appealed to the Supreme Court, which, in the May term, 1861, on errors of law occurring upon the trial, and not upon the merits, reversed the judgment and remanded the cause for trial. (*Judah* v. *Trustees, etc.*, 16 *Ind.* 56). Again the judgment was adverse to Mr. Judah, and he a second time appealed to the Supreme Court, which again, at the November term, 1864, reversed the judgment and ordered a new trial. (*Judah* v. *Trustees, etc.*, 23 *Ind.* 273). The suit ended in the retention of the fees by the attorney.

Returning to the Indiana University, we find an act approved January 27, 1847 (Laws 1847, p. 42), providing that, when students appointed from counties failed to attend any one session after their appointment, their appointment became vacated, and the county boards were authorized to appoint others in their places.

The act approved June 17, 1852 (Rev. 1852, vol. 1, p. 504), enacted that "the institution established by an act to establish a college in the State of Indiana, approved January 28, 1828, is hereby recognized as the University of the State."

It provided that the present Trustees, three of whom should reside in the county of Monroe, and their successors, should be a body corporate, with similar powers to those granted by former acts, to meet annually at Bloomington, at least three days preceding the annual commencement. Five were to constitute a quorum, and, in case of an emergency declared by the Faculty, if the others failed to attend at a called meeting, the resident Trustees were empowered to fill vacancies in the Board and Faculty, but appointments so made expired at the next meeting of the Board. The Governor, Lieutenant Governor, Speaker of the House of Representatives, Judges of the Supreme Court and Superintendent of Common Schools were constituted a Board of Visitors, three to form a quorum, and those not present were to be reported by the Board of Trustees in their annual report. It was made the duty of one of the Faculty, to be designated by a majority of the members thereof, to deliver a public lecture on the principles and organization of the University, its educational facilities (being careful not to disparage the claims of other institutions of learning in the State), in at least fifteen different counties, after due notice; but if the vacation was less than one month, then in three counties.

The lecturers were also to make geological examinations, and collect mineralogical specimens for the cabinet by voluntary donations. Notice of the commencement of each session was to be published in a newspaper in each of the cities of Indianapolis, Louisville and New Orleans.

A normal department for instruction in the theory and practice of teaching of such young persons, male and female, residents of the State, was authorized, as well as an agricultural department. In other respects the provisions of the act in reference to the government of the University were similar to those established by former laws.

An act supplemental to and amendatory of the second section of the last mentioned act was approved March 3, 1855 (Laws 1855, p. 201). It made some important changes. The Board of Trustees were to be eight in number, no two of whom were to be residents of the same county, excepting Monroe, from which two might be selected. The same powers were conferred upon them as upon the former boards, except the right to fill vacancies, which was vested in the State Board of

Education. Joseph S. Jenckes, of Vigo; Joel B. McFarland, of Tippecanoe; George Evans, of Henry; William M. French, of Clark; Ransom W. Aiken and Johnson McCullough, of Monroe; James R. M. Bryant, of Warren, and John I. Morrison, of Marion, were named as such Board, three of whom were to serve two years, two for three years, and three for four years, to be determined by lot at their first meeting, which was fixed for Monday, April 2, 1855. The Trustees, while actually employed in the service of the University, were to receive the same pay as members of the General Assembly, and all their prior contracts for rebuilding the main edifice were legalized.

An act approved March 7, 1857 (Laws 1857, p. 130), provided that scholarships founded upon subscriptions of individuals to the University fund might be transferred or sold by the holders for a valuable consideration.

The act approved March 2, 1859 (Laws 1859, p. 239), among general enactments for the sale of lands and the loaning of the funds, provided that out of the first proceeds the Board of Trustees should be entitled to receive an amount equal to the interest belonging to the University, to be applied to the discharge of the debts growing out of the rebuilding of the University, and to the purchase of a suitable library, philosophical apparatus, or proper furniture, in place of those destroyed by the burning of the University.

One of the members of the Board of Trustees, to be designated by the Board, was required to attend the sale of lands to prevent combinations injurious to the University, and was empowered to withdraw the lands, or a part of them, from sale whenever he should deem it for the interest of the institution so to do, but no member of the Board was to become the purchaser, either directly or indirectly of any University lands.

The act approved May 11, 1861 (Laws 1861, p. 88), authorized the Trustees to appropriate one thousand dollars out of the proceeds of the sales of University lands for the purpose of enlarging the cabinet, and appointed Professor T. A. Wylie, or such person as the Trustees might designate, to take charge of the appropriations and expend it in the purchase of specimens.

The State Geologist was created a member of the faculty, and directed in his reconnoissances to collect duplicate specimens of mineralogy and geology, and to deposit one set in the University cabinet; and the State Librarian was directed to transfer from the State Library to the library of the University a complete set of the journals of both houses, a copy of all laws enacted since the organization of the State, of all reports from the departments of the State, and of those received from the other States and the General Government, and of all other books where there were duplicates in the library, provided they could be spared, and the transfer be made without expense to the State.

In the same year, by the act approved May 31, 1861 (Laws 1861, p. 89), it was enacted that the contingent fee on the perpetual scholarships should be not more than one dollar each session; and the Trustees were authorized, whenever they should deem it for the best interest of the University, to purchase such scholarships at not more than 90 cents on the dollar, by giving notice in a Bloomington paper that they were ready to purchase, after which notice no person could claim any rights under such certificates, except to sell them.

An advance step was taken by the Legislature, in the act approved March 8, 1867 (Laws 1867, p. 20). The preamble of the act is as follows: "*Whereas*, The endowment fund of the University, located at Bloomington, Monroe County, is no longer sufficient to meet the growing wants of education, and make said University efficient and useful; and, whereas, it should be the pride of every citizen of Indiana to place the State University in the highest condition of usefulness, and make it the crowning glory of our present great common school system, where education shall be free, therefore," there was appropriated the sum of eight thousand dollars annually out of the State Treasury, to be paid semi-annually, commencing on the 31st day of March, 1867.

This appropriation seems to have been insufficient, for, by the act approved December 14, 1872 (Laws Spec. Sess. 1872, p. 4), it was recited that the incomes of the University were insufficient to meet current expenses, that the Board of Trustees, in order to keep the several departments in operation, had been compelled to borrow a large amount of money, to-wit: $8,000. Therefore, an appropriation of that amount was made, in order to pay and discharge the debts so incurred.

The general appropriation act of March 10, 1873 (Laws 1873, p. 8), appropriated the sum of $12,000 for the year commencing April 1, 1874, but the same Legislature, by the act of February

19, 1873, after declaring that the income of the endowment fund, together with the amount appropriated by the act of 1867 had "become wholly inadequate to meet the growing wants of public education, and is not sufficient to enable said University rightly to provide for the education of all who are seeking instruction within her walls, and to accomplish her true mission as the head of our present great system of common schools, *where education shall be free to all,*" made an appropriation of $15,000, to be paid semi-annually thereafter from the 30th of September, 1873.

The general appropriation act of 1877 (Laws 1877, p. 8), gave $14,000 to the University, but exacted that out of that amount should be paid the debts due on the Owen Cabinet, the salaries of the President at the rate of $2,500, and of the professors $1,500 each, per annum, and all expenses allowed to the Board of Trustees.

The annual appropriations thereafter were monotonously alike, and are passed over as unimportant.

The next great advance in University legislation, and the provision most likely to insure the fulfillment of the ideas of its founders, was through the "act to provide a fund for the permanent endowment of Indiana University, and for the endowment of the same," approved March 8, 1883 (Laws 1883, p. 82). Its importance will justify its insertion as a whole, rather than to attempt to state its substance:

"SECTION 1. *Be it enacted by the General Assembly of the State of Indiana,* That there shall be assessed and collected, as State revenues are assessed and collected, in the year of eighteen hundred and eighty-three, and in each of the succeeding twelve years, the sum of one-half of one cent on each one-hundred dollars' worth of taxable property in this State; which money when collected and paid into the State Treasury, in each of the years named in this act, shall be placed to the credit of a fund to be known as the Permanent Endowment fund of the Indiana University.

"SEC. 2. That whenever, after the first day of May, eighteen hundred and eighty-four, there shall have been paid into the State Treasury a sum of said Permanent Endowment Fund sufficient to pay off any of the interest-bearing indebtedness of the State, it shall be the duty of the Treasurer of State to pay off and cancel such indebtedness, and it shall be the duty of said Treasurer of State to continue to pay off and cancel said interest-bearing indebtedness which may be due, or which, by the terms of the contract creating such indebtedness, may be paid off, whenever there is a sufficient sum of said Permanent Endowment Fund in the State Treasury to pay off the same out of said Permanent Endowment Fund.

"SEC. 3. It shall be the duty of the Treasurer of State, immediately after paying off any of the interest-bearing indebtedness of the State, as provided for in section two of this act, to make and issue to the Trustees of said University, and to their successors in office, a non-negotiable bond of the State, in an amount equal to the sum drawn from the said Permanent Endowment Fund and used in said payment. Said non-negotiable bond shall be signed by the Governor and Treasurer of State, and attested by the Secretary of State and the seal of the State, and be made payable in fifty years after date, at the option of the State, and said bond shall bear five per cent. interest from date until paid; which interest shall be paid semi-annually, on the first days of May and November of each year, and the same shall be applied to the current and extraordinary expenses of said University and be paid to the Trustees thereof, under the same rules and regulations as is now required by law in the payment of revenues of said University. The non-negotiable bonds provided for in this act shall remain in the custody of the Treasurer of State.

"SEC. 4. That so much of said Permanent Endowment Fund as shall not at any time be absorbed by the non-negotiable bonds of the State, as contemplated in this act, shall be loaned by the Auditor of State at six per centum interest, payable annually in advance, in real estate security; and in making loans and disbursing interest collected the Treasurer of State and the Auditor of State shall be governed by the law now in force, regulating the manner of making loans of the University funds and paying out interest collected. except as otherwise provided in this act.

"SEC. 5. It shall be the duty of the Auditor of State to make a complete record of every mortgage and note executed on account of any loan from said permanent endowment fund in a book, to be kept in his office for that purpose; and on payment of any loan to said fund, said Auditor shall enter a record of satisfaction in full on the margin of the record of the mortgage in his office, and sign the same with his name; and he shall also, in like manner, enter satisfaction in full on the face of the mortgage, which mortgage, when presented by the mortgager, or any person holding title under him, to the Recorder of the county wherein the land mortgaged is situated, shall authorize the Recorder of said county to copy such entry on the record of his office.

"SEC. 6. If at any time hereafter the State shall need the loan of any part, or of all, of said permanent endowment fund, the State shall be a preferred borrower of so much of the fund as shall not be loaned at the time; but it shall be the duty of the Treasurer of State to cause to be executed, as an evidence of any such loan, a non-negotiable bond of the State for the amount so borrowed, in like manner as is provided in section three of this act: *Provided*, If at any time hereafter the said Indiana University shall be consolidated with any other educational institution or institutions of the State, or shall be removed from its present location for any cause whatever, the fund raised under the provisions of this act shall be held and used for the benefit of such institution as consolidated or changed, nothwithstanding such change or consolidation whenever so removed or consolidated: *Provided, further,* That after said date no further appropriation shall be made to said University.

"SEC. 7. Whereas an emergency exists for the immediate taking effect of this act, it shall be in force from and after its passage."

The general appropriation act of 1885 (Laws 1885, p. 47–189) gave the sum of $23,000, for the expenses of the current year, to the University, and the act approved March 6, 1885 (Laws 1885, p. 65) appropriated the further sum of $30,000, with which to build an engine house, to build fences and improve the college grounds, to supply the necessary piping and apparatus for lighting and heating the buildings, to replace the library and museum, and to supply the chemical, philosophical and natural science departments with the apparatus, fixtures and appliances therein needed. The law declared this necessary by reason of the total destruction of one of the buildings, with its contents, in July, 1883, to replace which the county of Monroe had, with great liberality, contributed the sum of fifty thousand dollars, with which sum the Board of Trustees had purchased a new site for the college campus, and erected two new buildings thereon for the use of the University.

The progress of legislation for the Indiana University has thus been traced through a century of wonderful growth in science, arts, public improvements and general wealth, in what was at the beginning a wilderness far from the refinements of civilization.

When the idea of establishing seminaries and colleges in the Northwest Territory was broached the savage red man claimed title to its soil, Spain and Great Britain claimed it by the right of discovery, the sparse settlements were exposed to all the terrors of Indian warfare, and the pioneer settler and his family lived in daily dread of the tomahawk and the scalping knife. The tides of war, both with the savage and with Great Britain, were for many years to ebb and flow over and hold in their vortex these exposed frontier settlements, and a decade was to elapse before Mad Anthony Wayne should break the backbone of savage supremacy by his skillful and dashing campaign subsequent to the defeat of Harmer and St. Clair; and a full quarter of a century was to be filled with breathings of war, pillage and slaughter, ere the founders of western empires were to find peace.

Beasts as savage as the Indian roamed throughout the dense forests and over the great prairies, adding to the terrors which surrounded the families which founded our infant State. The stately buffalo, the graceful elk and deer, furnished them with meat, and skins for clothing.

Ere the savage and the wild beast had disappeared before the footsteps of advancing civilization, log school houses, seminaries, colleges and universities were founded, and moccasined youth, in buckskin breeches or homespun garments, were among those seeking to sip from the fountain of learning.

How changed the times!

Now, the Indiana University stands among the leading institutions of learning which grace our fair land, in the midst of a dense population, close to the center of American empire, and challenges the admiration of the State whose fostering care has for a century been over her.

How much she has contributed to the rapid development of the State in virtue, education, wealth and power, who can tell?

Let the close of the next century of its existence answer.

THE INDIANA SEMINARY.

BY JUDGE DAVID D. BANTA.

On the nineteenth day of April, one thousand eight hundred and sixteen, the Congress of the United States passed an act to enable the people of the Indiana territory to form a Constitution and State Government, and to be admitted into the Union on an equal footing with the original States. Certain propositions were offered to the Convention of the territory when it met to frame a constitution "for their free acceptance or rejection," one of which was that an entire township "shall be designated by the President of the United States * * for the use of a seminary of learning, and be vested in the Legislature of said State, to be appropriated solely to the use of such seminary."

This act lies at the very foundation of the history of the Indiana University. It came as a free-will offering, and it is gratifying to know that it was accepted in a spirit as broad and liberal as that in which it was offered. The Convention to frame a Constitution for the new State met at Corydon on the 10th of June of the same year, and by the 30th of the month the work was done.

A liberal spirit animated the members of the Convention in favor of popular education. With the declaration that "knowledge and learning generally diffused through a community" is "essential to the preservation of free government," they imposed upon all future general assemblies of the State the duty of providing by law for a "general system of education, ascending in a regular gradation from township schools to a State university, wherein tuition shall be gratis, and equally open to all."

On the 30th of the month the Convention adjourned, its last act being a formal acceptance of the propositions made by Congress. Eleven days thereafter James Madison, the President, designated Congressional township number eight north, range number one west, in the "Vincennes District," which township two years after, in the organization of Monroe county, became a part thereof.

At the time of the admission the population of Indiana did not, it is believed, exceed seventy thousand.* The settled parts were confined to a narrow fringe of territory extending down the Ohio State line from Wayne County to the Ohio River and thence down that to the mouth of the Wabash, and thence up that to Vincennes. Less than a fourth part of the State was unsurveyed, and to nearly or quite all the unsurveyed parts the Indians still claimed title. From the Seminary Township to the nearest point on the southern Indian boundary line was but litle over four miles.

The four years succeeding the admission of the State were marked by a great growth in population. The census of 1820 gave as the number 147,178, an increase of a fraction less than twenty-thousand per year. The new emigrants finding the more desirable lands of the older counties taken up, pressed out upon the Indian border in search of new homes. In the acts of the General Assembly creating new counties, we may read something of the story of the State's growth. In 1818 nine new ones were organized, a number never exceeded in one year in the history of the State, and never but once equaled.

The central regions of the State were in possession of the Delaware Indians, whose braves were renowned as hunters and trappers, and who were loth to surrender a country celebrated for its game and fur-bearing animals as was theirs, to take their chances they knew not where. But at length, admonished by the increasing numbers of pioneer settlers crowding upon their borders, they consented, in 1818, to cede their lands to the United States, reserving, however, the possession till 1820, at which time the last of the tribe were removed to their new home west of the Mississippi. As the red men went out at one door, the white moved in at the other, and at the close of the year 1820, there was no part of the New Purchase, afterwards organized into a county, in which the smoke from at least one adventurous pioneer's cabin did not ascend.

*By a census taken in 1875 the number of free white inhabitants was found to be 63,897.

In 1815 the first white man, a "jovial fiddler" as well as fearless hunter, founded a home within the present limits of Monroe County, and in the year following the first cabins were built on the present site of Bloomington. Early in 1818 Monroe County was organized, and in April of the same year Bloomington was staked out adjoining the Seminary township on the north.

For an inland town of that day, Bloomington grew rapidly from the first, a circumstance largely due to the nearness of the Seminary township. At the close of its first year it contained 140 inhabitants, living in thirty hastily constructed log cabins. In the following year its population was doubled. By 1820 the public square was cleared of the last of its native forest trees; the first log court house was outgrown, and Col. John Ketcham was at work on a brick edifice, which still stands in the public square, an enduring monument to honest workmanship.

The Constitution inhibited the General Assembly of the State from providing for the sale of any lands set aside for educational purposes for four years next after the organization of the State government. The Assembly which was to meet in December, 1820, in Corydon, was the first having the power to take another step toward the establishment of such a school of learning as the Congress of 1816 had in mind.

There is evidence of the fact that many of the educated men of the new State looked forward with interest to the time when legislative action could be had. The pioneer settlers of Indiana were poor men, and it was with the utmost difficulty that most of them were enabled to clear and make farms, and at the same time maintain themselves and families. In those days the number of children in most families within the school ages was large, and never in the history of the State has there been a time when there was such a pressing need for common schools, and never was there less ability to maintain them. The poverty of the people forbade an expenditure for school purposes in any manner commensurate with the wants of the times, nor were there any public funds to supplement their efforts; and worse than all, there were but few teachers in the new State whose moral and educational qualifications fitted them to become instructors of its youth. Founding a school on the plan of the college by the State would not add to the pecuniary ability of the people to maintain their "township schools," but would not such a school become a center of learning whence the young men of the State, fully equipped for the work, would go forth to take their places in the school-houses of the land? And would not the State the more surely, in after years, reap the reward coming through the influence of scholarly men in the walks of professional life? So reasoned the friends of higher education in Indiana in 1820.

The men of Bloomington, it may well be surmised, were ripe for legislative action as soon as it could be had. Not a few of them had been drawn to the new town by the reserved township, and it is not strange that they met late in the fall of 1819 and selected one of their number to represent them at the session of the Legislature, which was to meet early in the following December, to press upon the attention of the members the necessity of legislation in that behalf. Dr. David H. Maxwell was chosen for that service, and they could not have chosen a better man. As a delegate from Jefferson County he sat in the convention of 1816, and had therefore some legislative experience. He had a talent for politics, whence came an extensive acquaintance with the public men of the State. He was plausible, conciliatory, level-headed, and a good judge of human nature. That rare accomplishment of seeming to follow, while actually leading, he possessed in a high degree; and, above all, he was through and through a friend to higher education. This was the first service he was called upon to render an institution to the furthering of whose interests he was ever after devoted. For thirty years, of all men outside the circle of those engaged as teachers, he gave the most of his time in its service and to better purpose. It is not too much to say that during all that time the institution as Seminary, College and University (for he was with it from the inception of the first until it had passed into the last), was the center of his best thoughts, the object of his highest aims. Dr. Maxwell was an ambitious man, ambitious for place and power in the political world, but he seemed to have subordinated his highest ambitions to the welfare of his cherished institution. Is not such devotion worthy of remembrance? Is there not something worthy of high commendation in all this? I doubt if in all his work for Seminary, College and University he ever thought of self. His efforts were unselfishly directed. Let history do justice to his name. So unremitting was he in his labors and to such good purpose were they directed that it can be said of him, as of no other, he was the father of the Indiana University.*

Notwithstanding the legislative mind was favorable to the organization of a State school, there was wide difference of opinion when it came to the details of the plan, and to such an extent was this carried that when the bill went to the Senate it was saved by the casting vote of the Lieutenant Governor, Ratliff Boon. On the 20th of January, 1820, by the signature of Jonathan Jennings, the first Governor of the State, it became a law, and the STATE SEMINARY FOR THE STATE OF INDIANA was duly chartered. Six citizens of the State, Charles Dewey, Jonathan Lindley, David H. Maxwell, John M. Jenkins, Jonathan Nichols and William Lowe, were named as Trustees, and empowered to select a site for a Seminary, to provide for the sale of not exceeding 640 acres of the reserved land, and as soon as they thought it expedient to erect a "suitable building for a State Seminary, and also a suitable and commodious house for a professor."

On the first Monday in June four of the six Trustees met in Bloomington, in obedience to the law for the purpose of selecting a site for the Seminary, but on account of the absence of Dewey and Lindley, they adjourned over to a day in July, which the record does not name. On that unnamed day five members met and proceeded to choose a Seminary site "about a quarter of a mile due south from Bloomington, on a beautiful eminence, and convenient to an excellent spring of water, the only one on the section selected that could with convenience answer the purposes of a Seminary."

Over twenty months passed away before the work of building was actually begun. Everything was in the green, and while a round-log cabin, or even a hewed-log one, could be run up in a marvelously short time by the pioneers of 1820, the erection of a brick Seminary, or even a brick house for a professor, they found to be quite another thing. The two buildings were begun, however, and ultimately completed. The professor's house was erected in the southwest corner of the campus, at a cost of $891. The Seminary edifice, 60 feet long and 31 wide, stood on the high ground, well in toward the center of the campus. It was two stories in height, and when new was considered

*See a fuller notice of Dr. Maxwell preceding the list of Trustees.

quite a pretentious building. It fronted to the east, had a chapel and two recitation rooms below, and an equal number of rooms above. It cost $2,400, and must have been substantially built, for it stood for nearly half a century, being used the greater part of the time for the preparatory school, and being endeared to the memory of thousands of students who pursued their grammar studies therein. In 18— it was pulled down to make room for a more pretentious edifice.

By the fall of 1823 the seminary was so near completion that it was thought advisable to elect a professor and take such other steps looking to the beginning of educational work as should be deemed proper. Accordingly, on the 20th of November, the Rev. Baynard R. Hall, a native of Pennsylvania, but for nearly or quite a year living with friends on White river, not far from Gosport, was chosen at a salary of two hundred and fifty dollars per year. Two terms a year were provided for of five months each, and the tuition fees were fixed at five dollars per term, but at the end of a year were raised to ten.

The choice could hardly have fallen upon a worthier man. His academic education he had received at Union College and his theological at Princeton. He was an excellent classical scholar and a persuasive and sometimes eloquent preacher. As a teacher he was enthusiastic, faithful and painstaking. Into the frontier life of the White River settlement, in which his lot was cast for a time after he first came to the State, he entered with a zeal that soon brought him to know all its peculiarities, a knowledge that stood him many a good turn while at the head of the State seminary. He became a skilled marksman with the rifle, he learned the art of rolling logs, he took lessons in manners practiced at wood-chopping and quilting frolics, he was an interested looker-on at pioneer camp-meetings, he clerked in a country store, ground bark in a tannery, preached some, and was, he himself says, "the very first man since the creation of the world that read Greek in the new purchase."

On the first of May, 1824, the seminary doors were opened for the reception of students, and ten boys were admitted. These, the first to drink at the fountain of learning opened by the bounty of the State, were Findlay Dodds, James F. Dodds, Aaron Furgason, Hamilton Stockwell, John Todd, Michael

Hummer, Samuel C. Dunn, James W. Dunn, James A. Maxwell and Joseph A. Wright. All these lived to manhood and rendered efficient service to society, one as a tanner, one as a merchant, three as physicians, two as ministers of the gospel and three as lawyers, and the latter, Joseph A. Wright, attaining to the honorable position of Governor of Indiana, and subsequently to that serving his country in a diplomatic position in a foreign land.

To the reader of to-day the attendance at the beginning must seem small, and so of the attendance all through the seminary period. The first year the highest number was thirteen; the second, fifteen, and the third, twenty-one. This was indeed a slow growth, but we need not go far to find the cause. While the population of the State had increased rapidly, having mounted up to a half million in 1825, and was still going upward, the condition of the individual was but little if any better than it had ever been before. The great war with the trees was at its fiercest, and every man or boy able to swing an ax or "pick trash" was listed as a soldier. The old English rule, "All summer in the field and all winter in the study," universally prevailed as far as the summer was concerned. A part only of the winter was given to study in the log school houses of the State. There were few parents of that day able to give their sons opportunity for acquiring a better education than could be had in the district schools.

For three years Baynard R. Hall was the sole teacher in charge of the State Seminary, during all of which time Greek and Latin were the only branches taught. During the second year the Board of Trustees made an order requiring "English Grammar, Logic, Rhetoric, Geography, Moral and Natural Philosophy and Euclid's Elements of Geometry" to be taught; but we have the authority of the President of the Board, Dr. David H. Maxwell, in a report made to the General Assembly, for saying that "during the first three years the Greek and Latin languages alone were taught." Those were the days when everything was subordinated to the study of the classics. Every person making any pretence to learning could on occasion quote Latin. Most literary efforts abounded in classical allusions. The statesmen of the period interlarded their Congressional speeches with quotations from the Latin authors, and so did the Governors of Indiana, in their annual messages to the legislators of the State. The law books of the time are copious in Latin, and editors of newspapers even did not disdain now and then to instruct their readers by a sentence from a dead language woven into their more stately editorials. Baynard R. Hall was a classicist. He made no pretence to scholarship in any other line. During the seminary period, the year is not known, the students, with the aid of their professor, organized a literary society, for which he compounded a name, the *Henodelphisterian*. He prescribed certain rules for its government, one of which was that every person on becoming a member must drop his every day name and choose a Greek or Roman cognomen, by which he was ever after to be known while within the Henodelphisterian hall. Accordingly, every member of the society was an Ajax, a Pericles, a Timoleon, and so on.

As the end of the third year approached, it became evident that additional teaching force must be brought in. The older boys were wanting something else besides Greek and Latin, and moreover the twenty-one students of the third year promised to be thirty or forty the fourth, and so it was determined to elect an additional professor, one who could teach the Mathematics, pure and applied, and such of the natural sciences as in that day were deemed of sufficient importance to engage the attention of aspiring youth. Accordingly, on the 10th of May, 1827, John M. Harney, a recent graduate from the Miami University, was elected to the new professorship at a salary of two hundred and fifty dollars per year, and at once entered upon his duties.

The wisdom of the act was soon made manifest. The Seminary not only held its old students, but gained others. During the spring and summer term the number in attendance was twenty-six, but on the opening of the fall term "about forty students were present," and the number increased at such a rate that Dr. Maxwell was enabled to write in January, "there is a probability there will be fifty or sixty students in attendance before the close of the year."

The curriculum of studies in the Indiana Seminary was little, if any, less extensive, than in any of the western colleges of the day. Hall was a skillful teacher of the languages, while Harney had a genius for Mathematics. No records remain of classes; no records even of the names of students in attendance, but the few old men yet living who were students during Seminary times, all speak in glowing terms of the activity of the professors and the application of the students.

Early in the month of November, 1827, a Board of five visitors, of whom James B. Ray, the Governor of the State, was one, and James Scott, a Judge of the Supreme Court, was another, met in Bloomington. This Board had power to personally inspect the "studies and progress" of each student, and the work seems to have been thoroughly done. "Every scholar was critically examined in the different branches of education in which he had been engaged," and while the report does not in so many words say it, yet it is apparent that the professors were as "critically examined" as were the students, but in a different way. But professors, as well as students, stood the test. "The manner in which both teachers and scholars acquitted themselves" won their highest praise. "There was but one opinion among the visitors—that more ability to teach was exhibited by the professors and apparent proficiency by the scholars than ever before witnessed on a similar occasion." What more could have been said?

This Board examined into other things besides the ability of the professors to teach and the proficiency of students, one of which was the salaries paid to the professors, and they wisely came to the conclusion that a salary of two hundred and fifty dollars per year was not enough, and so they said to the Board of Trustees, which was in session at the same time, whereupon that Board raised the salary of each to four hundred dollars.

The Board of Visitors, through their President, Judge Scott, made their report to the next General Assembly, which met in the following December, Governor Ray made his report in his annual message, and Dr. Maxwell, the President of the Board of Trustees, and member of the House of Representatives, made his report, and all the reports concurred in recommending that the Indiana Seminary be raised to the dignity of a college.

Early in the session a bill was introduced having that end in view, which was finally passed and signed by the Governor; and thus, by legislative enactment, on the 24th day of January, 1827, seven years and four days after the Indiana State Seminary had been chartered, it was merged into Indiana College.

HISTORY OF THE COLLEGIATE DEPARTMENT OF INDIANA UNIVERSITY.

INDIANA COLLEGE AND UNIVERSITY UNDER DR. ANDREW WYLIE'S ADMINISTRATION.

Indiana College was, as already stated, established by an act of the Legislature, passed January 24, 1828. It was enacted by the General Assembly of the State of Indiana, "That there shall be, and hereby is, created and established a college adjacent to the town of Bloomington, in the county of Monroe, for the education of youth in the American* learned and foreign languages, the useful arts and sciences, and literature, to be known by the name and style of the Indiana College, and to be governed and regulated as hereinafter directed." To carry into effect this ordinance, a Board of Trustees and a Board of Visitors were appointed. Among the first acts of this Board, at its meeting in Bloomington, May, 1828, was the election of a President and two professors for the college. Andrew Wylie, D. D., President of Washington College, Pa., was chosen President.

It was at the beginning of the college year, October, 1829, having the year before visited Bloomington, that Dr. Wylie entered upon his duties, and the State Seminary became Indiana College. Dr. Wylie was also Professor of Moral and Mental Philosophy, Political Economy and Polite Literature. At the same time the Rev. Baynard R. Hall, the Principal of the Seminary, was elected Professor of the Ancient Language, and John H. Harney, teacher in the Seminary, Professor of Mathematics and Natural and Mechanical Philosophy and Chemistry, and Mr. W. H. Stockwell appointed Superintendent of the Prepar-

*In the early days the bitterness of feeling with regard to everything English had not altogether subsided, hence the term "American" in this connection.

atory Department. Soon after the organization of the college another larger and more convenient building was contracted for, but it was not completed till 1836.

In the first catalogue of the Institution, published in 1831, there is given, in addition to the list of students, the course of studies and something with regard to its management and discipline. "The studies are so conducted that each student gives his undivided attention to one principal study till it is completed. This method was adopted by the President under the full conviction, founded on twenty years' experience, that it possesses many and decided advantages over that which is pursued in most colleges, of blending together a variety of studies. During the whole course, however, special attention is given to Rhetorical Reading, Composition, Elocution and English Grammar, and the exercises in these become the more frequent as the student advances." This system was, no doubt, well adapted to minds like the President's, who had, in phrenological language, a great organ of concentrativeness, but not to the average minds of students, nor to the condition of things as they then existed. It was partially changed in 1840.

In these early times the students were required to assemble every morning for prayers, shortly after daybreak, and to receive such intimations concerning their duty as the President might deem necessary. "The strictest attention is expected of the students to the rules of morality and good manners, as well as to the performance of their stated college duties. As to matters of religion, particularly the manner in which students entrusted to their care should spend the Sabbath, the Faculty are guided in every case by the will of the parent or guardian. A decent respect, however, to the sentiments and practices of the religious world is, in all cases, expected and required. It is the special care of the Faculty to inculcate, by precept and example, the pure principles of Christianity, free from the narrow views of sectarianism and perversions of fanaticism, and so to train the minds of their pupils that they may cherish enlightened piety and benevolence toward men."

In 1836 the seventh commencement exercises were held in the new college building. This edifice was not remarkable for architectural beauty. It resembled somewhat, in its outward appearance, an old-fashioned New England cotton mill.

For about three years all things connected with the college went on harmoniously, but some trouble arising in the Faculty and among the students, the cause and nature of which it is unnecessary to inquire into, resulted in the diminution of the number of students, and the resignation of Professors Hall and Harney. This took place in 1832. The vacancies thus created were supplied by the election of Ebenezer N. Elliott, a graduate of Miami University, as Professor of Natural Philosophy and Chemistry, and of Beaumont Parks, a graduate of Dartmouth College, as Professor of Languages. James D. Maxwell, a graduate of Indiana College, succeeded W. H. Stockwell as principal of the Preparatory Department. After the resignation of Mr. Maxwell, Joseph G. McPheeters, assisted by M. M. Campbell, took his place in the Preparatory Department.

In 1835 Professor Elliott received an invitation to the Presidency of Mississippi College. This he accepted, taking with him Mr. Maxwell, the Principal of the Preparatory Department, and Mr. David M. Elliott, a late graduate. At the next meeting of the Board, the vacancies thus caused were filled by the appointment of James F. Dodds, a graduate of Indiana College, as Professor of Mathematics; Augustus W. Ruter, a graduate of Allegheny College, Pa., Professor of Greek and French; T. A. Wylie, a graduate of the University of Pa., Professor of Natural Philosophy and Chemistry, and William R. Harding, a graduate of Trinity College, Dublin, Ireland, Principal of the Preparatory Department. Prof. Harding died after a little more than a year's service in the college.

Many of the students who attended the college in these early days were young men brought up on farms, and used to hard work. They came to Bloomington, generally on their own resources, depending on money they had earned or borrowed. It was not unusual for students to attend to their studies for a year and then absent themselves for the same length of time in order to earn money by teaching, or otherwise, and returning, would complete their college course. Out of this kind of material have many of the graduates, and some who were not graduates, been made, who have done honor to their alma mater and their country.

To show the difference between the present and past times, a few interesting items as to the manner of living are here stated. In this thickly wooded country fuel was cheap. Fields cleared of their timber were what the farmer desired, and hence fire-wood cost only the labor to prepare it, and to deliver it to the consumer. Magnificent tulip-poplar trees, many of them from four to six feet in diameter, and rising to the height of sixty to eighty feet before branching, were *deadened* and left in the fields to rot, their destruction often being hastened by fire; and valuable walnut trees were used for firewood and fence rails, and so of other trees, in order that open fields might be obtained for the agriculturist. The wages of a laboring man were low; from thirty-seven and a half to fifty cents a day was considered a fair price.

In an old record book it was stated that Joseph A. Wright was allowed for ringing the bell, making fire, etc., during the last session in 1828 (the sessions were then five months long), $16.25. We find also that Joseph A. Wright could do a higher class of work than that. In the same record it is stated that he was allowed one dollar for repairing the top of one of the chimneys. This same Joseph A. Wright was in 1850 a much esteemed and highly popular Governor of Indiana, and afterwards was United States Minister at Berlin.

Living in these early times was not expensive. Boarding could be obtained in 1830 for from $1.00 to $1.25 a week; in 1837 from $1.50 to $2.00 a week; these prices included fuel. As late as 1852 the price of boarding in private families was from $1.25 to $1.75 a week. This will not appear strange if we notice the prices of provisions in these early days before the railroad had reached the town. Beef could be bought for from two to four cents a pound; pork as cheap or cheaper; butter seldom more than ten cents a pound; chickens cost from seventy-five to eighty cents a dozen; eggs two or three cents a dozen; twenty-five cents would buy a three-gallon bucketful of eggs; turkeys cost twenty-five cents apiece; venison hams the same price, and flour and meal cheap in proportion. Students who preferred to board themselves, or to *batch*, as they called it, could live well on seventy-five cents a week. All imported delicacies, such as *store* sugar, so called to distinguish it from maple sugar, and *store* tea, to distinguish it from sassafras, sometimes called "grub hyson," were comparatively high priced. These articles had to be brought from "the River," *i. e.*, the Ohio, in wagons, and it took from seven to ten days to make the trip.

In 1828, on account of the *high* price of boarding, some charging as much as $1.75 or $2.00 a week, a large brick building, two stories high, was erected near the southwest corner of the campus. This building was given, rent free, to a person who engaged to furnish boarding and lodging at a lower price than was asked in the town. The plan, however, did not work well. A boarding club was then formed. The students in the club catered for themselves, and employed all necessary help. The general supervision of the club was entrusted to Professor M. M. Campbell. Under his management the plan succeeded very well. It was, however, in a few years discontinued.

Bloomington, for many years of its early history, was an isolated place. It was about fifty miles from Terre Haute, the same distance from Indianapolis, forty miles from Columbus, the then terminus of the Madison & Indianapolis Railroad, and nearly a hundred miles from New Albany. There was, in these times, not even a turnpike road leading to it. It sometimes happened, in the beginning of winter, that the clay roads leading to it were rendered impassable by the rain and frost, and sometimes for two weeks there would be no communication between Bloomington, and we might say, the outside world. The tri-weekly Louisville and Indianapolis mail, established by Messrs. John and Samuel Orchard, would be stopped for that length of time. We find, in some of the old catalogues of the University, special directions given to the students from the South as to the best way to reach Bloomington. They might land at Leavenworth, and taking the stage there for Paoli, and thence by Orchard's stage line, reach Bloomington in three days; or landing at Louisville, and taking the stage there could get to the end of their journey in two days. When the railroad from Madison to Columbus was finished, landing at Madison they could reach Columbus by rail, and if they did not happen to meet the tri-weekly stage to Bloomington, they could hire a private conveyance that would take them to the end of their journey. When the New Albany & Salem Railroad was finished, it was announced that students from the South could take the railroad from New Albany to Salem, and thence to Bloomington it was only twelve hours. On the completion of the railroad to and through Bloomington to Michigan City, in 1855, there was comparatively easy access to the University from all quarters.

In the year 1838, on the 15th of February, by an act of the General Assembly of the State of Indiana, the University was chartered. This charter, with the proper changes made, is similar to that of the college. The Board of Trustees was to consist of twenty-one members, any ten of whom would make a quorum. If no quorum was present, the President of the University was to be considered as a member of the Board till the absent member appeared. The Governor of the State was made ex officio Vice President. Governor Wallace was expressly mentioned, as he was Governor at the time; he and his successors were to occupy this position forever. By this act of the Legislature the college ceased to exist, and all its property, rights and privileges were turned over to the University. There is no mention made of a Board of Visitors in the University charter, but in the act providing for the government of the University, approved June 17, 1852, the Governor, the Lieutenant Governor, Speaker of the House of Representatives, the Judges of the Supreme Court and Superintendent of Public Instruction, were made a Board of Visitors, any three of them making a quorum.

In 1838, the last year under the college charter, a member of the Board brought charges against the President for maladministration; the principal charge seems to have been with reference to the purchase of books for the Library. It was asserted that more money than had been appropriated by the Board had been spent, and improper books had been bought. The President, however, was fully acquitted, and was thanked by the Board for what he had done, instead of being censured. When the Board of Trustees of the University was appointed by the Legislature, the member of the Board who brought these charges was left out. The fomenter of all these troubles succeeded in some degree in producing disaffection among the students and in the Faculty. This affair was considered by the Board of sufficient importance to warrant the publication of an address by them to the people, which was written by the Hon. Robert Dale Owen. From it we extract the following:

"The causes which have cast a temporary cloud over the prosperity of the Institution are such as very commonly affect seminaries of learning at some period of their existence; especially such as are endowed by public funds, and are thus placed under the supervision of the State Legislature. Unhallowed ambition to subserve its own private ends has sought to excite both within and without the halls of legislation, dissentions, heart burnings, and prejudices against the University.

"It too frequently happens that men in pursuit of evil purposes exhibit an industry and perseverance that would do them honor in a good cause, and so it was in the case before us. An individual who had been, during the existence of Indiana College, for a time, one of its Trustees, and who on account of the factious disposition he exhibited in that capacity failed to obtain a reäppointment on the Board of the University, stung by what he regarded as an injury and believing that the President of the University had exerted influence to procure his exclusion, he openly avowed his determination either to be reïnstated in office, or if not reïnstated to visit upon the President, at whatever cost, the effects of his disappointment. A vacancy in the Board of the University occurred during its first session, and the individual in question aspired to the situation. Immediately before the Board went into the election it was plainly intimated to them that the aspirant to the vacancy pledged himself to bury in oblivion all animosities if elected; but if rejected then the Institution and the President might look to themselves and must suffer the consequences.

"The Board rejected this threatening candidate. He, however, kept his word. Not satisfied to create and foment jealousies and jarrings at home and not content to sow in the minds of the students the seeds of disaffection to their instructors and to villify the President by injurious epithets and unfounded insinuations, he proceeded in a more tangible way and official form to prosecute his attacks."

At the next meeting of the Legislature he presented a petition in which formal charges were preferred against Dr. Wylie. The Legislature, after some discussion, referred the matter back to the Board of Trustees for decision. In April, 1839, a special meeting of the Board was called; there were eleven members present; the Board continued a week in session; the Prosecutor was called to bring forward his charges, with their specifications. "The examination," in the words of the address "was conducted according to the forms and regulations of criminal prosecutions. The trial was open to the public; the witnesses regularly sworn, and when demanded by either party, subjected to cross examination. The Board continued to sit till the prosecutor and defendant had brought forward all the testimony they desired." It was at the close of this investigation that the prosecutor with much eloquence and feeling said, "Gentlemen, it would seem as things now stand, that the prosecutor has become the defendant and the defendant the prosecutor." This peroration was received with an audible smile by the Board.

"The testimony adduced during the investigation"—the address goes on to say—"was of so decided a character that no impartial jury in the State of Indiana (it may be confidently asserted) would have left the jury box without returning a verdict of acquittal."

The Board expressed their opinion of the result in the following resolutions:

"*Resolved*, That the Board of Trustees have patiently investigated the charges against Dr. Wylie, President of the University, of mal-administration, and having heard for several days the prosecutor and the voluminous testimony introduced by him, as well as the testimony of Dr. Wylie, come unanimously to the following conclusion, to-wit: That the four charges and their specifications: 1st, of duplicity; 2d, of neglecting or refusing to obey the requirements of the By-Laws; 3d, of arbitrary and ungentlemanly conduct; and, 4th, of misrepresentation and falsehood, are wholly unsubstantiated by proof, and, in the opinion of the Board, untrue."

"*Also, resolved*, That although the Board have declined to investigate, officially, the ten charges and specifications of mal-administration of the college, believing that they have no authority to reverse or modify any of the proceedings of the College Board, yet, from individual examinations of the college records, it does appear that the gravest charges against President Wylie, and particularly in regard to the purchase of books, etc., have been fully investigated by the Board, and the President's conduct not only approved of, but a vote of thanks to him recorded for his faithful agency in the affair."

"The above resolutions were adopted by the Board without a dissenting voice. Even the gentleman (still a member of the Board) who had authorized his name to be placed along with that of the prosecutor on the accusing petition, joined, after he had heard the evidence, in the unanimous and honorable acquittal of President Wylie of each and every charge that had been brought against him."

The Faculty in 1839 was reduced to three, the President and two professors, and in 1840 the number of students was 64.* The deficiency was supplied by the election of Lieut. Jacob Ammen, a graduate of West Point, who, on account of his excellency as a mathematician and draughtsman, had been appointed Assistant Professor in the department of Professor Davies, the Professor of Mathematics and Engineering. During the short stay of Professor Ammen in the University, in addition to the duties of his special department, he organized a military company, which drilled in the afternoon, when the weather permitted. Arms were furnished by the Government, and an armory fitted up for their reception. After the resignation of Professor Ammen the department continued for some time, but for want of a proper leader it was soon discontinued. The other vacancy in the Faculty, the Professorship of Languages, was supplied at the same time by the election of John I. Morrison, a graduate of Miami University, and at that time Principal of the Salem Seminary, and well-known as an excellent teacher and scholar.

At the close of the year 1838 the Professor of Natural Philosophy and Chemistry laid before the Board a paper presenting the wants of the department. In the existing buildings there were no conveniences for experimental illustration. The Board promptly replied to the suggestions, and arrangements were made for the erection of a suitable building. This building was ready for occupation a little over a year after the application had been made to the Board.

The number of students had increased from 64, in 1840, to 115 in 1843. In 1843, June 5th, Professor Ammen resigned, and on September 25th of the same year Professor Morrison Mr. Henry Tanner, a graduate of the class of 1842, was selected

---

*We should not despise the day of small beginnings. We present here the number of graduates of Yale College from the year 1702, as given in an old Catalogue in the University Library, for the first twenty years, and also for the same length of time from the year 1830, that of the first graduating classes of Indiana University:

Yale:		1702....6	1707....5	1712....2	1717....5
		1703....1	1708....3	1713....3	1718....13
		1704....3	1709....9	1714....9	1719....4
		1705....6	1710....2	1715....3	1720....11
		1706....3	1711....3	1716....3	1721....14
Indiana University:		1830....4	1835....4	1840....5	1845....8
		1831....3	1836....8	1841....5	1846....10
		1832....5	1837....10	1842....6	1847....5
		1833....3	1838....11	1843....8	1848....6
		1834....4	1839....7	1844....3	1849....7

to take charge of the Mathematical Department to the close of the college year, September 30. This position Mr. Tanner filled with credit to himself, and to the entire satisfaction of the Board of Trustees. On the resignation of Professor Morrison, Professor Daniel Read, of Ohio University, was unanimously elected to fill the vacancy. On the following day Professor Alfred Ryors, of the same institution, was elected Professor of Mathematics and Civil Engineering.

All things in the management of the college affairs went on smoothly for several years thereafter. The members of the Faculty acted harmoniously, and the number of the students gradually increased. In 1842 a long-continued effort on the part of the Board of Trustees to establish a law school as a department of the institution was finally crowned with success by the election of Judge David McDonald Professor of Law, and his acceptance of the position. Thence, and for many years, the law school continued to increase the number of students in attendance upon the institution.*

We now revert to the closing years of President Wylie's administration.

Dr. Ryors, the Professor of Mathematics and Engineering, received an invitation from Ohio University to return as its President. This invitation Professor Ryors accepted. The Faculty and the Board expressed their estimation of the Professor by conferring upon him the degree of Doctor of Divinity. On the resignation of Dr. Ryors, Professor McCartney, of Easton, Pennsylvania, was elected in his place. Professor McCartney did not accept. Charles Marshall, a young man educated at the University of Virginia, received a *pro tem.* appointment. Mr. Marshall came highly recommended by Professor Courtenay, of the Mathematical Department of the University of Virginia, and formerly Professor of Engineering and Physics in the Military Academy, West Point, and Dr. William H. McGuffey, formerly of Ohio University, then of University of Virginia. In the minutes of the Board, in 1850, there is a notice to this effect: "That the Board, as yet, had not been able to judge of the propriety of confirming the *pro tempore* appointment of Professor Marshall, as there was but a bare quorum present." It is well remembered by the writer that

---

*For a particular notice of the law school see further on, at the close of the history of the Col. Dept. of the University.

when Professor Marshall appeared in Bloomington one at least of the Professors was by no means pleased with his youthful appearance. He was then not quite twenty years old, and not large for his age. This displeased professor thought that so young a person in the Faculty and among students, many of them several years older than himself, would not do. But the youthful professor soon showed himself equal to the occasion. Piqued, perhaps, at the cool reception, he tendered his resignation October 3, 1850. This resignation was accepted, and Professor Larabee, of Greencastle, was elected Professor of Mathematics, and a resolution* highly commendatory of Professor Marshall passed by the Board. The Board was soon after informed that Professor Larabee could not immediately accept, and asked the delay of a year. Professor Marshall was then earnestly requested to remain another year at least. This he consented to do.

The year 1850 opened auspiciously. There were in attendance about a hundred and sixty students in all the departments at the commencement of the college year September 22, 1850. About the first of November, Dr. Wylie had been taking his accustomed exercise with his axe in the woods, nearly a mile away from his dwelling, when he accidentally cut his foot. Unable to help himself, after bleeding and suffering for some time, some person passing in a carriage found him and took him home. The wound was properly attended to, and in a day or two he procured crutches, and contrary to the remonstrances of family and friends, he went to the college and attended to his classes. On Friday, he delivered, according to appointment, a lecture to the Agricultural Society of the town. He remained in the college till the time for the lecture in the afternoon. After the lecture he was quite exhausted; he expressed his thankfulness that he would now have two days rest. On Sunday evening symptoms of pneumonia appeared and on Tuesday morning following he breathed his last.† The formal announcement was made by Dr. Read, to the students on Wednesday, and on the following day the Faculty and students and a

---

*The following is the resolution of the Board passed on the occasion of Professor Marshall's resignation: "*Resolved*, That the Board had received with regret the resignation of Professor Marshall, and desire now to express to that gentleman, in the strongest terms their high sense of his merits and his services while acting as Professor of Mathematics in the University." This resolution was unanimously passed.

† See fuller account in the sketch of Dr. Wylie.

large concourse of friends and citizens followed the body to the grave. On the day after the funeral of the President, Dr. Read addressed the students assembled in the chapel and announced the arrangements made for carrying on the work of the University. The classes of the President were taken by Professor Read, in addition to work in his own department. The Freshman class was taken by Professor Wylie in classical studies, in addition to his ordinary work. All the Professors heartily coöperated in this division of labor, calling for no outside help, in order that the bereaved family of the President, if the Board should so order it, might receive the salary for the collegiate year, which had just commenced at the time of his death.

REORGANIZATION OF THE BOARD OF TRUSTEES BY THE LEGISLATURE, AND PRESIDENCY OF DR. RYORS.

In accordance with an act to reorganize the Board of Trustees of Indiana University, defining their powers and their duties, and providing for the election of a President and other officers, and pointing out their powers and duties, approved February 16, 1852, the following persons were present and installed in office as Trustees of the University by the President of the former Board, as required by law, viz.: John I. Morrison, George Evans, Michael Malott, Patrick J. R. Murphy, Thomas M. Adams, Nathaniel Browning, Johnston McCullough and Joseph G. McPheeters. Joseph G. McPheeters was chosen President. The Board then elected Dr. James D. Maxwell, Secretary of the Board, and Joseph M. Howe, Treasurer of the University. Among the first acts of this Board, at its first meeting in April, 1852, was to pass unanimously the resolutions expressing their high appreciation of the late President, and their regret at the loss the University had sustained, and their sympathy for the bereaved family.

In the Faculty report made at this meeting of the Board, several suggestions were made with regard to the condition of the University and its future prospects, presenting those measures and improvements to which public opinion most plainly points, and which, if adopted, will most fully meet the demand and wishes of the friends of education in Indiana, and most certainly commend the University to the favor and fostering care of the Legislature.

At this meeting of the Board, April 10th, 1852, John H. Lathrop, LL. D., Chancellor of Wisconsin University, was unanimously elected President to fill the vacancy caused by Dr. Wylie's death. At the June meeting of the Board, a letter was read from Dr. Lathrop, declining the acceptance of the position. At the close of the April meeting of the Board, Professor Wylie was made Superintendent of the University buildings and adjacent grounds, and the Faculty was requested to make him also their Chairman and acting President of the University till the President elect shall enter upon the duties of his office. At the request of the acting President, Judge McDonald delivered the Baccalaureate at the July Commencement. He took as his subject the "True Man," and made its application in the close to the late President.

The Board, after receiving the declination of Dr. Lathrop, elected Henry Barnard, LL. D., of Connecticut, President, and on the contingency of his not accepting, Rev. Dr. Alfred Ryors, President of Ohio University, was elected to take the place.*

Before referring to the recommendations of the Faculty with regard to the improvements to be made in the college curriculum, the committee of the Board state that they can not avoid an expression of their gratification at the prompt, faithful and judicious manner in which the Faculty acted in the painful emergencies in which they were severally placed by the decease of the President, and for the onerous labors which they cheerfully assumed without any extra charge to the University; the Board owe the expression of their approbation in strong and decided terms. The labors, particularly, of Professor Read, in attending to the whole studies of the Senior and Junior classes in the President's department, and of Professor Wylie in hearing the recitations of the Freshman class in Latin and Greek, (in addition to the duties of their own departments) ought not to be passed over without notice and approval. That in keeping up the recitations and all the public exercises of the University, the conduct of the Faculty is a valuable precedent in future contingencies which may arise, and in the opinion of the committee, merits the notice and commendation of the Board of Trustees.

---

* It is stated in the Annual Report, 1851-2, that a letter was received from Mr. Barnard, not long before the close of the term, in which he says that he was completely incapacitated for all bodily or mental labor by being thrown out of a carriage, and that there was no prospect of his being able to act or even to think for some time to come, and that he must therefore in justice to himself and the University, decline the appointment.

The committee, also, in accordance with the suggestions of the Faculty, recommended each of the following measures as calculated to render the University more useful and more popular:
1. A course of agricultural chemistry.
2. A normal seminary, with department for males and females.
3. Theoretical and practical engineering.
4. The adoption of a regular graduation of that class of students who take what is called the scientific course.

A committee consisting of John F. Morrison, Patrick J. R. Murphy and Joseph G. McPheeters, was appoined, and, on motion, Mr. Morrison was selected by the unanimous consent of the Board to present the subject to the Legislature.

In accordance with this resolution, Mr. Morrison presented the report at its session in 1852, then assembled. On the 3d of June he reported the presentation of the report, and that the Senate had ordered a thousand copies to be printed.*

In accordance with the report and recommendation of the Faculty, the Board of Trustees, having now the legal sanction, resolved that a Normal Seminary for males and females be established in connection with the University, and that a room be fitted up for a model school, as subservient to the Normal. It was also resolved that —— sum be appropriated, to be expended in purchasing a building for the use and accommodation of the Female Department of the Normal Seminary, and that a Department of Civil Engineering is hereby established in connection with the Chair of Mathematics.

In accordance with the resolution of the Faculty, a Normal Department was established. Dr. Reed, by the appointment of the Faculty and resident Trustees, undertook its management. Auxiliary to the Normal, certain rooms in the old Seminary Building were fitted up for the model school, and placed under the charge of (now Rev.) J. C. Smith, a graduate of the University. During the first year of the Normal Department there was an attendance of thirty-seven, fifteen of these females. The resolution of the Board to establish a separate Female Department of the Normal School was rescinded in

---

*In Laws and Regulations concerning Indiana University from 1827 to 1878, on p. 46, the act which grew out of this report is presented. On pp. 50 and 51 will be found the law with reference to the Normal Department and the Department of Agricultural Chemistry.

August, 1853. Not long after a resolution was passed to make the Monroe County Female Seminary, then under the care of Mrs. E. J. McFerson, its accomplished Principal, the Female Normal Seminary of the University. This resolution was never carried into effect. After the resignation of Professor Read in 1856, the Normal Department was discontinued, and in the following year the model school. The model school was hard to manage. The pay of the teachers was insufficient; hence it was impossible to retain competent instructors. It had a change of teachers nearly every year of its existence.*

Dr. Barnard not accepting the offered Presidency of the Institution, Dr. Ryors, President of Ohio University, who had been elected as contingent, became the President of Indiana University.

The prospects of the University were at this time very gloomy. To its most hopeful friends it looked as if the time was nigh at hand when its doors must be closed for want of funds. A long and tedious litigation, in which a considerable part of the endowment of the Institution was at stake, had come to an end, and that adversely to it, a brief account of which it is deemed proper to herewith give.

In 1804, while Indiana was still under territorial control, an act of Congress had reserved a township of land in Vincennes Land District for sale for the use of a seminary of learning. That township was two years afterward located in what is now known as Gibson County, and about the same time the Territorial Legislature incorporated the Vincennes University, appointing Trustees therefor, and empowering them to sell not exceeding 4,000 acres of the reserved lands. By virtue of this authority, the Trustees sold the land, and with the proceeds "erected a large, commodious and appropriate brick building" for college purposes, and then the matter stopped. No school was opened in the Institution under the control of the Board or by its direction.

It was an opinion shared in by many that under the act of 1804 the Gibson County township was to be considered as a mere reservation of land, and not a grant, and that the act of the Territorial Legislature incorporating the Vincennes University was without authority of law.†

---
*The teachers in the model school were J. C. Smith, 1852-54; A. L. Gilbert, 1854-55; D. Eckley Hunter, 1855-56, and Hiram Riddile, 1856-57.
†This was the view taken by Chief Justice Taney, of the U. S. Supreme Court, on the final adjudication, as appears from his dissenting opinion in 14 How., 27 p.

It was further an opinion that the enabling act of 1816, under which Indiana was admitted into the Union, granted to the new State the Gibson County lands. But if this were not true, it was argued that the Vincennes University had forfeited its charter by *non user;* and so the General Assembly, at the same session the act establishing the State Seminary was passed, appointed an agent to rent the Gibson County lands, and account for the rents to the State. Two years afterward the agent was empowered to sell the lands, and proceeds to be appropriated to the use of the Seminary. Other acts and laws were from time to time passed, all looking to the same end; and the lands were ultimately sold, the proceeds going to swell the endowment fund of the State Institution.

Thus matters continued up to 1838, when as many of the old Trustees of the Vincennes University as could be got together met and reorganized the Board by the election of officers. Six years thereafter they caused actions of ejectment to be commenced, in the Gibson County Circuit Court, against occupants of the land sold by the State. These legal proceedings are said to have created great feeling throughout Gibson County, and the General Assembly, in 1846, to relieve occupants of lands holding by titles derived from the State, passed an act authorizing one suit to be brought against the State, in the Marion Circuit Court, and providing further, that in event the judgment should be in favor of the Vincennes Board, would relinquish all claim to so much of the land as the State had sold, while the State would set apart to such Board of Trustees the funds derived from the sale of said township of land, as, also, the amount yet due of unpaid purchase money.

In accordance with this act an action was begun in the Marion Circuit Court, which resulted in a finding in favor of the Trustees of Vincennes University, and fixing the amount of the proceeds of the sales of the lands sold by the authority of the State at the sum of $30,099.96, and judgment was entered accordingly. The case was appealed to the Supreme Court of the State, and thence to the Supreme Court of the United States, and thence going back again to the Supreme Court of the State, where a final judgment was rendered in 1854, sustaining the judgment of the court below. The following General Assembly of the State assuming the payment of the debt by an act approved February 13, 1856, the troublesome question was forever put to rest, and the endowment saved to the State Institution.

This decision of the Court was regarded at the time as very injurious if not ruinous to the Indiana University. The effect showed itself in the diminished number of students, and in the general despondency produced.* The Faculty at this time coöperating with Dr. Ryors in the management of the Institution was as follows: Dr. Daniel Read, Professor of Languages. Rev. R. Milligan, Professor of Natural Philosophy and Chemistry, to which chair he had been called on the resignation of Professor Wylie, who had accepted a position in the Miami University, Oxford, Ohio. On the transfer of Professor Milligan, Professor M. M. Campbell was chosen Adjunct Professor of Languages and Principal of Preparatory Department, and Mr. J. Calvin Smith, A. M., head master of the lately organized Model school, and Mr. James Woodburn, a graduate of class 1842, and a well-known and competent teacher of Bloomington, was appointed acting Professor of Mathematics and Civil Engineering. Everything went on as prosperously as could be expected under the circumstances during the year of President Ryors' administration. President Ryors resigned August 3, 1853.

On July 31, a few days before Dr. Ryors' resignation, Dr. William M. Daily, who was then a member of the Board of Trustees, announced to the Board then in session, that Governor Wright, a member of the Board of Visitors, would be pleased to confer with them whenever it would suit their convenience. Dr. Daily was appointed to invite the Governor to meet with them on the following Monday. On the next Tuesday Dr. Daily handed in his resignation as Trustee to the Board, resigning, as he stated, for reasons satisfactory to himself. His place was immediately filled by the election of Cyrus L. Dunham, of Brownstown, who happened to be in town. On August 3, Governor Wright reported to the Board that he had had a conference for more than an hour with Dr. Ryors, and that the Doctor had no communication to make to the Board. On the evening of the same day the President of the Board laid before that body the resignations of the following members of the Fac-

---

* But the subsequent action of the Legislature restored confidence, and the supposed disaster proved the beginning of a new era of prosperity.

ulty: Dr. Ryors, President; Dr. Read, Professor of Languages; Mr. Milligan, Professor of Natural Philosophy. These resignations were accepted.

The Board, on the resignation of Dr. Ryors, passed the following resolution:

Resolved, That we deem this a proper occasion to tender to Dr. Ryors assurances of our highest respect for him as a scholar, instructor and as a christian gentleman, and that *we are fully satisfied with the manner in which he has discharged his duties as President of the University and as a Professor of Moral and Mental Philosophy;*

Resolved, That the Secretary be directed to furnish Dr. Ryors a copy of the foregoing resolution.

The Board then proceeded to fill the vacancies caused by these resignations.

DR. DAILY'S ADMINISTRATION.

On August 3, 1853, immediately after the resignation of Dr. Ryors, Dr. William M. Daily was chosen President of the University.

The professors for the vacant chairs were then chosen *viva voce.* Dr. Read was elected Professor of Languages; Dr. Ryors, Professor of Mathematics and Engineering; Professor Milligan, Professor of Natural Philosophy and Chemistry. Committees were appointed to inform these gentlemen of their election, and in a short time it was reported that all had accepted. But Dr. Ryors' name does not hereafter appear as connected in any way with the University. At this meeting Judge McDonald, Professor of Law, handed in his resignation. The Board, after expressing their regret that Judge McDonald deemed it necessary to resign, elected Judge James Hughes to fill the vacancy.

Professor Campbell resigned April 5, 1854. On the ground of his long and faithful services in the University, the Board granted him the privilege of sending his sons to the University free of tuition during his natural life. On Professor Campbell's resignation, James Woodburn was elected Adjunct Professor of Languages and Principal of the Preparatory Department, which position he held till his death, Sepember 8, 1865.

The inauguration of Dr. Daily was deferred till the next Commencement, and Governor Wright was invited to deliver the inaugural charge.

Everything went on prosperously till April 11, 1854, when the new college building, as it was then called, already re-referred to, was burnt. The fire occurring in the night, and during the vacation, when no one was in the building, many of the citizens knew nothing of it till the morning. This destruction seemed like a death blow to the University. Its small, though valuable, library, its chapel, recitation rooms, the neatly fitted up Philomathean and Athenian Society halls, with their libraries and furniture, had in the course of a few hours been annihilated—nothing left but rubbish and ashes. Though all connected with the University were distressed by this catastrophe, they were not disheartened or discouraged. When the question was proposed, "What shall we do?" the unanimous answer from Trustees, Faculty, students and citizens was "Rebuild, and put the University in a better condition than it ever was before." We find in an excellent address* delivered to the Philomathean Society by Dr. Reed, August 5, 1856, about two years after the fire, reference made to the conduct of the students on that occasion..

The professor referred to that *esprit de corps*, that community of feeling, without which no body of men can be effective—as the very life of our colleges, the element of their success.

He goes on to say: "When that old college building, uncomely in aspect though it may have been, but around which clustered so many sacred associations; when your society halls, adorned with so much taste from the savings of your pocket money; when your society libraries, collected with so much pains; when the college library, were all lying in the ashes—not a book saved; when dismay sat upon the countenances of all good citizens in that dark hour, some of you of this Senior class and of the two preceding ones, met with a little band of other students and sent forth to your fellow-students, then scattered in different parts of the State, the rallying call, and soon the response came back from Lafayette, from Terre Haute, from Evansville, from New Albany: 'We will to the last stand by our cherished alma mater.'" This first gave the assurance of hope that all was not lost.

---

*See also the eloquent reference to this catastrophe in the close of Dr. Daily's inaugural address.

Here follows an extract from the appeal which this noble band of young men sent forth to their fellow-students. It is dated April 12, 1854, shortly after the fire:

"At a meeting of the students remaining in Bloomington during the present vacation, a committee was appointed to address you in relation to the great calamity which has befallen our beloved *alma mater*.

"The main University edifice, with the chapel, where we have so often met, and our beautiful society halls and our libraries, are a smouldering mass of ruins.

"It is with sad hearts that we turn our eyes to the blackened walls, where clusters so many pleasant recollections of the past. You will, with us, be deeply afflicted by the tidings of this, our common misfortune.

"But the question arises, What shall we do as students? We are directed by the unanimous voice of those at this meeting to say to you, it is our resolution to remain as students of Indiana University. We will never desert her in this, her hour of trial."

Again, with a prophecy which has proved reality, they say:

"We have no doubt this calamity will be made the beginning of a greater prosperity than ever to the Indiana University.

"Let us, fellow-students, not be wanting; we can nowhere have better advantages. Let us be present and partake in the energy and spirit which this event awakens. Come, and bring with you as many others as possible."

We may safely say had there not been this *esprit de corps* of the students, Trustees, Faculty and citizens, the days of the University of Indiana would have been numbered. By the Vincennes suit the University had lost nearly $70,000. The State had not yet assumed this loss; its main college building had been burnt, and the land grant made in February 23, 1854, was not yet available, and we believe was very far from covering the loss sustained. These calamities almost simultaneously crowding upon the University were enough to discourage and destroy all hopes of resuscitation. But the Trustees, at their meeting not long after the fire (April 27, 1854), showed that they were neither discouraged or disheartened. Among their first acts was that there should be a Building Committee to superintend the reconstruction of the main college edifice, to consist: First, a part of the Board, of Messrs. John I. Morrison, Thomas M. Adams, Johnson McCullough; secondly, of the Faculty, of President Daily, Professors Read and Milligan, and of the citizens, John Orchard. *Resolved, further,* As soon as the plan of the building is determined upon, and the citizens of Bloomington and others have made a subscription of ten thousand dollars, and tendered the same to the Board through their committee, the Building Committee shall immediately make contracts for building, and shall select a competent superintendent. The cost of the new building was not to exceed eighteen thousand dollars; the President of the Board was to find a competent architect, which he did; the services of Mr. W. .Tinsley were secured for this purpose, and his proposed plan and elevation adopted.

At the meeting of the Board on April 27, 1854, a committee was appointed to prepare a scheme of scholarships. This committee, consisting of Messrs. Jenckes, McPheeters and Malott, made their report. The scholarships were so arranged that those paying one hundred dollars were entitled to a perpetual scholarship in the Preparatory and Academical Departments; those paying fifty dollars had in the same departments a scholarship for four years, and those paying twenty-five dollars a scholarship for two years. The subscriptions that had been made by the citizens, or should hereafter be made, were made convertible into scholarships. Money was borrowed and property mortgaged, and the building, considering time and place, was completed within a reasonable time. It was expected to hold the Commencement August, 1855, in the new building, but by some delay they were disappointed. The first Commencement in it took place August 6, 1856, and the whole building finished was formally dedicated November 30, 1856, by President Daily.

During the first two or three years of the Presidency of Dr. Daily there were many changes in the Faculty. The College, however, flourished, increasing in numbers and popularity. The President was indefatigable in his efforts to rebuild and maintain the standing of the University.

Professor Milligan resigned July, 1854, on account of sickness in his family, much to the regret of his associates in the Faculty and the citizens generally. General Ammen, at that time Professor in Bacon College, Kentucky, was elected to succeed Professor Milligan. Professor Ammen accepted, but remained only a short time and then returned to Georgetown, Kentucky. In 1854, Professor Elisha Ballantine, of Ohio University, was elected Professor of Mathematics, and on April 28, his letter of acceptance was received by the Board. Professor Ballantine succeeded Professor Milligan, who had been transferred from the chair of Mathematics to the chair of Natural Philosophy, on the resignation of Professor Wylie. At a called meeting of the Board April, 1855, Professor Wylie, then Professor in Miami University, was recalled to his former position, vacated by the resignation of Professor Ammen. The valuable donation of books made by Mr. Henry W. Derby, a well-known bookseller and publisher of Cincinnati, by which the loss of the small but valuable library, lately destroyed by fire, was almost replaced, is worthy of grateful mention. President Daily received from him the following letter:

"SEPTEMBER 25, 1855.
"*Rev. Wm. M. Daily, D. D., President of Indiana University.*

"DEAR SIR—Upon a recent visit to Bloomington, the calamity which had befallen the University in the total destruction of its library, was brought to my attention. In aid of repairing a loss so serious to an institution of learning, I beg you to select from our general catalogue of books to the amount of fifteen hundred dollars, which are hereby placed to your order.

"Respectfully, your obedient servant,
"H. W. DERBY."

The Faculty on receipt of this letter, passed the following resolution: "The thanks of the Faculty is hereby tendered to Mr. Derby for this generous and timely gift, the first of its kind made to the University since the great calamity in the destruction of its library. It was also directed that when the new library should be fitted up, there should be a special alcove devoted to its reception." The books were selected principally by Drs. Daily and Read and all labeled, "The Derby Donation." A valuable donation of law-books, made by a citizen of Fort Wayne, W. H. Jones, Esq., is also worthy of honorable mention. The exact number is not remembered, but it was not less than two hundred. Many of them were folios, some running back to the reign of Charles I, nearly all referring to old English laws.*

Dr. Read, Professor of Languages, presented his resignation December 4, 1855. During his connection with the University, his diplomacy and energy, particularly during the troubles arising from law-suits and the burning of the main building of the University, together with his excellence as a scholar and teacher, called forth from the Board a strong expression of regret and an earnest request from the Board that he would remain at least another year in the University. Dr. Read consented to remain. Professor Butler, of Wabash College, who had been elected Dr. Read's successor, did not accept, and Professor Ballantine was transferred from the chair of Mathematics to that of Languages. At this juncture, the name of Professor Daniel Kirkwood, then President of Newark College, Delaware, was presented for the chair of Mathematics. He accepted and thus all vacancies were filled. Professor Kirkwood did not take his place as a member of the Faculty till the last day of October, 1856, the preceding part of the term being filled satisfactorily by the temporary appointment of the Rev. Henry W. Ballantine, now of Orange, New Jersey.

After the vacancies in the Faculty had been thus satisfactorily filled the number of students gradually increased, and all things went on harmoniously to the close of Dr. Daily's Presidency.

On account of some untoward circumstances, resulting in a trial in an ecclesiastical court, in which charges were brought against Dr. Daily, and a popular clamor excited, which he feared might be injurious to the University, he handed in his resignation, January 27, 1859, which was accepted, and the following resolutions passed:

"*Resolved,* In view of the constant and untiring services rendered by Dr. Daily to the University, out of the proper sphere of his official duty, and made necessary by the calamity to which it was subjected by the destruction of its building and library, and the embarrassments resulting therefrom, he be, and is hereby allowed the sum of seven hundred dollars in addition to his regular salary, in full of such services."

---

*This very valuable collection of law-books of the 17th and 18th centuries, together with the extensive collection of the University, were totally lost in the fire of 1883.

"*Resolved*, That it is due to Dr. Daily to say that during the time of his connection with the University his administration thereof has met with our warmest and most cordial approbation."

Soon after, by a resolution of the Board, Prof. T. A. Wylie was directed to act as temporary President, and the Faculty was authorized to employ such assistance as may be necessary, and within their means.

The exercises of the University were conducted as usual after the resignation of its late President. About a dozen of the students, who were much attached to him, withdrew from the University, having called for honorable dismissals, which were granted. Indeed, nearly all the students were very much attached to the retiring President on the ground of his kindly disposition, and the interest he took in their welfare. It was widely circulated at this time that the University was fast falling into ruins, and soon there would be nothing of it left. Notwithstanding these predictions and efforts, stimulated by repeated visits of the ex-President, his friends within and without the University did not succeed in accomplishing their object. With rather more than ordinary manifestations of disorder and insubordination the storm was weathered, the commencement came, the degrees were conferred, and the Baccalaureate address delivered by the acting President.* During the last half of the college year (1858–59) the Rev. Caleb Blood, A. M., was appointed by the Faculty *pro tem*. Professor of Mental and Moral Philosophy and Belles Lettres, which position he filled to the satisfaction of all concerned, Messrs. Noah S. Given, A. B., and William T. Moffett, A. B., giving general assistance as tutors.

THE PRESIDENCY OF DR. LATHROP.

On July 13, 1859, John H. Lathrop, LL. D., was elected President of the University. As the records of the University after this date were destroyed by fire in 1883, what remains to be presented will depend on the annual reports, the Faculty minutes from 1859 to the present time, printed documents of va-

---

*The number of the students as given in the catalogue for the years 1859 and 1860 are 231 and 203. Leaving out the Law Department, which was not so much interested in these matters, the reduction in numbers was only 11.

rious kinds, and memory. Dr. Lathrop took his seat as President of the University September 20, 1859. At this time the turbulent spirit of the preceding year had disappeared, and a good spirit among the students generally prevailed. The Faculty, with the exception of the President, Professor Blood and the tutors, remained the same as in the preceding year. Professor Henry Bascom Hibben, A. M., had, at the last meeting of the Board in 1859, been elected Professor of Logic, Rhetoric and Belles Lettres. He took his seat as member of the Faculty January 6, 1860. Messrs. Charles Campbell, A. B., John H. Wilson and James C. Elliott were tutors, and Professor E. Marquis, Instructor in German, French and Hebrew. Dr. Lathrop delivered his Baccalaureate July 6, 1860. A few days after, July 11, the inauguration of the President took place. Governor Willard, his friend and former pupil, delivered the address of investiture, and Dr. Lathrop his inaugural, and before the adjournment of the Board, then in session, Dr. Lathrop resigned, having been connected with the college only one year. He accepted an invitation to a professorship in Missouri University, of which he had been the first President, serving there from 1842 to 1849, and then leaving because his views on the slavery question, which then was becoming a prominent subject in the political field, did not harmonize with the popular sentiment of that community.

THE PRESIDENCY OF DR. CYRUS NUTT.

Soon after the resignation of Dr. Lathrop, and before the Board had adjourned its annual meeting, Dr. Cyrus Nutt, of Greencastle, was elected President. The President-elect first met the Faculty, August 16, 1860, and arrangements were made for general college work during the next term. It was not till June 7, 1861, that his inauguration took place, Governor Oliver P. Morton making the address of investiture, and Dr. Nutt delivering his inaugural.

Dr. Nutt entered upon his duties amid favorable circumstances. In 1860 the number in the four regular classes (not counting the law students and Preparatory Department) was 99; in 1861, 112; in 1863, reaching the minimum, 67; then gradually rising till, in 1869, the number was 182.

In 1860 the Faculty consisted of the following persons: Dr. Nutt, President; Professors Ballantine, Wylie, Kirkwood, Woodburn; Judge Bryant, Professor of Law; H. B. Hibben, lately elected Professor of English Language and Literature, and E. Marquis, Professor of Modern Languages and Literature.

By a law approved May 11, 1861, the State Geologist, while he holds his office, was made a member of the Faculty of the University, and was directed to collect duplicate specimens of mineralogy and geology in his reconnoissances of the State, and deposit one set of the same in the cabinet of the State University. Professor Richard Owen was the first to receive this honorary appointment, and Professor E. T. Cox succeeded him as State Geologist and as a member of the Faculty.

At the close of the year 1861 Professor H. B. Hibben resigned his professorship and entered the army as a Chaplain. In 1854 he was appointed Chaplain in the Navy by President Lincoln, which position he still (1887) holds.

In 1863 Colonel Richard Owen, of New Harmony, then in the army, was elected to the Chair of Natural Philosophy and Chemistry. In the same year Professor E. Ballantine resigned, having accepted the position of Department Secretary of the American Board of Foreign Missions, and Professor M. M. Campbell, formerly Adjunct Professor of Languages, was invited by the resident members of the Board to take the vacated place *pro tem*. At the next meeting of the Board, Professor James D. Butler, of Wisconsin University, was again invited to the vacant chair. He, however, declined. The chair of Languages being thus vacated, Professor Wylie was transferred to the same, and Professor Owen was made Professor of Physics and Chemistry. This arrangement continued till 1868.

In 1866 Professor Kirkwood accepted the Professorship of Mathematics and Astronomy in Washington and Jefferson College, Pensylvania, and Prof. Cyrus M. Dodd, then of Washington and Jefferson College, was elected Professor of Mathematics in Indiana University. The next year Professor Kirkwood returned to Bloomington and resumed his former position in the University, and Professor Ballantine returning about the same time, was elected Professor of Greek Language and Literature, and Prof. C. M. Dodd of the Latin Language and Literature.

The Department of Ancient Languages being thus filled, Professor Wylie was made Professor of Natural Philosophy, and Dr. Owen, Professor of Natural Science and Chemistry.

In 1867 a Professorship of English Literature and the Theory and Practice of Teaching was established, and in 1868 the Hon. Geo. W. Hoss, late Superintendent of Public Instruction, was elected to that chair, and entered upon his duties in the following year, 1869. In 1871 Professor Hoss accepted a position as President of the Kansas Normal School, in Emporia. In 1871 he was recalled to Indiana University, to the Professorship of English Literature and Elocution, which he occupied till 1880.

Among the interesting events occurring during the administration of Dr. Nutt were the efforts made by the President, and other friends of the University, to locate the Agricultural College in Bloomington, in connection with the Indiana University.

By an act of Congress, of July 2, 1862, public lands belonging to the United States were donated to the several States and Territories which may provide colleges for the benefit of agriculture and the mechanic arts. This national grant was accepted by Indiana, March 6, 1865, and a Board of Trustees, with corporate name of the Trustees of the Indiana Agricultural College, was organized. Governor Morton was *ex officio* President. This Board received the land scrip of 390,000 acres, and sold it for $212,238.50, April 9, 1867. By careful management, this fund was increased to $340,000, and invested in non-negotiable State bonds bearing 5 per cent. interest, to be paid quarterly.

This was the prize for which the Indiana University contended. The cause of the University was ably advocated by many of its friends. Among others, President Nutt presented its plea very forcibly to the Legislature, and also in a lecture delivered in fifteen counties in southern Indiana. A synopsis of this lecture is given in the annual report of the University, made in the college year 1865–66.

The conditions of the grant were:

1. That at least one college must be organized, the leading object of which should be to teach such branches of learning as are related to agriculture and the mechanic arts.

2. If any portion of the fund, principal or interest, be lost, it shall be replaced by the State.

3. No portion of said fund, nor the interest thereon shall be applied directly or indirectly, under any pretense whatever, to the purchase, erection, preservation, or repair of any building or buildings.

4. The State shall provide within five years, not less than one college as described above.

Three plans were proposed for the disposition of this important trust:

1. The endowment of agricultural departments in some five of the leading colleges of the State, including a central institution of research at Indianapolis.

2. The founding of a separate Agricultural College.

3. The establishment of an Indiana State Agricultural College in connection with the Indiana University.

President Nutt showed very conclusively the impracticability of the first method proposed, the uselessness of the second, since the Indiana University was ready to carry out at once the conditions of the original grant, since the whole property of the University thus becomes subsidary to the State Agricultural College. By the union of the endowment of the Agricultural College with that of the State University, the whole endowment would be about $500,000, and would thus make an institution of which the State might be justly proud. These arguments had their weight, and all omens were favorable as to the location of the Agricultural College in Bloomington, till the last day of the meeting of the Legislature. But the gift of Mr. Purdue of $150,000, and the donation of one hundred acres of land appurtenant to the site of the Institution, by the citizens of Chauncey, and $50,000 from Tippecanoe, outweighed the proffered offer of the Indiana University, and located the Agricultural College in Lafayette, which, though not located in Monroe County, is in conjunction with the Normal at Terre Haute and Indiana University at Bloomington, a part of the University system of the State.

THE ADMISSION OF FEMALES TO THE UNIVERSITY.

A change in a long established custom with regard to the admission of females to all the privileges of the University was made in the college year 1867–68. In the preceding year, Mr. Jenkinson, then of Allen County, a member of the Board of

Trustees, offered a resolution to admit females to the same studies and the same standing as the males. For some time before this, the subject, "the coëducation of the sexes," had been agitated in various educational conventions, and Mr. Jenkinson was a strong advocate in its favor. Coöperating with others like-minded, he had been instrumental in opening the Fort Wayne Female College to males. The other members of the University Board were not prepared for the innovation; no member but himself approved of the resolution presented. At a subsequent meeting, Judge Rhoads offered a substitute for this resolution of Mr. Jenkinson, proposing to admit females to partial rights and privileges, but this was not agreed to by the Board. The original resolution was then pressed, and about the same time a petition was presented by Miss Sarah P. Morrison, asking that the law of the University should be so changed that females, with regard to their studies and privileges, should be put on the same footing as the males. This request of Miss Morrison, coming when the question was before the Board, had, without doubt, influence in the Board's deciding in favor of Mr. Jenkinson's resolution. The motion, however, was carried only by a majority of one; four in favor, three against it. Miss Morrison, who knew nothing of the agitation of this question by the Board, received a reply to her petition that the laws of the University with regard to this matter required no change, and that its doors, with all its rights and privileges, were open to females. Miss Morrison then entered the Sophomore Class at the beginning of the next year, 1868–9, and about nine weeks after a number of young ladies entered the Freshman Class, and before the end of the second term there were twelve female students.

We are not aware that any college before the year 1866, had admitted both sexes to the privileges, excepting Oberlin University, Ohio, and the Fort Wayne Female College, the former of which, as early as 1837, had the courage, in the face of public opinion, to open its halls to all the children of men without regard to sex or color. In the year 1868–9, the number of female students was about ten per cent. of the whole number of the students in the four college classes. In 1886 the number of female students is about thirty-three per cent.

THE CONNECTION BETWEEN THE COMMON SCHOOLS AND THE UNIVERSITY.

It is evident that the framers of the first Constitution of Indiana contemplated a system of education which should embrace the lowest and highest degrees of mental training. They had received from the General Government a large grant of land, the sixteenth section in each township, for the establishment of common schools, and a township of land in Monroe County for a State Seminary of learning. In the old Constitution of the State, adopted when Corydon was the capital, in the year 1816, we have in Article IX, section 2, these words: "It shall be the duty of the General Assembly, as soon as circumstances permit, to provide by law for a general system of education, ascending in regular gradation from the township school to a State University, wherein tuition shall be gratis and open to all." In the preceding section it is said that the "General Assembly shall pass such laws as shall be calculated to encourage intellectual, scientific and agricultural improvement, and encourage the principles of humanity, industry and morality." In the new Constitution, adopted February 10, 1851, Article VIII, the educational system seems to be limited to the common schools, the University being altogether ignored. But in 1852 amends were made for this omission, by the passing of an act with reference to the University, reading as follows:

"SECTION 1. *Be it enacted by the General Assembly of the State of Indiana:* The Institution established by an act entitled, An act to establish a college in the State of Indiana, approved January 28, 1828, is hereby recognized as the University of the State." This of course sanctions the idea that the Indiana University is at the head of the educational system of the State, and authorizes the action of the State Board of Education, taken May 5, 1873, as follows:

"*Resolved,* That the State Board of Education recommend the Trustees and Faculty of the Indiana University, in order to unite the high schools of the State and the University more closely together, to so modify the Preparatory course of study as to admit students to the Freshman class without the knowledge of Greek, putting in place thereof an equivalent in the increased amount of Mathematics and Science."

At a meeting of the superintendents and principals of schools of four hundred or more pupils, held in Indianapolis, May 7,

1873, for the consideration of matters pertaining to the welfare of the schools, the question, "How to harmonize the High School and University courses of instruction," elicited considerable discussion. The following resolutions were thereupon unanimously adopted:

"*Resolved*, That we, the members of the Convention of Superintendents of the High Schools of the State, respectfully represent that we fully approve the plan of uniting the high schools with the University by the method proposed, viz.: That the high schools shall prepare pupils in orthography, arithmetic, English grammar, geography, physiology, United States history, algebra, geometry, Latin grammar, Cæsar, and Virgil, which shall admit them to the Freshman class without the necessity of preparing them in the study of Greek, and that the study of the advanced mathematics be considered as an equivalent for the additional amount of Greek now required for admission.

"*Resolved*, That Mr. Gow present these resolutions to the Trustees of the University, at their meeting in June, as the expression of our views."

These resolutions having been presented, it was "ordered by the Board of Trustees of Indiana University, that the minimum standard of admission to the Freshman class in the University shall be a creditable examination in orthography, reading, geography, English grammar, United States history, composition, word analysis, physiology, algebra, geometry, Latin grammar, Latin prose composition, Cæsar and Virgil or their equivalents."

"Second, In order to bring the University into closer connection with the high schools of the State, we recommend the following plan: 'A certificate from certain high schools (the schools to be hereafter named by the State Board of Education) of a satisfactory examination, sustained in the Preparatory course, will entitle the bearer to admittance to the Freshman class, and no one will be admitted as a student in the University (except those admitted to select studies or on special examination) without such certificate from the authorities of the high schools.'"

This arrangement immediately went into effect, and twenty-one high schools in different parts of the State are mentioned as designated and commissioned by the State Board to prepare and examine students for admission to the Freshman class. The part of this arrangement that Greek should not be required for entrance into the Freshman class was quite an innovation, and was regarded by many scholars and literary institutions throughout the State with great disfavor, and as lowering the college standard and a step downward and backward. No evil seems, however, to have resulted from it; the Professor of Greek, the late Professor Ballantine, found that in a year after the change had been made he had the scholars as far advanced as under the old arrangement. This may be ascribed to the better and more uniform training in elementary instruction under the Professor himself than the pupil had under different instructors, some better and some worse, and each having his own peculiarities. The same may be said with regard to this innovation under the instruction of the present Professor of Greek, Mr. Hoffman.

In 1868 the military department of the University was revived. In Lieutenant (now General) Ammen's day, a military company of the students was formed—this was in the years 1839–42—and for a time, drilled every afternoon in the week, except Saturday and Sunday. On General Ammen's resigning in 1842, the military exercises were soon after discontinued. It was not till 1869 that the military department was put in working order, when arrangements were made for instruction in military science, and also for company and battalion drill. In this department, tactics, out-post duty, military engineering, and science of war, were to be taught; arms and accoutrements were obtained and Major General Eli Long was detailed by the President of the United States as Military Professor in the University. General Long occupied this position only for a year. He was recalled by the War Department from his position in the University and from the work so auspiciously commenced. The University was fortunate in securing the service of Colonel James Thompson, formerly Assistant Professor of Mathematics in West Point, as Professor of Military Science and Engineering, by whom this department was carried on with considerable spirit for two or three years. It so happened that many of the students of the military class, who lived at a considerable distance from the College, found it very inconvenient to attend the drill, and obtained permission to withdraw. While the military ardor was thus weakened, the zeal of the students took a new direction; the class of civil engineering was enlarged, and soon the military feature of Colonel Thompson's professorship became less and less prominent, while engineering, mechanical drawing, the construction of bridges, practical surveying, etc., became more and more popular. In 1875 the military features of this department altogether disappeared, and it became the department of civil engineering. This, all the scientific students were required to attend. There was an effort made by the Trustees about this time to establish a gymnasium; an appropriation was made to erect a building for this purpose in the college campus; but at a meeting of the Board not long after, it was thought that the money could be put to a better use, and the former action of the Board was rescinded.

THE MEDICAL DEPARTMENT.

In the Annual Report of 1870 mention is made among the wants of the University, of a gymnasium, and also another professional school—that of medicine—in which tuition shall be free for all. The Indiana Medical College, at Indianapolis, was, at a meeting of the Board in 1871, made the Medical Department of Indiana University, and in the Report for 1872, this Department appears as a part of its working force. The College building at Indianapolis had the appliances necessary for the different branches of the medical course. It had also access to the City Hospital, and all the opportunities necessary for teaching clinical medicine and surgery. There was also attached to the College a dispensary where gratuitous professional services were rendered, enabling the students to witness and take part in the management of such cases as presented themselves.

THE OWEN COLLECTION.

The appliances for instruction in physics, chemistry and natural science, were up to the year 1872, very meagre; the Trustees, always willing to go as far as their means would allow, were enabled by the grants made by the Legislature in 1867 and 1873, to put these departments, requiring so much and such expensive apparatus, on a much better footing than they ever had been before. In 1870, the large and extensive cabinet of the distinguished geologist, the late David Dale Owen, M. D., of

New Harmony, was offered for sale, and purchased by the University. The terms were made so favorable that the University was without difficulty able to purchase it. The negotiation with the family of the late Dr. D. D. Owen, was made by Professor B. E. Rhoads and Dr. H. Cloud, and the collection was packed and sent to Bloomington. It filled several cars. There was no room for it in the then existing buildings, and all that could be done was to hire a ware-room and store it away. To utilize it, rendered the erection of another building indispensable.

When it was determined that a new building should be provided for the Owen collection, it was thought advisable to erect one sufficiently large to accommodate the law school, library and other departments, for which there were not adequate accommodations in the old building. A plan was adopted in accordance with these suggestions. The corner-stone was laid July 2, 1873, Governor T. A. Hendricks and Lieutenant-Governor Leonidas Sexton delivering the orations. This building was in length, one hundred and thirty feet; in breadth, fifty feet; three stories high. The collection and chemical laboratory occupied the lower floor. The library, the physical department and analytical laboratory, the second floor. The law department, till its close in 1877, and afterwards the natural history and geological departments and modern languages the third floor. This building and nearly all its contents was destroyed by fire, being struck by lightning, in 1883, exactly ten years and eleven days after the laying of the corner-stone.

At the annual meeting of the Board, June 30, 1875, Dr. Cyrus Nutt resigned, having held the office of President for fifteen years. During his presidency there was on the whole a continued increase in the prosperity of the Institution, and a number of important changes made and measures adopted. In 1868 the College was opened to female students. In the year 1873 an important connection was made with the high schools of the State. In 1867 an annual grant of $8,000 was made to the University, and in 1873 another annual grant of $14,000. In the year before a grant of $8,000 was made for the payment of some debts of the University. In 1871 the Owen collection was purchased, and in 1872 the Indiana Medical College was united to the University, becoming its medical department. In 1873 a building was erected for the museum, the law, the physical, chemical, natural history, and modern language depart-

Erected 1855.

Erected 1873.
DESTROYED BY FIRE IN 1883.

ments, and also for the library. The number of students in the College proper and law school, exclusive of the medical school and preparatory department, averaged during Dr. Nutt's administration one hundred and sixty-six per annum. The lowest number, in 1863, (during the war) was seventy-nine, the highest, 1871, two hundred and fifty-eight. Dr. Nutt died August 23, 1875, less than two months after his resignation.

THE PRESIDENCY OF DR. LEMUEL MOSS.

After the resignation of Dr. Nutt, it became necessary to look for a successor. An alumnus of the University, residing in Chicago, suggested that Dr. Moss, who had lately resigned the Presidency of Chicago University, would be the man to fill the vacancy in this place. Inquiry was made respecting this retiring President, and the answers received were all favorable as to character and qualifications. It so happened that there was a called meeting of the Board of Trustees in Indianapolis, shortly before the end of the summer vacation, and while in session the Board was informed that Dr. Moss, whose name had been mentioned, was at that time in Indianapolis, with his family, on their way eastward. An interview was had with the Doctor, and shortly after, on the 13th of September, 1875, he was elected President of the University, and his course was diverted from the east and turned to Bloomington, at which place he arrived on Friday, the 17th. On the following day, the Senior Professor, President *pro tem*, introduced Dr. Moss to the students, and he then assumed his position as President of Indiana University. Under the preceding President, the University had prospered, and the incoming President entered upon his administration under very favorable auspices.

In the Annual Report of 1877 Dr. Moss presented to the Board of Trustees his views of the aims and wants of the University. Many, if not all, the excellent and appropriate suggestions then made were approved by the Board. The connection of the medical school with the University terminated in 1876, having continued five years.* In the following year the law department, established in 1842, was closed. The cause of the discontinuance of these schools seems to have been,

---

*The connection of the medical school with the University was little more than nominal, and of no advantage to either side, and was allowed to lapse, no one objecting.

that since, according to the decision of the Board, the tuition was free, it would have required an expenditure beyond the means at the disposal of the Trustees to secure the services of competent professors. In 1855 there was a so-called scientific course of three years, differing from the other courses by the omission of Greek and Latin. In 1867 the scientific course was changed to a four year course, and additional studies were required. This arrangement continued till the third year of Dr. Moss' Presidency, when three courses were established: 1. The course of ancient classics, leading to the degree B. A., Bachelor of Arts. 2. The course of modern classics, in which French or German was substituted for the Greek. The elements of Greek could, however, be taken in the Sophomore year. This course led to the degree, Bachelor of Letters, B. L. 3. The course in science was the same as the preceding as to languages; but special attention was given to the physical sciences in the Junior and Senior years. This course led to the degree, Bachelor of Science, B. S.

Courses of lectures called *Special Lectures* were introduced by Dr. Moss with the approval and support of the Board. These courses were not long, but were profitable to the students and the public, as may be inferred from the subjects and the distinguished lecturers by whom they were delivered.

The first course was delivered in November, 1877, by Professor George F. Barker, M. D., LL. D., of the University of Pennsylvania. His subject was "The Latest Discoveries and Most Recent Methods in Physics." The lectures were fully illustrated by experiments and eloquently delivered. The Professor exhibited the telephone, then in its infancy, and also the electric light produced by the galvanic battery. This light, otherwise produced, was then emerging from the halls of science and becoming a public illuminator.

In 1878 there was a highly instructive course of lectures delivered by President James B. Angell, of the University of Michigan, on "International Law, Illustrated by American History."

In February, 1880, the late Richard A. Proctor, B A., of Cambridge, England, so well known by his voluminous writings and as a popular lecturer, delivered a course of six lectures on astronomy. These eloquent and instructive lectures were illustrated by diagrams and the magic lantern.

In 1880 Professor William T. Harris, LL. D., then of St. Louis, delivered a course of six lectures on "The Philosophy and History of Education." In the following year, Professor Harris, now of Concord, Mass., was invited back to give a course of lectures in pedagogics to the Senior and Junior classes of the University. In the following winter of 1882, Miss Brace, a graduate of Vassar College, gave a five weeks' course in elocution to the Senior and Junior classes, together with several public exhibitions of her remarkable elocutionary powers. The year following she was elected Professor of Elocution in the University. Since this time, these special courses have been discontinued. The college year of 1882-3 terminated auspiciously. The last week was a festive occasion, closing with the usual commencement exercises. One evening was devoted to a levee and reunion of the Alumni and their friends. The College societies, the Philomathean, the Athenian and the Ladies' Hesperian, held their valedictory exercises some time during this week, thus closing this very prosperous year. It sometimes happens that calamity follows hard on prosperity. Just one month after the commencement, July 13, 1883, the College building, the corner-stone of which was laid by Governor T. A. Hendricks and Lieutenant-Governor Leonidas Sexton, July 2d, 1873, was a mass of ruins.

As there had been no one occupying the building for more than a week, there is no way of accounting for the fire but by a vivid flash of lightning, which occurred about 6 o'clock P. M. on the 12th of July, during a heavy fall of rain, which continued the whole night. The fire must have been smoldering in the building till 8 o'clock, when the alarm was given. The building was so pervaded by the smoke that no part could be entered except the museum, in the lower story, from which some tables, covered with specimens, were taken. The valuable library of about 13,000 volumes was completely destroyed, and also all the physical and chemical apparatus, and the valuable collections, together with the library of Professor, now President Jordan. Had it not been for the exertions of the firemen, and the heavy rain, the other building, only ten feet from it, must have met the same fate.

This calamity occurring during vacation, most of the professors were out of town. In the emergency, the resident trustees, professors and some influential citizens, met and discussed the situation. About the beginning of August the board of trustees in a called session, and, with the funds in hand, immediately proceeded to prepare the old college building* for the temporary reception of the professors who had lost their rooms and apparatus by the recent fire.

It was also resolved at this meeting of the board to select a new site, removed from the annoyance of the railroad, on which to rebuild the University. The board, after an examination of various situations, selected a tract of twenty acres, situate on the eastern border of, and overlooking the city, in what is known as "Dunn's woods." This they purchased from Moses E. Dunn, Esq., the grandson of the original proprietor. About the beginning of September the Commissioners of Monroe County voted to donate $50,000 to the University, for the purpose of erecting buildings; and by this generous grant, and the money received from the insurance companies, the trustees were enabled immediately to make preparations for building. Mr. George W. Bunting, of Indianapolis, was employed as architect. At the meeting of the board in November, 1883, the plans were submitted and adopted. Three buildings were at this time stipulated for. On Wednesday, April 2, 1884, the ground was broken. On June 10, in accordance with arrangements previously made, the corner-stone was laid. The day was unpropitious, and so rainy that the addresses were delivered in the Methodist Church, comparatively few assembling to witness the actual ceremony of putting the stone in place. The three buildings were named Wylie Hall, Owen Hall and Maxwell Hall. Wylie Hall, when the main building shall be erected, is intended for the Department of Physics and Chemistry. At present (1888), the Chemical Department occupies the first story, its proper place, while the second story is occupied by the Library and several other departments besides the Physical.

Owen Hall is intended for and is at present occupied by the Departments of Natural Science and the Museum. Maxwell Hall is a wooden structure. On its lower floor are the Chapel, a recitation room and the ladies' room. In the second story are five recitation rooms.

The commencement took place this year (1884), on June 11. The number of graduates was twenty-one; the whole number of

---

* The building erected in 1854-55.

WYLIE HALL.

MAXWELL HALL.

students, 143; this being the first year after the fire, compared with the preceding year, the diminution was only 23.

On November 8, 1884, the resignation of Dr. Moss was formally announced to the Faculty, and also that the Rev. Elisha Ballantine, LL. D., had been appointed President *pro tem*. All things connected with the University went on harmoniously and very prosperously, considering the great losses sustained by the destruction of the library, the museum, the physical and chemical apparatus, together with the buildings in which were the class-rooms of four professors, showing that the students and friends of the University had not lost their confidence in the institution by the disaster that had befallen it.

THE PRESIDENCY OF DR. DAVID S. JORDAN.

At a meeting of the Board of Trustees, January 1, 1885, Dr. David S. Jordan, Professor of Natural Science, was chosen President of the University, and Dr. Elisha Ballantine, vice President. A number of changes have been made in the management of the Institution and the courses of study since Dr. Jordan's inauguration. These changes, however, have been made so gradually that they have not appeared either abrupt or ostentatious. The ordinary business of the college was carried on in the old college during the erection of the new buildings. On the 3d of September, 1888, to the gratification of all concerned, the students assembled in their new and commodious halls, for prayers, lectures and recitations. Several new professorships have been instituted, and the Faculty increased in numbers, corresponding to the increased numbers of the students, and the requirements of the times.

The principal features of President Jordan's administration thus far have been the following:

"The development of special courses whereby each professor has some opportunity to give advanced instruction in the direction of his specialty, and the student has an opportunity to do something more than to secure the mere elements of a subject. The arrangement of the work is such that each student has a wide range of choice among elective studies, while at the same time he is required to take up special work of some one department and continue it for three or four years, thus making it the back-bone of his education. In the classical course such thoroughness has long been required in Greek and Latin, and in nothing else, while the modern substitutes for such a course as a rule, had no central axis, or subject to master.

For the arrangement of the studies, which may vary from time to time, see the annual reports of the University. The general course of study, which every candidate for the degree of A. B. must complete, is as follows:

GENERAL.—English, one year, daily.
  Mathematics, one year, daily.
  Some one Science (Biology, Chemistry, Physics), one year, daily.
  Ancient or Modern Languages, either one language two years, or two languages one year each, daily.
  English Prose Composition, once a week throughout the course.
SPECIAL.—Every student must select for a specialty a subject in which a four years' course is offered. The first year in each specialty is identical with some one of the required studies mentioned above.
COLLATERAL.—The head of each department may lay out in connection with his course, work in related subjects, such required collateral work not to exceed six terms of daily recitations, and to be specially arranged for each student.
ELECTIVE.—The remainder of his work—six terms of daily recitations—the student may elect from any departments in the University.

Freshmen may first take the required general studies without selecting a specialty. The order in which the required and general collateral studies are taken may vary with the conditions in each case. The student is to be guided in this case by the advice of the President, and after choosing a specialty by that of the professor under whom he desires to work. Sophomores, Juniors and Seniors must report to the professor in charge of the department in which they have chosen their specialty within a week after entering the University. They may change their specialty at the end of a term with the consent of the professors in the two departments concerned, but no changes as to the special collateral or elective studies will be permitted, after the beginning of a term, and no student will be graduated who has not finished all the work required for graduation in some department, no matter how much work he may have done in other departments.

Corresponding to the fourteen departments now fully organized and equipped, and each offering a four years' course to be pursued as a specialty, there are at present fourteen courses leading to the degree A. B. These courses are the same in extent and value. Each requires the same preparation for admission, and each requires four years for completion. Each one requires that the student shall have followed some special line of study for four years. It is intended that every graduate of the University shall have a thorough drill in some department of knowledge, while breadth of culture is encouraged by means of certain general studies required of all students, and by a wide range of elective studies during the Junior and Senior years."

THE LAW SCHOOL.

The organization of the Law School was agitated in 1835, if not sooner, early in the administration of the first President of the University. The earliest attempt to organize it as a department of the University must have been sometime between 1835 and 1837. A loose scrap of paper containing a note which the writer probably intended to transfer to the minutes has escaped destruction, on which is the following:

"*Resolved*, That in the opinion of the board a professorship of law should be established, to be connected with the college.

"That the law term should consist of four months, from December 1st to March 31st.

"That the salary of the professor shall be $300, to be paid as other salaries of the college officers, and that he also be entitled to dispose of lecture tickets for his own benefit, the price of which shall not exceed $10 per term.

"*Resolved*, That the board now proceed to the election of said professor."

Mr. Foster (who was a trustee from 1835 to 1838) was appointed teller, and on counting the votes it appeared that Isaac Blackford was unanimously elected professor.

There is no further trace of Judge Blackford's professorship. From some notes which had been taken from the old record book of the college, destroyed in the fire of 1883, mention is made of Charles Lewis having been chosen Professor of Law, September 20, 1837. We have no further notice of Mr. Lewis.

At the first-meeting of the board, after the college had been made a university, the following appeared on record in its proceedings under date of September 25, 1838: "On motion of Mr. Law the board proceeded to the election of a Professor of Law. The result of the election was that the Hon. Miles G. Eggleston was unanimously elected." Mr. Eggleston declined, owing to circumstances over which he had no control. Application was then made to several distinguished jurists, but no one was found willing to accept. The matter was then dropped till 1841, when Gen. Tilghman A. Howard was elected, and a very urgent letter was sent to the board requesting his acceptance. General Howard, however, declined this earnest request.

About a year after this the names of several distinguished jurists were presented to the board. Of this number David McDonald, who was a resident of Bloomington and a Judge of the Circuit Court, was duly elected, and on the following day his letter of acceptance was received. In the catalogue of 1841-42, the first announcement of the Law School is made by the professor,—but it does not appear that there was any class. In the following year, 1843, there was a graduating class of five, and in 1844, of eight. In the catalogue of this year an announcement was made, of which the following is an extract: "In establishing this department it is the design of the board of trustees to build up a law school that will furnish to gentlemen, intended for the bar, a complete course of legal education, but since time and experience are necessary in order to establish such an institution on a firm basis, and to give it such a character as will induce its success, it has been deemed advisable to adopt merely a temporary arrangement for the present year. * * * It is intended that the course of study shall occupy four sessions; the students will be divided into two classes, the Junior and Senior. * * * Any gentleman not wishing to study law as a profession may enter the Junior class for instruction in that part of the course which relates to international, constitutional and commercial law. * * * The professor will deliver a course of lectures on international and constitutional law, common law and equity jurisprudence. He will hold a moot court once a week in which the students will be exercised in drawing pleadings and arguing legal questions and law cases, previously given out, and on each of which he will afterwards deliver an opinion, as well as on the questions of law involved as on the manner of the arguments."

Under the direction of Judge McDonald, the Law School prospered. Students from all parts of the State and some from other States attended the classes.

In 1847 Judge W. T. Otto, a graduate of the University of Pennsylvania, well known in the State for his high attainments, both in law and general literature, was elected as Associate Professor of Law, and entered upon his duties in 1847. Judge Otto resigned in 1851, and Judge McDonald in 1853. Judge James Hughes succeeded Judge McDonald and held the office two years, when he obtained leave of absence to take his seat in Congress. During his absence his place was supplied by Judge A. B. Carlton. On the resignation of Judge Hughes in 1857, Col. James R. M. Bryant was elected Professor of Law, and held it till 1861, when he resigned to take a position in the army. Judge George A. Bicknell, a graduate of the University of Pennsylvania, succeeded Colonel Bryant, and continued till 1870. During the last year of his professorship he was assisted by John U. Pettit, of Wabash, who, having been elected Professor of Law, served one year. On their resignation in 1870, Samuel E. Perkins, of Indianapolis, long a Judge of the Supreme Court, was elected to the position, and began his service in the session ensuing, and held the place till 1872. At the time of the election of Judge Perkins, Bascom E. Rhodes was also chosen Professor of Law, and held this position till the close of the law school in 1877. Judge Delana R. Eckels, of Greencastle, succeeded Judge Perkins, who had resigned, and held this place for one year, when the Hon. D. W. LaFollette, of New Albany, took the the place of Judge Eckels, and in 1875, C. F. McNutt, of Martinsville, Ind., succeeded Judge Eckels, and, associated with Professor Rhoads, attended to the duties of the department till its close.

The law department was in a very flourishing condition when it was discontinued, there being forty-one students in attendance. By reason of legislative action cutting down the salaries of professors to such a point that competent professors could not be secured, this department of the University closed its doors. It is gratifying, however, to state that after a discontinuance of the Law School since 1876, the Trustees at a meeting of the Board in June, 1889, have made provision for the re-opening of this important department of the University by electing Judge David D. Banta, of Franklin, Professor of Law, who has now taken charge of the department.

The Law School opened propitiously, with about thirty students in attendance in September, at the beginning of the college year 1889-90.

SKETCHES OF THE PRESIDENTS OF THE INDIANA UNIVERSITY.

DR. ANDREW WYLIE, FIRST PRESIDENT OF INDIANA UNIVERSITY.

Andrew Wylie was born April 12, 1789, in Western Pennsylvania. He was the son of Adam Wylie, a native of County Antrim, in the north of Ireland, who emigrated to this country about the year 1776, and settled in Fayette County, Pa., then a new country and far west. His father was a hard-working farmer, and his son Andrew was in his youth accustomed to hard work. His early education was such as he received at the common school during the times he could be best spared from the labors of the farm. The early development of his mind was, in a great degree, due to his mother, who took special pains to imbue the minds of her children with the spirit of piety and the love of truth. The late Dr. William Wylie, of Newark, O., was one of these children. For a number of years Andrew Wylie was engaged in farming. After a hard day's work, he would spend the evening in storing his mind with some useful knowledge. It is to this vigorous exercise which he was compelled to undergo that his sound and healthy constitution is to be ascribed. Till his very last days he every day performed some manual labor out of doors. His favorite exercise was with the ax, in wielding which he had few superiors. From his childhood he was a great reader, reading whatever books he had access to—the Bible, some histories and a few religious works comprised such as he had to use. The writer has seen a manuscript geography, indicating that it had been well used, which he had copied, and probably modified, when a boy, either on account of the difficulty of procuring a copy, or to impress the subject better on his mind. When about fifteen he entered Jefferson

College, Canonsburg, then under the Presidency of Dr. Dunlap, through which he passed with great honor to himself, defraying his expenses by teaching or some other honest labor. In October, 1810, Mr. Wylie graduated with the first honor. Immediately after his graduation he was appointed tutor, and Dr. Dunlap resigning about a year after, he was unanimously elected by the Board of Trustees—the Faculty approving the act—President of the College; thus the youngest and lowest of the Faculty was made its head. In the year 1817 Dr. Wylie resigned the Presidency of Jefferson College and accepted that of Washington College, in a town by the same name about seven miles from Canonsburg, in the hope that the two institutions would be united. In this he was disappointed; the attempted union produced a series of troubles and difficulties, and was, no doubt, the cause of his resignation and removal. It was some time in the fall of 1829 that he, having been elected President of Indiana College, which had been chartered the year before, removed to Bloomington and took charge of the institution, which had been organized in 1820 and put in operation in 1824, under the name of the State Seminary, and had, just previous to the election of Dr. Wylie, been raised to the dignity of a college. The Seminary had been in active operation since 1824, under the superintendency of Professors Baynard R. Hall and John H. Harney.

Very different estimates have been put on the character of Dr. Wylie. He had many strong friends, and there were also some bitterly opposed to him. Those intimately acquainted with him will not find it difficult to account for this trait of character. He was tolerant, and patient to a fault, of everything but meanness and duplicity. A person in whom he had no confidence he would keep at arms' length, and although policy might dictate an opposite course, he would hardly treat one thus regarded with common courtesy. "He would never," to use his own expression, "throw a sop to Cerberus." On the other hand, to those in whom he had confidence no one was more affable. There was sometimes, however, an apparent want of civility, a brusk manner, which doubtless was the cause of some bad feeling toward him on the part of students and others. This arose from a trait of character often found with deep thinkers, when they have some subject of study constantly before their minds. Dr. Wylie, when in this mood, hardly noticed any one; he would brush past his nearest friends, even his wife and daughters, without recognizing them. Persons not knowing this peculiarity, when thus apparently slighted, with feelings hurt and pride wounded, would be deeply and often implacably offended.

Two characteristics of a good teacher Dr. Wylie had almost to perfection. He had learning and the faculty of communicating what he knew. No one understood better how to draw out the mind of the student. Under his training the pupil felt that he was really making progress and not blindly following a guide almost as blind as himself. Dr. W. H. McGuffey, of the University of Virginia, and the venerable nonagenarian, Dr. John W. Scott, now ('89) of Washington, D. C., and Gov. Henry A. Wise, of Virginia, were among his pupils before coming to Indiana, and General McKee Dunn and Judge Andrew Wylie, of Washington City, are among the earliest graduates of Indiana University.

As a writer, Dr. Wylie was clear and terse. His Baccalaureates and published writings are evidences of this. They are always interesting and instructive. Dr. Parvin, Professor in Jefferson Medical College, Philadelphia, and a pupil of Dr. W., thus speaks of the address of Dr. Wylie: "Of those published by him probably that which was delivered before the Philomathean Society, of Wabash College, July, '38, the subject of which was: 'The propriety of retaining the Greek and Roman classics in their place as a part of study necessary in the course of a liberal education,' was most widely known, and won for the author the highest praise. Asher Robins, of Rhode Island, one of the finest classical scholars ever a member of our National Senate, wrote to him soliciting a copy of the address. Daniel Webster wrote to him for the same purpose. Dr. Wylie's 'Eulogy on Lafayette,' delivered in Bloomington, elicited a letter from Webster, in which he spoke of the production in terms of the highest praise. Surely the students of Dr. Wylie are guilty of no blind idolatry, or no idolatry at all, when they declare that in ability he was one of the first men in all our country."

In addition to his Baccalaureate and other addresses, Dr. Wylie published, in 1839, a small treatise entitled "Sectarianism is Heresy." When President of Washington College, he published an "English Grammar." These and several sermons and some translations from Plato, published in a short-lived periodical, the *Equator*, are the principal writings of Dr. Wylie that have been printed. He left two works ready for the press, "A Treatise on Rhetoric," and one on "The Training of Youth."

Dr. Wylie was brought up a Presbyterian, and for many years was a pastor in that denomination, and much esteemed by his congregation in Western Pennsylvania. In 1841 he connected himself with the Episcopalians. We are at a loss to say what led him to select this denomination when we consider the liberality of his views and his opposition to sectarianism. Had he been influenced either by fear or by favor, or by any selfish motive, a more popular and influential body of Christians than the Episcopalians were, at that time in the State, would certainly have been his choice. However much some of his friends regretted the step he had taken, none of those intimately acquainted with him lost their confidence in his integrity or suspected him of any sinister motive in making this change.

His death took place November 11th, 1851, a full notice of which is given in the History of the University (page 57.)

REV. ALFRED RYORS, D. D., SECOND PRESIDENT, INDIANA UNIVERSITY.

Alfred Ryors was born in the city of Philadelphia, June 23, 1812. He was left an orphan at so early an age that he scarcely remembered his parents. After their death he found a home with his father's friends in Montgomery County, Pa., with whom he lived till 1823. In the summer of this year, he united with the Presbyterian Church, under the pastoral care of Rev. Robert Steel, D. D., with whom he began a course of classical study in preparation for the Gospel ministry. Assisted by the kindness and liberality of friends, and especially of Dr. Steel, he entered the Freshman Class of Jefferson College in 1831. Here he remained two years, when he left college and engaged as a teacher of Latin and Greek in the School of C. J. Halderman, at Bristol, Pa. Professor Halderman was an eminent mathematician and from him he received those lessons which gave direction to his future and contributed to his success as professor of mathematics. In the fall of 1834 he returned to Jefferson College, and graduated the following year, receiving, in a class of forty-three members, its first honors. Previously to taking his degree, he received and accepted the appointment of Principal of the Academic Department in LaFayette College, Easton, Pa. Here he remained only one year, having, in May, 1836, been elected Professor of Mathematics in the Ohio University. Notwithstanding his somewhat severe labors at Easton, he found time to prosecute a course of theological studies with a view to his regular introduction to the Gospel ministry. After completing his course of study, he was licensed to preach by the Second Presbytery of Philadelphia, in the fall of 1838, three years after his graduation.

Having been elected Professor of Mathematics in the University of Indiana, in the fall of 1843, he resigned the chair which he had held in Ohio University for more than seven years, and removed the following spring to Bloomington, Ind., the seat of the State University. This position he resigned in 1848, in order to return to the Ohio University, to the Presidency of which he had been elected. During his connection with the Indiana University he preached for more than two years to the Presbyterians of Bloomington, and it was at the request of this congregation that he was ordained by the Presbytery of Salem (now New Albany Presbytery), in 1845.

As Dr. Ryors succeeded Dr. W. H. McGuffey, that most popular and gifted instructor of young men, he had no ordinary ordeal to pass in the new and enlarged sphere of his labors. With what ability, zeal and success, both as a disciplinarian and instructor he filled this responsible position, his colleagues of the Faculty, as well as the students of the University, bear decided testimony. It was at the first meeting after his return to Ohio that he received from the University of Indiana the degree of Doctor of Divinity.

In the summer of 1852 he was invited to return to Indiana, having been elected President of the University which he had left four years before. Accepting the appointment, he resigned the post he held and removed to Bloomington in the fall, to remain only a year. Disappointed in the condition of the University, and opposed by disaffected intriguers and aspirants he determined to resign, and six months after his arrival he sent in his resignation, which, however, at the earnest request of the President of the board, he was induced to withdraw. At the next meeting of the board, at the close of the year, he again resigned, and accepted the invitation to supply for a while the pulpit of the First Presbyterian Church of Madison, Ind. He was called by this church in the May following to become their pastor. This call he declined, though still supplying their pulpit. A few weeks afterwards he was elected Professor of Mathematics in Center College, Ky., which position he held till he was removed by death, May 8, 1858.

Dr. Ryors in 1838 married Miss Louisa Walker, of Athens, Ohio, who still (1890) lives in Bloomington with her daughter, the wife of the Hon. R. W. Miers, one of the trustees of the University.

REV. WILLIAM M. DAILY, D. D., LLD., THIRD PRESIDENT OF INDIANA UNIVERSITY.

William M. Daily was born in Coshocton, Ohio, in 1812. This same year his father moved to Indiana and settled in Franklin County on a farm, near Brookville, the county seat. There he spent his childhood days, attending the country school when there was one. Having a frail constitution, it was thought when he was quite young that he would never be fit for manual labor. When he had learned all he could at the country school he was sent to Brookville, where he learned all that was taught there. At fifteen he left home to take charge of a school in an adjoining county, and began life for himself, which he preferred to do, although his father was in comfortable circumstances. He was baptized in infancy and grew up in the Methodist Episcopal Church. At sixteen he exhorted and preached, the people going for miles to hear the "boy preacher," as he was called. In 1831 he joined the conference; in 1833 he was ordained deacon; in 1835, elder. While discharging all the duties the church required of him as a minister, which were very laborious in those days, he kept up his studies, rising at four o'clock in the morning, that he might get a few hours at his books. In 1835–36 he was stationed at Bloomington, Indiana, where he discharged the duties of pastor and student in the Indiana University, graduating in 1836. In 1837 he was agent of the Preacher's Aid Society. In 1838 he was transferred to the Missouri Conference, and stationed in St. Louis. Soon after he was elected a professor in St. Charles College. He remained in Missouri till 1840, when he returned to Indiana in broken health, suffering from hemorrhage of the lungs. Having improved in health, in 1843, at the suggestion of Bishop Ames he was called to take charge of a congregation in Madison, Indiana. Here he met and was married to Miss Permelia A. Northcraft. In the winter of 1844–45 Mr. Daily was chaplain in the United States Congress, after which he was stationed at Rising Sun and Evansville. At this time he was made agent for Indiana Asbury (now DePauw) University, and afterwards Presiding Elder of the Bloomington and Madison districts. In 1852 Dr. Daily was a member of the general conference. In 1853 he was elected President of the Indiana University, when, after six years of hard labor, he resigned and returned to Madison in 1859. In 1862 he was appointed hospital chaplain at St. Louis, by President Lincoln, which position he held till the close of the war in 1865, when, as he was desirous of going south, at the request of General Yates he was appointed special mail agent.

He received the degree of A. M. in course from Indiana University, and the honorary degree A. M. from Augusta College, Kentucky, during the presidency of Bishop Bascom. He received the degree of D. D. from Indiana University in 1851, and LL. D. some years afterwards from the University of Louisville.

Dr. Daily became connected with the Louisiana Conference in January, 1869, and was appointed to the Baton Rouge District, and afterwards to the Upper Coast District. On each of these he served a term of four years. He was next appointed to the North New Orleans District. Not long after this appointment he was taken seriously ill, and in a few days departed this life. A few months after his death his remains were removed to Madison, Indiana, his old home.

Dr. Daily, during his connection with the University, delivered a number of Baccalaureates which were published. A volume of his sermons was published in Cincinnati.*

---
*Taken from the account published in the minutes of the M. E. Conference.

JOHN H. LATHROP, FOURTH PRESIDENT INDIANA UNIVERSITY.

John Hiram Lathrop, the fourth President of Indiana University was born in Sherburne, Chenango County, N. Y., January 22, 1799. He was fitted for college after the manner of the day by a neighboring clergyman, and entered Hamilton College in 1815. After the second year he availed himself of the larger opportunities of Yale College, entered its Junior Class and received his degree in 1819, in standing the salutatorian of the class. He accepted a tutorship in Yale, and thus obtained means for prosecuting the study of law in the Law Department of that Institution. He, however, finding the practice of the law uncongenial, decided to give his energies to the cause of education. He taught in various parts of New England, presided over a military academy at Norwich, Conn., and later over the Gardiner Lyceum, of Gardiner, Maine. In 1829 he was called to Hamilton College as Professor of Mathematics and Natural Philosophy. From this institution he received the degree of LL. D. In 1833 he married Miss Frances E. Lothrop, of Utica, N. Y., a niece of President Kirkland, of Harvard College. In 1835 he was advanced to the Professorship of Law, Civil Polity and Political Economy, in Hamilton College. In 1840 he was elected first President of the University of Missouri, at Columbia. Dr. Lathrop, though aware of the great sacrifice he made in leaving the East for this new and uncultivated field in the West, determined to accept the new trust, and after a journey of six weeks, he reached the remote station. Notwithstanding the fact that the University of which he was chosen President existed only in the appropriation of land made by Congress, Dr. Lathrop succeeded in calling it into real life, organizing it and making it a permanent and promising institution, with buildings unusually substantial for the period, and equipped with an able corps of instructors. When the slave agitation began in Missouri, which affected even educational establishments, President Lathrop, an unswerving friend of freedom, felt it due to himself to resign the charge he had so successfully conducted in Missouri. In 1849 he accepted the Chancellorship of Wisconsin University, at Madison. After ten years' service in Madison, he was induced to accept the twice-offered Presidency of Indiana Uni-

versity. After a year's service in that institution he received
an invitation to a Professorship in the University of Missouri,
which he had been instrumental in founding, preferring a Professorship to the cares of administration. In 1860 he returned
to Columbia, Missouri, and in 1865 he was a second time chosen
President. By an attack of typhoid fever, he died in the midst
of his labors in 1866. (Abridged from the Missouri Volume
of United States biographies of eminent self-made men.)

REV. CYRUS NUTT, D. D., LL. D., FIFTH PRESIDENT OF INDIANA UNIVERSITY.

Cyrus Nutt was born in Trumbull County, Ohio, September
4, 1814. He graduated at Allegheny College, Meadville, Pennsylvania, in 1831, and commenced his educational labors as
Principal of the Preparatory Department of his *Alma Mater*.
He was, not long after, called to a similar position in Indiana
Asbury (now DePauw) University, at Greencastle, Indiana.
While at the latter place he was licensed to preach the Gospel.
In 1837 he was elected Professor of Languages, and in 1841
he was made Professor of the Greek language and Literature,
and also of Hebrew. This post he occupied till the fall of
1843, when he took pastorial work in the Indiana Conference,
and was appointed to Bloomington Station. Here he remained
two years, when he removed to Salem. In the fall of 1848 he
was re-elected to his former position in Asbury University. In
1849 he was chosen President of Fort Wayne Female College.
In the following year he accepted the Presidency of Whitewater College. After five years' service in this situation he
resigned in order to resume his work in the ministry. In 1855
he was appointed Presiding Elder in the Richmond District.
In the fall of 1857 he was elected Professor of Mathematics in
Asbury University, and while in this department, for nearly
two years he was the acting President, till the inauguration of
President (afterward, Bishop Bowman). In 1859 Allegheny
College, his *Alma Mater*, conferred on him the degree of Doctor
of Divinity. In 1860 he was elected President of Indiana University, which post he held till the end of the college year,
1874-75.

The writer of this sketch of Dr. Nutt became acquainted with him in 1843, when he was pastor of the Bloomington M. E. Church. As a pastor, he was earnest, diligent and faithful, and courteous in his intercourse with all. In 1860 he was called to preside over the University as the successor of Dr. Lathrop. In this important post it can truthfully be said that in many excellent traits of character he was surpassed by none. He was diligent in his work and in his attention to the duties of his office, laboring wholly in the cause of religion and sound education.

In the year 1873 the honorary degree of LL. D. was conferred upon him by the University of Missouri, and also the same year by Hanover College, Indiana. For his administration as president, see the accompanying history of the University (p. 71).

Dr. Nutt married Miss Amanda Standiford, of Greencastle, April 26, 1838. He died a few weeks after his resignation, August 24, 1875, and was buried in Forest Hill Cemetery, at Greencastle.

REV. LEMUEL MOSS, D. D., SIXTH PRESIDENT OF INDIANA UNIVERSITY.

Lemuel Moss was born in Bullettsville, Ky., December 27, 1829. Was educated at Rochester University, N. Y., receiving the degree, A. B., in 1858. He graduated at the Rochester Theological seminary, 1860. The honorary degree of D. D. was conferred by his *Alma Mater* in the year 1868. From the year 1860 to 1864 Dr. Moss was pastor of the First Baptist Church, Worcester, Mass. In 1864 he became Secretary of the United States Christian Commission. From 1865 to 1868 he was Professor of Systematic Theology in the University of Lewisburgh, Pa. From 1868 to 1872 editor of the "National Baptist" and Professor of New Testament Interpretation in Crozier Theological Seminary, Upland, Pa., and in 1874–5 President of Chicago University. In 1875 Dr. Moss was elected President of Indiana University. Before entering Rochester University, in 1853, his life was spent as follows: About four years in his native State, Kentucky. He then lived ten years in Dearborn County, Ind. The rest of the time previous to 1853, in Ohio, principally in Cincinnati, as a printer.

OWEN HALL.

Photo-gravure, by Wm. B. Burford, Indianapolis.

THE LIBRARY.

Dr. Moss was the author of the "Annals of the Christian Commission," a large 8vo. volume, the editor of the "Baptist and the Centenary, 1876," and the writer of various reviews and magazine articles. As a man of excellent literary attainments Dr. M. had few superiors. He had also fine administrative ability. He resigned in November, 1884.

DAVID S. JORDAN, LL. D., SEVENTH PRESIDENT OF INDIANA UNIVERSITY.

David Starr Jordan was born January 19, 1851, at Gainesville, Wyoming County, N. Y. He was brought up on a farm. His father, Hiram Jordan, was born at Moriah, N. Y.; his mother, Huldah Hawley, at Whitehall, N. Y. Their son David soon showed his love for natural science. At an early age he was a botanist, and to gratify this taste he prepared for college, taking his first lessons in Gainesville Female Seminary. In 1869, he entered Cornell University and graduated in 1872 with the Master's degree, M. S. In 1875 he received the degree of M. D. from Indiana Medical College, Ph. D. from Butler University in 1877, and LL. D. from Cornell University in 1886. In 1871-2 he was Instructor in Botany at Cornell; in 1873 Professor of Biology in Lombard University, Galesburg, Ill.; in 1874 Instructor in Botany in the Anderson School of Natural History at Penikese; in 1875 in the Harvard Summer School of Geology at Cumberland Gap. In 1873-4 Dr. Jordan was also Principal of the Collegiate Institute at Appleton, Wis., and in the following year, 1874-5, Teacher of Science in the Indianapolis High School. From 1875 to 1879 he was Professor of Biology in Butler University, Irvington, Ind., and from 1879 to 1885 Professor of Biology in Indiana University, and was elected President of Indiana University at the close of 1884, entering upon his duties in this office January 1, 1885.

In 1877 Dr. Jordan became scientific assistant to the U. S. Fish Commission, and under its auspices explored South Carolina, Georgia and Tennessee, and in the following year North Carolina, and 1880, California, Oregon and Washington. He at the same time was special agent of the U. S. Census Bureau, in charge of the investigation of marine industries of the Pacific.

In 1882 he explored Lake Superior, in 1886 the Adirondacks, and also Iowa, Missouri, Arkansas and Texas; in 1888, Virginia, Tennessee and the Carolinas; in 1889, Colorado, Utah and Wyoming.

Dr. Jordan's scientific papers are chiefly on fishes. They number 250 titles, and are for the most part published by the U. S. Fish Commission, the U. S. National Museum, and the Smithsonian Institute. In very many of these Dr. Charles H. Gilbert is associated as collaborator. The principal are, "Manual of Vertebrates," now (1889) in its fifth edition; "Science Sketches," in 1888; "Synopsis of Fishes of North America," published 1883; "Review of the Flounders of North America and Europe," in 1889; "Review of the Sciænidæ," in 1889; "The Octroi at Issoire," 1888; "Catalogue of North American Fishes," 1885.

Dr. Jordan visited Europe in 1879, 1881, 1883, 1886, and studied in the museums of Paris and London. Since the commencement of Dr. Jordan's Presidency, and chiefly through his influence, the college course and general administration have been to a great extent remodeled, the number of professors increased, and a greater opportunity given to students for pursuing special studies and for practical work in the laboratories and in the field.

Dr. Jordan married Susan Bowen, daughter of Mr. S. S. Bowen, of Hinsdale, Mass., March 10, 1875. Mrs. Jordan died November 15, 1885. He subsequently (August 10, 1887,) married Jessie L. Knight, daughter of Mr. Charles S. Knight, of Worcester, Mass.

THE PROFESSORS AND INSTRUCTORS.

BAYNARD RUSH HALL

Was born in Philadelphia, Pa., in 1798, and graduated at Union College, N. Y. Moved to Indiana, then in the far west, about 1824; was ordained minister of the gospel in 1825; was the first Principal of the Indiana Seminary in 1824, and when the seminary received the college charter in 1828, Mr. Hall was elected Professor of Ancient Languages. This position he resigned in 1831. From Bloomington he removed to Bedford, Pa., where he opened a school, and became the stated supply of the church in that place. He continued there till 1838, when he removed to Bordentown, N. J., from Bordentown he removed to Trenton, from thence to Poughkeepsie, N. Y., and from thence to Newburgh, N. Y., in all of which places he taught school and preached the gospel. Finally he was chosen Principal of Park Institute, Brooklyn, and pastor of the Reformed (Dutch) Church. He died in Brooklyn, N. Y., January 23, 1863.

JOHN HOPKINS HARNEY

Was born in Bourbon County, Kentucky, February 20, 1806. He was left an orphan while quite young, and was taken into the family of Judge Benjamin Mills, his father's cousin, and law partner of Henry Clay, and by him brought up with his own sons. Mr. Harney spent six months at Miami University, where he graduated in 1827, receiving the degree of A. B., and in 1831 the degree A. M. Soon after his graduation he walked from Oxford, O., to Bloomington, and applied for the position of teacher of Mathematics in the State Seminary, lately established. He received the appointment desired. When the Seminary became the College of Indiana, Mr. Harney was elected Professor of Mathematics and Natural Science. This position he occupied till 1832. Removing to Hanover he was elected Professor of Mathematics and Astronomy. Four years afterward he was made Professor of Natural Philosophy and Chemistry and Geology. On leaving Hanover he went to Louisville, Ky., and became Professor of Civil Engineering in the Collegiate Institute of that city. In this Institute he was associated with Noble Butler, its Professor of Languages. From 1837 to 1844 Professor Harney was editor of the Louisville Democrat, which, under his editorship, became an influential and popular paper. Professor Harney, before coming to Bloomington, married Miss Wallace, a daughter of Rev. Mr. Wallace, a Presbyterian minister of Kentucky, and sister of William R. Wallace, a student of the college, and a poet of some reputation in those days. When Professor Harney first came to Bloomington he was under the care of the Presbytery, being a candidate for the ministry. Soon after leaving Hanover he left the Presbyterian Church, and joined a small local sect known as the Wilderites. Afterward he became an Independent, setting up for himself, and for sometime he preached in Louisville. About six months before he died he was received into the Episcopal Church. His death took place at Louisville, Ky., January 26, 1868.

The writer of this sketch is indebted for nearly all the statistics to the General Catalogue of Alumni of Hanover College, furnished through the courtesy of Professor Garritt, and for the general information to Judge D. D. Banta.

BEAUMONT PARKS, A: M.

Professor Beaumont Parks was born January, 1775, at Norwich, Conn., and, entering Dartmouth College at the close of the last century, he graduated about 1802 and received the degree of A. M. For ten years he practiced law, and in 1821 removed to Madison, Ind., and there opened one of the first classical schools west of the Alleghenies. After about ten years of successful teaching in Madison he was elected Professor of Languages in the Indiana University, which position he held for seven years.* Removing to Springfield, Ill., he opened a private academy, which was supported by the leading citizens of that place. The fact that many of his pupils have become eminent in the learned professions and in business attests his fidelity as a teacher. After a faithful service of twenty years, old age compelled him to relinquish his chosen pursuit, spending his declining years with his children. He died at the residence of his son, Judge S. C. Parks, April 8, 1870, without an hour's sickness, in the 96th year of his age.

---

*By act of the Legislature of January 25, 1827, Beaumont Parks was made one of the Board of Visitors of Indiana Seminary.

EBENEZER NEWTON ELLIOTT,

Born November 2, 1805, in Chester District, S. C., graduated at Miami University, Oxford, O., in 1830, receiving therefrom the degrees of A. B. and A. M. Professor Elliott received the honorary degrees of Ph. D. and LL. D. from Lewisburg University, Pa., and also from Oakland College, Miss. He was elected Professor of Mathematics and Physics in Indiana University in 1832. In 1836 he was chosen President of Mississippi College, and subsequently was President of Oakland Scientific School and President of Planters' College; also, of Ghent College and Washington Scientific School. Professor Elliott was a minister in the Southern Presbyterian Church and a surgeon in the Confederate army. He was the compiler and in part author of a large work published in Augusta, Ga., entitled "Cotton is King, and Pro-Slavery Arguments." In addition to this he contributed articles to various periodicals and was the author of many public addresses. Dr. Elliott married Mrs. Ann Nasby Willis October 2, 1832, in Boone County, Ky. Mrs. Willis was the daughter of Colonel John Grant, a nephew of Daniel Boone. Colonel Grant was a noted man in the early history of Kentucky, and Grant County was named for him. Dr. Elliott, now in his eighty-fourth year, is the sole survivor of his family. He lives with his brother and still enjoys life. His handwriting shows no sign of senility; he keeps well posted in the theology, literature, science and politics of the day, and enjoys visiting his friends and pedestrian rambles, waiting patiently till called to the eternal world.

WILLIAM RICHARD HARDING

Was born near Charleville, County Cork, Ireland, December 21, 1795. He graduated at Trinity College, Dublin, with distinguished honor. He was a "prize man," a rank corresponding to senior wrangler in the English universities. Mr. Harding came to America in May, 1836. In the same year he was elected principal of the Preparatory Department of Indiana College. On August 18, 1838, after a little more than a year's service, he died. Prof. Harding received his degree of A. M. from Augusta College. Though but a short time connected with the college, he had shown his excellence as a scholar and ability as a disciplinarian. His nephew, Prof. Harding, of Lehigh University, says of him: "He was a man of decided literary tastes and fond of writing. He wrote many short pieces, poems, etc., some of which gained extensive circulation through the country."

Prof. Harding, of Lehigh, also mentions as an interesting fact, stated in one of his nephew's letters from Bloomington, that there were two of his pupils commencing Latin, who went through the whole preparatory course, commencing with Historiae Sacrae. In addition to this they read Viri Romae, Cæsar and Sallust in the unprecedented time of ninety days' recitation. One of these was Chas. H. Hardin, of Columbia, Mo., and the other Edward Farquhar, of Logansport, Ind.

AUGUSTUS WASHINGTON RUTER.

Prof. Ruter was born in Philadelphia, Pa., February 22, 1811. He was the son of Rev. Dr. Martin Ruter. Prof. Ruter was a graduate of Augusta College, Ky., of the class of 1830, receiving the degrees A. B. and A. M. in course. Soon after graduation he engaged in teaching, and in 1836 was elected Professor of Greek and French in the Indiana University, and remained there till 1838. On leaving Bloomington he went to Wheeling, W. Va., and opened a female seminary. Continuing a few years in Wheeling, he removed to Pittsburg, Pa., and commenced the study of law. During his stay in Pittsburg he compiled a concordance or index to the laws of Pennsylvania. This was published by Alden & Fox, and is now in general use. In 1855 he moved to Texas, seeking a more congenial climate. He there was made President of Soule University, Chapel Hill, Texas. Prof. Ruter's health failing, he went to Lampasas Springs, where he died of consumption in 1869. Prof. Ruter was a member of the M. E. Church.

THEOPHILUS ADAM WYLIE

Was born October 8, 1810, in Philadelphia, Pa. He was the son of Rev. Samuel Brown Wylie, D. D., and Margaret Watson Wylie. He received his early education at the English Academy of Rev. Dr. S. W. Crawford, and commenced his classical education at the school of Wylie & Engles, Philadelphia. He entered the Junior Class of the University of Pennsylvania at its reorganization in 1828, under the Presidency of Dr. DeLancy. At the same time his father, Dr. S. B. Wylie, was elected Professor of Languages. He graduated in 1830, receiving the degrees A. B. and A. M. in course. Shortly after graduation he was one of the teachers in the Academy of the University of which Dr. Crawford was Principal. He became a student in the Theological Seminary of the R. P. Church, and in 1836 was licensed to preach. In the same year, after some correspondence with the Board of Trustees of Indiana College and its President, Dr. A. Wylie, he was offered a Professorship in Indiana University, and at his own request was elected *pro tem.* Professor of Natural Philosophy and Chemistry. In the spring of 1837 he left Philadelphia, and after ten days' journey reached the University in April, and commenced work at the opening of the second term, May 1. After a year's service he was made a permanent member of the Faculty. In 1852 he received an invitation to a Professorship in Miami University, Oxford, O., which was then in a flourishing state and looking up, while the Indiana University at that time was looking in the opposite direction. After remaining two and a half years at Miami he received an invitation to return to Bloomington to his former position in the University, then recovering from its severe calamity, the destruction of its main building in 1854, under the administration of President Daily. With various changes from Professor of Natural Philosophy and Chemistry to Professor of Languages, and in three years after, transferred to the chair of Natural Philosophy, he continued in the active service of the University till 1886, when he received the honorary title of "Emeritus," which he still ('89) holds. Professor Wylie, during the annual showers of honorary degrees, was not missed. He received from Miami University the degree D. D., and a year later from Monmouth College, and the following year from Princeton College, N. J., the same honorary title, and shortly after LL. D. from his *Alma Mater.* Prof. T. A. Wylie married Miss Rebecca Dennis, of Germantown, now in the city of Philadelphia, Pa., Nov. 5, 1838. They celebrated their golden wedding Nov. 5, 1888, receiving, among other kind remembrances, a valuable souvenir from the Faculty of the University.

JAMES FINDLEY DODDS, A. M., M. D.,

Was born November 1, 1807, in Lincoln County, Kentucky, and received his early education in the schools of his native county, in part, and in the schools of Bloomington, his parents moving to this place when he was in his thirteenth year. Dr. Dodds was among the first teachers in the Preparatory Department of the College. He graduated in 1834. In 1837 he was elected Professor of Mathematics. He did not long hold this position, owing to some financial and other difficulties in the College. That no fault was found with Professor Dodds is shown by the following resolution of the Board, passed April, 1840, on motion of Governor William Hendricks: "*Resolved*, That the Board of Trustees think it due to James F. Dodds, for some time Professor in the University, to testify to his industry and fidelity in filling the duties of his office. His dismission was not on account of any fault alleged against him, but as a matter of expediency, resulting from the very peculiar circumstances in which it took place." After leaving Bloomington he studied medicine in the Louisville Medical College, and also with Dr. Mitchell, of Corydon, with whom he practiced medicine for a year or two. On his return to Bloomington, he continued a practitioner in Monroe County till his death, which took place December 7, 1886. The funeral was arranged to take place on Thursday afternoon. On the morning of Thursday his wife, who had been sick for some time, died, and the funeral was postponed till Saturday in order that she might be laid to rest with him. The peculiarly solemn funeral services were conducted in the Presbyterian church, after which both were buried in the same grave. In December, 1838, Dr. Dodds had married Miss Mary Wylie, daughter of Rev. Andrew Wylie, D. D.

PROFESSOR JACOB AMMEN.

Jacob Ammen was born in Botetourt County, Virginia, was four years a cadet at the U. S. Military Academy, West Point (from July 1, 1827, to July 1, 1831), when he was graduated, and promoted in the army to second lieutenancy, 1st artillery; afterward served at the military academy as Assistant Professor of Mathematics and Assistant Instructor in Infantry Tactics for about a year, when he was ordered to the garrison at Charleston Harbor, S. C., during South Carolina's threatened nullification. He was stationed at Fort Trumbull, Conn., 1833-4. Recalled to West Point, he was, from 1836-7, Assistant Professor of Mathematics, and part of the time Principal Assistant Professor of Natural Philosophy, with the rank of First Lieutenant in the First Artillery. Resigning his military position, he was elected Professor of Mathematics in Bacon College, Georgetown, Ky. He continued here till 1839. In the following year he was Professor of Mathematics in Jefferson College, Miss. In 1840 he was elected Professor of Mathematics in the Indiana University, where he continued till 1843, and again returned to Jefferson College, Miss., where he remained till 1848, and from thence he removed to Georgetown, Ky., filling the chair of Mathematics and Astronomy in the college at that place. After leaving Georgetown, he was employed as a civil engineer at Ripley Ohio (from 1855-61). At the outbreak of the Rebellion, Professor Ammen again took up the sword. He organized a company of volunteers for the Twelfth Ohio, of which he was captain, April 18, 1861. In May he was promoted to the Lieutenant-Colonelcy, and in June, following, was commissioned Colonel of the Twenty-fourth Ohio Volunteers. He served in the Virginia campaign in 1861, was engaged in the battle of Cheat Mountain, September 12, and in the action at Greenbrier, October 3. In the Tennessee and Mississippi campaign of 1862, he commanded a brigade, and was engaged in the battle of Shiloh, April 6-7, 1862. The Comte de Paris, in his history of the war, highly praises the brigade of which Colonel Ammen was the organizer and commander. Colonel Ammen was made Brigadier-General, U. S. Volunteers, after this campaign. He was also in the advance upon, and at the siege of Corinth (April 8, 1862), and on the march through north Alabama, and the movement at Louisville, Ky., with the army of the Ohio. In 1862-3 he was placed in command at Covington, Ky., and afterward of Camp Dennison, O., of Camp Douglas, Ills., and of the District of Illinois, and in 1864, of the Districts of Middle Tennessee and Kentucky, and was in command of the District of East Tennessee till January, 1865, when he resigned. Since his resignation he has been County Surveyor of Hamilton County, O., and County Engineer. In 1874, in company with other officers of the army, he made an examination of the routes that had been surveyed for the inter-oceanic canal. At present (1884) he is a successful farmer at Beltsville, Md., and a near neighbor of his distinguished brother, Rear-Admiral Ammen.

(Compiled principally from General Cullum's Biographical Register of the Graduates of the U. S. Military Academy.)

MATTHEW MONROE CAMPBELL

Was born near Cumberland Gap, Tennessee, November 12, 1810. In 1818 the family moved from the Gap and settled on the large military claim which covered the southeast quarter of the city of Louisville, Ky. In 1829 he came to Bloomington, attracted there by the reputation of Dr. Andrew Wylie—who in the preceding year was made President of the University, and became a student under him, with a view to entering the ministry. He did not graduate till after the seventh year of his arrival in Bloomington. During one of these years he taught and for the last two years he assisted in the preparatory department, at the same time keeping up the studies of his class. In 1836 he graduated with honor and with a high reputation for a devout and consistent piety. Soon after graduating, he married Miss Martha McPheeters, and in 1837 he took a school in Mississippi at a salary of $1,200 a year. In 1840 he was called to take charge of the preparatory department of Indiana University, and though the salary was but $500, he, through his attachment to Dr. Wylie, whom he regarded as his personal friend, accepted the offer and hastened to return. Instead of finding a full faculty and only the usual amount of work, he found but two professors—death and a *college cyclone* had swept off all the others—and thus the work of six men devolved upon himself and the other two. On the ground of his assisting so frequently in teaching the regular college classes, he was made adjunct Professor of Languages. In 1853, his health failing, he retired to his farm. In 1863 he was called to fill a vacancy in the chair of languages, occasioned by the resignation of Prof. Ballantine. In 1859 Mr. Campbell was agent for the American Bible Society in Kansas, during which he exercised his talent as a lay-preacher of the gospel in the different places he visited. The famine and drought which prevailed in Kansas in 1860 terminated this agency. In 1861 he received from Governor Morton a chaplain's commission for the Eighty-second Regiment Indiana Volunteers, a position unsolicited by him. Not being an ordained preacher but only an elder in the Presbyterian church, he felt himself unqualified to accept. As he was directed to report immediately to headquarters, and as it was impossible to convene the Presbytery immediately, he applied to the Methodist Conference, then in session in Bloomington, which courteously received him and immediately licensed him to preach, regarding his Presbyterian ordination as sufficient. He immediately joined his regiment and continued with it till the end of the war. Prof. Campbell's last public service was as superintendent of the public schools of Monroe County, Ind., which office he held for four years; and now, a widower, without a home of his own, at the homes of his son and daughter, he spends his time teaching and training his grandchildren and other children, with the hope that they may become good and useful members of society. During three or four years past (since 1884) he has been nearly blind, but notwithstanding this great disadvantage, he has been laboring earnestly to direct the attention of our statesmen and people to the importance and advantage of correcting the orthography of the English language, showing, in several letters which he has published, the great saving of time there would be in the education of children and the advantage that there would be to all, even to the educated, in not being obliged to consult a dictionary for the correct spelling of a word. Prof. Campbell has published a number of open letters, calling the attention of statesmen and teachers and the public in general to the importance of the reform in the orthography and orthoepy which he proposes to make, and which he considers worthy of the attention of the rulers of the English speaking people in all parts of the world.

JOHN IRWIN MORRISON,

Born July 25, 1806, near Chambersburg, Franklin County, Pa. He had for his teachers in early youth the Rev. Samuel W. Crawford, D. D., afterward Principal of the Academy of the University of Pennsylvania, the Rev. Charles B. McKee and Rev. Robert Lusk, ministers of the Reformed Presbyterian Church. Mr. Morrison removed to Indiana in 1826, and settled in Washington County. He pursued his studies in Miami University, Ohio, and graduated there in 1829. Mr. Morrison was the founder of the Salem Female Institute in 1835. In 1839 he was elected State Representative. In 1840 he was Professor of Languages in the Indiana University, which place he occupied till 1843. From 1846 till 1855 he was a Trustee of the University, part of the time the President of the Board. In 1847-50 he was elected State Senator, and was appointed by the Senate, senatorial delegate to the constitutional convention, was chairman of the Committee on Education, and drafted substantially the article on education. Mr. Morrison has also the honor of being the author of section 8 of the law which created the office of "State Superintendent of Public Instruction." From 1856 to 1860 he was Treasurer of Washington County. During the war of the rebellion he was United States Commissioner, and from 1865 to 1867 Treasurer of State. In 1872 he removed from Indianapolis to Knightstown, Henry County, Ind. In that place he was President of the School Board from 1874 to 1877. Again we find him, in 1874-78, President of the Board of Trustees of Indiana University, taking an active part in fitting up the new building for the different departments which were to occupy it. Mr. Morrison united with the Presbyterian Church at Salem in 1830, under the ministry of the Rev. Benjamin Cressey. In 1832 he was married to Catherine Morris, daughter of Benoni Morris, of Washington County, Ind. John I. Morrison died at his home in Knightstown. Ind., July 17, 1882.

DAVID M'DONALD

Was born in the year 1803, on McBride's Run, near Millersburg, Bourbon County, Ky. In 1817, when he was fourteen years old, his parents removed to Indiana and settled in Daviess County, not far from Washington. In addition to the elementary instruction he received in Kentucky, he attended the school of Rev. Cyrus McIntire for a short time, where he received some instruction in Grammar and Rhetoric. This is about all the regular schooling he had. As he was fond of reading and had a disposition to study, he found means to gratify his taste for literature and the study of language. His future career has shown with what success.

In 1820 he connected himself with the religious body then known as New Lights, was licensed to preach, and officiated in this capacity for a number of years with great zeal. At the beginning of the year 1830 he commenced the study of law, devoting a certain number of hours every day to this work. At this time he also had charge of a school. In 1830 he was admitted to the bar. During the first year of his practice his income amounted to about $250, but after this his practice was always remunerative. In 1833 he was elected to the Legislature from the counties of Daviess and Martin, and in this year he was admitted to practice in the Supreme Court of Indiana. In 1834 he was elected Prosecuting Attorney for the Seventh Judicial Circuit; this included ten counties. In 1836 he was reëlected. In 1838 he was chosen Circuit Judge, and this office he held for two terms of seven years each. In September, 1841, he removed to Bloomington, and soon after was elected Professor of Law in Indiana University, in which office he continued till 1852. In November, 1851, the new constitution was adopted, which made sweeping changes in the judiciary. On this account, although urged to the contrary by his friends, he declined nomination. Not long after he was placed by the Whigs on the State ticket as a candidate for the Supreme Bench; but as the Whigs were in the minority he was not elected; his popularity, however, was shown by his receiving 5,000 more votes than any others on the same party ticket. In 1853 he commenced the practice of law in Indianapolis. In 1856 he was elected President of Indiana Asbury University, which honor he declined, for the same reason that he declined the degree of LL. D. conferred by Indiana University, viz., that he had not received a collegiate education. In 1854 he was severely afflicted by the death of a loved daughter. Not long after this he united with the Methodist Episcopal Church. In 1861 he was again subjected to a severe affliction by the death of his estimable wife.

In 1864 he was appointed Judge of the United States District Court for Indiana, which position he held till his death, August 26, 1869.

Judge McDonald was a man of pure morals and of strict integrity, beloved and respected by all who knew him. He was the author of "McDonald's Treatise," a legal work well-known and highly esteemed by the profession, and which still holds its place as a text-book of value. He wrote, also, a large portion of the opinions contained in Bissell's Reports of the U. S. Courts for the Seventh Circuit.

In 1828 Judge McDonald married Miss Mary R. Miller, of Lawrence County, Ill.

DANIEL READ, LL.D.

Daniel Read was born near Marietta, O., June 24, 1805, in the then almost wilderness of Ohio. He was emphatically a Western man, thoroughly identified with Western interests and Western progress, especially as regards education. He was educated at the University of Ohio, where he graduated with the honors of his class. . He then studied law and was admitted to practice in the courts of the State, but being elected to a professorship in his *Alma Mater* he accepted it, and this incident perhaps changed the whole current of his life work. He received his first commission as a teacher when nineteen years of age, on April 5, 1825, and continued either as a Professor or President in State Universities from that time till July 4, 1876, when his official career terminated as President of the University of Missouri, having served the cause of education continuously for more than fifty years. In the year 1843 he was elected Professor of Ancient Languages in Indiana University. In this situation he continued till the year 1856, when he was called to the same position in Wisconsin University, where he remained till 1866, when, on the death of President Lathrop, he was called to the Presidency of Missouri University, which position he held till his sudden death, October 3, 1878, put an end to his earthly career. During his connection with the University of Indiana he was chosen a member of the Constitutional Convention, held in Indianapolis in 1851, in which he took an active part in making the Constitution of the State of Indiana what it now is.

President Read was the oldest child of Ezra Read, of Urbana, O. There were in the family eight sons and one daughter. Dr. Read paid great attention to the education of his younger brothers and sister, all of whom were graduates of respectable colleges, and several of them distinguished in professional life. Two of his brothers were officers in the regular army of the United States. One of them was killed at the head of his regiment during the rebellion. Another brother was Captain in the navy, and was killed on the deck of the vessel commanded by him on the Mississippi River, near Baton Rouge. His sister, Mrs. E. J. McFerson, for a number of years during her widowhood, was principal of a ladies' seminary in Bloomington, Ind., which she conducted with great credit to herself and advantage to the community. General Theodore Read, Dr. Read's only son, the hope and pride of his family, was killed at Appomattox Bridge, in Virginia, in the spring of 1865, and in one of the battles immediately preceding the surrender of General Lee.

Dr. Read stood prominently before the country as a distinguished educator. During his administration the University of Missouri made immense strides in legislative recognition, increased endowment, assured stability and enlarged means of useful instruction, and largely augmented numbers of students. In private life, no family circle could have been more truthful and affectionate, no children could have shown more deference to a father's wishes, no father wiser or more constant and tender solicitude for his children's welfare. Dr. Read accepted reverently and devoutly the Christian religion. He drew inspiration from its sublime truths and precepts for his daily walk. He enjoyed the comforts and blessings promised to the believer, and endeavored to regulate his life in conformity to its laws. Prof. Read married Miss Alice Brice, of Athens, Ohio. He died in Keokuk, Iowa, October 3, 1878.

In making this brief sketch, the writer has made very free use of the memorial addresses made at the University of Missouri, on the occasion of Dr. Read's death, by Major James S. Rollins and R. L. Todd, Esq.

WILLIAM T. OTTO

Was born in 1816, in Philadelphia, Pa., and was educated in Philadelphia at the Academy of Wylie and Engles, and at the University of Pennsylvania in 1833. He studied law with the Hon. Joseph R. Ingersoll. In 1836 he removed to Indiana and engaged in the practice of law until 1844, when he was elected by the Legislature Judge of the Second Judicial Circuit, then embracing the counties of Floyd, Clark, Scott, Jackson, Washington, Orange and Harrison. He served in that capacity till 1852. During several years (from 1847–52) of his term of office he was Professor of Law, in conjunction with Judge David McDonald, in the Indiana University. Judge Otto received the degree of A. M. in course from the University of Pennsylvania, and the honorary degree of LL. D. from the University of Indiana in 1852. He was appointed Assistant Secretary of the Interior by President Lincoln, in which position he remained till 1871, when he was appointed the arbitrator on the part of the United States, under the treaty between the United States and Spain, which provided for the adjudication of claims of American citizens for wrongs and injuries committed against their persons and property by the Spanish authorities in Cuba. This position he resigned on his being appointed, in 1875, by the Supreme Court of the United States, as the Reporter of its decisions, resigning this office in 1884. Since that he was a delegate from the United States to the Universal Postal Congress, which met at the capital of Portugal in the spring of 1885.

CHARLES MARSHALL, PROFESSOR OF MATHEMATICS, 1849–52.

Charles Marshall was born October 3, 1830, at Warrenton, Fauquier County, Virginia; was educated at the University of Virginia, from which, in 1849, he received the degree of A. M. For three years, 1849–52, he was Professor of Mathematics in the University of Indiana, to which he came highly recommended by Professor Courtenay, formerly Professor of Natural and Experimental Philosophy at West Point, and afterward Professor of Mathematics in the University of Virginia; and also by Rev. Dr. W. H. McGuffey, then Professor in the same University. Though a young man when he came to Bloomngton, and boyish in his appearance, he soon commanded the respect of all, students, professors and citizens, by his courteous manner, his scholarship, and his aptness to teach. After resigning his position he studied law and practiced in the city of Baltimore, where he has since resided. At the beginning of the civil war he returned to Virginia and entered the Confederate army, in the spring of 1862, and was for a time on the personal staff of General Robert E. Lee, with the rank of first-lieutenant. In 1862 he was appointed Major and Aid-de-Camp on the staff of General Lee, and served under him in the army of Northern Virginia to the end of the war, having attained the rank of lieutenant-colonel. In 1865 he returned to Baltimore and resumed the practice of his profession. Colonel Marshall was on the staff of General Lee at his surrender at Appomattox.

ROBERT MILLIGAN

Was born in County Tyrone, Ireland, July 25, 1814. He died in his sixty-first year at Harrodsburgh, Kentucky, March 29, 1875. He was four years old when his parents emigrated from Ireland. The family settled in Trumbull County, Ohio, in a newly settled country. While a mere boy he had to assist in clearing the land. In this work, which he entered upon with his characteristic energy, he received some internal injury which compelled him to give up this mode of life, and thus, probably, was determined the current of his future life. When seventeen years old, he was sent to an adjacent county of Pennsylvania, to the Classical Academy of Dr. Gamble, a graduate of the University of Edinburgh, and an excellent teacher. When twenty-one years old he became a communicant in the Reformed Presbyterian church, in which he had been baptized. He was brought up in the strict religious training of that denomination. When twenty-three years old he opened a classical school in Flat Rock, Bourbon County, Kentucky. It was here, by the study of the Bible alone, he was compelled to change his religious views in some important particulars, and soon after he became a member of Mr. Irvine's congregation at Cane Ridge, Kentucky, by whom he was immersed. He left Flat Rock with the intention of going to Yale College. On his way he stopped at Washington, Pennsylvania, and was persuaded by friends there to pursue his studies at Washington College. The special inducement was that there was there a small band of Disciples, who made him their leader and teacher. He completed his course in Washington College in a single term and received the degree of A. B. This was in 1840. He was so much esteemed by the Professors and Trustees that he was elected to a Professorship. In 1842 he was formally ordained a preacher of the gospel by the venerable Thomas Campbell. Twelve years of his life were spent in Washington College, when it was determined by the Trustees to make the College more strictly denominational. The College had always been under Presbyterian control, but now it was to be under the

9—HISTORY.

immediate supervision of the Synod. Professor Milligan was assured that if he desired it he might remain in his position, but knowing that some would not be pleased with his remaining, he resigned his position and accepted, in 1852, the Professorship of Mathematics, and afterward, of Natural Philosophy and Chemistry, in Indiana University. This position he resigned, in 1854, on account of the health of his family, and accepted a Professorship in Bethany College, Virginia. Here he became a coöperator with Alexander Campbell in building up the Institution. In 1854 he entered upon his duties where, along with President Campbell and Messrs. Pendleton and Richardson, he was a coëditor of the *Millennial Harbinger*.

While Prof. Milligan was in Bethany College a strong effort was made to put Bacon College on a sure foundation. An endowment of $200,000 was secured and the name was changed to Kentucky University. Prof. Milligan was chosen President, and was induced to dissolve his relations with Bethany College, and to accept the offered Presidency. Here he labored with his accustomed zeal and success.

President Milligan, in addition to his many contributions to periodical literature, is the author of several works on religious topics. Among the first published, was a small volume on "Prayer." Then followed at different intervals, a volume entitled "Reason and Revelation," next a "Scheme of Redemption," a "Commentary on the Epistles to the Hebrews." "The Great Commission," and "Grace and Good Works." He left unfinished, "A Complete Analysis of the New Testament."

For many years before his death, President Milligan was an invalid. A severe attack of inflammatory rheumatism was followed by neuraligia of the brain, which afflicted him till his death.

President Milligan was a strong advocate of temperance. He would not follow the advice of the physicians in using whisky and brandy for a daily stimulus, as the only chance of prolonging his life. He considered the example he would set to the students and the community would do more harm than his prolonged life would do good.

Professor Milligan, married Miss Ellen Blaine Russell (Jan., 1842), daughter of Hon. Jas. Russell and a cousin of Hon. James Blaine.

JAMES WOODBURN

Was born in Chester District, S. C., September 11, 1817, and came to Bloomington with his father's family in 1826. He was educated at the common schools of the county. Entered the junior class of the University in 1840, was graduated in 1842, and in 1845 received the degree A. M. In 1846, Prof. Woodburn married Miss Martha Jane Hemphill. Immediately after graduation, he engaged in teaching. In 1853, under the Presidency of Dr. Ryors, he was acting Professor of Mathematics and Civil Engineering, and in the following year was called to fill the chair of Adjunct Professor of Languages and Principal of the Preparatory department. For eleven years he faithfully discharged the duties of his position, acting sometimes as county surveyor, and often taking part in educational institutes. In 1865 he returned home sick, from an Institute he had been attending, in Vincennes, and in the course of a few weeks, on the 8th of September, he died from the disease there contracted. Prof. Woodburn was a Ruling Elder in the Reformed Presbyterian church in Bloomington.

PROF. ELISHA BALLANTINE.

Elisha Ballantine was born at Schodack Landing, on the Hudson, N. Y., Oct. 11, 1809. He was well trained, in his parental home, in the primary schools and the University. He graduated in 1828 at Ohio University, at Athens; studied theology at Union Theological Seminary, Va., and afterwards, in 1834-5, at Halle and Leipsic, in Germany. He refused, as inconsistent with the precepts of the great Teacher whose minister he was, the degree of D. D., several times conferred on him. In 1878 he accepted the literary degree LL. D. from the University of Indiana, which he received the year of his resignation, 1878. His life was spent in the service of the church and the cause of education. He was Professor of Hebrew and Greek in Union Theological Seminary from 1831 till 1837; Professor of Languages in Ohio University from 1838 till 1840. From 1840 till 1848 he had charge of a congregation in Prince Edward County, Virginia; from 1848 till 1852 was pastor of the First Presbyterian Church, Washington, D. C. Being threatened with paralysis, and feeling himself unable to endure any mental strain, he rusticated for two years in a country place in

Virginia. In 1854 he was elected Professor of Mathematics in Indiana University. After filling this chair for two years, he was transferred to the chair of Languages, Dr. D. Kirkwood, of Newark, Delaware, having been chosen Professor of Mathematics. In 1863 Prof. Ballantine resigned his professorship in the University to accept a position as Secretary of the American Board of Foreign Missions. In 1866 he was Professor of Hebrew in Lane Theological Seminary, Cincinnati, Ohio. In 1867 he returned to Indiana University as Professor of Greek; since that time as professor and professor emeritus, he has, till his death, been connected with the University. During the last two years of his connection as a professor in active service he was assisted by his son, the Rev. Dr. W. G. Ballantine, now of Oberlin Theological Seminary.

Professor Ballantine was highly esteemed by all who knew him, as a scholar and as a Christian. He had taken the man Christ Jesus as his model, and came perhaps as near to that faultless character as but few of the human family have attained. Professor Ballantine was a sincere man; there was no dissembling about him. He was no flatterer; his words were the true representative of his thoughts. He was benevolent—kind to all with whom he was brought in contact. He was in constant demand when the desponding needed comfort, and when the dying needed a spiritual adviser. His services of this kind were freely rendered, and often sought by Christians of every name. He was highly esteemed by all classes—Protestant and Roman Catholic, Jew and Gentile. As a preacher, Professor Ballantine was plain and practical, often eloquent, never ostentatious.

As a literary man and scholar, Professor Ballantine stood in the first rank. He was thorough in his scholarship. In addition to his knowledge of the Greek and Latin, he was an excellent Hebrew scholar, and had also considerable knowledge of other Semitic dialects, and of modern languages he spoke and read the German language, and was an excellent French scholar.

Professor Ballantine resigned his professorship in Indiana University in 1878. After the resignation of Dr. Moss in November, 1884, he was made acting President. About the close of the year Dr. Jordan, Professor of Biology, was chosen President and Professor Ballantine Vice President and Professor of Greek. These positions he held till his death. On the morning of March 31, 1886, he, as usual, officiated in the chapel services, and seemed to be in perfect health and spirits. In the afternoon he engaged in his usual work in his garden, was suddenly taken ill, went into his house, and in a few moments expired, his daughter Anna being the only one present at his decease.

JAMES RAY M'CORKLE BRYANT

Was born in Philadelphia, June 25, 1802. His ancestors were true patriots, who fought for human rights and the foundation of the Republic. He was educated in Philadelphia at Gray & Wylie's Academy, and there prepared for his entrance into the University of Pennsylvania. After completing the preliminary studies, he studied law, and was admitted to the bar in 1835 by Chief Justice Cranch. For several years he held a position in the General Land Office at Washington, but subsequently moved to the West and settled at Crawfordsville, Indiana. Not long after he was elected to the State Legislature from Montgomery County, and in 1844 he was nominated on the Whig ticket for Congress, but was not elected. He afterwards represented Warren County in the Legislature for several terms. He was a member of the Constitutional Convention which met in Indianapolis in 1852. In 1838 he was appointed Aid-de-Camp to General John Tipton, with rank of Major. In 1856–'61 Major Bryant was Professor of Law in Indiana University. At the breaking out of the Rebellion he was among the first to enlist, and was appointed Lieutenant Colonel of the Tenth Indiana; at the battle of Rich Mountain, Va., he received a wound, from the effects of which he died February 25, 1866. He was a Whig in politics till 1856, from which time till his death he was a Republican, and always an uncompromising opponent of slavery, always on the side of the weak and the oppressed. He gave much of his time to the cause of education. He was himself a good classic scholar, well educated, and knew its value. He was honest and honorable in all his dealings, and made public profession of his Christian faith.

DAVID ECKLEY HUNTER

Was born January 6, 1834, at Princeton, Gibson County, Ind. His early education he received at the Gibson County Seminary, and in part at the University, but did not graduate. Leaving the college for the purpose of teaching, he found the work so attractive to him that he has been an enthusiastic teacher in the public schools, and at institutes, and taking great interest in everything connected with the education of youth. He was county examiner of Monroe County; superintendent of the Princeton schools, also of the Bloomington, Washington and Connersville schools. Professor Hunter is the author of several books for the use of schools, "Helps to History," published 1865; "Primary Charts," 1869; "Object Lessons in Arithmetic," in 1870; "Decalfa," 1870; "Morny Montray." 1884. Professor Hunter has delivered many addresses, on various subjects, "How the West Was Won," "Briers and Berries," "Down the Rapids," "The Race of Life." "A Lesson from the Hymn Book," "The Calycanthus," "Truth," "Davy Crocket," "Trial by Ordeal," "The Rechabites," "History of Indiana State Teachers' Association." In 1870 Mr. Hunter was President of the Indiana State Teachers' Association. President of Primary Section 1871, of Superintendent's Section 1872, Permanent Secretary of the State Teachers' Association since 1875. Mr. Hunter had charge of the model school of the University in 1856, and was Principal of Scientific Preparatory Department, 1866-7. Professor Hunter married Miss Elizabeth R., daughter of the Hon. P. L. D. Mitchell, of Bloomington, December 23, 1856. Professor Hunter's present residence ('89) is Bloomington.

DANIEL KIRKWOOD

Was born in Harford County, Maryland, September 27, 1814. His early education was limited. In 1834 he attended an academy in York, Pa., and afterward became a teacher in the same institution. In 1841 he was chosen Principal of the High School, of which John W. Forney and Thaddeus Stevens were directors. Afterward he removed to Lancaster, Pa., and took charge of the Lancaster City High School. In 1839 he was Principal of the Pottsville Academy. While in this place his "Analogy in the Periods of Rotation of the Primary Planets" was first published in Silliman's Journal of Science, and brought into notice by Professor Sears C. Walker, an astronomer of some distinction, to whom Professor Kirkwood had communicated it in a letter. This ingenious analogy, derived from La Place's nebular theory, attracted much attention, both in this country and in Europe. In 1851 Professor Kirkwood was chosen President of Delaware College, Newark, Del. In 1856 he was elected Professor of Mathematics in Indiana University, which position he occupied until 1886, with the exception of about two years, during which he filled the chair of Mathematics and Astronomy in Jefferson College, Canonsburg, Pa. He has been a frequent contributor to several scientific journals. Many of his articles have received high commendation both at home and abroad. A paper published by him in the proceedings of the Royal Astronomical Society of London first indicated the cause of the intervals between Saturn's rings. In 1851 he was made a member of the American Philosophical Society. The degree of A. M. was conferred on him by Washington College, Pa., and LL. D. by the University of Pennsylvania. The following are a few of his contributions to science: A "Treatise on Comets and Meteors," published by Lippincott & Co., Philadelphia; the "analogy," known as "Kirkwood's Analogy," already noticed; "On the Nebular Hypothesis," Silliman's Journal, 1860; "On the Zone of the Asteroids and the Approximate Commensurability of the Planetary Periods," Proceedings of the Royal Ast. Soc., vol. xxix.; "On the Formation and Primitive Condition of the Solar System," Proceedings of the Am. Philos. Soc., No. 87; "On the Meteors of January 2," proceedings of Am. Phil. Soc., November, 1873; "On Comets and Meteors," read before Am. Phil. Soc., November 19, 1863, and many others. For a more complete list of Professor Kirkwood's contributions to science, see "Circulars for Information," of the Bureau of Education, No. 4, 1873.

It might be also mentioned that Professor Kirkwood is author of the articles on astronomy in the annual supplements of Appleton's Cyclopedia, in which the progress of astronomy from year to year is given. In 1886 Professor Kirkwood resigned his professorship, having been connected with the University for nearly thirty years, and received from it the honorary title of Emeritus Professor.

Professor Kirkwood married Miss Sarah J. McNair, of Newtown, Pa. Professor and Mrs. Kirkwood left Bloomington for Riverside, Cal., October, 1889, where they now reside.

HENRY BASCOM HIBBEN

Was born December 23, 1829, at Uniontown, Pa. He completed his sophomore year at Jefferson College, Pa., and was graduated at Transylvania University September 1, 1848, from which University he received the degree of A. M. He then began his career as a teacher in Jeffersonville, Ind., being chosen Principal of the High School in that city. He next taught in Lawrenceburg Academy, and leaving this situation he took charge of a high school at Laurel, Ind. He afterward served as an itinerant preacher in the M. E. Church for two years, when he was elected to a professorship in Asbury (now DePauw) University, where he continued for five years, when he was elected Professor of English Literature in Indiana University in the year 1860. In 1861, on the breaking out of the war, he entered the service as an army chaplain, and served in this capacity for three years. He was present at the battle of Fort Donaldson, and was mentioned for faithful service in the official report of the battle of Shiloh. In 1864 he was appointed chaplain in the navy by President Lincoln. Professor Hibben is the author of several printed addresses—his last address (1883) was delivered before the Grand Army on memorial day, May 30th.

Rev. Mr. Hibben is still chaplain in the navy, at present (1884) stationed at the Marine Hospital, Philadelphia.

EMANUEL MARQUIS

Was born on the 6th of May, 1829, in Malchin, Grand Duchy of Mecklinburg. At the age of four years he attended the private school of Herr Ravi, a Polander, who instructed him in the elementary branches and prepared him for entering the flourishing Latin school of his native city, under the able management, both as to instruction and discipline, of its Rector, Carl Bütch. On leaving school Mr. Marquis had an award of honors in every department except Mathematics. During these years of severe study he found relief in practice on the piano, under the direction of his father, who was an excellent performer on that instrument. Though afflicted with inflammation of the eyes, brought on by hard study and candle light, he, contrary to the oculist's advice, pursued his studies with private teachers, acquiring in this way a knowledge of Greek,

French, English, Spanish and Hebrew. In 1850 he was engaged as a proof-reader and translator in the office of the "Norddeutsche Freie Presse," a daily paper published in Hamburg. In the same year he accompanied his mother to her native land, Sweden, in order to visit his numerous relatives and acquire a knowledge of the Swedish language. While in Carlscrone he exchanged instruction in German for recitations in Swedish with Magester Strömgren. While in Stockholm many kind services were rendered him in his business by the publisher, R. Bonnier. From Stockholm he returned to Hamburg in July, 1851, and from thence sailed to the United States, arriving at New York September 4. In 1852 he came to Indiana, supporting himself by giving lessons in music and modern languages. He was employed in Asbury (now DePauw) University as an instructor in German and French from 1856 to 1858. From Greencastle he removed to Bloomington in 1859. In 1860 the chair of Modern Languages was established, and Professor Marquis was invited to take charge of this department. In this position he continued till 1864. In 1860 he received the honorary degree of A. M. from the Indiana Asbury University. In 1865, having received an appointment as U. S. Consul at Napoleon Vendée, in France, he repaired to that place. He, however, soon resigned, and in 1866 returned to the United States, and moved back to Greencastle, where he has been engaged in private teaching and commercial pursuits. Professor Marquis has been a frequent contributor to the newspaper and periodical press.

GEORGE AUGUSTUS BICKNELL

Was born in Philadelphia, Pa., in 1817. His early classical education commenced in Wylie and Engles' Academy. From this school he entered the University of Pennsylvania as a sophomore in 1828, at the same time his teacher, Dr. S. B. Wylie, had been made Professor of Ancient Languages in the same institution. In 1831 he graduated, receiving the degree of A. B., and three years afterwards the degree A. M. He studied law in the law school of Yale College receiving the degree LL. B., and in 1864 the degree LL. D. was conferred by Indiana University. In 1846 he removed to Scott County, Indiana, and commenced his political ascent. He was elected Fence Viewer in 1847. In

1848 he was elected County Prosecutor, in 1850 Circuit Prosecutor, and in 1852 Judge of the Second Judicial Circuit, holding this last office twenty-four years by four successive elections. In 1861 he was chosen Professor of Law in Indiana University, which position he held till 1870. Judge Bicknell was elected to the Forty-fifth Congress and was re-elected to the Forty-sixth, as a Democrat, receiving 15,174 votes against 9,102 votes for Ara E. S. Long, National, and 1,757 votes for John F. Willy, Republican. Judge Bicknell belongs to the time-honored family of Bicknells, the ancestor of which, Zachary Bicknell, migrated to this country and settled at Weymouth, Mass., in 1635. It is said that in the nine or ten generations of this family, not one of the blood of the American branch has ever stood convicted of any crime or misdemeanor or fraud. Judge Bicknell's last four year term of service in congress terminated in 1881. In this same year he was appointed one of the Commissioners of the Supreme Court of Indiana, to hold for two years, an office of the same rank as a Judge of the Supreme Court.

Several important legal works and reported speeches are the result of Judge Bicknell's experience as a jurist and statesman. A commentary on the Bankrupt Law, which called for a second edition, was published in New York in 1841. During the twenty-four years of his time as Circuit Judge, at least 250 of his decisions have been published. During his term as Commissioner of Appeals, his decisions may be found in the reports of the Supreme Court, in vols. 73 to 103, inclusive. During his connection with the University as Professor of Law he published an octavo volume of 700 pages, called "Bicknell's Civil Practice." This work required the publication of a second edition in 1871. In 1866 "Bicknell's Criminal Practice," an 8vo. of 500 pages, was published; this also required a second edition in 1871. While in congress, from 1877 to March 4, 1881, many of his speeches and reports were printed. Judge Bicknell, May 28, 1840, married Elizabeth Haskins Richards, of Batso, N. J.

PROFESSOR RICHARD OWEN, M. D., LL. D.

Richard Owen was born January 6, 1810, at Branfield House, near New Lanark, Scotland. He received his early education under a private tutor, and later at the Grammar-school, at old

Lanark. He afterward spent three years at Hofwyl, Switzerland, at the Institution of Emanuel Fellenberg. On his return from Hofwyl, he attended the lectures of Dr. Andrew Ure, at the Andersonian Institute. In 1827 Mr. Owen sailed from Scotland in company with his father, Robert Owen, and on attaining his majority, he received his certificate of citizenship at the hands of Gen. William H. Harrison, the clerk of the Hamilton County Court. During President Polk's administration, at the breaking out of the Mexican war, he obtained a captain's commission in the 16th U. S. Infantry, in one of the ten regiments raised by act of congress, and served in the army during the greater part of the Mexican war. In 1861 Captain Owen accepted, from Governor Morton, a Lieutenant Coloneley in the 15th Indiana Volunteers. He served in West Virginia, in command of a Brigade under Gen. A. J. Smith. Later, while under the command of General Franklin, in 1863, he resigned and accepted a Professorship in Indiana University. Before his connection with the University, in the interim between the Mexican war and the war of the Rebellion, first as Major and afterwards as Lieutenant Colonel, he was connected with the Western Military Institute of Kentucky, as Professor of Natural Science. While in the Military Institute, Dr. Owen not only gave instruction in his own department, but shared with Colonel B. R. Johnson in the military training of the students, and as commandant was chiefly charged with the discipline of the Institution and with the management of the barracks. For three years he was engaged in the Literary department, of the University of Nashville. In Indiana University, Dr. Owen was Professor of Natural Philosophy and Chemistry, from 1863 to 1867. Professor of Natural Science and Chemistry from 1867 to 1879. During these fifteen years he gave instruction principally in Geology, Mineralogy and Chemistry, and during vacancies in the Modern Language Department, he taught German and French. Before becoming Professor in the Western Military Institute, Dr. Owen was, in 1849, the assistant of his brother Dr. David Dale Owen, in the United States Geological Survey of Minnesota. He was principally engaged in taking barometrical observations and making sketches, which were afterwards engraved for the large Fourth Report of the Survey. In 1859-60, before entering the Federal service, Dr. Owen made a geological survey of Indiana, the first year as assistant to his brother David Dale Owen, and in the following year as State Geologist. His report, with illustrations, was published by the State. While connected with the Indiana University, he made a survey of the mineral resources of portions of New Mexico and Arizona, at the request of Judge Watts, by whom the account of the exploration was published. Dr. Owen also made a geological examination of parts of North Carolina and of East Tennessee.

Dr. Owen also contributed largely to periodicals, both scientific and literary. Since his resignation in 1879 his researches have principally been in terrestrial magnetism and its effect on the formation of land on our globe. The results of these researches have been published partly in the proceedings of the A. A. A. S., and partly in "Science," a weekly journal.

From Dr. Owen's early home training, and the influence of a pious mother, he always manifested a religious spirit, while at the same time his father's skepticism and principles and opposition to Christianity had its effect upon him, causing him to doubt the truth of revealed religion. During his whole life he retained a spirit of liberality to all who conscientiously differed from him in his religious or political views. He always deprecated violence and extreme party spirit. He respected each man's individuality and peculiarity, when not interfering with another man's rights. It is not strange that, when in Bloomington, associating with God-fearing men in the town and in the faculty of the University, he professed his faith in the Divine Savior and became a member of and an office-bearer in the Presbyterian church. Dr. Owen died March 25, 1890, at New Harmony, from the effects of poison accidentally taken, while engaged in his philosophical studies with youthful ardor. In 1887 he contested for a high prize offered by the Belgium Government, which he did not win, but was one of the few of whom honorable mention was made. Dr. Owen married Miss Annie Neif, daughter of Joseph Neif.

PROF. AMZI ATWATER

Was born November 9, 1839, at Mantua, Portage County, Ohio, and commenced his classical education at the Eclectic Institute, which afterwards became Hiram College. On leaving the Institute he attended the Northwestern Christian University (now Butler), at Indianapolis, and remaining there a short time he entered the Junior class of Indiana University in 1864. In his senior year he was appointed Principal *pro tem.* of the Preparatory Department of the University, taking the place of Prof. James Woodburn, the Principal of this department, who died shortly before the commencement of the college year, 1865–6. In 1866 he graduated, receiving the degree A. B., and three years later the degree A. M. After graduation he was made adjunct Professor of Languages and Principal of the Preparatory Department of the University. This position he held until 1868, when he was elected Professor of Latin and Greek in Hiram College. While holding that position he was called to the pastorate of the Disciples' Church, at Mentor, Ohio. In 1870 he was elected Professor of Latin in Indiana University, and returned to Bloomington, where he has since remained, and has, since 1888, been Vice President of the University.

Professor Atwater is well known as an able and interesting lecturer, especially on educational topics. He lectured in the northeastern portion of the State in the interest of the University in the summer of 1875, and has since frequently lectured on these and kindred subjects before literary societies and institutes in the adjacent States.

He married Miss Cortensia Munson.

CYRUS MORRIS DODD

Was born in Broadalbin, N. Y., in 1826. His mother was a Harrison, of the New Jersey Harrisons, his father a lineal descendant of Daniel Dodd, who came from England and settled in Bradford, Conn., in 1646. His children went to Newark, N. J., among the first settlers of that city. The family has furnished its full proportion of men of superior talents and education, and has maintained during two centuries the old Puritan characteristics of piety and morality, of energy and of thrift.

Cyrus Dodd's first ten years were spent in Newark. When ten years old he went to Bloomfield, New Jersey, where he spent his boyhood and prepared for college in the old brick academy. His earliest training was given by his father, who was ambitious to give him a good education. When seventeen years old he began to earn his own schooling by teaching, for which occupation he seems to have had a natural instinct, which was stirred by his observation of the prevailing imperfect methods and results. In 1845 he entered the sophomore class of Williams College. His intention had been to go to Princeton for the junior class of which he had been prepared, and to which all of his family and all of his friends had gone or were going. But the hills of Williamstown and Dr. Mark Hopkins were the attractions which took him to Williams College. After a year of study there, he left to teach for several years in New Jersey and Maryland. In 1854 he returned to the college and entered the third term of the junior year, graduating in 1855. After teaching about two years in Salem, N. J., he married Miss Mary C. Latham, of Williamstown, and went to New Brunswick, N. J., where he taught for a year. He then entered the Presbyterian Theological Seminary at Allegheny City, Pa., where he remained a year and a half, teaching about half the time, and writing editorials for his support. About this time he received a call to the Latin chair of Jefferson College at Cannonsburgh, Pa., where he remained five years. He was then, in 1886, elected to the chair of mathematics in Indiana University, vacated by Professor Kirkwood, continuing in this position a year, and on the return of Professor Kirkwood, its former occupant, to the University, Professor Dodd was transferred to the chair of Latin Languages and Literature. In 1867 Professor Dodd received a call from his *Alma Mater* to the chair of mathematics, which he accepted, and soon after removed to Williamstown, where he still resides. Professor Dodd was not only an able mathematician and an excellent classical scholar, but he was well versed in English literature. He was a great lover of books, as his well selected library attests. Professor Dodd could work not only extraordinarily well with his head, but also with his hands; was skillful in the use of physical apparatus. He could print a book and then bind it as well as if brought up to these arts; could build a house and make its furniture as well as the trained carpenter or cabinet maker. His principal enjoyment, however, was in books, especially in poetry. He considered mathematics and poetry akin. Bryant was a favorite poet with him. He considered it an honor that he could count him among his friends. The "*Dies Iræ*" was made, as a painter would say, quite a study with Professor Dodd. He had, perhaps, collected more versions of this wonderful hymn than any person in the country. His three daughters, in their love of literature and poetry, seem to be following in the footsteps of their father. During his absence from Bloomington, while in New York engaged with Professor Wylie in purchasing books for the University library, Professor Dodd's dwelling was burned, and many of his valuable books as well as manuscripts were destroyed.

A sadder loss has lately (1887) befallen the Professor by the decease of his accomplished daughter Alice.

GEORGE WASHINGTON HOSS

Was born November 6, 1824, in Brown County, Ohio. The family removed, when he was twelve years old, to Marion County, Indiana. Until he was twenty-one, he worked on the farm, acquiring such education as the county schools afforded and his limited time permitted. He then entered Indiana Asbury University occasionally interrupting his regular studies by teaching, in order that he might gain means for completing his college course. He graduated in 1850, receiving the degrees of A. B. and A. M. In 1872 he received the honorary degree of LL. D. from Indiana University. In the year of his graduation he was elected Principal of the Muncie Academy. Two years after this he removed to Indianapolis, where he resided for many years. In 1855 he was teacher of Mathematics in Indiana Female College. In the next year he was first literary teacher in the Institution for the Blind. This position he occupied for two years, and then was made President of the Female College, which he held for one year, when he accepted the position of Professor of Mathematics in Butler University, where he continued eight years.

In 1864 he was elected Superintendent of Public Instruction. Two years before this he had succeeded to the editorship of the Indiana School Journal, which he conducted during his term of office till 1871, when he turned it over, with a subscription list increased to 1,600, to Professor W. A. Bell, who still (1886) ably edits and publishes it.

Superintendent Hoss entered upon the duties of his office of Superintendent of Public Instruction in March, 1865, well fitted for the post by his zeal and energy and his practical experience as a teacher. His capability is well indicated by his actions as well as his reports. He was an advocate for the law which the General Assembly had passed in favor of local taxation of corporations for the support of common schools, in opposition to the adverse decision of the Supreme Court, which had declared the law unconstitutional. Through his able advocacy of his position in his report, the General Assembly of 1867 enacted a new law authorizing special tuition taxes, and this law now stands.

In 1865 Superintendent Hoss was elected President of the State Teachers' Association. Two years later he issued a call to the Faculties of the colleges to organize a collegiate association to coöperate with the Teachers' Association, about to meet in New Albany.

In 1866 Superintendent Hoss was reëlected and served till 1868, when he resigned to enter upon the Professorship of English Literature in Indiana University, President Hobbs, of Earlham College, being appointed his successor.

Professor Hoss resigned his professorship in 1872, having accepted the Presidency of the State Normal School at Emporia, Kansas. After a year of service there he was recalled to Indiana University as Professor of English Literature and Elocution. This position he held with credit to himself and profit to the University till 1880, when he resigned and removed to Topeka, Kansas, where he became proprietor and editor of the Educationalist, the leading school journal of Kansas. In 1884 he was elected Professor of English Classics and Oratory in Baker University, Baldwin, Kansas, which position he now (1888) holds.

In addition to the able and carefully prepared reports as Superintendent of Public Instruction and two minor reports made to the Governor, his official publications, Dr. Hoss has prepared several small books for the use of schools. He married Miss Harriet J. Mitchell, of Portland, Maine.

SCOTT BUTLER

Was born at Indianapolis, February 9, 1844. He received his education at the Northwestern Christian University, now Butler University, so named from Professor Butler's father. He graduated in 1868, receiving the degrees A. B. and A. M. not long after. He studied two years in Germany; on his return he engaged in teaching. From 1868 to 1871 he was Principal of the Preparatory Department of the University of Indiana. Soon after leaving Indiana University, he was made Professor of Latin in Butler University, Irvington, Ind. This position he still (1889) holds. In 1862-5 he served as a private soldier in the U. S. Signal Service. Mr. Butler married Miss Julia Dunn, of Indianapolis, November 3, 1868.

ELI LONG

Was born at Versailles, Ky., June 16, 1837, graduated at the Military School near Frankfort, Ky., in 1855. Soon after he was appointed Second Lieutenant in First U. S. Cavalry, and served six weeks at Lecompton, Kan., during the troubles in that region. In the summer of 1857 he was with his regiment on the Cheyenne expedition, and was afterwards in command of General Sumner's body-guard in the fight with the Indians in 1857-58, and in the same years mail escort on the SantaFe road, from Fort Riley. In 1860 Lieutenant Long served on the Kiowa and Comanche expedition, under Major Sedgwick. In 1861 he prevented loss and serious damage to the Government by surprising and capturing near Fort Lyon a well armed company of thirty-eight men and fifty horses, on their way to join the Confederate General Price in Missouri. On this trip Lieutenant Long moved one hundred and twenty miles in thirty-two hours, with the loss of but one horse, and was promoted to be First Lieutenant, March 21, and to Captain, May 24, 1861, In February, 1862, Captain Long reported to General Buel at Louisville, Ky., was in the skirmish at Tuscumbia creek, near Corinth, Miss., took part in the battle of Chaplain Hills, near Perryville, Ky., remained on duty with his regiment as General Rosecran's escort until the battle of Stone river, when he was wounded in the shoulder while leading his command in a charge made by his regiment. He was, for gallant conduct, appointed Colonel of the Fourth Ohio Volunteer Cavalry. Shortly after receiving this command Colonel Long led in a charge against the enemy, in which fifty prisoners and many horses were captured. In June, 1863, Col. Long was appointed to command a brigade of the First, Third, Fourth and Tenth Ohio Volunteers and Second Kentucky Volunteer Cavalry regiments. He participated in most of the cavalry affairs at Mur-

freesboro, Tenn. He commanded his brigade at the defeat of
the rebels at Elk river, was at the battle of Chickamauga and
at the discomfiture of General Wheeler's command, by which
Chattanooga was secured to the United States forces. He was
also at the engagements at McMinnville and Farmington, Tex.,
and at the former place he received a wound. General Long
was favorably mentioned in the official reports for his gallant
conduct at McMinnville, and also for his expedition during the
battle of Missionary Ridge, where he destroyed thirty miles
of railroad. With his brigade, he participated in the complete
rout of General Wheeler at Calhoun. In 1864 he took part
with his command in the reconnoisance of Dalton with the
Sixteenth Army Corps. In connection with the Seventeenth
Army Corps, under General Blair, went to Kingston, Georgia,
defeating General Roddy on the way. He joined the army under
General Sherman, and participated in nearly all the army
operations under his command in 1864. In August, 1864, he
was appointed Brigadier General of Volunteers. Returning
after leave of absence, owing to his wounds, he rejoined his
command at Nashville, Tenn. After this he went South, and
with 1,250 men in line, took Selma, Ala., with many prisoners
and munitions of war.

General Long was frequently mentioned in reports for gallant
conduct. He retired as Major General, U. S. Army, but was
reduced to the grade of Brigadier General by act of Congress,
1875. In 1868 was Professor of Military Science and Civil Engineering
in Indiana University; afterward studied law at Cincinnati,
and was admitted to practice in Brooklyn, N. Y., in
1870.

JOHN UPFOLD PETTIT

Was born in Onondaga County, New York, September 11, 1820;
was educated in the Onondaga County schools, afterward in
Cazenovia Academy, Madison County; attended Hamilton College
for some time, and afterward Union College, Schenectady,
during the presidency of Dr. Nott, graduating B. A. in 1839.
Mr. Pettit studied law with Dr. Selkanoff, and also attended
the law school at Pompey, New York, under Daniel Gott.
After removing to Indiana he continued his study of law with
the Hon. D. D. Pratt, of Logansport, and in 1841 was admitted
to the bar, commencing the practice of law in Wabash, Indiana,

in the same year. He was elected to the State Legislature in 1844. In 1850 he was appointed U. S. Consul at Maranhao, Brazil. Mr. Pettit was appointed by Governor Wright Judge of the 8th Judicial District. Resigning this office he was, in 1854, elected representative to Congress from the 11th Congressional District. This position he held during the 34th, 35th and 36th Congresses, and in 1864 was again elected to Congress and chosen Speaker of the House. In 1869–70 Judge Pettit was Professor of Law in Indiana University, from which, in 1871, he received the degree LL. D. In 1872 he was elected Judge of the 17th Judicial District.

At the outbreak of the rebellion he engaged actively in recruiting soldiers. In 1862 in less than three weeks he mustered thirty-five hundred men, and in the following year assisted in organizing the Orphans' Home, at Knightstown, Indiana. In 1865, after others had failed, he was largely instrumental in procuring a commutation of the sentence of Bowles and Milligan, who had been condemned to death by the United States Military Commission for treasonable conspiracy in Indiana. On May 2 an order came from President Johnson to carry into effect the sentence, without delay. The date fixed was June 2, 1865. Judge Pettit was dispatched to Washington by Governor Morton to secure from the President a commutation of the sentence. Through the energy of Judge Pettit, acting under the earnest direction of Governor Morton, the sentences of these men were commuted. Judge Pettit was a ripe scholar, and a great reader. He was well acquainted with history, poetry, and the current literature of the day. He excelled in his knowledge of law. Very few appeals were taken from his decisions, and very rarely did the Supreme Court fail to affirm his judgments. In religion he was an Episcopalian. At the time of his death, which occurred March 21, 1881, at Wabash, Indiana, he had been appointed paymaster to disburse the principal due to the Miami Indians.

Judge Pettit married Miss Brenton, who survives him.

JOHN A. REUBELT

Was born February 22, 1819, in a village of Franconia in Germany. He received his theoretical education in his native land and when twenty-one years old came to America. As no degrees in course, in the American sense of the expression, are conferred in Germany, he of course received none, but in or about 1858 he received the honorary degree of A. M. from Dickinson College, Carlisle, Pa., and sometime afterwards the degree D. D. from Baldwin University, Ohio. Nearly all the time since his arrival in America, he has been engaged in teaching; he has been employed in schools of every grade and has filled different chairs in colleges and universities. In 1868 he was professor of modern languages in Indiana Asbury University, and in 1869-70 in Indiana University. In 1870 he removed to Henderson, Ky., where he was for some years Principal of a classical school. Dr. Reubelt has written much for various quarterlies and monthlies, and other periodicals. He translated Gess' "Person of Christ," published at Andover, 1870, and translated into German "Greeley's Great Conflict," and in the same language edited a "Manual of Natural History," and published many other smaller works and tracts in both languages. Dr. Reubelt is now (1889) Principal of an academy at Ghent, Ky.

HERMANN BALTHASAR BOISEN

Was born in Flensburg, Schleswig-Holstein, Germany, December 11, 1846. He received his education at the Gymnasium of Plön and at the University of Würzburg. He came to America in 1869, and went first to St. Paul, Minnesota. He remained in Minnesota about a year, teaching a part of the time. In 1870 he came to Indiana. He engaged first in institute work, and in the fall took charge of a school in Belleville. His enthusiastic work in the institutes had attracted the attention of some of the teachers in DePauw—then Asbury—University, and when inquiry was made concerning a teacher of modern languages for Indiana University, he was highly recommended, and Dr. Owen was then commissioned to visit him and offer him a temporary place in the University. He accepted the place and began his work in November, 1870. So well did he succeed in his work that in the following year the place was made permanent. In July, 1873, he was married to Miss Louise Wylie, of Bloomington. In 1874, having been elected to take charge of the advanced course in the State Normal School at Terre Haute, he left the University, only to return again in 1876, the advanced course having been abolished because the expense of maintaining it was too great in proportion to the number of students. In 1880 he again resigned his place in the University, and in November of the same year he was appointed by President Chadbourne to the Chair of Modern Languages in Williams College, Mass. Dr. Chadbourne resigned soon afterward and the trustees did not confirm the appointment, but left it to the new President to fill the place as he pleased. Without inquiry as to the success of Professor Boisen's work, and without reference to the promise made by Dr. Chadbourne that the appointment should be made permanent if his teaching was satisfactory, Dr. Carter chose another for the place. Sensitive in the extreme, Professor Boisen felt most keenly the injustice with which he was treated. He was now forced to give up a trip to Europe, and spend the summer at Martha's Vineyard, where there was a summer institute. In the fall he went to Boston, where he gave private lessons, and also prepared two books for publication. The "First Course in German" was written for use in his own classes, and not a very large edition was published. Since his death Professor Bernhardt has enlarged it and added a second volume, and it is now used in many schools. Being appointed a Director of the Martha's Vineyard Summer Institute, he spent a second summer at Cottage City, and completed the manuscript of his second book, "The Preparatory Book of German Prose," which is quite extensively used. In 1882 he was appointed Sub-Master of the Elliott School in Boston. The work in this school gave him great pleasure, but it also took all his time and he could accomplish but little outside work, and he had planned to do a great deal. Accordingly in 1883 he very gladly accepted a call to the Lawrenceville School in New Jersey, for there he would have leisure for other work. The beginning of the work at Lawrenceville was greatly saddened by the death of his brother, Christian, a young man of noble character. His own health was not so good as in former years, but he went to work with his accustomed energy and earnestness. His love for the boys under his care was untiring. Everything he could do to make them happier and better was done, and they appreciated his love for them and his devotion to their interests. As soon as he was fairly settled in his new home he began to work upon his first volume of Language Lessons, a book for use in the public schools. But suddenly he was taken violently ill; the doctor said his heart was affected. In two or three days he was up, and insisted on going to school. He heard all his classes on Monday, January 21, 1884. About eight o'clock that evening, almost without warning, he had left us. The stone that marks his last resting place, after names and dates, bears this inscription:

"Erected by his colleagues and pupils of the Lawrenceville School as a tribute to his worth as a man and his genius as a scholar."

BASKIN E. RHOADS

Was born in 1834, near Philadelphia, Pennsylvania. In the following year the family moved to Parke County, Indiana, and settled near Rockville. In 1840 they removed to Waveland, Indiana. He received his early education in the Waveland Academy, where he resided till the death of his father, in 1875. At sixteen years of age he was prepared to enter college, but on account of delicate health he learned the art of tanning with David Mann. After becoming master of the art he returned to the Waveland Academy, and after studying six months he taught in the Huxford school house. He returned after three months and spent another term in the Academy, when he was chosen Principal of the Newport School, where he taught and studied, preparing himself for the Junior Class of Wabash College, which he entered in 1858 and graduated in 1860. Soon after graduation he was chosen Professor of Natural Science in the Clinton Institute, and early in 1861 was put in charge of the Rockville public school, where he remained till the summer of 1862.

From 1862 till 1870 he practiced law in Newport. In 1864 he was chosen Representative of Vermillion County. He served in the Legislature with great distinction, in the regular and special sessions. As a member of the Committee on Education he drafted the present School Law, which was passed, and presented by himself to Governor Morton, who signed it in his presence. The law was passed with but little alteration from the original draft.

Judge Rhoads also introduced and warmly supported the bill for organizing the Normal School at Terre Haute, in consideration of which the teachers of the State unanimously chose him to deliver the annual address at their meeting in LaFayette, in 1866. In 1868 he was elected Professor of Greek in the Indiana University but declined, preferring to study law. He was elected a Trustee of the University, serving from 1868 till he resigned in 1872. When a Trustee he, in connection with Dr. Cloud, of Evansville, was the committee (Dr. Cloud entrusting the whole management of the affair to him) to purchase the large and valuable collection of minerals and geological specimens which Dr. David D. Owen had collected in his surveys as United States Geologist and had obtained by exchange and purchase. The sum paid for it was $20,000.

In 1870 Judge Rhoads was elected Professor of Law in Indiana University, which chair he filled till 1877. On his resignation the school was closed.

He then traveled for some time in Europe, and while there made the acquaintance of many men, eminent in law and science. He studied with great care the financial and economic questions presented there, and made a specialty of the matter of State control of railroads, as presented in Belgium and in Germany.

In 1868 Mr. Rhoads was elected Judge of the Court of Common Pleas, in the district composed of Montgomery, Fountain, and Vermillion Counties, but by some frauds in the Covington district, he was counted out. The perpetrator of this fraud has since confessed it. In April, 1881, Judge Rhoads was appointed by Governor Porter, Judge of the Superior Court of Vigo County.

In addition to Judge Rhoad's distinction as a scholar, lawyer and politician, he has also some claim to distinction as a scientist. In 1862 Judge Rhoads made a geological tour among the hills of Sand Creek, and there unearthed a stone, in which was imbedded a fossil never before classified. This fossil was sent to Professor Meek, the paleontologist of the Smithsonian Institute, who pronounced it new and valuable. It is figured in the Fifth Volume of the Illinois Geological reports. Dana and Agasiz pronounce it the first discovery of the kind, and hence entitled to the discoverer's name—*Eupachyerinus Tuberculatus Rhoadsii*.

JAMES THOMPSON

Was born September 27, 1828, in Franklin, Delaware County, N. Y. His opportunities for intellectual culture were good, and as he was endowed with a mind of superior character, he made good use of his advantages. He attended the Delaware Literary Institute and Fredonia Seminary. When nineteen years old he was appointed a cadet in the U. S. Military Academy at West Point. He was graduated with honor July 1, 1851, standing No. 6 in a large class. He was promoted to Brevet Lieutenant, Second Artillery, on the same day. He served in the garrison at Newport Barracks, Ky., in 1851. In 1852 he served at Fort Wood as Second Lieutenant, Second Artillery. He was next ordered to Fort Moultrie, S. C., where he continued till 1854. August 19, 1856, he was married to Miss Julia M. Taliaferro, of Newport, Ky. From 1854 to 1857 Lieutenant Thompson was Assistant Professor of Mathematics in the Military Academy. In 1859 he was in the garrison at Fort Independence, Boston Harbor, Mass. In 1860–61 he was on frontier duty at Fort Brown, Texas, and in the latter part of 1861 at Fort Hamilton, N. Y. While at Fort Brown the Rebellion was inaugurated, and Lieutenant Thompson was one of the first prisoners of war. He was paroled and came to Newport, where he remained until exchanged. He served during the whole of the War of the Rebellion—in defense of Fort Pickens in 1861, in the Manassas campaign, and in battle of Bull Run, July 21, 1861. Before this campaign he had been promoted to a captaincy for gallant conduct. He next served in the defenses about Washington, D. C. Next we find him in the Peninsular campaign (Army of the Potomac), engaged in the siege of Yorktown, at the battle of Williamsburg in 1862, in the battle of Fair Oaks May 31, 1862, in skirmishes on the 25th to 29th of June, 1862, near Seven Pines, and in the battle of Glendale, June 30, 1862. For his meritorious and gallant services at this battle he was brevetted Major. On the following day he fought at the battle of Malvern Hill, and on the next day in a skirmish at Harrison's Landing. For about a month he was absent on sick-leave. After this he served as Chief of Artillery in defense of Cincinnati during the rebel raid in September, 1862. He next served in the department of Ohio, and while in the army of Kentucky he was engaged in the defense of Franklin, Tenn., and in the battle of Chicamauga, Ga., in September, 1863. He organized an artillery regiment in Kentucky in 1863 and 1864, and was on mustering and disbursing duty at Louisville, Ky. (March to May), 1864, and on the same duty at Cincinnati,

Ohio, immediately afterward. In September, 1864, he was in the garrison at Fort Point, Cal., and on mustering and disbursing duty at San Francisco, Cal., in 1865, and on recruiting service in January, 1866, at the same place. Major Thompson was brevetted Lieutenant Colonel March 13, 1865. Such is the account given of Colonel Thompson in the U. S. Army Register. In 1860 he was Commissioner of Education for Tennessee under General Howard, and had charge of the educational interests of the freedmen. It was under his superintendence that Central Tennessee College at Nashville was founded. The freedmen, for whose mental and moral condition he has done so much, loved him, and gave his name to the chapel of the College. In 1859 failing health compelled his retirement from the army, or, as expressed by the official Army Register, "he was retired from disability resulting from long and faithful service." In 1870 he was offered and accepted a Professorship of Military Science and Civil Engineering in Indiana University. He remained in Bloomington until 1876, when his health became so bad that he resigned and returned to Newport.

Colonel Thompson, the brave soldier and the man of science, was an humble follower of Christ and an active member in the Methodist Episcopal Church. Both in Bloomington and as a member of Grace Church, Newport, Ky., with which he had connected himself in 1866, he held a number of church offices; and in all these offices, whether as steward, Sunday-school teacher or superintendent, he discharged all the duties devolving upon him with energy and zeal. During the last years of his illness he suffered much. On Friday, February 13, 1880, he departed this life. In the words of his pastor, Rev. M. Mullenix, to whose obituary notice we are indebted for a part of this sketch, "Colonel Thompson was one of the wisest, truest and purest men we have ever known."

JUDGE SAMUEL E. PERKINS.

Samuel E. Perkins was born in Brattleboro, Vt., on the 6th of December, 1811. He was left without parents or property when five years old, and was adopted into the family of William Baker, a respectable farmer of Conway, Mass., with whom he lived and labored till he was twenty-one. During this period, by the aid of three months' schooling a year in the State free schools during the winter months, and by devoting rainy days and evenings to books, he secured himself a good English education and made a beginning in the study of the dead languages. After he had reached his majority he pursued his studies in different schools, working mornings and evenings and during vacations to raise money for tuition and support. The last year of this course of studies was spent in the Yates County Academy, New York, of which Seymour B. Gookins, a brother of Judge Gookins, of Terre Haute, was Principal. Sometime about 1834 he attended the Fellenburg Academy at Shelburn, Mass. After this he studied law in Penn Yan, N. Y., writing in law offices for his board and tuition.

In the fall of 1836 he came alone on foot to Indiana. He was not acquainted with any one in the State. He arrived at Richmond and spent the winter reading law in the office of Judge Borden. In the following spring he was admitted to the bar at Centreville, the county seat of Wayne County, but opened his office in Richmond. He became editor of the Jeffersonian, a lately established Democratic paper. He soon found himself in this place in the midst of a large and lucrative practice.

In 1843 he was appointed Prosecuting Attorney by Governor Whitcomb for that judicial district, and in 1844 was one of the electors who gave the vote of the State to Polk. In 1841 he was nominated by Governor Whitcomb to a seat on the Supreme Bench, but was not confirmed. The same thing occurred the following year. On the adjournment of the Legisture Judge Perkins received from the Governor the appointment for one year to the Supreme Bench. On the reëlection of Governor Whitcomb Judge Perkins was renominated and his nomination was confirmed by the Senate. When called to the Supreme Bench he was but thirty-four years old. While on the Supreme Bench he prepared the Indiana Digest, a volume of over 800 pages, requiring great research, and one then of great use to and highly esteemed by the Indiana bar. In the following year he prepared "The Indiana Practice," in size and appearance like the "Digest." In 1852 he was elected and in 1858 reëlected to the Supreme Bench, and again in 1876. In 1857 he received the appointment of Professor of Law in the

Northwestern (now Butler) University, and in 1870 was chosen Professor of Law in the Indiana University, which post he occupied till 1872.

Judge Perkins was a man of large intellect and endowments. He was a profound thinker, a bold, incisive and scholarly writer, and an enlightened and impartial Judge.

Judge Perkins was married twice, first in 1838 to a daughter of Joseph Pyle, of Richmond, Ind. His second wife was also a daughter of Joseph Pyle.

Judge Perkins died at the close of the year 1880.

TILGHMAN HOWARD MALLOW

Was born in Johnson County, Indiana, December 20, 1841. Died at his father's residence in Johnston County, August 13, 1872. Professor Mallow received his early education in the district schools of his native county. In 1867 he entered the freshman class of the University and when in this class, on account of excellence as a scholar, he assisted in the Preparatory Department. Immediately after his graduation he was made adjunct Professor of Language and Principal of the Preparatory Department. He held this position for one college year, his life of much promise being cut off by consumption.

REV. JOHN L. GAY, A. M.,

Was born in Iredell County, North Carolina. He was prepared for college at the Wilkesburg and Beford Academies, and entered the North Carolina University in 1831, where he remained three years, but through feeble health was compelled to leave before graduation. After the recovery of his health he studied law and practiced at the bar in Alabama for four years. Abandoning that profession he was ordained a deacon in the Episcopal church in 1843. In 1845 he was advanced to the priesthood, and has continuously exercised his office as a clergyman ever since—first in Alabama then in Florida, and then in the diocese of western New York. From western New York he went successively to Tennessee, North Carolina and Delaware, thence to Canada, in the diocese of Quebec, and after that to Indiana, thence to Kansas, and from Kansas to Missouri, where he has resided and labored for more than eight years, in Fayette, his present (1887) home. His life has been laborious yet uneventful, mainly occupied as a missionary clergyman of the Protestant Episcopal church. He has spent forty-four years of his life in this service, as an humble laborer in the Lord's vineyard. Before Professor Gay studied law, he was Professor of Languages in Alabama University. In 1871–72 he was Professor of English Literature in Indiana University.

DELANA R. ECKELS

Was born August 19, 1806, in Fleming County, Ky., was educated in Flemingsburg, and in those early days, when colleges and academies were rare, Judge Eckels, by his own study and self-training, acquired the knowledge necessary for the practice of the law. He was admitted to the bar in 1827, and for sixteen years was a Judge on the Federal and State Bench. He was chosen Professor of Law in the University, a position he occupied in 1872-3.

Judge Eckels served one year in the Mexican War as a captain, and was in the campaign under General Johnson in Utah. In 1827 he served one session in the Legislature. He was the first Mayor of the city of Greencastle, and organized and conducted the free schools at their establishment in 1853.

In 1827 he connected himself with the Christian Church, and has, during his long life, served his country and his God as a teacher, soldier, advocate, statesman, judge and Christian.

Judge Eckels died November 5, 1888, at Greencastle, Ind.

GEORGE PARROTT.

George Parrott was born at Dayton, Ohio, August 12, 1832; was graduated at the Ohio Wesleyan University, Delaware County, Ohio, July, 1852, and received the degree A. M. in 1855. Subsequent to his graduation Mr. Parrott was for sixteen years engaged in the traveling ministry of the Methodist Episcopal Church. For three years he was President of Vincennes University, and in 1872–3 was Professor of English Literature in the the Indiana University at Bloomington. Since 1873, from failure of his voice, he engaged in business in the Parrott Manufacturing Company, at Dayton, Ohio, of which he is at present (1883) its secretary and treasurer. During the war he was connected for a time with the Christian Commission, stationed at Murfreesborough, Tennessee. While in Indiana he was the special correspondent of the Cincinnati Daily Gazette and Daily Times. In 1879 he retired from the ministry. Professor Parrott was an acceptable and eloquent preacher in the M. E. Church, and was frequently called on for public addresses before societies. At the invitation of the Faculty he preached the annual sermon at the Ohio Wesleyan University, in 1872.

DAVID W. LA FOLLETTE

Was born in Floyd County, Indiana, September 13, 1825, and is one of eleven children, of Robert and Martha La Follette, who emigrated from Kentucky to the Territory of Indiana, November 5, 1804. He was brought up in poverty, and in early life learned that honest toil is the surest road to prosperity. He received his early education in the county schools, and by his labor he acquired the means to defray his expenses, while obtaining a professional education. He commenced the study of law with the Honorable W. A. Porter, of Corydon, Indiana, and continued there till the fall of 1848, at which time he entered the Law Department of the State University. In February, 1849, he graduated, receiving the degree of LL. B. In the same year he was admitted to the bar and commenced practice at Corydon, Indiana. In 1852 he was elected District Attorney for the Court of Common Pleas. He removed to New Albany in 1855, where he formed a partnership with James Collins, and in 1858 was elected Judge of the Court of Common Pleas of Floyd County. In 1872 he was appointed Judge of the Criminal Circuit Court of Floyd and Clark Counties, but declined, and accepted the appointment of Prosecuting Attorney of the same district. In 1873 Judge La Follette was appointed one of the Law Professors of the Indiana University, and filled the chair during the collegiate year to the entire satisfaction of the Board of Trustees. Since then he has devoted his time to the practice of his profession in the city of New Albany, Indiana, and for two years was City Attorney (1881). In 1886 he was Prosecuting Attorney of the Circuit Court, City Attorney of New Albany, and has been President of the New Albany City School Board for eight years.

Judge La Follette is an elder in the Christian Church. He married Catharine R. Goldsberry April 17, 1850, who died November 2, 1862, leaving a daughter. October 20, 1863, he married Harriett A. Williams.

MISS MARGARET HEMPHILL M'CALLA.

Miss McCalla received her early education in the Monroe County Female Seminary, of which for so many years Mrs. E. McFerson, now of Evansville, was the accomplished principal. Miss McCalla's life has been devoted to teaching. Her first position was in the seminary of which she had been a pupil. From 1867 to 1873 she was principal of the Ninth Street School, Evansville. For four years she was assistant in the preparatory department of Indiana University, and for more than a decade the superintendent of the city graded schools. These schools, seldom numbering less than 600 under her administration, were kept in excellent order, and well instructed. For a number of years Miss McCalla was the only lady superintendent of the public schools of the State. After having filled this responsible position for about sixteen years, which she has held with so much credit to herself and advantage to the community, she has now (1890) retired to private life.

MISS SARAH PARKE MORRISON, A. M.,

Was born in Salem, Ind., and educated in the Salem Seminary, of which her father, the Hon. John I. Morrison, was proprietor and founder. She completed a course of study at the Indianapolis Commercial College in 1882, and also at Mt. Holyoke Seminary, Massachusetts, where she graduated in 1857. She afterward, in 1868, entered Indiana University and graduated, in 1869 receiving the degree A. B., and three years after the degree A. M. Since graduating, Miss Morrison has been engaged in teaching and other literary and religious work. She was pupil teacher at Vassar College, was one of the instructors at the summer school for teachers at the State Normal, Terre Haute. From 1873 to 1875 she was connected with the University, first as tutor, and afterward as adjunct Professor of English Literature. Since 1875 she has been busily engaged in temperance and religious work, and in studying and writing.

Miss Morrison was the first of her sex to formally apply for admission to the University on the same terms as were afforded to young men.

WALTER R. HOUGHTON.

W. R. Houghton was born October 3, 1845, near Mt. Pleasant, Ind. His present (1889) residence is Chicago, Ills. He received his early education at Mt. Pleasant, and afterward at Washington, Daviess County, Ind. Before entering college he taught school, giving great satisfaction to all concerned. As a student of the University, he entered as a Freshman in 1866, was one year absent from the college, and graduated with high honor in 1871. Immediately after graduation he was elected to teach Greek and Latin in the Bedford Male and Female College Seminary. After a year's service in Bedford, he was invited to take charge of the Freshman Class in Indiana University. The following year he was elected by the Trustees Principal of the Preparatory Department, in which position he continued till 1884. The Trustees, at the recommendation of the Faculty, conferred on him the degree A. M., a year before the usual time in which students who pursued, after graduation, a literary course, received it. As Principal of the Preparatory Department, Professor Houghton showed himself to be a thoroughly competent instructor, and an excellent disciplinarian; not only attending to the duties of the school, but doing a great amount of work in the study of History and Governmental Science. Professor Houghton's efforts at objective teaching in History attracted the attention of the College Board, and the President of the Board (John I. Morrison) suggested the embodiment in the form of a publication, both for the school room and for original work. This novel method of presenting "History" also attracted the attention of Attorney-General Baldwin (then unacquainted with Professor H.) who urged him to undertake the Constitutional History of the United States by administrations. This work was not undertaken at that time, owing to the pressure of other matters. For several years Professor H. was engaged in compiling information on Historical and Governmental subjects, to be used in future publications. In conjunction with Professor Herman B. Boisen, the Professor of Modern Languages in the University, the plan was laid for uniting the High Schools with the State University. The plan was adopted and the result secured, but the originators remained unknown. Professor Houghton is the author of several works, some of which are here mentioned.

1. "Portrayal of United States History, Literature and Geography." This was designed for reference and the school room. It has been adopted in various counties of the Eastern and Western States. Published by Hussey & Co., Chicago.

2. "A Conspectus of the History of Political Parties and the Federal Government," issued in map and atlas form. This has elicited highly complimentary testimonials. It was favorably reviewed in "The Nation" and other periodicals. It was highly commended by Lossing, the historian; by Garfield, Randall and Arthur. This was published by Townsend MacCoun, of New York.

3. A biographical work, "The Lives of Blaine and Logan," of which 20,000 copies were sold. Published by Clark & Co., Chicago.

4. "History of American Politics," which has been used as a text-book on Constitutional and Political History in the Indiana University, and in other schools of the State. This work contains an ingenious mechanical representation of the *machinery* of the U. S. Government, and also of the separate States.

5. "A Map of United States History," consisting of a map of the country containing leading events, located in the States in which they occur. Published by Andrews & Co., Chicago.

6. "A Map of Political History," published by H. M. Clark, Chicago.

Professor Houghton is the editor of several other works and pamphlets. March, 1884, he contracted with a publishing house of Chicago to enter upon work for them, but remained in the Indiana University till the close of the college year, when his resignation was accepted. And now, having made arrangements so that his works can be published without his special supervision, he will turn his attention to teaching.

WILLIAM GAY BALLANTINE.

The younger son of Professor Elisha Ballantine, was born at Washington, D. C., December 7, 1848. His early education and training he received from his father. In 1862–3 he was in the Senior Preparatory Department of Indiana University. January 5, 1865, he entered the Freshman Class of Wabash College, Indiana, where he completed his Freshman and Sophomore Years. He then entered the Junior Class of Marietta

College, from which he graduated in 1868, receiving the degrees A. B. and A. M. in course. Professor Ballantine entered the Union Theological Seminary in 1869, completed the course in that Institution, and was, in 1875, licensed to preach the gospel, and, in 1880, was ordained. Shortly after graduation he went abroad and spent some time in England and Germany. In the fall of '72 he was a student in the University of Leipsic. Returning in 1873, he became *pro tem.* Professor of English Literature in Indiana University. Leaving Bloomington, he accepted a Professorship of Chemistry and Natural Science in Ripon College, Wisconsin, which he held from 1873 to 1876. In 1876-78 he was Associate Professor of Greek in Indiana University. He accepted a Professorship of Hebrew and Greek Exegesis in Oberlin Theological Seminary in 1876, which he held till 1878, and in the next year became Professor of the Old Testament Language and Literature in the same Institution. In 1885 Professor Ballantine received the honorary degree D. D. from Marietta College. In 1885-86 he was Professor in the Chicago Summer School of the Institute of Hebrew. Since the year 1884 he has been one of the editors of the *Bibliothera Sacra.*

From February to August, 1873, Professor Ballantine was Assistant Engineer of the American Palestine Exploring Expedition. The greater part of this time was spent in the Land of Moab.

August 17, 1875, Professor Ballantine married Miss Emma Frances Atwood, of Waupun, Wisconsin.

JAMES KIRKWOOD BECK.

Professor Beck was born July 11, 1850, at Hamburg, Clark County, Ind. Was educated at Barnet's Academy, Charleston, Ind. Entered the Freshman Class of Indiana University, and graduated in 1874, receiving the degrees A. B. and A. M. in course. Soon after graduation he was an assistant in the Preparatory department of the University, and in 1889 Principal of the department, and in 1890 Associate Professor of Latin and Greek in the University. Professor Beck married Miss Falena Adams, of Bloomington, a graduate of the class of 1876.

THOMAS CHARLTON VAN NUYS, M. D.

Dr. Van Nuys was born March 24, 1844, in Switzerland County, Ind. Received his education at different schools in the county of his birth, at the Universities of Berlin and Strasburg, and the Chemical Institute of Wiesbaden. He studied medicine at the Medical College of Ohio, from which he received the degree M. D. Since graduation he practiced medicine and lectured in the city of Evansville, where he resided for some time. In 1874 he was elected Professor of Chemistry in Indiana University, a position he still occupies (1889). Dr. Van Nuys is the author of a work on "Chemistry and Microscopy of the Urine." In the year 1875 he was married to Miss Mary Elizabeth Hunter, daughter of General Morton C. Hunter, of Bloomington, Ind.

CYRUS F. M'NUTT

Was born in Johnson County, Ind., July 29, 1837; was educated at Franklin College, Ind., entering in 1856, but did not graduate, although he received the honorary degree of A. M. in 1878 from that college. Mr. McNutt was elected Professor in the Law Department in 1875, and continued till the close of the Law School in 1877. He is a resident and practicing lawyer of Terre Haute, Ind.

OWEN BENNER CLARK

Was born January 11, 1850, in Warsaw, Ind. He received his early education at the Warsaw Union School, and at the Preparatory Department of Chicago University. Entering that University, he graduated in 1872, receiving the degree, A. B., and three years after, the degree, A. M. After graduation, in 1873–4, he attended the Chicago Medical College, and afterwards, the Baptist Union Theological Seminary. In 1872–3 he was Principal of the Winnatka Institute, and the following year, '74–'5, Principal of the Preparatory Department, University of Chicago. In 1876–8 he was Professor of English in Antioch College, Ohio. In 1878 he was elected Professor of Greek in Indiana University. In 1880 he was transferred to the chair of English Language and Literature, which position he still holds. During the summer of this year he made a tour through England, Scotland and France. Before his connection with Indiana University he was agent for the "Nation," during the year 1875-6. With this exception, Professor Clark's whole work has been devoted to education. In the year 1885-6, having leave of absence, he spent in Harvard University, as a graduate student, receiving upon examination the degree, A. M. During this time at Harvard he was holder of the Morgan Fellowship.

Professor Clark married, Miss Mary Elizabeth Morris, of Warsaw, Ind., December 31, 1874.

JOHN GRAY NEWKIRK

Was born in Greenfield, Ulster County, N. Y., December 5, 1847. Was educated at Cornell University, where he received the degree of A. B. in 1873. He studied law at the Albany (N. Y.) Law School, and received the degree LL. B. in 1874. In 1880 Professor N. was elected Professor of History in Indiana University, which position he has held till 1886.

WILLIAM RUSSELL DUDLEY

Was born March 1, 1849, at Guilford, New Haven County, Conn. His present residence is at Cornell University, Utica, N. Y. During the absence, in 1887, of Dr. Jordan, Professor of Biology in the University, Professor Dudley had the charge of his department.

Professor Dudley received his early education at Guilford, Conn., and his collegiate education at Cornell University, graduating in 1874, B. S., and in 1876 the degree of M. S. He attended the Agassiz Summer School in 1874 and the Harvard Summer School of Botany in 1876. Ever since his graduation he has been engaged in teaching. From 1874 to 1876 an instructor in Cornell University; from 1876 to 1885 Assistant Professor of Botany in Cornell, and since that time Assistant Professor of Cryptogamic Botany (1887). He was Professor of Botany at Martha's Vineyard Summer Institute in 1878 and 1879. Professor Dudley is the author of "Bulletin of Cornell University" (science), vol. ii., part i.; "The Cayuga Flora," 170 pages, and two maps (1886). He has also contributed a number of papers to the scientific magazines. He has twice been elected to a professorship in Indiana University, but each time declined the offered position.

ANNA THANKFUL BALLANTINE.

The present residence of Miss Ballantine is Fisk University, Nashville, Tenn. The place of her birth was Prince Edward Court House, Virginia. She came to Indiana with her parents, the Rev. Dr. E. Ballantine and wife, in the year 1854. She received her early education at the Female Seminary, Monroe County, Ind. She afterwards attended the Ohio Female College, at Glendale, where she graduated in 1861, receiving the degree A. B. Her occupation for a number of years has been teaching; for some time a teacher of Latin in Glendale College. On her return to Bloomington was an assistant in the Latin Preparatory Department of the Indiana University. At present she occupies the responsible position as principal of the Ladies Department in Fisk University, Tenn.

WILLIAM TAYLOR JACKSON

Was born October 25, 1839, in Willoughby, Lincolnshire, England. His earlier education was at Richmond and Boston, England. After coming to this country he attended Western College, Toledo, Iowa, from which he received the degree A. M. in 1867. He graduated in 1864 at Michigan University, receiving the degree A. B. Studying theology at Yale College he received the degree B. D., and in 1879 the honorary degree of Ph. D. The general occupation of Professor Jackson since graduation has been the ministry and teaching. He was Principal of Westfield Seminary and Professor in Westfield College, Illinois, in 1864-70; Principal of Greenhill Seminary, 1870-72 and 1875-78; Principal of Fostoria Academy, Ohio, 1879-80; Acting Professor of Modern Languages, Indiana University, 1880-81. Professor Jackson is the author of an "Exposition of the Ethical Systems of Seneca and Kant."

RUFUS BYRAM RICHARDSON.

Rufus B. Richardson was born in Westford, Mass., April 18, 1845. Received the degree of A. B. from Yale College in 1869, and also in 1878 the degree of Ph. D. From 1879 to 1872 was a student in the Theological Seminary of Yale College; from 1874 to 1878 was tutor in the College. In 1880 he was elected Professor of Greek in Indiana University, which position he held till 1882, when, to the regret of the Faculty and students, he resigned, accepting the professorship of Greek in Dartmouth College, which position he now (1885) holds. Professor Richardson served one year in the Sixth Massachusetts Regiment during the War of the Rebellion. He has been a contributor of various articles in the "New Englander" and other periodicals.

SAMUEL GARNER.

Samuel Garner was born November 16, 1846, in St. Mary's County, Md. He received the degree B. A. from St. John's College, Annapolis, Md., in 1871, and Ph. D. from Johns Hopkins University in 1881. Since his graduation his principal occupation has been teaching. From 1874 to 1876 he was a bank clerk in the Traders' National Bank, Baltimore. In 1879–80 he was instructor in Romanic Languages, Johns Hopkins University. From 1881 to 1887 he was Professor in Indiana University; from 1881 to 1886, Professor of Modern Languages, and from 1886 to 1887, of Romance Language. Professor Garner is the author of a work entitled, "The Gerundial Construction in the Romanic Languages," and also the writer of numerous articles contributed to the "American Journal of Philology" and "Modern Language Notes" and other papers and journals. At present (1889) Dr. Garner is Professor in the U. S. Naval Academy, Annapolis, Md.

HORACE ADDISON HOFFMAN

Was born July 30, 1855, at Auburn, DeKalb County, Indiana. He received his early education at the country schools and at the Auburn High School. After leaving the High School he taught for five winters. Entering Indiana University in 1877, he graduated A. B. in 1881. The next year after graduation, he was Assistant in the departments of Latin and Greek, and in 1883–84 he was absent on leave, spending the year as a graduate student in Classical Philology, in Harvard University, from which, in June, 1884, he received the degree of A. M. On his return to Bloomington he was elected Professor of the Greek Language and Literature in Indiana University, which position he at present (1890) holds.

Professor Hoffman married Miss Anna Bowman, June 13, 1888, at her home, Monticello, Indiana.

AUGUSTUS ARMAGNAC, PH. D.,

Was born March 5, 1839, in the West Indies. He first entered Madison University, Hamilton, New York, but afterward entered Princeton College, New Jersey, where he graduated in 1861, receiving the degrees A. M. and Ph. D. Since graduation he has been a teacher and before his connection with Indiana University was Principal of the Irving Institute, a flourishing boarding school at Tarrytown, New York.

He was elected Professor of Greek in 1882, and served in that capacity until the close of the college year of 1883–1884, when he resigned and returned to resume his former position in Tarrytown, where he still resides. He was married in 1870 to Miss Harriet D. Rowe.

MISS MARIA PORTER BRACE,

Was born at Penn Yan, Yates County, N. Y., was educated at Vassar College, Poughkeepsie, from which institution she received the degree of A. B., in 1872. Miss Brace having a remarkable talent for elocution, was engaged as a teacher of that art and an instructor in reading, in Vassar College. In the year 1882 she gave a four weeks' course in elocution to the Senior and Junior classes of the University, and in the same year she was elected Professor of Elocution, resigning in 1883. She also gave instruction in elocution in Chicago and in New York.

SAMUEL BROWN WYLIE,

Was born June 26, 1854, at Oxford, Butler County, Ohio. In May, 1855, his parents and family returned to Bloomington, his father having been recalled to a professorship in the University. Mr. Wylie received his early education at the Bloomington Public Schools, and at the Academy of Professor E. P. Cole. In 1867 he attended the Classical Academy of the

Rev. Dr. J. W. Faries at Philadelphia, Pa. Soon after his return in 1872, he entered the Freshman Class of the University and graduated in 1876, receiving the degree B. S. In 1882, he received from the University *pro merito* the degree M. S. Soon after graduation he became assistant in the department of Physics and Chemistry. During the absence of the Professor of Chemistry, for one year, the Professor of Physics was called upon to take charge of the department, in addition to the duties of his own room. Mr. Wylie and Mr. W. E. Moffet were selected as assistants, and by them the principal part of the work was carried on. In 1881-82, the Professor of Chemistry being absent for one year, through ill health, Mr. Wylie was entrusted with the whole department, assisted by Mr. J. N. Corr, at present an assayer in Colorado. After the destruction by fire of the laboratory, his services were not required for a year. This year he spent in the philosophical and chemical apparatus establishment of J. W. Queen & Co., Philadelphia. On his return from Philadelphia the Professor of Chemistry found that an assistant in his department was not necessary; he then continued his studies for a short time in Johns Hopkins University, and not long after his return to Bloomington received the appointment of Professor of Physics in Geneva College, Beaver Falls, Pa.

In 1876 he married Miss Seabrook Mitchell, of Bloomington.

W. J. BRYAN.

William Julian Bryan was born November 11, 1860, at Bloomington, Ind. He was the son of Rev. John Bryan, of the United Presbyterian Church.

Professor Bryan received his early education in the Bloomington High School; entered Indiana University in 1880, receiving the degree A. B. in 1884, and the degree of A. M. on the presentation of a thesis on "The Polar Logic of Heraclitus."

After his graduation in 1884, Professor Bryan was appointed Tutor in the University; in 1885 Associate Professor of Philosophy, and in 1887 Professor of Philosophy. In 1886-7 he spent a year in Berlin in the study of philosophy and the German language, and having returned he now (1890) occupies his chair in the University.

Prof. Bryan married Miss Charlotte Lowe, of Indianapolis.

ALLEN BEARDEN PHILPUTT.

Mr. Philputt was born May 6, 1856, at Flatcreek, Tenn. In 1876 he entered the Freshman Class of the Indiana University and graduated in 1880, receiving the degree A. B., and in '87 A. M. (*pro merito*). During his Senior year Mr. Philputt frequently preached to the "Disciples" in the town and country adjacent, and after graduation was chosen minister of the Christian Church in Bloomington. For some time he was a member of the School Board of Bloomington. In 1884 he was appointed Instructor in Latin and Greek in the University, and in the following year Associate Professor. He spent a year at Harvard University, and on the completion of his studies there, returned to Bloomington. In 1888 he resigned his position in the University and accepted a call to the charge of a congregation in Philadelphia. Mr. Philputt married Miss Anna Maxwell, daughter of Dr. J. D. Maxwell, of Bloomington, Ind.

JOHN C. BRANNER.

John Casper Branner was born July 4, 1850, at New Market, Jefferson County, East Tennessee. Was educated at Maryville College, East Tennessee; also attended school at Ithaca Academy, completing his education at Cornell University, Ithaca, New York, taking the degree B. S. in 1874. The degree Ph. D. was conferred in course by Indiana University in the year 1885. In this same year he accepted the Professorship of Geology and Botany in the University. Ever since his graduation in Cornell University he has been practically engaged in the study and extension of his favorite science, Geology, and Natural History in general. He became Assistant Geologist on the Imperial Geological Survey of Brazil (S. A.), in the year 1884; also, Assistant Geologist, Engineer and Interpreter of the São Cyriaco Gold Mining Company, Minas Geraes, Brazil; and Special Commissioner of Mr. Thomas A. Edison to South America and the West Indies; Special Agent of the United States Department of Agriculture; Assistant in the Geological Survey of Pennsylvania, and Professor of Geology in Indiana University; Special Assistant of the United States Geological Survey, in 1886; Director of the State Geological

Survey of Arkansas, and Collaborateur of the Polyglot Geological Dictionary.

Dr. Branner is the author of many valuable articles contributed to the transactions of various philosophical societies, and to scientific periodicals, a concise summary of which is here given:

1. The Course and Growth of the Fibro-Vascular Bundles in Palms, with illustrations; American Philosophical Society, 1883.
2. Rock Inscription in Brazil, with illustrations; *American Naturalist*, 1884.
3. The Pororoca or Bore of the Amazon, illustrated; *Science*, 1884.
4. Preliminary Report on the Cotton Insects of Brazil; United States Department of Agriculture Report, 1884.
5. Cotton in Brazil; United States Department of Agriculture, 1885.
6. Insects Injurious to Cotton in Brazil; Annual Report of Bureau of Entomology, United States Department of Agriculture, 1886.
7. The Reputation of the Lantern Fly, illustrated; *American Naturalist*, 1885.
8. A Gitiranaboia *Liberal Mineiro*, Ouro Preto; Brazil, 1885.
9. Inscripções em Rochedos do Brazil; published by Instituto Archeologico, Pernambuco, Brazil, 1885.
10. Glaciation of the Lackawanna Valley; A. A. A. S., 1885.
11. Glaciation of the Wyoming-Lackawanna Valley, with two maps; American Philosophical Society, 1886.
12. Geographical and Geological Explorations in Brazil; *American Naturalist*, 1886.
13. Miniature Geological Map of Indiana, in the international colors; 1886.
14. Thickness of the Ice in Northeastern Pennsylvania, during the Glacial Epoch; *American Journal of Science*, 1886.
15. Topographic Map of the Lackawanna Valley of Pennsylvania, scale $1''=1600'$ (two sheets); Geological Survey of Pennsylvania, 1887.
16. Notes upon a Native Brazilian Language; A. A. A. S., 1886.
17. Topographical Survey and Map of Bloomington, Indiana and Vicinity.

18. Notes upon the Glacial Striæ Observed in the Wyoming-Lackawanna Region of Pennsylvania; Lackawanna Institute, Scranton, Pennsylvania, 1887.
19. Geology of the Sergipe-Alagôas Basin, illustrated; (Brazil), 1887.
20. The Sandstone Reefs of the Brazilian Coast; 1887.

Dr. Branner is a member of the American Philosophical Society, Fellow of the American Association for the Advancement of Science, of the Indiana Academy of Science, and of the American Institute of Mining Engineers, Honorary Member of the Brazilian Instituto Archeologico Alagoano, Corresponding Member of the New York Academy of Science and of the Instituto Archeologicó e Geographico Pernambucani, of Brazil. Also, a contributor to the *American Journal of Science*, the *American Naturalist*, and to the proceedings of various scientific bodies.

On June 22, 1883, Dr. Branner married Susan Dow Kennedy, of the Class of 1879 of Vassar College, at Oneida, New York. The present residence of Dr. Branner is Bloomington, Indiana.

In 1887 he was called to be the Director of the State Geological Survey of Arkansas, and, shortly afterward, having received leave of absence from Indiana University, he entered upon the duties of that position, and has since been conducting the survey with marked ability. It is expected that his absence from the University of Indiana will only be temporary, and will not exceed the two years for which leave of absence was granted.

CHARLES HENRY GILBERT.

Formerly, from 1880 to 1884, an assistant in the Department of the Natural Sciences and the Modern Languages, accepted a position in Cincinnati as Professor of Biology, but has now (1888) been recalled to Indiana University as Professor of Zoölogy. Professor Gilbert was born December 5, 1859, in Rockford, Illinois. He received his collegiate education in Butler University, Indianapolis, graduating B. A. in 1879. From Indiana University he has received the degrees, *pro merito*, M. S. and Ph. D. He has been engaged in giving instruction in his favorite branches in Bloomington and Cincinnati ever since his graduation. As a scientist, he was employed by the United States Fish Commission on the steamer Albatros. He is the author of many papers on Ichthyology. Professor Gilbert married Miss Julia R. Hughes, a daughter of the Rev. Levi Hughes.

RUFUS LOT GREEN

Was born in Rush County, Indiana, March 3, 1862. Professor Green received his early education at the district school in Center Township, near the place of his nativity, and at the high school in Knightstown. He entered Indiana University in 1879; graduated in 1885, receiving the degree of B. S. Part of this time (1881–'82) was spent in the study of Mathematics at Cornell University. Soon after graduation, in 1885, he was appointed Instructor in Mathematics in Indiana University, and the following year Associate Professor of Pure Mathematics and Secretary of the Faculty, on the resignation of Professor Atwater. August 12, 1886, Professor Green married Miss Emma Edwards, of Knightstown, Indiana.

JOHN MERCER PATTON

Was born in Richmond, Virginia, August 30, 1859. His present residence (1887) is Ashland, Hanover County, Virginia. Professor Patton graduated from the Virginia Military Institute in 1880, and afterward was a student in Berlin University (Germany), and also at the University of Madrid. From Indiana University he received the degree A. M. Since his return to the United States he has been engaged in teaching modern languages. For some time he was assistant professor at the Virginia Military Institute, with the title of Captain of Engineers. In the year 1885-86 he was Associate Professor of German in Indiana University.

JOSEPH SWAIN.

Professor Swain was born June 16, 1857, at Pendleton, Indiana. He entered the Freshman Class of the Indiana University in the fall of 1879 and graduated in 1883, receiving the degree B. L. Two years after, he received the degree M. S. For two years afterwards he was Dr. Kirkwood's assistant in the Mathematical Department, and for one year an assistant of Dr. Jordan in the Department of Natural History. The next year he was appointed Associate Professor of Mathematics.

and, on the resignation of Dr. Kirkwood, Professor of Mathematics and Astronomy. The collegiate year 1885-6 was spent in the study of Mathematics and Astronomy in the University of Edinburgh (Scotland). During the summer vacation Professor Swain conducted a party of teachers and students in a continental tour. Joseph Swain is a member of the Society of Friends. September 22, 1885, Professor Swain married Miss Fannie H. Morgan, of Knightstown, Indiana.

RICHARD GAUSE BOONE

Was born September 9, 1849, in Spiceland, Henry County, Indiana, and received his early education in the Spiceland Academy. Soon after leaving school he engaged in teaching, at first in the common schools. Afterwards he was made Superintendent of the city schools of Frankfort, Indiana. He was also President of the Board of Directors of the Indiana Teachers' Reading Circle. He was elected Professor of Pedagogics, in Indiana University, in June, 1886. The college year of 1887-88 was spent by him at Johns Hopkins University, on leave of absence granted for the purpose of study, and with that exception he has, ever since his election, filled the duties of his chair. He is well known throughout the West in educational circles, is a popular lecturer before institutes, and always in demand. In July, 1874, he was married to Mary E. Stanley, of Amo, Indiana.

RICHARD HEATH DABNEY.

Professor Dabney is a native of Tennessee. Was born at Memphis, March 29, 1860. He received his collegiate education at the University of Virginia, from which he received the degree of Master of Arts, in 1881. Soon after he went to Germany and attended lectures, pursuing his studies at the Universities of Munich, Berlin and Heidelberg. At Heidelberg he took the degree of Ph. D., in 1885. On his return from Germany he was elected, in 1886, Professor of History in Indiana University. Dr. Dabney delivered a course of nine lectures on the causes of the French Revolution, at Washington and Lee University, Lexington, Virginia, in March and April, 1886, which have been published in a volume bearing the same title. Dr. Dabney, in 1889, was called to a professorship in the University of Virginia, which he accepted, and resigned his chair in Indiana University. He married Miss Mary Bentley, of Richmond, Virginia, in June, 1888. She spent the greater part of the first year of their married life with her husband in Bloomington, and shortly before his removal to Virginia returned to her former home to await him, but suddenly, and before his arrival, her bright young life was ended.

HANS CARL GUENTHER VON JAGEMAN.

Born August 2, 1859, at Grottkau, Prussia. Educated at the Nuremburg Gymnasium. Attended Johns Hopkins University in 1884. In 1876 he received the degree Ph. D., *pro merito*, from the University of Leipsic. From 1884 to 1886 he was Professor of Modern Languages in Earlham College, Richmond, Indiana. In 1886 he was elected Professor of the Germanic Languages in Indiana University. Dr. von Jageman has contributed articles on Philology and kindred subjects to the Proceedings of the Philological Society.

He married Miss Frances A. Whitman, of Williamstown, Mass. Professor von Jageman resigned in 1887, and accepted a professorship in Harvard University.

ARTHUR BURNHAM WOODFORD

Was born in West Winsted, Connecticut, October 7, 1861. Was a student at Yale College, where he received the degree of Ph. B. He was for some time a student of the University of Michigan; afterwards, of the University of Berlin (Germany), and of the Ecole des Sciences Politiques at Paris.

He received, *pro merito*, the degree A. M. from the Indiana University, and was elected Professor of Political and Social Science in 1886.

Professor Woodford married Miss Margaret C. Bowditch, of New Haven, Connecticut, August 19, 1885. He remained in the position to which elected until June, 1889, when he resigned and returned to the East.

JAMES ALBERT WOODBURN

Was born in Bloomington, Indiana, November 30, 1856. He received his early education at the public school of Bloomington, and entered the University in 1872, graduating in 1876.

Upon the presentation of a thesis in 1885, he received, *pro merito*, the degree A. M. Ever since graduation Professor Woodburn has been engaged in teaching. He was first assistant in the Grayville, Illinois, public schools, afterwards one of the teachers in the Preparatory Department of Indiana University, and assistant in the High School, Secretary of the Indiana University Alumni Association, Professor-elect of History in Indiana University, and in 1887 was a student in Johns Hopkins University, Baltimore, and in 1888 became Associate Professor of Rhetoric and Composition. Professor Woodburn is the son of Professor James Woodburn, the subject of a preceding sketch. During the college year of 1888-9 he was absent on leave, attending lectures in Johns Hopkins University.

PERCEY BENTLEY BURNET.

Mr. Burnet was born September 10, 1861, at Vincennes, Indiana. He received his early education at Vincennes, and graduated from the Vincennes University, June, 1880, and from Indiana University in 1884. Received from Indiana University the degree of A. M. in 1887. During the winter after his graduation he attended the business college at Cleveland, Ohio. In July, 1885, he spent sometime in Germany, and in the following year in Paris, and on his return to the United States he received the position of assistant in the Department of German in Indiana University. Having resigned this position, Mr. Burnet traveled in South America, spending some time in Buenos Ayres. Afterwards, crossing the Andes on *mule-back*, he spent some time in Chili in a medical laboratory, in the preparation of medicines. After visiting Rio Janeiro, Mr. Burnet designs to return home and renew his occupation as a teacher. Lately (1889) he has been commissioned to obtain English, French and German speaking persons for work on the great railroad to the Pacific.

GUSTAV FRIEDRICK KARSTEN

Was born May 22, 1859, at Petershagenfeld bei Tiegenhof, West Prussia. He received his early education at Tiegenhof high school, afterwards at the Marionburg Gymnasium, finishing his scholastic education at the universities of Leipsic, Königsberg, Heidelberg, Geneva, Freiburg and Tübingen. He received the degree B. A. at the Marionburg Gymnasium, Prussia; the degree Ph. D. at Freiburg University, Baden, Germany. Since completing his education he has been traveling, lecturing and teaching; was Privat-docent of Germanic and Romance Philology at Geneva University, Switzerland, and is now (1889) Professor of Romance Philology at Indiana University. Professor Karsten was Secretary of the phonetic section of the Modern Language Association of America, and is the writer of various treatises, mostly Philological: "Zur Geschicte der alt-französischen Konsonantenverbindungen. Freiburg, 1883." "Speech Unities and their Role in Sound Change, and Phonetic Laws," in the Transactions of the Modern Language Association of America, 1888; and, also, of various articles and reviews in Philological periodicals in America and Europe. The Professor has also in an advanced state of preparation, "Editio princeps of Jehan de Lanson," an old French Epopee of the thirteenth century.

JOSEPH P. NAYLOR.

Professor Naylor is a native of Ohio. He was born at Pennsville, April 4, 1853. Attended Adrian College, at Adrian, Michigan, but did not graduate. Intending to turn his attention to civil engineering, he made Mathematics and Surveying his principal studies. He received the degree Master of Science, *pro merito*, from Indiana University. Professor Naylor lived for two years in Columbus, Ohio. While there he studied Physics under Prof. T. C. Mendenhall, then of the Ohio State University, now President of the Rose Polytechnic Institute, Terre Haute, Indiana. While in Columbus he was employed as draftsman, and had charge of the pattern department of the Capital City Car Works, and also for a time was employed with the Columbus Watch Factory. From Columbus he moved to Indianapolis, and for two years taught Physics in the Indianapolis High School. From Indianapolis he came to Bloomington, having received an appointment as Assistant Professor of Physics in the State University, and, on the resignation of the Professor, he became the occupant of the vacated chair. Professor Naylor's collegiate training in Engineering, and under Professor Mendenhall, and in the watch factory, has eminently fitted him for the duties of the Department of Natural Philosophy and the Physical Laboratory of the University. On the 25th of November, 1880, Professor Naylor married Miss Maria J. Murrey, of McConnellsville, Ohio.

JOHN STERLING KINGSLEY

Was born at Cincinnatus, in Cortland County, New York, April 7, 1854. He received his collegiate degrees, A. B. and A. M., from Williams College, and the degree of Sc. D. from the College of Princeton, New Jersey. He also attended the Brooklyn Polytechnic Institute. Teaching has been his occupation since graduation, both in the college and through the press. In 1888 he was elected Professor of Zoölogy in the University. He is also editor of "Standard Natural History," in six volumes, and of the American Naturalist.

Professor Kingsley married Mary Emma, daughter of John Franklin and Caroline Louise (Chase) Read, of Salem, Massachusetts.

Professor Kingsley resigned at the end of the college year, and accepted a professorship of Biology in the University of Nebraska, at Lincoln.

DAVID A. CURRY

Was born February 15, 1860, at Bloomington, Indiana. He received his early education in the common schools of Monroe County and of Winchester, Kansas. He is an alumnus of Indiana University, graduating Bachelor of Arts in 1883. Since graduating he has been engaged for several years in teaching, first in the common schools and later in the High School of Greensburg, Indiana.

In 1887 he was elected Assistant in the Latin Department of Indiana University, and during the college year 1888-9 took post graduate studies in Harvard University, and resigned in 1888 to commence studying for the ministry in the United Presbyterian Theological Seminary at Xenia, Ohio.

March 6, 1886, he married Miss Jennie Foster, of Bloomington, and their son, David Foster Curry, born May 9, 1888, received the cup presented to the first child of the class of 1888.

WILLIAM WESLEY SPANGLER,

Librarian of Indiana University, and Secretary of the Board of Trustees, was born near Auburn, Dekalb County, Indiana, November 15, 1855. He was educated at Auburn, and at the Canton, Ohio, high school, and the Northwestern Normal, at Ada, Ohio, and Indiana University. Having completed the required studies, he received the degrees A. B. and B. L. He has been an assistant on his father's farm, near Auburn, assistant director of European tours, Secretary and Librarian, and assistant teacher in Indiana University, business manager of the "Indiana Student," and may be called a professional tourist. In 1879 he tramped 350 miles in Switzerland and adjacent parts; in 1880, 740 miles in Southern California and the Sierras; in 1881, 400 miles in Switzerland and Italy; and, in company with four others, scaled the Matterhorn to its apex, after which he again visited Italy. In 1882 he tramped seventy-five miles in the White Mountains. In 1883 he assisted Dr. D. S. Jordan in his third summer tramp in Europe; conducted, personally, the fourth University tramping party of fifteen among the Alps. He went on another tour to the Northwest in 1888, on which trip he had the great misfortune of losing his wife by death. In 1889 he conducted a fifth party on a tour of Europe. In 1882, associated with Messrs. Gordon and Bryant, he reëstablished the "Indiana Student," a monthly educational paper. He is engaged in preparing a card catalogue of the University Library, and has acquired a fine reputation among college Librarians. June 10, 1885, he married Miss Ida Smell, of Muncie, Indiana, who died after a short illness while with him in the far Northwest.

ALUMNI OF THE COLLEGIATE DEPARTMENT OF INDIANA UNIVERSITY.

1830.

JAMES WILSON DUNN, born near Danville, Kentucky, Mercer County (now Boyle County), September 14, 1807. Died at Logansport, Indiana, April 23, 1873. Was educated, as there were no public schools in the territory of Indiana, in a log cabin school-house, on his father's farm, in Jefferson County, to which place his father and family had emigrated in 1809. When the State Seminary was organized in 1824, and located in Bloomington, he was sent to that Institution, and when the Seminary became the College in 1828 he entered the College and graduated in 1830 with the first graduating class, receiving the degrees A. B., and three years afterward, A. M. After graduation he studied law and located at Logansport, soon after that town was estabblished. He did not, however, continue to practice law long, but engaged in various business enterprises. In 1863 or 1864 he was made Lieutenant Colonel of a regiment of Indiana volunteers, raised for temporary service in a great emergency, and served in Tennessee. Though not a member of any church he was a principal supporter of the Presbyterian Church of Logansport.

MICHAEL HUMMER, born in Fayette County, Kentucky, April 11, 1802. At the time of his death he resided at Wyandotte, Kansas. He was educated at the Academy of John I. Morrison, Salem, and one year at Oxford, Ohio. Entered the Sophomore class of Indiana College, and received on graduation the degrees, A. B. and A. M. in course. Graduated at Princeton, N. J., Theological Seminary. Occupation, minister of the Gospel. Was elected President of Des Moines College, Iowa. Superintendent of Public Instruction, Kansas. Mr. Hummer was stated supply at LaFayette, Indiana, in 1836–7. Pastor at Stevenson, Ill., and missionary preacher at Davenport, Iowa, Washington, Kansas, Lawrence, Kansas, and Wyandotte, Kansas, 1870–77.

JAMES S. ROLLINS was born in Richmond, Madison County, Kentucky, Wednesday, April 19, 1812. At the time of his death his home was Columbia, Boone County, Missouri. Educated at Richmond Academy, Kentucky. When fifteen years old he entered Washington College, Pennsylvania, Sophomore Class, and on entering the Senior Class, in the fall of 1829, he accompanied Dr. Andrew Wylie, the late President of Washington College, he having been elected President of Indiana College, to Bloomington, Indiana. Entering the Senior Class of Indiana College, he graduated October 30, receiving the degrees A. B. and A. M. in course. This was the first graduating class of the college. He also received the honorary degree LL. D., in 1872. Mr. Rollins studied law at the Transylvania University, Lexington, Kentucky, and graduated there in 1834, receiving the degree LL. B. Occupation and position, the practice of law and agricultural pursuits. During the Black Hawk War, in 1832, Mr. Rollins was Aid de Camp, with the rank of Major, to Major General Richard Gentry. He was commissioned as Colonel of a volunteer regiment, by Governor H. R. Gamble, of the Union army during the Rebellion, but having just before been elected to the 37th Congress, he did not serve in the army. Major Rollins, for the period of sixteen years, represented the county of Boone, and was a Senator in the General Assembly of Missouri from his district. In 1848 and 1857 he was the Whig candidate for Governor of Missouri. In the latter canvass his Whig friends claim that he was fairly elected. All his life Mr. Rollins has been the friend and advocate of common school education by the States. He was the author of the bill locating the University of Missouri in Boone County, and by his efforts as a member of the Legislature, he secured its passage, and from this time to the end of his life he was the steadfast friend of the University, and was the author and eloquent advocate of nearly every bill intended to promote its prosperity, its endowment and its usefulness. For the last fifteen years he has been the active and vigilant President of the Board of Curators of the Institution. In the 37th Congress he was the able advocate of the passage of the law of 1852 making large grants of land for the benefit of agricultural and mechanical colleges in the different States. After leaving Congress he again became a member of the Legislature of the State of Missouri, and was the author of the bill making the Agricultural and Mechanical College a department of the State University, securing the passage of the same after a struggle of four years against the most violent opposition, and under which bill about $400,000 was added to the endowment of the University. In May, 1872, the Curators of the University passed highly commendatory resolutions with regard to the services of Mr. Rollins, both to the cause of education and the State. Reference was made to the position he took on the slavery question. Although born in the South, and himself a large slave owner, and representing the strongest slave district in Missouri, he, when in Congress, advocated, in a powerful speech, and voted for the 13th Amendment to the Constitution of the United States abolishing slavery. He sustained President Lincoln in his efforts to put down the Rebellion. Although not a member of any church, he was a firm believer in the Christian religion, and throughout his whole life an advocate of all the agencies promotive of morality, and peace, and temperance; in a word, of everything calculated to improve and elevate the standard of social intercourse among men. He was not only an eloquent speaker, but a clear, able writer, as many of his speeches and addresses testify. Mr. Rollins was married to an accomplished lady, Miss Mary E. Hickman. Of his eleven children eight survive (1889).

1831.

WILLIAM HAMILTON STOCKWELL, born April 3, 1811, at Flemingsburg, Kentucky. Died February 9, 1875, at Orange, New Jersey. Degrees A. B. and A. M., Indiana University, and M. D. Transylvania University, Kentucky. Occupation and position, practicing physician at New Orleans. For sometime editor of a medical journal at New Orleans. While living in Indiana was elected State Senator, and was proposed as member of Congress, but declined the candidacy. On removing to New Jersey, he was made Superintendent of the public schools. Dr. Stockwell spent several years in travel and observation in Europe. Two sons and two daughters survive him.

LEWIS BOLLMAN, born May 24, 1811, at Williamsport, now called Monongahela City, Pennsylvania. Residence Bloomington, Indiana. Died September 3, 1888. Educated at Washington College, Pennsylvania. Degrees A. B., A. M., and LL. B., in 1846, Indiana University. Occupation, lawyer, reporter, farmer and writer. Position, first statistician of the Department of Agriculture. Reporter of the proceedings of the Indiana House of Representatives, for about twelve winters. Mr. Bollman originated the plan of taking crop and stock statistics, now used in the Department of Agriculture, and in several States. Mr. Bollman, also, originated the Ohio and Mississippi Railroad, and also, the P. V. & C. R. Railroad, running along the Monongahela River, Pennsylvania. He considers the most useful work of his life to have been, the part he took in procuring the stock, and in the work done for Bloomington division of the Louisville, New Albany and Chicago, Railroad. Mr. Bollman has written much for the press; essays on agricultural topics; also, a work entitled " A Month at Mr. Johnstones," in which he gives his views on literary, agricultural, educational, religious topics, and on nature.

THOMAS MILLER, born 1811, near Middletown, Washington County, Pennsylvania, and died in 1841. Educated at Washington College, Pennsylvania. In 1831 entered Indiana College, received degrees A. B. and A. M. Occupation, tutor in Transylvania University, Lexington, Kentucky, where he studied law. Was professor of mathematics and ancient languages in Columbia College, Missouri. Afterwards, practiced law, and was also editor of a paper in Columbia, associated with Major James S. Rollins. Position, Aid-de-camp of General Richard Gentry, who fell in the battle of Lake Ocheeclohe, December, 1837. Mr. Miller was a fine scholar, a brilliant orator and writer. His health failing, he undertook a trip to the Rocky Mountains, but before reaching his destination he died, and was buried by his companions on the plains.

CHARLES McMICKEN RANDALL, was born Berks County, Pennsylvania, 1808. Educated at Washington College, Pennsylvania, and entered Indiana College, 1830, graduated A. B. and A. M. Received the degree, LL. B. from Transylvania University, Kentucky. Occupation, a successful practioner of law in New Orleans, where he died of cholera.

1832.

WILLIAM MCKEE DUNN. Born December 12, 1814, in Jefferson County, Indiana Territory. Resided since 1863 at Washington, D. C., until his death, July 24, 1887. Educated in the common schools of Jefferson and Montgomery Counties, Indiana. Degrees A. B. and A. M. in course, and honorary degree A. M., from Yale College, and A. M. and LL. D. from Hanover College. Mr. Dunn studied law, and was admitted to the bar in 1839, at Lexington, Ky. He has held the following official positions: A member of the Indiana House of Representatives in 1837-38, and again elected in 1868. In 1850-51 was a member of the State Constitutional Convention. In 1858-59 a member of the Thirty-Sixth and Thirty-Seventh Congresses. He entered the army in 1861, and served as aid on General McClellan's staff in West Virginia. In 1863 he was commissioned a Major and Judge Advocate of the United States Volunteers of the Department of Missouri. In 1864 he was promoted to be a Colonel and Assistant Judge Advocate in the regular army, and in March, 1866, was brevetted Brigadier General, for faithful, meritorious and distinguished services. In 1886 he was a delegate to the Philadelphia Loyalists' Convention. December 1, 1875, he was appointed Judge Advocate General of the Army. He held this place till 1882, when he was placed on the retired list. It should have been mentioned that before entering the bar General Dunn had been Professor of Mathematics in Hanover College, and that he took great interest in educational work, was a Trustee of Indiana University, and for many years a Trustee of Hanover College, devoting much of his time to the public schools of Madison.

GEORGE GILL PORTER. Born August 6, 1797, in Chester District, South Carolina. Died in Clinton, Indiana, August 5, 1841. Educated at Paris, Kentucky, and Center College, Kentucky. Degrees A. B. and A. M., from Indiana University. Studied theology and was licensed to preach at Murphreesboro, Tennessee, October 3, 1835, and was ordained at Waveland, Indiana, April 3, 1838, by the Crawfordsville Presbytery. Preached the Gospel and taught school. Married Mary Knox Rutherford in Tennessee.

JOSIAH PORTER. Born April 10, 1802, in Chester District,

South Carolina. Died at his residence, Chatham, Illinois, January 11, 1887. Educated at Paris, Kentucky, and Center College. Degrees A. B. and A. M. Studied theology at Lane Seminary, Ohio,; was a member of its first class. Occupation, a minister of the Gospel. In active service twenty years; afterwards honorably retired. Since, and at present (1886), a farmer. For some time agent of the American Bible Society, and during the War distributed hundreds of Testaments to the soldiers. Mr. Porter was licensed to preach at Murphreesboro, Tennessee, October, 1835; was ordained (1838) an evangelist, at Waveland, Indiana, by the Crawfordsville Presbytery. He was an early and earnest advocate of the temperance cause, having joined the society in 1829. He never used tobacco in any form. Since entering his eighty-fifth year he has not plowed any, an exercise in which he engaged every year from early boyhood. Mr. Porter married Martha W. Thormlow, July 18, 1860.

JAMES MORELAND STAGG. Born November 11, 1810, at Harrodsburg, Kentucky. Died November 2, 1827, at Port Gibson, Mississippi. Degrees A. B. and A. M. Occupation, attorney at law. Studied under Judge Blackford. Practiced in Indianapolis, and removed thence to Port Gibson.

ANDREW WYLIE, born February 28, 1814, Cannonsburgh, Pa. Residence, Washington, D. C. Educated at Jefferson College, Cannonsburgh, Pa., and Bloomington. Degrees, A. B. and A. M. Occupation, student of law, Transylvania University, Kentucky, and removing to Pittsburgh, Pa., continued the study of law under the distinguished lawyer, Walter Forward. Was admitted to the bar in 1838. In 1848 removed to Washington, D. C., continuing the practice of law in the city and in Virginia. Position: Was appointed by President Lincoln, March, 1863, one of the Justices of the Supreme Court of the District of Columbia, which office he held until honorably retired in 1884. Judge Wylie was Judge of the Court in several celebrated cases. He was noted for his impartiality and ability. Among other cases he presided at the trial of Mrs. Surat's son, the Confederate conspirator, and also in the Star Route trials. Judge Wylie married Miss Caroline Bryan, of Alexandria, Va., a niece of Judge Barbour, of the Supreme Court.

1833.

SAMUEL ALEXANDER, born November 9, 1808, Fleming County, Kentucky. Residence, Clinton, Hinds County, Mississippi, at the time of his death. Educated in the common schools of Fleming County, Kentucky. On graduating, received the degree A. B., and three years after A. M. Mr. Alexander studied medicine at the Physiopathic Medical College of Ohio, and received therefrom the degree M. D. Since then has been a practicing physician. Position: Dr. Alexander was for many years an Elder in the Presbyterian Church; a school trustee for forty years and always an active laborer in the cause of religion and temperance, a Sabbath-school teacher, and for fifty-two years a prohibitionist, ably advocating religion and temperance by his voice and pen. By paying strict attention to the laws of health he was as strong and vigorous in his seventy-fifth year as in the prime of life. Dr. Alexander had nearly reached his eightieth year when he died.

JOHN LEWIS KETCHAM, born April 3, 1810, Shelby County, Kentucky. Died April 20, 1869, at Indianapolis, to which place he had removed, soon after graduation. Mr. Ketcham lost his life, by an accidental fall through the hatchway in the store of Alford Talbot & Co. He was the son of Colonel John Ketcham, a well known inhabitant of Monroe County, a man famous in Southern Indiana for his public spirit, his hospitality, his generosity and his industry, and also, for his anti-slavery principles, when these principles were dangerously unpopular. Mr. J. Lewis Ketcham studied law under Judge Blackford. The only political office Mr. Ketcham held was "Justice of the Peace," and this for but one term, as he desired to devote himself to his profession. In the practice of law, he was at different times associated with Messrs. N. B. Taylor, Lucian Barbour, D. W. Coffin and James L. Mitchell, with whom he was connected at the time of his death. Mr. Ketcham was characterized by his kindness and piety, by his ability as a lawyer, and his zeal as a christian. He was punctual in his attendance at church and church-meetings, and in his daily worship. He was connected with and an elder in the Second Presbyterian church, (New School), of which the Rev. Henry Ward Beecher was the first pastor. Mr. Ketcham was, when the accommodations of the Second church had become too restricted, one of the founders of the Fourth church. In 1836 Mr. Ketcham married Miss Jane Merrill, daughter of Samuel Merrill, of Indianapolis.

JAMES DARWIN MAXWELL, born May 19, 1815, Hanover, Jefferson County, Indiana. Residence, Bloomington. Educated in the county schools. Degrees, A. B. and A. M. Indiana University, and M. D. Jefferson Medical College, Philadelphia. Dr. Maxwell soon after graduating, was made a tutor in the University. In 1836, went with Professor Elliot of Indiana University, and became a teacher in Mississippi College, of which Professor Elliot had been elected President. Returning to Bloomington, he studied medicine with his father Dr. D. H. Maxwell for a short time, and then went to Jefferson College, Philadelphia. Occupation, practitioner of medicine. Position, Secretary of Board of Trustees of Indiana University, and for many years a member, and for some time President. Dr. Maxwell married Miss Louisa Howe of Bloomington in 1839.

1834.

JAMES FINDLEY DODDS, A. B. and A. M. See Faculty list.

WILLIAM H. B. CUSTIS, born December 28, 1814, Accomack County, Virginia. Residence, Accomack Court House, Virginia. Educated, Margaret Academy, Accomack. Degrees, A. B. and A. M. Occupation, farmer. Position, Mr. Custis served three terms in the House of Delegates, Virginia, from 1843—1847. Was a member of the convention of 1861. After the war, was twice elected to the House of Representatives of the Congress of the United States. In March, 1869, was appointed clerk of the Circuit Court and County Court of Accomack, by Brev. Major General George Stoneman, a position he still holds. (1882).

JOSEPH GLASS MCPHEETERS, born in Fayette County, Kentucky, January 1, 1810, died at his residence, in Bloomington, Monday, April 2, 1888, of paralysis. Degrees A. B., A. M. and M. D., from Transylvania University, Lexington, Kentucky. Occupation, physician and surgeon. Soon after graduation Mr. McPheeters had charge of the Preparatory Department of Indiana College, assisted by M. M. Campbell. Dr. McPheeters, from the time of his graduation till his death, took an active interest in the affairs of the University. From 1851 to 1856 he was a Trustee, and part of this time President of the Board. On the breaking out of the War of the Rebellion in 1861, he entered the army as Surgeon of the 14th Indiana Volunteers, and was honorably discharged in August, 1864. During a part of his service he was on staff duty as Medical Director in the 33d Regiment of Indiana Volunteers under General Beard, and afterwards on the staff of General Whitaker, and of General Jas. B. Stedman. Dr. McPheeters was regarded as one of the most useful and efficient surgeons in the army.

In early life he married Miss Clara Dunn. He was a kind and affectionate husband and father, a member of the Presbyterian Church, and a public-spirited citizen.

THOMAS JEFFERSON WILSON died at his residence in Logansport about 1877. Educated in the common schools of Gibson County. Degrees: A. B. and A. M. Occupation: In 1848, taught school in Bloomington, was Probate Judge of Cass County for four years, and also a farmer. For many years he was a leading member in the Presbyterian Church at Logansport. Was much respected by all who knew him. Was in his disposition retiring and diffident.

1835.

*PARKER CAMPBELL, born in 1815, at Washington, Pennsylvania, died March 28, 1882, at Jacksonville, Florida. Degrees A. B. and A. M. Occupation and position, sugar planter in Louisiana and banker in Richmond, Virginia. Major in the Confederate Army. Was engaged in the battles of Lookout Mountain, Tennessee, Manassas, Virginia, Knoxville, Tennessee, and others.

DAVID MITCHELL ELLIOTT, born August 21, 1816, in Preble County, Ohio, died December 21, 1839, in Preble County, Ohio. Educated at Morning Sun and Miami University. Degrees A. B. and A. M., and M. D. from Cincinnati College, 1837. Occupation: Practiced medicine at Aurora, Indiana, with Dr. Sutton. Dr. Elliott was considered a very promising young physician. Was a member of the Associate Reformed Church.

JOHN PURCELL, Elizabethtown, Ohio.

JOHN SELREE WATTS, born in Boone County Kentucky, January 19, 1816, died June 11, 1876, at Bloomington, Indiana. Educated in the Preparatory Department of Indiana College. Degrees A. B. and A. M. Occupation and position: Studied law under Judge Sullivan at Madison, Indiana. In 1858 he was elected Prosecuting Attorney in the Judicial District. In 1866 was elected Representative for Monroe County. Under the administration of President Fillmore, he was appointed one of the Associate Judges of New Mexico, which position he resigned during President Pierce's administration, and engaged in the practice of the law, for which his command of the Spanish language especially qualified him. During Lincoln's administration he was elected a Delegate from New Mexico, and was one of the delegates to the Baltimore convention which nominated Mr. Lincoln for his second term. Under President Johnson he was confirmed by the Senate as Chief Justice of New Mexico. He was a strong and decided Union man during the Rebellion, and rendered valuable services to his country in conveying important messages from Sante Fe to Washington, at great personal expense and risk. Judge Watts married Miss Elizabeth Howe, of Bloomington, in May, 1837.

1836.

MATTHEW M. CAMPBELL, A. B. and A. M. in course. See the Faculty list.

WILLIAM M. DAILY, A. B. and A. M. See the Faculty list of Presidents.

WILLIAM HARRISON JONES, born October 11, 1813, in Daviess County, Indiana. Residence, Bloomington. Educated at common schools of Daviess County. Degrees, A. B. and A. M. Occupation, teacher, and bookseller. Served four years in the Union army, and while connected with the Veteran Reserve Corps, was detailed to serve as clerk in the Provost Marshal's office, Indianapolis. Mr. Jones was in the battle of Fort Donelson, siege of Corinth and the battle of Stone River; was also in the line of battle near Perryville, in the reserve corps. Education, religion and temperance had always an able advocate in W. H. Jones.

*JESSE WILLIAM LOWE, born March 11, 1814, in Rowan County, North Carolina; died April 3, 1868, at Omaha, Nebraska. Educated at Bloomington, Indiana. Degrees A. B. and A. M. Occupation and position, an active business man. Settled in Omaha in 1853, and was chosen the first Mayor of the city. As a capitalist, he did much for the prosperity of the city of Omaha.

JOHN JOHNSTON MCCLURKIN, born June 6, 1813, in Chester District, South Carolina. Residence, Orange, Fayette County, Indiana. Educated at Winsboro and Chester, South Carolina. Degrees A. B. and A. M. Occupation, teaching and preaching. Mr. McClurkin was licensed to preach April 12, 1841. For eight years he was pastor of a Reformed Presbyterian congregation in Gibson County, Indiana. For twenty years a pastor in Mercer County, Pennsylvania, and since pastor of a congregation of the same denomination in Fayette County, Indiana.

ADDISON LOCKE ROACHE, born November 3, 1817, Rutherford County, Tennessee. Residence, Indianapolis, Ind. Educated at McKnights Academy, Rutherford, Tennessee. Degrees A. B. and A. M. Occupation, attorney at law. Position, member of Legislature in 1847; Judge of the Supreme Court of Indiana in 1852. In 1859 appointed Trustee of Indiana University. Mr. Roache studied law with Gen. T. A. Howard, of Rockville, where he practiced law till 1858 when he removed to Indianapolis. Mr. Roache drafted the original resolution for founding the Public Library in Indianapolis.

LLOYD THEOPHILUS POSEY, born March 13, 1817, Opelousas Parish, Louisiana. Occupation, lawyer. Mr. Posey studied law under Henry Eddy, of Shawneetown, Illinois, and afterward became partner of Mr. Eddy. Mr. Posey is a member of the Presbyterian Church. He married Georgiana T. Posey, of Henderson, Ky.

ANDREW JACKSON THICKSTUN, born February 28, 1815, New Jersey. Died November 23, 1854, Council Bluffs, Iowa. Educated by an elder brother till he entered college, degrees A. B. and A. M. Occupation and position, studied law, teacher and preacher of the Gospel; Prosecuting Attorney for Sullivan County and local preacher of the M. E. Church. The last five years of his life an itinerant preacher. Was a member of the law firm of Rousseau & Thickstun—L. H. and R. H. Rousseau the other members. Mr. Thickstun gave up the practice of law because he thought he could not be religious and practice *successfully*. He left the Indiana Conference with the intention of settling in Nebraska. Was taken ill at Council Bluffs and died in eighteen hours. Mr. Thickstun was not an eloquent preacher but was well versed in the law, and was regarded as the real power of the firm. He was conscientious in the discharge of duty. On a certain occasion, a storm raging while he was on his way to the chuch, he found but one man present when he entered the pulpit. He took for his text the words of Nathan to David: " Thou art the man." His audience was attentive. He did not meet his hearer for some years; he found him a converted man, who told him that his first serious thoughts were occasioned by the sermon Mr. Thickstun had addressed to himself. Mr. Thickstun married Mary Gaines Rousseau in 1839..

1837.

JOHN DALE, born, 1812, in Cumberland County, Pennsylvania; died, 1871, at Providence, Illinois. Educated at Oxford, Ohio. Degrees A. B. and A. M. Occupation and position, minister of the gospel. Principal fields of his work were Knightstown, Indiana; Kokomo, Indiana; Tipton, Indiana; Pleasant Hill, Illinois; Virginia, Illinois; Fairburg, Illinois, and Providence, Illinois. Was Chaplain of the 75th Indiana volunteers at the time the battles at Chattanooga, Tennessee, were fought.

SAMUEL LEVI GEIGER, born January, 1817, at Louisville, Kentucky; died in the spring of 1875, in Louisville, Kentucky. Educated in Louisville, Kentucky. Degrees A. B. and A. M. Occupation and position, studied law under Chancellor George M. Bibb of the Chancery Court. Did not practice law, but made farming his principal life occupation. Engaged for sometime in steamboating, and later in manufactures in the city of Louisville. Was elected several times a Representative of Jefferson County, Kentucky, to the Legislature. Was Chairman of the Board of Trustees of the Lunatic Asylum at Anchorage, Kentucky. Was a lay member of the Episcopal church, and during the services, Sunday morning, was stricken with apoplexy and died the same evening.

RICHARD HENRY HOLMAN, born February 24, 1817, at Veraestau, near Aurora, Indiana; died at Veraestau, December 27,

1841. Educated at the Aurora Seminary and Rising Sun Seminary. Degrees A. B. and A. M. Occupation, student of law under his father, Judge Holman, and within two years had reached the front rank in his profession at the bar of the county seat of Dearbon County, then one of the ablest in the State. By his incessant labor he brought on the disease of which he died, in the 24th year of his age.

ERASMUS D. C. MCELRATH. Degrees A. B. and A. M. Residence, Mississippi.

GEORGE L. MCAFFEE, born June 11, 1815, in Mercer County, Kentucky. Residence, Long Grove, Hardin County, Kentucky. Educated in the Mercer County common schools. Degrees A. B., A. M. and M. D., Louisville Medical Institute, 1845. Occupation and position, practicing physician for thirty-five years. At present (1883) agriclturist. Was elected without opposition to the State Legislature, 1866, from Hardin County, Kentucky. Delivered a eulogy on the occasion of the death of Governor Helm, in the House of Representatives, which was highly spoken of by Senator Jesse D. Bright, and other distinguished persons.

JOSEPH F. NICHOLS, born September 6, 1816. Died August 17, 1843, near Kaskaskia, Illinois. Educated, at Bloomington, Indiana. Degrees, A. B. and A. M. and M. D., Louisville Medical Institute, 1840. Occupation, practicing physician.

JOHN W. H. PARKER, born April 2, 1819, Accomack County, Virginia. Residence, Onancock, Accomack County, Virginia. Educated at Margaret Academy. Degrees, A. B. and A. M., LL. B., William and Mary College, Virginia. Occupation, practice of law. Position, member of Senate of Virginia, for four years.

HUGH THOMPSON REID, born October 5, 1811, near Liberty, Union County, Indiana. Died August 21, 1874, at Keokuk, Iowa. Educated, Miami University, Oxford, Ohio, and Lane Seminary, near Cincinnati, Ohio. Degrees, A. B. and A. M. Occupation and position, attorney at law. District Attorney of Iowa Territory. Visitor to the West Point Military Academy. Member of the Society of the Army of the Tennessee. Colonel of the 15th Regiment Iowa Volunteers. Brigadier-General of Volunteers, (1861-65). President of Des Moines

Railroad Company, Keokuk, and of Hamilton Bridge Company. General Reid was in many battles, during the civil war. At the battle of Shiloh, he received a wound in the neck, which induced paralysis and Bright's disease, of which he died,—at the battle of Corinth, Mississippi. Had command of Post Bolivar, Tennessee; Cairo, Illinois; Lake Providence, Louisana, and the battle there, and also, at Hatchie. He gave information to Admiral Porter, which led to the capture of Yazoo City, Mississippi. When commanding the port at Columbus, Kentucky, he caused the arrest of the Knights' of the Golden Circle. General Reid was a successful prosecutor and land lawyer. He was the attorney employed in defending Joseph Smith, the Mormon leader, when he was assassinated. General Reid may be said to have been the builder of the railroad, from Keokuk to Fort Dodge, (near 250 miles). He was also, a vestryman in St. John's Episcopal Church.

GEORGE SEAMAN SHEETS, born August 22, 1818, Madison. Died January 4, 1852, Madison. Educated, at school of Beaumont Parks, Madison. Degrees, A. B. and A. M., Ind. Univ. and LL. B., Harvard University, Cambridge, Massachusetts. Occupation, lawyer.

WILLIAM WILLIS, born April, 1818, Belleview, Kentucky. Died May, 1843, at Belleview, Kentucky. Educated, Petersburg, Kentucky, and Rising Sun Academy. Degrees, A. B. and A. M. Occupation, farmer. A member of the Presbyterian Church. Was a man of great influence among his neighbors and bore an irreproachable character.

1838.

E. L. ARMSTRONG, Newton, Ohio. Degrees, A. B. and A. M.

WILLIAM C. HILLIS, born September 20, 1820, Jefferson County, Indiana. Residence, Des Moines, Iowa. Educated, Madison, Indiana. Degrees, A. B. and A. M. Occupation and position, attorney at law. Representative in Indiana Legislature. Prosecuting attorney 4th. Circuit, Missouri, for eight years. Judge of Criminal Court, of Des Moines, four years.

SAMUEL FRANKLIN MAXWELL, born July 29, 1817, Madison, Indiana. Died June 15, 1877, Rockville, Indiana. Educated, Bloomington Schools. Degrees, A. B. and A. M. Occupation and position, lawyer, and for several years Judge of the Court of Common Pleas, 1853–61, of Parke and Vermillion Counties, Indiana, for Parke, Vigo and Sullivan, 1865–69. Judge Maxwell's death was caused by tetanus, arising from a wound in his hand.

JOHN WILSON MORRISON, born October 23, 1813, Chester District, South Carolina. Died January 5, 1867, Lake Forest, Illinois. Degrees, A. B. and A. M. Occupation, preaching the gospel. Position, pastor of the Reformed Presbyterian Church, Bloom, Illinois, for twenty-two years. His tombstone has on it this inscription: "A Prairie Missionary, an Eloquent Preacher and Faithful Pastor."

SAMUEL C. PARKS, born March 25, 1820, Middlebury, Vermont. Residence, Rawlins, Wyoming Territory. Educated, at Madison, Indiana. Degrees, A. B. and A. M., and A. M. from Jacksonville College, 1844. Occupation and position, taught school for six years, studied law and practiced till September, 1863. Member of Constitutional Convention of Illinois. In 1863 was appointed by President Lincoln, Associate Justice of Idaho, resigned in 1865. Was appointed Associate Justice of New Mexico, served one term of four years, was at his own request transferred to Wyoming Territory, in 1882. At present (1883), Judge of the Third Judicial District of Wyoming Territory. It is perhaps worthy of note that Judge Parks has served as Judge, in three different territories. Judge Parks is the son of Professor B. Parks, of the University of Indiana.

JOSHUA PRESSLER, A. B. and A. M., Concordia, Louisana,

J. J. PRESLER, A. B. and A. M., Mississippi.

HOWARD STAPP, born July 20, 1819, Madison, Indiana. Residence, Galveston, Texas. Education: Was a pupil of Beaumont Parks, afterward Professor of Language in Indiana University. Degrees A. B. and A. M. Occupation and position, attorney at law in Indiana. Admitted to the bar, 1840; in Boonville, Missouri, 1841. In 1848 returned to Madison and practiced law there. In 1858 crossed the plains to California, via Salt Lake City, San Bernardino and Los Angeles to San Francisco. Followed mining for eight years. In 1866 returned via Nicaragua and New York to Texas as an employé in the Internal Revenue Department. At present (1883) a cotton planter. Took an active part in the Presidential canvass of 1848 and 1852 for General Taylor and General Scott. A member of the Christian Church.

JAMES MCGREADY TOWNSEND, born February 19, 1820, Morganfield, Kentucky. Residence, San Bernardino, California. Educated at Morganfield, Kentucky. Degrees A. B. and A. M. Occupation and position, teacher and farmer; steward in the church; engaged actively in educational, church and temperance work, before leaving Clay and Vigo Counties, Indiana, and also in California.

GEORGE EDWARD WEST, born November 25, 1819, Salem, Massachusetts. Residence, Lafayette, Indiana. Educated at Salem, Massachusetts. Degrees A. B. and A. M. Position, four years in United States Navy. Occupation after leaving the navy, milling and merchandising. Resigned position in United States Navy on account of sickness caused by African fever.

CRAIG RITCHIE WYLIE, born April 25, 1819. Died July 23, 1840, near Louisville, Kentucky. Educated, Preparatory School Indiana College. Degree A. B. Occupation, teaching. Intending to study law. The third son of President Wylie.

1839.

JOHN A. CLEMENT, born in 1814, in Gibson County, Indiana, died March 8, 1845. Educated at Princeton, Indiana, Seminary, Mr. Brydon, Principal. Degrees A. B. and A. M. Occupation, teacher in high school, Casey County, Georgia. During a vacancy in the Department of Mathematics in the University (1839-40) Mr. Clement had charge.

SETH MARSHALL LEAVENWORTH, born July 30, 1821, at Milltown, Harrison County, Indiana, died November 21, 1868, at Mt. Vernon, Indiana. Degrees A. B. and A. M. Occupation: Studied law with Mr. Edson, of Mt. Vernon; engaged in trade; since 1857, cashier First National Bank of Mt. Vernon.

ADAM MARSHALL, born in 1807, in Fairfield District, South Carolina, died at Idana, Kansas, December 21, 1866. Educated at Winsboro College, South Carolina. Degrees A. B. and A. M. Occupation, teaching. Was an elder in the Reformed Presbyterian Church.

ELAM HAMILTON WAUGH, born December 25, 1815, in Iredell County, North Carolina. Residence, Longmont, Boulder County, Colorado. Educated at home by his mother and father. Degrees A. B. and A. M., and, from Elective Medical Institute, Cincinnati, M. D. Occupation, for five years a teacher, for thirty-four years a practitioner of medicine. Position, elder in the Presbyterian Church; delegate to General Assembly in May, 1878, meeting in Pittsburgh, Pennsylvania, and also to the meeting in Minneapolis in 1886. In 1862 he was made Physician to the City of Leavenworth, and for some time was Superintendent of the schools. Dr. Waugh married Miss Margaret Dodds, of Bloomington. In July, 1840, he moved to Kansas Territory. During the troubles which took place in the effort to make Kansas a slave State, he lost his second son, Addison, in the Quantrel raid upon Lawrence. His eldest son, Newton, who had enlisted to fight with the Indians, was killed in a battle with the Utes, in Idaho. A third son, Morris, who had left home for the Far West in 1866, was never heard of afterwards.

In 1865 Mrs. Waugh died, and soon after her eldest daughter, leaving the two youngest surviving. In 1871 Dr. Waugh married Delia E. Olney, and moved to Clinton, a small town west of Lawrence, in 1873, and in 1880 moved to Colorado, near Longmont.

THOMAS D. WEIR, A. B., A. M., Salem.

FRANCIS WEST, born August 13, 1822, at Salem, Massachusetts; died August 3, 1840, at Indianapolis. Educated at Salem, Massachusetts. Degree A. B. This young man, of fine talents, and much esteemed by his teachers, by his early death disappointed the expectations of a brilliant career in life.

GEORGE GROVER WRIGHT was born in Bloomington, March 24, 1820, the eighth child of a family of five sons and four daughters. Residence, DesMoines, Iowa. Educated at Bloomington. Entered the Preparatory Department when about fourteen years old. Degrees A. B., A. M. and LL. D. in 1866. The degree LL. D. was also conferred by Iowa College, at Grinnell; the Wesleyan University, Mt. Pleasant, Iowa; Simpson Centenary College, Indianola, Iowa, and Iowa State University. Occupation and position: Studied law with his brother, Governor Joseph A. Wright, at Rockville. In 1840 was admitted to practice in Indiana. On moving to Kesauqua, Iowa, commenced practice. At this time his pecuniary capital was zero. In 1865 Judge Wright removed to DesMoines, his present residence (1889). In 1847 he was elected Prosecuting Attorney for Van Buren County. In 1848, State Senator, as a Whig, by a majority of 140 in a county having a Democratic majority of about 250. In 1852 was voted unanimously by the Whigs for the United States Senate, but was left in the minority, as the district was overwhelmingly Democratic. He then returned to the practice of law. In 1855 was elected Chief Justice of the State Supreme Court, by the Legislature. This position he held till 1860, when he declined a reëlection the fall before, by the people, according to the Constitution of 1857. In 1860, a vacancy on the bench occurring, by death, Governor Kirkwood requested Judge Wright, to fill the unexpired term. Judge Wright was elected for the unexpired term that fall, and in 1865 was again reëlected for a term of six years. In 1870, while occupying this place, he was elected United States Senator, and entered upon the duties of his office March 4, 1871. Having served as Senator for six years, he declined a reëlection, and in March, 1877, returned to the practice of his profession, not however, engaging in general practice, but giving his attention only to cases in the United States Supreme Court. In 1865, in connection with two others, he opened a law school in DesMoines. Three years after, at the request of the Regents of Iowa University, this law school was made a department of this institution. Here he continued to teach and lecture till January, 1871, resigning this place on account of his approaching duties as Senator. Recently he has engaged to return to his law professorship for a short term each year. For ten years past he has nearly all the time taken an active part in political campaigns, generally in Iowa, sometimes in other States. Judge Wright has been a diligent worker, not only within but outside of his professional duties. He has lectured two hundred times or more, before societies and colleges on commencement occasions, before lyceums, for the benefit of library associations, school libraries, and for many benevolent, literary, church and like associations. Among these should be mentioned the eloquent address delivered in the M. E. Church, before the Alumni of Indiana University, June 11, 1889. Judge Wright's ambition has been, not to accumulate wealth, but rather to bring up a good family, and to acquire the means to do it. In these aims he has been successful. Three of his sons are lawyers, two of them associated with himself in the practice of law, and the third at Sioux City, all eminent citizens. It is pleasant and profitable to contemplate such a life as Judge Wright's—a self-made man, born in poverty—his father dying when he was five years old, his mother left with but little property, and that unproductive. All the children, as soon as they were able, had to work for their living. His distinguished brother, Governor Joseph A. Wright, was glad to undertake any menial work about the college, or elsewhere, while he was a student, but was unable, through want of means, to complete the course of study. In order to help his widowed mother and the younger members of the family, he gave up for a time the studies in which he delighted. George, the subject of this sketch, at an early age was attacked by rheumatism, which afflicted him severely for seven years, and left him a cripple for life. When about fourteen years old he first went to school, having been taught to some extent by his mother and brothers at home. His name first occurs in a MS. list of the students in the winter term of 1834–5. His honesty, prudence and temperance in all things, with the talents God gave him, have made him a distinguished citizen of his adopted State. Judge Wright is a member of the Methodist Episcopal Church, and heartily thanks the Giver of all good for the blessings he has received, and for the care of a good mother, and for the lessons he received from his teachers, and especially from the President of the University, Dr. A. Wylie. Judge Wright married Hannah M. Dibble, October 19, 1843.

1840.

JOHN ROBERT CRAVENS, born November 22, 1819, at Madison. Residence, Madison, Indiana. Educated in the Madison schools, at a school in Xenia, Ohio, and also at Harrisonburgh, Virginia. Degrees A. B. and A. M. Occupation, attorney at law. Took an active part in the political issues of the day. Positions: Paymaster in United States Army for four years, school trustee of the city of Madison, and for nine sessions State Senator. Mr. Cravens is a member and trustee of the Second Presbyterian Church.

JOHN WILLIS DUNBAR, born May 3, 1819, at Dunbarton, Mississippi, died December 11, 1846, at Dunbarton, near Natchez, Mississippi. Educated at Jefferson College, Washington, Mississippi, but did not graduate. Mr. Dunbar also received instruction from the celebrated orator, S. S. Prentiss. Degrees A. B. and A. M. Occupation: After graduation he studied law, intending to prepare himself for political life, but his failing health terminated in death. Mr. Dunbar was a popular man among his fellow students. An address he delivered while a student at college was so much esteemed by the students and his friends that they published it.

WILLIAM K. EDWARDS, born near Louisville, Kentucky, about the year 1820. Died in 1878. Mr. Edwards entered the Freshman Class in 1836. Degrees A. B. and A. M. Studied law at Transylvania University, Kentucky. Was a pupil of Judge Mayes and Judge Robertson. He graduated LL. B. in 1842. Occupation: Mr. Edwards located in Terre Haute and commenced the practice of his profession. Position: In 1845 he was elected to the Legislature. He served three subsequent sessions of the Legislature; in 1873 was Speaker of the House of Representatives. Mr. Edwards was noted as a painstaking, laborious worker as a legislator, and was particularly distinguished as a parliamentarian. He was the first Mayor of Terre Haute after its organization as a city under the act of 1853. This office he held to the satisfaction of the community for two terms. In 1855 he was appointed a Trustee of Indiana University; was President of the Board from 1855 to 1857, and with the exception of the years 1859–61 was a Trustee till the time of his death. He was also Secretary of the Rose Polytechnic Institute; he delivered the address at the laying of its corner stone. Col. Edwards was also a Director of the Terre Haute & Chicago, and Terre Haute, Indianapolis & Vandalia Railroads, and also a Director of the First National Bank of Terre Haute. He was the best known and, perhaps, the best posted Odd Fellow in the State, of which he was Past Grand Master. He was also a prominent Mason, and at one time Master of the Social Lodge No. 86. Col. Edwards was designated by the late Chauncey Rose as one of the executors of his will, and was especially entrusted by that philanthropist with the carrying out of his various schemes of an educational and charitable character.

Indebted to Prof. Byers for the above notice.

MATTHEW ELDER, born January 3, 1813, in Chester District, South Carolina. Residence, Guthriesville, York County, South Carolina. Educated at the schools of Messrs. McMillan, Donnelly & Sheene. Degrees A. B. and A. M. Occupation: For twenty-four years a teacher; nine years Professor of Ancient Languages in Yorkville Female College, and also Professor of Natural Science; now, in his seventieth year (1882), a farmer in York County, South Carolina. Position, an elder in the Associate Reformed Presbyterian Church. Mr. Elder's intention was to study for the ministry, but was prevented by a severe spinal affection. Mr. Elder, by his public addresses and contributions to the papers, has been a zealous advocate of temperance.

ZENAS KELL M. HOGE, born 1821, in Gibson County, Indiana, died about four years after graduation. Educated at Princeton, Indiana, Seminary. Degrees A. B. and A. M. Occupation, farmer.

1841.

RICHARD TAYLOR ALLISON, born June 6, 1823, in Jefferson County, Kentucky, near Louisville. Educated at private schools, principally the school of Mr. Robert B. Smith. Degrees received, A. B. and A. M., and the degree LL. B. from Transylvania University. Occupation: After leaving the University he studied law, pursuing the study with much interest, both at home and in the offices of attorneys in Louisville, and at the Transylvania University. After studying the profession he commenced the practice of law under favorable auspices in Baltimore, Maryland, but, his health failing, he spent the winter of 1848-49 in the West Indies. On his return to Baltimore he was appointed by his uncle, President Taylor, Paymaster in the United States Navy, and in this capacity served in the Pacific and East Indies, in China and Japan, and notably in the squadron which, under Commodore Perry, constituted the Japan expedition, which opened Japan to the world. When the Civil War broke out in 1861, he was stationed at the Navy Yard in Washington. Resigning his office April 20, 1861, he went South and was appointed Paymaster in the Marine Corps of the Confederate States, and served in this capacity throughout the war. After the war was over he returned to Baltimore, where he has resided ever since, filling different positions; amongst others he was Clerk of the Superior Court of Baltimore City. At present (1886) he is resting from his labors, feeling that he has grown rusty in law, and, having reached the grand climacteric, it is too late for him to study anew and to resume the practice of law. Mr. Allison says of himself that he has some pleasant hobbies which he rides moderately; he haunts the libraries and reads a good deal, but he can not call it study. He ascribes one of his chief pleasures and resources to his love of books and reading, for which he is indebted in a great degree to Indiana University and to its late revered President, Dr. Andrew Wylie, and in a lesser degree to the Philomathean Society. Mr. Allison married Miss Maria Key Taney, daughter of the late Roger B. Taney, Chief Justice of the United States.

JOHN FINLEY DODDS, born February 24, 1819, at Georgetown, Kentucky. Residence, Logansport, Indiana. Educated in the Bloomington common schools. Degrees A. B. and A. M. Occupation, lawyer. Positions: Judge; County Auditor; Collector of Internal Revenue, Ninth District, Indiana; member of the Presbyterian Church.

ALBERT ROBINSON SHANNON, born June 28, 1822, in Shelby County, Kentucky. Residence, Carmi, Illinois. Educated at Illinois College, Jacksonville, Illinois. Degrees A. B. and A. M., and LL. B. from Transylvania University, Lexington (1844). Occupation, merchant.

CHARLES BENJAMIN THOMAS, born in 1823, at Charleston, South Carolina, died at Lexington, Kentucky, December 14, 1873. Degrees A. B. and A. M. Occupation, lawyer. Position, Judge of Fayette Circuit Court at the time of his death. Judge Thomas was Judge Advocate in the Army of the Confederate States, with the rank of Colonel.

JOHN HOSEA WYLIE, born February 14, 1823, at Washington, Pennsylvania, died March 10, 1855, at Likna Plantation, Hawai, Sandwich Islands, where he had gone for health. Educated in Bloomington schools. Degrees A. B. and A. M., and M. D. from Louisville University. Occupation, physician, at Richmond, Indiana.

1842.

ISAAC BENJAMIN GWATHMEY, born November 4, 1822, Shelbyville, Kentucky. Died May 5, 1856, St. Louis, Missouri. Educated at Thomas Elliott's School, afterwards went to Bacon College, Kentucky. Entered Junior Class, Indiana University. Degrees, A. B. and A. M., and LL. B., Harvard Law School, 1867. He removed from Louisville to St. Louis, where he practiced law for three years before his death. He had just then begun to establish himself, and to be regarded as one of the leading men at the bar. Mr. Blackwood his eulogist said, "that the bar had lost a prominent member, the community a useful citizen, and society that bright ornament a christian gentleman."

SAMUEL MILLEN, born March 22, 1818, Chester District, South Carolina. Died October 11, 1871. Educated, public school, Chester District. Degrees, A. B. and A. M. Occupation, minister of the gospel in the United Presbyterian Church. Position, pastor of Shiloh Congregation, Indiana, for three years; Clayton, Indiana, for seven years and Smith Creek, Illinois, fifteen years. Mr. Millen was connected with the christain commission during the rebellion.

GEORGE HOLIBIRD MUNSON, born April 18, 1825, Litchfield County, Connecticut. Died August 11, 1855, at his residence, Bedford, Indiana. Educated, Salem Academy. Degrees, A. B., A. M. and LL. B. Occupation, attorney at law, in partnership with the late George G. Dunn. Mr. Munson was not a member of any church, though a daily reader of the Bible, and always ready to help the needy.

DAVID WASSON STORMONT, born September 26, 1820, Princeton, Indiana. Residence, Topeka, Kansas. Educated, Princeton Seminary. Degrees, A. B., A. M. and M. D., from University of Pennsylvania. Occupation, practice of medicine.

HENRY TANNER, born April 28, 1817, London, England. Residence, Paris, Edgar County, Illinois. Educated, in London. Degrees, A. B., A. M. and LL. B. Occupation, attorney at law. After the resignation of Professor Ammen, Mr. Tanner was formally appointed Professor of Mathematics, *pro tem.* till the end of the year. At the close of Mr. Tanner's term of service, the board expressed on their minutes, their entire satisfaction with the creditable manner, in which he had filled so responsible a position.

JAMES WOODBURN, A. M. See list of professors.

1843.

RICHARD CLOUGH GWATHMEY, born November 9, 1824, Jefferson County, Kentucky. Died August 6, 1885, at San Bernardino, California. Educated at Mr. Thomas Elliott's school and at Bacon College. Entered Sophomore Class Indiana University, degrees A. B. and A. M. During the rebellion Mr. Gwathmey was loyal to the Union. Both he and his brother (of class 1842) were opposed to slavery, and on the side of emancipation when the question was raised in Kentucky, previous to the war. Mr. Gwathmey was the inventor of an instrument, the cyclophore; the patent was at first refused. Mr. Gwathmey appealed to the Supreme Court, plead his own cause and gained the suit.

WILLIAM H. HEAD, born 1822, Chester District, South Carolina. Residence, Bryan, Texas. Educated at Louisville, Mississippi. Degrees A. B. and A. M. Occupation, attorney at law for some time; afterward minister of the gospel in the Baptist Church. Position, President of Concord Institute, Shiloh, Louisiana; President of the Hazlehurst Academy, Mississippi.

JOHN ABRAHAM HENDRICKS, born March 7, 1823, Madison, Indiana. Killed at the battle of Pea Ridge, Friday, March 7, 1862. Educated, at the common and classical schools of Madison, Indiana. Degrees, A. B. and A. M. Occupation, practicing law. Engaged for a short time in the lumber and sash business, and afterwards in law. Position, Captain in regimental service, 16th Regiment United States Infantry, under the "Ten Regiment Bill" in the Mexican War, and in active service on the Rio Grande. Lieutenant-Colonel, 22d Indiana Volunteers, in the war of the Rebellion.

JAMES SCOTT HESTER, born 1825, Monroe County, Indiana. Died 1879, Nashville, Indiana. Educated, public school, Bloomington, Indiana. Degrees, A. B. and A. M. Occupation, lawyer. Position, member of committee to devise State code, 1852. Colonel in Union Army. Elected Judge of Circuit Court of Bartholomew and Brown Counties. Mr. Hester attended the law school of the University for two years.

HUGH AIKEN MCKELVEY, born March 23, 1818, at Chester, South Carolina. Residence, 544 Fairfield Avenue, Bridgeport,

Connecticut (1887). Educated at Sparta, Illinois. Degrees, A. B. and A. M. Occupation: Teaching and preaching; pastor seven years; missionary in Minnesota four years; appointed Superintendent of Freedman's School, in 1864, at Natchez and Baton Rouge. Married Miss Harriet Fletcher, of Jamestown, New York, September 22, 1852. After her death Mr. McKelvey married Mrs. H. M. Finch, of Sharon, Connecticut, August 28, 1866.

JOHN ORCHARD MCKINNEY. A. B. and A. M. Dentist. Died. A dentist by profession.

STAFFORD CURRY MILLEN, born March 1, 1812, in Chester District, South Carolina. Died April 13, 1874, Iredell County, North Carolina. Educated, Fishing Creek Academy, Chester District, South Carolina, Mr. Wylie the principal. Afterward at the Seminary of Rev. Hugh McMillan, Xenia, O. Degrees, A. B. and A. M., and in 1861 the honorary degree D. D. from Indiana University. Studied theology at Due-West Theological Seminary, South Carolina. Occupation, a preacher of the gospel. Position, pastor of several congregations in the Presbyterian Church. President of Concord Female College, Statesville, North Carolina. Rev. Dr. Millen was originally a member and minister of the Associate Reformed Presbyterian Church. Afterwards joined the Presbyterian Church and became pastor of the church at Taylorsville. At the time of his death was pastor of the Concord Church, Iredell County, North Carolina.

SAMUEL THEOPHYLACT WYLIE, born January 2, 1825, Washington, Pennsylvania. Died January 25, 1850, Cincinnati, Ohio. Educated, preparatory department Indiana University. Degrees, A. B. and A. M. and LL. B. Occupation, lawyer, Cincinnati, Ohio. Mr. Wylie was a young man of fine talents and bid fair to become distinguished in his profession.

1844.

ROBERT NEWTON FEE, born December 3, 1822, Chester District, South Carolina. He resided at Lewiston, Nez-Percé County, Idaho Territory, where he died, March 12, 1887. Educated, Bloomington, Indiana. Degrees, A. B. and A. M. Occupation, preaching and occasionally teaching school. For five years a missionary and teacher among the Indians. Position, a minister of the gospel. For some time superintendent of the public schools in Iowa, and for a short time non-commissioned Chaplain at Camp McClelland, Davenport, Iowa. Rev. R. N. Fee married Miss Isabella G. Monteith, September 6, 1848.

GABRIEL MONROE OVERSTREET, born May 21, 1819, Oldham County, Kentucky. Residence, Franklin, Indiana. Educated, Franklin College, Indiana. Degrees, A. B. and A. M., Indiana University. Occupation and position, attorney at law. Prosecuting attorney, city councilman and State Senator. Elder of the Presbyterian Church. Private in the war of the Rebellion. Married November 20, 1849, to Sarah S. Morgan.

PAUL SIEG, born March 24, 1817, Shenandoah County, Virginia. Died April 6, 1861, Corydon, Indiana. Educated, Corydon, Indiana. Degrees, A. B. and A. M.: M. D. Louisville Medical Institute, 1856. Occupation and position, farmer, teacher, and druggist. A minister in the Methodist Episcopal Church. Principal of Corydon Seminary, 1851–56. In 1860 editor of the *Corydon Argus*. From 1846 to 1850 taught in Louisiana. Was instrumental in securing the passage of the school law of the State.

1845.

JESSE IANTHUS ALEXANDER, born October 10, 1824, Gosport, Indiana. Died May 30, 1871, at Terre Haute. Educated, at Bloomington Preparatory. Degrees, A. B. and A. M. Occupation and position, lawyer; State Senator, six years. United States Collector of Internal Revenue, 7th District Indiana. Two years Captain in Mexican War. Colonel Alexander served with his command three years in the army of the Tennessee and for one year in command of 1st Brigade, 3d Division, 17th army corps. Was engaged in the battles of New Madrid and Island No. 10, Corinth, Iuka, Jackson Walnut Hills, Vicksburgh; the Yazoo expedition and Missionary Ridge and other.

BEZA KILL ARCHER, born July 5, 1822, near Princeton, Indiana. Died at Princeton, Indiana, May 13, 1847. Educated, at Princeton Seminary and Hanover College. Degrees, A. B., (Mr. A. on account of a severe mental and bodily affliction, was unable to attend, the last term of the Senior year, but on account of his excellence as a student, was regarded as entitled to a diploma). Occupation, for a short time, a druggist, then a teacher. Position, principal of the Gibson Seminary, Princeton, Indiana. A member of the Reformed Presbyterian Church.

JOHN ALEXANDER CAMPBELL, born March 21, 1825, Johnson County, Indiana. Died August 8, 1860, suddenly while filling a synodical appointment at Somonauk Congregation, Illinois. Educated, at Bloomington, and the Preparatory Department, Indiana University. Degrees, A. B. and A. M. Mr. Campbell studied theology in the Seminary of the United Presbyterian Church, Oxford, Ohio. Occupation and position, teacher at Dayton, Pennsylvania, and Lebanon, Pennsylvania, and preacher of the gospel.

GEORGE ABRAHAM HAUSER, born April 16, 1820, Salem, North Carolina. Died at Hope, his home, soon after graduation, having returned home sick. Educated, at the Moravian School, Salem, North Carolina. Degree, A. B. Was a member of the Moravian Church.

JOHN A. MILLEN, born June 21, 1826, Chester, South Carolina. Died November 7, 1849, Bedford, Indiana. Educated, Monroe County Schools. Degrees, A. B. and A. M. Occupation and position, for a short time teacher in Louisiana. Practiced law in Bedford, till the time of his death. Member of the Presbyterian Church.

ROBERT QUINCY ROACHE, born June 16, 1824, Rutherford, County, Tennessee. Residence, California, Moniteau County, Missouri. Educated, at Bloomington, Indiana. Degrees, A. B. and A. M. Occupation, commercial business and banking. Position, served one term as Judge of Circuit Court.

WILLIAM E. SIMPSON, born October 19, 1823, Brunswick County, Virginia. Died April 25, 1846, Paoli, Indiana. Degree, A. B. Mr. Simpson was a young man of fine personal appearance and address, of excellent mind, and much esteemed by both professors and students. He was a member of the Presbyterian Church.

BARTON W. WILSON, A. M. Lawyer. Greensburg.

1846.

THOMAS P. CONELLY, born November 19, 1817, Mount Sterling, Kentucky. Died November 10, 1865, Spencer, Indiana. Educated, in part at Wabash College. Degrees, A. B. and A. M., Indiana University, and M. D. from Cincinnati Eclectic College of Medicine. Occupation and position, preacher of gospel in the Christian Church. For some time principal of the Bedford High School. Practiced medicine in Fayetteville, Indiana, and afterwards in Spencer, Indiana, preaching on the Lord's day. He held a public discussion on "Materialism," with Dr. N. Fields of Jeffersonville; which debate he afterwards published. His defence of the "Conscious existence of the soul after death, was regarded as a true triumph of truth." He also held several other public discussions. Mr. Connelly was highly respected, as a patriot and christian by all who knew him.

JONATHAN CLARK, born August 3, 1828, Fayette County, Kentucky. Residence, Paducah, Kentucky. Educated, Louisville, Kentucky, at the schools of R. M. Smith, John Harney, and Noble Butler. Degrees, A. B. and A. M., and M. D. from Louisville University. Occupation, physician.

THOMAS A. GRAHAM. A. B. and A. M. Jasper, Indiana.

ALEXANDER MCCAUGHAN, born 1821. Died October 15, 1845. Was a member of the senior class at the time of his death.

SAMUEL N. D. MARTIN, born January 11, 1825, Livonia, Indiana. Residence, Winnebago Agency Nebraska. Educated, at a private school Livonia, also, at Paris, Illinois. Degrees, A. B. and A. M. Occupation, preaching the gospel and teaching. Position, missionary of Presbyterian Board of Foreign Missions at Ningpo, China, from 1850–58. Superintendent of boys' boarding-school. Home missionary for six years in Texas, and for eight years in Indiana, Illinois and Missouri. For two years superintendent of government boarding-school among the Nez-Percés, Indian reservation Idaho Territory. For four years missionary in Kansas. At present (1882), superintendent Government Industrial Boarding-school for the Winnebago Indians, at Winnebago, Nebraska.

WILLIAM ALEXANDER PARSONS MARTIN, born April 10, 1827, in Livonia, Indiana. Residence, Peking, China. Educated at

Livonia and at Indiana University. He entered the University in 1843. Degrees A. B. and A. M. Dr. Martin received the degree D. D. from Layfayette College, Easton, Pennsylvania, in 1869, and LL. D. from New York University in 1870. By the Imperial decree he has been made a Mandarin of the third rank. Occupation and position, studied theology for three years at the Presbyterian Theological Seminary, New Albany. In 1850 went as missionary to China, and since 1857 has been in the service of the Chinese government. In 1867 was made Professor of International Law, in the Imperial College at Peking, and since 1869 has been its President. In 1858, Dr. Martin assisted as interpreter for the Hon. W. B. Reed, United States Minister, in negotiating the new or second treaty with China. In 1859 he accompanied the United States Embassy to Peking. Four years afterwards he made Peking his permanent residence. The following are some of the books of which Dr. Martin is author or editor: "The Chinese, their Education, Philosophy and Letters." This work was first published in China, and afterwards republished by the Harper Brothers, of New York. "History of the Classic Ages of China." "Les Vestiges d'un Droit International dans l'ancienne Chine"—(Revue de Droit International). Natural Theology and Evidences of Christianity. Chinese. Reprinted in numerous editions in China and Japan. Natural Philosophy. Chinese; 7 volumes. This work contained the first formal treatise on chemistry, and the first regular course of Physics ever published in the Chinese language. A new edition of this work was called for, or, rather, a new work entitled, "Mathematical Physics," was published in 1885. "The Chinese, their Education, Philosophy and Letters." Shanghai and London, 1885. New York, 1881. The following translations were made by Dr. Martin, or under his direction: Wheaton's International Law, De Marten's Guide Diplomatique, Woolsey's International Law, Bluntschle's International Law. All the works the Chinese possess thus far, on international law, are directly or indirectly from the pen of Dr. Martin. Fawcet's Political Economy. The first systematic work on the subject in the Chinese language. Dr. Martin has lately been made an Associé de l'institut de droit International de l'Europe, and Membre Correspondent de la Societé de la Legislation Compareè de Paris. In the way of adventures, Dr. Martin reports the following: He was once taken prisoner by Chinese pirates, who soon released him, because, as they said, they had learned to regard missionaries as "good men." Whether this happened in connection with the two important battles he witnessed, he does not state. Dr. Martin was the first foreigner in recent times to make the inland passage from Peking to Shanghai, *via* the Grand Canal, visiting, *en route*, the Chinese Jews in Honan, and the tomb of Confucius in Shantung. Dr. Martin is still (1889) President of the Imperial College, Peking (the Tungwen College). The catalogue of 1888, of about one hundred pages, published by Imperial authority, is in English and Chinese. There are four English-speaking Professors, two French, one German and three Chinese, with seven Chinese Tutors. Two in Mathematics, one in Chemistry, two in English, one in Russian and one in French. Many of the students have received posts of official duty at home (in China) and abroad.

ROBERT RUFUS ROBERTS, born November 7, 1824, in Henderson, Kentucky. Died at Brazil, Indiana, January 22, 1880. Educated, at Henderson and afterwards at the Newburg Schools. Degrees, A. B. and A. M. Occupation, Mr. Roberts first employment was cashier in the Evansville Bank. He then became a farmer, and lastly, a dealer in coal in Newburg and at Brazil, where he lost his life by a boiler explosion. Mr. Roberts was a prominent member of the Methodist Episcopal Church. He married Miss Martha C. Parrett of Evansville, daughter of the Rev. Robert Parrett, November 20, 1849.

WASHINGTON M. SHARP. A. B. and A. M. Abbeville, S. C.

DAVID SHUCK, born April, 1821, Harrison County, Indiana. Residence, Lecompton, Kansas. Educated, at common schools of Harrison County. Degrees, A. B. and A. M., and D. D., from Hartsville University. Occupation, teaching and preaching, in Louisiana, Mississippi, Indiana, Illinois and Kansas. Position, elder in the church. Professor in, and for fifteen years president of Hartsville University. Dr. Shuck took a course of lectures in medicine at Louisville University. He entered the ministry in 1853.

HOMER WHEELER, born May 13, 1819, Alexander, Genessee County, New York. Died, San Francisco, California, November 10, 1878. Educated in common schools of New York and

Indiana, and Nashotah Theological Seminary, Wisconsin. Degrees, A. B. and A. M. Occupation, teacher and minister of the gospel. Position, Rector of St. John's Parish, Bristol, Indiana. In 1854, of St. Peter's Church, Ashtabula, Ohio. Professor of Mathematics, Racine College, Wisconsin, during the presidency of Rev. Dr. Roswell Park. In company with Rev. Dr. Falk, Mr. Wheeler organized the Mission of Holy Innocents. Afterward he officiated as Chaplain of St. Luke's Hospital, Racine, and at the same time took charge of St. Stephen's Mission Chapel. Mr. Wheeler, while a student at Indiana University, was baptized by the Rev. Andrew Wylie, D.D., the President, in the college chapel, W. A. P. Martin and S. N. Martin, his classmates, standing up with him as sponsors. Mr. Wheeler's health failing, he went to California, and died soon after his arrival in San Francisco.

1847.

RUSSELL BIGELOW ABBOTT, born August 8, 1823, Franklin County, Indiana. Residence, Albert Lea, Minnesota. Educated in district school, Franklin County. Degrees, A. B. and A. M., and honorary degree of D. D. (Galesville University). Occupation, teaching and the ministry. Positions, principal of school in Muncie, of the Henry County Seminary at New Castle and White Water Presbyterial Academy. Ordained minister, 1857. For seven years pastor of Brookville Church; for two years of Knightstown. In 1866 Principal of St. Paul Female Seminary, Minnesota. Pastor, since 1869, of church at Albert Lea, and President of Albert Lea College since 1882, under care of the Synod of Minnesota. Author of several published addresses and sermons.

DAVIES BATTERTON, born February 16, 1823, Bloomington, Indiana. Died April 19, 1858, Greensburg, Indiana. Educated in Bloomington schools. Degrees, A. B. and A. M. Occupation, editor and druggist. Positions, County Superintendent and member of the Indiana Legislature.'

JOHN OLDHAM BULLOCK, born 1832, Louisville, Kentucky. Died, 1856, Columbus, Kentucky. Educated, Louisville, Kentucky. Degrees, A. B. and A. M. Occupation and position, attorney at law. Co-editor of a Democratic paper in Louisville. As a political writer he was distinguished for his ability.

In Columbus, Kentucky, where he practiced law, he acquired a high position at the bar, and was regarded as one of the most promising men in that section of the state. He was alike distinguished for his talents and intrepidity.

ROBERT BARR CAMPBELL, born July 30, 1820, Clark County, Indiana. Died November 4, 1849, Bloomington, Indiana. Educated; Bloomington, Indiana. Degrees, A. B. and A. M. At the time of his death was a student of theology at the Theological Seminary of the Associate Reformed Presbyterian Church, Oxford, Ohio.

THEOPHILUS PARVIN, born January 9, 1829, Buenos Ayres, South America. Residence, Philadelphia, Pennsylvania. Education, Easton, Pennsylvania. Degrees, A. B. and A. M., and from the University of Pennsylvania, M. D., and from Hanover College, the honorary degree LL. D. Occupation, teacher and physician. Position, professor in the Medical College, Ohio, 1864–69. Professor in the University of Louisville, 1869–72, in Indiana Medical College, Indianapolis, 1881. Dr. Parvin was president of the American Medical Association in 1879, and professor of Obstetrics, in Jefferson Medical College, Philadelphia, since 1883 to the present time 1890. Dr. Parvin has been a contributor to the medical literature of the day, and is the author of many lectures and addresses, and treatises on medical subjects.

1848.

ORLANDO CLARKE, born November 6, 1824, Vernon, Indiana. Died April 2, 1876, at Vinton, Iowa. Educated, in part at Hanover College, Indiana. Degrees, A. B. and A. M. Mr. Clarke studied theology for three years at Princeton Theological Seminary, New Jersey, where he was licensed to preach, and afterwards, studied at New Haven Theological Seminary. Was stated supply in different congregations in Ohio, Missouri and Iowa. Was ordained as a minister of the Congregational Church at St. Louis, January 5, 1865. Was for a short time chaplain in the army. In 1862–64, superintendent of Blind Asylum, Iowa City, and afterward in 1875–76, he held the same office in the Blind Asylum, Vinton, Iowa, where after a short illness he died. Rev. Mr. Clarke was in his attainments, scholarly; in his sentiments elevated, and in his care and government of the pupils, wise, tender and loving.

ROBERT FULLERTON, born February 13, 1819, in Lincoln County, Tennessee. Died September 12, 1849, Lincoln County. Educated in Viney Grove Academy, Tennessee. Degree, A. B. Occupation, principal of a high school in Limestone County, Alabama, at the time of his death. Member of Reformed Presbyterian Church, and intended to study for the ministry.

ISAAC WASHINGTON LOVE, born October 2, 1820, near Mauckport, Indiana. Died May 28, 1859, Corydon, Indiana. Educated in Harrison County, Indiana. Degrees, A. B. and A. M. Occupation, attorney-at-law. Mr. Love was a member of the Methodist Episcopal Church.

ROBERT M. OVERSTREET, born December 23, ——, in Oldham County, Kentucky. Residence, Emporia, Kansas. Educated in Franklin schools. Degrees, A. B. and A. M. Occupation and position, minister of the Presbyterian Church. Mr. Overstreet was a member of the Kansas Legislature. He was stationed at Beaver, Indian Territory, as a Stated Supply by the Presbyterian Board. An interesting letter by Rev. Mr. Overstreet was published in "The Church at Home and Abroad," on this new and interesting field for Home Missions.

JEFFERSON CLAY THORNTON, born January 9, 1827, in Salem, Indiana. Residence, Warrensburg, Missouri. Educated in Salem, Indiana, and New Albany, Indiana. Degrees, A. B. and A. M. Occupation, preacher and teacher. After completing his theological studies, Mr. Thornton had charge of a congregation in St. Charles, Missouri, for a short time, and then accepted a call from a church in Liberty, Missouri. In 1853 he was elected a Professor in William Jewell College. In 1859 Mr. Thornton, through failing health, had to give up pastoral duties for several years. He visited his friends in Paoli, Indiana. In 1871 he returned to Missouri and preached occasionally as health would permit. At present (1888) Mr. Thornton is a member of the Kansas Presbytery, though without charge, and lives at Warrensburg, Missouri. Mr. Thornton, in 1854, married Miss Kate Bird, of Liberty, Missouri.

WILLIAM THEODORE WYLIE, born March 2, 1829, in Kakaskia, Illinois. Residence, Butler, Butler County, Pennsylvania.

Educated at Dr. McMillian's Academy, Xenia, Ohio, and Dr. Faires', Philadelphia, Pennsylvania. Degrees, A. B. and A. M. Occupation, teaching and the ministry. Position, pastor at Milton, Pennsylvania, at Newcastle, Pennsylvania, at Bellefonte, Pennsylvania. President of Wilson College for women, Chambersburgh, Pennsylvania. Mr. Wylie is an ardent advocate of temperance. The author of the Bellefont system of church collections; compiler of "Lessons and prayers for the school and family." Originator and publisher of "*The Christian Giver*, a monthly devoted to systematic benevolence," and a series of tracts on christian giving.

1849.

MICHAEL STEELE BRIGHT, born January 6, 1830, in Madison, Indiana. Died November 4, 1868, on the Ohio River. Degrees, A. B. and A. M. Occupation, studied law with his father Senator Michael S. Bright, and practiced law till 1854. Position, was for some time Judge in County Court, Superior, Wisconsin. In 1862 moved to Chicago. In 1863 moved to New York City and established the banking house of Bright & Co. Mr. Bright met his death in a collision of steamers on the Ohio River, between Cincinnati and Madison, in his exertion to save others. An eloquent eulogy was pronounced before the Gold-board of New York, by Dr. T. A. Hoyt.

ALVAH JOHNSON, born November 5, 1825, in Warrick County, Indiana. Residence, Evansville, Indiana. Educated at Boonville, Indiana. Degrees, A. B. and A. M. Mr. Johnson studied law with Judge W. T. Parrett, and commenced the practice in Boonville, in 1852, in connection with Judge L. Q. De Bruler of Rockport. Was elected and served for four years as Recorder of Warrick County. Was afterward elected Treasurer of the county in 1858, and served four years. In 1862 was a union candidate for Congress, in the first Congressional District, but was not elected, though the usual Democratic majority was much reduced. Mr. Johnson took an active part in defense of the integrity of the Union during the rebellion. Removing to Evansville he was appointed Provost Marshall of the 1st Congressional District and was engaged till the end of the war mustering in the 143d and 144th Regiments of Infantry, and was honorably discharged at the end of the war. Occupation, at present (1889), and for some years past, is dealing in real estate. In June 1869 he made a tour of Europe, from Scotland through England, France, Germany, Switzerland and Italy, in company with Professor Richard Owen. Mr. Johnson on his return united with the Cumberland Presbyterian Church in Evansville, of which he was made a ruling elder and trustee, and also, superintendent of the Sabbath School. In June, 1852, Mr. Johnson married Miss Jane Parrett, daughter of Rev. Robert Parrett.

CHARLES McLEAN, born November 7, 1832, in Baltimore, Maryland. Residence, 2704 Chestnut street, St. Louis, Missouri. Educated at private school, Madison, Indiana. Occupation, merchant.

WILLIAM EDWARD McLEAN, born October 12, 1831 in Frederick, Maryland. Residence, Terre Haute, Indiana. Educated at common schools of Bloomington and Terre Haute. Degrees, A. B. and A. M. Occupation, attorney at law. Position, Prosecuting Attorney; member of House of Representatives and State Senate, and Secretary of Senate of Indiana; Colonel of 43d Regiment Indiana Volunteers during the entire war. Col. McLean was engaged with his regiment at the battle of New Madrid, the capture of Island No. Ten, assault on Fort Pillow, battle of Helena, capture of Little Rock, Arkansas, capture of Memphis, Tennessee, and in the engagements of the "Banks Expedition," and battle of Jenkins' Ferry. Married Miss Juliette Barnes.

JAMES McDOWELL MILLER, born September 25, 1825, in Crawford County, Indiana. Residence, Iuka, Mississippi. Educated at common schools of Crawford County, and at Livonia Academy, Indiana. Degrees, A. B. and A. M. Occupation, merchandizing, teaching, preaching and farming. Position, School Superintendent, United States Census Enumerator, 1870 and 1880, State Statistician; correspondent of the Agricultural Bureau, author of several articles on temperance, spiritualism, agriculture, etc.

BLACKFORD BONDINOT MOFFATT, born August 24, 1825, in Vincennes, Indiana. Died a few years after graduation. Educated at Terre Haute. Degrees, A. B., A. M. LL. B. Occupation, attorney at law.

JAMES WOODWARD, born October 4, 1828, London, England. Residence, Carbon, Adams County, Iowa, in 1883. Educated in Louisville, Kentucky. Degrees, A. B., A. M. and LL. B. Occupation, for some years a merchant; for the last seven a teacher. Position, since 1852 a minister in the Methodist Episcopal Church. Mr. Woodward is a zealous preacher of the gospel, and was an active opponent of slavery in pro-slavery times and on pro-slavery ground.

1850.

ROBERT GASTON ELLIOTT, residence, Lawrence, Kansas. Came to Indiana University from College Corner, Ohio. Soon after graduating went to Kansas. Was in the territory during the time the great conflict took place between the slaveholders and the friends of freedom for the occupancy of the territory. Mr. Elliott, in connection with Judge Miller, class 1852, was editor and proprietor of the *Kansas Free Press* which was destroyed by the border ruffians. Mr. Elliott was Railroad Commissioner of Tree Culture. (From Φ. Δ. Θ. Catalogue.) He was also a member of the Board of Trustees of State University at Lawrence.

SAMUEL STEELE ELLIOTT, died May 2, 1863, Morning Sun, Ohio. Degrees, A. B. and A. M. Occupation, principal of the Knoxville, Tennessee, Academy, and afterward of the High School at Morning Sun. (Φ. Δ. Θ. Catalogue).

ROBERT CHARLES FOSTER, born August 8, 1831, Philadelphia, Pennsylvania. Residence, Bloomington, Indiana, since 1844. Educated in Philadelphia Public Schools. Degrees, A. B. and A. M. Position, County Auditor and Clerk of Circuit Court of Monroe County; Representative of Monroe County in State Legislature 1877; School Trustee of Bloomington; Secretary of Board of Trustees of Indiana University for nearly twenty-five years; cashier for some years of First National Bank, Bloomington; member and treasurer of the Presbyterian Church. Married Miss Agnes McCalla.

ARA EDWARD SPENCE LONG, born November 30, 1825, Princess Ann, Sommerset County, Maryland. Residence, Columbus, Indiana. Educated in the Public Schools. Degrees, A. B., A. M. and LL. B., Northwestern Christian University (now Butler), 1859. Occupation and position, teacher, merchant, lawyer and farmer; postmaster at Columbus four years during Pierce's administration. After resigning this office practiced law for five years; afterward became farmer. Was for a year assistant treasurer of Bartholomew County. Was Republican candidate for Congress to fill the term of Mr. Kerr (deceased). Nominated by the National party for Congress against Judge Bicknell, but in both cases was defeated.

LITTLETON JOHN POWELL, A. B., Spencer, Ind. Soon after graduating was accidently killed at a barn raising, Occupation, farmer, Spencer, Ind. (Φ. Δ. Θ. Catalogue.)

JAMES STREAN, born August 21, 1824, Columbiana County, Ohio. Died September 7, 1851, Monroe County Indiana. Educated in the Ohio and Indiana Public Schools. Degree A. B. Occupation, farmer and miller. Died from overwork building a mill. (Φ. Δ. Θ. Catalogue.)

PETER M. VAIL, degrees, A. B. and A. M., Dearborn County.

JOHN HENRY WISE, born July 19, 1829, in Accomack County, Virginia. Residence, San Francisco, California. Educated in Accomack, Virginia, and Washington City, D. C. Degrees, A. B. and A. M. Occupation and position, on the Coast Survey from spring of 1853 till 1861. Inspector and gauger and Deputy Collector in the Custom House at San Francisco. Director of the Free Library of San Francisco. Chairman of the Democratic State Central Committee, which position he still holds (1882). From 1861 to the present time, wool and commission merchant (of the firm of Christy & Wise). Was elected a member of the Board of Supervisors of San Francisco.

GEORGE DUGDALE WISE. A. B. and A. M. Lawyer. Washington, D. C.

OBADIAH JENNINGS WISE, born April 10, 1821, in Accomack County, Virginia. Died February 9, 1862. Educated in Washton, D. C., and studied under a private tutor in Rio Janeiro, Brazil, his father being United States Minister at that place. Degrees, A. B. and A. M., and from William and Mary College, Virginia, LL. B. Soon after his graduation at William and Mary College he was Secretary of Legation at Berlin and Paris, and on his return became editor of *Richmond Enquirer*. At the breaking out of the Rebellion joined the Confederate army as Captain of the Light Infantry Blues, and served under his father, General Henry A. Wise, in West Virginia, during the summer and fall of '61. Was in several engagements. He fell mortally wounded at the battle of Roanoke Island, North Carolina, on February 8, '62, was captured and died in the hospital the following day. Capt. Wise, while editor of the *Richmond Enquirer*, took a very prominent and active part in National and State politics.

JOHN JAMES WISE, born January 11, 1830, in Accomack, Virginia. Residence, Accomack C. H., Virginia. Educated, in part, at Dickinson College, Carlisle, Pennsylvania. Degrees, A. B. and A. M. Occupation and position, physician; County Treasurer for four years, Captain in C. S. A. army. Engaged in all the battles of the seven days around Richmond, and in the siege of Petersburg.

ALEXANDER YATES, born November 30, 1830, in Hines County, Mississippi. Killed at the battle of Vicksburg. Educated at county school. Degrees, A. B. and A. M., and from Cambridge, Massachusetts, LL. B., and from Medical School, New Orleans, M. D., in 1856. Occupation and position, practicing physician, Brigadier General in Confederate army. Was in most of the battles fought in the siege of Vicksburg, where he was killed.

1851.

NELSON KENDALL CROWE, born December 15, 1830, at Princeton Indiana. Residence, Wellsville, Ohio. Educated at Princeton Academy, Indiana. Degrees, A. B. and A. M. Occupation, minister of the gospel. Position, pastor of Hill Prairie Reformed Presbyterian Church, Marissa, Illinois; of Walton Presbyterian Church, Walton, New York; of Savannah Presbyterian Church, Savannah, Ohio; of Radnor Presbyterian Church, Radnor, Ohio; of Kingston Church, Delaware, Ohio. Was sent by the General Synod of the Reformed Presbyterian Church to Alexandria, Virginia, in the Freedmen's Mission, and labored there till the close of the war. Was delegate to the General Assembly, Pittsburg, Pennsylvania; Post Chaplain at Giesboro, D. C., in 1863; author of the History of the Freedmen's Mission of the Reformed Presbyterian Church, and of many public addresses, and of many lectures; one of the committee of the National Reform Association when presenting their cause to President Lincoln.

DAVID SMITH FARIS, born November 11, 1830, near Bloomington, Indiana. Residence, Sparta, Randolph County, Illinois. Educated in the district school and at home. Degrees, A. B. and A. M. Occupation, preaching the gospel. Position, pastor of Bethel Congregational Reformed Presbyterian Church, Sparta, Illinois.

WILLIAM HENRY, born June 7, 1830, in South Carolina. Died April 18, 1856, Bloomington, Indiana. Educated, in part by Rev. James Faris, Monroe County, Indiana. Degrees, A. B. and A. M. Occupation, studied theology in the Associate Reformed Presbyterian Seminary, under Dr. Claybaugh, Oxford, Ohio. Position, minister in the Associate Reformed Presbyterian Church.

JOHN MAGILL JOHNSON, born June 9, 1826, in Liberty Township, Crawford County, Indiana. Residence, Marengo, Crawford County, Indiana. Educated in the common schools of Crawford, Orange and Harrison Counties. Degrees, A. B. and A. M. Occupation, teaching, preaching and farming. Position, ordained elder in the church of the United Brethren. Principal of the Marengo Academy. For some time pastor of the church in Marengo. Mr. Johnson was author of a discourse giving account of the origin, doctrine and progress, of the church of the United Brethren in Christ, for the Centennial Exposition at Philadelphia. He has also labored in the temperance cause.

JOHN CALVIN SMITH, born October 29, 1831, in Bloomington, Indiana. Residence, Rose Point, Lawrence County, Pennsylvania. Educated in Monroe County, Indiana. Occupation, taught at Bedford Seminary for one year, and conducted the model school in connection with Indiana University. Position, for four years professor of mathematics, Geneva College, Ohio. Ordained and installed pastor at Newcastle, Pennsylvania, May, 1863. Member of board of trustees of Geneva College. Mr. Smith's original congregation has become four, of one of which, Slippery Rock, he is still pastor (1882).

REDICK MCKEE WYLIE, born May 22, 1831, in Bloomington,

Indiana. Residence, Bloomington, Indiana. Educated in the Bloomington schools. Degrees, A. B. and A. M. Occupation, farmer and merchant. Married Miss Madeline Thompson.

1852.

GEORGE P. KETCHAM, A. B. and A. M. Dentist. Bedford.

DAVID HUME MCDONALD, born in Washington, Indiana. Residence, Quincy, Owen County, Indiana. Educated at Bloomington Academy. Degrees, A. B. and A. M., and M. D. by the University of Louisville. Occupation, practitioner of medicine. Position, local preacher of the Methodist Episcopal Church.

CURRAN EMMETT MCDONALD, born August 20, 1833, in Daviess County, Indiana. Residence, 270 East Tenth street, New York, N. Y. Educated principally in Bloomington schools and Preparatory Department of University. Degrees, A. B., and A. M. Occupation, attorney in patent cases and solicitor of patents.

NEWTON F. MALOTT, born February 13, 1832, in Leesville, Indiana. Died at his residence, Vincennes, Indiana, of paralysis, April 23, 1888. Educated in Bedford County Seminary. Degrees, A. B., A. M. and LL. B. (1854). Occupation, attorney-at-law. Positions, Judge of Circuit Court since 1870, and Trustee of Indiana University (1863). An important decision was made by Judge Malott with regard to the legal existence of the 29th of February, in opposition to the old legal opinion that it was not to be regarded as a legal day. Judge Malott was an exemplary citizen and upright judge.

JOSIAH MILLER, born November 12, 1828, in Chester District, South Carolina; died January 7, 1870, in Lawrence, Kansas. Degrees, A. B. and A. M. Occupation, Attorney at Law, receiving the degree of LL. B. from law school at Poughkeepsie, New York. Position, editor of *Central Illinois Times*, Bloomington, Illinois. On removing to Kansas, editor of the *Kansas Free State*, Lawrence, Kansas. In 1857 was elected Probate Judge of Douglass County. In 1861, State Senator, which office he resigned and accepted that of Postmaster of Lawrence, which he held till 1863, when he became Paymaster in the United States army, with rank of Major. In 1866 was a member of the Legislature. The *Kansas Free State* was an anti-slavery journal, and was destroyed by order of the Territorial government, May 21, 1856, having been indicted by a pro-slavery jury as a nuisance. Shortly after this Judge Miller was captured by the pro-slavery forces, and was tried for treason against South Carolina by Buford's band of invaders. On his release, he canvassed Iowa and other portions of the West for J. C. Fremont. To Judge Miller Kansas is indebted for its seal with the appropriate motto, "*Ad astra per aspera.*" Judge Miller married Miss Agnes Carlisle, of Bloomington, January 3, 1854.

THOMAS WHEELER, born March 15, 1821, in London, England. Came to Indiana in 1822. Residence, Sandborn, Indiana. Educated at Vanderburgh County schools. Degrees, A. B. and A. M. Occupation and position, physician. In the War of the Rebellion was surgeon of the 79th Illinois Infantry, and served during the time of enlistment in the Army of the Cumberland.

ANDERSON MCELROY WYLIE, born December 12, 1833, at Bloomington, Indiana. Residence, Newtown, Bucks County, Pennsylvania. Educated at Bloomington. Degrees, A. B. and A. M. Occupations, taught three years in Philadelphia; studied three years in the Episcopal Seminary, Virginia, and ever since a preacher of the gospel. Positions, for twelve years a minister of the Episcopal Church, and afterwards, a minister of the Presbyterian Church. Spent parts of two years in England, lecturing and writing; was a constant correspondent for some time of New York and Philadelphia periodicals, and author of several published sermons and other discourses. Mr. Wylie was pastor of Presbyterian Church in Nyack, New York, for some years, and afterwards of the church in Newtown, Pennsylvania. At present (1889) residing in Brooklyn, New York.

1853.

JOHN CALVIN KNOX FARIS, born April 11, 1833, at Bloomington, Indiana. Residence, Topsham, Vermont. Educated at home by his father, Rev. James Faris. Degrees, A. B. and A. M. Occupation, preaching since 1859. Positions, in 1864–5, Missionary to the Freedmen, Natchez, Mississippi; in 1870, pastor of a congregation in Ohio; from 1874 till the present time (1882) pastor in Topsham, and for three years superintendent of the Topsham schools.

WILLIAM WILSON MCMILLAN, born May 13, 1827, at Selma, Alabama. Residence, Olathe, Kansas. Educated at Fayetteville, Indiana. Degrees, A. B. and A. M. Occupation, preaching and teaching. Taught in Sharon College for five years. Preached in Baltimore. Pastor of Reformed Presbyterian Church in Olathe, Kansas.

1854.

JOHN J. HIGHT, born December 4, 1834, in Bloomington, Indiana. Died at Cincinnati, December 18, 1886. Educated at Bloomington, Indiana. Degrees, A. B., A. M. and Honorary Degree D. D. Occupation, preacher in Methodist Episcopal Church. Chaplain in the army, and assistant editor of the *Western Christian Advocate*. Dr. Hight was received into the Indiana Conference in 1854. Was ordained a deacon in 1850, and elder in 1858. His first pastoral charge was at Princeton, Indiana, in 1858. He served two years as pastor of Robert's Chapel, and one year as pastor of John Street Church, in New Albany, and four years a presiding elder in the New Albany district. In 1862 he was appointed chaplain of the 58th Indiana Regiment, in which position he distinguished himself in his assiduous attention to the wounded and his tender consolation to the dying. He was often called to the dangerous duty of gathering the wounded from the battle field. It is said that he fought with his regiment at the battles of Chickamauga, and also, at Stone River. After his retiring from the army he became the centenary agent in behalf of education in Indiana. After his service as presiding elder he was stationed at Evansville, and afterward at Bloomington. In July, 1875, he was appointed to the assistant editorship of the *Western Christian Advocate* which position he filled with marked fidelity and success. He was a delegate to the General Conference in 1872 and in 1880. Dr. Hight was a trustee of Indiana Asbury University. He was the author of an elaborate article on the "Tabernacle," for the Complete Text Pictorial Bible. He gave of his means for charitable and religious purposes, on the basis of one tenth of his annual income. He was cut off in the vigor of life and usefulness, in the fifty-second year of his age.

A sort of paralysis felt first in his hand, by slow degrees affected his whole nervous system, and finally terminated in his death. Dr. Hight was twice married. His first wife was Miss Mary E. Arnold, of Bloomington, whom he married in 1856. She lived only about a year after marriage. He married his second wife in 1867, Miss Mary E. Mitchell, who with one daughter Ida Gertrude survive him.

LEWIS A. KELLAR, A. B. and A. M., New Albany.

JOHN H. KETCHAM, was born December 29, 1832, in Monroe County, Indiana. Residence, Martinsville, Indiana. Educated in district schools of Monroe County. Degrees, B. S. and A. M. Occupation and position, regular minister of the Methodist Episcopal Church. A pastor in different congregations; Presiding Elder. Since graduation, a member of the Indiana Conference, having filled the first leading charges in the Conference, and in 1882, pastor of the church in Martinsville.

WILLIAM HERSCHEL LEMON, born October 14, 1832 in Lawrence County, Indiana. Residence, Winchester, Jefferson County, Kansas. Educated at home. Degrees, A. B. and A. M. Occupation, student, teacher and physician. Position, President of Sugar Grove Institute, Tippecanoe County, Indiana, for three years, 1854–58. Assistant Surgeon 54th Indiana Volunteers for prisoners at Camp Morton, Indiana. Surgeon 82d Indiana Volunteers during the last three years of the Rebellion. Orator of the Society of Alumni, 1861. Dr. Lemon was engaged in the battles of Nolinsville, Stone River, Tullahoma, Chattanooga (was made prisoner of war there and confined in Libby prison four months), Tunnel Hill, Buzzard Roost, Resacca, Burnt Hickory, Kenesaw, Pine Mountain, Jonesboro, Kingston, at Savannah, Branchville, Bentonville, and in many skirmishes during his march to the sea. Dr. Lemon has in press a work entitled, "Ithuriel, the Days of the Demiurge," and also several works in MS. ready for the press.

THEODORE READ, born April 11, 1835, at Athens, Ohio, died on the field of battle, near Richmond, Virginia, April 6, 1865. Degrees, A. B. and A. M. Occupation and position: attorney at law; Prosecuting Attorney, Bloomington District. Held an official position in the Department of the Interior, at Washington, D. C., till 1860. Resigning, he practiced law at Paris, Illinois. When the call was made by President Lincoln for 75,000 men for three months' service, at the commencement of the War of the Rebellion, he joined the army as a private, and was made Assistant Adjutant General, with the rank of Captain, at the close of the three months' service, and assigned to duty under General Brooks, in the Army of the Potomac. Was engaged in the battles from Manassas to Yorktown and the Chickahominy, the battles at Harrison's Landing and Antietam. Was severely wounded at Fredericksburg. After his wound was healed, he mustered forces in Pennsylvania to oppose the invasion of Pennsylvania by General Lee at Gettysburg. He passed through the battles of the Wilderness and Spottsylvania unharmed. Was again wounded at Cold Harbor. Was in Butler's advance on Richmond, when Fort Harrison was taken. Here he was wounded a third time. Being no longer able to serve, he returned home. During his absence from the army he married a young lady of Cleveland. He returned to the army in 1864, when, on the ground of his eminent services and skill as an officer, and at the request of his division, he was promoted from the rank of a Major to that of Brigadier General. After the fall of Petersburg and Richmond, the more effectively to cut off the enemy's retreat, a portion of the army was put by General Grant under the command of General Read, at his own request. The enemy was met in overwhelming numbers, and the battle was most strongly contested, and, just as victory was achieved, he fell, mortally wounded, and was buried on the ground where he shed his blood. General Read was the oldest son of Professor Daniel Read, of the University of Missouri, formerly Professor of Languages in Indiana University.

[Condensed from a sketch by Hon. J. W. Foster.]

ROBERT LOUDEN RUDDICK, born February 8, 1834, at Columbus, Indiana, died September 23, 1871, at Keokuk, Iowa. Educated at Columbus, Indiana. Degree, A. B. Occupation, speculator, pork packer, iron merchant, cattle dealer and real estate broker.

1855.

DAVID DEMAREE BANTA, born May 23, 1833, in Johnson County, Indiana. Residence, Franklin, Indiana. Educated in the county schools and Franklin College. Entered Indiana University. Degrees, B. S. and, in 1887, LL.B. The honorary degree of LL. D. was conferred by Franklin College in 1888. Occupation, in 1856, Principal of Monroe County Female Seminary; since 1857, lawyer, District Attorney, Common Pleas Court, 1858–'60, and again from 1862–'64; Division Revenue Assessor from 1865–'68; County School Examiner, 1866–'70; Trustee of Franklin Schools, 1868–'70; Judge of the 16th Judicial Circuit, 1870–'76; Trustee of Indiana University, 1877–'89; President of the Board of Trustees, 1882–'89; Dean of the Indiana University Law School since 1889; Vice-President of Citizens' National Bank (Franklin) since 1889. Married Mrs. Melissa Elizabeth Perrin, June 16th, 1856. Judge Banta is the author of "History of Johnson County, Indiana," "The History of the Presbyterian Church of Franklin," "Making a Neighborhood," and of numerous papers and sketches published from time to time in the magazines and newspapers, relating chiefly to local historical and out-of-door subjects. The Department of Law, after thirteen years suspension, has been reopened, and Judge D. D. Banta chosen Dean and Ernest W. Huffcut, Professor.

WILLIAM CYRUS BARBER, born December 11, 1830, in Madison, Indiana; died September 28, 1859, at Cincinnati. Educated at Madison schools. Degrees, A. B. and A. M. Mr. Barber was an invalid nearly all the time from his graduation till his death. He was an enthusiast on the subject of education, and no doubt his close application to study and want of exercise hastened his death.

ROBERT BROWN CARNAHAN, born January 1, 1835, at Lafayette, Indiana; died at Lafayette, February 27, 1861. Educated at common schools of Lafayette. Occupation, was for some time Deputy County Treasurer. At the time of his death was a member of the Protestant Episcopal Church.

JOHN A. CARTWRIGHT, born November 17, 1830, in North Jackson, Ohio. Residence, Delphi, Indiana. Educated at Common schools and Mount Vernon College. Degree, B. S. Occupation and position, teacher. Principal of Sugar Grove Institute for three years; Superintendent of the Delphi public schools, three years; County Examiner of Carroll County, three years; Mayor of the city of Delphi for four years; Auditor of Carroll County, eight years; President of the School Board for eight years; Chairman of the Central Democratic Committee for twelve years; at present (1883) manager of the Delphi Lime Company, and a successful agriculturist and stock raiser.

JOHN WATSON FOSTER, born in Pike County, Indiana, 1836. Residence (1888), Washington, D. C. Educated in the Evansville schools. Degrees, A. B. and A. M. Delivered the valedictory oration. Studied law at Harvard University. Occupation and position, attorney at law for a short time in Evansville. Entered the Union army in 1861 as Major of the Twenty-fifth Indiana Volunteers. Promoted to Lieutenant-Colonel after the battle of Fort Donelson, and to Colonel of the Sixty-fifth and One Hundred and Thirty-sixth Indiana Volunteers after the battle of Shiloh. Commanded a division of cavalry in the army of Ohio, in the Kentucky and Tennessee campaigns. Was the first to enter Knoxville after it was taken by the Union forces. Was mustered out at the expiration of service in 1864. Col. Foster was editor of the *Evansville Journal* till 1869, when he was appointed postmaster of Evansville from 1869 to 1873. Was chairman of the Republican State Central Committee in the political campaign in 1872. Was appointed by President Grant Envoy Extraordinary and Minister Plenipotentiary to Mexico in 1873. Remained in that mission till 1880, when he was promoted and transferred by President Hayes as Envoy and Minister Plenipotentiary to Russia, and was reaccredited as such by President Garfield in 1881. He was appointed minister to Spain February, 1883. This office he resigned in 1885. On his return to Washington he resumed the practice of law. In addition to these civil offices Col. Foster was chosen permanent Vice-President of the American Bible Society in 1880. He is also an honorary member of the Geographical, Historical and Scientific Societies of Mexico and Russia, and a ruling elder in the Presbyterian Church. Col. Foster married Miss Mary Parke McFerson, daughter of Mrs. E. J. McFerson, then of Glendale, Ohio, in 1859.

MELLVILLE CRAVEN HESTER, born January 20, 1834, in Scott County, Indiana. Residence, Charlestown, Clark County, Indiana. Educated at Indiana Asbury University, Greencastle, Indiana. Degrees, A. B. and A. M. Occupation and position, attorney at law. Prosecuting Attorney and Judge of Criminal

Circuit Court, by appointment of the Governor. Was a member of the Methodist Episcopal Church.

ROBERT ROBERTS HITT, born January 16, 1834, in Urbana, Ohio. Residence, Washington, District Columbia, (1881.) Educated at Rock River Seminary and Indiana Asbury University. Degrees, A. B. and A. M., Indiana University. Occupation, literature, law, reporting, and diplomacy. Position, Secretary of Legation at Paris, Assistant Secretary of State.

AARON LYTLE JONES, born in Shreve, Wayne County, Ohio. Residence, Valparaiso, Indiana. Educated at Valparaiso Schools. Degrees, B. S. Occupation and position, attorney at law. First Lieutenant and Quartermaster, 7th Indiana Cavalry Volunteers.

JOHN CHAPMAN MILLER, residence Nineveh, Indiana. Degrees, B. S. and A. B., and A. M. Bethany College, Virginia. Occupation, professor Northwestern Christian University, 1870–76, director of, since 1879. Minister of Christian Church, Spencer, Indiana, 1865–67, and in Nineveh, 1867–70. Since 1870 farmer.

ROBERT I. MORRISON, born November 3, 1835, in Salem, Indiana. Residence, Knightstown, Indiana. Educated at Washington County Seminary. Degrees, A. B., A. M. and LL. B. Occupation, civil engineer. Position, Chairman United States Linear Surveys, and afterwards United States Deputy Surveyor in Minnesota Territory from April, 1861, to July 15. Cashier Indiana State Treasury 1865–1871. United States Assistant Engineer River Improvements, 1873 to 1877.

ACHILLES VAWTER PENDLETON, born June 5, 1833, in Jennings County, Indiana. Residence, Nineveh, Indiana. Educated in the common schools. Degrees, A. B. and A. M. Occupation: The winter after graduation Mr. Pendleton taught school in Jennings County, and the next year he taught in Johnson County. He continued in this occupation till 1859. In the winter of 1859-60 he went to Vicksburg, Mississippi, and took charge of the books of a company then engaged in building a levee. Returning in the spring to his home, he again became a teacher. In early life he became a member, and afterwards a minister, of the Christian Church. In 1863 Mr. Pendleton was elected a member of the Legislature, and served during the stormy session of that year. In 1874-76 he accepted the nomination for Congress, and became the candidate of the Greenback party. In the latter years of his life Mr. Pendleton withdrew from politics, and engaged with great success in farming, himself and farm being models for the surrounding country. His education, and his experience in church and state have made him a prudent adviser in the community in which he lives.

Mr. Pendleton, March 20, 1862, married Rebecca S. Forsythe.

WILLIAM CALVIN LINTON TAYLOR, born May 22, 1836, at Lafayette, Indiana. Residence, Lafayette, Indiana. Educated at Lafayette, Indiana. Degrees, A. B. and A. M. Occupation, practice of law. Positions, District Attorney, First Lieutenant, Captain, Major, Lieutenant-Colonel and Colonel in the 20th Indiana Volunteers. Colonel Taylor was engaged in the battles of Hatteras Bluff; in the engagement of the Merrimac, the Congress and Cumberland; also in the battles of Orchards, Mechanicsville, Glendale, Malvern Hills, Harrison's Landing, Bull Run, Chantilly, Fredericksburgh, Chancellorsville, Gettysburg, Manassas Gap, Locust Grove, Mine Run, Kelly's Ford, the Wilderness, Spottsylvania, Cold Harbor, Deep Bottom, Strawberry Plains and Siege of Petersburg; and in many skirmishes, reconnoisances and picket fights. Colonel Taylor participated in all the campaigns of Generals McClelland, Burnside, Hooker, Mead and Grant, when these officers had command of the Army of the Potomac. Was also in the rear guard in McClelland's retreat from Richmond, fighting almost constantly for seven days and nights, and also in the van of General Grant's advance to Petersburg and Richmond. Colonel Taylor is the author of a Treatise on Municipal Law. Married Miss Elizabeth McPheeters, of Bloomington, Indiana, daughter of Dr. J. G. McPheeters.

1856.

HENRY WATKINS BALLANTINE, born November 6, 1838, in Prince Edward County, Virginia. Residence, Bloomfield, New Jersey. Educated by his father. Entered the Junior Class of the University. Degrees, A. B. and A. M. In the fall of 1856 Mr. Ballantine took charge of the classes in Mathematics, awaiting the arrival of Dr. Kirkwood, Professor elect. Toward the close of the year he entered the Union Theological Seminary, New York City, and received therefrom the degree B. D. January 9, 1861, he was ordained by the Salem Presbytery (Indiana), minister of the gospel, as an evangelist. In 1862 he went as a Missionary of the American Board of Commissioners of Foreign Missions to Bombay, India, and was employed there until 1865, when, on account of the ill health of his wife, he returned home. For some months he supplied the pulpit of the Baldwin Presbyterian Church, Terre Haute. Afterward he received an invitation to become pastor of the Presbyterian Church of Marietta, Ohio. This position he occupied from 1865 to 1869. From this place he was called to the pastorate of the First Presbyterian Church, Bloomfield, New Jersey. This position he still (1889) holds. In 1870 he was appointed *pro tem.* Professor of Latin in Indiana University. Mr. Ballantine married Miss Mary Elizabeth Loomis, of Suffield, Connecticut.

SAMUEL LYBRAND BINKLEY, born February 17, 1836, at Tarlton, Ohio. Died at his home, Barnesville, Ohio, September 24, 1887. Educated in high school, Tarlton, Ohio; Mt. Pleasant, Kingston, Ohio; Ohio University, Athens, Ohio. Degrees, A. B. and A. M. Occupation, teaching, the ministry and foreign missionary work. Mr. Binkley, shortly after graduation, was Principal of the Methodist Episcopal Seminary, Bloomington. He was at the same time appointed class leader and a licensed exhorter. He then entered the Garrett Biblical Institute to prepare for mission work. After leaving the institute he labored in the Southeast Indiana Conference for six months in order to prepare himself practically for his work in the foreign field. Mr. Binkley served in Moorefield, Poseyville and Patoka Circuits, and was, at his earnest desire, appointed missionary to Fuchau, China. Shortly before sailing he was ordained elder by Bishop Simpson. His work in China was short, for just as he began to be able to use the native language he was compelled, through the serious illness of his wife, to return home; this was in March, 1864. Leaving this work, so auspiciously commenced, was regarded by Mr. Binkley as the hardest trial of his life. Returning to the Indiana Conference he served Robert's Chapel, New Albany, Mt. Vernon, Vincennes, the Centenary Church, New Albany, and Martinsville. In 1876 he was transferred to the East Ohio Conference. He was stationed at Kingsville, Ohio, Alliance, Ohio, and Prospect-Street Church, Cleveland. After a short rest, on account of health, he served in Saybrook and afterward in Barnesville, Ohio, where he died. Rev. Mr. Binkley married Miss Elizabeth R. Carter, of Bloomington, September 16, 1859. (Much of this sketch is from the "Memorial" of Mr. Binkley.)

MADISON EVANS, born October 24, 1834, in Warrick County, Indiana. Died March 5, 1866. Degrees, A. B., A. M. and LL. B. Occupation, teacher and lawyer. Positions, tutor in Wisconsin State University; Principal of one of the New Albany schools; Professor in the (then) Northwestern University, now Butler University; after resigning this position he studied law.

JOSEPH SHERBURNE JENCKES, born April 4, 1834, in Terre Haute, Indiana. Residence, Indianapolis (1889). Educated at Vigo Collegiate Institute, Terre Haute. Degrees, A. B. and A. M., and B. L. Cincinnati College, Honorary Degree, B. D., Kingan College, Ohio, and LL. D., Indiana University. Occupation, for ten years a lawyer, since a clergyman. Position, in 1868 member of the Episcopal general convention from Kentucky, and 1880 from Iowa. For thirteen months with Captain's pay, a Chaplain in the army. In 1879 Chaplain of the Iowa Legislature. Professor of history and political economy in Griswold College, Iowa, and in the theological seminary of the same institution, professor of ecclesiastical history, homiletics and systematic divinity. In (1882) rector of St. John's church, Cincinnati, Ohio, and in (1888) rector of Saint Paul's church, Indianapolis, Indiana.

RICHARD MORRIS JOHNSON, born May 18, 1832, in Little Mounds, Warrick County. Residence, Hyde Park, Illinois. Educated at Little Mounds School. Degrees, A. B. and A. M. Occupation, for nine years a teacher and school superintendent. Principal of Bedford School, afterward of Ladoga School, and professor of mathematics in New Albany Female College. For one year editor of a daily paper. For several years a manufacturer of chemical fire apparatus. Spent three summers in Colorado, as correspondent of the *Chicago Tribune*, and while there discovered and secured from the Government the Tomichi Hot Springs, the largest and probably the hottest in the world, and possessed of remarkable medical properties.

Mr. Johnston is a member of, and deacon in, the Christian Church.

THOMAS J. WOLFE, born January 25, 1832, in Sullivan County, Indiana. Residence, Merom, Indiana. Educated at the common schools of the county. Degrees, A. B. A. M. and LL. B. Occupation, a merchant and afterward a lawyer till 1870, since that time attorney at law. Married Lucia R. Smith of Monroe County, August, 1859.

HIRAM ALLEN, JR. A. B. and A. M. Delphi. Lawyer.

JAMES M. BROWN. B. S. Nebraska. Lawyer.

STEPHEN GIRARD BURTON, born January 22, 1835, in Perryville, Kentucky. Residence, Lebanon, Kentucky. Educated, for three years, at Indiana Asbury University. Degrees, A. B., A. M. and LL. B., Indiana University. Occupation, lawyer, politician, minister. Position, deacon in Protestant Episcopal Church for six years, and then resumed the practice of law. A member of the Indiana Legislature for four years. Centennial orator, July 4, 1876, at San Antonio, Texas. The address was published by the committee.

JAMES M. CLARK. A. B. and A. M. Minister. Demorestville, Canada West.

HIRAM WILBUR CLOUD, born September 7, 1833, in Henderson, Kentucky. Died May 5, 1875, at Evansville. Educated at Asbury University. Degrees, A. B. and A. M., Indiana University, and from Louisville Medical College, M. D. Occupation, chemist and druggist. Position, Trustee of Indiana University; President of Henry Female College, New Castle, Kentucky; President, Secretary and Treasurer of School Board at Evansville, at different periods, for ten years. Married Miss Sarah M. Akin, of Bloomington, in 1859.

ALFRED E. GRAHAM, born November 22, 1837, in Bloomington, Indiana. Residence, Martinsville, Indiana. Educated in Bloomington public schools. Degree, B. S. Occupation, banker. Was clerk in Pay Department of United States Army.

GEORGE WASHINGTON LEE, born February 5, 1832, at Bloomington, Indiana. Residence, Greencastle, Indiana. Educated in public and private schools of Putnam County, and at Indiana Asbury University. Degrees, A. B. and A. M., Indiana University. Occupation, teaching. Positions, School Examiner of Clark County for seven years; Superintendent of Greencastle City Schools for nine years; Principal of Academy for Males in Newcastle, Kentucky, and Principal of Charleston Public Schools for ten years; Superintendent of Bloomington Public Schools for two years. Mr. Lee married Miss Isabel M. Cole, December 15, 1859.

AUGUSTUS DAVIS LYNCH, born September ⋆, 1835, at Georgetown, Ohio. Residence, Indianapolis, Indiana. Educated, till through the Junior Year, at Asbury University. Degrees, A. B., A. M. and LL. B., from Indiana University. Occupation, teacher, student of law, banker. Positions, Principal of Bloomington M. E. Female College; Professor of Mathematics in Brookville College, and afterwards President; Superintendent of Shelbyville Public Schools; Cashier for ten years of First National Bank, Shelbyville; in 1876 appointed National Bank Examiner for Indiana; resigned in 1881 to accept the Presidency of the First National Bank, Indianapolis. Enlisted in the 68th Indiana Regiment in 1862. Author of addresses on education and on financial topics. Married Miss Laura V. Hitt, August 20, 1861.

HAMILTON SAMUEL McREA was born January 4, 1833, New Middleton, Indiana; died April 26, 1887, Marion, Indiana. Was educated at Corydon public schools, and at Friendship Seminary. Degrees, A. B. and A. M. Occupation, teacher and lawyer. Was district prosecutor. In 1861 was a member of the Legislature. This position he resigned to enter the army; entered as a private, was mustered out as a Captain in 1865. At Vevay was School Superintendent and also Township Trustee; School Superintendent also at Muncie. Captain McRea fought at Richmond August 30, 1862; Collinsville, Tennessee, October 11, 1863; Snake Creek Gap, Georgia, May 10, 1864, and at Resaca, Georgia, May 27, 1864, where he was wounded. In 1883 was elected Superintedent of the Marion schools, which position he held till his death. Married Miss Montgomery. Mrs. McRae was associated with her husband in Muncie as teacher in the graded schools. She is at present a teacher in Purdue University.

URIAH MULLIKIN, born February 5, 1836, Williamsburg, Indiana. Residence, Nineveh, Johnson County, Indiana. Educated in part at Franklin College. Degrees, A. B. and A. M. Occupation, merchant and farmer.

JOHN DODDS PERING, born November 27, 1835, Bloomington, Indiana. Residence, Clay Centre, Kansas. Educated at Bloomington. Degrees, A. B. and A. M. Occupation, student of theology, Princeton Seminary, and at the Presbyterian Theological Seminary of the Northwest at Chicago. Minister of the gospel and agent for Presbyterian Board of Publication. Position, tutor of Hebrew in Chicago Theological Seminary. Ordained to the ministry October 23, 1862. Pastor at Foreston, Iowa, and stated supply in various places in Iowa, Indiana and Kansas. Now (1888) stated supply Oak Hill Church.

DAVID ALMORO ROBERTSON, born September 7, 1834, in Paris, Ind. Residence, Hartsville, Indiana. Educated in part at Indiana Asbury University. Degree, B. S., Indiana University. Occupation, teacher for two years. Afterward a minister in the Methodist Episcopal Church. A member of the Southeast Indiana Conference. Entered the ministry at Columbus, Indiana. Served during the war in the United States Christian Commission. Married Miss R. H. Maxwell, of Moore's Hill, Indiana, August 8, 1861.

WILBUR FISK STONE, born December 28, 1832, in Litchfield, Connecticut. Residence, Denver, Colorado. Educated in public schools of several States; two years in Rushville Academy, Indiana; four years in Asbury University. Degrees, A. B., A. M. and LL. B. (Indiana University). Occupation, editor and lawyer. Positions, several times member of the Colorado Legislature; four years Assistant United States Attorney; President for four years of Public School Board; member of Constitutional Convention of Colorado, 1876; Judge of the Supreme Court of Colorado; Ecclesiastical Chancellor of the Episcopal Diocese of Colorado. Judge Stone was one of the early Pike's Peak pioneers, and a frequent contributor to the Colorado press and author of many literary addresses. As an early settler, Judge Stone has had many adventures and battles with the Indians in Colorado and Montana from 1860 to 1865. Judge Stone married Miss S. Saddler, of Bloomington, Indiana.

SAMUEL M. THOMAS. A. B. and A. M. Delphi. Physician.

STEPHEN THRASHER, born February 24, 1833, in Pendleton County, Kentucky. Residence, Port Gibson, Mississippi. Educated in public schools, Shelbyville, Indiana. Degrees, A. B. and A. M. Occupation and position, attorney-at-law; Lieutenant-Colonel in Confederate army during the Civil War; served in Virginia; was engaged in twenty-three battles and was several times wounded.

JOSHUA HOWE WATTS. Residence, White Oaks, New Mexico. Educated in Bloomington schools. Degrees, A. B. and A. M. Occupation and positions, mining engineer and United States Mineral Surveyor; Lieutenant-Colonel during the war; Adjutant General of the Territory under Governor Lew Wallace.

GEORGE C. WILSON. A. B. and A. M. Owensboro, Kentucky. Teacher.

JACOB VANCE WOLFE, born October 7, 1833, in Merom, Indiana. Residence, Lincoln, Nebraska. Educated at the public schools of Sullivan County. Degrees, A. B., A. M. and LL. B. Occupation and position, lawyer, teacher, editor, farmer and legislator; a teacher at Glendale Female College, Ohio; President of the Major Female College, Bloomington, Illinois; Principal of Gosport high school. Mr. Wolfe married Eliza Ellen Batterton, of Bloomington.

1858.

JOSEPH BARRETT ATKINSON, died November, 1862. Educated in schools of Mt. Vernon, Indiana, and at Indiana Asbury University. Degree, B. S., Indiana University. Lieutenant Indiana Infantry, 1861-2. Attorney at law, Greenfield, Ind. Was wounded at the battle of Hatchie, and died from the wound.

CASWELL RIDDLE BURTON, born, 1831, in Lawrence County, Indiana. Died September, 1862, at Woodsonville, Kentucky. Educated at Hartsville. Degree, B. S., and M. D. at Michigan University, 1861. Occupation, practice of medicine. Position, Lieutenant of Co. G, 50th Indiana Volunteers. Fell mortally wounded at Woodsonville, Kentucky.

JOHN S. CARTER, born June 15, 1837, in Bloomington, Indiana. Residence, Auburn, Shawnee County, Kansas. Educated at public schools of Monroe County. Degree, B. S. Occupation and position, farmer and stock raiser; deacon in the Baptist Church.

DAVID S. CHAMBERS, born March 19, 1836, Philomath, Union County, Indiana. Residence, New Castle, Indiana. Educated,

New Castle Academy. Degrees A. B. and A. M. Occupation, study and practice of law. Position, Captain in Union Army, 36th Regiment, Indiana Volunteers. Two terms, from 1864-68, member of the Legislature of Indiana. Prosecuting Attorney of Circuit Court for five years. Elder in Presbyterian Church. Was wounded in the head at the battle of Shiloh, and also wounded in the shoulder at the battle of Chickamauga. Engaged in battles of Stone River, Lookout Mountain and in the battles of Sherman's March, from Chattanooga to Atlanta, Georgia. In 1876 Democratic-Greenback nominee for Congress, and in 1880 Democratic elector on the Hancock and English ticket.

FRANCIS RILEY DORMAN, born March 22, 1834, in Manchester, Indiana. Residence, Lawrenceburg, Indiana. Educated at common schools and Indiana Asbury University. Degrees, A. B. and A. M., Indiana University. Occupation, teacher, farmer, and merchant. Position, twice elected Sheriff of Dearborn County, Township Trustee and Member of School Board. Trustee of Lawrenceburg City Schools. President of Lawrenceburg Lecture Assembly. Married Miss Geneva Jordan, March 25, 1865.

NOAH S. GIVEN, born September 30, 1833, in Dearborn County, Indiana. Residence, Lawrenceburg, Indiana. Educated at common schools and at Franklin College, three years. Degrees, A. B. and A. M. and LL. B., Indiana University, in 1859. Occupation, lawyer. Position, Prosecuting Attorney. Representative in the State Legislature in 1863 and 1873, and also Senator in 1875. Elected Judge of 7th Judicial District in 1878. County Examiner and School Trustee of the city of Lawrenceburg for five years. Judge Given married Miss Mary Martin.

LUCIEN GREATHOUSE, born June 7, 1842, at Carlinville, Illinois, died July 22, 1864, near Atlanta, Georgia. Educated in the common schools of Kentucky and Illinois. In 1855 entered McKendree College, Lebanon, Illinois, and Indiana University at the age of fifteen. Degrees, A. B. and A. M. Occupation and position, studied law, but before entering on the practice of his profession he enlisted in the three months' service, on the first call made for men to put down the rebellion. He was chosen Captain of his company. In the volunteer service he rose from the ranks to the position of Brigadier General. General Greathouse was distinguished for his bravery. It was said of him he never said "go," but "follow," always leading his men to the front. He was engaged in forty pitched battles, and always stood among the foremost for his courage and daring. He lost his life in the storming of a rebel stronghold near Atlanta, in one of the last campaigns of the war, July 22, 1864. General Sherman, in one of his official reports, said: "Where all have been so brave it seems invidious to mention one name, but we must speak of Colonel Lucien Greathouse. He is the bravest of the brave." He was buried with military honors. His remains repose in the cemetery of Vandalia. A beautiful monument, erected by the officers and men of his regiment, marks the place.

SAMUEL JAMES KAHLER, born January 20, 1834, in Center County, Pennsylvania. Residence, Fresno, Fresno County, California. Educated, two years, at Franklin College, Indiana. Degrees, A. B. and A. M., Indiana University. Occupation and position, Professor of Mathematics and Natural Science, for three years, at Moore's Hill College. Professor Kahler entered the North West Indiana Conference in 1862. In 1870 he was transferred to Kansas, and in 1883 to California, where he engaged in itinerant work in the conferences there. In 1873 he was elected and served as Representative of Dickinson County, Kansas. He served also as County Commissioner.

JAMES L. MITCHELL, born, 1834, in Shelby County, Kentucky. Residence, Indianapolis. Educated at Bloomington, Indiana. Degrees, A. B. and A. M. Occupation, lawyer. In the army during the war. Position, Adjutant 70th Regiment, Indiana Volunteers; Mayor of Indianapolis, 1873; Alumni orator Indiana University, 1860; served in the Department of the Cumberland under General George H. Thomas; with General Sherman's army in the battles from Chattanooga to Atlanta, and afterwards on the staff of General Lovel H. Rousseau.

ROBERT CAMPBELL MCKINNEY, born December 7, 1832, in Livonia, Indiana. Residence, Fort Bragg, California. Degrees, A. B. and A. M. Occupation, student of Theology and graduate of Princeton, New Jersey Theological Seminary; minister of the gospel. Position, pastor Brownstown congregation, 1874–78; stated supply at Hebron, Livonia, Orleans, and at Norton, Kansas; now (1888) Home Missionary at Fort Bragg, California.

WILLIAM TELL MOFFET, born July 27, 1837, in Bloomington, Indiana. Residence, Morning Sun, Iowa. Educated at public schools. Degrees A. B. and A. M. Occupation, the ministry. Position, Clerk of United Presbyterian Synod of Illinois, nine years; Superintendent of the United Presbyterian Board of Missions; member of Monmouth College Senate for eighteen years.

ALEXANDER DOWNING LEMON, born August 17, 1834, in Lawrence County, Indiana. Residence, Phœnix, Maricopa County, Arizona. Educated at district schools, Monroe County. Degrees, B. S. and LL. B. Occupation, attorney and counselor at law. Position, Superintendent of public schools; District Attorney; member of Legislature, and Presidential Elector. Author of an address on the "Political Issues of the Day," published in 1868; "Facts for the People," 1872; "Influence of Popular Education," 1874; centennial oration, published by the citizens of San Diego County, California, July 4, 1876; funeral oration on the death of Garfield, delivered September 4, 1881, in Phœnix, Arizona, and published by request.

WILLIAM M. SPRINGER, born May 30, 1836, Sullivan County, Indiana. Residence, Springfield, Illinois. Educated, Illinois College, Jacksonville and Indiana Asbury University, Greencastle. Entered the Junior Class of Indiana University, and received therefrom the degrees A. B. and A. M. Occupation, student of law and lawyer. Position, Secretary of State Constitutional Convention of Illinois, 1862. Member of State Legislature of Illinois in 1871-2. Was elected to Forty-fourth, Forty-fifth and Forty-sixth Congress, and was re-elected to the Forty-seventh Congress by a majority of 1,058 over two opposing candidates. Contributed an article on "Postal Telegraphs" in *North American Review* May, 1881. Mr. Springer is regarded as one of the ablest parliamentarians in the country.

1859.

CHARLES M. CAMPBELL, born March 10, 1842, Bloomington, Indiana. Residence, Boulder, Colorado. Educated, Bloomington, at home by his father, Prof. M. M. Campbell. Degrees, A. B. and A. M. Occupation, student of theology and a graduate of Presbyterian Theological Seminary at Allegheny, Pennsylvania, 1864, and minister of the gospel. Position, pastor and stated supply at Valmont and Denver. County Superintendent of the schools of Boulder County and of the State of Colorado. Served as Justice of the Peace. High Private in the United States Marine Corps. Chairman of Republican County Central Committee of Boulder County, Colorado. Tutor in Indiana University 1859–60.

JOHN A. CONWELL, residence, Aurora, Indiana. Degree, B. S. From Cincinnati College, LL. B. Occupation, lawyer. Position, Clerk of Circuit Court of Dearborn County. On the editorial staff of the *Cincinnati Daily Commercial*.

JAMES WHITCOMB GORMAN, born July 10, 1839, in Bloomington, Indiana. Died February 19, 1863, at the Bates House, Indianapolis. Degrees, A. B. and A. M. Educated in private schools in St. Paul, Minnesota. Occupation, attorney and counselor at law. Position, entered the army in August, 1862; Assistant Adjutant General (rank and commission as Captain) on the staff of General Gorman. Was in the battles of Antietam, South Mountain and at the capture of Duval's Bluff, Arkansas, in 1863.

JOHN A. MULLANEY, B. S., San Francisco, California. Teacher.

WILLIAM E. SWEENY, born August 6, 1837, in Bucyrus, Ohio. Residence, Hebron, Indiana (1883). Educated at home. Degree, B. S. Occupation, civil engineer, farmer and merchant. A contributor of many articles, on various topics, to the journals.

THOMAS DIGGS THARPE, born 1835, in Marion, Indiana. Residence, Marion, Indiana. Educated at Marion Academy and common schools. Degrees, A. B. and A. M. Occupation and position, studied law, but did not continue in the practice; recently (1882) engaged in school work, superintending the schools in Marion; a minister in the Methodist Episcopal Church, of the Northern Indiana Conference; in 1885 was pastor of Simpson Methodist Episcopal Church, Fort Wayne; had for a time charge of an academy, also of a normal school. Served in the army, on Staff Brigade. In this service, through loss of health, became incapacitated for hard work. At present (1883) comparatively well, and, when able, engaged in literary and religious work.

1860.

GEORGE FRANCIS ADYE, born March 11, 1837, at Jamestown, New York. Came with the family to Indiana in 1839. Residence, Newtonville, Indiana. Educated in the common schools of Spencer County, though principally self taught, commencing his preparation for the University when about seventeen years old. Degrees, B. S. and M. D., from the Cincinnati Medical College, in 1865, and also from the Eclectic Medical Institute, Cincinnati, in 1870. Occupation, teaching, and study of medicine, under Dr. Willard Gage, and the practice of medicine and surgery. Position, School Director, and County Examiner in Newtonville; First Lieutenant of Home Guards during the Morgan raid. When a student of Indiana University Dr. Adye became a member of the Methodist Episcopal Church. He after leaving the University became a Baptist. He was the author of many articles for the press advocating temperance, female suffrage and Republicanism.

Dr. Adye was called out during the "Morgan raid," and was in the battle of Painter's Creek, near Owensboro, Kentucky, a battle fought and gained by the Home Guards.

Dr. Adye married Miss Elizabeth Dugan, February 26, 1861.

DAVID ENOCH BEEM, born June 24, 1837, at Spencer. Residence, Spencer, Indiana. Educated in the common county schools. Degrees, B. S. in 1858, A. B. in 1860 and A. M. in 1863. Occupation, lawyer and banker. Position, Captain, Co. H., 14th Indiana Volunteers, from 1861 to 1864. During the Rebellion, served with the Army of the Potomac. Participated in the battles of Winchester, Antietam, Fredericksburg, Chancellorsville, Gettysburg, Spottsylvania, and in other minor engagements.

JACOB S. BROADWELL, born August 14, 1840, at Cincinnati, Ohio; died at Bloomington, March 29, 1869. Entered the Freshman Class in 1856, a student from Oxford, Indiana. Degrees, A. B. and A. M. Occupation, lawyer. Was Prosecuting Attorney of a Judicial Circuit of Indiana. Mr. Broadwell married Miss Alice S. Buskirk, of Bloomington, February 16, 1863.

JAMES COUCH ELLIOTT, born January 6, 1830, in Sparta, Illinois. Residence, Swanwick, Perry County, Illinois. Educated,

Union Academy, Sparta, Illinois. Degrees, A. B. and A. M. Occupation, for three years student of theology. Position, minister of the gospel. Pastor of the United Presbyterian Church in Wyoming, Wisconsin, from 1863 to '68. In 1868 pastor of congregation in Swanwick, Illinois. Was clerk of Presbytery of Wisconsin, and also of Illinois. Member of the Board of Directors of Monmouth College, from 1871 to 1876, and also of the United Presbyterian Theological Seminary, Momouth, Illinois, from 1865 and 1868; and of Xenia, Ohio, from 1875 to '79. Mr. Elliott has ready for the publishers, a history of the United Presbyterian Presbytery of Southern Illinois. (1882).

HARRISON HIGHT, born 1841, in Bloomington. Residence, Spencer, Indiana. Degrees, A. B. and A. M. Occupation, teaching and preaching. Position, Elder in the Christian Church.

EDWIN RUTHVEN HATFIELD, born September 2, 1837, Newtown, Ohio. Died at Evansville, Indiana. Educated at common schools, Perry County, Indiana. Degrees, B. S. (1858), A. B. (1860), A. M. (1863). Occupation, attorney at law. Position, Prosecuting Attorney of the Second Judicial Circuit of Indiana, from October, 1872, to October, 1876. Both Mr. Beem and Mr. Hatfield after passing through the Scientific Department, remained two years longer and received the degree A. B.

LEVI SMITH JOHNSON, born 1837, in Spencer, Indiana. Died April 13, 1882. Educated at the Spencer common schools. Degree, B. S. Occupation and position, attorney at law. Served three years in the army during the Rebellion, was First Lieutenant, Company F, 71st Indiana Volunteers. Was engaged in all the marches and battles with his command, during his connection with the army.

JOHN MILTON McCOY, Residence, Dallas, Texas. Degrees, A. B., A. M. and LL. B. Occupation, attorney at law, practiced some years in Bloomington, and afterward in Dallas, where he held the office of City Attorney. Married Miss Laura Henderson of Bloomington.

HARRISON McNEIL, residence, Indianola, Iowa. Degrees, A. B. and A. M. Occupation, lawyer.

JAMES FRANKLIN ROBERSON, born September 9, 1836, in Crawford County, Indiana; died December 11, 1862, at Grantsburg, Indiana. Educated in the common schools of Crawford County. Degree, B. S. Occupation, teaching. Teacher in public schools of Paoli; also in Leavenworth, where he was taken by the disease of which he died. Mr. Roberson was distinguished while at the University by his mathematical talents, and was a contributor to the mathematical journals, and solved several problems for which prizes were given. In religion, a member of the Presbyterian Church.

ROBERT KENNEDY SMITH, born November 12, 1839, at Versailles, Indiana; died at Chaplin Hills, Kentucky, October 8, 1862. Educated in the common schools of Versailles, Indiana. Degree, B. S. Occupation and position: After graduation engaged in the drug business; in the spring of 1861 entered the army as Lieutenant of the 22d Infantry; was made Captain of the company, and soon after was killed at the battle of Chaplin Hills.

JOHN HEMPHILL WILSON, born February 11, 1836, in Monroe County, Indiana. Residence, Monmouth, Illinois. Educated in Monroe County schools. Degrees, A. B. and A. M. Occupation and position, Professor of Latin in Monmouth College, 1861-64; of Mathematics, 1864-76, and of Greek since 1876.

WILLIAM BENTON WOLF, born February 4, 1838, at Merom, Sullivan County, Indiana. Residence, Oaktown, Knox County, Indiana. Educated in the district schools of Sullivan County, and University Model School, Monroe County. Degrees, A. B. and A. M. and LL. B. Occupation, merchant for twelve years and farming since.

1861.

JOHN D. ALEXANDER, born February 6, 1839, in Bloomington, Indiana. Residence, Bloomfield, Indiana. Educated at the common schools. Degrees, A. B. and A. M. Occupation, taught school for one year. Went into the army in 1862, where he served three years. He then attended the law school of Michigan University (winter of 1865-66); since that time an attorney at law. In September, 1880, was elected a ruling elder in the Cumberland Presbyterian Church. In the fall of 1886 was chosen by the Synod a Trustee of Lincoln University,

Illinois. In the same year was elected Representative of Greene County to the State Legislature. From 1881 to 1885 was Prosecuting Attorney of the Fourteenth and Fifteenth Judicial Circuits. Served in the War of the Rebellion from 1862 to 1865. Was Captain of Co. D, 97th Regiment of Indiana Infantry Volunteers. Was engaged in the battles at Vicksburg, Resaca, Dallas, Big Shanty, New Hope Church, Lost Mountain, Kenesaw Mountain, Griswoldville, Savannah, Columbia and Bentonville. April, 1865, was appointed by General Logan, Acting Assistant Inspector General of Second Brigade, First Division, Fifteenth Army Corps, on the staff of General Robert F. Catterson. Was married December 8, 1886, to Miss Mary M. Rogers, of Bloomington, Indiana.

HENRY C. BARTON. B. S. Louisville. Student of law.

HANFORD BENEDICT, born June 26, 1837, in Sullivan County, New York. Residence, Springport, Indiana. Degrees, B. S., and M. D. from Michigan University. Occupation, physician and druggist.

SAMUEL WYLIE DODDS, born May 22, 1841, in Corydon, Indiana; died November 7, 1861, in St. Louis. Educated in Bloomington. Degree, A. B. Occupation and position, enlisted in the Union Army soon after graduation, Eighteenth Regiment, Company H. Went with his company to join Gen. Fremont's army in Missouri. Was sent to take care of a dying comrade, R. D. Wylie; was taken sick himself, and died in hospital at St. Louis. Mr. Dodds was a member of the Presbyterian Church by baptism and profession of faith, and a young man of more than ordinary talents.

ROBERT S. EDGAR. Residence, Coultersville, Illinois. Degrees, A. B. and A. M., M. D., Rush Medical College, Chicago, Illinois, 1870. Occupation, physician. Married Miss Jane Alexander, of Bloomington.

SAMUEL A. EMISON. B. S. Indianapolis. Lawyer.

SIMEON GREEN, born March 13, 1836, in Harrison County, Indiana. Residence, Paoli, Indiana. Educated in the common schools and academy, Corydon, Indiana. Degree, B. S. Occupation, teacher, agriculturist, surveyor, architect and builder. Position, elder in the Paoli Presbyterian Church.

BURTON GRAEM HANNA, born November 17, 1840, in Bowling Green, Indiana. Residence, Shelburn, Sullivan County, Indiana. Educated in graded schools of Terre Haute; one year at Wabash College, Crawfordsville. Degrees, A. B. and A. M. Occupations, teaching, farming, engineering and law. Positions, Prosecuting Attorney in Fourteenth and Twenty-first Judicial Circuits; deacon in Christian Church. Mr. Hanna was shipwrecked on steamship "Golden Rule," on return from California, near Greytown, in the spring of 1865.

SAMUEL JABEZ KIRKWOOD, born January 29, 1840, Monroe County, Ohio. Residence, Wooster, Ohio. Educated in the public schools, Woodsfield, Ohio, and at Miller's Academy, Washington, Ohio, and one term in Washington College, Pennsylvania. Degrees, A. B. and A. M., Indiana University; Ph. D. Lafayette College, Easton, Pennsylvania, and LL. D. Columbian University, Washington, D. C. Occupation, teaching. Position, Superintendent of the public schools, Cambridge, Ohio; also at Bucyrus, Ohio, and Tiffin, Ohio. Professor of mathematics, Wooster, Ohio. Dr. Kirkwood has lately (May, 1887) been called to the presidency of Cole College, Cedar Rapids, Iowa.

HENRY CLAY LEGG, degree, A. B. Needmore, Brown County. Occupation, farmer.

BYFORD ERNEST LONG, residence, Brownstown, Indiana. Degrees, A. B. and A. M. Occupation, lawyer. Position, Captain Sixty-seventh Regiment, Indiana Volunteers during the rebellion.

JOHN HENRY LOUDEN, born November 24, 1835, in Louden County, Pennsylvania. Residence, Bloomington, Indiana. Educated at Dunlapville, Indiana. Degrees, A. B., A. M. and LL. B. Occupation, attorney at law. Married Miss Lizzie Hemphill March 18, 1863.

RICHARD M. JOHNSTON MILLER, residence, Princeton, Indiana. Degree, B. S. Occupation, lawyer. Position, enlisted in 1862. Served through the war. Mustered out Captain Company B, Sixty-fifth Indiana Volunteers. County Clerk Gibson County for five years.

JAMES SILVESTER NUTT, born February 18, 1839, Greencastle, Indiana. Residence, Greencastle, Indiana. Educated at Whitewater College, Centreville, Indiana, and at Indiana Asbury University. Degrees, A. B. and A. M. (Indiana University.) Occupation and position, Principal of Third Ward School, Terre Haute, Indiana. Superintendent Public Schools Rising Sun, Indiana, and attorney at law.

JOHN CHALMERS ORCHARD, born November 3, 1840, in Bloomington, Indiana. Died June 26, 1881, Bloomington. Educated at Bloomington. Degrees, A. B. A. M. and LL. B. Occupation, student of law and merchant. Position, Trustee of the Public School and Trustee of the Methodist Episcopal Church, Bloomington. Sergeant-Major Indiana Volunteers.

JOHN ROBERTS, born November 14, 1838, in Pittsburg, Pennslyvania. Residence, Chicago. Educated at High School, Madison, Indiana. Degrees, A. B., and A. M. Occupation, lawyer. Position, Prosecuting Attorney Fifth Judicial District Indiana. Corporation Counsel of Madison, Indiana. Delivered the oration at the B Θ Π Convention, Indianapolis. In 1876 and '77 was in the lecture field. In 1887 addressed the Alumni Association of Indiana University. In 1875 traveled extensively in Europe. Mr. Roberts was Journal Clerk of the Indiana Legislature in the session of 1870–71. December 27, 1877, Mr. Roberts married Miss Lou B. Keuthav.

JOHN CRUDEN ROBINSON, born February 29, 1840, in Rush County, Indiana. Residence, Spencer, Indiana. Prepared for college in Fayetteville Academy, under Professor Thrasher, now of Butler University. Degrees, A. B. and A. M. Occupation, teacher, farmer and lawyer. Position, elected Judge 1876. District Attorney 1866. Prosecuting Attorney 1868 and 1870.

BENJAMIN FRANKLIN ROGERS, born March 31, 1840, in Monroe County, Indiana. Residence, Rich Pond Grove, Warren County, Kentucky. Educated at the public school. Degrees, A. B. and A. M. Occupation, teaching and preaching. Position, Principal and Proprietor of Rich Pond Academy. Elder in Christian Church.

JAMES HENRY ROGERS, born 1838, in Bloomington, Indiana. Died at Bloomington. Educated at district school. Degrees,

A. B., A. M. and LL. B. Occupation and position, lawyer. Prosecuting Attorney. County School Superintendent.

JOHN WATTS, A. B. and A. M. Lawyer, Santa Fe.

JOHN W. WELCH, born April 2, 1832, at Edgar County, Illinois. Residence, Hindsboro, Illinois. Educated, Paris Seminary, Paris, Illinois. Occupation, a teacher, afterwards a dealer in cattle. Position, member of the Methodist Episcopal Church and an earnest believer in the doctrines of Evangelical religion.

THOMAS W. ZOOK, B. S., Waynetown, Indiana. Mr. Zook was killed in battle.

1862.

NAPOLEON BONAPARTE ARNOLD, born September 18, 1840, in Columbus, Indiana. Residence, Topeka, Kansas. Educated at Bloomington. Degrees, A. B., A. M. and LL. B. Occupation, lawyer.

HENRY BUNGER, born October 13, 1838, in Bloomington, Indiana; died December 16, 1862, in Bloomington. Educated at Monroe County district school. Degree, B. S. Occupation, studied law for a short time, and then entered the army as private in Captain Wylie's company, 82d Regiment, Indiana Volunteers. Was appointed company clerk. Secretary of Sabbath School in Walnut Street, Presbyterian Church. Was engaged in battle at Perryville. Before leaving for the field a flag was presented to the company, through Dr. Nutt. Mr. Bunger was selected to receive and respond to his address.

DANIEL BRIDGE. A. B. and A. M. Minister. Sidney, Ohio.

JAMES MELVILLE FARIS, born April 14, 1840, in Bloomington, Indiana. Residence, Coultersville, Illinois. Educated at Bloomington public school. Degrees, A. B. and A. M. Occupation, preaching, performing military duty and teaching. Position, pastor of the Reformed Presbyterian congregation at Topsham, Vermont; pastor of Reformed Presbyterian congregation, Church Hill, Illinois; private in 117th Regiment, Indiana Volunteers; teacher in Union Academy, Dayton, Pennsylvania.

NOAH MONROE GIVAN, born December 1, 1840, in Dearborn County, Indiana. Residence, Harrisonville, Missouri. Educated at Manchester Academy and Franklin College. Entering

Indiana University Senior Class received the degrees A. B. and A. M. in course. Occupation, Principal of Lawrenceburg graded schools the first year after graduation; Deputy County Treasurer the next two years. In 1864–5, editor of the *Lawrenceburg Register*, and in 1867–8, editor of the *Harrisonville Herald*, Missouri. Was admitted to the bar at Lawrenceburg, Indiana, May 19, 1863. He was School Examiner in 1866, which position he resigned and removed to Missouri. In 1877 was elected Judge of the Seventh Judicial Circuit of Missouri. In 1880, reëlected to the same position, which he still (1886) holds. In 1878 he was elected Grand Master of Masons of Missouri; afterward was elected and served as Grand High Priest of the Grand Royal Arch Chapter of Missouri from 1878 to 1880. Judge Givan married Lizzie C. Jackson, August 7, 1862.

JOHN HOOD, born November 17, 1838, in Washington County, Illinois. Residence, Cedar Rapids, Iowa. Educated at Sparta, Illinois. Occupation and position, teacher and preacher; pastor of a Presbyterian congregation in Sparta. In 1878 Rev. Mr. Hood accepted a call to the Second Presbyterian Church of Cedar Rapids, Iowa; during the war, was Captain of a company; was in several engagements; was held a prisoner by the rebels for twenty-two months; resigned his pastorate in 1875, and became an agent of the Bible Society. Mr. Hood married Miss Mary Gault, of Sparta, April 24, 1871, who died July 24, 1886, leaving three daughters.

HOWARD C. LAFORCE, born in 1842, at Bedford, Indiana. Residence, Bedford. Educated in Bedford schools. Degrees, A. B. and A. M., and M. D. from Jefferson Medical College, Philadelphia. Occupation, physician and surgeon. Position, surgeon in the 179th Regiment, Ohio Volunteers. Was at the battle of Nashville, and in several minor engagements.

LEONARD WOODS MCCORD, B. S., lawyer, Indianapolis.

HUGH DUNN MCMULLEN, born December 11, 1836, at Manchester, Indiana. Residence, Aurora, Indiana. Educated at Indiana Asbury University. Degree, B. S. (Indiana University). Occupation and position, practice of law, and politics; Prosecuting Attorney one term; State Legislature one term; was Chairman of the Judiciary Committee, in 1883, in the

Legislature; was nominee of the Democratic Convention of 1886 for Attorney General.

HENRY H. MATHIAS, born January 30, 1838, at Jackson, Louisiana. Residence, Greencastle. Educated in part at Indiana Asbury University. Degrees, A. B. and A. M. One of the Professors of Law in DePauw University, 1881. Served three years in the War of the Rebellion in the 71st Regiment, Indiana Volunteers.

JAMES V. MITCHELL, born October 15, 1842, in Martinsville. Residence, Martinsville, Indiana. Educated at Indiana University Preparatory, 1857-58; Northwestern Christian University, 1858-59. In August, 1859, St. Mary's of the West, a Roman Catholic college, Cincinnati, Ohio, where he remained five weeks. Returned to the Northwestern Christian University and continued there a short time. In 1860 returned to Indiana University, where he remained till the breaking out of the war in 1861. When the first call for troops for three months' service was made, Mr. Mitchell enlisted in Company K, Seventh Regiment, Indiana Volunteers. Col. Eb. Dumont had the command. The regiment was ordered to West Virginia. At the expiration of the term of service Mr. Mitchell, in August, 1861, returned to the Indiana University; in September, 1861, degree B. S. Occupation, studied law in the office of Lucien Barbour and J. D. Howland. In August, 1863, commenced the practice of law in Martinsville, and was admitted to the bar September, 1863. In 1868 was elected Representative of Morgan County. Mr. Mitchell, supposing that the means used for ratifying the Fifteenth Amendment to the United States Constitution was forced by the Republicans, during the absence of a quorum, as nearly all the Democratic members had resigned, he withdrew from the party, regarding this as an act of usurpation, and as he was the only Republican who refused to endorse this action, he was ostracised. The next General Assembly, in 1871, being Democratic, he was elected to succeed General Robert Milroy as Trustee on the part of the State of the Wabash and Erie Canal. This office Mr. Mitchell held three years. In 1872 the Republicans gained the ascendancy in the State Legislature, and elected James S. Hinton, a colored politician of Indianapolis, to succeed him as Canal Trustee. "Verily," as Mr. Mitchell remarks, "the wheels go round." In 1871-72 Mr. Mitchell was part owner and editor of the *Morgan County Gazette*, and advocated the election of Horace Greely for President of the United States. Mr. Mitchell was twice married; first to Miss Ada Draper, July, 1863, at Bloomington, who died in California, November, 1869, whither she had been removed for health; second, to Mrs. E. F. Lawson, of Cincinnati, Ohio, July, 1872.

JOHN HENRY O'NEALL, born October 30, 1837, in Newburg, South Carolina. Residence, Washington, Indiana. Educated in county schools of Greene and Daviess Counties. Degree, B. S. Occupation and positions, attorney-at-law; Representative in the Legislature of the State in 1867, and subsequently State's Attorney; elected to Congress in 1866.

THOMAS CARTER PERING, born June 7, 1840, in Bloomington. Residence, Bloomington, Indiana. Educated in the district schools. Degrees, A. B. and A. M. Occupation, express and railroad business; freight and ticket agent, Bloomington station.

1863.

CYRUS BUCKMAN BATES, died July 13, 1865, at Pekin, Illinois. Educated at Illinois College. Degree, B. S. Occupation, student of law.

WILLIAM TURNER CATHCART, born at Bloomington. Residence, Golconda, Pipe County, Illinois. Educated in Bloomington schools. Degrees, A. B. and A. M. Occupation and position, teaching; School Examiner in Tenth Judicial District, Arkansas; Principal of the Golconda (Illinois) School. Joined the 82d Indiana Regiment in time to march with Sherman to the sea and take part in the campaign of the Carolinas. Mr. Cathcart married Miss Alice Cox, of Morgantown, in 1875.

THOMAS BENTON DEARBORN, born in 1830, at Northfield, New Hampshire; died August 10, 1879, at Milford, New Hampshire. Educated at Tilton, New Hampshire, where he commenced his classical studies. Entered the preparatory department of college at Jacksonville, Illinois. Degrees, A. B. and A. M., Indiana University; M. D. from Dartmouth College, 1865. Occupation, teaching; student of medicine in office of his uncle, Dr. Dearborn, and his brother, Dr. S. Dearborn, and also in Medical College, New York City; practitioner of medicine in

Milford, New Hampshire. Position, Principal of high schools in Augusta and Carthage, Illinois. Dr. Dearborn was a member of a family of physicians. On his return from Illinois, whither he had gone for health, the train was wrecked, and injuries were received which produced his disease and death. He trusted in the Savior, and had the hope of the righteous in his death.

CURRAN ALONZO DEBRULER, born November 11, 1843, at Jasper. Residence, Evansville, Indiana. Educated in the common schools of Dubois County. Degrees, B. S. and LL. B. Occupation, attorney at law.

DANIEL CARGILL FARIS, born June 21, 1843, in Bloomington, Indiana. Residence, West Barnet, Vermont. Educated at the district school. Degrees A. B. and A. M. Occupation, teacher of the freedmen one year; student of Theology four years; preacher twelve years. Position, Home Missionary in Minnesota for two and a half years.

ISAIAH FARIS, born April 25, 1846, near Bloomington, Indiana. Residence, Waukesha, Wisconsin. Educated at district school. Degrees A. B. and A. M. Occupation, student of Theology and preacher. Position, teacher of the freedmen, Natchez, Mississippi; pastor of the Reformed Presbyterian Church, Walnut City, Iowa, 1870–77; of Vernon Reformed Presbyterian Church, Wisconsin, 1878.

JAMES THOMAS MELLETTE, born October 31, 1837, in Henry County, Indiana. Residence, New Castle, Indiana. Educated at Marion Academy, Grant County. Degrees A. B. and A. M. Occupation, attorney at law. Member of the Legislature.

SAMUEL IRVIN PERING, born July 24, 1842, in Monroe County, Indiana. Residence, Silverdale, Cowley County, Kansas. Educated at Monroe County district school. Degrees A. B. and A. M.; Master of Accounts from Eastman's College, Poughkeepsie Occupation, for fifteen years boot and shoe merchant; since, stock farming. Member of the Presbyterian Church.

CHARLES W. SAPPENFIELD. B. S. Parkville, Ind.

ROBERT M. WEIR, residence, Bloomington, Indiana. Educated at common school, Bloomington, Indiana. Occupation, student of medicine, and in the army. Degrees, A. B. and A. M., and M. D. at University, Michigan, 1866. Position, private, Co. K,

138th Regiment, Indiana Volunteers. Dr. Weir is now (1887) a practicing physician in Bloomington.

WILLIAM B. WILSON, born January 14, 1839, in Monroe County, Indiana. Residence, Indianapolis. Educated in the common schools. Degrees, A. B. and A. M. Occupation, teacher. Position, Superintendent Owen County schools; Superintendent of schools at Spencer and at Edinburg, Indiana; Superintendent of Indiana Institute for the Education of the Blind.

JAMES S. WILSON, born April 14, 1841, in Monroe County, Indiana. Residence, Paxton, Illinois. Educated at schools of Monroe County. Degrees A. B. and A. M. Occupation, teacher till 1871. Position, Vice-President First National Bank, Paxton, Illinois; Elder and correspondent of the United Presbyterian Church, Paxton, Illinois.

1864.

BARTHOLOMEW H. BURRELL, born March 13, 1841, Jackson County, Indiana. Residence, Brownstown, Indiana. Degrees, B. S. and LL. B. (1866.) Occupation, studied law with Judge Emerson, whose partner he became after graduation. Position, Township Trustee, State Senator 1877-79 and member of Presbyterian Church. Married Miss Maggie F. Throop, October, 1864.

JAMES HIRAM FOSTER, born March 12, 1844, Petersburg, Indiana. Residence, Sunny Side, Arkansas. Educated in the Evansville public schools. Degrees, A. B. and A. M. Occupation, merchant.

SIDNEY B. HATFIELD, born January 30, 1842, Mead County, Kentucky. Residence, Boonville, Indiana. Educated at common schools. Degrees, A. B., A. M. and LL. B., 1866. Occupation, attorney at law. Position, District Attorney 1866-68; Prosecuting Attorney Second Judicial Circuit 1880; Clerk Perry County 1872-76.

ARCHIBALD WARRISTON JOHNSTON, born November 26, 1844, Hopedale, Ohio. Residence, 2,128 Columbia avenue, Philadelphia. Educated Geneva Hall, Northwood, Ohio. Degrees, A. B., A. M., M. D. Jefferson Medical College, Philadelphia. Occupation and position, Student of Theology at the Reformed

Presbyterian Seminary, Allegheny, Pennsylvania; graduated 1868; Pastor of East Craftsburg Reformed Presbyterian Congregation from 1868 to 1871; Student of Medicine, Jefferson Medical College in 1873, graduated 1875; since graduation, a practitioner of medicine.

ARTHUR CALVIN MELLETTE, born June 23, 1842. Henry County. Residence Watertown, South Dakota, at present, 1889, Pierre, South Dakota. Educated at Marion Academy, entered the Sophomore Class of Indiana University. Degrees, A. B., A. M. and LL. B. from Law Department in 1866. Occupation, Lawyer in Muncie, Indiana; In military service a short time before the close of the war; for a number of years editor of the *Muncie Times* and in 1872-74 was representative in the State Legislature; removed to Springfield, Dakota, where he was Register of the land office. The land office being removed to Watertown, D. T., then a mere hamlet, Mr. Mellette moved with it. In this office he continued several years. Soon after the inauguration of President Harrison Mr. Mellette was made Governor of the territory, the capital of which was Bismarck. On the divison of the territory, he was chosen by acclamation and was afterward by election, Governor of South Dakota. Pierre was made the temporary capital. Mr Mellette married Miss Margaret Wylie, of Bloomington, Indiana.

RUFUS N. RAMSEY, born May 20, 1839, in Trenton, Illinois. Residence, Carlyle, Illinois. Educated, three years at Jacksonville College. Five terms at McKendree College. Degrees, A. B and A. M., Indiana University. Occupation and position, attorney at law, for seven years. Banker since 1871. Member of the Educational Board for six years. (1880). County Clerk eight years and Presiding Officer of the borough of Carlyle. Mr. Ramsay has taken great interest in local politics, participating.in all Congressional, State and County conventions; was the centennial orator in 1876.

AMOS M. ROSS, B. S. Andersonville. Physician.

SAMUEL HENRY WEED, born November 5, 1863, in Ogdon, Henry County, Indiana. Residence, Colona, Henry County, Illinois. Educated at public schools of Monroe and Boone Counties. Degrees, A. B. and A. M. Occupation, in military sevice in 1864, a private of Company K., 133d Indiana Volunteers. A teacher for three winters. Studied theology, 1865–1868. Pastor of United Presbyterian Church, in Colona from 1866 to 1879. A delegate five times to the United Presbyterian General Assembly. Mr. Weed secured the organization of the Colona United Presbyterian Congregation in 1867, and the building of the church in 1868, and also, of Pleasant Unity Church in 1869. Mr. Weed has also served as Town Clerk, School Trustee and also Notary Public. By a disease of the lungs contracted while in the army, Mr. Weed for some years has been almost incapacitated from public speaking. Since laying down his charge, he has become a printer. He married Miss Mary Jane Davidson of Rock Island, Illinois.

1865.

ELLIS STONE GORMAN, born January 8, 1845, in Bloomington. Residence, St. Paul, Minnesota. Educated at private school. St. Paul. Degree, B. S. Occupation, lawyer, admitted to bar, Madison, Indiana, 1886. In (1886) practicing at Wichita, Kansas.

PHILIP HOLLAND, A. B. and A. M. Arcola. Physician. Degrees, M. D.

EZEKIEL M. McDONALD, born October 7, 1845, in Crawfordsville, Indiana. Died January 2, 1873, St. Paul, Minnesota. Educated at Earlham College, Richmond, Indiana. Degrees, A. B. and A. M. Occupation, student in law school of Judge David McDonald, and commenced practice in partnership with his father Honorable Joseph E. McDonald and A. L. Roach. On account of his failing health he relinquished his practice and in a vain hope of restoration he removed to St. Paul, Minnesota, where he died.

WALTER S. ROBERTS, born November 26, 1844, in Madison. Residence, Clearwater, Kansas. Educated at Hanover, Indiana. Degree, B. S. Occupation student of law, admitted to the bar at Madison, 1866. In (1886) practicing law at Wichita, Kansas.

ROBERT STEELE RYORS, born in Bloomington, 1846. Residence, Linn, Osage County, Missouri. Educated at Indiana University, and United States Naval Academy. Degree, B.

S. Occupation, lawyer. Position, Prosecuting Attorney, 1876 till 1880. Was chosen Presidential Elector on the Republican ticket in 1876. Resigned to become the Republican candidate for the Legislature. Was elected State Senator from the 21st District in 1886 and reëlected in 1888.

GREENBERRY HITE SACK, born November 5, 1841, at Greensburg, Decatur County, Indiana. Residence, Warrensburg, Missouri. Educated at Laurel (Ohio) graded school, and at Acton, Marion County, Indiana. Degrees, B. S. and LL. B. Occupation, practiced law for short time in Shelbyville, Indiana; taught in Centerview, Missouri, in 1866-67, and was Principal of Seminary in Warrensburg, Missouri, 1868-69, and since (1885) engaged in the practice of law. Since 1867 a member of the Christian Church.

HIRAM PETER WEBB, born March 14, 1842, in Sangamon County, Illinois. Residence, Albany, Linn County, Oregon, (1887). Educated in the district schools of Sangamon County and at North Sangamon Academy, in Menard County. Degrees, A. B., A. M. and LL. B. Occupation and position, teacher; lawyer; Clerk of Circuit Court; County Treasurer, in Nebraska; banking; Representative in Legislature. Mr. Webb had charge of the public schools in Canyon City. It was in 1868 that he moved from Illinois to Nebraska, and in the fall of the same year was appointed Clerk of the Court, which office he held about three years. He was then elected County Treasurer of Gage County, and was reëlected three times, holding the office eight years. Was engaged in banking for about six years, then moved to Oregon (November, 1878), and engaged in mining for about a year. In 1882 was elected Representative from Douglas County, and in 1882 went heartily into the active work of the ministry of the Methodist Episcopal Church, having for some time before been a local preacher. At first Mr. Webb was a supply in the Roseburgh Circuit. After two years' service as pastor, he was appointed to Albany, Oregon, where he is now (1887) closing his second year's work. October 21, 1873, Mr. Webb married Jennette Mayfield, at Beatrice, Nebraska.

LEVI B. WILSON, A. M., Crawfordsville, lawyer; a local preacher of the Methodist Church. Died.

1866.

AMZI ATWATER. (See list of Professors.)

JAMES PHILIP BAKER, born August 27, 1844, in Bartholomew County, Indiana. Residence, Indianapolis, Indiana. Educated in the common schools of Bartholomew County and Columbus City, Indiana. Degrees, A. B. and A. M. Occupation, teacher for two years; since a student of and an attorney at law.

BEDFORD AUGUSTUS BRADLEY, A. B., New Albany, merchant.

HOSEA V. FERRELL, born March 13, 1844, in Williamson County, Illinois. Residence, Carterville, Williamson County, Illinois. Educated at Clark Seminary, Aurora, Illinois. Degrees, B. S. and, from St. Louis Medical College, M. D., 1877. Occupation, physician and surgeon. Dr. Ferrell served through the War of the Rebellion, in the Union Army, as a First Lieutenant. Was wounded at the battle of Stone River. Was also President of Williamson Medical Society, and of Southern Illinois Medical Association, and author of various medical and surgical papers.

OMER TOUSEY GILLETT, born June 28, 1845, at Terre Haute, Indiana. Residence, Iowa City, Iowa. Educated, Indianapolis, at the Northwestern Christian University. Degrees, A. B. and A. M., and, from College of Physicians and Surgeons, New York, M. D. Occupation and position, study and practice of medicine; Secretary of Medical Faculty of State University, Iowa, and an Assistant Professor of Surgery in University of Iowa.

RANSOM E. HAWLEY, born July 8, 1844, at Putnamville, Indiana. Residence, Washington, Daviess County, Indiana. Educated at village school, Putnamville, and Wabash College, Crawfordsville. Degrees, A. B. and A. M. Occupation, three years in Lane Theological Seminary, Cincinnati, Ohio. Position, minister of Presbyterian Church, Cincinnati, Ohio, until 1873; Kentland, Indiana, 1874; Cleves, Ohio, 1880; Washington, Indiana, 1880; pastor of church, Oakland City, Indiana, 1887, and pastor at St. Paul, Minnesota, 1889. In the army through the severe campaign of 1863-64 in East Tennessee. A private in Co. A, 78th Indiana Volunteers, and afterward in Regiments 115 and 133. Was wounded in guerilla fight, Uniontown, Kentucky, August, 1862.

NATHAN D. MILES, born April 2, 1841, in New Lebanon, Indiana. Residence, Nicholasville, Kentucky. Educated at common schools, New Lebanon Academy, three years; Indiana Asbury University, one year. Degrees, B. S. and LL. B., 1867, Indiana University. Occupation, practice of law, politics, and farming. Position, Representative of Sullivan County, in Indiana Legislature 1868. Reëlected 1869, by a majority of 2,300. On removing to Kentucky, in 1871, was elected to represent Jessamine County, Kentucky, for two years. Mr. Miles married Mrs. Kittie Roberts (nee Hemphill,) March 1, 1871.

GEORGE WASHINGTON PAYNE, born October 1, 1843, in Monroe County, Indiana. Died October 4, 1873, Monroe County, Indiana. Educated at common schools. Degree, B. S. Occupation, teacher and farmer.

WILLIAM LANCASTER POLK, born May 8, 1844, in Bullitt County, Kentucky. Residence, Vicksburgh, Mississippi. Educated at Franklin College, Indiana. Degree, B. S. Occupation, planter and Civil Engineer. Mr. Polk married Miss Alice Howe, of Bloomington, February, 1867.

WILLIAM C. SANDEFUR, born March 31, 1839, in Johnson County, Indiana. Residence, Franklin, Indiana. Educated at Edinburg, Indiana. Degrees, B. S. and LL. B. Occupation, lawyer. Position, Official Court Stenographer. Treasurer of Board of Trustees Methodist Episcopal Church, Franklin. Prosecuting Attorney. Color Guard, Company I, 70th Regiment, Indiana Volunteers. Engaged in all the battles of the Regiment, including Sherman's March to the Sea.

JOSEPH W. WALKER, born April 18, 1845, in Wenham, Essex County, Massachusetts. Residence, Indianapolis, Indiana. Educated at Warren High School, Warren, Rhode Island. Degrees, A. B. and A. M., in course, LL. B. Central Law School, Indiana, graduating in law, at the head of a class of thirty-six. Occupation and position, dealer in real estate, afterward, attorney at law. For about five years after graduation, traveled extensively in Europe and the United States. At present engaged with Mr. W. H. Ripley in preparing an analytical digest of decisions of the Supreme Court of Indiana.

1867.

VINSON CARTER, born July 16, 1840, at Mooresville, Indiana. Residence, Indianapolis. Educated at Earlham College, Richmond, Indiana, and Northwestern Christian University, Indianapolis. Degrees, B. S., and LL. B. in 1867. Major Carter served in the army during the Rebellion in the 12th Indiana Volunteers. Was wounded at the battle of Richmond, Kentucky, August 30, 1862. Served as State military agent for Indiana from March, 1863, to August, 1865, in the Department of the Cumberland, and Military Division of the Mississippi. In the church militant, he is a Presbyterian elder and Sunday school superintendent. Was Chairman of the House Committee on the Judiciary. Major Carter, October 1, 1867, married Miss Emma Maxwell, of Bloomington, daughter of Dr. James D. Maxwell.

WILLIAM C. DRAPER, born in 1850, at Bloomington, Indiana. Residence, Ellettsville, Indiana. Educated in Bloomington public schools. Degree, B. S. Occupation, before commencing the practice of law, which he had studied, he engaged in the lumber business. His health failing, he went to California; his father dying, he returned to Ellettsville and continued his business as proprietor of the flour mill. In 1873 he again became a lumber merchant in connection with the management of a saw-mill.

FRANK J. HALL, born February 16, 1844, in Rush County, Indiana. Residence, Rushville, Indiana. Educated, common schools; Farmer's College, College Hill, Ohio, 1864-65. Degrees, B. S. and LL. B. (1869). Occupation, lawyer.

CASSIUS F. HUNTER, born September 25, 1847, at Cambridge, Ohio. Residence, Junction City, Kansas. Educated in Cambridge schools, Ohio. Degrees, B. S. and, from Jefferson Medical College, Philadelphia, (1871), M. D. Occupation, student and practitioner of medicine.

CYRUS BURT HUTCHISON, born September 23, 1846, at Cambridge, Ohio. Residence, Cambridge, Guernsey County, Ohio. Educated in Cambridge public schools and at Washington and Jefferson College, Pennsylvania. Degrees, A. B. and A. M. Occupation, teacher. Position, County School Examiner.

HENRY CLAY MEREDITH, born July 17, 1843, at Cambridge City, Indiana; died July 7, 1882, at Cambridge City. Educated at Friends' Boarding School, Greenmont, Indiana, and Fairview Academy, Groves, Fayette County, Indiana. Degrees, A. B. and A. M. Occupation and position, Chief Clerk in the office of the United States Surveyor General, Helena, Montana Territory. Editor of the *Cambridge City Tribune* and *Farmer and Stock Breeder*. Member of House of Representatives, 1881, and Aid-de-Camp on the staff of General Meredith in 1864-65.

ROBERT DALE RICHARDSON, born January 13, 1847, in Spencer County, Indiana. Residence, Evansville, Indiana. Educated at Rockport (Indiana) High School. Degrees, B. S. and LL. B. (1868). Occupation, attorney at law. Position, Trustee of City Schools of Evansville, 1866-77; Trustee of Indiana University since April, 1879, and at the present time (1888). Mr. Richardson was lately elected Judge of the First Judicial District. Mr. Richardson married Miss Mary Eva Bollman, of Bloomington, June 26, 1867.

1868.

ANDREW JACKSON ARNOLD, born 1843, in Columbus, Indiana. Residence, Topeka, Kansas. Degree, B. S. Occupation, druggist. Position, enlisted in 2d Indiana Cavalry 1862. In service till close of the war. A prisoner for eight months at Andersonville. Mr. Arnold married Miss Louisa Campbell, daughter of Professor M. M. Campbell.

JESSE RICHARDS BICKNELL, born November 13, 1848, Lexington, Indiana. Residence, Jacksonville, Florida. Educated at private school, New Albany. Degrees, A. B., A. M. and LL. B., and from Nashotah Theological Seminary, Wisconsin, B. D. 1874. Occupation, the ministry. Position, Assistant Minister Indianapolis, 1875-77. Missionary at Muncie, Indiana, 1877-80. Assistant at St. John's Episcopal Church, Jacksonville, Florida. During the yellow-fever epidemic in 1888, the Rev. Mr. Bicknell remained at his post ministering to the sick and dying, both before and after his own almost fatal prostration by the disease.

JOHN MILTON BROWN, born February 12, 1844, in Jackson

County, Indiana. Residence, Shelbyville, Indiana. Educated at Clear Spring High School, Indiana. Degree, B. S. Occupation and position, merchant and dealer in lumber. A member of the Methodist Episcopal Church. Served eighteen months in the Union Army.

AMBROSE M. CUNNING, Martinsville. Lawyer.

HENRY CLAY DUNCAN, born January 16, 1845, in Leatherwood, Lawrence County, Indiana. Residence, Bloomington, Indiana. Educated at district schools, Lawrence County. Degrees, A. B., A. M. and LL. B., 1870. Occupation, lawyer. Position, private in the army during the Rebellion. Member of Christian Church. Prosecuting Attorney 10th Judicial District.

DAVID McKENDREE GUNN, born December 17, 1839, in Floyd County, Indiana. Died May 22, 1873, Montrose, Wright County, Minnesota. Educated at Minneapolis, Minnesota. Degree, B. S. Occupation and position, teacher and civil engineer. A member of the Methodist Episcopal Church.

JAMES H. JORDAN, born December 21, 1842, at Woodstock, Virginia. Residence, Martinsville, Indiana. Educated, common schools and Wabash College, Crawfordsville, Indiana. Degrees, B. S. and LL. B. (1871). Occupation, attorney at law and in the Union Army. Position, Prosecuting Attorney. Was in the battles of Antietam, Gettysburgh, Fredericksburg, South Mountain, Chancellorsville and others.

ALLISON MAXWELL. Residence, Indianapolis, Indiana. Educated in Bloomington schools. Degrees, A. B., A. M. and, from Miami Medical College, M. D. Occupation, teacher and physician. Position, tutor in Indiana University, 1868–70; connected with H. H. Bancroft's publishing house, San Francisco, California, 1870–72; House Physician, Cincinnati Hospital, for one year; elected Coroner of Marion County, 1880; Professor of Theory and Practice of Medicine in Central College of Physicians and Surgeons at Indianapolis, 1886-87.

GEORGE MATTISON ROBERTS, born in 1847, in Sullivan County, Indiana. Residence, Bucklin, Mo. Educated at Union Christian College, Merom, Indiana. Degree, B. S. Occupation, physician and druggist.

JAMES WILLIAM ROBERTS, born August 19, 1841, in Sullivan County, Indiana. Residence, Bucklin, Missouri. Educated at Union Christian College, Merom, Indiana. Degree, B. S. Occupation and position, attorney at law; Prosecuting Attorney.

SAM. BELL WAKEFIELD, born December 4, 1848, at Mackvell, Kentucky; died at San Francisco, June, 1887. Educated in common schools, Savannah, Missouri. Degrees, A. B. and A. M. Occupation and position, student of medicine, 1871–74; mining in Nevada; since, 1874 to 1883, Vice-President of San Francisco Stock Exchange Board; January 12, 1885, was elected President of the Board. Mr. Wakefield was a member of the Methodist Episcopal Church.

1869.

GEORGE WASHINGTON ALFORD, born September 28, 1846, in Alfordsville, Indiana. Residence, Loogootee, Indiana. Educated at common schools of Daviess County, Indiana. Degrees, B. S. and LL. B., 1869. Occupation, lawyer. Publisher of *Tribune*, Loogootee, Indiana. Member of Christian Church. Postmaster for ten years. Present address (1889) Washington, Indiana.

JAMES DARWIN ALLEN, born September 25, 1849, in Bloomington, Indiana. Residence, Buffalo, Wilson County, Kansas. Educated at Bloomington Public Schools. Degree, A. B. Occupation, merchant.

JOHN HOMER BOTHWELL, born November 20, 1848, in Maysville, Illinois. Residence, Sedalia, Missouri. Educated at Clay County Public Schools. Degrees, B. S. and from the Law School, Albany, New York, in 1871, LL. B. Occupation, student of law two years. Attorney at law, Sedalia, Missouri. Mr. Bothwell has been popular and successful in his profession.

WILLIAM DALLAS BYNUM, born June 26, 1846, Newberry, Indiana. Residence, Indianapolis. Educated, received his primary education at the common schools. Received from the Indiana University degree B. S. Studied law in the office of Honorable W. Mack, of Terre Haute, was admitted to practice. Commenced the practice of his profession at Washington, Indiana. Was the City Attorney from 1871 to 1875. Was Mayor of the City of Washington, Indiana, from 1875 to 1879. In February, 1875, he was appointed a Trustee of the State

Normal School at Terre Haute. In 1876 was chosen Democratic Elector. In May, 1881, he removed from Daviess County to Indianapolis. In 1882 was elected Member of the State Legislature, and at the opening of the session in 1883 was elected Speaker of the House. Was elected to the Forty-ninth Congress, and reëlected to the Fiftieth Congress, as a Democrat, receiving 22,882 votes, against 21,108 votes for Harris, Republican. Was a member of the Ways and Means Committee of the Fiftieth Congress. In 1879 Mr. Bynum delivered the annual address to the alumni of Indiana University. He also delivered a eulogy on Thomas A. Hendricks, Vice-President-elect, in the House of Representatives. An able speech has lately been made by Mr. Bynum on the tariff question. Mr. Bynum married Miss Rachel Dixon, of Henderson County, Illinois, October 4, 1871.

MATTHEW T. CAMPBELL. Residence, Topeka, Kansas. Educated at Bloomington. Degrees, B. S. and LL. B., 1869. Occupation, attorney at law. Position, member of Board of Education for two years; represented 62d District, Kansas, in Legislature, 1877-78. Married Miss Louise Adams, Waterville, Kansas.

JAMES M. CRAIG, born January 27, 1845, at Bloomington, Indiana. Residence, Garnett, Kansas. Educated in the com-schools of Monroe County. Degrees, B. S. and LL. B., 1872. Occupation and position, druggist; Probate Judge for four years; County Treasurer of Anderson County, Kansas. Member of the United Presbyterian Church.

AARON ASBURY CRAVENS, born July 26, 1844, in Washington County, Indiana. Residence, Hardinsburg, Indiana. Educated at May's Academy, Salem, Indiana. Degree, B. S. Occupation, teacher; editor; lawyer; farmer. Position, School Superintendent of Washington County; author of a volume of "Speeches and Lectures"; Presidential Elector, 1884.

T. WYCKLIFF DENTON, B. S., Vernon, Indiana; lawyer.

ROBERT E. EVELEIGH, born August 31, 1848, at Bloomfield, Indiana. Residence, Bloomfield, Indiana. Educated at Bloomfield. Degree, B. S. Occupation, student of medicine; druggist; layman in the Cumberland Presbyterian Church. Mr. Eveleigh married Miss Emma Freeland, November 16, 1888.

ROBERT MELLVILLE GAMBLE, born September 6, 1841. Residence, Anaheim, California. Educated in the common schools of Monroe County. Occupation, merchant. Position, private soldier in the army. Engaged in the battles of Shiloh, Tennessee, Perryville, Kentucky, Chickamauga, Atlanta and Lovejoy Station, under the command of Rosencranz and Sherman. Married Miss Rachel Alexander, of Bloomington, Indiana.

HENRY M. GILMORE, B. S., Bloomington; lawyer.

ELI HOCH, B. S., Winamac; druggist.

ALFRED RYORS HOWE, born November 3, 1849, at Bloomington. Residence, Bloomington, Indiana. Educated in Bloomington schools. Degree, A. B. Occupation, merchant and manufacturer. Residence, 1887, Louisville, Kentucky. Married Miss Mary Frazee, of Louisville, Kentucky.

GEORGE W. JOHNS, born March 7, 1849, at Albion, Illinois. Residence, Fairfield, Wayne County, Illinois. Educated in Albion common schools. Degrees, B. S. and LL. B. Occupation and position, attorney at law, Carmi, Illinois, and two years at Fairfield, Illinois; ten years member of the firm Forth, Robinson & Co., bankers. Mr. Johns was Colonel and Aid on the staff of General Cullom during the war. In 1873, Journal Clerk of the House of Representatives (Illinois), and also of the Twenty-eighth General Assembly. Secretary of the Illinois Republican Convention, and also Vice-President of another convention.

BENJAMIN FREELAND MCCORD, born December 23, 1845, at Martinsville, Indiana. Residence, Lincoln, Illinois. Educated by his father, Rev. Mr. E. McCord. Degrees, A. B. and A. M. Occupation and position, Professor of Mathematics, Lincoln University; minister of Cumberland Presbyterian Church. Professor McCord married Miss Rose Fitch, January, 1873.

E. MORGAN MCCORD, born January 29, 1848, at Centerville, Indiana. Residence, Martinsville, Indiana. Occupation, lawyer.

SAMUEL H. MCCORMICK, B. S., Worthington. Physician.

SAMUEL EARLY MAHAN, born August 4, 1846, Pleasant Garden, Indiana. Residence, Bayfield, Wisconsin. Educated in Terre Haute public schools and by private teacher. Degree,

B. S. Occupation and position, student of medicine two and one-half years. Farmer. Connected with an Indian agency till 1881. Merchant. First Lieutenant and Adjutant One Hundreth and Forty-ninth Regiment, Indiana Volunteers. On General R. E. Granger's staff as aid. Clerk of the Bayfield County School Board.

ALLEN KING MELTON, B. S., Carrizo Springs, Texas. Teacher.

SARAH PARKE MORRISON. See list of professors.

ISAAC NATHAN NEELD, born July 26, 1866, Bloomington, Indiana. Residence, Indianapolis, Indiana. Educated in district school, Van Buren Township, Monroe County. Degree, A. B. Occupation, general commission merchant, provisions, grain.

CYRUS NEWLAND NUTT, born December 21, 1848, Greencastle, Indiana. Died at his residence, New Albany, Indiana, December 23, 1884. Degrees, A. B., A. M. and M. D., medical department University of New York. Occupation and position, student of medicine. Began practice of medicine in one of the hospitals on Blackwell's Island. Afterward he engaged as surgeon on a merchant vessel of New York and sailed for Europe, where he visited the hospitals of London and other cities. Dr. Nutt, when sixteen years old, volunteered in the Union Army as a drummer boy. Was at the battle of Nashville, and was praised for his bravery. . After the death of his father, President Nutt, he and his widowed mother made their home in New Albany, where he had built up a large and profitable practice.

JOHN LLOYD PITNER, born October 12, 1846, Jerseyville, Illinois. Residence, Bloomington, Indiana, 1882. Educated in the Illinois common schools. Degrees, B. S. and LL. B, 1871. Occupation and position, teacher, attorney at law, minister of the Methodist Episcopal Church, soldier in the Union Army from December, 1863, till close of the war. Mr. Pitner has delivered many eloquent orations on different occasions. He was the alumni orator in 1882.

GEORGE W. SANDERS, A. B., Indianapolis. Real estate agent.

LUTHER SHORT, born May 14, 1845, Springville, Indiana. Residence, Franklin, Indiana. Educated in Indiana Asbury University and Butler University. Degree, B. S., Indiana University. Occupation and position, lawyer, editor and proprietor of the *Franklin Democrat*. Private in the Forty-third Indiana Infantry; took part in all the battles in which the regiment engaged.

ASHER LABOYTEAUX SLUSS, born November 10, 1848, Bloomington. Residence, Brownsville, Saline County, Missouri. Educated in Bloomington schools. Degrees A. B. and A. M.

FELIX W. THOMAS, born 1844, at Connersville, Indiana. Residence, Winamac, Indiana. Educated at Monticello and Winamac. Degree, B. S. Occupation, lawyer.

WILLIAM HOWARD TRIPPETT, born April 18, 1847, in Gibson County, Indiana. Residence, Princeton, Indiana, Educated in Owensville graded schools. Degrees, B. S. and LL. B. Occupation and position, lawyer, Prosecuting Attorney Eleventh Judicial Circuit, 1877-80.

1870.

SAMUEL D. BUTZ, born May 4, 1850, at Liberty, Illinois. Residence, near Edinburg, Indiana. Educated at Illinois College and Northwestern Christian University. Degrees, A. B. and A. M. Occupation and position, druggist, farmer, deacon, and treasurer of the Baptist Church.

WALTER A. FOLAND, born March 12, 1846, at Dayton, Ohio. Residence, Benson, Minnesota. Educated in Terre Haute public school. Degrees, A. B., A. M. and LL. B., 1873. Occupation and position, attorney-at-law, Alumni orator, 1873. Married Miss Laura Woodburn, of Bloomington.

GEORGE W. MCDONALD, born January 24, 1848, at Attica, Indiana. Residence, Attica, Indiana. Educated in Attica schools and Wabash College. Degrees, A. B., A. M. and LL. B., 1873. Occupation, attorney-at-law.

ROBERT W. MIERS, born January 27, 1848, near Greensburg, Indiana. Residence, Bloomington, Indiana. Educated in public schools and Hartsville Academy. Degrees, B. S. and LL. B. Occupation and position, Prosecuting Attorney, 1874 to 1878; Member of Legislature 1877 and 1878; member of Board of Trustees of Indiana University since 1882; appointed Judge for the unexpired time of Judge Wilson, deceased; nominee of the Democratic convention for Secretary of State. Mr. Miers is a member of the Presbyterian Church. He married Miss Belle Ryors, of Bloomington.

SAMUEL THOMPSON QUICK. Residence, Edinburgh, Indiana. Degrees, A. B., A. M. and, from Eclectic Medical Institute, Cincinnati, M. D. Occupation, physician. Married Miss Elizabeth Dodds, of Bloomington, Indiana, in 1872.

AUGUSTUS ORWIG REUBELT, born July 15, 1849, at Orwigsburgh, Pennsylvania. Residence, Winamac, Pulaski County, Indiana. Educated at Orwigsburgh, Pennsylvania, and Trenton, Tennessee, and Greencastle, Indiana. Degrees, A. B. and A. M. Occupation and position, teacher; Professor of Mathematics and German, Ghent College, Kentucky; Superintendent of Public Schools at Lebanon, Vevay, Winamac, and Corydon in Kentucky. Private in Co. I, 43d Regiment, Indiana Volunteers. Elder in Christian Church. Mr. Reubelt married Miss Jennie Warner, of Brazil, Indiana, December 29, 1875.

ARTHUR P. TWINEHAM. Residence, Princeton, Indiana. Degrees, A. B. and A. M. Occupation and position, lawyer; City Attorney, 1874–76; Chairman of the Republican Convention; Superintendent of the Public Schools, Rockville, Indiana.

JULIUS W. YOUCHÉ, born March 4, 1848, Canal, Winchester, Ohio. Residence, Crown Point, Lake County, Indiana. Educated in Ohio public schools and Heidleburg College, Tiffin, Ohio. Degrees, A. B. and A. M.; LL. B., Michigan University, 1872. Occupation and position, teacher; attorney at law; Superintendent of Public Schools, Crown Point, Indiana; Prosecuting Attorney of the 31st Judicial Circuit of Indiana, 1876–80; Trustee of Indiana University since 1885.

1871.

THOMAS GREENE ALFORD, born March 26, 1852, Alfordsville, Indiana. Residence, Indianapolis, Ind. Educated in the district schools of Daviess County. Degree, B. S. Occupation and position, teaching in district schools; Principal of Vevay High School and Superintendent of Vevay City Schools, 1881, and Principal of High School in Indianapolis, 1888.

SUSANNA R. (HAMILTON) ANDERSON, born in Leesville, Indiana. Residence, Quincy, Indiana. Educated in Bloomington. Degree, B. S. Occupation, teaching.

HELEN (ALFORD) BERRY, born in Alfordsville, Indiana. Residence, Loogootee, Indiana. Educated in Daviess County public schools. Degree, B. S. Occupation, teacher and housewife. Member of the Church of Christ, Loogootee.

E. LOUISA (WYLIE) BOISEN, born in Bloomington. Residence, Bloomington. Educated at Mrs. McFerson's Ladies' Seminary, Bloomington, at Rev. Dr. J. W. Scott's Female Seminary, Oxford, Ohio. Graduated at Glendale Female College. Degree, B. S., Indiana University. Occupation, teaching, Missouri State University, 1872-73; teacher of drawing in the Bloomington public schools since 1884. Married Prof. H. B. Boisen, of Indiana University, July 16, 1873. Visited Germany with her husband in 1873.

JOHN WOODRUFF CULMER, born January 28, 1847, in Allegheny County, Pennsylvania. Residence, Prairieton, Vigo County, Indiana (1881). Educated at Springville, Indiana. Degree, B. S. Occupation and position, minister of the Methodist Episcopal Church.

JAMES HENRY DUNN, born September 30, 1849, at New Albany, Indiana. Residence, Louisville, Kentucky. Educated at Chicago University. Degree, A. B., Indiana University. Occupation, merchant. Mr. Dunn married Miss Lizzie Harbison, March 9, 1880.

LIZZIE (HARBISON) DUNN, born near Bloomington, Indiana. Residence, Louisville, Kentucky. Educated at Bloomington Seminary. Degree, B. S. Married (see above).

ELLA (FELLOWS) EWING, born July 14, near Bloomfield, Indiana. Residence, Princeton, Indiana. Educated at Bloomington Female Academy and in the graded schools. Degree, B. S. Occupation, teacher of Music. Miss Fellows married John W. Ewing, October 16, 1873.

JAMES MILLIGAN FOSTER, born September 22. 1850, at Cedarville, Ohio. Residence, Cincinnati, Ohio. Educated in Cedarville public schools. Degree, A. B. Occupation and position, teacher in Cedarville for two years; four years at Reformed Presbyterian Theological Seminary, Allegheny, Pennsylvania; pastor of Reformed Presbyterian Church, Cincinnati (1882); Superintendent of Public Schools, Cedarville; public lecturer on National Reform. Married Miss Laura Turner, of Bloomington.

LAURA L. (TURNER) FOSTER, born at Bloomington. Residence, Cincinnati, Ohio. Educated in Bloomington public schools. Degree, B. S. Occupation, teacher for five years. Married Rev. James M. Foster.

WALTER R. HOUGHTON. See Faculty list.

ALEXANDER KILPATRICK, born January 20, 1848, at Bloomington. Residence, Valencia, Pennsylvania. Educated at Morning Sun, Iowa. Degrees, A. B. and A. M. Occupation and position, a teacher for two years; student of theology for four years; minister of the Reformed Presbyterian Church since 1877.

CLARA ELIZA McCORD, born at Centerville, Indiana. Residence, Lincoln, Illinois (1882). Educated at Bloomington, Indiana. Degree, B. S. Occupation, teaching.

JAMES E. McCOLLOUGH, born April 1, 1847, at Hamilton, Ohio. Residence, Princeton, Indiana. Educated in the common schools of Hamilton County and Spencer County, Indiana. Degrees, B. S. and LL. B. Occupation, attorney at law. Married Miss Emma Turner, of Bloomington.

FRANK BUELL McDONALD, born May 24, 1850, at Crawfordsville, Indiana. Died at Washington, D. C., January 7, 1887. Educated at Indianapolis and by Professor Pickett, of Attica. Degrees, A. B. and A. M. Occupation and position, study and practice of law; at the time of his death was Pension Office Examiner in Washington.

TILGHMAN H. MALLOW. See Faculty list.

COLUMBUS NAVE. A. B. and A. M. Attica. Lawyer.

LESTER L. NORTON, born July 26, 1848, in Marion, Indiana. Residence, Indianapolis. Educated at Marion and Antioch schools. Degrees, B. S. and LL. B. Occupation, lawyer.

JAMES ROBERT OVERMAN, born October 14, 1847, in Lawrence County, Indiana. Residence, Evansville, Indiana. Educated at Bedford schools. Degree, B. S. Occupation, 1871–81, farming; in 1881 to 1883 traveled extensively, visiting Cuba, Yucatan, Mexico and the Southern States; in 1882, California, Wyoming, Utah, Idaho, Oregon and Colorado. Occupation, a manufacturer. In 1887 was elected Auditor of Lawrence County.

DAVID L. RICHARDSON, born November 17, 1843, in Spencer, Indiana. Residence, Dallas, Texas. Educated at Spencer County schools. Degree, B. S. Occupation, commission merchant. Since 1877, dealer in hardware and agricultural implements.

1872.

WILLIAM S. BROWN, born June 11, 1847, in Jackson County. Residence, Kansas City, Missouri. Educated at Clear Spring common schools. Degrees, A. B., A. M. and LL. B. Occupation, lawyer. At present (1889) is engaged in real estate and loan business, letting contracts for buildings, etc.

THOMAS JEFFERSON CLARK, born April 19, 1846, in Bruceville, Knox County. Residence, Vincennes, Indiana. Educated at Bloomington common schools. Degrees, A. B. and A. M. Occupation and position, Principal of the Vincennes high school, 1873. Minister of Christian Church, Vincennes, for the last seventeen years. Mr. Clark has been a diligent and successful minister; has had 732 accessions to his church; has preached 2,250 sermons; attended 235 funerals, and united in marriage 224 couples. Mr. Clark married Miss Emma Jennings, of class 1873.

ORLANDO H. COBB. B. S. and LL. B. Residence, Vincennes. Lawyer.

GEORGE WILLIAM COOPER, born May 21, 1851, in Bartholomew County. Residence, Columbus, Indiana. Educated at Columbus common schools and private tuition. Degrees, A. B., A. M. and LL. B. Mr. Cooper completed his college course and law studies in four years. Occupation and position, lawyer; Prosecuting Attorney for Bartholomew and Brown counties; Mayor of Columbus; City Attorney in 1887. Mr. Cooper has always been an active politician. In almost every county of the State he has advocated the reunion of the States in feeling as well as in force—a reformation of the tariff to a revenue basis. He was elected Congressman of the Fifth District on the Democratic ticket in 1888. Mr. Cooper married Miss Sina

E. Greene, of Bloomington. Both Mr. and Mrs. Cooper are active members of the Christian Church.

BENJAMIN HARRISON CRAVENS, born November 25, 1868, in Washington County. Residence, Hardinsburg, Washington County, Indiana. Educated at Salem Academy. Degree, B. S. Occupation, principally farming; took an active part in the political contest of 1884; Treasurer of Washington County. Mr. Cravens married Miss Susan McIntosh, of Hardinsburg, March, 1880.

GEORGE W. CUMMINGS, born 1848, in Illinois. Residence, 32 Vesey street, New York (1889), formerly a resident of St. Louis. Degrees, A. B. and A. M. Educated in Terre Haute schools. Occupation, lawyer; recently, newspaper correspondent; when at St. Louis, published the *Official Railroad Guide;* spent one year at St. Louis Law School; practiced law three years; his health failing, went to Colorado and engaged in mining, but got neither health or wealth. He then returned to Missouri, and soon after went back to Colorado; this time he improved in health, but not otherwise. In 1882 went to Chicago, where, with two friends, he organized the American Press Association, which has engaged his attention till the present time (1889). Mr. Cummings married Miss Josephine de Fontaine in 1879.

JOHN W. EWING, born February 14, 1850, in Patoka, Gibson County, Indiana. Residence, Princeton, Indiana. Educated in Gibson and Pike Counties common schools and at Owenville graded schools. Degrees, B. S. and LL. B., 1873. Occupation and position, attorney-at-law, Treasurer of School Board of Princeton, School Trustee two terms. Mr. Ewing was the first mayor of the City of Princeton, Indiana. He married Miss Ella Fellows of Class 1871, October 16, 1873.

EMORY EVANS GRINNELL, born 1852, in Burlington, Vermont. Residence, Woodys, Kern County, California, formerly Peabody, Marion County, Kansas. Educated in Morgantown public schools. Degree, B. S. Occupation, teacher, student of law, wool grower, ranchman, and Principal of the Graded Schools. Mr. Grinnell married Matilda Gunnarson.

JAMES P. HALE, born April 15, 1846, at Bluffton. Residence, Bluffton, Indiana. Educated in Bluffton schools. Degree, B. S. Occupation and position, County Surveyor, 1872-75;

teacher; admitted to the bar 1876; attorney at law; Prosecuting Attorney for four years; Mayor of Bluffton five years. Mr. Hale married Miss Delia E. Wilson, June 10, 1880.

ELISHA ASBURY HAMILTON, born December 28, 1851, at Orleans. Residence, Whitehall, Illinois (1889). Educated in part at Greencastle. Degrees, A. B. and A. M., Indiana University, and B. D. from Drew Theological Seminary, 1875. Occupation and position, for three years a theological student; entered the Illinois Conference, 1875; minister in the Methodist Episcopal Church. Has been pastor in Wapella, Gibson City, Rantoul, Tolono, Monticello, LeRoy and Whitehall, all towns of Illinois. Mr. Hamilton married Lura Wolfe, of Clinton, Illinois, September 24, 1878.

FREDERICK HEINER, born September 2, 1852, in Bath County, Kentucky. Residence, Indianapolis. Degrees, B. S. and LL. B. Occupation and position, lawyer; Librarian of Supreme Court; was nominated as Judge on the Democratic ticket, but not elected.

MARY (HANNAMAN) JAMES, born in Indianapolis. Residence, Duluth, Minnesota (1889). Educated at the Methodist Female College, Indianapolis. Degrees, A. B. and A. M. Occupation, postmistress at Aberdeen, Dakota. After marriage moved to Columbia, Dakota Territory. Miss Hannaman married Mr. John R. James, of Columbia, Dakota Territory, at Watertown, Dakota Territory. Mrs. James was Class Historian at the reunion of Class 1872, June 10, 1889.

JOHN H. KENDALL, born July 19, 1851, Jamestown, Ohio. Residence, Tarentum, Pennsylvania. Educated at Cedarville, Ohio. Degrees A. B. and A. M. Occupation and position, studied theology at the Reformed Presbyterian Theological Seminary in Philadelphia. Licensed to preach in 1876 and ordained minister of the gospel the same year. Pastor of the Reformed Presbyterian Congregation at Ryegate, Vermont, for nearly ten years. After giving up his charge in Ryegate he traveled in Great Britain and Ireland. On returning, accepted a call from the Reformed Presbyterian Congregation at Tarentum, Pennsylvania.

HICKMAN NEW KING, born October 2, 1840, Jennings County. Residence, Petersburg, Indiana, 1889. Educated in Jennings and Morgan County schools. Degree, B. S. Mr. King entered college in 1866, the next year he taught, returned in 1868, entered the Junior Class; taught in 1870–71, entered Senior Class, graduating in 1872. Occupation and position, minister and elder in the Methodist Episcopal Church. Served in the army during the late war. Was honorably discharged after a three years' service. Was in the battle of Pea Ridge, Arkansas, Perryville, Kentucky, Murfreesborough, Missionary Ridge, Kenesaw Mountain.

SAMUEL LILLY, born May 11, 1841, New Lisbon, Henry County. Residence, Fowler, Ind. Educated in New Lisbon common schools. Degrees, A. B. and A. M. Occupation and position, teacher, Principal of LaGrange school, 1872–73; of Bluffton schools, 1873–75; of Worthington schools, 1875–76; of Gosport, 1876–88; now (1889) Principal of Fowler schools. Mr. Lilly married Miss Mary M. Gray, of Gosport, July 1, 1874.

WILLIAM E. McCORD, born March 21, 1850, Centreville, Indiana. Residence, Martinsville, Indiana. Educated in the schools of Bainbridge, Gosport and Clayton. Degrees, A. B., A. M. and LL. B. Occupation, attorney at law and farmer. Mr. McCord married Miss Mary Callis October 31, 1883.

JOHN BROWN MALOTT, born 1846, at Bedford. Residence, Erie, Lawrence County, Indiana. Educated in Bedford schools. Degree, B. S. Occupation and position, teacher, farmer, dealer in live stock, surveyor, soldier in Company A, Sixty-seventh Regiment of Indiana Volunteers, Union Army. Was engaged in the battles of Mumfordville, Kentucky (was taken prisoner with the regiment), and Chickasaw Heights, Arkansas Heights, Port Gibson, Champion Hills, Black River Bridge, and Jackson, Mississippi, and was wounded in the charge on the works at the siege of Vicksburg, Mississippi. Mr. Malott has always been an advocate of temperance, religion, and republican institutions.

JOSEPH EDWIN MELLETTE, born 1848, in Henry County. Residence, Watertown, South Dakota. Educated in Muncie schools. Degrees, A. B. and A. M. Occupation and position, study and practice of law; Prosecuting Attorney for four years in Muncie. Mr. Mellette married Miss Ella Dunn, of Bloomington.

EDMUND MOONEY, born 1869, in Johnson County. Residence, Columbus, Indiana. Educated in Columbus public schools. Degree, A. B. Occupation, merchant and manufacturer. Mr. Mooney married Miss Laura Henley, of Bloomington, September, 1887.

JOSEPH SHANNON NAVE, born September 19, 1851, at Attica. Residence, Attica, Indiana. Educated in Attica schools. Degree, B. S. Attended the Law School of Michigan University. Occupation and position, lawyer, Representative of Fountain County, 1879–1883.

PIERCE NORTON, born September 3, 1850, at Marion. Residence, Indianapolis. Educated in Marion schools. Degrees, A. B. and LL. B. Occupation and position, studied law, in addition to the University course, in the office of Joseph E. McDonald; Deputy Prosecuting Attorney of the city court; in 1882 was elected Judge of the Criminal Court of Marion County, till the expiration of his four years' term; in 1885 traveled in Europe. Judge Norton married Miss Maud E. Lynn, April 14, 1887.

ROBERT ALEXANDER OGG, born December 14, 1848, in Noble County, Ohio. Residence, Greencastle, Indiana. Educated at the public schools and at Summerfield, Ohio, high school. Degree, B. S. Occupation and position, teacher. In Ellettsville, two years; Mitchell, four years; Professor in DePauw Female College one year, and New Albany high school seven years. At present (1889) Superintendent of the public schools in Greencastle. Local minister in the M. E. Church. An efficient and active member of the Teacher's Association of Southern Indiana. Was its President in 1886. Mr. Ogg married Miss Louise H. Hutchinson, of Mitchell, December 25, 1877.

RICHARD LEE ORGAN, born December 8, 1850, in Wayne County. Residence, Carmi, Illinois. Educated at Fairfield school. Degrees, B. S., LL. B., 1873. Occupation and position, attorney at law; loan and real estate business; State Senator in 1884, for four years.

FRANCIS KELLOGG RAYMOND, born January 3, 1852, in Cambridge City. Residence, Winfield, Kansas. Educated at Miami University, Oxford, Ohio. Degrees, A. B. and A. M., Indiana University. Occupation and position, attorney at law; assistant city editor *Indianapolis News;* 1872 to 1880, Law Reporter; official Stenographer Thirteenth Judicial District, Kansas, since 1881. Mr. Raymond married Miss M. K. Brown, September 13, 1881.

CHARLES H. STRONG, born December 20, 1848, in Ellettsville. Residence, Garnett, Kansas. Educated at Monroe County schools. Degrees, A. B. and A. M., B. D. from United Presbyterian Theological Seminary, Xenia, Ohio. Occupation and position, student of Theology; preacher of the gospel; pastor of First United Presbyterian Church, Garnett, Kansas; author of a history of the Waldensian Church. Mr. Strong married Miss Emma Blair, of Bloomington.

DAVID THOMAS WORLEY, born November 4th, 1841, in Scott County. Residence, Newtonia, Missouri. Educated at Orleans, Indiana. Degree, B. S. Occupation and position, teaching, farming, stock raising; Principal of graded and high schools. Was a soldier in the War of the Rebellion. Fought at Stone River, Shiloh, Chattanooga, Franklin and Nashville, Tennessee, Atlanta, Georgia. Lost his left arm at Averasboro, North Carolina. Mr. Worley married Sarah C. Baker, Mason County, Illinois, August 19, 1873.

The compiler is indebted to Mrs. James, the Class Historian in 1889, for many interesting items in these sketches of Class 1872.

1873.

HERMANN GLEASON BRADFORD. Residence, Louisville, Kentucky. Degree, B. S. Occupation, jeweler and book-keeper in a jewelry store, Louisville, Kentucky.

JOHN BUNYAN CAMPBELL, born March 11, 1856, at Bloomington. Residence, Toledo, Ohio. Educated at home by his father, Professor Campbell, of Indiana University, and in the district schools. Degrees, A. B. and A. M. Occupation and position, music teacher and composer; organist in Parks Chapel, Methodist Episcopal Church, Indianapolis, in 1879; Professor of Music in Wesleyan University, Delaware, Ohio. Mr. Campbell exhibited when a mere child a superior musical talent, and has from his graduation made music his profession.

EMMA R. (JENNINGS) CLARK, born at Cataract, Owen County. Residence, Vincennes, Indiana. Educated in the Owen

County schools. Degree, B. S. Miss Jennings married Rev. Thos. J. Clark, of Class 1872.

WEBSTER DIXON, born January 9, 1854, at Paris, Indiana. Residence, Columbus, Indiana. Educated at Vernon Academy. Degrees, A. B. and A. M. Occupation and position, lawyer; Clerk of Indiana House of Representatives in 1879; Prosecuting Attorney in the Ninth Judicial Circuit of Indiana; Democratic candidate for Representative of Jennings County in 1870; held a joint debate with Mr. Overmeyer, Republican candidate; orator of the Σ. X. Fraternity in 1880.

SANFORD HUTCHISON DRYBREAD, born September 17, 1848, in Bartholomew County, Indiana. Residence, Taylorsville, Indiana. Educated in Bartholomew County schools, Williamsburg High School, and graded school, Columbus. Degree, B. S. Occupation and position, attorney at law; formerly proprietor of a flouring mill at Taylorsville; Justice of the Peace in Bartholomew County.

ALFRED W. FULLERTON, born March 2, 1850, in Monroe County, Indiana. Residence, Spencer, Indiana. Educated in the public schools of Monroe County. Degrees, A. B. and LL. B. Occupation, attorney at law.

THERESA (LUZADDER) GREGORY, born November 8, in Guernsey County, Ohio. Residence, Brooklyn, Morgan County, Indiana. Educated in Bloomington graded schools. Degree, B. S.

JAMES FRANKLIN HEADY. Residence, Glendale, Ohio. Degrees, A. B., A. M. and, from Miami Medical College, M. D. Occupation and position, practitioner of medicine; resident physician at Cincinnati Hospital.

JAMES ROSS LATIMER, born July 14, 1851, Bloomington. Residence, Londonderry, Guernsey County, Ohio. Educated in the Monroe County common schools. Degrees A. B. and A. M. Occupation, teaching and studying theology. Position, pastor of the Reformed Presbyterian Church, Londonderry, Ohio, 1882. Professor of Greek in Geneva College for some time.

WILLIAM BROWN McCLINTIC, born November 9, 1852, Peru, Indiana. Residence, Peru, Indiana. Educated in the Peru

High School. Degrees, A. B. and A. M. Occupation, for six years in the United States Postal Service. Since, attorney at law.

JAMES DARWIN MAXWELL, JR., born July 14, 1850, Bloomington. Residence, Bloomington, Indiana. Educated in Bloomington Academy. Degrees, A. B. and A. M., and from Miami Medical College, Ohio, M. D. Dr. Maxwell also studied medicine at Bellevue Medical College, New York.' Occupation and position, practicing physician; Coroner of Monroe County.

GILES S. MITCHELL, residence, Cincinnati, Ohio. Degrees, A. B. and A. M., Indiana University, and M. D., Medical College, Ohio. Member of Cincinnati Academy of Medicine. Fellow of the Cincinnati Obstetrical Society. Dr. Mitchell also attended medical lectures in the Universities of Vienna and Strasburg. In '1875–76 Dr. Mitchell traveled extensively in Europe.

JOHN S. NEWBY, born December 20, 1848, Mooresville. Residence, Martinsville, Indiana. Educated in Mooresville High School. Degrees A. B. and A. M. Occupation, attorney at law.

ROBERT M. PIATT, born April 7, 1840, in Boonville, Indiana. Residence, Witchita, Kansas. Educated at Collegiate Institute, Rockport, Indiana. Degrees A. B. and A. M. Occupation and position, lawyer; Secretary of the School Board at Boonville; Deputy Prosecuting Attorney. Mr. Piatt married Miss Alma Fellows, Class 1874.

JOHN A. RAMSEY, residence, Chase City, Virginia. Degrees, A. B. and A. M. Occupation and position, teacher; student of Theology; ordained minister of the United Presbyterian Church, and missionary to, and teacher of, the freedmen, Chase City, Virginia. Mr. Ramsey married Miss Bryan, daughter of Rev. John Bryan, of Bloomington.

WILLIAM FRANCIS LEWIS SANDERS, born September 12, 1849, in Maxville, Indiana. Residence, New Albany, Indiana. Educated at Spencer County common schools and at home. Degree, B. S. Occupation and position, teacher and author; Principal of Owensville graded schools, 1873 to 1876; teacher in Bloomington high school and in the college Preparatory Department, 1876 to 1879; Assistant Principal in the high school, New Albany; author of "Analysis by Diagrams;" "The Structure of the English Sentence and Sentential Analysis by Diagrams," and a "Chart of the English Verb." In 1889 Superintendent of the Connersville schools.

NEWELL SANDERS, born July 12, 1850, in Owen County, Indiana. Residence, Chattanooga, Tennessee. Educated at Owen County schools. 'Degree, B. S. Occupation and position, for four years book-seller in Bloomington; since, a manufacturer of plows and other agricultural implements; member of the Board of Education of the city of Chattanooga. Inventor of the Chattanooga patent chilled plow. Mr. Sanders married Miss Corinne Dodds, October 28, 1873.

CORINNE (DODDS) SANDERS, born July 4, in Bloomington, Indiana. Residence, Chattanooga, Tennessee. Educated at Bloomington public schools. Degree, B. S. In addition to her domestic duties, Mrs. Sanders has been an assistant to her husband in business matters, in book-keeping and in manufacturing. In company with her husband, she is now (1889) visiting the great Exposition in Paris, France, more for improvement than amusement.

BURNET MILTON SHORT, born December 31, 1853, at Springville. Residence, Fredonia, Kansas. Educated at Springville District School. Degrees, A. B. and A. M. Occupation and position, lawyer; elected Mayor of Fredonia, Kansas, in 1878; reëlected 1879. Mr. Short made an address at Fredonia, at a Masonic celebration, which was published.

THOMAS J. TERHUNE, born March 8, 1848, in Greene County, Indiana. Residence, Lebanon, Indiana. Degrees, A. B. and A. M., LL. B. (1874). Occupation and position, lawyer; elected Judge in 1878.

1874.

WILLIAM WIRT BECK, born February 9, 1851, in Warren County, Kentucky. Residence, Walla-Walla, Washington Territory, formerly Franklin, Tennessee. Educated in private school. Degrees, A. B. and A. M. Occupation, teaching, until 1879; preacher of the gospel, working zealously and successfully in Washington Territory.

BARON D. CRAWFORD, born January 11, 1849, in New Albany. Residence, Plymouth, Indiana. Educated in New Albany public schools. Degrees, A. B. and A. M. Occupation and position, attorney-at-law; Prosecuting Attorney for two terms in the Fourth Judicial Circuit, Indiana. Mr. Crawford, before entering college, and in vacation, while at college, supported himself by his trade, a bricklayer.

JOHN F. DILLON, born August 21, 1852, in Southern Indiana. Residence, Pierre, South Dakota. Degrees, B. S. and LL. B. Occupation, practice of law, five years in Jasper, and since in Pierre, South Dakota. Mr. Dillon is the author of "Pleading and Practice in Dakota." Mr. J. F. Dillon married Miss Emma Sherritt, of Portersville, Indiana.

CHARLES HALL DILLON, born December 18, 1853, in Dubois County, Indiana. Residence, Mitchell, South Dakota. Educated at Dubois High School. Degrees, B. S. and LL. B. Occupation, practice of law, four years, in Jasper County; in 1880 moved to Mitchell, Dakota; at present (1882) attorney at law and banker. Mr. C. H. Dillon married Miss Maud Tripp, of Yankton, South Dakota.

JAMES HERVEY DOWD, born January 15, 1846, in Vinton County, Ohio. Residence, Hebron, Indiana. Educated in the public schools and Valparaiso College. Degree, A. B. Occupation, teaching for two years; afterwards a dry goods merchant.

ALMA (FELLOWS) PIATT, born at Bloomfield. Residence, Boonville, Indiana (1881). Educated in the public schools of Bloomington. Degree, A. B. Occupation, practical domestic economy. Married Robert M. Piatt, Class '73, October 29, 1874.

WILLIAM S. FISH, born January 6, 1856, at Bloomington, Indiana. Residence, Anaheim, Los Angeles County, California. Educated in Bloomington graded schools. Degree, A. B. Occupation and position, member of engineer corps of the Southern Pacific Railroad; compositor in printing office, and viticulturist.

WILLIAM JOHN FRAZER, born March 22, 1853, at Paoli, Indiana. Residence, Shelbyville, Illinois (1888). Educated in Paoli schools. Degree, B. S. Occupation and position, student of law; teacher; student of theology, Princeton (New Jersey) Theological Seminary, for three years; stated supply at Worthington; pastor of Presbyterian Church, Bedford, Indiana, 1882; stated supply at Shelbyville, Illinois. The scientific course not requiring classical studies, Mr. Frazer devoted three years to the study of Greek with private tutors.

PIERRE GRAY, born May 2, 1853, New Madison, Darke County, Ohio. Residence, Indianapolis. Educated in the Union City schools. Degree, A. B. Occupation and position, student of law in the office of his father, Isaac P. Gray, lawyer. In November, 1875, admitted to practice at Randolph County bar, October 24, 1876, admitted to the Supreme Court of Indiana, in 1875–76 City Civil Engineer, City Attorney in 1882, in 1885–89 Secretary of Governor Isaac P. Gray.

LOUISA S. GREGG, born July 23, Delaware, Ohio. Residence, Columbia City, Indiana. Educated in the public schools of Columbia City and Fort Wayne. Degree, A. B. Occupation, teaching.

ALFRED HARRISON HARRYMAN, born October 27, 1849, Mooresville, Indiana. Residence, No. 134 Van Buren street, Chicago, 1888. Educated at Mooresville, Indiana. Degrees A. B., A. M. and LL. B. Occupation, journalist. Mr. Harryman, in 1881–83, was city editor of the *Columbus Democrat*, 1883–85, editor of the *Martinsville Republican*, managing editor of the *Muncie Daily News*, 1885–86, editor of the *Current*, 1886–88. Mr. Harryman, outside of his literary work, took an active part in the campaigns of 1880 and 1886 in making speeches in Indiana, Ohio and Illinois under the direction of the Republican State Committees of these States. Mr. Harryman was the alumni poet at the reunion of Class '76.

JAMES W. HEAD, residence, Shelbyville, Kentucky. Degrees, A. B. and A. M. Occupation and position, lawyer, Prosecuting Attorney. In 1881 a prominent candidate for Judge of Shelby County and the Quarterly Courts of Kentucky.

ANNA MARY (BUSKIRK) HILL, born at Bloomington, September 4. Residence, Bloomington, Indiana. Educated in the Bloomington public schools and seminary. Degrees A. B. Married Mr. Nathaniel Hill, of Class '75.

CRAIG HUNTER, born October 4, 1853, in Bloomington, Indiana. Residence, Topeka, Kansas. Educated in Bloomington, one year at Notre Dame University. Degree, A. B. Occupation and position, attorney-at-law; at present (1883) chief clerk of General Roadmaster's office, of the Topeka & Santa Fé Railroad. Member of the Baptist Church.

SAMUEL MITCHELL JEFFERSON, born July 28, 1849, in Kent County, Delaware. Residence, Covington, Kentucky. Educated in Illinois common schools and Eureka College, Illinois. Degree, A. B. Occupation and position, minister of the gospel; pastor of Christian Church, Lafayette, Indiana, 1874–77; pastor of Fourth-street Christian Church, Covington, Kentucky, 1877–82; Recording Secretary of the Christian Foreign Missionary Society. Author of several published addresses and contributor to religious periodicals.

SARAH BELLE (LATIMER) KELLEY, born in Monroe County. Residence, Bloomington, Indiana. Educated in Monroe County common schools. Degree, B. S. Occupation, a teacher for several years.

MARY CAROLINE McCOLLOUGH, born in Bloomington, Indiana. Residence, Bloomington, Indiana. Educated in Bloomington schools. Degree, B. S. Member of Presbyterian Church.

JOHN HENRY McMILLAN, born October 29, 1851, in Cedarville, Ohio. Residence, Monmouth, Illinois (1887). Educated in Cedarville High School. Degree, A. B. Occupation and position, teacher, Professor of Greek and Mathematics, Smith's Grove College, Kentucky; Superintendent of the Cedarville Schools; Principal of Xenia High School; County School Examiner; Professor of Latin, Monmouth College, Monmouth, Illinois. Professor McMillan married Miss Ida Lizzie Woodburn, of Bloomington, in 1876, of Class '75.

DAVID HOWE MAXWELL, born in Bloomington. Residence, Bloomington, Indiana. Educated in Bloomington High School. Degree, A. B. Occupation, farmer.

LAURA (HENLEY) MOONEY, A. B., Columbus, Indiana. Married Mr. Ed. Mooney, Class '72.

CHARLES T. MOORE, born January 19, 1854, in Washington County, Illinois. Residence, Okawville, Illinois. Educated at McKendree College, Lebanon, Illinois. Degree, A. B. Occupation, teacher; Principal of Nashville (Illinois) public schools; since 1872, attorney at law.

MARGARET IRENE (DODDS) ROSE, born February 17, at Bloomington, Indiana. Residence, Muncie, Indiana. Educated in Bloomington graded schools. Degree, B. S. Married Mr. T. Rose, Class '75.

DAVID NEWTON TAYLOR, born September 13, 1850, at Harrodsburgh, Indiana. Residence, Terre Haute, Indiana. Educated at Lincoln University, Illinois. Degrees, A. B. and LL. B. Occupation, lawyer. Democratic candidate (1880) for Legislature for Vigo County. Was defeated by a small majority, but 200 ahead of the State (Democratic) ticket.

JESSE DAY TRUEBLOOD, born June 24, 1849, in Parke County, Indiana. Residence, Danville, Illinois. Educated in the Parke County common schools and Bloomingdale Academy. Degrees, A. B. and LL. B. Occupation and position, lawyer; by birth a "Friend," he joined the Presbyterian Church while at the University; was admitted to practice in the Supreme Court of Illinois in 1876, and in the United States Circuit Courts and District Courts for State of Illinois in 1877.

CHARLES WHITTED, born December 12, 1853, at Springville, Indiana. Residence, Owensburg, Indiana. Educated in public schools. Degree, B. S. Occupation, hardware merchant; and dealer in stock.

GEORGE WASHINGTON WIGGS, born December 2, 1853, at Hollandsburgh, Ohio. Residence, Union City, Indiana, in Chicago, Illinois (1886). Educated at high school, Union City, Indiana. Degree, B. S. Occupation, agent of Charles H. Cummings, grain exporter, Philadelphia; contributor to the *Waverly Magazine*, Boston, Massachusetts, and to the New York, Cincinnati and Indianapolis dailies; in commission business; member of Chicago Board of Trade; formerly proprietor of the weekly magazine, *The Current*. Mr. Wiggs married Anna May Oldfield, a frequent contributor to *The Current*.

1875.

DEWITT CLINTON BARNETT, born June 19, 1850, in Edinburg, Indiana. Residence, Harrisonville, Cass County, Missouri. Educated at high school, Nineveh, Indiana, and Northwestern

Christian University (now Butler). Degree, A. B. Occupation and position, teaching and preaching. In 1883, attorney at law, Kansas, Missouri. Removed shortly after to Harrisonville, Missouri. In 1878–79, Mr. Barnett was Principal of the high school in Knightstown, Indiana. Has lectured on political, religious and educational subjects, and has contributed many articles on these subjects; and, also, articles of fiction, poetry and travel, for several journals.

EDWIN WILSON BLACK, born July 3, 1852, in Paoli, Indiana. Residence, Terre Haute, Indiana. Educated at Paoli schools. Degree, A. B. Occupation, attorney at law.

LUTHER B. BUNNEL, born May 23, 1849, in Warren County, Ohio. Residence, Wichita, Kansas. Educated at Earlham College, Indiana. Degrees, A. B. and LL. B. Occupation, real estate, mortgage and loan business. Position, Trustee of First Presbyterian Church, Wichita.

JERRY COLLINS, born in County Cork, Ireland, 1850. Residence, Fort Benton, Montana Territory. Educated at public schools of Wabash, Indiana, and Kokomo, Indiana, (school of Prof. Hopkins). Degree, B. S. Occupation, editor and publisher. First, of the *Wabash Courier;* second, *The Logansport Pharos,* and since 1881, *The Fort Benton River Press,* Montana Territory. Position, Secretary of the Montana Press Association. Wedded to newspaper work. Married (1879) to Miss Letta E. Fitzgerald, of Logansport.

ALBERT DAVIS, born February 13, 1849, in Billingsville, Franklin County, Indiana. Residence, Cowles, Nebraska Territory. Educated at common schools. Degrees, B. S. and LL. B. Occupation, attorney at law and wool grower.

SAMUEL CLELLAND DODDS, born January 29, 1854, in Bloomington, Indiana. Residence, Bloomington, Indiana. Educated at Bloomington high school. Degree, B. S. Occupation, for four years book-seller and stationer; and since manufacturer of furniture, more particularly chairs. Deacon in the Walnut Street Presbyterian Church, and Superintendent of the Sabbath School. Mr. Dodds married Miss Nellie Winters, of Bloomington.

WASHINGTON C. DUNCAN, born June 24, 1851, Marion County, Indiana. Residence, Nashville, Indiana. Educated in the

Brown County common schools. Degree, B. S. Occupation and position, student of law at Indiana University, lawyer, Prosecuting Attorney of the Ninth Judicial District of Indiana, member of Legislature, 1886, and one of the Educational Committee.

LILIAN MAY FOLAND, born, Spartansburg, Indiana. Residence, Terre Haute, Indiana. Educated in Terre Haute public schools and at Bloomington. Degree, B. S. Occupation and position, teaching, assistant teacher in Terre Haute High School.

JOSEPH E. HENLEY, born April 21, 1856, Orange County, Indiana. Residence, Bloomington, Indiana. Degree, A. B. Occupation and position, teacher, attorney at law, City Clerk of Bloomington, Indiana, 1879-81, Deputy City Attorney, 1881, Professor of Greek and German, Smith's Grove College, Kentucky, School Superintendent, Shoals, Indiana.

NATHANIEL USHER HILL, born June 21, 1851, Brazil, Indiana. Residence, Bloomington, Indiana. Educated in Ladoga Academy and Howard College, Kokomo. Degrees, B. S. and LL. B. Occupation, attorney at law and banker. Mr. Hill married Miss Anna Buskirk, Class '74.

EDWIN RANDOLPH HITT, born at Vincennes, Indiana, September 12, 1852. Residence, Vincennes, Indiana. Educated at Vincennes University and at Earlham College, 1870-71. Degree, A. B. Occupation, teaching, Sunday-school Superintendent. Mr. E. R. Hitt is the youngest son of the late W. W. Hitt, M. D., of Vincennes.

ELIZABETH G. HUGHES, born at Logansport, Indiana. Residence, Bloomington, Indiana. Educated in Oxford Seminary. Degrees, A. B., M. S. *pro merito*, 1887. Occupation, teaching, post-graduate student in Indiana University, 1885, in Department of Biology.

HIRAM M. LOGSDEN, born June 28, 1852, in Spencer County, Indiana. Residence, Rockport, Indiana. Educated in Spencer County schools. Degree, B. S. Occupation, lawyer.

JAMES F. MCGREGOR, born May 6, 1848, in Ritchie County, West Virginia. Residence, Cory, Indiana. Educated in Mt. Vernon, Indiana. Degrees, A. B. and B. D. from Drew Theological Seminary. Occupation and position, student of theology; minister in Methodist Episcopal Church.

JOHN MCGREGOR, born December 9, 1853, in Switzerland County, Indiana. Residence, Madison, Indiana. Educated in Jennings County common schools and Friends' Academy. Degree, B. S. Occupation and position, study and practice of law; attorney for City of Madison.

WILLIAM J. MCLEOD, A. B., Gunnison, Colorado. Lawyer.

IDA ELIZABETH (WOODBURN) MCMILLAN, born October 21, in Bloomington. Residence, Monmouth, Illinois. Educated in Bloomington High School. Married. Prof. J. H. McMillan, Class '74.

SILVESTER ALONZO MONTGOMERY, born December 13, 1850, in Lincoln County, Tennessee. Died March 10, 1881, near Carmi, Illinois. Educated by his father, Rev. Mr. Montgomery, and at the Enfield (Illinois) School. Occupation, teacher at Grayville, Illinois. Was School Superintendent. A member of the United Presbyterian Church.

JOHN BENONI MORRISON, born October 31, 1851, in Salem, Indiana. Residence, Indianapolis, Indiana. Educated in Indianapolis High School and Earlham College, Indiana. Degrees, B. S., and from Philadelphia Dental College, D. D. S. Occupation and position, study of dentistry at Knightstown and at Philadelphia; practice of dentistry at, and Professor of Clinical Dentistry in, Indiana Dental College, Indianapolis. Valedictorian of Class of '79, Philadelphia Dental College.

RAYMOND NAVE. A. B. Attica, Indiana. Lawyer.

FRANCIS MARION PARKER, born February 13, 1844, in Cumberland County, North Carolina. Residence, Bloomfield, Indiana. Educated at Greene County schools. Degree, B. S. Occupation, teaching, land surveying and civil engineering.

THEODORE FRELINGHUYSEN ROSE, born December 18, 1849, in Fairfield, Indiana. Residence, Muncie, Indiana. Educated at public schools. Degree, B. S. Occupation and position, attorney at law; City Attorney of Muncie for four years. Mr. Rose married Miss Margaret Irene Dodds, daughter of Dr. J. F. Dodds, of Bloomington.

WILLIAM W. SPENCER, born October 7, 1851, in Jefferson County, Indiana. Residence, Indianapolis, Indiana. Educated at public schools and Friends' High School, Jennings County, Indiana. Degrees, B. S. and LL. B. Occupation, attorney at law.

DAVID FRIZZELL WHITE, born January 11, 1849, in Casey, Illinois. Residence, Brookville, Indiana. Educated at Brookville schools. Degree, B. S. Occupation, practicing law. Mr. White has devoted some time to lecturing on temperance.

WILLIAM STUART WHITTINGILL, born January 16, 1853, in Warrick County, Indiana. Residence, Selvin, Indiana. Educated at high schools of Boonville, Oakland City and Gentryville. Degree, B. S. Occupation, teaching and attorney at law. In 1880 was Republican candidate for Representative, and though defeated, ran far ahead of the strength of the party in the county. Engaged in the study of social questions and political economy. Member of the Methodist Episcopal Church.

JAMES R. WILLIAMS, born December 27, 1851, in Burnt Prairie, White County, Illinois. Residence, Carmi, Illinois. Educated at home and county schools of Carmi and Enfield, Illinois. Degree, A. B., and from Union College of Law, Chicago, LL. B. Occupation and position, lawyer: Master in Chancery for two years.

WARREN B. WILSON. A. B. Chicago, Illinois. Lawyer.

1876.

GEORGE BANTA, born July 16, 1857, in Covington, Kentucky. Residence, Menasha, Wisconsin. Educated at Franklin Academy, and Franklin College through Junior year. Degree, A. B. Occupation and position, teacher; law student, 1876–78; local insurance agent, 1878–81; special insurance agent, National Insurance Company, Hartford, 1881–82; special agent Standard Fire Insurance Company, of England, till 1884; State agent, for State of Wisconsin, for Phenix Fire Insurance Company, of Brooklyn, New York; President of Φ. Δ. Θ. Fraternity, 1880–82; editor of "Flying Leaves," a book of 300 pages of literary selections. Mr. Banta married Ellen Lee Pleasants, June 16, 1886.

LENA (ADAMS) BECK, born February 20, at Standford. Residence, Bloomington, Indiana. Educated at Bloomington High School. Degree, A. B. Occupation, for two years a teacher; since a wife, mother and housekeeper, having married Prof. J. K. Beck. Mrs. Beck is an active and eloquent member of the Methodist Episcopal Church.

WILLIAM THORNTON BRANNAMAN, born at Clear Spring, Jackson County, July 15, 1846. Educated at Clear Spring school. Degree, B. S. Occupation and position, attorney at law; Prosecuting Attorney of the 42d Judicial Circuit of Indiana from 1882 to 1885.

ALICE FLORINE (RICHARDS) BRUNSON, born February 14, at Clear Spring. Residence, Eagletown, Indiana. Educated at Clear Spring school. Degree, B. S. Occupation, teaching and housewifery.

JOHN WILSON BURTON, born August 3, 1854. Residence, Marion, Illinois. Educated in Johnson County public schools and at Carbondale. Degree, A. B. Occupation and position, attorney at law; City Attorney of Carbondale, Illinois; Master in Chancery for Williamson County, Illinois, and Clerk of Appellate Court (1884).

CHARLES THOMAS CARPENTER, born December 9, 1858, at Palmetto, Tennessee. Residence, Oswego, Kansas. Educated at Palmetto Academy. Degree, A. B. Occupation and position, book-keeper and clerk in a store; now banker (July, 1886); Assistant Examiner of LaBette County teachers; deacon in Presbyterian Church; Librarian of American Bible Society. Was on one of Professor Jordan's European tramps.

HARRY WHITNEY DURAND, born October 26, 1856, at Rockford, Indiana. Residence, Chattanooga, Tennessee. Educated in Bloomington schools. Degree, A. B. Occupation and position, teacher; lawyer; Secretary of the Chattanooga Methodist Episcopal Conference. Mr. Durand is an active worker in the temperance cause.

WILLIAM BOYER DURBOROW, born January 1, 1853, in Philadelphia, Pennsylvania. Residence, Williamsport, Indiana. Educated at Wabash College, Crawfordsville. Degree, B. S. Occupation, attorney at law.

HARBERT HARRISON EDWARDS, born August 3, 1851, at Mitchell, Indiana. Residence, Bedford, Indiana. Educated at Franklin College, Indiana. Degree, B. S.. Indiana University. Occupation, dealer in grain.

CHARLES WINFIELD FIREBAUGH, born in Bucyrus, Ohio. Residence, Austin, Texas. Educated at Illinois State Normal University, Normal, Illinois. Occupation and position, selling hardware in Texas (1881). Member of Presbyterian Church.

FINLEY MILLIGAN FOSTER, born December 1, 1853, in Cedarville, Ohio. Residence, Bellefontaine, Logan County, Ohio. Educated in Cedarville (Ohio) High School. Degree, A. B. Occupation and position, study of theology and the ministry; pastor of the Bellefontaine Reformed Presbyterian Church.

ROBERT FRANCIS GRAHAM, born April 22, 1853, in Richland, Indiana. Residence, Greeley, Colorado. Educated at Richland Academy. Degrees, A. B. and, from Miami Medical College, M. D. Occupation and position, physician; assistant physician in Cleveland Hospital for the Insane; resident physician in Cincinnati Hospital, and afterward practiced in Rushville, and now practicing in Greeley, Colorado.

SAMUEL ERNEST HARWOOD, born December 20, 1848, near Nashville, Tennessee. Residence, Attica, Indiana. Educated at home; private school; Andrew College, Trenton, Tennessee, and at Southern Illinois College, Carbondale. Degree, A. B. Professor Harwood has been a teacher almost continuously since his graduation, and a member of the Methodist Episcopal Church. He was principal of a seminary at Grand Tower, Illinois; superintendent at Carbondale, Illinois, at Spencer and at Attica. He commenced teaching before he was nineteen years old. He was eight years in passing through college, earning money by teaching in order to pay his way. Prof. Harwood married Miss Carrie E. Howe, of Bloomington, May, 1878.

GEORGE THEOPHILUS HERRICK, born November 24, 1849, in Allen County, Indiana. Residence, Wabash, Indiana. Educated in public schools and Fort Wayne College, Indiana. Degree, A. B. Occupation and position, teacher, county school superintendent and attorney-at-law.

OLÉ ANNA (WILLSON) HOOD, born in Bloomington, Indiana.

Residence, New Castle, Indiana. Educated in Bloomington graded schools. Degree, A. B. Occupation, for some time a teacher in the graded schools of Bloomington. Married Rev. Mr. Hood (Class '81), pastor of the Presbyterian Church, New Castle, Indiana.

FLORA CAROLINE KENDALL, born January 13, in Galesburg, Illinois. Residence, Oakland, California. Educated at public schools, Lombard University, Galesburg, Illinois, and Smithson College, Logansport, Indiana. Degrees, A. B. and A. M., *pro merito*. Teaching in the public schools. Professor of music, Oakland, California.

JOHN ISAAC MCLAUGHLIN, born June 8, 1849, in Senecaville, Ohio. Residence, Solsberry, Indiana. Educated at Solsberry district school and Bloomington High School. Degree, A. B., and B. D. at Garret Biblical Institute. Occupation and position, teaching and studying Theology; Principal of Bloomfield High School; minister in the Methodist Episcopal Church.

PERRY GEORGE MICHENER, born September 15, 1852, in Connersville, Indiana. Residence, Connersville, Indiana. Educated at Fayette County schools. Degree, B. S. Occupation, lawyer. A teacher for two years previous.

HENRY CLAY MONTGOMERY, born July 4, 1852, in Marshall County, Tennessee. Died December 18, 1878. Educated at Palmetto Academy, Tennessee. Degree, A. B. Occupation, manager of the hardware house of Montgomery Bros.

EDGAR ALLEN SHIELDS, born July 9, 1853, in Paddy's Run, Butler County, Ohio. Residence, Muncie, Indiana. Educated at Indiana University Peparatory Department. Degrees, A. B. and A. M., *pro merito*. From Jefferson Medical College, Philadelphia, M. D., in 1880. Occupation, physician. Appointed, January, 1877, member of the Pension Board of Examining Surgeons, at Muncie, Indiana. Married Miss F. May Barbour, September 6, 1880.

NEWTON BROADUS SMITH, born July 19, 1851, in Jefferson County, Kentucky. Residence, Kokomo, Indiana. Educated at Howard County common schools, Williamstown graded school, and student at Howard College, Kokomo. Degree, A. B. Occupation and position, student of law, Indiana University, and, also, at Virginia University; attorney at law; a member of the Christian Church, an advocate of temperance, and a Democrat.

IDA MAY (PARKS) WALKER, born in Bedford Indiana. Residence, San Buena Ventura, California. Educated at Bedford and Franklin schools. Degree, B. S. Married John A. Walker, Cashier of Ventura Bank, December 31, 1877.

FLORA (BRYAN) WEIR, born April 24, Pittsburgh, Pennsylvania. Residence, New Castle, Indiana, 1889, formerly of Leavenworth and Baxter Springs. Educated in the Bloomington public schools. Degree, A. B. Class Historian of 1876. Miss Bryan married Mr. J. Crawford Weir, a student, but not a graduate of the University. Mr. Weir is now (1889) Superintendent of the New Castle schools.

JAMES ALBERT WOODBURN, A. M. See Faculty list.

SAMUEL BROWN WYLIE, M. S. See Faculty list.

JOHN ALFRED BECK, born February 4, 1850, Beck's Mill, Indiana. Residence, Beck's Mill, Indiana. Educated in the public schools and Professor May's Academy, Salem, Indiana. Degree, B. S. Occupation and position, teacher, Superintendent of the schools of Washington County, 1882.

BENJAMIN FRANKLIN BENNETT, born May 31, 1854, Adams, Indiana. Residence, Greensburg, Indiana. Educated in the district schools and Greensburg High School. Degree, A. B. Occupation, studying and practicing law.

ANDREW SPENCE DICKEY, born September 7, 1850, Fayette County, Indiana. Residence, Tipton, Indiana. Educated in the Tipton public schools and Waveland Academy. Degree, A. B., and from the Central College of Physicians, Indianapolis, M. D. Occupation and position, teacher in the Tipton schools 1877–78, physician and surgeon, elder in the United Presbyterian Bethsaida Church.

ALLAN CATHCART DURBOROW, JR., born November 10, 1857, Philadelphia, Pennsylvania. Residence, Chicago, Illinois. Educated in the Williamsport High School, for two years at the Wabash College, Crawfordsville, and three years at the Indiana University. Degree, A. B. Occupation, mercantile pursuits, represented the Athenian Society as anniversary orator, 1876.

ALBERT DICKSON GOURLEY, born November 18, 1853, Bloomington, Indiana. Residence, Bloomington, Indiana. Educated in the county public schools. Degree, A. B. Occupation, farming, teaching occasionally and at present, 1886, of the firm of Baldredge & Gourley, millers.

RICHARD BUTLER HAWKINS, born November 19, 1855, Newport, Kentucky. Residence, Louisville, Kentucky. Educated in the Newport public schools. Degree, A. B., and from Cincinnati Law School, LL. B. Occupation, lawyer.

ORRIN ZEIGLER HUBBELL, born March 30, 1856, Kelso, Huntington County, Indiana. Residence, Butler, Indiana. Educated in the Butler graded schools. Degree, A. B. Occupation and position, teacher and lawyer, Superintendent Butler graded schools, Deputy Prosecuting Attorney Thirty-fifth Judicial Indiana Circuit, author of a number of addresses, reported and published in full.

ROBERT J. KIRKWOOD, born October 13, 1854, Madison, Indiana. Residence, Washington, D. C. Educated in the district schools and Hanover College. Degree, A. B. Occupation, a manufacturer, in employment of the United States, student in the National Law School, Washington, D. C.

SAMUEL HARVEY MITCHELL, born July 7, 1846, in Washington County, Indiana. Residence, Salem, Indiana. Educated in Tampico graded schools, Prof. May's graded school, Salem. Degree, A. B. Occupation and position, Principal of Hardinsburg graded schools, minister in Christian Church, 1879-81; lawyer; two terms member of the Indiana Legislature. From 1869 Mr. Mitchell, by mechanical work and teaching, procured the means for obtaining a collegiate education.

DAVID BENTON PIERSON, born October 29, 1854, in Frazeysburg, Ohio. Died March 7, 1877, at Bloomington, Indiana. Educated at home by an elder brother. In consideration of Mr. Pierson's diligence as a student, though dying before commencement, his name was enrolled among the alumni. Mr. Pierson was a member of the Methodist Episcopal Church.

CHARLES RICHARDSON, born July 19, 1853, near Columbus, Indiana. Residence, Plymouth, Indiana. Educated in Plymouth high school. Degree, A. B. Occupation, special agent and adjuster for fire insurance company.

JOSEPH BOSTON RODDY, born February 10, 1834, in Chester District, South Carolina. Died in Bloomington, Indiana, September, 1879. Educated in Monroe County schools. Degree, A. B. Occupation and position, a teacher; Captain, Thirty-first Regiment, Indiana Volunteers; was wounded at Resaca, Georgia. Was an elder in the United Presbyterian Church at the time of his death. Mr. Roddy entered Indiana University in 1860; left to go to the war in 1861; served until its close, in 1864. Commenced farming, but by reason of his wound he was compelled to leave the farm. He then entered the University to prepare for teaching. Mr. Roddy married Mary Harbison, March, 1867.

ELLSWORTH SADDLER, born October 18, 1858, in Monroe County, Indiana. Residence, Martinsville, Indiana. Educated in the Monroe County schools. Degree, A. B. Occupation, attorney-at-law.

WARREN CARNAHAN SHERMAN, born September 2, 1855, in Mount Pleasant, Indiana. Residence, Rossville, Kansas. Educated in Washington, Indiana, schools, Degree, A. B. Occupation and position, attorney-at-law, Deputy Prosecuting Attorney for Shawnee County, Kansas; merchant, dealer in heavy hardware implements. Canvassed part of Kansas in the interest of the prohibitory law, speaking in Topeka, Manhattan, Clay Centre, and also in Indiana.

ELLIS MILLIGAN SLUSS, born May 11, 1856, in Bloomington, Indiana. Died January 6, 1887. Educated in public schools, Bloomington. Degree, A. B. Occupation, mercantile; salesman in McCalla & Co.'s dry goods house, Bloomington, and afterward in the house of Marshal Field, Chicago, Illinois.

RICHARD DENNIS SPECK, born June 21, 1858, in Wyandotte, Kansas. Residence, Wyandotte, Kansas. Educated in Wyandotte High School. Degree, A. B. Occupation, clerk in the ticket agent office of the Kansas Pacific Railroad. Mr. Speck married Miss Mary Fletcher, June 30, 1885.

WILLIAM LAMBERN TAYLOR, born July 16, 1850, in Wolcottville, Indiana. Residence, Indianapolis, Indiana. Educated at Wolcottville Seminary and Hillsdale College, Michigan. Degrees, A. B. and, from Central Law School, Indiana, LL. B. Occupation, attorney at law.

THEODORUS WILLIAM JOHN WYLIE, JR., born May 26, 1858, in Bloomington. Residence, Frankfort, Kentucky (1889). Educated in Bloomington graded schools and private school. Degree, A. B. Occupation and position, four years in the United States Railway Mail Service; afterward (1882) in the United States Land Office, Watertown, Dakota Territory; in (1884) office of the *Kentucky Herald*, Newport, Kentucky; now, 1889, clerk in United States Engineer Office, Frankfort, Kentucky. Mr. Wylie married Miss Fanny Thompson, of Newport, Kentucky, June 28, 1882.

1878.

JOSEPH ADDISON ARNOLD, born December 22. 1857, in Columbus, Indiana. Residence, Columbus, Indiana. Educated at Columbus public schools. Degree, B. S. Occupation, study of law and journalism. Mr. Arnold married Miss Hattie Arwine.

ENOCH ALBERT BRYAN, born May 10, 1855, in Bloomington. Residence, Vincennes, Indiana. Educated at home and at the public schools. Degrees, A. B. and A. M., *pro merito*. Occupation, teaching; Superintendent of the Grayville graded schools. At present (1888) Professor of Latin and Greek, and President of Vincennes University.

HENRY A. BURTT, born October 8, 1852, in Utica, Indiana. Residence, Jeffersonville, Indiana. Educated at the Brownsboro Academy, Oldham County, Kentucky. Occupation, studied law for two years, and attorney at law. Degrees, B. S. and LL. B. from the Louisville Law School, 1880.

ANNA (DENNIS) CARRIER, born at Marshalton, Pennsylvania, December 20th. Degree, A. B. Educated at Westchester, Pennsylvania, and at Poughkeepsie, New York. Degree, A. B. Occupation, a teacher for three years. Married to Rev. A. C. Carrier, of Chicago Northwestern Seminary, July 16, 1885. Mrs. Carrier spent a year in Berlin, Germany, with her husband.

DALE J. CRICKENBERGER, born December 31, 1855, in Harrisburg, Virginia. Residence, Anderson, Indiana. Degree, B. S. Occupation, attorney at law and Deputy Secretary of State.

FLORA DILLON, born in Jasper County, Indiana. Residence, Bloomington. Education, Bloomington High School. Occupation, dentistry. Miss Dillon studied her profession at the Tennessee Medical College, and in the dental department took the degree D. D. S. She is at present (1890) a successful practitioner in Bloomington.

DAVID HUME ELLISON, born October 7, 1851, near Leesville, Indiana. Residence, Leesville, Indiana. Educated in the Leesville High School. Degree, B. S. Occupation and position, Principal of Leesville High School. Mr. Ellison (1889) is Superintendent of the Mitchell schools.

JAMES C. FLOYD, born November 14, 1855, St. Paul, Indiana. Residence, Indianapolis, Indiana. Educated in the public schools of St. Paul and Moore's Hill College. Degree, A. B. Occupation, for some time a piano tuner, afterward entry clerk. A member of the Methodist Episcopal Church.

ALEXANDER GWYN FOSTER, born September 21, 1858, Evansville, Indiana. Residence, El Paso, Texas. Educated in Brooklyn, New York, Polytechnic Institute. Degrees, A. B., A. M. and LL. B. from Law School in Indianapolis. Mr. Foster delivered a poem before the Φ. Δ. Θ. Convention October, 1880.

HENRY ANDERSON LEE, born November 19, 1854, Hamilton County, Indiana. Residence, Detroit, Michigan. Educated in the district schools and Anderson Select School, of which Mr. Joseph Franklin was Principal. Degree, A. B. Occupation and position, student of law, editor of a county paper, the *Republican Ledger*, for a year, then returned to the practice of law.

SIMPSON LOWE, born December 15, 1854, near Harrodsburg, Monroe County, Indiana. Residence, Bedford, Indiana. Educated at Harrodsburg school. Degree, A. B. Occupation, teaching and practice of law; Prosecuting Attorney in 1886; reëlected, 1888.

SOPHIE HORTENSE LUZADDER, born at Dover Hill. Residence, Bloomington, Indiana. Educated at graded and high schools, Bloomington. Degree, A. B. Occupation, teacher in the common and graded schools; also, in the Sunday School.

MILES ROBERT MCCLASKEY, born July 2, 1852, in Lagrange. Residence, Lagrange, Indiana. Educated at Lagrange High School and Preparatory Department Indiana University. Degree, A. B. Occupation, teacher, traveling agent and farmer.

LUCIE ALICE MAXWELL, born in Bloomington. Residence, Bloomington, Indiana. Educated at Bloomington graded schools. Degree, A. B. Assistant in the library of the University.

LOUIS MUNSON, born February 15, 1859, in Mitchell, Indiana. Residence, Chicago, Illinois, now (April, 1889) at Banning, California. Educated at Mitchell graded schools. Degree, A. B. Occupation, teaching, attorney at law, and journalism. Mr. Munson went to California as an invalid. He has been unable, through disease, to exercise his fine talents in his profession.

LEONIDAS D. ROGERS, born May 21, 1858, near Bloomington. Residence, Bloomington, Indiana. Educated at country school. Degrees, A. B. and Master of Accounts from Eastman's Business College, Poughkeepsie, New York. Occupation, commercial business and insurance agency.

QUINCY SHORT, born November 12, 1853, near Springville, Indiana. Residence, Springville, Indiana. Educated in country school. Degree, A. B. Occupation, teaching, preaching and farming. Lawrence County Evangelist of the Christian Church in 1882.

FRANKLIN PIERCE SMITH, born July 9, 1854, in Salem. Residence, Bedford, Indiana. Educated at Salem. Degree, A. B. Occupation, teaching; Principal of Salem High School (1882), now (1888) Principal of High School, Orleans; Superintendent of the Methodist Sunday School.

FRANCIS M. SPRAKER, born February 6, 1850, in Decatur County, Indiana. Residence, Logansport, Indiana. Educated at Kokomo, Indiana, and Hartsville University. Degree, A. B. Occupation, Principal of the Graded Schools, Sardinia, Decatur County, Indiana, for two years, and afterward Principal of the North Side School, Logansport, Indiana.

FREDERICK TREUDLEY, born September 24, 1852, in New Brighton, Pennsylvania. Residence, Union City, Indiana, now (1889) Youngstown, Ohio. Educated at Hiram College, Hiram, Ohio. Occupation, teaching, first year after graduation, Ellettsville schools; second year, Principal of High School, Union

City, and since then Superintendent of Public Schools, Union City. Mr. Trendley married Miss Mary Moss, of Bloomington.

BENJAMIN VAIL, JR., born June 23, 1854, in Wilmington, Indiana. Residence, Washington, D. C. Educated at Aurora, Indiana, High School. Degree, A. B. Occupation and position, journalist; clerk in the United States Department of the Interior, April, 1881; promoted to place of Special Examiner, United States Pension Office, February 1, 1882. Author of "The Poet's Tribute to Garfield" (published by Moses King, Cambridge, Mass.) and other poems.

ELLEN WARD, born March 27, in Winchester, Indiana. Residence, Winchester, Indiana. Educated in Winchester public schools. Degree, A. B. Occupation and position, teacher in Kokomo public schools; member of the Methodist Episcopal Church.

JEPTHA DUDLEY WHISENAND, born February 9, 1855, in Monroe County, Indiana. Residence, Des Moines, Iowa. Educated in Harrodsburg graded schools. Degree, A. B. Occupation and position, teacher; Principal of the Valley Mills graded schools, Marion County; student of law at Chariton, Iowa, in Col. Bartholomew's office; clerk in First National Bank, Chariton; practitioner of law, Des Moines, Iowa. For more than a year before removing to Des Moines was a partner of Col. Bartholomew.

1879.

DAVID WALTER BELL, born August 17, 1858, in Wheeling, West Virginia. Residence, Wheeling West Virginia. Educated at Poughkeepsie, New York. Degrees, A. B. and A. M. Occupation and position, student of law, Columbia College Law School, New York City, lawyer. Principal of Ellettsville, Indiana, public school before beginning the study of law.

IDA BELL (KENNEY) BROWN, born in Knox County, Missouri. Residence, Owensburg, Indiana. Educated at Bloomington. Degree, A. B. Occupation, teaching. Married Mr. Brown, of Owensburg.

FREDERICK EUGENE DICKENSON, born August 31, 1853, in Wolcottville, Indiana. Residence, Wolcottville, Indiana. Edu-

cated at Wolcottville school. Degrees, A. B. and A. M., *pro
merito*. 1886, B. D. Chicago Baptist Theological Seminary. In
1886 ordained to the gospel ministry by a representative counsel of the Baptist churches, at Lagrange, Indiana. This church
at Lagrange Mr. Dickenson was instrumental in organizing,
and is its pastor, (1888).

FRANKLIN PIERCE FOSTER, born January 8, 1856, in Newton-Stuart. Indiana. Residence, Harold, Hughes County, South
Dakota. Educated at Mitchell, Indiana. Degree, A. B. Occupation and position, teaching; Principal of the Chesterfield,
Indiana, graded school, 1883; attorney at law; in 1888 Representative in the State Legislature.

CHARLES HARRIS, born November 19, 1859, in Albion, Illinois.
Residence, Oberlin, Ohio. Educated in the Albion public
schools. Degrees, A. B. and A. M., *pro merito*, and from the
University of Leipsig, Germany, Ph. D. Occupation and position, teacher in the Albion schools until 1881, and, also, Principal. Since, a student at the University of Leipsig until his
graduation. Mr. Harris's principal study at Leipsig was Philology. On his return, in 1883, he became Professor of Modern
Language in Vincennes University. In 1886 he was elected
Professor of German and French in the Normal School of
Southern Illinois. Now (1887) Professor of German and French
in Oberlin College, Ohio. Professor Harris married Miss Mary
Ballantine McCalla, of Bloomington, Indiana.

BENJAMIN FRANKLIN HATFIELD, born December 25, 1855, in
Perry County, Indiana. Residence, Boonville, Warrick County,
Indiana. Educated at high school of Rockport and Preparatory Department of Indiana University. Degree, A. B., M. D.
Ohio Medical College, March, 1882. Occupation, physician;
practitioner at Velpen, Pike County, Indiana.

FRANK ECKLEY HUNTER, born January 11, 1858, Bloomington,
Indiana. Residence, El Paso, Texas, 1887. Educated in Peru,
Indiana, Princeton, Indiana, graduated at Bloomington High
School in 1875. Degree, A. B., and from Central Law School,
Indianapolis, LL. B., April, 1882. Occupation, attorney at law
and Prosecuting Attorney of his district.

WILLIAM JAY KING, born January 14, 1859, Houstonville, Lincoln County, Kentucky. Residence, Voorhies, Piatt County,

Illinois. Educated in the Bloomington schools. Degree, A. B. Occupation, teaching, publisher of Beebe (Arkansas) *Times*, at present (1888) merchandizing. Mr. King died at Bloomington, May, 1889.

FREDERICK PIERCE LEONARD, born at Mt. Vernon, Indiana, November, 4, 1858. Residence, Mt. Vernon, Indiana. Educated in the public schools of Mt. Vernon. Degree, A. B., Indiana University, B. L., University of Michigan, 1881. Occupation, attorney at law and Prosecuting Attorney in 1886.

JOHN EDGAR MCCLOSKEY, born October 23, 1854, at LaGrange, Indiana. Residence, LaGrange, Indiana. Educated in the LaGrange High School. Degree, A. B. Occupation and position, attorney at law, President of the Addisonian Society of LaGrange, Trustee in the First Presbyterian Church.

ROBERT MILTON PARKS, born July 20, 1858, in Bedford, Indiana. Residence, Bedford, Indiana. Educated in Franklin (Indiana) High School. Degree, A. B. Occupation, student of philology; recently (1882) in Harvard University, Cambridge. In 1883 a student in the Royal Bavarian University, Munich, Germany.

EARLY WHITTEN POINDEXTER, born January 8, 1854, in Kecksville. Residence, Bloomfield, Indiana. Educated in common schools of Martin County, and in the Bedford schools, Lawrence County. Degree, A. B. Occupation and position, teacher; Superintendent of Schools at Owensburg and at Bloomfield. At present Associate Principal of Bloomfield Normal School.

WOODFIN D. ROBINSON, born January 27, 1857, in DeWitt County, Illinois. Residence, Princeton, Indiana. Educated at Owensville, Indiana. Degrees, A. B., Indiana University, and LL. B., Michigan University, 1883. Occupation and position, Principal of Owensville school for two years; student of law, Virginia University, one session; County Superintendent of Gibson County (1888).

JAMES P. STUNKARD, JR., born December 31, 1885, in Brazil, Indiana. Residence, Terre Haute, Indiana. Educated in Terre Haute High School and Smithson College, Logansport, Indiana. Degree, A. B. Occupation and position, student of law under Judge B. E. Rhoads, at Terre Haute, in 1880; afterward attended the Indiana Central Law School, Indianapolis; was admitted to the Terre Haute bar in 1881, and began the practice of law in the fall of 1882.

LILLIE HARRIET (ADAMS) TELFER, born in Monroe County. Residence (1889), Indianapolis. Educated in Bloomington High school. Degree, A. B. Occupation, 1879–80, teaching. Miss Adams married Rev. Mr. Telfer, of the Methodist Church.

MARY HELEN (MOSS) TREUDLEY, born in Zanesville, Ohio. Residence, Youngstown, Ohio (1889). Educated in public schools and at Ladies' Seminary, Lewisburg, Pennsylvania. Degree, A. B. Occupation, woman's work in general. Miss Moss married Professor Treudley, of Class '78.

MINNIE (COFFIN) WALLINGFORD, born in Salem, Indiana. Residence, Minneapolis, Minnesota. Educated in Bloomington, Indiana. Degree, B. S.

1880.

WILLIAM FRANCIS AXTELL, born December 28, 1855, at Solsberry, Greene County, Indiana. Residence, Washington, Indiana. Educated in Bloomington High School. Degree, A. B. Occupation, teacher in the public schools, Principal of Washington (Indiana) High School in 1886. Married Miss Kate Bollenbacher.

WILLIAM THEODORE BLAIR, born May 1, 1856, at Bloomington, Indiana. Residence, Bloomington, Indiana. Educated in the Bloomington public schools. Degree, B. L. Occupation, hardware business, at present, 1885, a dealer in shoes, in 1888 was elected Auditor of Monroe County. Married Miss Waldron, of Bloomington.

DAVIS CARPENTER BUNTEN, born in July, 1858, at Terre Haute, Indiana. Residence, Terre Haute, Indiana. Educated in the Terre Haute High School. Degree, A. B. Occupation, in railroad office, at present, 1883, assistant paymaster of the Vandalia railroad.

JOHN PRICE CARR, born 1854, in White County, Indiana. Residence, Oxford, Indiana. Degree, A. B. Occupation, editor and publisher of the *Oxford Tribune*.

CYRUS EDGAR DAVIS, born December 17, 1856, in Washington County, Indiana. Residence, Bloomfield, Indiana. Educated in the schools of Paoli and Salem. Degree, A. B., LL. B. from Michigan University. Occupation, lawyer, in partnership with his classmate, W. W. Moffett.

LINCOLN DIXON, born February 9, 1860, at Vernon, Indiana. Residence, North Vernon, Indiana. Educated at the Jennings Academy. Degree, A. B. Occupation and position, attorney at law, Reading Clerk of the House of Representatives in the Legislature of 1880, reëlected Prosecuting Attorney of Scott and Jennings Counties, represented the University of Indiana at the State and Interstate Oratorical Contest, 1880.

LOTTIE ELIZABETH FARIS, born in Bloomington, Indiana. Residence, Bloomington, Indiana. Educated at Bloomington graded and high schools. Degree, A. B. Occupation, for two years after graduation, teaching.

JOHN FREMONT GODDARD, born October 2, 1858, in Wilford, Indiana. Residence, Greensburg, Indiana. Educated at the common schools of Center Grove and Springhill, and Moore's Hill College. Degree, A. B. Occupation, farming; clerk from August, 1880, till June, 1881; lawyer, giving special attention to claims.

HARRY GRAY, born June 14, 1861, in Grayville, Illinois. Residence, Grayville, Illinois. Educated at Grayville schools. Degree, A. B. Occupation, grain merchant until January, 1882. Since, banker.

WILLIAM HARRY HAWLEY, born April 9, 1858, in College Corner, Ohio. Residence, College Corner, Butler County, Ohio. Educated at Preparatory Department of Miami University, Oxford, Ohio, 1874–76; Monmouth College, 1876–77. Degree, A. B., M. D. at Cincinnati Medical College. Practitioner at College Corner (1888).

KATE M. HIGHT, born in Bloomington, Indiana. Residence, Bloomington, Indiana. Educated at Bloomington graded and high schools. Degree, B. L. Occupation, teaching; a teacher in the Bloomington graded school.

HILARY QUINCY HOUGHTON, born June 16, 1855, in Daviess County, Indiana. Residence, Loogootee, Martin County, Indiana. Educated at common schools, Daviess County. Degree, A. B. Occupation, attorney at law.

FRANCIS PRESERVED LEAVENWORTH, born September 3, 1858, at Mt. Vernon, Indiana. Residence, Haverford College, Pennsylvania, 1888. Educated in Mt. Vernon High School. Degrees, A. B. and A. M., *pro merito*, 1888, and P. A. (Practical Astronomy), University of Virginia. Occupation and position, student under Professor O. Stone and assistant in the Cincinnati Observatory. Prof. Stone being made director in the Leander McCormick Observatory, University of Virginia, Mr. Leavenworth accompanied him as his assistant, 1882–86. In 1887, Professor Leavenworth was chosen Professor of Astronomy in Haverford College, Swarthmore, Pennsylvania. In these positions Professor Leavenworth has done much work in Practical Astronomy. He has computed the orbits and ephemeris of the asteroids 223 and 241, for 1881 and 1884, respectively; he has made accurate drawings of the nebula of Orion; has discovered 270 nebulæ and nine double stars; has assisted in the computation of the elements of the orbit of Tuttle's comet; he has assisted in the observation of the approximate position of 6,000 stars (23° S. D.) In 1881 he made the astronomical observations for determining the western and southern boundary of the "Panhandle" of Indian Territory. Professor Leavenworth married Miss Jennie C. Campbell, daughter of Professor M. M. Campbell, of Topeka, October 11, 1883.

JENNIE C. (CAMPBELL) LEAVENWORTH, born at Bloomington. Residence, Swarthmore, Pennsylvania. Educated in the high school at Bloomington. Degree, A. B. Occupation, teacher, Secretary of the Kansas Historical Society. Married Professor Leavenworth.

WILLIAM WILEY MOFFIT, born February 19, 1853, in Owen County. Residence, Bloomfield, Indiana. Educated in the Spencer High School. Degree, A. B. Occupation, lawyer, partner of C. E. Davis.

ELLEN ELIZA MUNSON, born in Orleans, Indiana. Residence, Mitchell, Indiana. Educated at the Mitchell High School. Degree, A. B. Occupation and position, teacher, Principal of the Mitchell High School (1888).

FANNIE CAROLINE (ALLEN) PALMER, born in Bloomington, Indiana. Residence, Columbia City, Missouri. Educated in Bloomington graded schools, course of modern classics. Degree, B. L. Miss Allen married Mr. Palmer.

JOHN LAW PATTERSON, born June 30, 1858, in Terre Haute, Indiana. Residence, Terre Haute, Indiana. Educated in Terre Haute public schools. Degree, A. B. Occupation, lawyer.

WILLIAM HARVEY PAYNTER, born November 11, 1858, in Salem, Indiana. Residence, Salem, Indiana. Educated in Salem High School and Professor May's Academy. Degree, A. B. Occupation, attorney at law; Deputy Prosecuting Attorney for the Forty-second Judicial District. Mr. Paynter delivered a political speech for Hancock and English at Pekin, Indiana.

ALLEN B. PHILPUTT, A. M. See Professors' list.

EDWARD CRITTENDEN SIMPSON, born February 21, 1860, in Paoli, Indiana. Residence, Buffalo, Wyoming Territory. Educated in Paoli High School. Degree, A. B. Occupation, Deputy in the Clerk's, Treasurer's and Auditor's offices in the Paoli Court House. In May, 1881, elected Clerk of Paoli; re-elected, 1882. In 1883 appointed assistant under Attorney General for Second Congressional District of Indiana.

WINFIELD CHRISTIAN SNYDER, born March 4, 1851, at Beck's Mill, Indiana. Residence, Salem, Washington County, Indiana. Educated at Salem, Indiana. Degree, B. S. Occupation and position, teaching for two years; elected, June 4, 1883, County Superintendent of Washington County; previously Principal of the Graded Schools.

WILLIAM WESLEY SPANGLER. See Professors' list.

THOMAS BEATTIE STEWART, born October 1, 1854, in Glenwood. Residence, San Francisco, California. Educated at Richland Academy, Rush County. Degree, A. B. Occupation and position, minister of the Gospel; pastor of the Second United Presbyterian Church, San Francisco. Author of a poem, "The Coming Conflict, or a Plea for Prohibition." Also, of poems and articles in different periodicals. Mr. Stewart married Miss Sarah L. Wylie of Bloomington, June 7, 1883.

DAVID LAFAYETTE VANDAMENT, born August 29, in Manilla, Rush County. Residence, Bainbridge, Indiana. Educated at Spencer graded schools. Degrees A. B. Occupation and position, teacher until 1882; since, a minister of the gospel; Associate editor of the *Christian Witness;* Secretary of the Church Council.

ALBERT WEATHERLY. A. B. Kansas City, Missouri. Salesman.

WILLIAM HENRY WELLS, born March 9, 1853, in Clark County. Residence, Wichita, Kansas. Educated at common schools and Preparatory Department of Lexington University, Kentucky. Degrees, A. B., M. D. from the University of Louisville, Kentucky. Occupation and position, teaching; study and practice of medicine; Principal of the Utica graded schools. In an elective course, "The Thesis on the Diseases of Children," by Dr. Wells was awarded the first prize.

GEORGE W. WOODS, born November 9, 1858, in Knightstown. Residence, Indianapolis. Educated at the Knightstown schools. Degree, B. L. Occupation, lawyer.

1881.

CHARLES BANTA, born October 16, 1859, at Franklin, Indiana. Present residence, Mt. Vernon, New York, 1889, Postoffice address, No. 67, Wall street, room 24, New York City, N. Y. Educated in the Franklin High School. Degree, A. B. Occupation, law student, taught school in the winter of 1881–82, became an insurance agent, in 1886 was appointed Inspector for the Phœnix Insurance Company, Brooklyn, and of the Fire Association of New York, in 1887, and the Mutual Insurance Company of New York, in 1888, and at present (since March 1, 1889,) Inspector for the Middle States Inspection Bureau, and an occasional writer for the *Insurance World.* Mr. Banta married Miss Martha Evelyn Graham, of Richland, Indiana, October 14, 1885, a former student of the University.

WILLIAM EDWARD BEACH, born October 8, 1860, at Lafayette. Residence, Lafayette, Indiana. Educated in the Lafayette public schools and Purdue University. Degree, B. L. Occupation, heavy hardware business. Married Miss Gertrude Burnett, of Washington, D. C., on the 20th of December, 1888.

CHARLES ALBERT BURNETT, born January 9, 1861, Terre Haute, Indiana. Residence, Washington, D. C. Educated in the Indianapolis public schools and Terre Haute High School.

Degrees, A. B. and A. M., *pro merito*, in 1886. Occupation, clerk in the United States Geological Survey and student of law in Washington, D. C., where he received the degree, LL. B.

DANIEL GREEN DUBOIS, born October 25, 1857, Nashville, Indiana. Residence, Evanston, Illinois, 1883. Educated in the Nashville schools. Degree, A. B. Occupation, teaching and student of theology in Garrett Biblical Institute.

ROBERT G. GILLUM, born January 22, 1856, at Greenville, Augusta County, Virginia. Residence, Terre Haute, Indiana. Educated in Virginia. Degree, A. B. Occupation, teaching. At present (1886) an Instructor in the Indiana State Normal.

MARY BALLANTINE (MCCALLA) HARRIS, born at Bloomington, Indiana. Residence, Oberlin, Ohio, 1888. Educated in the Bloomington High School. Degree, B. L. Married Professor Charles Harris (Class '79), of Oberlin, Ohio.

FRANK CARTER HOOD, born in 1858, at Greensburg, Indiana. Residence, New Castle, Indiana. Educated in the Greensburg High School. Degree, A. B. Occupation, studied theology in seminary at Princeton, New Jersey. Now (1886) pastor of the Presbyterian Church in New Castle, Indiana. Mr. Hood married Miss Ole Wilson, of Class '76, Indiana University.

HORACE ADDISON HOFFMAN. See professors' list.

JACOB P. LINDLEY, born May 23, 1852, near Monrovia, Indiana. Residence, Bloomington, Illinois. Educated in the West Union High School, Monrovia, Friends' Private School at Plainfield, the Poplar Ridge Seminary, near Carmel, Indiana, the New Providence Academy, Iowa, and also a year at the Illinois Industrial University, Champaign, Illinois. Having entered the Select Class of Indiana University in 1876, in 1881 he received the Degree, A. B., and in 1883, LL. B. from Illinois Wesleyan University. Occupation and position, attorney at law. For the last four years (1886) Professor in the Law Department in the Wesleyan University. Mr. Lindley married Sylvia J. Benson.

MARY ELIZABETH LYON, born at Xenia, Ohio. Residence, Fairburg, Illinois. Educated in the common schools. Degrees, B. L. and B. S. Occupation, teaching. Position, Principal of

Knightstown High School, teacher of natural science in Waukegan (Illinois) High School, and also at Fairburg (Illinois) High School.

CHARLES LESLIE MCKAY, born at Appleton, Wisconsin, April 21, 1855. Died near Cape Constantine, Alaska, April 19, 1883. Educated at Appleton Collegiate Institute, Wisconsin. Dr. David S. Jordan was his teacher while at this Institution, and finding that he had a remarkable talent for learning and a taste similar to his own, he took a peculiar interest in him. Under this influence young McKay decided to be a naturalist, and, as a preparatory step, he entered the Natural History Department of Cornell University. After spending some time at Cornell, he became a pupil of his friend, Dr. Jordan, in Butler University, and afterward in the University of Indiana, in 1879, where he graduated in 1881, receiving the degree, B. S. Before graduation he acted as assistant to Professor Dudley, of Cornell, who temporarily occupied the place of Dr. Jordan, then in California. In the winter of 1881, he was for a short time assistant to the United States Fish Commission. In the spring of the same year he received the appointment as Signal Officer at Nushagak (Fort Alexander), on Bristol Bay, Alaska. He graduated with the Class of '81, receiving from the Faculty the distinction of "Graduated With Honor." Mr. McKay made ichthyology an especial study. He had, before leaving for Alaska, nearly ready for publication a monograph of the freshwater sunfishes. An outline of this work was published in the proceedings of the United States National Museum for 1881, with descriptions of three new species, which he had discovered. Mr. McKay left for San Francisco in June, 1881, and proceeded directly to Alaska, where he remained at Nushagak, with but a single white companion till his death in 1883. The National Museum has received from him large collections of birds, fishes, plants, minerals, skins and skeletons of mammals and Indian relics. On the 17th of April, 1883, Mr. Clark, the agent of the Alaska Commercial Company, at Nushagak, Mr. McKay's only white associate during his two years in Alaska, communicated the sad news to his father, Mr. Hector McKay. He informed his father that he left in company with a native, each of them in a single canoe. They passed the night at an Indian village, sixteen miles from the station. The next day being stormy, they lay over in the village. On the morning of the 19th, as it was calm, they left the village to cross over the bay, a distance of twelve miles. When about two-thirds of the way across, a strong wind sprang up. Mr. McKay, in his canoe, was left behind, and was never seen again. Search was made, broken pieces of the canoe were found, his gun and rubber boots and other articles were picked up on the beach, about a mile from the village they had left in the morning. Thus, in the prime of life this young and enthusiastic naturalist was suddenly cut off. The above account is taken and abbreviated from a notice of Mr. McKay by President David S. Jordan, published in the *Indiana Student*, November, 1883, p. 2.

FANNIE BELL MAXWELL, born at Bloomington, Indiana. Residence, Albert Lea, Minnesota. Educated in the Bloomington High School. Degree, B. L. Occupation, 1888, teacher of French and German, Albert Lea, Minnesota.

STEPHEN W. MEADE, JR., born February 14, 1857, at Atlanta, Illinois. Residence, Lake Charles, Louisana. Educated in the Fort Branch High School. Degree, A. B. Occupation and position, Principal of High School, Morgantown, 1881, student of law in the office of P. Maier. In 1888 lawyer in Lake Charles, Louisiana.

EDGAR MARTIN MICHENER, born October 29, 1857, in Fayette County, Indiana. Residence, Connersville, Indiana. Educated in the district schools and Connersville High School. Degree, B. L. Occupation, farming and teaching.

JAMES OSMAN MULKY, born September 15, 1859, Bloomington, Indiana. Residence, Chicago, Illinois. Educated in the Bloomington graded schools. Degree, B. L. Occupation, merchants' clerk, 1888, dealer in coal, Chicago, Illinois.

JOHN LEWIS POWERS, born May 28, 1858, at Muncie, Indiana. Residence, Muncie, Indiana. Degree, A. B. Occupation, lawyer.

ALFRED WILLIS SCOTT, born November 8, 1856, Fayette County, Indiana. Residence, Lincoln, Nebraska. Educated in the public schools of Fayette County and Spiceland Academy, Henry County. Degree, A. B. Occupation and position, attorney at law, member of the Legislature in 1886, a member of the Educational Committee. Married Miss Alice Long, a class mate.

ALICE (LONG) SCOTT, born at Columbus. Residence, Lincoln, Nebraska. Educated in the Columbus High School. Degree, A. B. Married Alfred Willis Scott, August 29, 1883.

JOHN C. SHIRK, born March 14, 1858, Brookville, Indiana. Residence, Brookville, Indiana, having moved from Petoskey, Emmet County, Michigan. Educated at the district schools. Degree, B. L. Occupation and position, assistant cashier in the Brookville bank till January, 1883. Since, President of Petoskey bank. Now, 1888, banker at Brookville. Mr. Shirk is a Trustee of the Baptist Church.

HARRY HAMILTON SIMS, born February 13, 1860, at Utica, Clark County. Residence, Jeffersonville, Indiana. Educated at Utica. Degree, A. B. Occupation, teacher. In 1888, a merchant. One of the Indiana University tourists in 1881. Mr. Sims is a member of the Methodist Church.

FRANK PHILO TAYLOR, born December 27, 1859, at Wolcottville. Residence, Tulare, California. Educated in the Wolcottville High School. Degree, A. B. Occupation, teacher, student of law and in 1888 attorney at law.

A. ROWLAND VAN FOSSEN, born June 4, 1856, at Norristown, Ohio. Residence, St. Louis, Missouri. Educated in the Hopedale Normal School, Harrison County, Ohio. Degree, A. B. Occupation and position, teaching, Superintendent of Cedarville public schools. In 1883, stock collector for the Ohio Anti-Liquor Alliance. Afterward connected with the *Midland*, published at St. Louis, Missouri. In 1886 a student of theology in the United Presbyterian Theological Seminary, Alleghany, Pennsylvania.

CHARLES WILBERFORCE WILEY, born at Martins Ferry, Belmont County, Ohio, July 20, 1858. Residence, South Bend, Indiana. Educated at Edgerton, Ohio, and at home. Degree, A. B. Occupation, teaching one year after graduation, afterward studied law, commenced practice of law at Fort Wayne, then removed to South Bend.

FRANCIS WOODARD, born May 30, 1853, at Coloma. Residence, Coloma, Parke County, Indiana. Educated at home and Terre Haute. Degree, B. L. Occupation, student in Yale College Theological Seminary, in 1888, pastor of a church at Gridley, Illinois.

ROBERT ARCHER WOODS, born January 5, 1861, at Princeton, Indiana. Residence, Princeton, Indiana. Educated in the Princeton graded schools. Degree, B. S. Occupation, student of law, in 1883, Deputy Clerk of Gibson County, druggist at Princeton, Indiana, in 1888.

NANCY MARGARET WOODWARD, born at Springville. Residence, Martinsville, Indiana. Educated in the public schools of Monroe County. Degree, B. S. Occupation, Principal of Martinsville High School. Member of the Methodist Church.

1882.

WILLIAM HAMILTON ADAMS, born in 1860, in Monroe County, Indiana. Residence, Bloomington, Indiana. Educated in the Bloomington graded schools. Degree, A. B. Occupation, in the dry goods business, partner in the firm of Adams, Hall & Company.

FREDERICK R. ALBERTSON, born July 2, 1860, at Canton, Indiana. Died at Bridgeport, Indiana, May 16, 1887. Educated in Blue River Academy, near Canton. Degree, A. B. Occupation, teaching, nurseryman.

HARRY ARCHIBALD BUERK, born May 8, 1862, at Paoli, Indiana. Residence, New Albany, Indiana. Educated in the New Albany public schools. Degree, A. B. Occupation, in 1883, student at Harvard University, Cambridge, Massachusetts, attorney at law, 1888, New Albany.

GEORGE WASHINGTON CROMER, born May 13, 1857, Columbus, Indiana. Residence, Muncie, Indiana. Educated in the Preparatory Department of Wittenburg College. Degree, A. B. Occupation and position, student of law and editor and proprietor of the *Muncie Times*, Prosecuting Attorney, Muncie, Indiana.

WILLIAM JAMES DAVIS, born February 5, 1856, in Goldsboro, North Carolina. Residence, Elizabethtown, Indiana, in 1887. Educated in the Sand Creek Seminary at Azalia, Indiana. Degree, A. B. Occupation, teaching.

CHARLES ORTON DUBOIS, born March 29, 1856, in Brown County, Indiana. Residence, Nashville, Indiana. Educated in the Morgantown graded schools. Degree, A. B. Occupation and position, Principal of Ellettsville school, student at Indiana State Normal, Terre Haute, farmer in Brown County.

JOHN H. FOSTER, born January 31, 1862, at Evansville. Residence, Washington, D. C., in 1883. Educated in the Evansville common schools and private academy. Occupation, student of law, Columbian University, D. C.

LUTHER CALVIN FRAME, born April 17, 1856, at Senecaville, Ohio. Died at his home in Solsbury, Indiana, July 14, 1886. Educated at the school of Mr. Ogg, B. S., Solsberry, and at Bloomington High School. Entered University in 1878. Degree, A. B. Occupation and position, teaching, elected a teacher in the New Albany High School; after a year's service Principal of the Bloomfield High School. This position he held till ill health compelled him to return home, and in a few weeks he died. As a student, as a teacher and as a Christian, Mr. Frame held a high rank.

MILTON BENTON HOTTEL, born May 1, 1860, in Harrison County, Ohio. Residence, Salem, Indiana. Educated in the Fredericksburg schools. Degree, A. B. Occupation, clerk in Fredericksburg and attorney at law. Mr. Hottell married Miss Harris, of Salem, in May, 1888.

AQUILA C. HUFF, born at Troy, Perry County, August 26, 1856. Residence, Troy, Perry County, Indiana. Educated in the district schools and St. Meinrad. Degree, B. S. Occupation, teaching.

SAMUEL HALL KIDD, born October 21, 1861, at Princeton. Residence, Princeton, Indiana. Educated in the Princeton High School. Degree, B. L. Occupation, lawyer. Married Miss Minnie Moore, of Indianapolis in 1888.

HARRIETT PAINE MOSS, born at Zanesville, Ohio. Residence, Chicago, Illinois. Educated in Philadelphia and Chicago. Degree, B. L. At present, 1883, studying music.

FRANK LEWIS MULKY, born June 8, 1863, Bloomington, Indiana. Residence, Leavenworth, Indiana. Educated in the Bloomington graded schools and high school. Degree, B. L. Occupation, teaching, General Agent of the Ætna Life Insurance Company, in 1888, Leavenworth, Indiana.

ALEXANDER F. OLINGER, born May 20, 1855, Harrison County,

Indiana. Residence, New Middleton, Harrison County, Indiana. Educated at the common schools of Harrison County. Degree, B. L. Occupation, teacher, author of a school chart, presenting a new method of teaching fractions.

BEATRICE OLIVIA SANDERS, born June 29, at Quincy. Residence, Bloomington, Indiana. Educated in the Bloomington High School. Degree, B. L. Occupation, teaching. A member of the Baptist Church.

ALICE CARRIE SHORT, residence, Vincennes, Indiana. Educated in the Vincennes University. Graduate and Valedictorian. Degree, B. L. Occupation, teacher in Bedford High School. In 1888, teacher in graded school, Franklin, Indiana.

SAMUEL EDWIN SMITH, born August 31, 1861, Gosport, Indiana. Residence, Gosport, Indiana, Educated in the Gosport High School. Degree, B. L., M. D. from the University of Louisville. Occupation, physician.

JOHN LAFAYETTE STEPHENSON, born July 29, 1858, at Campbellsburg, Indiana. Residence, Campbellsburg, Indiana. Educated at Salem, Indiana. Degree, A. B. Occupation, teaching, farming. Resident graduate at Indiana University in 1883-84. Married Miss Hattie Martin, of Campbellsburg, October 30, 1884.

ELLA ALPINE (TURNER) LIVELY, born at Bloomington, Indiana. Residence, Bloomington, Indiana. Educated in the Bloomington schools. Degree, B. L. Occupation, teaching. Married Mr. David Lively in the spring of 1888.

1883.

BENJAMIN FRANKLIN ADAMS, JR., born September 29, 1861, in Monroe County. Residence, Bloomington, Indiana. Educated in the Bloomington public schools. Degree, A. B. Occupation, Civil Engineer and merchant, Superintendent of the Methodist Sunday School. Married Miss Anna Brant of Parsons, Kansas, daughter of the Rev. J. E. Brant, December 4, 1888.

ALBERT MONROE ADAMS, born March 29, 1858, in Rockville. Indiana. Residence, Rockville, Indiana. Educated in the Bloomingdale Academy and Preparatory Department Indiana University. Degree, B. L. Occupation, teaching.

CHARLES McLANE AUSTIN, born November 20, 1859, in Morgantown, West Virginia. Residence, Muncie, Indiana. Educated in the Muncie High School, Degree, A. B. Occupation, Principal of the Albany school, Delaware County.

SARAH (DILLON) BOYLE. Degree, A. B. Residence, Bloomington, Indiana.

EDWIN CORR, born December 31, 1860, in Monroe County, Indiana. Residence, Bloomington, Indiana. Educated in the common schools. Degree, B. L., and from DePauw University LL. B., in 1885. Occupation, teacher for two years, student of law, and in 1888 Attorney at Law.

DAVID A. CURRY. (See Faculty list.)

JENNIE (FOSTER) CURRY, born in Rushville. Residence, (1888) Xenia, Ohio. Education in the Knightstown High School. Degree, B. L. Occupation, teaching in the Bloomington and Knightstown public schools. Mrs. Curry was Principal of the Greensburgh High School. Miss Foster married Prof. D. A. Curry April 6, 1886.

O. P. FLOYD. Residence, Omaha, Nebraska. Degree, B. L. Occupation, merchant.

CLARENCE LaRUE GOODWIN, born December 23, 1859 in Warren County, Kentucky. Residence, Los Angeles, California. Education, Henderson (Kentucky) High School and at Butler University. Entered the Junior Class of Indiana University. Degree B. L. Occupation, teacher one year, studying law at Indianapolis, Attorney at Law, reporter on the *Indianapols Journal* and *Times*. Since August 1886 associate editor of the *Los Angeles Evening Express*. Mr. Goodwin represented the Indiana University in the State oratorical contest in 1882, and also the Interstate contest the same year. Mr. Goodwin married Harriet A. Kuhn of Greensburgh, Pennsylvania, November 17, 1885.

ELIZABETH LONG. Residence, Columbus. Degree, B. L.

JULIETTA M. MAXWELL, born in Bloomington, Indiana. Residence, Bloomington, Indiana. Education in the Bloomington High School. Degree, B. L.

ALONZO DALE MOFFETT, born October 10, 1859, in Owen County, Indiana. Residence, White Cloud, Kansas (1887).

Educated at Spencer schools. Degree, A. B. Occupation, eacher. Position, Superintendent of Tipton public schools, 1884-85; Bowling Green schools, 1885-86; White Cloud, Kansas, 1886. Returned to the University in 1888, and in 1889 received the degree, A. M., *pro merito*. Mr. Moffett married Hester Alverson, of Spencer, Indiana.

ARAMINTA ELIZABETH SIMS, born Greentown, Indiana. Residence, Utica, Clark County, Indiana. Educated at Utica schools and Greentown schools. Degree, B. L. Occupation, teaching.

KATE S. SNYDER, born Rockport, Indiana. Residence, Rockport, Indiana. Educated at Rockport. Degree, A. B. Occupation, for some time after graduation, teaching. In 1885, a student of medicine, Michigan University, Ann Arbor.

WILLIAM HALLECK SNYDER, born March 1, 1859, Rockport, Indiana. Residence, Rockport, Indiana. Educated at Rockport schools. Degree, A. B. Occupation, teaching. January, 1886, a student of Medicine at Ann Arbor, Michigan.

IDA (SMELL) SPANGLER, born in Muncie, Indiana. Died August 12, 1888, at Tacoma, Washington Territory. Educated at Muncie schools. Degree, A. B. Married Mr. W. W. Spangler, Librarian Indiana University, June 10, 1885, whom she assisted in his work. She visited Europe twice, once in the summer of 1883, and the second time in 1888. On a tour with her husband to the Pacific, she was taken with typhoid fever and died in the twenty-seventh year of her age, having been married about three years. Mrs. Spangler, when a student, was exemplary in every respect—diligent, punctual and successful in the aquisition of knowledge. About a year before her death she connected herself with the Presbyterian Church, in Bloomington, under the pastorate of Rev. Mr. Minton.

ROBERT SCOTT STEVENSON, born January 15, 1859, Bellefontaine, O. Residence, Madison, D. T. Educated in Cambridge City High Schools. Degree, A. B. Occupation, student of theology in Chicago Theological Seminary. Now (1889), and since 1886, pastor of a Presbyterian church in Madison, S. D. Married Kate Hoover, of Bloomington, Ind.

JOSEPH SWAIN. See Professor's List.

1884.

JAMES REUBEN BECKETT, born March 8, 1861, Daviess County, Residence, Washington, Indiana. Educated at Washington High Schools. Degree, A. B. Occupation, lawyer. After graduating he lived for three years on the Kansas frontier. Returned to Washington in the fall of 1888.

OSCAR EDWIN BRADFUTE, born January 21, 1862, Meadow's Brook, near Cedarville, O. Residence, Cedarville, O. Educated at district schools. Degree, B. A. Occupation, farming and stock raising. Mr. Bradfute, in the fall of 1888, was elected by the county a member of the Board of the Agricultural Society of Greene County. Mr. Bradfute is a member of the United Presbyterian Church and Sabbath school superintendent.

WILLIAM JULIAN BRYAN. See Faculty List.

HARRY B. BURNETT, born September 10, 1861, Vincennes. Residence, Cleveland, O. Educated at Vincennes University. Degree, B. L. (Indiana University). Occupation, teaching for short time. Studied law at Indianapolis, 1885-86. Engaged in real estate business at Minneapolis. In 1888 came to Cleveland and commenced dealing in lumber. In the fall of 1886 was stenographer to the Republican State Central Committee, Indianapolis.

PERCY BENTON BURNETT. See Faculty List.

PHILIP KEARNEY BUSKIRK, born September 11, 1862, in Bloomington. Residence, Bloomington, Indiana. Educated at Bloomington schools and at Racine, College, Racine, Wisconsin. Afterwards entered Indiana University. Degree, B. L. Occupation, for some time a hardware merchant, studied law; now, (1889), attorney at law and Vice-President of the First National Bank, Bloomington.

SILAS DELMAR CONGER, born November 23, 1855, in Salem Centre, Indiana. Residence, Holdrege, Nebraska. Degree, B. A. Occupation, student of theology in Northwestern Theological Seminary, Chicago. Rev. Mr. Conger was in 1888 stated supply of a Presbyterian congregation at Holdrege, Nebraska, and is now its pastor (1889). Mr. Conger married Miss Mary Bardshaw.

PRUDENCE (ARNOTT) CRAIG, born in Hanover, Jefferson
County. Residence, Noblesville, Indiana. Educated at Madison
public schools. Degree, B. L. Occupation, teacher of art;
also, a teacher in the primary and High School and principal
of the New Harmony High School. Married October 10, 1889,
John C. Craig, of Noblesville.

JOHN LOCKWOOD GENTLE, born October 1, 1860, in Southport,
Indiana. Died January 29, 1889, at Southport. Educated
at Southport High School. Degree, B. A. Occupation, soon
after graduation, taught school at Freelandsville. At the time
of his death Mr. Gentle was a student of theology in Yale
Theological Seminary, and about to commence the studies of
the third year. In June, July and August, 1888, he was an
evangelist in Drummond and Mason, Wisconsin. He had been
recommended by the Association of the Western District of
New Haven (Rev. Dr. Harris was the moderator) as a suitable
candidate for the ministry. When at Minneapolis he was
prostrated by disease. He was brought home, where for a
short time he improved. About the beginning of 1889 he
grew worse and died. A post mortem examination showed
that his disease was *cerebral hemorrhage*.

JOHN NICHOLAS HUFF, born December 5, 1853, near Troy,
Spencer County. Died at his home March 16, 1887. Educated
at the district school of his native place, entered the Junior
Class of the Preparatory Department of Indiana University in
1877, and the Freshman Class in 1879. On his graduation in
1884 he received the degree, B. L. Occupation, teaching. His
first school was at Williamsville, Illinois. He left this on being elected Principal of a school in Springfield, Illinois, and after a years' service there was transferred to the High School in
the city of Springfield. Through ill health he was compelled
to give up his position and return to his home. His strength
was not equal to his energy, and in a short time he died.
Death did not find him unprepared. After affectionately bid-
ding farewell to each of the members of the family, he departed this life. Mr. Huff was an exemplary member of the
Baptist Church.

OSCAR LYNN KELSO, born October 10, 1854, in Ireland, Indiana. Residence, Richmond, Indiana. Educated at county
schools and Indiana State Normal, graduating in 1879. En-

tered the Junior Class in 1883. Degree, B. S. Occupation, teaching, first as Principal of Anderson High School, and next Principal of the Richmond High School. Mr. Kelso married Miss Carrie E. Bollenbacher, of Bloomington, Indiana.

LEWIS O. LEONARD, born October 6, 1862, in Smithville, Indiana. Residence, Portland, Oregon. Educated at Smithville schools. Degree, B. L. Occupation, clerk in railroad office.

1884.

FRANK LINCOLN McCOY, born February 9, 1862, near Greensburg. Residence, Paxton Block, Omaha, Nebraska. Educated at district schools, graduating at Greensburg High School. Degree, B. A., and from Cincinnati Law School, LL. B. Occupation, attorney at law. Commenced study of law in the office of Miller & Gavin, at Greensburg; completed the study at the Cincinnati Law School. Mr. McCoy, after graduating at the Indiana University, traveled in Canada and the Eastern States. After being admitted to the bar, he moved to Omaha, Nebraska, and commenced practice with Mr. Olmsted. In politics, Mr. McCoy is a Republican; in religion a Presbyterian, member and Trustee of the Westminster church; member, also, of the College Fraternity, B. Θ. Π.

SETH EUGENE MEEK, born April 1, 1859, in Hicksville, Ohio. Residence, Cedar Rapids, Iowa. Educated at Bryan, Ohio, and Valparaiso, Indiana. Degree, B. S. Mr. Meek at college was a diligent student of Natural History. After graduation he was, for a time, an assistant in the Smithsonian Institute, Washington, and also in the Academy of Natural Sciences, Philadelphia; assistant, also, to the New York Fish Commission. In 1885–86, holding a fellowship in Cornell University, he continued his studies in that institution. In December, 1886, he was elected Professor in Eureka College, Illinois, and continued there until January, 1888, when he was chosen Professor of Biology in Coe College, Iowa. Prof. Meek is the author of several scientific papers in the proceedings of the Philadelphia Academy of Natural Sciences, and also in the Smithsonian publications. He married Miss Ella Emma Tourner, of Bloomington, Indiana, December 25, 1886.

JOHN BOYD MILLER, born April 12, 1862, in Fayetteville, Indiana. Residence, Glenwood, Rush County, Indiana. Educated at common schools and Fairview Academy. Degree, B. L. Occupation, during 1885, traveling; for a time an insurance agent; in 1886 a student of medicine at Glenwood, Indiana.

CHARLES HENRY MOSS, born November 3, 1864, at Worcester, Massachusetts. Residence, Minneapolis, Minnesota (1889). Educated at the Bloomington schools. Degree, B. A. Occupation, has been engaged in merchantile pursuits; at present (1889) manager of branch office and warehouse of J. H. Leslie & Co., Minneapolis, Minnesota. Mr. Moss married Miss Nellie Florence Bates, of Chicago, Illinois, July 5, 1888.

ADAM CARL PATTON, born October 4, 1860, at Richland Township, Rush County. Residence, Greeley, Weld County, Colorado. A graduate of Greensburg High School; went through the Freshman year at Monmouth College, Illinois. Degree, A. B. Occupation, lawyer. Mr. Patton married Miss Nellie Davis, of Greeley, Colorado, February 21, 1889.

SAMUEL GILMORE RAMSEY, born April 13, 1862, at Fairhavens, Ohio. Residence, College Corner, Ohio. Educated at Miami Training School, Oxford, Ohio. Degree, B. L. Occupation, student in the Ohio College of Dental Surgery, Cincinnati, and for some time after in the Cincinnati Business College, and afterward, till 1888, a book-keeper at College Corner, and now (1889) a druggist. Mr. Ramsey has been twice elected Town Clerk.

WILLIAM A. RAWLES, born December 24, 1863, at Remington, Jasper County. Residence, Sedalia, Missouri. Educated at Remington and Bloomington schools. Degree, A. B. Occupation, teaching; Principal of Mitchell High School, assistant in Preparatory Department Indiana University, Principal of Vincennes High School.

DAVID CHAMBERS STEWART, born September 5, 1860, at Bellbrook, Ohio. Residence, Morgan street, St. Louis, Missouri. Educated at Richland Academy. Degree, A. B. Occupation, student in the United Presbyterian Theological Seminary, Xenia, Ohio. In 1887 licensed to preach. In 1889 pastor of United Presbyterian church in St. Louis, Missouri.

THOMAS WILLIAM WILSON, born October 18, 1860, at New Harmony. Residence, New Harmony, Indiana. Educated at Posey County schools and Preparatory Department of the University. Degree, B. L. Occupation, student in Miami Medical College, Cincinnati, Ohio, receiving therefrom March, 1887, the degree, M. D.; now (1889) a practioner of medicine in Posey County. Mr. Wilson was a delegate to the American Medical Association, Cincinnati, June, 1888.

1885.

CHARLES FREDERICK BAIN, born February 25, 1859, at Martinsville Indiana. Died April 28, 1887, at Martinsville. Educated at Martinsville schools and Preparatory Department Indiana University. Degree, B. A. Occupation; was engaged in the study of law at the time of death.

MABEL BANTA, born Franklin, Indiana. Residence, Franklin, Indiana, (1887). Educated at Franklin High School in 1881. Degree, A. B. Occupation, a teacher for a year in Franklin public school, and for two years Assistant Principal in the High School.

IRA COLEMAN BATMAN, born January 20, 1862, at Lawrence County, Indiana. Residence, Bloomington, Indiana. Educated at Bedford schools. Degree, B. L. Occupation, in 1886, a teacher in the High School, Columbia City, Indiana; in 1887 practiced law in Grant, Nebraska, his former residence; in 1888 attorney for the city of Bloomington. Mr. Batman married Miss Mary T. Waldron, of Bloomington.

MINNIE BELL BRYAN, born at Bloomington. Residence, Bloomington. Educated at Bloomington schools. Degree, B. L. Occupation, study and practice of music and painting.

JOHN WESLEY CARR, born December 13, 1859, at Bedford. Residence, Anderson, Indiana (1890). Educated in the Greene County schools. Degree, A. B. Occupation, teaching; Principal of the Bloomington High School; in 1890 Principal of the Anderson schools. Mr. Carr married Rachel Ashcraft, of Robinson, Indiana, in 1878.

PHILLMER DAY, born September 8, 1856, at North Madison, Jefferson County, Indiana. Residence, Vincennes, Indiana

(1887). Educated at district schools of Ripley County, and High School, Bloomington, Indiana. Degree, A. B. Occupation, teaching and preaching; Principal of Osgood schools; pastor of the Baptist Church, Vincennes, Indiana.

MOREY MCKEE DUNLAP, born July 7, 1860, at Franklin, Indiana. Residence, Bloomington, Indiana. Educated at Hopewell Academy, near Franklin, Indiana. Degree, B. L. Occupation, lawyer. In the spring of 1885 represented Indiana University in the Inter-Collegiate oratorical contest, in Indianapolis, ranking second in honors. On May 3, 1887, was elected Mayor of Bloomington, Indiana. On November 10, 1885, was married to Miss Minnie V. Davis, of Bloomington.

EDWARD CHURCHILL FITCH, born May 11, 1862, at Vandalia, Illinois. Residence. Albion, Edwards County, Illinois. Educated at Albion public schools; also, a graduate of Evansville High School (Latin course) in 1881. Degree, B. L., modern classic course. Occupation, student of law (1887), County Superintendent of Edwards County schools, Illinois (1886–90). E. C. Fitch is a popular orator; made Fourth of July orations in 1885 and 1886, and also on Memorial Day; was selected to deliver the address at the reunion of Sixty-sixth Illinois Regiment of Volunteer Veterans, and was elected an honorary member of that regiment.

RUFUS L. GREEN. See Professor's List.

ELMER ELLSWORTH GRIFFITH, born September 1, 1861, at Vevay, Indiana. Residence, Frankfort, Indiana. Educated at Vevay public schools. Degree, A. B. Occupation, teaching; Superintendent of Frankfort public school. Delivered an instructive lecture in the college chapel May, 1889, on Erasmus.

MARTIN LUTHER HOFFMAN, born August 26, 1859, near Auburn, DeKalb County, Indiana. Educated in the district school and High School at Auburn, and by private study. Degree, A. B. Occupation, teacher in the Indianapolis High School. Teacher in Minneapolis, Minnesota (1890).

MARY EDNA (LONG) PENCE. Degree, A. B. Teacher, Columbus. In 1890 Denver, Colorado.

JAMES ZWINGLE ALEXANDER MCCAUGHAN, born February 16, 1864, at Morning Sun, Iowa. Residence, Amboy, Indiana (1887). Educated at Morning Sun Academy, Iowa. Degree,

B. A., Indiana University. Occupation, teaching. In 1890, Principal of Amboy Academy.

WILLIAM CHRISTOPHER MASON, born September 25, 1863, at Grand View, Indiana. Residence, Rockport, Spencer County, Indiana (1887). Educated at Grand View common schools. Degree, B. A. Occupation, the study and practice of law. Married October 31, 1886, Anna Hardy, of Rockport, Indiana.

DORA BELLE (MERRIFIELD) WINBORN, born at Valparaiso, Indiana (1887). Residence, Murfeesboro, North Carolina. Educated at Valparaiso High School. Degree, B. L. Occupation, since graduation, has been engaged in teaching.

. WESLEY WALKER NORMAN, born February 10, 1863, at Heltonville, Indiana. Residence Aurora, Indiana. Educated at Bloomington High School and Preparatory Department of University. Degree, B. S. Occupation, teaching; 1885-86 Principal of Aurora High School; 1886-87, Principal of Dillsborough schools. Now, 1890, a student at Naples, Italy.

LUCIAN RHORER OAKES, born May 3, 1861, at LaPlata, Missouri. Residence, Topeka, Kansas (1887). Educated at Valparaiso High School. Degree, A. B. Occupation, poultry fancier until 1887; in 1887 State agent for the Novelty Wood Works, of Union City, Pennsylvania.

KATE NORVELL PEARSON, born December 16 at Bloomington, Indiana. Residence, Abilene, Kansas (1887). Educated at Bloomington graded schools. Degree, A. B. Occupation, Principal of High School at Bluffton, assistant in the High School of Abilene, Kansas. Miss Pearson is a contributor to the *New Moon*, a magazine published at Lowell, Massachusetts, and has written some for other periodicals.

JAMES McBRIDE PHILPUTT, born September 17, 1860, at Flat Creek, Bedford County, Tennessee. Residence, New York (1887). Educated at Campbellsburg, Indiana. Degree, A. B. and A. M., *pro merito*, 1888. Occupation, student of theology in the Union Theological Seminary, New York (1887); pastor of Church of the Disciples, One Hundred and Sixty-ninth Street, New York. Married Miss Nellie C. Pettit, of New York, October, 1888.

WILLIAM HARRISON RUCKER, born January 25, 1861, at Murfreesborough, Tennessee. Residence, Lawrenceburg, Indiana.

Educated at Athens, Alabama. Degree, B. S. Occupation, teaching; Principal of Lawrenceburg High School. Mr. Rucker married Miss Blanch Dorman, daughter of the Hon. Frank R. Dorman, of the class of 1858 (Indiana University).

SUSAN ISOLA (McCAUGHAN) RUSSEL, born December 8, at Morning Sun, Iowa. Residence, Bloomington, Indiana. Educated at Morning Sun High School and Academy. Degree, B. L. Occupation, housekeeping. Married December 30, 1885, Mr. Henry Russel, of Monroe County, Indiana.

ROBERT ELMER SCOTT. Degree, A. B. Teacher, New London. Now lawyer at Indianapolis.

NEWTON RAMSAY SPENCER, born March 6, 1855, at Portland Mills, Indiana. Residence, Johnson City, Kansas. Educated at common schools and Waveland Institute. Degree, A. B. Occupation, for a short time a teacher; afterwards a student at law; admitted to practice at the bar of the Superior Court, Marion County, June 29, 1886. Mr. Spencer's father was a student, but not a graduate of the University, in 1847-49. November 26, 1885, Mr. Spencer married Miss Viola Banks, at Greenfield, Indiana. Miss Banks was a student of the University in 1882-83.

JOHN EDWARD WILEY, born April 17, 1856, at Waverly, Indiana. Residence, Franklin, Johnson County, Indiana (1887). Occupation, teaching. Degree, A. B., A. M., *pro merito*, 1889. Mr. Wiley is the author of a story entitled, "The Tornado," a tale of horror; also, of an educational book entitled, "Books and Reading for Pupils," a graded course of reading. Mr. Wiley (1885-89) is one of the teachers in the Preparatory Department of the University.

MARTHA ELLA WILSON, born at Bloomington. Residence, Bloomington, Indiana. Educated at Bloomington graded schools. Degree, B. L. Occupation, taught school for one year.

GRACE HELEN WOODBURN, born at Bloomington. Residence, Bloomington. Educated at Bloomington public schools. Degree, A. B. Occupation, teacher; Principal of the New Harmony High School, Posey County, Indiana, in 1885-86, and Principal of the High School at Bloomington. Appointed, 1887.

1886.

WALLACE BRUCE CAMPBELL, born June 8, 1857, near Kenny, DeWitt County, Illinois. Residence, Roberts, Ford County, Illinois. Educated at district schools of Varna, Illinois, and Wabash College, Senior Preparatory in 1879; Freshman Class Indiana University, 1880; Sophomore and Junior at Wabash College, 1881 and 1882; Senior Class at Indiana University, graduating B. S. Occupation and position, teaching, studying law and journalism. Mr. Campbell had charge of the Botany and Geology in the Ladoga Normal School in the summer of 1885. Was assistant in the Botanical Laboratory of Indiana University under Prof. John C. Branner in the last term of 1886. Studied law with White & Humphrey, at Crawfordsville, and was admitted to the bar June 8, 1887. Was elected Principal of the Paxton High School in the fall of 1886, but resigned soon after on account of ill health.

MAY DILLON, born in Ireland, Dubois County, Indiana. Residence, Bloomington, Indiana. Educated at Bloomington public schools. Degree, A. B.

CHARLES LINCOLN EDWARDS, born December 8, 1863, Oquawka, Illinois. Residence, Minneapolis, Minnesota. Educated at Lombard University, from which he received the degree B. S. Degree B. S. and A. M. in 1887 *pro merito*. Occupation, student of zoölogy at Johns Hopkins University, Baltimore. Position; editor of Scientific Department of *Reason*, published in Minneapolis. Mr. Edwards' thesis on receiving the degree A. M. was the "Effect of Warmth on the Irritability of the Muscles and Nerves of a Frog." In May, 1888, he contributed to the *Journal of Psychology* an article on the "Winter Roosting Colonies of Crows;" to the *American Naturalist*, "The Relation of the Pectoral Muscles to the Power of Flight in American Birds," and in the Proceedings of the National Museum, along with Dr. Jordan, "A Review of the Tetraodontidae."

CHARLES BENJAMIN ELLIS, born March 12, 1863, Bradford. Residence, Bradford, Indiana. Educated at Bradford Schools. Degree, A. B. Occupation, lawyer.

CARL H. EIGENMANN, born March 9, 1863, Flehkingen, Baden, Germany. Residence, San Diego, California. Educated at the primary schools of Baden, Germany; after coming to America (May, 1877), at the High School of Rockport. In 1882 he entered the Freshman Class of the University, and on graduating received the degree B. S., and in 1887 A. M. *pro merito*. Occupation and position. In college Mr. Eigenmann turned his attention especially to zoölogy and botany, and on graduating he was made acting instructor in these branches. After leaving the University he spent a year and a half in Harvard University, Cambridge, Massachusetts. On leaving Harvard, he studied in the Marine Laboratory at Woods Hole. He then went to California and pursued his studies in the Biological Laboratory at San Diego. Mr. Eigenmann has contributed a number of interesting and important papers to science and literature. These contributions are principally ichthyological, and are published in the proceedings of different scientific societies—the Academy of Natural Science, Philadelphia; the National Museum of the United States; the Annals of the New York Academy of Science. Mr. Eigenmann married Miss Rosa Smith, August 20, 1887, a helpmeet not only in domestic economy but in scientific ichthyology. Mrs. Eigenmann is a joint contributor with her husband of scientific papers to the periodicals.

BARTON WARREN EVERMAN, born October 24, 1853, at Albia, Iowa. Residence, Indiana State Normal School, Terre Haute, Indiana. Educated at Howard College, Kokomo, Indiana. Degree, B. S. and A. M., *pro merito*, 1888. Occupation and position, teacher; Professor of Natural Science in Indiana State Normal School; County Superintendent of schools; now Superintendent of Bird Migration for the District of Indiana and Michigan; assistant in Museum of Indiana University, and also in the United States Fish Commission. Professor Everman is the author of a book entitled, "Animal Analysis," for use in high schools and colleges; also, of various scientific papers, especially on birds and fishes. Professor Everman married Meadie Hawkins (Mrs. Meadie Hawkins Everman), of the class of '87, October 24, 1875.

CHARLES BENJAMIN ELLIS, born March 12, 1863, at Bradford. Residence, Bradford, Indiana. Degree, A. B. (ancient classics). Occupation, lawyer.

JOEL CHURCHILL FITCH, born November 29, 1863, at Vandalia, Illinois. Residence, Albion, Edwards County, Illinois. Educated at common schools of Albion, Illinois, and of Evansville. Degree, A. B. (philosophical course). Occupation, student of law and lawyer. Married Miss A. Alvaretta Springer, a classmate.

ALICE ALVARETTA (SPRINGER) FITCH. Degree, B. P. (History).

MORTON WILLIAM FORDICE, born May 26, at Russelville, Putnam County, Indiana. Educated at Russelville schools. Degree, B. S. (in biology). Occupation, farmer.

JOSEPH ELIAS ALVIN HEINEY, born May 21, 1860, at Andrews, Indiana. Residence, Nebraska City, Nebraska. Degree, Ph. B. (course of history—political science). Occupation, teacher; position, Principal of Rochester High School in 1886-87, and in Nebraska City High School in 1887. Mr. Heiney married Miss Joanna Painter, of Monrovia, Indiana, August 9, 1888.

WILSON J. MCCORMICK, born February 3, 1861, at Greensburg, Ohio. Residence, LaGrange, Indiana. Educated at Wolcotville. Degree, A. B. (ancient classics). Occupation and position, School Superintendent at New Harmony; attorney at law. Mr. McCormick has delivered many addresses, generally on national topics. The Decoration Day address of 1889 was printed and largely circulated. On the occasion of the Centennial of Washington's inauguration the addresses were delivered by Senator J. S. Drake and Mr. McCormick at the LaGrange Opera House.

JEROME MCNEIL, born September 25, 1857, at Laurel, Clermont County, Ohio. Residence, Moline, Illinois. Educated at Antioch, College. Degree, B. S. (in biology), Indiana University. Occupation and position, teaching; Superintendent of High School, Moline, Illinois. Mr. McNeil married Alfreda Sophia Alderson.

KATE MILNER, born Rockport, Indiana. Residence, Rockport, Spencer County, Indiana. Educated at Rockport High School. Degree, A. B. (modern classics). Occupation, teaching; position, Principal of Rockport High School.

CHARLES NEWTON PEAK, born March 9, 1858, in Ripley County. Residence, North Vernon, Indiana. Mr. Peak completed his Preparatory course at Indiana University. Degree, Ph. B., Indiana University. Occupation and position, teaching; Principal of New Marion graded schools, two years; tutor in M. H. Coll; for one term Principal of Aurora High School, two years, and Superintendent of the North Vernon schools, two years. Mr. Peak married Maggie M. Harper, August 25, 1887.

CHARLES EDGAR SIMS, born March 21, 1864, Greentown, Howard County. Residence, Columbus, Ohio. Educated at the graded schools of Greentown and Utica. Degree, A. B. (ancient classics) of class, and LL. B. from Louisville Law School. Occupation, teaching, student of law and practicing attorney.

FRANK T. SINGLETON. Ph. B. (History and Political Science). Martinsville.

ALICE ALVERETTA (SPRINGER) FITCH. Ph. B. Wolcottville.

VIOLA CURTIS STUCKEY. B. A. (ancient classics). Lynnville.

JOHN CARR WELLS, born September 17, 1861, Clear Spring, Indiana. Residence, Clear Spring, Indiana. Educated one year at De Pauw. Degree, A. B. (ancient classics). Occupation, attorney at law. Mr. Wells was the winner of the Cobden medal in 1886 at the University.

TEMPLE WEST, born May 8, Pike County, Indiana. Residence, Rockport, Indiana. Educated at Rockport Public Schools. Degree, Ph. B. Occupation, teaching, for two and a half years in Rockport; in Minneapolis city schools, 1889.

JOSEPH WOODS WILEY, born July 19, 1860, Boone County. Residence, Elizaville, Boone County, Indiana. Educated at Antioch. Degree, Ph. B. (History Course). Occupation, teaching. Position, Superintendent of public schools, Lebanon. Mr. Wiley married Miss Maud Lane, of Lebanon, Indiana, May 31, 1888.

1887.

ERNEST PERCY BICKNELL, born February 23, 1862, Knox County. Residence, Indianapolis. Educated at the common schools. Degree, A. B. Occupation, journalism; before entering college, a teacher. Mr. Bicknell married Cora B. Scott, of Knox County, December 25, 1886.

WILLIS STANLEY BLATCHLEY, born October 6, 1859, North

Madison, Connecticut. Residence, Terre Haute, Indiana. Educated at Bainbridge, graded schools, Putnam County. Degree, A. B. Occupation, instructor in biology and chemistry, Terre Haute High School. Mr. Blatchley married Clara A. Fordyce, of Russellville, Putnam County, May 2, 1882.

MARTHA (WALLINGFORD) CADWELL, born in Harrodsburg. Residence, Neponset, Illinois. Educated at graded and High Schools of Bloomington. Degree, A. B. Married Mr. Charles A. Cadwell, December 22, 1887.

ALONZO ALVIN DeLARME, born April 13, 1859, Jefferson County, Pennsylvania. Residence, Dubois, Clearfield County, Pennsylvania. Educated at Mt. Pleasant Classical and Scientific Institute. Degree, A. B. (Greek Course). Occupation. Was pastor of the Baptist Church at Spencer, Indiana, for one year; a student in Crozer Theological Seminary, Chester, Pennsylvania, for three years; pulpit supply in Grace Baptist Church, Wilmington, Delaware, and Moderator of Clearfield Baptist Association. Before entering the University was principal of Clearfield County Normal School.

CHARLES AMBROSE DUGAN, born February 17, 1862, at Sedan, DeKalb County. Educated at Fort Wayne College. Degree, A. B. Occupation, teaching; Superintendent of schools in Delaware County.

MRS. MEADIE (HAWKINS) EVERMAN, born at Berrien Springs, Michigan. Residence, Terre Haute, Indiana. Educated at Butler University, Irvington. Degree, B. A. (course taken, Biology). Miss Hawkins married Prof. B. W. Everman, of the class of '86.

WILLIAM I. FEE, born 1865, at Bloomington. Residence, Bloomington. Educated at Bloomington public schools. Degree, A. B. Occupation, farming and the dry-goods business.

JAMES WILLIAM FESLER, born September 29, 1864, at Morgantown. Residence, Indianapolis. Educated at Franklin public schools and Franklin College. Degree, A. B. Occupation and position, lawyer and Prosecutor.

GOTTHARD WALDEMAR GÖRLITZ, a German from Herrnhut, Saxony. Mr. Görlitz was for some time since graduation a pastor of the Lutheran Church, Newark, New Jersey.

DAVID KOPP GOSS, born November 19, 1861, in Monroe County, near Gosport. Residence, Lebanon, Indiana. Educated at the district schools and the Gosport High School. Degree, A. B. Occupation, Superintendent of Lebanon city schools. Mr. Goss married Miss Alice Bell Diven (a student of the University), from Anderson, December 26, 1887.

CYRUS LAURON HOOPER, born November 7, 1863, at Rockport. Residence, New Harmony, Indiana, Educated at Illinois public schools. Degree Ph. B. and A. M., on presentation of a thesis, in 1888. Occupation, a teacher; three months in Champaign County, Illinois; five months in Wisconsin; Principal of the Spencer schools, and afterward Superintendent of the New Harmony school. Mr. Hooper is a writer for various periodicals.

WALTER GRESHAM HUDSON, born December 13, 1866, at Indianapolis. Residence, Rockport, Indiana. Educated at Rockport High School. Degree, A. B. Occupation, manager of the "leading insurance, real estate and loan agency."

ANDREW MORTON MALCOLM, born November 26, 1862, near Pittsburgh, Carroll County, Indiana. Residence, Albia, Monroe County, Iowa. Educated, three years in Washington Academy. Degree, A. B. Occupation, since graduation, a student of theology, and occasionally, teaching. Mr. Malcolm married Miss Altha Rose Martin, August 17, 1887.

IDA MAY MANLEY, born August 18, at Bloomington. Residence, Bloomington. Educated at graded schools of Bloomington. Degree, A. B.

JAMES AUSTIN MITCHELL, born March 13, 1856, at Bridgeton, Park County. Residence, Bloomington, Indiana. Educated at Bloomingdale Academy and Indiana State Normal School, class of '82; special student in the University of Michigan, 1884-86. Degree, A. B., A. M., *pro merito*. Occupation, assistant in the Preparatory Department of the University; Superintendent of the Sunday School of the Presbyterian Church. Mr. Mitchell married Mary A. Hickles, of Terre Haute, June 20, 1888. Mr. Mitchell engaged in training Normal classes during the summer vacations. In 1882-84 he was principal of South Wabash Academy.

ROBERT NURLAND, born May 16, 1866, New Albany, Indiana. Residence, Bedford, Indiana. Educated at Bedford Public Schools. Degree, A. B. (Modern Language Course). Occupation, teacher, Principal of Bedford High School (1887–89).

ALBERT RABB, born February 25, 1863, Fountain County. Residence, Indianapolis. Educated at Common Schools and Preparatory Department of the University. Degree, B. A., and from the University of Virginia, LL. B., in 1889. Occupation, in 1887–88, teaching; lawyer at Indianapolis (1889). Mr. Rabb was Assistant Principal in the High School at New Castle in 1887–88.

ELMER BRYAN STEWART, born August 16, 1865, Richland. Residence, Richland. Educated at Richland Academy. Degree, B. A. Occupation, from 1887 to 1889, Professor of Mathematics in Vincennes University; in 1889, Student of Theology in the United Presbyterian Theological Seminary, Xenia, Ohio.

JOE CURRY STRICKLAND. Degree, A. B., New Marion.

EDGAR TAYLOR, born at Smithville May 8, 1866. Residence, Smithville. Educated at New Albany High School in 1883. Degree, A. B. Occupation, teaching. Position, Principal of the High School at Paoli and also at Rensselaer.

FRANK M. WALTERS, born August 30, 1862, Switzerland County. Residence, LaPorte, Indiana. Educated at the County Schools of Switzerland County and at Vevay High School. Degree, B. A. Occupation, teacher; Principal of Monticello High School for a year; since that time teacher of Natural Science in LaPorte, Indiana.

Mr. Walters married Miss Jennie E. Horning, a student of the University, June 22, 1887.

LULU ADDIE WILSON, born at Bloomington, Indiana. Residence, Bloomington, Indiana. Educated in the Bloomington Schools. Degree, A. B. Occupation, teaching. Miss Wilson is a member of the United Presbyterian Church.

ALUMNI OF THE LAW DEPARTMENT.

1844.

FRANCIS PATRICK BRADLEY, born at Newry, Pennsylvania, 1817. Died in Louisiana about 1876. Degree, LL. B. Occupation, attorney at law; practiced at Washington, Indiana. Was a volunteer in the army during the Mexican war and served on the staff of Colonel J. H. Lane. For several years Mr. Bradley was a clerk in the land office of the Trustees of the Wabash and Erie canal. He was also a contractor on public works. On the breaking out of the Mexican war he assisted in raising a company of volunteers who served in the regiment of Colonel Lane. Mr. Bradley, in 1850, was married to Mary W. Brett. Mrs. Bradley died in 1854, leaving a son and a daughter.

JOSEPH BLAIR CARNAHAN, born in Nicholas County, Kentucky, 1815. Died at Washington, Indiana, 1848. Was educated at the Washington, Indiana, schools. Studied law at Indiana University, and received the degree LL. B. Occupation, attorney at law. Mr. Carnahan was a successful practitioner in Southern Indiana. He took an important part in politics as a Whig. Was justly noted for his zealous and energetic efforts in behalf of the religious, social, moral and commercial advancement of the community in which he lived. Mr. Carnahan was a member of the Presbyterian Church and a popular temperance lecturer.

JOHN M. CLARK. LL. B. Vincennes.

CLARENDON DAVISSON was born December 10, 1817, Xenia, Ohio. Died September 10, 1878, Brighton Island, Georgia. Educated at Xenia, Ohio; attended the Law School of Indiana University, and on graduating received the degree LL. B. For two years he practiced law at Petersburg. Moving to Bloomington he edited the town paper, *The Herald*. He was afterwards connected with the editorial corps of the Indianapolis *Journal*, Chicago *Tribune* and St. Louis *Democrat*. In 1861 he was appointed Consul at Bourdeaux, France. When in Bourdeaux he was made an honorary member of the Historical and Geological Society of France. Afterwards he became a member of the Geological and Statistical Society, New York. Mr. Davisson, during his consulship, rendered the United States Government great service by the influence he had in the south of France. It was mainly through him that the war steamers, Yeddo and Osacca, built by the Confederates, were prevented sailing from France. On Mr. Davisson's return from France he went to New Orleans, where he was on the editorial staff of the New Orleans *Republican*, and was connected with the Board of Education for two or three years.

JONATHAN K. KENNY. LL. B. Terre Haute.

1845.

SAMUEL HAMILTON BUSKIRK, born January 19, 1820, at New Albany. He received his early education at the common schools of Bloomington; attended the University, but did not graduate in the Collegiate Department; from the Law Department he received the degree, LL. B., in course, and in 1871, the honorary degree, LL. D.; from 1848 to 1854 he was a member of the Legislature; from 1862-65, Speaker of the House; in 1870, one of the Judges of the Supreme Court of Indiana. Judge Buskirk was the author of "Buskirk's Practice." For many years he resided in Bloomington. The last years of his life were spent in Indianapolis, where he died April 3, 1879.

GRAFTON F. COOKERLY, born August 18, 1818, at Frederick, Maryland. Residence, Terre Haute, Indiana. Educated in part at Indiana University. Degree, LL. B. Occupation, attorney at law; twice elected Mayor of Terre Haute; was a member of the Constitutional Convention in 1850, and twice elected a member of the Indiana Legislature.

WILLIAM B. HAGINS, born December 9, 1815, at Winchester, Kentucky. Residence, Portland, Jay County, Indiana (1887). Educated at private school and self taught. Degree, LL. B.

Occupation, attorney at law, and since the war of the Rebellion, fire insurance agent. Mr. Hagins has held the office of Notary Public, and Justice of the Peace, occasionally; was often called upon to act as Circuit Judge *pro tem*. Mr. Hagins, through disability, was unable to enter the army and fight for the Union, of which he was an enthusiastic friend. He was a Republican in politics, and a friend and supporter of religion.

WILLIS ARNOLD GORMAN, born January 12, 1814, near Flemingsburg, Kentucky. Died May 20, 1876, at St. Paul, Minnesota. Educated at home. Was admitted to the bar about 1834. Degree, LL. B. Occupation and position, attorney at law; an active politician of the Democratic party; Representative in the Indiana Legislature in 1837; member of Congress in 1849; re-elected in 1851; in 1853 was appointed by President Pierce the first Governor of Minnesota; in 1857 was a delegate to the Constitutional Convention of Minnesota; was Major in the Third Regiment of Indiana Volunteers in the Mexican War, and soon after was made Colonel of the Fourth Indiana Regiment; was engaged in the battles of Buena Vista and Huamantla, Atlixco, Puebla, Tlaxcala, El Peñol and some others; was military Governor of the city of Puebla; in 1861 was Colonel of the first Minnesota Infantry. For meritorious services in the first battle of Bull Run, was made Brigadier General, and during the civil war was in the following battles: Ball's Bluff, South Mountain, Antietam; afterwards was ordered to the Southwest; returned to St. Paul and practiced as City Attorney until his decease. On the 23d of May he was buried with civil and military honors.

JOHN M. COWEN. Frankfort, Indiana.

JAMES SCOTT HESTER. See Collegiate Department, 1843.

GEORGE H. MUNSON, Bedford, Indiana. See Collegiate Department, 1842.

DAVID K. SMYDTH, born October 29, 1819, Monroe County, Indiana. Died February 18, 1852, Milwaukee, Wisconsin. Educated at the Common Schools and at the University. Degree, LL. B. Occupation and position, attorney at law in Spencer, Indiana, and in Milwaukee, Wisconsin.

JAMES WILSON, Crawfordsville, Indiana.

SAMUEL THEOPHYLACT WYLIE. See Collegiate Department, year 1848.

1846.

V. M. BELL, Mount Carmel, Illinois.

LEWIS BOLLMAN. See Collegiate Department, Class 1831.

JOHN DARROCK, born July 8, 1820, Orange County. Residence, Morocco, Newton County, Indiana. Educated at Parke County Seminary. Degree, LL. B. Before entering the University he studied law in the office of Howard & Wright, in Rockville, for two years. Occupation, practiced law in Parke County for about two years, and since has been farming. Mr. Darrock was appointed Swamp Land Commissioner of Jasper County, and after holding this office eighteen months resigned. On January 18, 1844, Mr. Darrock married Caroline, daughter of Austin M. Puett, of Parke County, by whom he had six children, five sons and one daughter. Mrs. Darrock died July 2, 1853. On the 18th of October, 1855, he married Cecelia M., daughter of Benjamin Henkle, by whom he has had thirteen children, six sons and seven daughters, ten of whom are now living (1887). Mrs. Cecelia Darrock died January 17, 1878.

ALEXANDER MCCLELLAND, born January 1, 1800, County Derry, Ireland. Died September 8, 1876, Monroe County. Educated in Ireland. Degree, LL. B. Occupation, merchant and book-keeper. Mr. McClelland served during the Mexican War in the Commissary Department.

T. R. OSBORN, LL. B., Danville, Illinois.

ISAAC A. RICE, LL. B., Waveland, Indiana.

HENRY TANNER. See Collegiate Department, Class 1842.

1847.

NATHANIEL TIMOTHY HAUSER, born March 8, 1822, near Salem, in Stokes (now Forsythe) County, North Carolina. Mr. Hauser's present residence (1883) is Glenco, McLeod County, Minnesota. Educated at the common schools of Stokes County, and in part at the Moravian Academy, Salem, North Carolina. Leaving North Carolina when about 12 years old, and coming with his parents to Indiana, when schools were few and far between, he educated himself, till he entered the Law Department of the University, from which he received the degree LL. B. Since graduation he has practiced law and farmed on a small scale. From 1856 to 1860 he was Judge of Common Pleas in Bartholomew County. Was a private in a hastily organized company to oppose the "Morgan Raid" in Southern Indiana. During the war of the rebellion he was a war Democrat, supporting the cause of the Union unconditionally. Mr. Hauser was a Master Mason of the third degree and afterwards a Royal Arch Mason. Is a member of the church of his parents, the Moravian. In July, 1864, Mr. Hauser removed from Bartholomew County to Minnesota.

MILTON HIGHT, born February 7, 1823, Bloomington, Indiana, where he resided till the time of his death, November 3, 1887. Educated at the Bloomington schools and Collegiate Department of the University. Entered the Law School and received the degree LL. B. Occupation and position: For some years a merchant, afterwards a miller; was also a Justice of the Peace, and Treasurer of the University for some time, and a school trustee. Mr. Hight married Miss Sarah McCalla, of Bloomington.

DANIEL CAREY STOVER, born Nevember 18, 1822, Botetourt Court House, Virginia. Residence, Ladoga, Indiana. Educated at Wabash College. Degree, LL. B. Occupation and position, lawyer; Indiana State agent, 1859-61; in 1851 member of Indiana Legislature; on the committee that revised the statutes of Indiana, 1852; Elder in the Christian Church since 1847; President of Indiana State Christian Ministerial Association; organized a Christian Church in Denver, Colorado.

BARTON W. WILSON. See Collegiate Department, Class 1845.

1848.

A. H. EVANS. Delphi.

MORTON CRAIG HUNTER, born February 5, 1825, Versailles, Indiana. Residence, Bloomington, Indiana. Educated at Versailles and Wilmington, Indiana. Degree, LL. B. Occupation and position, lawyer, member of Indiana Legislature, Representative in Congress, Colonel in the army, Brevet General; was in all the battles under General Thomas from Stone River to Chicamauga, and from thence with General Sherman in all his battles to the close of the war, including his march to the sea. Shortly before the severe illness with which General Hunter was afflicted he was widely spoken of as the Republican candidate for Governor of Indiana. General Hunter married Miss Adeline Labertew, of Bloomington.

D. C. LANE.˙ LL. B. Indianapolis.

JOHN G. MCCALLUM. LL. B. Switzerland County.

W. K. PARISH, LL. B., Elizabethtown.

LARKIN REYNOLDS, born October 19, 1823, Mooresville, Indiana. Died August 13, 1855, Bloomington, Indiana. Educated in Common Schools. Degree, LL. B. Occupation, attorney at law. Member of Methodist Episcopal Church.

GUSTAVUS H. VOSS, born in 1821, Cincinnati, Ohio. Died at Indianapolis March 11, 1883. Educated at Woodward College, Cincinnati. Degree, LL. B. Occupation and position, practiced law at Palestine, Indiana, thence removed to Noblesville, where he served as District Attorney. In 1868 he moved to Indianapolis, and was a member of the law firm of Ray, Voss, Davis & Holman, until within two years of his decease. He was the proprietor of a fine stock farm in Hamilton County.

1849.

FREDERICK T. BROWN, a native of Bloomington. Residence, Greencastle. Educated in the Common Schools and at Mr. Cornelius Pering's Academy in Bloomington. Degree, LL. B. Occupation and position, attorney at law, Prosecuting Attorney and Judge.

T. H. BRUNER, LL. B., Ripon, Kansas, formerly of Princeton, Indiana.

WILLIAM WELLINGTON CARSON was born in County Mayo, Ireland, of Cromwellian stock. His father was hospital sergeant of the North Mayo Militia. He was quite young when he emigrated with his parents to Cobourg, Ontario, Canada. He received his early education in Canada. After removing to Fort Wayne in 1840 he took an irregular classical course in Mr. McJunkin's School. He afterwards engaged in teaching, and at the same time studied law. Being admitted to the bar, he commenced the practice of his profession at Decatur, Adams County, in 1846. He at the same time acted as Deputy Clerk and Recorder under the Hon. Samuel L. Rugg. To perfect himself in his profession, he attended the Law School of Indiana University in 1848–49, under the Professors Judge McDonald and Judge Otto. Leaving Decatur, he returned to Fort Wayne, and was elected Prosecuting Attorney. In 1850 he was appointed City Attorney of Fort Wayne, which position he held till 1857. In 1858 he was nominated by the Democratic party for Judge, but was defeated. In 1860 he was County Attorney during the construction of the present court house. In 1864 he was elected State Senator, and re-elected in 1866, and resigned in 1869; when, in company with his family he visited Europe. Mr. Carson made a good record while a Senator. He was the author of the constitutional amendment in relation to the Wabash & Erie Canal, and of the act of 1867 for the incorporation of cities. He voted for the bill presented by Judge Hughes, which made an appropriation of eight thousand dollars to the University. In 1870 he was elected Judge of the Court of Common Pleas for the counties of Adams, Allen, Huntington and Wells. In 1875 he was appointed Judge of the Judicial District, vacated by the resignation of Judge Lowry. On the expiration of the term he resumed the practice of law.

JAMES ASLIN ELSTON, born September 24, 1828. Died November 8, 1849. Mr. Elston was a graduate of Wabash College in 1846. In 1849 received the degree of LL. B. from Indiana University. At the time of his death he had just commenced the practice of law.

JOHN GREER, born at Dayton, Ohio, October 21, 1828. Residence, Topeka, Kansas, (1885.) Graduated in 1849. Degree, LL. B. Occupation, attorney at law and editor of the Topeka Tribune. From 1861-'66 was a member of the last Territorial Legislature of Kansas, and of the Wyandotte Constitutional Convention that formed the present Constitution of Kansas, and Consul to Mexico from 1869-'71. Mr. Greer was in the battle of Little Blue, Mo., and was severely wounded. The battle was fought October 22, 1864. Mr. Greer has lectured extensively on various subjects, such as Agriculture, Horticulture, Temperance, The Forces of Nature and Evolution.

DAVID W. LAFOLLETTE, LL. B. See professors' list.

MURRAY, LL. B., Vincennes.

WILLIAM C. WILSON, born November 22, 1827, at Crawfordsville, his residence (1882.) He graduated with high honor at Wabash College and received the degree A. B. in 1847, and A. M. in 1873. Mr Wilson was admitted to the practice of law in the First Circuit Court of Indiana, January, 1849. This same year he attended the Law School of Indiana University, and received the degree of LL. B. On June 2, 1849, he was admitted to the Supreme Court of Indiana, and on April 18, 1876, to the Supreme Court of the United States. He began the practice of law in Lafayette, March, 1850. He was appointed Assessor of Internal Revenue for the Eighth District of Indiana; this office he held during 1866. In August, 1867, he was appointed Postmaster at Lafayette, which office he held till April 1869. On the 17th of April, 1861, Mr. Wilson volunteered as a private, four days later he was mustered into the United States' service as Captain of Company D, 10th Regiment, Indiana Volunteers, and in the following May 10, was promoted to the rank of Major of the regiment. On July 11, he was wounded at the battle of Rich Mountain. Not long after, December, 1861, he was appointed Colonel of the 40th Regiment, Indiana Volunteers, which he had raised, and was mustered into the United States' service. In April, 1864, he was appointed Colonel of the 13th Regiment, Indiana Volunteers, and was discharged from service with the thanks of the Commander-General in September, 1864. Colonel Wilson was selected by the soldiers of Tippecanoe County to command the regiment at the soldier's reunion at Indianapolis on the 15th of October, 1875, and received for the regiment the prizes awarded by Governor Morton on that occasion. Col. Wilson was selected by the Army of the Cumberland to deliver the annual address before that body on July 7, 1876, at the Academy of Music, in Philadelphia. This address was received with high encomiums by the press throughout the country. Col. Wilson was elected Councilman for the Third Ward of Lafayette, and served till he was appointed Assessor of Internal Revenue. Col. Wilson was a Republican, but not

a politician. He cast his vote for General Taylor and General
Scott, always voting till 1876. He gave his time assiduously
to his profession. During his long practice he has been engaged in thirty-two capital cases, and no client of his has ever
been executed. The nation, always good to its defenders, has
placed Col. Wilson's name on the roll of invalid pensioners,
for wounds received in the service of his country.

WILLIAM A. BUGH. LL. B. Decatur, Illinois.

GEORGE ABRAHAM BUSKIRK, born August 10, 1829, Bloomington, Ind. Died July 22, 1874. Educated at Bloomington public schools and at the University, leaving while a Freshman to
enlist for the Mexican war. Printer and student of law in his
brother's (S. H. Buskirk's) office. Degree, LL. B. Occupation and position, lawyer; elected Judge of Common Pleas
Court in 1856; in 1867 elected Land Agent of State; in 1866
elected Representative to the State Legislature; in 1869 chosen
Speaker; 1871 organized the First National Bank, Bloomington. Enlisted a private in the Mexican war, in the First Indiana Regiment of volunteers; was transferred to the Third
Regiment under Colonel Lane; fought at the battle of Buena
Vista. As State agent opened an office at New York, and had
control of the funds for the payment of the State debt. Was
appointed, during the rebellion, Colonel of the Indiana Legion,
and also Judge Advocate. In 1869, while Speaker, he strongly
advocated the passage of the 15th amendment to the Constitution.

AMBROSE B. CARLTON, born December 18, 1825, Lawrence
County, Indiana. Residence, Terre Haute, Indiana (1883).
Educated in common schools and academy. Degree, LL. B.
Occupation and position, attorney at law, editor, author; has
twice held the office of Circuit Judge and twice Prosecuting
Attorney; was member of Indiana General Assembly, and in
the year 1883 chairman of the United States Utah Commission
of five; author of law book on Homicide, 1881; was tempora-
rily Professor of Law in Indiana University, 1856–57. Of late
Mr. Carlton has paid a good deal of attention to belles lettres.
His favorite books are Shakspeare and the Bible.

ADEN G. CAVENS, born October 24, 1827, Lawrence County,
Indiana. Residence, Bloomfield, Indiana. Educated at As-

bury University. Degree, LL. B. Occupation and position, attorney at law; a member of Nebraska Territorial Legislature, 1860-61; Captain Company E, 59th Indiana volunteers, 1861-62; afterward Major, Lieutenant Colonel and Colonel, 97th Regiment, till the close of the war. While Captain in 59th Indiana Regiment under General Pope was at New Madrid, Fort Pillow and the advance on Corinth. While Lieutenant Colonel was at the siege of Vicksburg; in battle at Jackson, Mississippi, and at Missionary Ridge. Went to the relief of General Burnside in the winter of 1863. In the Atlantic campaign was in the battles of Resaca, Dallas, Big Shanty Station, Kennesaw Mountain, at Atlanta July 22, 1864, and at Ezra Chapel, on the right of Atlanta, at Jonesboro and Lovejoy; commanded a prominent battalion at Kingston, in North Carolina; joined his regiment at Goldsboro and was in pursuit of Johnson at the close of the war. Was mustered out at Washington in 1865.

RICHARD ANDREW CLEMENTS, born July 20, 1827, Montgomery County, Maryland. Died September 16, 1867, Washington, Indiana. Degree, LL. B. Occupation and position, attorney at law, Representative of Daviess County in 1858-59, Prosecuting Attorney for the district for several years, and on the death of his father, Judge R. A. Clements, Sr., was appointed to fill the vacancy on the bench. In the fall of 1866 was elected Circuit Judge.

ISAAC W. LOVE. See Collegiate Department, 1848.

ROBERT HUSTON MILROY, born June 11, 1816, in Washington County, Indiana. Residence, Olympia, Washington Territory. Educated in the Norwich University, Norwich, Vermont, where he graduated, receiving the degrees A. B. and A. M., and delivered the valedictory oration. In 1850, LL. B., Indiana University. Occupation and position, attorney at law, in the army, Indian Agent, Washington Territory, President Judge of the Eighth Judicial Circuit, Captain in the Mexican war and Major-General in the late war, serving in the army from the first to the last day of the war. General Milroy was an Elder in the Presbyterian Church. Judge Gould thus writes of General Milroy: "He has a striking military air, being over six feet in stature, as straight as an arrow in form, and he has a sharp and piercing eye. He was beloved by all of his soldiers. In private life, of strict integrity and of a pure and unsullied character."

SHERIDAN P. READ. Degree, LL. B. Paris, Illinois.

ROBERT A. SMITH, born June 13, at Boonville, Indiana. Residence, St. Paul, Minnesota. Educated principally at the Indiana University. Degree, LL. B. Occupation and position, lawyer, Auditor of Warrick County, Indiana; from 1850 to 1853, Private Secretary of Governor Gorman; from 1853 to 1856, Treasurer of Ramsey County, Minnesota. Since leaving the public office, from 1856 to 1868, banker. Mr. Smith was one of the Aldermen of St. Paul.

ELIAS WILLITTS, born August 12, 1826, Wayne County, Indiana. Died in Monmouth, Illinois, November 1, 1881. Educated at Centreville, Indiana, and Quincy, Illinois. Occupation, attorney at law. During the last eleven years of his life Mr. Willitts was Probate Judge. He was a member of the Swedenborgian Church.

ALFRED WHEELER, born October 10, 1824, in Ridgeway, Orleans County, New York. Was educated at the common schools of New York and Indiana; two years at Indiana University Collegiate Department. Graduated LL. B. from the Law School. Since graduation his principal employment has been as a printer, publisher and editor; occasionally a teacher, book-keeper, merchant and speculator. In 1882, a member of the Tribune Printing Company, in South Bend, Indiana. For two terms, 1867–1875, he has been Auditor of St. Joseph County. Mr. Wheeler has traveled in nearly every State and Territory in the Union, and in British Columbia and Canada.

SIMEON K. WOLFE, born February 14, 1824, in Floyd County, Indiana. Residence, New Albany, Indiana. Educated in Floyd County common schools. Degree, LL. B. Occupation and position, attorney at law, member of State Senate in 1860 to 1864, member of Congress 1873–1875, Judge of Floyd and Clark Circuit Court, 1880; editor of the Corydon Weekly Democrat; in 1856, Presidential elector. In conjunction with Mr. Norman, of the New Albany Ledger, was delegate to the Charleston National Convention, an opponent of disunion and an advocate of the war policy of the North.

1851.

THOMAS BIGHAM, LL. B., Otumwa, Wapello County, Iowa.

MARMION H. BOWERS, born April 29, 1829, at Moore's Hill, Indiana. Died March 3, 1872, at Austin, Texas. Educated at Hamilton College, Ohio. Degree, LL. B. Occupation and position, attorney at law and politician. Went to Texas in 1852, and in 1854 located at Austin; 1861, Captain of the 16th Infantry, Texas Volunteers; Representative in Texas Legislature, 1864; State Senator of the twelfth Texas Legislature. Mr. Bowers had a high reputation as a patriot statesman. Though enfeebled by consumption and unable to stand, he did not absent himself from the Senate, but contended bravely for an honest government and an upright administration.

IGNATIUS BROWN, born August 11, 1831, at Indianapolis. Residence, Indianapolis, Indiana. Educated at Marion County Seminary. Degree, LL. B. Occupation, attorney at law and abstractor of titles to real estate.

MICHAEL FINK BURKE, born March 10, 1829, in County Limerick, Ireland; died May 22, 1864, at Washington, Indiana. Judge Burke received his academical education in Ireland, his professional education in Indiana University Law School, receiving the degree LL. B. Occupation, practice of the law. Was for some time Judge of the Circuit Court.

JESSE M. GALE, born June 18, 1828, in Crawford County, Ohio. Residence, Angola, Steuben County, Indiana. Educated at Collegiate Institute, LaGrange, Indiana. Degree, LL. B. at Indiana University and National Law School, Ballston Spa, New York. Occupation, attorney at law and banker; for twenty years actively engaged in the temperance cause. Member of the Alpha Literary Society, of Angola.

JONAS GEORGE HOWARD, born May 22, 1825, in Floyd County, Indiana. Residence, Jeffersonville, Indiana. Educated in the common schools and at Indiana Asbury University. Degree, LL. B. Occupation and position, lawyer and member of the State Legislature in 1863. In 1868, Presidential elector, and also in 1876.

DAVID MILTON JONES, born February 15, 1828, in Vermillion County; died August 14, 1865, at Newport. Educated four years at Wabash College. Studied law with Hon. H. S. Lane and Judge S. C. Wilson, of Crawfordsville. Entered Indiana Law School. On graduating, received the degree LL. B. Occupation, attorney at law. Position, was Representative from Vermillion County in 41st General Assembly of Indiana. Mr. Jones was an ardent Republican, took an active part in the campaigns of 1856 and 1860, and made numerous eloquent addresses in support of the war.

JOHN STOCKTON LEEDON, born August 1, 1826, Bucks County, Pennsylvania. Residence, Urbana, Ohio. Educated at Springfield (Ohio) Academy. Degree, LL. B. Occupation, practice of law in the Ohio Court and the District and Circuit Courts of the United States.

JOHN WALTER LOPP, born November 14, 1828, Harrison County, Indiana. Residence, Mauckport, Indiana. Educated at the public schools. Degree, LL. B. Occupation and position, farmer and attorney at law. Member of the Legislature of Indiana of 1865 and '67, and the special session of 1865.

BLACKFORD BOUDINOT MOFFATT. See Collegiate Department, Class 1849.

ELIPHALET D. PEARSON, born December 18, 1829, Springville, Indiana. Residence, Bedford, Indiana. Educated in common schools and Indiana University. Degree, LL. B. Occupation and position, practicing law, editor of White River *Standard*, Prosecuting Attorney, and Judge of the Tenth Judicial Circuit for six years. This upright Judge and excellent citizen died July 3, 1890.

JAMES COLLINS THOM, born December 29, 1824, Scott County, Indiana. Died August 30, 1865, Madison, Indiana. Educated at Hanover College, from which he received the degree B. S. Degree, LL. B., Indiana University. Occupation, teacher; afterwards attorney at law in Madison. Being lame he could not serve in the army, but was active and efficient in doing all in his power for the soldier and his cause.

JAMES WOODARD. See Collegiate Department, Class 1849.

BEZALEEL E. WRIGHT, LL. B., Richland.

1852.

JOHN PAUL BAIRD, born in April, 1829, Shelby County, Kentucky. Died in April, 1882. Educated in Franklin College, but did not graduate. Degree, LL. B. Occupation, attorney at law; one of the most able lawyers that ever practiced at the Terre Haute bar. He was a member of the Legislature. He was a Colonel in the Eighty-fifth Indiana Regiment, in the Army of the Cumberland, and went with Sherman as far as Marietta, Georgia, when ill health compelled him to resign.

SAMUEL ALEXANDER BONNER, born December 5, 1826, in Wilcox County, Alabama. Residence, Greensburg, Indiana. Educated at Miami University, Oxford, Ohio, and at Centre College, Kentucky. Degree, LL. B. Judge Bonner received degree A. B. from Centre College and A. M. from Miami University. Occupation and position, lawyer, Representative in the State Legislature in 1855, Common Pleas Judge in 1856–60, Circuit Judge in 1877. Judge Bonner is an elder in the Presbyterian Church.

WILLIAM M. CONNELLY, LL. B., Spencer, Indiana.

JOSEPH FOX DRAPER, born at Haw Patch, near Columbus, Indiana. Died June 19, 1876, in Chariton County, Missouri. Mr. Draper was self-educated. Degree, LL. B. Occupation, was for some time a merchant and farmer, practiced law in Chariton. On the breaking out of the war, Mr. Draper was the first to enlist in the township where he resided. He raised three companies of volunteers, served in the 12th Indiana Regiment, served in Virginia with the 12th Indiana, under Col. W. H. Link, and was Captain of Company K, 12th Indiana.

JAMES THOMAS EMBREE, born January 27, 1829, Princeton, Indiana. Died August 3, 1867, Princeton Indiana. Educated at Princeton common schools and Indiana Asbury University, from which he received the degree A. B. in 1850. Degree, LL. B., Indiana University. Occupation and position, lawyer at Princeton from 1852–61. Major and Lieutenant-Colonel 58th Indiana Volunteers for two years, and was afterward a lawyer and farmer; was engaged in the battles of Stone

River, Chickamauga, Lookout Mountain and Shiloh. As a lawyer, Mr. Embree held a high rank in south-western Indiana.

WILLIAM HENRY GREEN, LL. B., Mt. Vernon.

LEWIS COBB STINSON, born February 17, 1825, Evansville, Indiana, died September 16, 1875, at Evansville. Educated at common schools of Vanderburgh County, and at Evansville. Degree, LL. B. Occupation and position, attorney at law. Prosecuting Attorney in Evansville District; for some time taught school. Member of the General Baptist Church, of which his father was a minister.

STEPHEN C. TABOR, LL. B., Mt. Vernon.

HENRY D. WISE, LL. B., Vincennes.

REUBEN SAMUEL RAGAN, born March 10, 1819, Mercer County, Kentucky. Residence, Greencastle, Indiana. Degree, B. S., Wabash College, and LL. B., Indiana University. Occupation and position, lawyer and fruit grower. Representative in the State Legislature of Indiana for two terms. Mayor of Greencastle. Colonel on Governor Morton's staff. Deacon and elder in the Presbyterian Church.

1853.

WILLIAM H. BROWNLEE, born January 8, 1832, Princeton, Indiana. Residence, Brookfield, Missouri. Educated at Gibson County Seminary. Degree, LL. B. Occupation and position, lawyer, and of late years lawyer and banker. Judge of Linn County Probate Court, 1862-66. Judge Common Pleas, 1870-74.

FRANCIS L. NEFF, born 1832, Boyle County, Kentucky. Killed June 24, 1864, at the battle of Kennesaw Mountain. Educated in part at Indiana University. Degree, LL. B. Occupation and position, attorney at law; till 1861, Prosecuting Attorney. Enlisted in the Union army in 1861, and was a private, lieutenant, adjutant, captain, major and lieutenant-colonel; was engaged in the battles of Fort Donaldson, Pittsburg Landing, Stone River, Chickamauga and Kenesaw Mountain, where he lost his life.

FIELDING PRICKETT, born December 21, 1827, in Brown County, Ohio. Residence, Albion, Indiana. Educated at Lagrange Collegiate Institute, Lagrange, Indiana. Degree, LL. B. Occupation and position, attorney at law.

JOSEPH C. THOMPSON, born September 18, 1826, Blairsville, Pennsylvania. Residence, Quincy, Illinois. Educated at Lebanon, Ohio. Degree, LL. B. Occupation and position, attorney at law, member of Constitutional Convention of Illinois, 1862-63. County Judge of Adams County, 1873-77.

1854.

JOSEPH COX, born March 21, 1821, in Orange County, Indiana. Residence, Dallas, Texas. Educated at Friends' School, Lick Creek, Orange County. Degree, LL. B. Occupation and position, attorney at law, and in Indiana, Tennessee and Texas farming; State Senator in Indiana Legislature, 1853; Township Trustee in Paoli. Major in the Confederate Cavalry, 2d Texas Regiment. Was at the battle of Shiloh, at the capture of Holly Springs, at the battles around and in the retreat from Corinth, at the battle of Chickamauga. Was captured on a scouting expedition in Tennessee, in December, 1863, and held a prisoner of war at Nashville and Johnson's Island, in Lake Erie, till the close of the war. Returned to Paoli, entered the practice of law till April, 1880. Removed to Dallas, Texas, where he engaged in his profession with commendable success.

JOHNSON D. CURL. LL. B. Lagrange County.

JONATHAN H. JONES. LL. B. Marion County.

ELHANAN W. LAFOLLETTE. LL. B. Montgomery County.

CURRAN EMMETT MCDONALD. A. M. and LL. B. See Collegiate Department, Class of 1852.

NEWTON F. MALOTT. A. M. and LL. B. See Collegiate Department, 1852.

WILLIS G. NEFF, born August 30, 1828, Boyle County, Kentucky. Residence, Greencastle, Indiana. Educated in county schools. Degree, LL. B. Occupation and position, Recorder of Sullivan County, 1857; Prosecuting Attorney, 1860-62; four times elected to represent Putnam County in the Legislature; 1871, chairman of the Committee of Ways and Means and of the Judiciary; delegate to the National Convention in 1876 at St. Louis; a member of the Christian Church.

PASCAL S. PARKS. LL. B. Martinsville.

JOHN J. PAYNTER. Degree, LL. B. Omaha, Nebraska.

JOHN MCCARTNEY. LL. B. Indiana, Pennsylvania.

1855.

ROBERT BELL, born in 1829, in Lawrence County, Illinois. Residence, Mount Carmel, Illinois. Educated in the Mt. Carmel select schools. Degree, LL. B. Occupation and position, attorney at law, Circuit Judge, President of the Illinois Southern Railroad Company, President of the St. Louis, Mt. Carmel and New Albany Railroad Company, Special Internal Revenue Agent in California in 1876, Republican candidate for Congress in the Nineteenth Illinois District in 1878, United States Committeeman to examine Atlantic and Pacific Railroad in New Mexico, 1881; member of Republican State Central Committee of Illinois since 1878.

SAMUEL W. HILL. LL. B. Bloomfield.

JACOB L. PAYNTER, born November 7, 1833, in Washington County, Indiana. Residence, Salem, Indiana. Educated in the Washington County district schools. Degree, LL. B. Occupation, farmer and teacher. Mr. Paynter is the inventor and patentee of a straw cutter, 1881.

HENRY CLAY RIPPEY, born April 29, 1830, at Lewisville, Henry County, Indiana. Residence, Tallahassee, Leon County, Florida. Educated in the Leesburg public schools and Indiana University. Degree, LL. B. Occupation and position, lawyer, land agent and editor; Enrolling Clerk Iowa Senate, 1864; member of House of Representatives, Iowa, 1867-8, and Journal Clerk; Major of the Forty-sixth Iowa Infantry; also a judge in Florida, having removed there in 1874.

1856.

GEORGE W. DEAN. LL. B. Springfield, Illinois.

OLIVER J. GLESSNER, born October 11, 1828, Frederick, Maryland. Residence, Shelbyville, Indiana. Degree, LL. B. Occupation and position, lawyer, Judge of the Eighth Judicial District from 1864 to 1868, State Senator from 1870 to 1874. See Indiana Biography, Volumn 1, 7th, 45.

ROBERT I. MORRISON. Degree, A. M. See College Department, Class 1855.

DAVID SHEEKS, born May 9, 1830, in Lawrence County, Indiana. Residence, Austin, Texas. Educated at the Indiana Asbury University. Degree, LL. B. Occupation and position, practicing attorney at law; Judge of District Court, Texas.

1857.

DAVID DEMAREE BANTA. Degree, A. M. See College Department, 1855.

HENRY P. BRAZEE. LL. B. Cannelton.

JAMES W. BROWN. LL. B. Marion.

EDMUND JAEGER, born September 22, 1833, Mandack, Rhenish Bavaria, Germany. Residence, Keokuk, Iowa. Educated at Mandack public schools and Normal Institute. Degree, LL. B. Occupation and positions, lawyer, banker, Alderman, Vice President of School Board, Probate Judge, Auditor, and Mayor of Keokuk, Iowa.

BURR H. POLK, born January 15, 1835, at Taylorsville, Kentucky. Residence, Lincoln, Nebraska. Educated in the town and county schools, and for a term at the William Jewett College, Liberty, Missouri. Degree, LL. B. Occupation, attorney at law till the rebellion; served in the army during the war; after that was a merchant in Vicksburg till the year 1876; since a broker and speculator in Western lands; in 1868-69 he was Mayor of Vicksburg. Mr. Polk went to the war as Captain Company F, 33d Indiana; subsequently was appointed Captain and Assistant Adjutant General by President Lincoln; afterward was, at the request of General Grant, promoted by President Lincoln to the rank of Major; by President Johnson was brevetted Lieutenant Colonel and Colonel; continued Adjutant General for some time after the war; served on the staffs of Generals Baird, Stoneman, Rousseau and Thomas, in the Army of the Cumberland; was appointed First Lieutenant in the regular army after the war, but having gone into business, declined the position. In 1879 General Polk traveled in Europe, and gave an account of his travels in a series of letters to the Evansville *Journal* and Vicksburg *Herald*. These letters were subsequently published in book form under the title of the "Big American Caravan in Europe." General Polk, it should have been stated, took an active part in the battles of Wild Cat, Chickamauga, Mission Ridge and Nashville.

OMER F. ROBERTS, born June 17, 1834, in Dearborn County, Indiana. Residence, Aurora, Indiana. Educated at Lawrenceburg, under Prof. B. T. Hoyt. Degree, LL. B. Occupation and position, lawyer, member of Indiana Legislature two terms, Judge of the 7th Judicial Circuit of Indiana for six years and seven months.

GEORGE W. THOMPSON, LL. B., Owensville.

1858.

NEWTON BURWELL, born August 1, 1836, in Fairfield County, Ohio. Residence, Bluffton, Indiana. Educated in Fairfield County, and after at Bluffton. Degree, LL. B. Occupation and position, practiced law from 1858 to 1876; entered North Indiana Conference on trial, and remained in the ministry till April, 1871; withdrew and became a dealer in lumber; Prosecuting Attorney; Representative in State Legislature, 1865; member Board of School Trustees, Bluffton, and local preacher in Methodist Episcopal Church.

STEPHEN GIRARD BURTON, A. M. See Collegiate Department, class of 1857.

BENJAMIN F. CAVINS, born March 25, 1838, at Bloomfield, Indiana. Residence, New Albany, Indiana. Educated at Indiana Asbury University. Degree, LL. B. Occupation and position, practice of law for ten years; since, a minister in the Baptist Church. Enlisted as a private soldier in the army; was in the battles of Chickamauga, Resaca, Kennesaw Mountain, and in the disastrous raids of Stoneman and McCook, south of Atlanta.

ANDREW JACKSON LEE, LL. B., Starville, Texas.

ELI K. MILLEN, born February 26, 1837, in Monroe County,

Indiana. Residence, Bloomington, Indiana. Educated at Bloomington public schools. Degree, LL. B. Occupation and position, attorney at law; Prosecuting Attorney from 1858 to 1861.

HOSEA MURRAY, LL. B., Springhill.

WILBUR FISKE STONE, A. M. See Collegiate Department, Class 1857.

JAMES B. TURNER, LL. B., Elizabethtown, Illinois.

1859.

THEODORE W. FRY BRYANT, LL. B., Williamsport.

RICHARD L. COFFEY, born May 7, 1835, in Monroe County, Indiana. Residence, Nashville, Indiana. Educated in Franklin College, Indiana. Degree, LL. B. Occupation and position, attorney at law, Judge of Court of Common Pleas of Eighth District, and State Senator from the counties of Bartholomew, Brown and Monroe (1882).

SAMUEL W. CURTIS, LL. B., Brazil, Indiana.

LUTHER MARTIN DEMOTTE, born September 23, 1838, at Bloomington, Indiana. Died June 1, 1875, at Grayville, Illinois. Educated at Bloomington public schools and Preparatory Department of Indiana University. Degree, LL. B. Occupation and position, editor and attorney at law. In the war of the rebellion he was Lieutenant, and for special service in the Signal office was promoted to the rank of Captain. At the close of his life he was a member of the Christian Church.

NOAH S. GIVEN. See Collegiate Department, Class 1858.

HENRY CLAY HILL, born December 13, 1834, at the Hill homestead, Greene County, Indiana. Died May 4, 1865, at Bloomfield, Indiana. Educated at the common schools of New Lebanon and Bloomfield. Degree, LL. B. Occupation, in 1855-56, a teacher. After graduation he practiced law, and was a successful and highly esteemed member of the bar till his health failed, and his disease, consumption, soon ended his life on earth. Mr. Hill served for some time as County School Superintendent, taking great interest in educational work. He was a steward in and an influential and exemplary member of the Methodist Episcopal Church. His addresses, which he was often called upon to make professionally and otherwise, were of a high order of merit. Mr. Hill married (June 25, 1861) Miss Emma, the youngest daughter of M. and A. Ritter, of Bloomfield, who still survives, and mourns her loss, sorrowing, yet rejoicing that he died in the full assurance of faith in his Savior.

JOHN RANDOLPH ISENHOWER, born May 6, 1833, near Ellettsville, Monroe County. Residence, Bloomfield, Indiana. Educated in Monroe County schools. Degree, LL. B. Occupation and position, attorney and counselor at law; member of the State Legislature; served both at special and regular sessions of the Legislature of 1872-3; School Examiner in Greene County. Mr. Isenhower married Sallie L. Lester, of Bloomfield, September 29, 1863.

ALEXANDER D. LEMON. See Collegiate Department, Class of 1858.

AMOS H. LUTHER, LL. B., Des Moines, Iowa.

AUGUSTUS DAVIS LYNCH. See Collegiate Department, Class of 1857.

JAMES BOLEYN MULKY, born October 4, 1826, Harrison County. Residence, Bloomington, Indiana. Educated in Harrison and Monroe County schools. Degree, LL. B. Occupation and position, attorney at law; in the army at different times; served as Major, Colonel and Provost Marshal, both in the Mexican war and during the rebellion. In June, 1846, he volunteered in Company A; 2d Regiment, Indiana volunteers, for the Mexican war. Fought at Beuna Vista, where he received a slight wound. In the war of the rebellion he fought at Richmond, Kentucky, in 1862. Major Mulky was appointed Register in Bankruptcy by Chief Justice Chase. Was congressional delegate to the Republican National Convention at Chicago in 1868, and in the convention at Philadelphia in 1872, and also national convention at Cincinnati in 1876. Colonel Mulky married Miss Coffey, of Monroe County.

URIAH MULLIKIN. See Collegiate Department, Class 1857.

PLEASANT ALONZO PARKS, born November 12, 1828, in Lawrence County. Died February 11, 1875. Educated at county schools and Bedford schools. Degree, LL. B. Occupation, attorney at law, practicing in Bedford and the District Courts. Though physically weak, Mr. Parks was industrious, energetic and talented.

STEPHEN THRASHER. See Collegiate Department, Class 1857.

GEORGE WALLACE THROOP, born October 10, 1836, at Millgrove, Owen County, Indiana. Died December 7, 1862, at Stockton, Indiana. Degree, LL. B. Occupation, attorney at law.

NICHOLAS VAN HORN, born July 14, 1834, in Darke County, Ohio. Residence, Indianapolis. Educated in common schools of Northern Indiana. Degree, LL. B. Occupation and position, attorney at law; Prosecuting Attorney 17th Circuit, 1866 to 1868; assistant U. S. Assessor 11th District of Indiana; Lieutenant Company A, 47th Indiana Volunteers; served for four years in the army, was at the battles of Stone River, Riddles' Point and Nashville. An elder in the Church.

THOMAS JEFFERSON WOLFE. See Collegiate Department, Class 1856.

*1861.

DANIEL M. BAKER, born January 26, 1842, in Brown County, Indiana. Residence, Chariton, Iowa. Educated at Chariton schools. Degree, LL. B. Occupation and position, lawyer, editor of Chariton *Leader* nine years, miner four years in Montana Territory; 1866 and 1867 served in Iowa Legislature, 16th General Assembly; 1876 Mayor of city of Chariton, President of Board of Trustees of State Asylum for the Feeble-Minded, author of History of Lucas County, Iowa; a Democrat in politics.

JAMES A. BARNETT, born February 2, 1837, at Camden, Ohio. Residence, Wellsville, Franklin County, Kansas. Educated at Wabash College. Degree, LL. B. Occupation, farmer and stock-raiser, served two terms in Kansas Legislature, entered the army as a private in 1861, left it a captain. Married, December, 1862, Miss Sarah R. Harrison, daughter of Hon. James H. Harrison, Ladoga, Indiana.

---

* There was no graduating class in 1860.

AMBROSE CLINTON CARLTON, born February 2, 1832, at Bedford, Indiana. Residence, Bedford, Indiana. Educated in the Bedford High School. Degree, LL. B. Occupation and position, engaged for some time in teaching, attorney at law, editor and farmer, was a private in the army.

THOMAS BARTHOLOMEW DONICA, born January 25, 1832, in Lawrence County. Residence, Ellenton, Manatee County, Florida; in 1887, at Bedford. Educated in the Bedford High School. Degree, LL. B. Occupation, commenced the practice of law at Bedford, Indiana; through failure of health engaged in farming; for the last three years, since 1884, a cultivator of fruits and vegetables in South Florida.

LEVI HANSON, born December 25, 1827, in Lawrence County, Indiana. Residence, South Granger, Monroe County, Indiana. Educated in the Wabash College and Northwestern Christian University, and completed the full course at Indiana University, but graduated at the Northwestern Christian University (now Butler), receiving the degrees, A. B. and A. M.; degree, LL. B., Indiana University. Occupation and position, teaching, preaching and farming; evangelist and elder in the Christian Church.

1862.

GEORGE O. ISEMINGER, born May 16, 1841, Bloomington, Indiana. Residence, Bedford, Indiana. Educated at Mt. Pleasant and Chariton, Iowa. Degree, LL. B.

MARION MOONEY, LL. B., Columbus, Indiana.

JAMES MORGAN, LL. B., Olathe, Kansas.

JOHN STILWELL HEADY, born April 27, 1836, in Switzerland County, Indiana. Residence, Mount Sterling, Indiana (1887). Educated at Hartsville College in 1862-3. Degree, LL. B. Occupation, attorney at law. Mr. Heady married Margaret Stickler.

1863.

EDWARD C. BUSKIRK, born in 1834 at Bloomington, Indiana. Residence, Washington, D. C. Educated at Bloomington schools. Degree, LL. B. Occupation and position, lawyer, and Judge of Marion County Court in 1874-78.

CURRAN A. DEBRULER, A. M. See Collegiate Department, Class 1863.

JAMES SYLVESTER NUTT, A. M. See Collegiate Department, Class 1861.

ALFRED RYORS, born February 27, 1843, at Athens, Ohio. Residence, Chicago, Illinois. Educated at Centre College, Kentucky. Degree, LL. B. Occupation, lawyer.

TREVANION TEEL WEIR, born April 1, 1834, at New Albany, Indiana. Died February 6, 1876, at Wabash, Indiana. Educated at Greencastle. Degree, LL. B. Occupation, lawyer.

JACOB VANCE WOLFE. See Collegiate Department, Class 1857.

1864.

NAPOLEON BONAPARTE ARNOLD, A. M. See Collegiate Department, Class 1862.

ORLAN FRANKLIN BAKER, Died at Vincennes. Residence, Spencer, Indiana. Degree, LL. B. Occupation, lawyer, City Attorney of Vincennes in 1863–65, member of the House of Representatives in 1866–68, editor of Vincennes *Times*, author of "The Primitive Dwellers, a History of the Population, Aboriginal and Colonial," and "Annals of Vincennes" (Φ. Δ. Θ. Catalogue). Mr. Baker married Miss Nora Aley, of Bedford.

WILLIAM M. HOGGATT, LL. B., Paoli.

MADISON EVANS, A. M. See Collegiate Department, Class 1856.

JASPER N. LEE, LL. B., Terre Haute.

JOHN H. LOUDEN, A. M. See Collegiate Department, Class 1861.

JOHN MILTON MCCOY, A. M. See Collegiate Department, Class 1860.

HENRY A. PARSONS, LL. B., Manchester.

JAMES P. RANKIN, born September 8, 1831, near Middleton, Tennessee. Residence, Pulaski, Giles County, Tennessee. Educated at county schools and Union University, Murfreesboro, Tennessee. Degree, LL. B. Occupation, merchant, residing in Giles County, except four years during the war, which were spent in Indiana. A Unitarian in faith. A man of high principles and morality, an advocate of independent thought, and one who desires the elevation of mankind.

DANIEL OLIVER SPENCER, born September 1, 1842, Bloomington, Indiana. Residence, Bloomington, Indiana. Educated at Bloomington public schools. Degree, LL. B. Occupation, court and general reporter for the Monon railroad. Mr. Spencer served in the army; was Corporal and acting Sergeant Major in Company H, 18th Regiment, Indiana volunteers. Was orator at the State Encampment of the G. A. R. at Indianapolis, February, 1888. He took an active part in the battle of Pea Ridge, March, 1862. Mr. Spencer, as a stenographer, reported the trial of Prof. Strunk, at New Albany, in October, 1886. This report was published in pamphlet form by the New Albany *Ledger*. Mr. Spencer has not only reported for several newspapers, but has also delivered many public lectures on "Elocution," "Mind Reading," "Justification by Faith," and the "Final Perseverance of the Saints, Baptized Believers," etc., etc., at the Masonic Orphans' and Widows' Home and at Prof. Chase's Female High School. For these two last lectures he was complimented by a rising vote of thanks. In 1888 made an active canvass as a stump orator for the Democracy. In October, 1886, Mr. Spencer married Miss Belle Holmes, of Louisville, Ky.

WILLIAM B. WOLFE. See Collegiate Department, Class of 1860.

1865.

ISAAC NEWTON CAREFS, born July 30, 1840, near Salem, Indiana. Died February 9, 1867, Washington County, Indiana. Educated at Salem Academy. Degree, LL. B. Occupation and position, lawyer, Prosecuting Attorney, 4th District, Indiana.

GEORGE WOODSON EASLEY, born December 15, 1844, Clark County Missouri. Residence, Hannibal, Missouri. Educated in public schools, Missouri. Degree, LL. B. Occupation and position, attorney at law, Linn County, Missouri, General Attorney of the Hannibal & St. Joseph Railroad Company. Member of Legislature of Missouri, in 1876-7, Chief-of-staff to Gen. Van Cleve, with rank of Lieutenant-Colonel (1882.)

JOHN CHALMERS ORCHARD, A. M., LL. B. See Collegiate Department, Class 1861.

JAMES H. ROGERS, A. M., LL. B. See Collegiate Department, Class 1861.

GREENBERRY SACK, B. S., LL. B. See Collegiate Department, Class 1865.

CHRISTOPHER THOMPSON, LL. B., Russellville, Kentucky.

1866.

EDWARD B. BARNARD, born April 7, 1841, died January 15, 1882. Degree, LL. B. Occupation, printer, foreman in Louisville *Journal* office, political writer, and publisher of newspapers. His last paper was called the Olney *Times*; married Miss Lizzie Gray, of Olney, Illinois, in 1872. Mrs. Barnard died March 18, 1882, leaving three children.

DANIEL M. BROWNING, born at Benton, Illinois, October 11, 1846. Residence, Benton, Illinois. Educated at the schools of Benton. Degree, LL. B. He graduated with distinction in the Law Department of the University; was examined before the Supreme Court of Illinois in June following, and was admitted to the bar before he was twenty years of age. He was elected County Judge in November, 1869, at the age of twenty-three years and was re-elected in 1873 and 1877 without opposition, which position he resigned upon being elected Circuit Judge of the First Judical Circuit in June, 1879. Judge Browning has a reputation for his suavity, dignity, learning and good sense rarely equalled, and also is of exceptional good social qualities. As a Mason, Judge Browning, entering the Benton Lodge in 1868, has served as Worshipful Master, and as District Deputy Grand Master, He was chairman of the Committe of Appeals and Grievances. In 1878 was elected Junior Grand Warden, and has reached the rank of Grand Master (1883.) Judge Browning married Tirzah Bell Naylor, of Cincinnati, in 1868, and has three children (1887.) He now has a large and lucrative practice in Benton.

(Taken; with slight modifications, from the *Advocate*, Bloomington, Illinois, of October, 1886.)

BARTHOLOMEW BURRELL, B. S., LL. B. See Collegiate Department, 1864.

JOSEPH S. DAILY, born May 31, 1844, in Wells County. Residence, Bluffton, Indiana. Educated in public schools of Wells County; studied law in the office of N. Burrell, Esq. Degree, LL. B. Occupation and position, lawyer, District Attorney, Prosecuting Attorney Tenth Judicial Circuit, 1870–74; Representative Wells and Adams counties; director and attorney of the Delphi, Bluffton & Frankfort railroad. Member of the Universalist Church.

BENJAMIN F. GARRISON, LL. B., Carthage, Missouri.

HOWARD HART, born October 25, 1841, at Putnamville, Indiana. Residence, Cloverdale, Indiana. Educated in the county schools. Degree, LL. B. Occupation, farmer and proprietor of a saw mill.

SIDNEY B. HATFIELD, A. M. and LL. B. See Collegiate Department, Class of 1864.

CHARLES KROFF, born December 11, 1837, in Monroe County, Ohio. Residence, Hermitage, Hickory County, Missouri. Educated at Captina, Ohio: Columbus, Indiana; Milford, Indiana, and Indiana Asbury University. Degree, LL. B. Occupation and position, practice of law, dealer in real estate, and also engaged in farming and stock raising. During the war was Sergeant, Second Lieutenant, Aid de Camp and Assistant Adjutant General, while a member of Company F, 11th Regiment, Indiana volunteers. County Attorney of Hamilton County, Missouri, and Prosecuting Attorney; member of Centennial Committee. In the army for four years; participated in the battles of Fort Henry, Fort Donaldson, Pittsburg Landing, siege of Corinth, battle of Port Gibson, Champion Hills, Mississippi, siege of Vicksburg, Lake Tasse, Louisiana, and Hall Town, Winchester, Fisher's Hill, Tim's Brook and Cedar Creek, Virginia.

ARTHUR CALVIN MELLETTE, A. M., LL. B. See Collegiate Department, Class 1864.

THOMAS MONROE MOONEYHAM, born October 17, 1844, at Benton, Illinois. Residence, Benton, Illinois, Franklin County. Educated at McKendree College, Illinois. Degree, LL. B. Occupation, practiced law till 1880, since which time he has engaged in milling, farming and stock-raising. Position,

Clerk in Circuit Court in 1872-76, and member of the Legislature from 1876 to 1888.

GEORGE D. ORNER, born April 24, 1845, in Hunterdon County, New Jersey. Residence, Medicine Lodge, Kansas. Educated at Lambertville Academy, New Jersey. Degree, LL. B. Occupation and position, lawyer, special agent of Postoffice Department, United States Revenue Collector, member of Legislature of Kansas in 1881, regent of State Normal School of Kansas in 1882, member of Company C, 33d Indiana Regiment, and participated in the principal battles under Sherman from Chattanooga to the sea.

SAMUEL A. ROBBINS, LL. B., Laporte.

PETER WILSON, born October 16, 1840, at Carlisle, Indiana. Residence, Butler, Bates County, Missouri. Educated at Carlisle Academy, and one year at Indiana Asbury University. Degree, LL. B. Occupation, attorney at law.

1867.

WILLIAM W. BARR, born May 8, 1847, in Centre County, Pennsylvania. Residence (1886), Carbondale, Illinois. Educated in common schools. Degree, LL. B. Occupation, attorney at law. Position, Master in Chancery of Franklin County, Illinois; State's Attorney; member of the Illinois Legislature.

JOHN M. BOYLE, LL. B., Vincennes.

JUDSON P. CUMMINS, born November 26, 1838, in Jackson County, Indiana. Residence, Hugoton, Stevens County, Kansas. Educated at Clear Spring, Indiana. Degree, LL. B. Occupation and position, attorney at law, Auditor of Adams County, Iowa (1870-75); County Superintendent Steven County, Kansas, 1887. Mr. Cummins was First Lieutenant, Company H, Regiment 120, Indiana volunteers, and Brevet Major (1865); Judge Advocate military district of New Orleans (1865); fought in the battles of Atlanta, Campagne, Columbus, Franklin and Nashville, in Georgia, and Kingston, North Carolina. Mr. Cummins married Nancy Emmons, May, 1858, who lived but eight months after marriage. He then married Sarah Gates, in 1862, who died in 1883.

VINSON CARTER, B. S. See Collegiate Department, Class of 1867.

PATRICK O. FLYNN, born March 25, in Greenup County, Ohio. Residence, Walton, Indiana. Educated at Hartsville University, Indiana. Degree, LL. B. Occupation and position, teacher, in the postal service, lumber merchant, and in 1882 a shipper of live stock. Mr. Flynn was a private in the Union army. Was in the battle of Richmond, Kentucky, August 29, 1865; taken prisoner when in General Kirby Smith's command. Mr. Flynn is a school trustee, and a member of the church of United Brethren.

NATHAN K. GRIGGS, LL. B, Beatrice, Nebraska.

JOSEPH PHILIP JONES, born January 27, 1843, in Owen County, Indiana. Residence, Martinez, California. Educated at Willamette University, Salem, Oregon, receiving the degree B. S. Degree, LL. B. Occupation and position, attorney at law, practicing at Martinez since 1870; for two years a miner in North California; for two years District Attorney of Contra Costa County, California, elected in 1875; in 1880 elected Representative of Contra Costa County in the State Assembly.

JAMES E. KENTON, born April 7, 1841, at Zanesfield, Logan County, Ohio. Residence, Kansas City, Missouri. Educated in Ohio common schools and Earlham College, Richmond, Indiana. Degree, LL. B. Occupation and position, practiced law till 1875; since then in the mercantile business. In 1882 he was Secretary and Trustee of the Kansas City Paper Company. He was deacon in the Calvary Presbyterian Church, Springfield, Missouri, till he removed to Kansas City.

WILLIAM H. MARTIN, LL. B., Rensselaer, Indiana.

NATHAN D. MILES, B. S., LL. B. See Collegiate Department, Class 1866.

WILLIAM B. ROBINSON, born in 1839 in Knox County, Indiana. Residence, Vincennes, Indiana. Educated in Knox County, New Lebanon Academy. Degree, LL. B. Occupation and position, practicing law; Mayor of the city of Vincennes for four years, and Clerk of Knox County Circuit Court.

WILLIAM C. SANDEFUR, B. S., LL. B. See Collegiate Department, Class 1866.

WARDER W. STEVENS, born September 30, 1845, in Elizabethtown, Kentucky. Residence, Salem, Indiana. Educated in the

Corydon Seminary. Degree, LL. B. Occupation and position, lawyer; at present (1883) editing and publishing a newspaper and farming; Auditor of Washington County one year.

HIRAM P. WEBB, A. M., LL. B. See Collegiate Department, Class 1865.

1868.

DAVID M. ALSPAUGH, born September 11, 1842, in Crawford County. Residence, Salem, Indiana. Educated in the common schools and Professor Bolc's Academy, Paoli, Indiana. Degree, LL. B. Occupation and position, attorney at law. He entered as private in Company E, First Regiment Indiana Cavalry, in August, 1861, and was in all the engagements in which the company took part; was wounded at Saline River, Arkansas, January 28, 1864. He was in command of the company when mustered out September 12, 1864, and was commissioned First Lieutenant by Governor Morton on February 20, 1865, in Company F, One Hundred and Forty-fourth Regiment, Indiana Volunteers. Trustee of Methodist Episcopal Church at Salem, Indiana, and also of the Salem graded schools.

SAMUEL ALBERT BOYLES, born July 7, 1841, at Huntingburgh' Residence, Olivet, South Dakota. Educated in the common schools, and in part in Indiana University, leaving it to enter the army. Degree, LL. B. Occupation and position, attorney at law and editor; at present (1883) Clerk of the United States District Court at Yankton, Dakota; member of the Dakota Legislature in 1881; County Attorney of Clay County, Illinois; First Lieutenant of Eighteenth Indiana Volunteers, in which regiment he served through the war of the rebellion. Mr. Boyles was engaged in twenty-seven battles and skirmishes, the most notable of these being Pea Ridge, Arkansas. He took part in the whole series of battles during the Vicksburgh campaign, including the siege of Jackson. In 1881 he was chairman of the Judiciary Committee in the Dakota Legislature. He took an active part in the G. A. R. organization, and delivered several addresses which have been published.

JESSE TOWELL COX, born March 21, 1821, in Orange County, Indiana. Died August 26, 1882, Paoli, Indiana. Educated in Friends' School, at Lick Creek, Orange County. Degree, LL. B.

Occupation and position, practice of law in Kokomo, Bloomington, and Groesbeck and Dallas, Texas; hospital steward and surgeon in the Union army; was made prisoner at the surrender of Munfordville, Kentucky, 1862; was stationed at Memphis in charge of the hospital; went, under General Sherman, to the Yazoo County and operations in Mississippi; with General Banks up Red river, and afterward to Mobile, where he was mustered out. Mr. Cox was the first advocate of the free school system in Orange County, where it met with much opposition, but aided by his brother and others, public opinion was changed, and the schools were established. (Joseph Cox, Class of 1856, and Jesse T. Cox, of Class of 1868, were twin brothers. In the war of the rebellion Joseph joined the Confederate army, while Jesse enlisted in the Union army. This opposition did not interfere with their brotherly affection.)

JOHN FIELDS, born April 14, 1848, in Lawrence County, Indiana. Residence, Colorado Springs, Colorado. Educated at McKendree College, Lebanon, Illinois. Degree, LL. B. Occupation and position, attorney at law, a Republican in politics, a soldier in the ranks—11th Missouri infantry—for 38 months, from June, 1861, till August, 1864; a participant in fourteen battles, including siege of Corinth, Vicksburg, Island No. 10, Iuka, Mississippi, etc; was in the Red River Company in 1864, under A. J. Smith, who was then on detached service in the 33d Missouri infantry.

FRANK R. OGG, born September 13, 1845, in Lawrence County, Indiana. Residence, Olathe, Johnson County, Kansas (1887). Educated at Mitchell, Indiana, schools. Degree, LL. B. Occupation, attorney at law. Mr. Ogg was for four years Prosecuting Attorney of Johnson County, Kansas, and for the same length of time postmaster; for two years Mayor, and at present (1887) attorney for the A. & S. F. R. R. Co. and the Southern Kansas R. R. Co. Mr. Ogg married Mary E. Daggy, of Bedford, Indiana, November 14, 1869.

JEREMIAH F. PITTMAN, born March 12, 1842, in Orange County, Indiana. Residence, Bloomington, Indiana. Educated at Leavenworth High School, Mr. Harris, Principal, and at Hon. Francis Wilson's High School. Degree, LL. B. Occupation and position, practicing attorney and Prosecuting Attorney, Tenth Judicial Circuit; Recorder of Orange County,

Indiana; Master Commissioner of the Monroe Circuit Court; enlisted in Company F, 50th Regiment, Indiana Volunteers; was in all the engagements of that regiment during the rebellion. In 1887. Mr. Pittman was Pension Examiner in Michigan.

CYRUS W. PRICE, LL. B., Bennettsville.

ROBERT D. RICHARDSON, B. S., LL. B. See Collegiate Department, Class 1867.

ROBERT R. TAYLOR, LL. B., Bloomfield.

GEORGE SHEEKS, born December 25, 1826, at Mitchell, Indiana. Died January 28, 1879, at Shoals, Indiana. Educated at Asbury University. Degree, LL. B. Occupation and position, lawyer and banker; Treasurer of Lawrence County; in the army for three years; First Lieutenant, Captain and Acting Quartermaster on the staff of General Hovey; was at the siege of Vicksburg, the battles of Fort Donaldson and Shiloh, and many others of less note.

WILLIAM A. TRAYLOR, born February 5, 1843. Residence, Jasper, Indiana. Educated in the common schools and by private teachers. Degree, LL. B. Occupation and position, attorney at law; elected State Senator in 1878 from the district composed of Dubois, Martin and Orange counties; Delegate to the Democratic National Convention in 1880, at Cincinnati; chairman of the Democratic Central Committee of Dubois County.

1869.

GEORGE W. ALFORD, B. S., LL. B. See Collegiate Department, Class 1869.

WILLIAM I. BAKER, born July 2, 1841, in Bartholomew County, Indiana. Residence, Bloomfield, Indiana. Educated in Bartholomew County public schools and at Earlham College, Indiana. Degree, LL. B. Occupation, attorney at law; in 1887 merchant in Lynden, Whatcom County, Washington State.

MATTHEW T. CAMPBELL, B. S., LL. B. See Collegiate Department, Class 1869.

T. WYCLIFF DENTON, B. S., LL. B. See Collegiate Department, Class 1869.

HENRY M. GILMORE, B. S., LL. B. See Collegiate Department, Class 1869.

FRANK I. HALL, LL. B. See Collegiate Department, Class 1867.

DALLAS S. HOLMAN, LL. B., Frankfort, Indiana.

THOMPSON H. JOHNSON, born February 13, 1847, in Greene County, Indiana. Residence, Cleveland, Ohio. Educated at U. C. College, Merom, Indiana. Degree, LL. B. Occupation and position, in 1870 was County Attorney for Conley County, Kansas; in 1872 was Probate Judge, elected for two terms.

FRANCIS BLACKBURN POSEY, born April 28, 1848, at Petersburg, Indiana. Residence, Petersburg, Indiana. Educated at Blythewood Academy and Indiana Asbury University. Degree, LL. B. Occupation and position, attorney at law, Prosecuting Attorney, and Elector of First District of Indiana in 1880.

WILLIAM THOMAS SCOTT, born October 30, 1845, in Union County, Kentucky. Residence, York, Nebraska. Educated in Brandenburgh, Kentucky. Degree, LL. B. Occupation, attorney at law. Mr. Scott was a member of the Nebraska House of Representatives in 1879. In 1887 he was Prosecuting Attorney for the district of York County, and is Mayor of the city of York. Mr. Scott married Sarah J. Miller December 5, 1872.

OSCAR WILDER SHRYER, born April 15, 1847, at Bloomfield, Indiana. Residence, Bloomfield, Indiana. Educated at Hanover College, Hanover, Indiana. Degree, LL. B. Occupation, attorney at law, banker and teacher.

JACOB S. SLICK, born January 4, 1848, at Dayton, Ohio. Residence, Rochester, Fulton County, Indiana. Educated at Normal School, Lebanon, Ohio. Degree, LL. B. Occupation, attorney at law.

JOSEPH C. WRIGHT, LL. B., born April 13, 1844, at South Bend. Died at Worthington, February 11, 1872. Educated in public schools of South Bend, and graduated at Notre Dame, Indiana. Occupation, for a year he practiced law; his health failing, he then worked at carriage-making. He was elected City Clerk, and while in this office he died. Though not a professing Christian, he was highly esteemed for his moral character. In 1870 he married Miss Emma J. Phillis.

1870.

JAMES FINLEY ALLEN, born October 5, 1844, near Sullivan, Indiana. Died March 15, 1876. Received the degree B. S. at Indiana Asbury University (now DePauw) in 1867, and in 1870 the degree LL. B. at Indiana University. Occupation, attorney at law. He was a member of the Methodist Episcopal Church.

JAMES GALLAGHER BAIN, born April 29, 1844, at Martinsville, Indiana. Residence, Martinsville, Indiana. Educated at Earlham College, Richmond, Indiana. Degree, LL. B. Occupation and position, Lieutenant in Company C, Thirty-third Regiment, Indiana Volunteers; was in all the battles and campaigns of the Army of the Cumberland from the first battle of Wild Cat, Kentucky, in November, '61, till the last in North Carolina in 1865. For the past ten years (since 1883) editor and proprietor of the *Republican*, Martinsville, Indiana, and since 1872 postmaster.

JESSE RICHARDS BICKNELL, A. M., LL. B. See Collegiate Department, Class 1868.

JAMES WHITCOMB BROWN, born 1846, near Pulaski, Indiana. Residence, DeWitt, Nebraska. Educated at Wabash College and Chicago University. From the latter he received the degree A. B. Degree, LL. B. Occupation, attorney at law. Position, Captain of Company H, 46th Regiment, Indiana volunteers; was engaged in all the battles and campaigns of his regiment. October 19, 1870, married Miss Mattie H. Hiatt, at Crawfordsville, Indiana.

WILLIAM HENRY CLARK, born January 27, 1836, in Shelby County, Kentucky. Residence, Tipton, Indiana. Educated at Danville Academy and Christian University, 1861–62. Degree, LL. B. Occupation and position, practice of law, pension agent, Town Clerk of Tipton, member of the Christian Church, member of the Pythonia Society; was a political prisoner in the barracks at Louisville, Kentucky, and a newspaper correspondent in 1863. Mr. Clark married Miss Ophelia P. Jesse, of Shelby County, Kentucky.

HENRY CLAY DUNCAN. See Collegiate Department, Class of 1868.

JOHN R. EAST, born May 11, 1845, in Harrodsburg, Indiana. Residence, Bloomington, Indiana. Educated at the public schools of Monroe County, Degree, LL. B. Occupation and position, attorney at law, Prosecuting Attorney, appointed by Governor Williams, 1878–79; Clerk of the Monroe County Court from 1876–80; Sergeant in Company I, 59th Regiment, Indiana volunteers, and was in Sherman's army during his march to the sea; was at the battle of Alto, Georgia, the Union forces commanded by General J. M. Carre, the rebels by General Hood, and saw the signal from General Sherman at Kennesaw Mountain to General Carre to "Hold the fort," an event which gave origin to the popular hymn. Mr. East is a member of the M. E. Church, and has lately distinguished himself as an able politician.

PERRY W. GARD, born November 30, 1883, in Switzerland County, Indiana. Residence, Frankfort, Indiana. Educated in the public schools. Degree, LL. B. Occupation and position, lawyer; first Mayor of the city of Frankfort, and afterward member of the City Council. At present, Illustrious Grand Master of the Grand Council of Indiana.

LEWIS CASS GARRIGUS, born April 29, 1844, in Parke County, Indiana. Residence, Russellville, Kentucky. Educated in the common schools of Parke County and Terre Haute High School. Degree, LL. B. Occupation and position, attorney at law; county attorney of Logan County, Kentucky, from 1874 to 1878, and Commissioner of Sinking Fund of the Louisville and Nashville Railroad. Was in the Confederate army from 1862 to close of the war. In 1877 Mr. Garrigus was called on to speak at the reunion of Hood's Confederate Texas Brigade at Waco, Texas, and on this occasion held up the American flag, and called on the ex-Confederates to give three cheers for the old flag, the flag of our fathers and our country, and entitled to our love, and received, much to his gratification, a hearty response, making him, though a stranger, the hero of the hour.*

CAREY WAYLAND HENDERSON, born May 11, 1844, at Putnamville, Indiana. Died March 7, 1880, at Washington, D. C. Degree, LL. B. Occupation and position, attorney at law; clerk in Postoffice Department, Washington; also clerk in the Indiana Legislature. Was chosen first Mayor of the city of Bloomington.

JAMES T. HERRICK, born November 4, 1846, in Boone County, Indiana. Residence, Wellington, Kansas. Educated at Valparaiso College. Degree, LL. B. Occupation and position, lawyer. Was elected Probate Judge in 1874. At the same time acted as City Treasurer. At present, 1883, is City Attorney and member of the City Board of Education, and for ten years past Trustee of the Methodist Episcopal Church of Wellington.

GEORGE W. JOHNS. See Collegiate Department, Class of 1869.

JOHN C. MCCARTY, born November 25, 1834, in Meade County, Kentucky. Residence, El Dorado, Butler County, Kansas. Educated at common and private schools of Indiana and Kentucky. Degree, LL. B. Occupation, attorney at law; during the rebellion served as pilot in the Mississippi squadron; was in service at the siege of Vicksburg. Mr. McCarty married Anna Bently, October 28, 1874.

JOHN L. PIERCE, born March 1, 1848, near Lafayette, Indiana. Residence, Lebanon, Boone County, Indiana. Educated at Lebanon Presbyterian Academy. Degree, LL. B. Occupation and position, attorney at law in Lafayette, Indiana, until 1871, and since in Lebanon; Clerk of the town of Lebanon, and in 1882 Mayor of the city of Lebanon.

JAMES E. SAYERS, LL. B., San Francisco.

ASHER LABERTEW SLUSS. See Collegiate Department, Class of 1869.

GEORGE W. SMITH, born August 18, 1846, Putnam County, Ohio. Residence, Murphysborough, Jackson County, Illinois. Educated at McKendree College, Lebanon, Illinois; B. S. from McKendree College. Degree, LL. B. from Indiana University. Occupation, attorney at law. Position, Republican Elector for Nineteenth Congressional District of Illinois.

ALANSON STEPHENS, born December 22, 1840, in Harrison County, Indiana. Died August 31, 1880, at New Albany, Indiana. Principally self-educated. Degree, LL. B. Occupation and position, attorney at law; was Sergeant-Major Third Indiana Cavalry; served in the army of the Potomac; was engaged in all the battles and skirmishes of that army from Bull Run to Appomattox Court House.

JOHN J. STEPHENSON, LL. B., Bowling Green.

SAMUEL A. WISE, LL. B., Vincennes.

1871.

JOHN W. BUSKIRK, born at Bedford. Residence, Bloomington, Indiana. Educated in the common schools. Degree, LL. B. Occupation and position, lawyer, District Prosecutor of Eighth Common Pleas District. Mr. Buskirk was a member of the Legislature; as a soldier he was in the battles of Chickasaw Bluffs and Arkansas Post. Married Florence J. Williams, of Bloomington, December 17, 1889.

WILLIAM P. CLARK, LL. B., Oskaloosa, Illinois.

CHESTER C. CULP, LL. B., East Enterprise.

WILLIAM HENRY DAGUE, born December 17, 1842, in Washington County, Pennsylvania. Residence (1888), Fowler, Benton County, Indiana. Educated at Kokomo high school. Degree, LL. B. Occupation and position, attorney at law six years; for the last seven years, a banker; from 1865-70, owned, published and edited the Monticello *Herald*; for a year, Postmaster at Monticello; member and Trustee of the Fowler Presbyterian Church. In 1876 Mr. Dague married Miss Mary A. McKeehan, at Indianapolis.

SAMUEL DALTON, born March 30, 1843, in Orange County, Indiana. Residence, Winfield, Cowley County, Kansas. Educated at the Mitchell high school. Degree, LL. B. Occupation and position, attorney and counsellor at law; on several occasions has acted as Judge, *pro tem*. Mr. Dalton enlisted as a private in the United States army of volunteers, on February 17, 1862, was at the siege of Corinth, Vicksburg, Atlanta, and in Sherman's army in its march to the sea and to Washington; re-enlisted as a veteran in February, 1864, and was honorably discharged July 21, 1865. In politics he is a Republican. Mr. Dalton married Elma B. Boyd, of Orange County, Indiana, December 17, 1872.

ANDREW DAY, born October 15, 1843, in Jackson County, Indiana. Residence, Washington, D. C. Educated in Jackson County schools. Degree, LL. B. Occupation and position, teacher, attorney at law; Third Auditor's office; Treasury Department, Washington; Sergeant-at-Arms, Iowa State Senate, 1878; Superintendent of Public Schools, Lucas County, Iowa, 1876-77. Mr. Day lost his right arm in a charge made on Hood's army, December 15, 1864, at Nashville, Tennessee.

LEMUEL LEVI DILLY, born October 22, 1839, in Martin County, Indiana. Residence, Loogootee, Indiana. Educated at Mt. Pleasant, Greenville, Illinois, and Bedford, Indiana. Degree, LL. B. Occupation and position, lawyer for four years; since, a farmer, United States Assistant Assessor, Justice of the Peace, census enumerator; private, Company D, 22d Regiment, Illinois Volunteers; was at the battles of Belmont, November, 1861, Island No. 10, Corinth, Mississippi, Stone River, Talahoma and Chickamauga, where he lost his right arm.

WILLIAM HENRY DOWDELL, born July 11, 1842, in Dearborn County, Indiana. Residence, Lawrenceburgh, Indiana. Educated at Southwestern Normal School, Lebanon, Ohio. Degree, LL. B. Occupation and position, lawyer, and in 1864-5, Quartermaster Clerk.

NATHAN WARD FITZGERALD, born March 4, 1846, in Dearborn County, Indiana. Residence, Washington, D. C. Educated in the public schools, and took a partial course in the Collegiate Department of Indiana University. Degree, LL. B. Occupation and position, practicing attorney in the highest courts, State and National; editor of the Washington *World;* commander of the First Battalion of the National Rifles.

INMAN H. FOWLER, born June 7, 1834, at Eaton, Ohio. Residence, Spencer, Indiana. Educated in part at Wabash College, Indiana. Degree, LL. B. Occupation and position, attorney at law; State Senator in 1876 for the district composed of the counties of Owen and Clay, and served during the special sessions of 1877-79.

JOHN GRAHAM, born November 22, 1844, at Bloomington, Indiana. Residence, Bloomington, Indiana. Educated at the Bloomington schools. Degree, LL. B. Occupation and position, lawyer; Librarian of Supreme Court; Joint Representative of Monroe and Brown counties in 1883. Mr. Graham died at Indianapolis, June, 1890.

ALBERT L. GRIMES, LL. B., Mount Vernon, Illinois.

GAINES H. HAZEN, born October 26, 1847, in Newburgh. Residence, Boonville, Warrick County, Indiana. Educated at High School, Newburgh. Degree, LL. B. Occupation, attorney at law.

FRANCIS B. HITCHCOCK, born June 3, 1846, in Terre Haute, Indiana. Residence, Flora, Illinois. Educated in Terre Haute schools. Degree, LL. B. Occupation and position, attorney at law; also editor; Deputy County Clerk, Clay County, Illinois, 1867; editor of Clay County *Union*, 1866–67; editor Marion County *Republican*, 1868; associate editor Southern Illinois *Journal*, 1878–82, and since 1880 sole editor and proprietor. Was hospital steward during the war.

JAMES H. JORDAN. See Collegiate Department, Class of 1868.

JAMES B. KENNER, born November 5, 1846, in Hancock, Maryland. Residence, Huntington, Indiana. Educated in Roanoke Classical Seminary. Degree, LL. B. Occupation and position, attorney at law; member of Indiana Legislature in 1881; was chairman of the Committee of Ways and Means, and the author of the bill to re-submit the constitutional amendments, overthrown by the Supreme Court of Indiana; elected by the Legislature Trustee of the Deaf and Dumb Institute, in 1876. Private soldier on the Union side during the rebellion. Author of a work on "The Law and Practice in Indiana on Drainage," and of many essays on political and legal topics, and of many public addresses.

DAVID A. KOCHENOUR, born February 7, 1844, in Harrison County. Residence, Brownstown, Jackson County, Indiana. Educated at Hartsville University, Hartsville, Indiana. Degree, LL. B. Occupation, attorney at law.

GEORGE H. KOONS, born April 2, 1848, near New Castle. Residence, Muncie, Indiana. Educated in the common schools of Henry County and New Castle Academy. Degree, LL. B. Occupation and position, teacher, and Principal of the Middletown Academy; since 1874 attorney at law.

JAMES E. MCCOLLOUGH, B. S., LL. B. See Collegiate Department, Class 1871.

ROBERT W. MIERS, B. S., LL. B. See Collegiate Department, Class 1870.

THOMAS G. MAHAN, born March 23, 1844, in Orange County, Indiana. Residence, Orleans, Indiana. Educated at the Orange County schools. Degree, LL. B. Occupation and position, attorney at law and teacher. He was a private in the army, and was in many battles under Sherman; was twice wounded at Richmond, Kentucky, and rendered a cripple for life August 31, 1862.

GEORGE A. MAHAN, born August 6, 1852, in Marion County, Missouri. Residence, Hannibal, Missouri. Educated at Bethel College, Palmyra, Missouri, and at Washington and Lee University, Lexington, Virginia, in 1869. Degree, LL. B. Occupation and position, lawyer, City Counsellor for city of Hannibal in 1874–75, and State's attorney for Marion County since 1879.

DENNIS H. PALMER, LL. B., Logansport.

JOHN LLOYD PITNER, B. S., LL. B. See Collegiate Department, Class 1869.

JOHN K. RHINEHART, born December 16, 1841, at Rogersville, Ohio. Residence, Bluffton, Wells County, Indiana. Educated at Roanoke Academy. Degree, LL. B. Occupation and position, lawyer; member of School Board, Bluffton, for six years. Deputy Clerk of Wells County.

DAVID A. ROACH, born July 13, 1843, in Parke County. Residence, Crawfordsville, Indiana. Educated in Harmonia College, Russellville, Indiana. Degree, LL. B. Occupation and position, attorney at law; Prosecuting Attorney for Twenty-second Indiana Circuit, 1876–78.

GEORGE H. RYMAN, born July 7, 1846, at Lawrenceburg, Indiana. Residence, Grafton, Nebraska. Educated in schools of Lawrenceburg, Connersville and Ladoga. Degree, LL. B. Occupation and position, attorney at law, at Indianapolis, and afterward at Grafton, Nebraska. Private, Ninth Indiana Cavalry, Company H. Was in the battles at Nashville, Tennessee, and Franklin, Tennessee, and in all the battles of the Hood campaign; enlisted in 1863 and served until close of the war. Entering so young into the army greatly interfered with his education. Mr. Ryman is a member of the Baptist Church.

JAMES A. STEPHENSON, LL. B., Ladoga.

WILLIAM JOHNSON THROOP, born December 10, 1841, at Paoli. Residence, Paoli, Ind., (1887). Educated at Paoli High School. Degree, LL. B. Occupation, for the first eight years, farmed and practiced law; since that time an attorney at law.

JOSEPH P. THROOP, LL. B., Paoli, Ind.

WILLIAM HOWARD TRIPPETT. See Collegiate Department, Class 1869.

ARGUS D. VANOSDOL, born September 18, 1839, in Jefferson County. Residence, Madison, Indiana. Educated at Madison. Degree, LL. B. Occupation and position, attorney at law; Captain in Federal Army, 1861.

1872.

GEORGE ANDREW ADAMS, born June 4, 1849, at Morgantown, Indiana. Residence, Martinsville, Indiana. Educated at common school and High School of Martinsville. Degree, LL. B. Occupation and position, attorney at law, teacher, trustee and steward in Methodist Church.

WILLIAM B. C. ARMSTRONG, born January 17, 1849, in Knox County, Indiana. Residence, Washington, Indiana. Educated in common schools of Knox County, and in part at Bloomington in the University. Degree, LL. B. Occupation, attorney at law; for two years after graduation, in the office of General Shackleford and S. R. Hornbrook.

CHARLES NIMROD BECKHAM, born February 4, 1849, at Elk Creek, Spencer County, Kentucky. Residence, Louisville, Kentucky. Educated in primary schools of Spencer and Nelson counties, Kentucky, and Washington and Lee University, Va. Degree, LL. B. Occupation and position, attorney at law; a soldier in the Confederate service during the rebellion; was in Morgan's raid in Indiana and Ohio; was captured with Morgan when he surrendered, and remained from July, 1863, to February, 1865, in military prison in Camp Chase, Ohio; was exchanged, and surrendered with General R. E. Lee at the final dissolution of the Confederacy; served under General Wharton as Orderly at the battle of Perryville, Kentucky, October, 1862, and carried the orders for the last charge made on that field.

NELSON J. BOZARTH, born July 13, 1849, at Rochester, Indiana. Residence, Valparaiso, Indiana. Educated at Valparaiso College and at West Point Military Academy, New York. Degree, LL. B. Occupation and position, attorney at law, cadet at West Point; when fifteen years old, Orderly in Ninth Illinois Cavalry; wounded at the battle of Nashville; has been Prosecuting Attorney of Thirty-first Judicial District of Indiana, and in 1882 was City Attorney of Valparaiso. Mr. Bozarth lost his books and papers, and nearly lost his life, in the great fire in Chicago in 1871.

JAMES S. CAMPBELL, LL. B., Indianapolis.

JAMES M. CRAIG, A. M., LL. B. See Collegiate Department, Class 1869.

GEORGE W. COOPER, A. M., LL. B. See Collegiate Department, Class 1872.

FRANK C. DONALDSON, born September 26, 1852, at Terre Haute. Residence, Terre Haute, Indiana. Education, graduate of Terre Haute High School. Degree, LL. B. Occupation, attorney at law. Has delivered several addresses on public occasions and lectures to literary societies, and made earnest Republican speeches during the political campaigns.

DAVID ELEY, born February 27, 1841, in Adams County. Residence, Decatur, Adams County, Indiana. Educated at National Normal School, 1871. Degree, LL. B. Occupation, attorney at law until 1880; since engaged in agriculture and horticulture.

CLARKSON ERWIN, LL. B., Nashville, Indiana.

SAMUEL A. EMISON, B. S., LL.B See Collegiate Department Class 1861.

WILLIAM F. GALLIMORE, LL. B., Paragon, Indiana.

COLUMBUS BYRON HARROD, born April 13, 1849, in Scott County, Indiana. Residence, Scottsburg, Scott County, Indiana. Educated at the Friends' Academy, Blue River, 1867-69.

Degree, LL. B. Occupation and position, attorney at law; a leading member of the bar. Took an active part in the canvass for Garfield in 1880. For four years a justice of the peace. Mr. Harrod is a member of the Christian Church.

GEORGE W. HART, LL. B., Lee, Indiana.

CHARLES L. HENRY, born July 1, 1849, in Hancock County. Residence, Anderson, Indiana. Educated at Asbury University, Greencastle. Degree, LL. B. Occupation and position, attorney at law; State Senator from Madison and Grant counties (1882).

EDWARD G. HENRY, born 1850, in Pleasant, Switzerland County. Residence, New Albany, Indiana. Educated at Hanover College, Indiana. Degrees, B. S. and A. M. from Hanover, and LL. B., Indiana University. Occupation, attorney at law.

JOHN COREY HUNTER, born October 27, 1847, at Versailles, Indiana. Residence, Socorro, New Mexico, in 1883. Educated at Bloomington Seminary. Degree, LL. B. Occupation and position, attorney at law until 1881; mining in New Mexico and Arizona since 1881. Master in Chancery, Second Judicial District, United States Court.

JEFFERSON McANELLY, born in Hancock County, Ohio. Residence, Loveland, Laramie County, Colorado. Educated at Ohio Wesleyan University, Delaware, Ohio. Degree, LL. B. Occupation and position, attorney at law and Auditor of Clay County, Indiana.

DAVID WILSON McKEE, born December 14, 1845, in Rush County. Residence, Connersville, Indiana (1887). Educated at home and in the public schools. Degree, LL. B. Occupation and position, attorney at law, an elder in the Presbyterian Church, and Sunday-school Superintendent. Delegate to the General Assembly at Buffalo. Mr. McKee is a leading and successful practitioner of law, commencing to practice in Brookville in 1873, and he afterward went in partnership with Jos. J. Little, Esq.; removed to Connersville in 1886. Mr. McKee married Miss M. Ella McKee, of Woodford County, Kentucky, in June, 1873.

WILLIAM D. MAY, born September 4, 1847, at Rome, Perry

County. Residence, Avoca, Lawrence County, Indiana. Educated at Rome Academy. Degree, LL. B. Occupation, United States Internal Revenue Gauger, collecting and insurance agent. For some time he has been engaged in teaching in Dubois and Perry counties, Indiana.

LEANDER P. MITCHELL, born February 5, 1849, at Mechanicsburg, Henry County. Residence, New Castle, Indiana. Educated at Northwestern Christian University (now Butler), Indianapolis. Degree, B. S., Butler University; LL. B., Indiana University. Occupation, attorney at law.

LESTER L. NORTON, B. S., LL. B. See Collegiate Department, Class 1871.

TRUMAN FAYETTE PALMER, born January 7, 1851, at Orland, Steuben County. Residence, Monticello, Indiana. Educated at Battle Ground and Clinton schools. Degree, LL. B. Occupation, attorney at law.

BRIEL F. SMITH, LL. B., Goshen.

JAMES HENRY LANE TIBBETTS, born September 12, 1848, at Manchester. Residence, Alhambra, Illinois. Educated at Manchester schools, and one term at Litchfield, Illinois. Degree, LL. B. Occupation, attorney at law till afflicted with loss of hearing; since a farmer.

1873.

WILLIAM S. BROWN, A. M., LL. B. See Collegiate Department, Class 1872.

FRANCIS M. CHARLTON, born November 25, 1852, in Switzerland County, Indiana. Residence, Lebanon, Indiana. Educated at Vevay high schools and Moore's Hill College. Degree, LL. B. Occupation and position, practicing attorney at Boone County Circuit Court, and Prosecuting Attorney of the Twentieth Judicial Circuit of Indiana (1882).

MARCELLUS A. CHIPMAN, born September 27, 1852, at Noblesville. Residence, Anderson, Indiana. Educated in public schools. Degree, LL. B. Occupation, attorney at law.

ORLANDO H. COBB, B. S., LL. B. See Collegiate Department, Class 1872.

BENJAMIN FRANKLIN DAVIS, LL. B., Lebanon.

NATHAN GROVE DOWDELL, born April 21, 1849, at Elizabethtown, Ohio. Died July 8, 1874, at Lebanon, Ohio. Educated at Southwestern Normal School, Lebanon. Degree, LL. B. Occupation and position, lawyer; Quartermaster U. S. Army during the Rebellion; a Republican, advocate of temperance, member of the Methodist Church, and a friend of education, the church, and the country.

WESLEY E. DRUMM, LL. B., Clinton, Missouri.

JOHN W. EWING, B. S., LL. B. See Collegiate Department, Class 1872.

WALTER A. FULAND, A. M., LL. B. See Collegiate Department, Class 1870.

RICHARD A. FULK, LL. B., Bloomington, Ind.

ZACHARY TAYLOR HAZEN, born March 15, 1848, in Ripley County, Indiana. Residence, Versailles, Indiana. Educated at Brookville College, Ohio, and Moore's Hill College. Degree, LL. B. Occupation, attorney at law.

GEORGE WILSON HOLMAN, born September 30, 1850, at Sevastopol, Kosciusko County. Residence, Rochester, Indiana. Educated in the public schools and at Notre Dame for two years. Degree, LL. B. Occupation, practice of law; admitted to the bar, June, 1873.

FREDERICK HEINER, B. S., LL. B. See Collegiate Department, Class 1872.

BENTON KNAPP, LL. B., Liberty, Union County.

PERRY OLIVER JONES, born April 5, 1847, in Marshall County, Indiana. Residence, Plymouth, Indiana. Educated in common schools, Rochester Academy, and Valparaiso College. Degree, LL. B. Occupation and position, attorney at law: State Attorney for two terms; Mayor of City of Plymouth: member and Trustee of the Methodist Church.

ZUINGLIUS K. MCCORMACK, LL. B., Indianapolis.

GEORGE W. MCDONALD, A. M. See College Department, Class 1870.

JOHN REED MCMAHAN, born December 4, 1848, in Crawford County, Indiana. Residence, Muncie, Indiana. Educated in the public schools, Marengo Academy and at Orleans. Occupation, for some time (from 1866 to 1872) a teacher; after graduation, attorney at law.

PIERCE NORTON, A. M., LL. B. See Collegiate Department, Class 1872.

NEWTON BEN. O'NEILL, born in 1853 at Lanesboro, Illinois. Died at Bloomington, Indiana, in 1873. Educated in part at a Roman Catholic School, Helena, Arkansas, where he was rewarded with a medal and at an examination with several prizes. Occupation: taught school for some time; read law with his uncle, John Marshall; afterward attended the law school of Indiana University, where he died shortly before the termination of the term.

RICHARD LEE ORGAN, B. S., LL. B. See Collegiate Department, Class 1872.

SAMUEL O. PICKENS, born April 26, 1846, in Owen County, Indiana. Residence, Spencer, Indiana. Educated in the public schools of Owen County. Degree, LL. B. Occupation and position, attorney at law; Prosecuting Attorney of the Fifteenth Judicial Circuit of Indiana for two terms.

WILLIAM H. POLLARD, born April 17, 1841, at Campbellsburg, Washington County. Residence, Ozark, Christian County, Missouri. Educated in the common schools. Degree, LL. B. Occupation and position, attorney at law, Prosecuting Attorney for two years in Christian County, Missouri; Assistant Assessor of Internal Revenue, Third Division, Second District, Indiana; served four years and four months in the 13th Regiment, Indiana Volunteers; was in all the battles around Petersburg, Virginia; was severely wounded August 14, 1864; also, was in the battle of Rich Mountain, Virginia, July 11, 1861; at Winchester, Virginia, March 23, 1862; Suffolk, Virginia, in 1863, and at the siege of Fort Wagner, South Carolina, in 1863; battle of Cold Harbor, Virginia, June 1, 1864; at the explosion of a mine at Petersburg, July 31, 1864; was the Republican nominee for Chief Clerk of the Missouri Legislature in 1881.

CHARLES NEWTON SPENCER, born February 2, 1843, at Milltown. Residence, Columbus, Indiana. Educated at Hartsville University, graduating A. B. and A. M. Degree, LL. B., Indiana University. Occupation and position, teacher and afterward attorney at law; in the late war he was a member of the 23d Indiana Volunteer Infantry, and, as a private soldier, participated in its hardships and battles; was unfitted for manual labor by a wound in the right arm. He is a member of the Church of the Disciples.

WILLIAM H. WOODWARD, born December 27, 1846, at Caledonia, Pulaski County, Illinois. Residence, Carbondale, Illinois. Educated in the public schools and Southern Illinois College. Degree, LL. B. Occupation and position, attorney at law, member of Illinois Legislature; entered the army at the age of 15 years as private in Company D, 56th Illinois Volunteers; was in all the battles around Vicksburg; was in Sherman's army from Lookout Mountain to Washington City; was in ten general engagements during the war, and in very many skirmishes; is the sole survivor of the family. His father was Captain of Company A, 2d Illinois Regiment, and was killed at Buena Vista, Mexico. His only brother was Lieutenant in the 11th Illinois Regiment and was killed at Fort Donaldson.

1874.

SAMUEL W. AXTELL, born June 17, 1850, in Knox County, Ohio. Residence, Bloomfield, Indiana. Educated in Greene County Normal School. Degree, LL. B. Occupation and position, County Superintendent of Public Schools of Greene County since 1876.

EDWARD ALEY, LL. B., Scottsburg. Died, 1876.

JOHN H. BURFORD, born Sunday, February 29, 1852, at Parkville. Residence, Crawfordsville, Indiana. Educated at Waveland Collegiate Institute. Degree, LL. B. Occupation and position, attorney at law. (After graduation continued studies at Indianapolis.) Prosecuting Attorney, Twenty-second Judicial Circuit, at Crawfordsville (1880–82), having located there in 1877. A teacher before studying law. In 1878 Mr. Burford was a candidate for Prosecuting Attorney, but was defeated by a small majority of seventeen, by the combined Democratic and Greenback votes.

ELI B. CARESS, born March 29, 1849, in Salem. Residence, Seymour, Indiana. Educated at Salem Academy. Degree,

LL. B. Occupation and position, attorney at law; deacon in Presbyterian Church since 1876.

FABIUS M. CLARKE, born June 10, 1853, in Manchester, Indiana. Residence, Topeka, Kansas. Degree, LL. B. Occupation, lawyer.

EDGAR DEAN CRUMPACKER, born May 27, 1853, in Laporte County, Indiana. Residence, Valparaiso, Indiana. Educated at Valparaiso College, graduating B. S. Degree, LL. B. Occupation, teacher for two years; attorney and counsellor at law (1882).

OSIANDER FAIRHURST, born January 19, 1849. Died February 3, 1878. Educated at Northwestern Christian University. Degree, LL. B. Occupation, attorney at law.

ALFRED W. FULLERTON, A. B., LL. B. See Collegiate Department, Class 1873.

FRANCIS M. GIDEON, born February 21, 1849, in Christian County, Missouri. Residence, Washington, D. C. Educated at Springfield Academy, Missouri, and Abingdon College, Illinois, from which he received the degree of B. S. in 1871. Degree, LL. B. Occupation and position, lawyer; two terms City Attorney of Kokomo, Ind.; Clerk in Postoffice Department at Washington; in 1867 was appointed Probate Clerk of Christian County, Missouri; entered the army at fifteen years of age; was chosen Major of Ninety-Ninth Missouri Regiment when seventeen years old; he served till close of the war; was wounded on the forehead at the battle of Boonville, Missouri.

JOHN S. NEWBY, A. B., LL. B. See Collegiate Department, Class 1873.

ALLEN DAVID NORMAN, born in Marion, Illinois. Residence, Springfield, Illinois. Educated at Braden's School, Carbondale, Illinois. Degree, LL. B. Occupation, attorney at law.

ROBERT M. PIATT, A. B., LL. B. See Collegiate Department, Class 1873.

EMERSON SHORT, born December 2, 1848, at Springville, Lawrence County, Indiana. Residence, Bloomfield, Indiana. Educated at Bedford High School, Indiana University till Senior year. Degree, LL. B. Occupation, attorney at law.

THOMAS J. TERHUNE, A. B., LL. B. See Collegiate Department, Class 1873.

JOHN A. ZARING, born October 30, 1848, in Scott County, Indiana. Residence, Salem, Indiana. Educated in the public schools of Washington County; three years' course at Indiana University. Degree, LL. B. Occupation, attorney at law.

1875.

DANIEL O. BARKER, LL. B., Emporia, Kansas.

SIMPSON M. BEECHER, LL. B., Los Angeles, California.

DANIEL W. BEECHER, LL. B., Los Angeles, California.

DAVID W. BAIRD, LL. B., Fort Wayne.

JAMES COURTLAND BLACKLIDGE, born September 19, 1849, at Brookville, Franklin County. Residence, Kokomo, Indiana, Educated at Brookville College. Degree, LL. B. Occupation, attorney at law. During the ten years since graduation, Mr. Blacklidge has attained, by his industry, perseverance and talents, after overcoming many obstacles, a high position among the lawyers of the State.

GEORGE L. EVERBACH, born December 13, 1846, at Heilbron, Kingdom of Wurtemberg, Germany. Residence, Louisville, Kentucky. Educated at Möckmühl, Germany, 1851–59; Heidelberg, 1859–63; Louisville, Kentucky, Commercial College, 1866–68. Degree, LL. B. Occupation and position, attorney and counsellor at law, since, 1875. Enlisted in the Federal Army, as Clerk in the Engineer Department, under General Thomas. Volunteered and took an active part in the battle of Nashville, in the winter of 1864. Was stationed at Nashville, Atlanta and Savannah during military service. Honorably discharged in 1866. Engaged for some time in farming, afterward, in commercial business, and studied law and was admitted to the Louisville bar in 1875.

MAJOR W. FUNK, born October 29, 1849, at Milltown, Crawford County. Residence, Corydon, Indiana. Educated at Marengo Academy, and at the graded schools in Canton, Indiana. Degree, LL. B. Occupation and position, Judge of Harrison Circuit Court by appointment, three different terms.

Received the Democratic nomination, in 1881, for Prosecuting Attorney.

JAMES B. HARPER, born November 21, 1848, in Allen County, Indiana. Residence, Fort Wayne, Indiana. Educated at the Fort Wayne Methodist College. Degree, LL. B. Occupation and position, attorney at law, United States Commissioner for District of Indiana. Valedictorian of the law class of 1875. In 1882 junior member of the law firm of Robertson & Harper, Fort Wayne.

WINFIELD SCOTT HUNTER, born December 22, 1848, at Callensburg, Clarion County, Pennsylvania. Residence, Jasper, Dubois County, Indiana. Educated at the Buffaloville and Marengo schools. Degree, LL. B. Occupation and position, attorney at law; entered the army at the age of 15; served in the Thirteenth Regiment Indiana Cavalry, Company L, as private; was in the battles of Huntsville, Alabama, and Nashville, Tennessee, Mobile and defences; in Grierson's raid and in many skirmishes.

HARVEY W. LETSINGER, born May 24, 1849, in Greene County. Residence, Bloomfield, Indiana. Educated in the Sullivan County schools. Degree, LL. B. Occupation and position, attorney at law; Deputy Treasurer and Prosecuting Attorney of Greene County. A member of the Methodist Church.

E. MORGAN McCORD, B. S., LL. B. See Collegiate Department, Class 1869.

MAHLON R. NEAL, born February 7, 1851, in Clay County. Residence, Bloomfield, Indiana. Educated in the Farmersburg and Sullivan schools. Graduated in Sullivan Normal School. Degree, LL. B. Occupation, teacher, merchant and lawyer; candidate for Representative on Republican ticket in 1876.

ARTHUR J. PALMER, born September 3, 1852, at Kokomo, Indiana. Residence, Lebanon, Indiana. Educated at the Frankfort Seminary. Degree, LL. B. Occupation, attorney at law.

ROBERT ADAM PARRETT, born April 24, 1852, at Russellville, Putnam County. Residence, Newport, Indiana. Educated in the Newport public schools; three years at Indiana Asbury University (now DePauw). Degree, LL. B. Occupation, attorney at law.

LEWIS C. PARRISH, born October 20, 1850, in Owen County, Indiana. Residence, Ravanna, Missouri. Educated in the Owen County public schools. Degree, LL. B. Occupation and position, Principal of schools at Lovilia, Iowa, and also at Ravanna, Missouri; attorney at law; for two years a traveler.

WILLIAM MICHAEL STANLEY, born September 7, 1841, in Danzig, Germany. Residence, Chicago, Illinois. Educated in Germany. The first English school he entered was the Indiana University. Degree, LL. B. Occupation, attorney at law. Mr. Stanley was a private in the army and also a seaman in the United States navy during the late war. Mr. Stanley is a devoted student of books and men and things.

JOHN G. STEWART, LL. B., Richland.

WILLIS TANDY, born September 10, 1850, in Ghent, Kentucky. Residence, Ghent, Kentucky. Educated in Center College, Kentucky, receiving, on graduating, the degree A. B., and from Ghent College the degree A. M., and from Indiana University the degree LL. B. Occupation and position, teacher of mathematics from 1875 until 1878; since, attorney at law in Ghent.

NEWTON M. TAYLOR, born October 3, 1847, at Attica. Residence, Danville, Indiana. Education: a graduate of Indiana Asbury University, from which he received the degree B. S. in 1879; degree LL. B., Indiana University. Occupation and position, attorney at law; in 1880, Prosecuting Attorney of the Nineteenth Judicial District Circuit.

1876.

RICHARD BENSON, LL. B., Rushville.

ALBERT DAVIS, B. S., LL. B. See Collegiate Department, Class 1875.

JOHN F. DILLON, B. S., LL. B. See Collegiate Department, Class 1874.

CHARLES HALL DILLON, B. S., LL. B. See Collegiate Department, Class 1874.

JAMES ROBISON FUNK, born December 31, 1847, at Militown. Residence, Fredericksburg, Indiana. Educated and received diploma from National Normal Business Institute, Lebanon, Ohio. Degree, LL. B. Occupation, attorney at law.

BENJAMIN TERRY HALSTEAD, born March 30, 1850, at Brooklyn, New York. Residence, Harbor Springs, Michigan. Educated at Michigan Agricultural College, receiving the degree B. S. Degree, LL. B. Occupation and position, till 1879 teacher; since attorney at law; in 1878, Superintendent of schools; Justice of the Peace in 1882–86; Prosecuting Attorney of Manitou County, Michigan, in 1884–86; member of the Board of Trustees of Harbor Springs graded schools in 1884–88.

NATHANIEL U. HILL, B. S., LL. B. See Collegiate Department, Class 1875.

ALFRED GRAHAM HOWE, born April 4, 1853, in Monroe County, Indiana. Residence, Knoxville, Tennessee, ('87). Educated at Bloomington, Indiana. Degree, LL. B. Occupation, attorney at law; married Mary B. Jennings, of Shelbyville, Indiana.

TERRENCE MCCLEARY, LL. B., Rochester.

WILLIAM E. MCCORD, A. M., LL. B. See Collegiate Department, 1872.

BENJAMIN FRANKLIN MASON, born April 3, 1849, in Wayne County. Residence, Hagerstown, Indiana. Educated at Hagerstown high school and at Richmond. Degree, LL. B. Occupation, attorney at law.

WILLIAM RILEY MYERS, born August 26, 1852, near Keithsburg, Illinois. Residence, Smith Centre, Smith County, Kansas. Educated at Marengo Academy, Crawford County. Degree, LL. B. Occupation, attorney at law.

CLARENCE WIRT STEPHENSON, born March 25, 1851, at Pendleton. Residence, Wabash, Indiana. Educated at Indiana Asbury University, and received on graduating the degree A. B. Degree, LL. B., Indiana University. Occupation, attorney at law; Mayor of Wabash City (1882). Married Miss Fannie S. Town, May 28, 1879.

SYLVESTER STARK, LL. B., Terre Haute.

WALTER B. SWAINE, born in Knightstown, Indiana, 1854. Died April 10, 1880, at Knightstown. Educated in the

Knightstown public schools. Entered the Law Department of the University in 1874. Degree, LL. B. Occupation and position: Mr. Swaine was a successful and unusually promising lawyer, practicing in Henry and Rush counties, Indiana.

DAVID NEWTON TAYLOR, A. M., LL. B. See Collegiate Department, Class 1874.

JESSE DAY TRUEBLOOD, A. M., LL. B. See Collegiate Department, Class 1874.

OWEN JASON WOOD, born August 10, 1853, at Crown Point, Lake County, Indiana. Residence, Montevideo, Chippewa County, Minnesota. Educated in Crown Point High School. Degree, LL. B. Occupation and position, attorney at law; Prosecuting Attorney Twelfth Judicial District, Minnesota, 1879–83.

CALVIN RUTER WORRALL, born May 24, 1855, in Marion, Iowa. Residence, Bloomington, Indiana. Educated in part at Indiana Asbury (now DePauw) University, leaving at the end of the junior year. Degree, LL. B. Occupation, attorney at law; politician. Delivered the valedictory of Law Class, 1876. Member of Legislature, 1886, and one of the educational committee.

CLINTON CALVERT WORRALL, born June 19, 1857, in Marion, Iowa. Residence, Bloomington, Indiana. Educated for four years at DePauw University, Greencastle. Degree, LL. B. Occupation, attorney at law. Has traveled as a professional tourist extensively through the United States.

GAYLORD GRISWOLD BARTON, born April 11, 1844, at Washington, Indiana. Residence, Washington, Indiana. Educated at grammar school, Madison University, Hamilton, N. Y., and public schools of Daviess County, Indiana. Degree, LL. B. Occupation and position, attorney at law; Deputy Clerk for six years of Daviess County Court, before entering the Law Department; after graduation he made a tour through Ireland, England and France before admission to the bar; Mr. Barton was admitted as an attorney of the Daviess County Court, October 9, 1887.

ALBERT MILO BEATTIE, born June 10, 1853, at Ruggles, Ohio. Residence, New London, Huron County, Ohio. Educated at Geneva, Ashtabula County, Ohio. Degree, LL. B. Occupation and position, attorney at law; teacher; in 1880 was elected Mayor of New London, Ohio. (1882) Mr. Beattie is a member of the Baptist Church.

LUTHER B. BUNNELL, A. B., LL. B. See Collegiate Department, Class 1875.

MATTHEW F. BURKE, born December 8, 1855, at Washington, Indiana; Residence, Washington, Indiana. Educated at Washington public schools and at St. Louis University. Degrees, A. B., St. Louis University; LL. B., Indiana University.

ISAAC N. CLAYBURG, born October 6, 1847, at Richland County, Ohio. Residence, Mansfield, Ohio. Educated at Savannah Academy, Ashland County, Ohio, and Smithville High School, Wayne County, Ohio. Degree, LL. B. Occupation, attorney at law.

JOHN J. DILLE, born November 18, 1857, at Antioch, Indiana. Residence, Huntington, Indiana. Educated at Northern Indiana Normal School. Degree, LL. B. Occupation, attorney at law; partner of J. B. Kenner, of Law Class, 1871, with a large and lucrative practice.

JAMES WESLEY DOUTHIT, born January 15, 1848, in Decatur County, Indiana. Residence, Rensselaer, Indiana. Educated at Hartsville University; B. S., Hartsville University. Degree, LL. B. Occupation, attorney at law.

ARNOLD F. FARRER, born May 29, 1857, at Peru. Died June 17, 1877, at Peru, Indiana. Educated at high school of Peru. He attended law school in Chicago the year preceding his attending the Indiana University, where he received the degree LL. B. Mr. Farrer's death was caused by the accidental discharge of a revolver he was examining a few days after his graduation.

BARTON STONE HIGGINS, born August 11, 1849, at Milford, Decatur County. Residence, Lebanon, Boone County, Indiana. Educated in Boone County common schools; afterwards a year and a half at Ladoga Academy and six months at Notre Dame. Degree, LL. B. Occupation, attorney at law.

WALTER S. MENDENHALL, born October 28, at Richmond. Residence, Indianapolis. Educated at the Friends' Boarding School, Providence, Rhode Island. From this institution he received the degree A. B. Degree, LL. B., Indiana University. Occupation, attorney at law and book-keeping.

JAMES W. MORRISON, born December 15, 1853, at Middle Fork. Residence, Frankfort, Indiana. Educated at Wabash College. Degree, LL. B. Occupation, attorney at law.

MCHENRY OWEN, born in Owen township, Jackson County. Residence, Leesville, Indiana. His early education was at Clear Spring, Jackson County. He entered the Junior Law Class in 1874. During the college year, 1875–6, he took a select literary course, and the year following returned to the Law Department, graduating with the class of 1877. During his first year the old-time spelling school was revived, and became popular in Bloomington, and he succeeded in taking about all the prizes in such contests. During his three years' course he was a member of the Philomathean Literary Society. He began the practice of law at Brownstown in August, 1877, and so continued there till 1881, two years of which time he was Deputy Prosecuting Attorney. October 8, 1879, he was married to Miss Ada E. Smith, daughter of W. K. Smith, of Leesville, where, in addition to mercantile and agricultural pursuits, he was editor of the *Leesville Graphic* until October, 1886, when he was, under the Civil Service Rules, appointed a special examiner of the pension office. He served in such capacity until June 30, 1889, when, because of a change of administration, he was not reappointed. While acting in such capacity he was stationed at different cities in the State of Ohio. In September, 1889, he removed to Bedford, Indiana, and resumed the practice of law.

ARNOLD J. PADGETT, born October 28, 1855, Daviess County. Residence, Washington, Indiana. Educated in the Washington High School. Degree, LL. B. Occupation, attorney at law; in 1882, Prosecuting Attorney.

NOAH JEFFERSON SHECKELL, born October 8, 1852, in Crawford County. Residence, Tekamah, Burt County, Nebraska. Educated at Hartsville University, receiving therefrom the degrees, B. S. and M. S. Degree, LL. B., Indiana University. Occupation and position, attorney at law; Police Judge of Tekamah, Nebraska, and County Attorney since 1874.

WILLIAM W. SPENCER, B. S., LL. B. See Collegiate Department, Class 1875.

ELBRIDGE GERRY WILSON, LL. B., Paoli, Indiana.

NON-GRADUATE LAW STUDENTS.

The names without class indication are Juniors. Those marked Sen. (Senior), attended the Senior Class and were for the most part practicing lawyers, or students not intending to graduate.

		Year.
William Addison	Lawrenceville, Tenn..Sen.	1874
James W. Allen	Rockville	1848
Edward B. Allen	Terre Haute	1850
Andrew J. Arnold	Bloomington	1877
Perri S. Askren	Corydon	1872
Samuel D. Ayres	Frankfort	1872
Daniel Barbour	Terre Haute	1848
William Borland Barnes	Bloomington	1857
Zachariah T. Barton	Princeton	1876
John S. Bays	Worthington	1871
David Enoch Beem	Spencer	1859
A. L. Benham	Lebanon	1853
Richard Benson	Rushville...........Sen.	1876
Edward W. Black	Terre Haute	1876
Augustine W. Blair	Randolph, N. C	1844
I. W. Blasdell	Lawrenceburg	1853
James B. Boyle	Butler	1876
Louis M. Boyle	Stewartsville	1863
John T. Breckinridge	Booneville	1852
John H. Bradley	Laporte	1871
Peter A. Brady	Campbell, Ill	1873
Lawson T. Brannaman	Clear Springs	1874
Charles F. Brenton	Fort Wayne	1870
Charles A. Brown	Grandville, Ill	1845
William Brown	Howard County	1850
D. Gray Brown	Bloomington	1870
Daniel R. Browning	Spencer	1863
Leander S. Burdick	Bedford	1873

David V. Burns	Sharpsville	1866
Alfred D. Buskirk	Worthington	1874
Samuel W. Buskirk	Bloomington......Sen.	1874
Samuel D. Buttz	Quincy, Ill	1870
H. D. Caldwell	Sullivan	1853
James W. Canine	Galveston	1877
David R. Carpenter	Cainsville, Mo	1874
C. D. Cavins	Bloomfield	1853
William Charles	Grayville, Ill	1853
James T. Chittenden	Hartsville	1856
J. Chord	South Bend	1853
John E. Cline	Lanesville	1856
Thomas R. Cobb	Bedford	1854
Jonathan Cobb	Pine Village	1858
George W. Collings	Rockville......Sen.	1875
David A. Combs	Bloomington, Ill	1853
Samuel W. Conboy	Butlersville	1877
Henry E. Cook	New Albany	1867
Oliver H. Cook	Huntington	1877
George W. Cornelius	Wayne......Sen.	1847
John M. Cowan	Frankfort......Sen.	1845
Baron D. Crawford	New Albany......Sen.	1875
Chilton A. Darnell	Bainbridge......Sen.	1848
James R. Davidson	Rensselaer	1871
William H. Davis	Poseyville	1874
James Davis	Jamestown	1877
Thomas W. Denton	Butlersville	1868
Samuel F. Denton	Butlersville	1870
W. S. Denton	Indianapolis......Sen.	1877
Alman H. Dickey	Indianapolis	1873
Webster Dixon	Vernon	1873
Matthew Donaldson	Walkertown	1871
Joseph M. Dorr	Valparaiso	1856
W. P. Douthit	Franklin	1853
Sandford H. Drybread	Nineveh	1873
Washington C. Duncan	Nashville......Sen.	1877
Samuel H. Dunn	Spencer	1869
Harry Durand	Bloomington	1877
William B. Durborow	Williamsport	1877
M. S. Durham	Terre Haute	1853
William H. Edwards	Mitchell	1867

Eli Edwards	Mitchell	1871
James W. Eller	Bloomington	1870
Henry W. Elwyn	Oakland City	1870
Weston Emison	Vincennes	1866
William N. Engard	Thorntown	1872
James P. Ennis	Martinsville	1871
J. C. Farris	Rensselaer	1850
George W. Fellenger	Terre Haute	1876
Amos Frost	Vernon	1844
Eli C. Galbreth	Greenfield	1871
S. George	Maxwell, O	1876
J. Wright Gladish	Petersburg	1877
John C. Graham	Washington	1853
James H. Green	Lanesville	1856
Samuel Griffin	Ogden	1868
Enos P. Gwinn	San Francisco, Cal	1873
Eli B. Hamilton	Terre Haute	1866
William S. Harbert	Terre Haute	1866
Oliver A. Harker	St. Louis, Mo.	1867
Albert G. Harris	Macon, Ill	1868
Ben. F. Harris	Richmond Sen.	1875
B. F. Harrison	Georgetown	1876
Joseph M. Hart	Baton Rouge, La.	1870
George W. Hart	Lee	1871
J. McD. Haskell	Marietta, O.	1850
William S. Hastings	Laporte	1854
Ed. Ruthvin Hatfield	Concordia, Ky	1859
David J. Heffron	Washington	1869
*James Scott Hester	Bloomington Sen.	1844
Willis Hickman	Spencer	1877
William S. Hillyer	New Albany	1850
Virgil M. Hobbs	Salem	1875
J. McG. C. Holden	Perrysville Sen.	1848
David Holland	Henry	1848
William G. Holland	Bennington	1870
Jesse L. H. Holman	Aurora	1851
Melville C. Hoss	Bloomington	1874
John W. Horner	Lanesville	1873

*J. Scott Hester is mentioned as one of the graduating class in the proceedings of the Board, and as a resident graduate of the Law Department in Catalogue, 1845; his name is omitted in the list of graduates of Law Department in Catalogues of 1875, 1885 and 1886.

David O. House	Harrodsburg		1873
George P. Huckely	Rome		1863
Anderson B. Hunter	Johnson	Sen.	1848
M. Craig Hunter, Jr.	Bloomington		1875
William H. H. Hunter	Versailles		1859
Nathaniel Huntington	Laporte		1851
Barnes Hutson	Vandalia	Sen.	1875
John Ingles	Centre Point		1874
J. W. Irwin	Elkhart		1847
Joseph S. Jenckes, Jr.	Terre Haute		1857
George A. Johnson	New Castle		1850
Thomas J. Johnson	New Harmony		1865
Charles E. Johnston	Spencer	Sen.	1877
Henry C. Jones	Versailles		1873
Alexander C. Jones	Brookville	Sen.	1875
Lewis A. Keller	New Albany		1855
Calvin Kelsey	Bloomfield		1853
J. Edgar Kenton	Bloomington		1866
David M. Kinsall	Omaha, Ill		1875
George A. Kirland	Indianapolis		1865
W. D. Lee	Terre Haute		1853
Jacob P. Lindley	Eldora, Iowa		1877
Richard T. Long	Charlestown		1855
Robert McAfee	Bedford		1856
A. M. McElhaney	Randolph		1853
A. V. McKee	Greensburg		1853
George W. McKeaig	Louisville, Ky		1851
William E. McLean	Terre Haute		1851
Paul A. McMinn	Darlington		1851
Joseph T. McMinn	Logansport		1866
William Malott	Cicero		1875
Philip A. Marquam	Lafayette	Sen.	1848
James L. Mason	Brownsville		1855
James E. Matthews	Bloomington		1859
James W. Mavity	Titusville		1869
Christian P. Mayer	Palestine		1859
David H. Maxwell	Rockville		1848
E. W. Meeks	Fort Wayne	Sen.	1877
James A. Mershon	Bloomington		1875
Josiah Miller	Chester, S. C.		1853
John Millen	Bloomington		1847

James L. Mitchell	Bloomington	1859
William W. Moffett	Spencer	1877
Sylvester A. Montgomery	Carmi, Ill	1874
William B. Montgomery	Linden.	1875
Calvin C. Morrical	Laporte	1857
Francis M. Moyer	Elizabethtown, Ill.....Sen.	1877
Augustus O'Bryan	Delphi	1870
Andrew S. Oliphant	Terre Haute	1870
T. S. Osborn	St. Louis, Mo	1853
Gabriel M. Overstreet	Franklin ....Sen.	1847
George W. Parrish	Cuba	1865
Anderson Percifield	Nashville	1874
Jehu W. Perkins	Lebanon	1872
William E. Pinney	Laporte	1872
Joseph T. Pressley	Rush	1851
Jacob M. Ranard	Whitehall	1862
Robert B. Ranard	Whitehall	1864
Theodore Read	Bloomington	1855
Edward P. Richardson	Petersburg	1870
Aurelius W. Roberts	Bruceville	1854
Marcellus P. Roberts	Bruceville	1856
James W. Roberts	Buckland, Mo	1866
Melville C. Robertson	Paris	1864
Middleton G. Robertson	Deputy	1877
Alfred Rogers	Bloomington ....Sen.	1863
G. E. Ross	Logansport	1877
Valentine C. Rucker	Farmington, Mo	1866
William Rude	Morgantown	1877
Isaac N. Senter	Lawrence County	1845
D. W. Shafer	Franklin	1852
Henry Shannon	Thornton	1853
Samuel R. Shannon	Carmi, Ill.	1871
David Shelby	Eugene	1851
Harvey E. Shields	Terre Haute	1868
Charles N. Shook	Versailles	1847
Samuel W. Short	Springville	1847
Burnet W. Short	Springville	1847
Thales Short	Springville	1876
Leander Simons	Warren	1877
John S. Smith	Rushville	1868
Benjamin F. Smith	Fort Wayne	1877

Newton B. Smith	Kokomo	1877
William C. Smith	Kokomo	1877
Robert F. Stanley	Beech Grove	1871
William P. Stanley	Beech Grove	1871
B. C. Stewart	Richland	1852
Carroll S. Tandy	Ghent, Ky	1875
J. T. Taylor	Elizabethtown, Ill	1876
A. M. Thompson	Fort Wayne	1852
David H. Thompson	Little York......Sen.	1875
Charles A. Thompson	Delphi	1875
George W. Thornton	Lumpkin, Ga	1853
Thomas V. Thornton	Bedford	1870
Hiram S. Tousley	Fort Wayne ......Sen.	1848
Thomas J. Tuley	New Albany	1864
Leander J. S. Turney	Fairfield, Ill......Sen.	1848
Arthur P. Twineham	Terre Haute	1872
John Van Trees	Washington	1853
James W. Walker	Rushville	1851
A. Hinkston Welch	Pendleton	1875
Joseph W. Wharton	Worthington	1871
David F. White	Fairfield	1877
Erie Woolery	Bedford	1870
Charles Whitted	Springville	1876
James Wilkins	Washington	1857
James R. Williams	Carmi, Ill	1875
George Wilson	Lafayette	1877
Thomas S. Wood	Wilmington	1845
LeRoy Woods	New Castle	1868
Alexander Yates	Utica, Miss	1851
Henry A. Yeager	Fort Branch	1870

SUPPLEMENT TO COLLEGIATE DEPARTMENT.

Supposing that the catalogue would have been published in 1888, no effort was made to bring it up to the present time. To supply the deficiency, to some degree, the following lists of Professor selected since 1887, and graduates from the same date, are subjoined:

LIST OF PROFESSORS APPOINTED SINCE THE CLOSE OF THE CATALOGUE IN 1887.

J. STERLING KINGSLEY, D. Sc. A graduate of Williams College. Professor of Zoölogy. Resigned in 1889, and accepted a professorship in the State University, Lincoln, Nebraska.

HENRY BEMAN MITER, A. M. Resigned, 1890. Professor of Rhetoric and Oratory.

CARL OSTHAUS of the University of Göttingen. Associate Professor of German, 1888.

JAMES AUSTIN MITCHELL, A. B., 1888–90. Instructor in Preparatory Department till its close.

JAMES ELLIS HUMPHREY, A. B., of Harvard University. Instructor in Botany, 1888–89.

ROBERT JUDSON ALEY, A. B., 1888–89. Instructor in Mathematics.

CHARLES HENRY GILBERT, PH. D. Professor Gilbert was Assistant Professor in Biology and German from 1880 to 1884. Accepted a Professorship in Cincinnati Medical College; returned to Indiana University in 1890.

THOMAS MCCABE, PH. D. Professor of Germanic Languages and Literature, 1890.

JEREMIAH WHIPPLE JENKS, PH. D., 1890. Professor of Economics and Social Science.

EARL BARNES, 1890. Professor of History.

DAVID DEMAREE BANTA, B. S., LL. B., Indiana University, LL. D., Franklin, Dean of the Department of Law, 1890. See sketch of, among Alumni, 1855.

GEORGE WILLIAM SANDERSON, A. M., LL. B., 1890. Professor of Rhetoric and Oratory.

ERNEST WILSON HUFFCUT, B. S., LL. B., 1890. Professor-elect of Law.

FRANKLIN FULLER GUNN, A. B., 1890. Associate Professor of Latin and Greek.

EDWARD HOWARD GRIGGS, A. B., 1890. Instructor in English.

ROBERT EDWARD LYONS, A. B., 1890. Instructor in Chemistry.

CHARLES MARION CARPENTER, A. B., 1890. Instructor in Mathematics. Professor Carpenter has lately accepted the position of Principal of the High and Graded Schools of Bloomington.

LOUIS RETTGER, A. B. Instructor in Mineralogy and Histology.

The following are the courses of study pursued in the University, in the year 1890:

I. Greek, Professor Hoffman.

II. Latin, Professor Atwater, and Professor Gunn, Associate.

III. Romance Languages, Professor Karsten.

IV. Germanic Languages, Professor McCabe, and Professor Osthaus, Associate.

V. English Language and Literature, Professor Clark, and Edward Howard Griggs, Instructor.

VI. Rhetoric and Oratory, Professor Sanderson.

HISTORY OF INDIANA UNIVERSITY.   373

VII. History, Professor Barnes. American History, Professor Woodburn.

VIII. Economics and Social Science, Professor Jenks.

IX. Philosophy, Professor Bryan.

X. Pedagogics, Professor Boone.

XI. Mathematics, Professor Swain. Professor Green, Associate, John A. Miller, Instructor.

XII. Physics, Professor Naylor; A. Lee Foley, Instructor.

XIII. Chemistry, Professor Van Nüys, and Robert E. Lyons, Instructor.

XIV. Geology, Professor Branner and Professor Jordan.

XV. Zoölogy, Professor Gilbert, and Louis Retger, Instructor.

XVI. Botany, Professor Campbell.

XVII. Law, Professor Banta, Dean, and Professor Huffcut, Professor.

GRADUATES OF 1888.

Robert Judson Aley ....*Math.   Spencer.
Myrtie Alma (Logan) Beale ....Gr.   Clarksburg.
J. Frank Benham ....Chem.   Richmond.
Idelle Bicknell ....Ger.   Bicknell.
Clara Amelia (Sluss) Bicknell......Ger.   Bloomington.
George M. Braxton ....Soc.   Bloomington.
Jennie Bryan ....Gr.   Bloomington.
Charlotte A. (Lowe) Bryan ....Gr.   Indianapolis.

*The different departments in which the specialty of each student is taken are indicated by the abbreviations, thus:

Bot.	Botany.	Math.	Mathematics.
Chem.	Chemistry.	Ped.	Pedagogics.
Eng.	English.	Phil.	Philosophy.
Geol.	Geology.	Phys.	Physics.
Ger.	Germanic Languages.	Rom.	Romance Languages.
Gr.	Greek.	Soc.	Social Science.
Hist.	History.	Zoöl.	Zoölogy.
Lat.	Latin.		

25—History.

Lawrence V. Buskirk, Ph. B ....Soc.   Bloomington.
Oscar Chrisman ....Hist.   Gosport.
David A. Cox ....Chem.   Evansville.
Daniel Driscol............................Phil.   Bedford.
Frank Brown Foster ....Gr.   Morning Sun, O.
William Harper Foster................Gr.   Morning Sun, O.
Harry E. Gabe ....Eng.   Bloomington.
William E. M. Golden.................Eng.   New Harmony.
Jennie Taylor (Fry) Griggs ....Rom.   Indianapolis.
Robert Foster Hight ....Zoöl.   Bloomington.
Joseph Henry Howard...............Ger.   Indianapolis.
Ralph Jones ....Phil.   Franklin.
Philip H. Kirsch ....Biol.   Crawfordsville.
Frank Felix Lodeman ....Ger.   Ypsilanti, Mich.
Benj. Franklin Mathews..............Gr.   Shelbyville, Ky.
Josie Millen ....Ger.   Wichita, Kan.
Albert Miller..............................Chem.   New Harmony.
Louella T. Morris ....Ger.   Milton.
Willard L. Morrison...................Phil.   Alpha.
Haidee C. Nuckols ....Ger.   Bloomington.
Henry J. Ratts...........................Phil.   Wakeland.
Ella Rawles ....Eng.   Bloomington.
John S. Shannon ....Hist.   Greensburg.
Kate Shannon............................Gr.   Clarksburg.
Sophia May Sheeks....................Eng.   Bloomington.
Elbert Jeter Stalker ....Gr.   Bedford.
Glenn Leslie Swiggett ....Phil.   Cambridge City.
Joseph F. Thornton ....Ger.   Bedford.
Maud F. VanZandt ....Eng.   Bloomington.
Alfred Scott Wartthin ....Eng.   Greensburg.
Lora Wilson ....Lat.   Bloomington.

GRADUATES OF 1889.

Albert R. Abel ....Hist.   Boundary.
Emma Bain.................................Eng.   Martinsville.
Alfred Herbert Beldon ....Hist.   Tampico.

*Charles Harvey Bollman	Zoöl.	Bloomington.
John Robert Brill	Hist.	Centre Valley.
Joseph C. Bryan	Phil.	Bloomington.
Charles M. Carpenter	Math.	Manchester.
Homer Bliss Dibell	Soc.	Wolcott.
Fletcher Bascom Dresslar	Phil.	Waverly.
Bert Fesler	Zoöl.	Indianapolis.
Edward Howard Griggs	Math.	Indianapolis.
Charles Elmer Heiney	Ger.	Andrews.
William W. Holmes	Hist.	Lima.
Thomas M. Honan	Soc.	Seymour.
James B. Hughes	Hist.	Redwood City, Cal.
Russell King	Ger.	Indianapolis.
Henry Clinton Kinzie	Hist.	South Bend.
Effie Lemonds	Ger.	Rockport.
Theodore J. Louden	Hist.	Bloomington.
Robert Edward Lyons	Chem.	Bloomington.
Ada McMahan	Gr.	Huntingburg.
William A. Millis	Phil.	Paoli.
James L. Mitchell, Jr	Lat.	Indianapolis.
Webster V. Moffett	Hist.	Spencer.
Fred. Segal Monical	Phil.	Brooklyn.
Frederick V. Moss	Phys.	Noblesville.
William Alonzo Mussett	Phil.	Grayville, Ill.
John Roscoe Mutz	Chem.	Edinburg.
Creed Myers	Gr.	Gosport.
Christian Newman	Ger.	Mt. Vernon.
Jonathan Truman Perigo	Math.	Boonville.
John B. Phillips	Ger.	Holt, Mich.
Charles E. Remsberg	Soc.	West Lebanon.
Charles A. Rhetts	Gr.	Salem.
Willard Robertson	Hist.	Brownstown.
Bessie Rogers	Ger.	Bloomington.
Ella Ryan	Ger.	Bloomington.
Joseph H. Shea	Hist.	Lexington.
Frederick C. Test	Zoöl.	Lafayette.
Arnold Tompkins	Ped.	Greencastle.
Howard L. Wilson	Gr.	Arcadia.

*Deceased.

GRADUATES OF 1890.

William M. Andrews	Bot.	Bloomington.
Earl Barnes	Ped.	Mortville, N. Y.
Regina Bitner	Ger.	Warsaw.
Eugene W. Bohannon	Ped.	Boonville.
Caroline H. Brown	Hist.	Indianapolis.
Richard Ellsworth Call	Geol.	Des Moines, Iowa.
A. Harvey Collins	Hist.	Salem.
Ella M. Corr	Eng.	Bloomington.
James B. Cook, Jr	Soc.	Glenwood.
William R. Cravens	Chem.	Bloomfield.
Schuyler C. Davisson	Math.	Galveston.
Frank Mayo Drew	Zoöl.	Bunker Hill, Ill.
Charles H. Drybread	Chem.	Nineveh.
Arthur Lee Foley	Phys.	Gem.
George A. Gordon	Gr.	Cedar Rapids, Ia.
Nellie M. Gordon	Gr.	Cedar Rapids, Ia.
Frank C. Groninger	Hist.	Camden.
William James Hannah	Soc.	Davison, Mich.
Samuel B. Harding	Gr.	Indianapolis.
Frank H. Hatfield	Chem.	Boonville.
James Harvey Hayworth	Math.	Greencastle.
Robert Hessler	Chem.	Connersville.
Walter Dunn Howe	Lat.	New London, Conn.
Jesse Wesley Hubbard	Hist.	Bloomington.
Manson U. Johnson	Soc.	Summittville.
Everett Orville Jones	Zoöl.	Red Wing, Minn.
Jessie Knight Jordan	Ger.	Bloomington.
Isaac Anderson Loeb	Soc.	Anderson.
Ida Louden	Eng.	Bloomington.
Charles Roll Madison	Hist.	Bloomington.
John Anthony Miller	Math.	Kokomo.
Peter Benton Monical	Chem.	Orangeville.
Hiram W. Monical	Ped.	Brooklyn.
Maurice G. Moore	Chem.	Vincennes.
George D. Morris	Rom.	Knoxville.
Charles A. Mosemiller	Ger.	Jeffersonville.
Edward O'Donnell	Soc.	Mitchell.

J. Frank H. Post	Chem.	Murphysboro', Ill.
Josephine Pittman	Ger.	Bloomington.
Alpheus J. Reynolds	Hist.	Maxwell.
Henry Wilson Rouff	Phil.	Indiana, Pa.
John Everett Shepardson	Ped.	Shoals.
Edwin E. Starbuck	Math.	Bridgeport.
Charles W. Stewart	Hist.	Marengo.
Bedford Vance Sudbury	Hist.	Bloomington.
Alice Test	Ger.	Richmond.
John B. Wisely	Eng.	Terre Haute.

THE FIRST COLLEGE CATALOGUE.

This catalouge is dated Bloomington, Indiana, August 17, 1831. It gives a list of the Board of Trustees—a list of the Visitors at that time—the Faculty, together with statements respecting the studies of the College and Preparatory Classes, the manner in which the studies are conducted and the general discipline of the Institution. It closes with a catalogue of the students and their places of residence. Without any distinction of classes, generally, only the surnames are given:

Mr. Alexander	Bloomington, Ind.
Allen	Louisville, Ky.
Allison	Spencer, Ind.
S. Anderson	Washington County, Pa.
Wm. Anderson	Indianapolis, Ind.
W. I. Anderson	Monroe County, Ind.
Ezra Baker	Wabash County, Ill.
Ed. Baker	Wabash County, Ill.
L. Bollman	Williamsport, Pa.
Barbour	Vigo County, Ind.
Bowles	St. Mary's Parish, La.
Campbell	Louisville, Ky.
Carr	Buck County, Pa.
Curry	Harrison County, Ky.
Dagger	Bottetourt County, Va.
Denson	Lawrence County, Ind.
Dodds	Monroe County, Ind.
Downing	Harrison County, Ky.
Dunn	Hanover, Ind.
Evans	Owen County, Ind.
Freeland	Monroe County, Ind.
Givens	Oldham County, Ky.

Harney..Bloomington, Ind.
Jones..Bloomington, Ind.
Ketcham ....Monroe County, Ind.
Kyle..Madison, Ind.
S. Leffler ....,Ohio County, Va.
I. Leffler ....Ohio County, Va.
Lowe...Bloomington, Ind.
Marsh ....New Albany, Ind.
Maxwell ....Bloomington, Ind.
McCoy...Clark County, Ind.
McClure ....Madison, Ind.
McPheeters ....Fayette County, Ky.
Miller ....Washington County, Pa.
Mitchell ....Shelby County Ky.
S. Mitchell ....Columbus, Ind.
Nichols ....Monroe County, Ind.
Pettit..Washington, Miss.
I. Porter ....Bloomington, Ind.
S. Porter..Bloomington, Ind.
Posey ....Corydon, Ind.
C. Randal...Burks County, Pa.
A. Randal...Burks County, Pa.
J. Randal ....Burks County, Pa.
Richie ....Cannonsburg, Pa.
Roach ....Bloomington, Ind.
Thickston...Harrison County, Ind.
Throop ....Bloomington, Ind.
Townsend...Putnamville, Ind.
Turnstall..Jeffersonville, Ind.
Seward ....Bloomington, Ind.
Small..Wayne County, Ind.
Smith..Monroe County, Ind.
Wylie ....Bloomington, Ind.
Walker..Brook County, Va.
Watts ....Dearborn County, Ind.
Wallace..Bloomington.
Yandes ....Indianapolis, Ind.
Yewell..Oldham County, Ky.

LIST OF STUDENTS, ETC.

When the State is not given, Indiana is understood. Se. or Sen. stands for Senior; Ju. for Junior; So. for Sophomore; Fr. for Freshman; Pr. for Preparatory; Irr., Irregular, and Sel., Select, mean the same—those students who were not in the regular classes, and took select studies. This list of those who attended, but are not graduates of Indiana University, is taken from a nearly complete file of the annual catalogues of the University. In the "*First College Catalogue,*" printed entire (see p. 378) graduates and non-graduates are presented indiscriminately.

Joseph Abel	Bloomington	Pr.,	1845
Charles C. Ackelmire	Brazil	Fr.,	1877
Samuel Adams	Brown County	Pr.,	1852
William B. Adams	Reinsville	Pr.,	1855
Andrew J. Adams	Reynolds	Pr.,	1860
James Watts Adams	Nashville	Pr.,	1866
George A. Adams	Morgantown	Sel.,	1871
Emma Adams	Bloomington	Pr.,	1876
Joseph E. Adams	Bloomington	Pr.,	1877
Jennie Adams	Bloomington	Pr.,	1882
William H. Adkins	Hopeville	Pr.,	1860
James M. Adkins	Bloomington	Pr.,	1867
Ella J. Adkins	Bloomington	Pr.,	1878
Charles C. Agar	Princeton	El.,	1878
Ransom W. Akin	Bloomington	Pr.,	1861
William O. Albertson	Orleans	Pr.,	1866
Joseph Aley	Little York	Fr.,	1870
William Alexander	Bloomington	Pr.,	1835
J. W. Alexander	Gosport	Pr.,	1845
Jackson H. Alexander	Gosport	Irr.,	1848
James M. Alexander	Gosport	Irr.,	1847
James W. Alexander	Gosport	Irr.,	1847
W. J. Alexander	Greene County	Irr.,	1850
John Alexander	Bloomington	Irr.,	1853

HISTORY OF INDIANA UNIVERSITY. 381

William M. Alexander ....Bloomington.........Irr.,		1853
James II. Alexander ....Bloomington.........Pr.,		1853
Joseph P. Alexander ....Bloomington.........Fr.,		1854
William S. Alexander ....Bloomington.........So.,		1861
Thomas F. Alexander...........Sparta, I................Fr.,		1862
John Arthur Alexander ....Bloomington.........Fr.,		1867
Joseph S. Alexander ....Bloomington.........Pr.,		1867
Joseph B. Alford ....Alfordsville...........Fr.,		1867
James M. Allen....................Rockville..............So.,		1846
J. W. Allen .... Monroe County......Pr.,		1850
William J. Allen..................Bloomington.........Pr.,		1852
Harry P. Allen .... Rockville..............Fr.,		1864
Robert A. Allen ....Bloomington.........Pr.,		1867
Paris W. Allen ....Mount Meridian.....Pr.,		1867
Hamlet Allen.......................Washington...........Fr.,		1872
Jesse Allen..........................West Newton ....Pr.,		1876
Joseph Allen ....Bloomington.........Pr.,		1879
Lizzie S. Allen ....Bloomington.........Pr.,		1881
Mrs. E. A. Allen..................Hartsville..............Fr.,		1882
Eli A. Allen ....Hartsville..............Se.,		1882
John Allison ....Floyd County ....Irr.,		1848
William T. Allison .... .Point Commerce.....Fr.,		1854
Deborah Allison ....Bloomington.........Pr.,		1879
Jessie Allison......................Bloomington.........Pr.,		1881
Emma Allison ....Bloomington.........So.,		1882
William Alloway ....Utica.....................Pr.,		1857
Henry B. Alvord ....Indianapolis ....So.,		1860
Jeremiah Anderson ....Greensburgh .... Fr.,		1838
Wesley Anderson ....Monroe County......Pr.,		1838
William W. Anderson...........Monroe County......Pr.,		1846
John K. Anderson ....Monroe County......Pr.,		1848
Hiram Anderson...................Compton ....Pr.,		1851
James M. Anderson ....Covington ....Irr.		1850
George Anderson ....Covington ....So.,		1854
Milton Anderson ....Harrodsburg.........Pr.,		1855
John H. Anderson ....Evansville ....Pr.,		1857
Vincent Anderson ....Gosport ....Pr.,		1860
William A. Anderson ....Lewisburg, W. Va..Irr.,		1865
Marcellus H. Anderson ....Rockville..............Pr.,		1865
Andrew J. Anderson............Ireland ....,....Pr.,		1874
Leman C. Anderson.............Bloomington.........Pr.,		1876

Lewis H. Anderson	Bloomington	Pr.,	1880
Sarah Anderson	Bloomington	So.,	1881
Edgar Andrews	Bloomington	Pr.,	1879
Lizzie B. Andrews	Bloomington	Pr.,	1880
David E. Andrews	Bloomington	Pr.,	1880
Birdie Andrews	Bloomington	Fr.,	1884
William E. Angerman	South Bethany	Pr.,	1881
John H. App	Evansville	Pr.,	1859
Thomas Applegate	Louisville, Ky	Pr.,	1837
James P. Applegate	Jeffersonville	So.,	1859
Thomas J. Applegate	Corydon	Pr.,	1867
A. G. Archer	Monroe County	Pr.,	1838
Robert Archer	Bloomington	Pr.,	1854
Samuel A. Archer	Bloomington	Pr.,	1860
Royal M. Archer	Bloomington	Irr.,	1865
James Archibald	Brookfield	Fr.,	1866
S. M. Ardell	Scotland	Pr.,	1879
Edward W. Argenbright	Gosport	Pr.,	1848
John Armer	Warrick	Pr.,	1851
Zachary T. Arms	Danville, Pa	Jr.,	1881
David F. Armstrong	Fayetteville	Fr.,	1846
John Armstrong	Lawrence	Irr.,	1848
James P. Armstrong	Springville	Fr.,	1853
Felix Armstrong	Springville	Fr.,	1859
John S. Armstrong	Springville	Fr.,	1864
William Armstrong	Vincennes	Sel.,	1871
Willis E. Armstrong	Camden	Sel.,	1877
Jeanette Armstrong	Bloomington	Pr.,	1880
Thomas H. Arnold	Columbus	Irr.,	1852
George W. Arnold	Columbus	Pr.,	1852
William Arnold	Bartholomew Co	Pr.,	1845
Benjamin F. Arnold	Columbus	Pr.,	1860
Frank Arnott	Bloomington	Pr.,	1881
Enoch S. Arwine	Nashville	Pr.,	1862
Albert Ashcraft	Dresden	Fr.,	1882
William R. Asher	Martinsville	Se.,	1883
Henry S. F. Ashford	Bloomington	Pr.,	1867
Francis M. Ashford	Bloomington	Sel.,	1871
James S. Athon	Indianapolis	Irr.,	1864
Archibald M. Auld	Bogart Sands	Pr.,	1863
Henry J. Austin	New Albany	Pr.,	1855

Carrie W. Austin	Bloomington ....Pr.,	1882
Francis A. Avard	Covington, Ky ......Fr.,	1859
Guy C. Avery	St. Paul ....Pr.,	1863
Milan Axe	Valparaiso ....Pr.,	1858
Charles J. Axtell	Solsberry ....Sel.,	1872
Samuel W. Axtell	Bloomington ....Sel.,	1873
Martha Axtell	Bloomington ....Pr.,	1879
Isaac L. Ayres	Marion ....Sc. So.,	1865
William Z. Aydelott	New Albany ....Irr.,	1851
Horace P. Bachman	Logansport............Irr.,	1871
Theodore Bailey	Terre Haute..........Pr.,	1838
Paris Bailey	Monroe County......Pr.,	1838
Henry Bailey	Charlottesville........Pr.,	1842
William P. Bailey	Washington............Irr.,	1852
Ellard D. Bailey	Vernon ....Fr.,	1881
James Bain	Martinsville...........So.,	1869
Samuel J. Baird	Bruceville.............Fr.,	1857
I. S. Baker	Vernon ....Pr.,	1839
Joseph M. Baker	Hillsborough, O......Pr.,	1853
Volney T. Baker	Orleans ....Fr.,	1857
Thomas Hart Benton Baker	Pekin.....................Pr.,	1858
Samuel W. Baker	Bloomington ....So.,	1867
Sumner W. Baker	Warsaw................So.,	1867
Joseph H. Baker	Stockwell..............Sel.,	1873
Eli C. Baker	Louisville, Ky........Sel.,	1875
William H. Baker	Louisville, Ky........Sel.,	1875
Jesse T. Baker	Bloomington ....Pr.,	1876
Arthur R. Baker	Bloomington ....Pr.,	1880
Samuel Logan Baker	Greensburgh ....Jr.,	1881
Frank W. Baker	Andrews................Fr.,	1883
A. H. Baldwin	Harrison County....Sci.,	1842
Eli M. Baldwin	Lawrence County ...Irr.,	1846
William C. Ball	Terre Haute ....Pr.,	1863
Robert R. Ball	Portland Mills ....Pr.,	1875
Henry Ballantine	Ahmednugger, H'n.Pr.,	1863
William G. Ballantine	Bloomington ....Fr.,	1864
John Q. A. Ballard	Bloomington ....Pr.,	1838
Wesley Ballard	Bridgeport ....Irr.,	1845
James G. Ballee	Simpsonville, Ky....Pr.,	1837
Viola Banks	Greenfield.............Fr.,	1882
Lovina Banks	Greenfield.............Fr.,	1883

Abraham T. Banta	Pleasureville .... Pr.,	1861
Orson Barber	Terre Haute..........Sen.,	1838
John Barber	Madison ....Irr.,	1853
Frederick Barbour	Terre Haute..........Pr.,	1863
Obadiah F. Barker	Scotland ....Pr.,	1848
Henry Barkman	Crothersville ....Fr.,	1880
John K. Barkman	Hardensburg ....Pr.,	1880
Frederick Barnard	Hancock...............Pr.,	1848
Bowland Barnes	Bloomington ....Pr.,	1847
William B. Barnes	Bloomington ....Irr.,	1852
William O. Barnett	Rockport ....So.,	1871
W. P. Barnhill	Salineville, O........Pr.,	1878
Florence Barnhill	Unionville ....Pr.,	1879
P. David Barr	Bloomington ....Pr.,	1856
Michael V. Barr	Grandview, Ill.......Fr.,	1867
John M. Barrett	Milton...................Irr.,	1846
David Barrow	Bloomington ....Fr.,	1876
Andrew W. Barrow	Unionville ....Pr.,	1878
Spurgeon Barrow	Unionville ....Pr.,	1878
Richard F. Barter	Mount Vernon ......Fr.,	1860
Charles R. Basham	Louisville, Ky. ......Pr.,	1865
John L. Bartmes	Vincennes ....Pr.,	1866
Samuel T. Bartmes	Vincennes ....Pr.,	1868
William H. Bass	Boston, Mass.........Irr.,	1852
Henry Caldwell Barton	Louisville, Ky ....Se.,	1859
Philip H. Barton	Washington...........So.,	1859
Joshua Barwick	Brookville ....So.,	1837
Joseph S. Barwick	Brookville ....Jr.,	1837
Franklin Bass	Mitchell ....Fr.,	1867
Samuel W. Baswell	Bloomington ....Fr.,	1858
John Basye	Troy ....Irr.,	1851
William Basye	Troy ....Irr.,	1852
Booker F. Bates	Troy ....Irr.,	1844
James H. Bates	Troy ....So.,	1846
Thomas W. Bates	Troy ....Pr.,	1848
Henry S. Bates	Bloomington ....Pr.,	1866
Laura E. Bates	Unionville ....Pr.,	1880
Olive N. Batman	Bedford ....Pr.,	1882
Orris Batson	Carlisle................Pr.,	1842
J. Batterton	Bloomington.........Irr.,	1839
Granville Batterton	Bloomington.........Pr.,	1841

Williamson Batterton	Bloomington..........Pr.,	1845
George Batterton	Bloomington..........Se.,	1857
David H. M. Batterton	Bloomington..........Fr.,	1863
Milton Batterton	Bloomington..........Fr.,	1870
Frank Batterton	Greensburg............Sel.,	1877
J. H. Baugh	Monroe County......Pr.,	1838
Harvey P. Baugh	Monroe County......Pr.,	1839
Joseph Baugh	Monroe County ....Pr.,	1850
Morris C. Baum	Evansville............So.,	1875
Sylvester Bayless	Franklin...............Irr.,	1846
John S. Bays	Point Commerce.....Pr.,	1868
Lou. Emma Baxter	Bloomington.......Jr.,	1881
Theodore F. Beach	Baltimore, Md........Pr.,	1847
Schuyler C. Beard	Vincennes..............So.,	1882
Charles Beardsley	Elkhart................Jr.,	1868
Lillie Beatley	Bloomington..........Pr.,	1878
David S. Beatty	Indianapolis ....Se.,	1839
Marshall Beatty	Owensburg............Sel.,	1871
Mary E. Beatty	Bloomington..........Sel.,	1873
William Beatty	Bloomington..........Pr.,	1875
Preston Beck	Bolivar, Mo...........Fr.,	1841
Jeptha L. Beck	Pinhook ....Pr.,	1856
William L. Beck	Sellersburg............Pr.,	1876
Andrew Jackson Beckett	Washington...........So.,	1852
Reuben Becketts	Washington...........Pr.,	1856
Charles N. Beckham	Bloomington ....Sel.,	1871
Orlando B. Beckham	Bloomington ....Fr.,	1870
William A. Beckner	Wabash ....Pr.,	1846
John H. Beeson	Mooresville ... .Sel.,	1872
Silas Beezley	Leesville ....Pr.,	1851
William N. Beezley	Medora ....Jr.,	1880
Stephen Belding	Washington...........Fr.,	1861
Hugh W. Bell	Ogden ....Pr.,	1851
Ashley M. Bell	Hamburg, Ark.......So.,	1870
Fannie Bell	Wheeeling, Va.......Sel.,	1876
Charles R. Bell	Bloomington..........Pr.,	1879
Thomas Bellows	New Providence.....Fr.,	1869
George Bellows	New Providence .....Fr.,	1869
Thomas Benbridge	Lafayette ....Fr.,	1856
Hanford Benedict	Luray...................So.,	1860
Erasmus Bennett	Bloomington..........Pr.,	1866

Perry Bennett	Lebanon	Pr.,	1868
Louisa N. Bennett	Harrodsburg	Pr.,	1880
William M. Berry	Bloomington	Fr.,	1855
Thomas B. Berry	Bloomington	Pr.,	1856
James R. Berry	Bloomington	Fr.,	1858
Viola Berry	Bloomington	Pr.,	1881
Robert C. Bethel	Newburg	Sel.,	1874
Albert Bettinger	Tell City	Jr.,	1873
Thomas Bigham	Portland Mills	So.,	1848
Morris Birkbeck	New Harmony	Fr.,	1847
Frederick N. Birkey	Salem	Fr.,	1854
Christopher Bisher	Monticello	Pr.,	1864
Silas F. Bishop	Bardstown, Ky	Pr.,	1864
Deming Bishop	Bloomington	Pr.,	1867
John H. Bishop	Mt. Carmel	Pr.,	1880
William B. Blackstone	Hebron	Sel.,	1878
James Blair	Monroe County	So.,	1838
William W. Blair	Monroe County	Sel.,	1848
E. Fayette M. Blair	Bloomington	Fr.,	1842
James W. Blair	Sparta, Ill	Fr.,	1853
Robert R. Blair	Orleans	Pr.,	1875
Isabel Blair	Princeton	So.,	1875
Maria Blair	Princeton	So.,	1877
Agnes M. Blair	Bloomington	Pr.,	1880
Ada L. Blair	Bloomington	Fr.,	1881
H. Blake	Franklin	Sci.,	1845
Jacob W. Blaisdel	Dearborn	So.,	1852
Henry E. Blemker	Huntingburg	Fr.,	1857
Eli Van Buren Blount	West Kinderhook	Pr.,	1856
Brazillai M. Blount	West Kinderhook	Se.,	1859
Joshua D. Boardman	Moorefield	Irr.,	1852
Eli P. Boardman	Moorefield	Pr.,	1852
George Bodé	Bloomington	Pr.,	1878
Lillie C. Boggs	Bloomington	Pr.,	1882
Anton F. E. Boisen	Nordburg, Ger	Sel.,	1872
Christian Boisen	Leek, Germany	Fr.,	1879
George Bollenbacher	Bloomington	Pr.,	1867
Julia E. Bollenbacher	Bloomington	Sel.,	1877
Carrie E. Bollenbacher	Bloomington	So.,	1879
Sallie Bollenbacher	Bloomington	So.,	1880
Jacob I. Bollenbacher	Bloomington	Pr.,	1881

Samuel M. Bollenbacher	Bloomington	Pr.,	1881
Fannie C. Bollenbacher	Bloomington	Pr.,	1882
Gotthold Bollinger	Tell City	Fr.,	1872
Henry Bonebrake	Georgetown	Pr.,	1848
Edward Bonham	Fairfield, Ill	Pr.,	1848
John A. Bonham	Hartford City	Fr.,	1882
Wal. W. Bonner	Spring Hill	Ju.,	1881
A. J. Boone	Lebanon	So.,	1845
John R. Boone	Louisville, Ky	So.,	1861
John Borden	Providence	So.,	1842
William Borden	Providence	Se.,	1842
John G. Borland	Bedford	Irr.,	1852
John E. Borland	Bloomington	Fr.,	1856
Alexander S. Borland	Bloomington	Pr.,	1863
Minnie Borland	Bloomington	Pr.,	1879
Walter H. Borland	Bloomington	Pr.,	1880
Walter N. Borland	Bloomington	Pr.,	1882
Samuel R. Bottorff	Jeffersonville	Pr.,	1855
Jonathan Bottorff	Charleston	Fr.,	1867
Daniel Bowers	Russelville	Pr.,	1847
J. M. Botts	Clay County	Irr.,	1845
Alexander O. Bowland	Bloomington	Pr.,	1838
F. M. Boydon	Martin County	Pr.,	1850
H. P. S. Boyle	Danville, Ky	Pr.,	1837
James B. Boyle	Butler	Pr.,	1876
John W. Boynton	Oxford	Pr.,	1854
Daniel Bowers	Putnam County	Ju.,	1851
Henry Bowles	Evansville	Pr.,	1848
John W. Bowman	Yazoo, Miss.	Jr.,	1852
Laura Bowman	Middletown	Pr.,	1878
Edgar Bowser	Warsaw	So.,	1888
Thomas M. Boyd	Lawrence County	Irr.,	1851
David M. Boyle	Cynthiana	So.,	1888
John H. Boyer	Carmi, Ill	Pr.,	1866
Fountain Bozeman	Poseyville	Pr.,	1866
Virgil P. Bozeman	Poseyville	Pr.,	1866
James M. Brackinridge	Warrick County	Pr.,	1845
J. Thomas Brackinridge	Booneville	Irr.,	1848
George W. Brackinridge	Booneville	Pr.,	1848
Walter S. Bradfute	Bloomington	Pr.,	1880

Lizzie L. Bradfute	Bloomington .... Fr.,	1881
W. J. Bradley	Lexington. .... Pr.,	1840
Joseph C. Bradley	Martinsville.......... Pr.,	1857
James C. Bradley.	Martinsville .... Pr.,	1858
Charles S. Bradley	Washington, D. C... So.,	1860
Richard Bradley	New Albany. .... Pr.,	1866
S. Stokely Bragg	Martinsville .... Pr.,	1876
Louis W. Branam...	Bloomington .... So.,	1866
Lawson F. Branaman	Clear Spring .... Sel.,	1873
Daniel H. Branaman	Clear Spring .... So.,	1884
Anna L. Brant	Bloomington .... So.,	1884
Mollie Bratney	Bloomington .... Pr.,	1876
Iredell Bray	Monroe County ..... Pr.,	1847
William Bray	Monroe County ...... Fr.,	1847
Alexander C. Bray	Bloomington .... Pr.,	1868
John W. Bray	Whitehall............. Pr.,	1868
Jane E. Bray	Bloomington .... So.,	1869
H. Frank Braxton	Paoli .... Pr.,	1854
Henry P. Brazee	Cannellton .... So.,	1852
Jesse Breakiron	Bloomington .... Fr.,	1871
Zachary T. Breckinridge	Boonville .... Fr.,	1864
John A. Breckinridge	Boonville .... So.,	1864
Joseph M. Breech	Lebanon .... Pr.,	1867
William M. Brenton	Peru .... Pr.,	1877
Theodore M. Brenton	Edinburg .... Pr.,	1876
James F. Brett	Washington .... Fr.,	1846
Benjamin Bridge	Lafayette .... Pr.,	1845
Hayden Bridwell	Lawrence County... Pr.,	1868
Lafayette Bridwell	Springville .... Pr.,	1863
Richard A. Bright	Madison .... Fr.,	1850
Robert J. Bright	Madison .... Fr.,	1850
L. L. Broadus	Connersville........... So.,	1879
Oliver G. Brockett	Carmi .... Fr.,	1872
Hannah E. Brooks	Loogootee .... Sel.,	1871
Grace Brooks	Loogootee .... Pr.,	1875
Felix G. Brown	Bedford .... Pr.,	1837
Joseph F. Brown	Indianapolis........... Fr.,	1838
E. K. Brown	Indianapolis .... Se.,	1839
C. H. Brown	Edgar County, Ill... Pr.,	1839
Jacob I. Brown	Bloomington .... Pr.,	1839
H. W. Brown	Mercer County, Ky.Pr.,	1839

Edwin W. Brown.................Edgar County, Ill...Se.,	1839
Isaac M. Brown ....Monroe County......Pr.,	1861
Lazarus M. Brown...............Logansport ....Pr.,	1844
Frederick Brown.. ....Owen County........Pr.,	1848
James M. Brown.................Clinton ....Sen.,	1857
Tilghman A. Brown..............Gosport.................Pr.,	1859
Joseph J. Brown.................Louisville, Ky........Irr.,	1865
Jasper N. Brown.................Rosewood.............Pr.,	1866
Milton F. Brown............. .....Bloomington ....Fr.,	1872
Charles Brown (deceased).....Whitehall.............Fr.,	1872
Thomas L. Brown................Bloomington ....Pr.,	1875
Cynthia A. Brown................Whitehall..............Pr.,	1878
Eva K. Brown....................Bloomington ....Pr.,	1879
Mary E. Brown....................Paragon .... Pr.,	1881
W. B. Brown................ ....McVille......... ......Pr.,	1882
Salado Brown ......,..............Whitehall..............Pr.,	1882
John M. Brown ....Louisville, Ky........Pr.,	1838
Ira Browning ....Bloomington ....Pr.,	1850
Finley Browning............... Bloomington ....Pr.,	1852
Rufus Browning.................Bloomington .... Pr.,	1853
Enos Browning....,...............Bloomington ....Pr.,	1857
Daniel R. Browning.............Spencer..................Fr.,	1862
Columbus Browning ....Bloomington ....Fr.,	1865
David W. Browning.............Bloomington ....Pr.,	1867
Andrew E. Browning.. ....Bloomington ....Pr.,	1882
James P. Brownson..............Valparaiso ....Pr.,	1851
Charles M. Brucker..............Tell City...............So.,	1880
Theresa H. Brucker..............Tell City...............Pr.,	1880
Flora B. Brucker ....Tell City...............Pr.,	1880
John Bruner ....Harrodsburg ....Sel.,	1852
J. C. Bruner................. ....Patoka ....Irr.,	1865
Lizzie M. Bryan ....Bloomington ....Sel.,	1873
Joseph C. Bryan ....Bloomington ....Pr.,	1882
Mollie Bryan ....Bloomington ....So.,	1882
James G. Bryant..................Hebron ....Pr.,	1851
Edward B. Buchanan............Logansport............Pr.,	1846
James Buchanan..................Columbus.............Sel.,	1871
Robert A. Buchanan.............Rossville ....Pr.,	1881
Anna C. Buchanan..............Rossville......... ......Fr.,	1882
Charles A. Buck ....College Corner, O...Jr.,	1881
Elijah W. Buckner...............Martinsville...........Pr.,	1862

26—HISTORY.

James M. Buckner	Stinesville	Pr.,	1867
Thomas J. Buckner	Gosport	Pr.,	1880
Salmon A. Buell	Lawrenceburg	So.,	1846
Julius O. Buell	Lawrenceburg	Fr.,	1859
Charles H. Bunce	Portland, Ky	Pr.,	1865
Loring Bundy	New Castle	Jr.,	1870
Richard J. Bullett	Louisville, Ky.	Irr.,	1852
Richard E. Bunger	Bloomington	Irr.,	1857
Alfred R. Bunger	Bloomington	Fr.,	1867
William M. Bunger	Bloomington	Fr.,	1869
Omer G. Bunger	Bloomington	Pr.,	1882
Thomas N. Bunnell	Monticello	So.,	1860
Isaac N. Bunnell	Salt Lake City	Sel.,	1878
George Bunton	Terre Haute	So.,	1880
William D. Burford	Nyesville	Pr.,	1882
Alexander Burge	Linton	So.,	1871
Helen Burgoon	South Grange	Pr.,	1881
Thomas Burke	Bloomington	Fr.,	1872
Agnes Burk	Bloomington	Pr.,	1882
Alexander S. J. Burnett	New Albany	Pr.,	1858
Luther Burnett	Ossian	Fr.,	1871
Fred Lange Burnett	Washington, D. C	Fr.,	1883
David V. Burns	Sharpsville	Fr.,	1866
Charles P. Burns	New Providence	Pr.,	1879
John A. Burns	Bloomington	Pr.,	1882
Hugh Burrell	Brownstown	Pr.,	1867
Edward Burson	Laporte	Fr.,	1871
Florence L. Burtt	Tarrytown, N. Y	Fr.,	1883
William Burton	Terre Haute	Irr.,	1848
William A. Burton	Mitchell	Fr.,	1857
Hugh F. Burton	Mitchell	So.,	1859
Joseph A. Burton	Mitchell	Fr.,	1859
Martin A. Burton	Bedford	Pr.,	1862
David P. Burton	Gosport	So.,	1868
George T. Burton	Georgia	So.,	1871
William H. Burton	Georgia	So.,	1871
Charles H. Burton	Mitchell	Sel.,	1874
Frank I. Burton	Mitchell	So.,	1881
Henry A. Burtt	Utica	Fr.,	1871
Laura H. Burtt	Utica	Pr.,	1877
Charles E. Bushfield	Utica	Fr.,	1872

Edward Buskirk	Bloomington	Irr.,	1846
Thomas C. Buskirk	Orangeville	Pr.,	1861
Joseph V. Buskirk	Gosport	Sci.,	1865
David C. Buskirk	Gosport	Pr.,	1867
David W. Buskirk	Bloomington	Jr.,	1871
Samuel W. Buskirk	Bloomington	Fr.,	1871
Frank Buskirk	Bloomington	Fr.,	1871
Harriet A. Buskirk	Bloomington	Sel.,	1871
George A. Buskirk, Jr	Bloomington	Sel.,	1874
M. Belle Buskirk	Paoli	Sel.,	1874
Lillie B. Buskirk	Bloomington	So.,	1875
J. L. Buskirk	Gosport	Pr.,	1879
Ella C. Buskirk	Bloomington	Pr.,	1880
Mattie Buskirk	Bloomington	Pr.,	1880
Lois Buskirk	Paoli	Pr.,	1882
David F. Butcher	Bloomfield	Fr.,	1872
Mollie Butcher	Stanford	Pr.,	1877
James D. Butcher	Bloomington	Pr.,	1882
George H. Butler	Bloomington	Pr.,	1846
William Butler	Bloomington	Jr.,	1852
Hugh R. Butler	Nashville	Pr.,	1862
Amos W. Butler	Brookville	So.,	1879
Flora N. Buzzaird	Bloomington	Pr.,	1881
Clara Buzzaird	Bloomington	Pr.,	1883
Thomas J. Byers	Whitehall	Fr.,	1867
Dewey L. Byers	Annapolis	Pr.,	1880
Leander F. Cain	Caldwell	Pr.,	1877
L. F. Cain	Bloomington	Pr.,	1881
John H. Caldwell	Leavenworth	Fr.,	1861
Gad C. Caldwell	Leavenworth	Sci.,	1864
Alexander W. Campbell	Monroe County	Pr.,	1855
Robert H. Campbell	Monroe County	Pr.,	1858
William D. Campbell	West Station, Miss.	Pr.,	1867
William P. Campbell	Bloomington	Pr.,	1867
Arthur Lee Campbell	Bloomington	Fr.,	1868
William I. Campbell	Como, Tenn	Pr.,	1868
Robert H. Campbell, Jr	Bloomington	So.,	1869
James M. Campbell	Bloomington	Fr.,	1869
John Campbell	Normandy	Fr.,	1869
George P. Campbell	Bloomington	Sel.,	1873
Mary A. Campbell	Bloomington	Fr.,	1873

Charles Campbell	Nineveh	Pr.,	1876
Haucher Campbell	Belleville	Pr.,	1878
Wallace B. Campbell	Melvin	Fr.,	1881
Mary H. Campbell	Gosport	Pr.,	1881
Edward W. Cannon	Jefferson Co., Ky	Irr.	1840
Hiram O. Cannon	Georgetown, Ky	Irr.,	1848
Robert J. Cantrell	Benton, Ill	Fr.,	1864
William S. Cantrell	Benton, Ill	So.,	1870
Nathan H. Carithers	Centre Point	Pr.,	1880
George S. Carlisle	Louisville, Ky	Pr.,	1842
William R. Carlton	Ellettsville	Pr.,	1859
John M. Carlton	Butler, Mo	So.,	1860
John M. Carlton	Ellettsville	So.,	1861
Oliver R. Carlton	Bloomington	Pr.,	1863
Andrew Carmichael	Brookville	Pr.,	1856
William T. Carmichael	Becks Grove	Fr.,	1869
John R. Carmichael	Hobbieville	Fr.,	1871
Solomon E. Carmichael	Cincinnati	Fr.,	1873
William L. Carnahan	Lafayette	Pr.,	1854
John Carney	Vernon	Fr..	1864
Isaac Caruthers	Jackson County	Pr.,	1845
Rufus Carpenter	Carpentersville	So.,	1861
David R. Carpenter	Crainsville, Mo	Fr.,	1873
Theodore S. Carr	Terre Haute	Jr.,	1871
E. Bruce Carr	Leipsic	Jr..	1871
John Pinckney Carr	Oregon	So.,	1879
Walter B. Carr	Bloomington	Pr.,	1864
Herman Carr	Columbus	Fr.,	1882
Henry W. Carr	Bloomington	Pr.,	1882
J. M. Carter	Clinton, Miss	So.,	1885
Elihu Carter	Monroe County	Pr.,	1838
James Carter	Bloomington	Pr.,	1841
James F. Carter	Monroe County	Irr.,	1847
Lorenzo D. Carter	Fayetteville	Irr.,	1848
Thomas Carter	Monroe County	Irr.,	1850
John Carter	Monroe County	Fr.,	1852
William A. Carter	Bloomington	Fr.,	1855
Thomas B. Carter	Winona	Fr.,	1861
John C. Carter	Bloomington	Pr.,	1862
Joseph W. Carter	Centerfield	So.,	1869
Ollie Carter	Bloomington	Pr.,	1874

Thomas Carter	Bloomington ....Pr.,	1876
Fannie O. Carter	Bloomington ....Pr.,	1880
Oliver C. Carter	Bloomington ....Pr.,	1881
John H. Cartmell	Chalmer's Station...Fr.,	1859
Baldwin H. Cartright	Carlisle ....Fr.,	1839
Homer Carter	Annapolis............So.,	1882
James S. Case	Delphi ....Fr.,	1859
John S. Case	Delphi ....Fr.,	1859
William G. Casey	Raglesville ....Pr.,	1856
John Cassidy	Washington ....Sel.,	1845
Samuel R. Cathcart	Bloomington ....Pr.,	1868
Thomas C. Catherwood	Carlisle ....Irr.,	1844
Samuel M. Catlin	Georgetown...........Pr.,	1854
Nora Chadwick	New Harmony ......Pr.,	1878
William W. Chambers	Monroe County......Pr.,	1846
John E. Chambers	Spencer.................Jr.,	1871
Shadrack Chandler	Brown County........Pr.,	1842
Andrew W. Chandler	Williamsport..........Pr.,	1846
Robert A. Chandler	Williamsport..........So.,	1874
Edward R. Chapin	Valparaiso ....Fr.,	1856
Dewitt Q. Chappell	Petersburg ....Pr.,	1882
Maggie B. Chappell	Remington.............Pr.,	1882
Daniel Charles	Philipston..............Fr.,	1861
Francis M. Charles	Grayville, Ill ....Fr.,	1864
A. B. Charpie	Bloomington ....Se.,	1881
Aaron G. Chase	Bloomington ....Pr.,	1857
George G. Chase	Bloomington ....Pr.,	1867
Leroy G. Chase	Bloomington ....Fr.,	1869
Lizzie R. Chase	Bloomington ....Fr.,	1872
Aaron Chatterton	Ohio County ....Sel.,	1845
John A. Chenowith	Shoals ....Fr.,	1871
Daniel Chenowith	Shoals ....So.,	1873
Samuel Albert Chenowith	Shoals ....So.,	1877
Edward Cherrill	Carthage, Ill ....So.,	1859
Lulu Cherry	Bloomington..........Pr.,	1880
Sallie Cherry	Bloomington..........Pr.,	1882
Charles H. Chitty	Lawrence County...Pr.,	1844
John S. Chipman	Bloomington..........Pr.,	1845
Draper K. Chipman	Bloomington ....Pr.,	1859
Marcellus A. Chipman	Noblesville............Pr.,	1868
John Wesley Chord	Bloomington ....Irr.,	1844

James S. Christie	Madison	Pr.,	1867
Thomas I. Christy	New Winchester	Fr.,	1870
Warden P. Churchill	Louisville, Ky	Fr.,	1847
James Churchill	Albion	Pr.,	1850
George H. Cissna	Watseka, Ill	Pr.,	1868
Isaac Claman	Bloomington	Fr.,	1865
J. M. Clark	Vincennes	Pr.,	1835
Robert Clark	Monroe County	Irr.,	1841
David M. Clark	Bloomington	Pr.,	1853
John N. Clark	Golconda	Pr.,	1864
Wesley F. Clark	Waveland	Fr.,	1872
Flora A. Clark	Bloomington	Fr.,	1873
Orrin S. Clark	Attica	Fr.,	1876
Belle Clark	Bloomington	Pr.,	1879
Carrie Clark	Bloomington	Pr.,	1879
Ella W. Clark	Warsaw	Fr.,	1881
Laura Clarke	Bloomington	Pr.,	1882
A. J. Claypool	Connersville	Irr.,	1850
E. F. Claypool	Connersville	Irr.,	1850
John G. Clendenin	Paoli	Ju.,	1846
Charles E. Clevenger	Winchester	So.,	1863
Lewis H. Clevenger	Larwill	Pr.,	1882
Charles W. Clifton	Rensselaer	Pr.,	1874
Philemon Clugston	Larwill	So.,	1883
George M. Cobb	Greensburg	Ju.,	1835
Samuel Cobb	Lawrence County	Pr.,	1848
Thomas R. Cobb	Lawrence County	Pr.,	1848
Jonathan W. Cobb	Pine Village	Pr.,	1858
Virgil A. Cobb	Pine Village	Se.,	1860
Leverett Cochran	Bloomington	Pr.,	1861
Jasper H. Coffee	Ellettsville	So.,	1860
Emma Coffee	Clear Creek	Pr.,	1881
Silas Coffey	Spencer	Fr.,	1861
George W. Coffey	Owensboro, Ky	So.,	1866
Edgar Coffey	Ellettsville	Fr.,	1873
Nelson G. Coffin	Vermillion County	Irr.,	1841
Simpson W. Coffin	Vermillion County	Irr.,	1847
John E. Coffin	Bloomington	Pr.,	1879
Milton Cogswell	Noblesville	Irr.,	1844
Francis B. Cogswell	Noblesville	Irr.,	1852
Alonzo Cole	Bloomington	Fr.,	1860

Edward A. Cole	Charleston	Fr.,	1871
Charles A. Cole	Peru	Jr.,	1877
Martin B. Cole	Seymour	Pr.,	1882
James M. Coleman	Morgantown	Fr.,	1868
Oliver S. Colleer	Columbus	Pr.,	1864
Josephus Collett	Eugene	So.,	1850
Archibald B. Collings	Bellmore	Pr.,	1862
George W. Collings	Parkville	Pr.,	1862
Walter S. Collins	Columbia City	Pr.,	1866
Slaughter I. Collins	Newburg	Pr.,	1866
James M. Collins	Charlestown	Fr.,	1870
John E. Collins	Bloomington	Pr.,	1875
E. E. Collins	Cedarville	Pr.,	1879
William Collins	Bloomington	Pr.,	1880
Columbus Combes	Utica	So.,	1865
John M. Combes	Charlestown	So.,	1862
Samuel A. Colpitts	Bloomington	Pr.,	1882
Samuel W. Conboy	San Jacinto	So.,	1882
George W. Conclasnre	Valeene	Fr.,	1857
Wayne E. Condict	Lamar, Mo	So.,	1873
S. Pierce Condict	Lamar, Mo	So.,	1873
Mercell D. Condiff	Gosport	Irr.,	1848
John W. Conduit	Columbus	Irr.,	1844
Henry C. Conduit	Mooresville	Sel.,	1864
William E. Conley	Bloomfield	Fr.,	1871
Walter W. Conley	Bloomfield	Sel.,	1872
James D. Conlon	Cambridge City	Jr.,	1881
Michael T. Connaughton	Black Oak Ridge	Pr.,	1867
Ella Connelly	Bloomington	Pr.,	1882
D. A. Connover	Gosport	Irr.,	1850
William J. Conrad	Corydon	Pr.,	1867
Allen B. Constantine	Jewett	Pr.,	1860
Joseph Cook	Parke County	Pr.,	1838
John W. Cook	Springville	Pr.,	1846
Norvell L. Cook	Evansville	Pr.,	1856
James M. Cook	Cleona	Fr.,	1865
Joseph M. Cook	Cleona	So.,	1866
William C. Cook	Newport	Pr.,	1876
Henry E. Cook	Evansville	Jr.,	1883
Frederick W. Cook, Jr	Evansville	Jr.,	1883
James W. Cookerly	Bloomington	Pr.,	1838

John Cookerly	Bloomington	Pr.,	1867
Charles S. Cookerly	Bloomington	Pr.,	1868
Rose A. Cookerly	Bloomington	Pr.,	1878
Nannie C. Cookerly	Bloomington	Pr.,	1879
Charles W. Cooper	Merom	Pr.,	1844
Joseph Cooper	Tippecanoe	Pr.,	1846
Thomas Cooper	Fairfield, Ill	Irr.,	1848
James Cooper	New Harmony	Irr.,	1848
David Cooper	Bloomington	Pr.,	1879
E. Calvin Cooper	Sparta, Ill	So.,	1859
Samuel D. Cooper	Bloomington	Fr.,	1860
George H. Cooper	Greenfield	So.,	1881
Laura M. Cooper	Portland Mills	Pr.,	1881
James P. Cope	Butlerville	Sel.,	1871
Orlando Cope	Butlerville	So.,	1867
Anatole Cormier	St. Martinsville, La.	Sel.,	1879
Pembroke S. Cornelius	Dearborn County	Jr.,	1848
Isaac N. Carr	Bloomington	Jr.,	1881
W. Ulysses Corsaw	Bloomington	Pr.,	1867
Stephen M. Carrington	Liberty	Pr.,	1874
Logan M. Cox	Stanford	Pr.,	1852
Paris J. Cox	Stanford	Pr.,	1852
William H. Cox	Lafayette	Pr.,	1856
Alexander Cox	Door Village	Pr.,	1857
William L. Cox	Bloomington	Pr.,	1859
Isaac M. Cox	Bloomington	Pr.,	1859
John C. Cox	Paoli	Fr.,	1861
Nathaniel D. Cox	Unionville	Pr.,	1866
John C. Cox	Cynthiana	So.,	1867
Ezekiel S. Cox	Azalia	Fr.,	1867
Lindley H. Cox	Azalia	Pr.,	1867
George W. Cox	Unionville	Pr.,	1868
Andrew J. Cox	Unionville	Pr.,	1868
Rachel E. Cox	Paoli	So.,	1869
James F. Cox	Bloomington	Fr.,	1873
William Cox	Bloomington	Pr.,	1876
Frank E. Cox	Bloomington	Pr.,	1877
Nelson Crabb	Louisville, Ky	Pr.,	1853
Henry W. Crabb	Bloomington	Fr.,	1859
Frank A. Crabb	Scotland	Pr.,	1876
James R. Crabb	Owensburg	Pr.,	1879

J. Loring Craft	Rising Sun	Fr.,	1859
Israel T. Craft	Rising Sun	So.,	1860
J. M. Craig	Mauckport	Pr.,	1835
Sarah F. Craig	Bloomington	So.,	1869
Daniel M. Craig	Bloomington	Fr.,	1871
Noble Crane	Jackson	Pr.,	1853
David M. Crane	Levonia	Fr.,	1870
Richard H. Crane	Loogootee	Pr.,	1876
John W. Crandel	Mooresfield	So.,	1882
Andrew J. Cranor	Union City	Fr.,	1871
C. Spencer Crary	Olney, Ill	Pr.,	1866
John L. Crawford	Princeton	Fr.,	1857
John Crawson	Oxford	Pr.,	1857
Anna R. Crecelius	Loogootee	Fr.,	1872
Robert A. Cree	Bloomington	Sel.,	1865
Clara Crew	New Marion	Pr.,	1878
Paul Crews	Fayette, Mo	Fr.,	1864
Jacob J. Crickenbarger	Middletown	Fr.,	1873
Wm. L. Crittenden	Columbus	Irr.,	1846
Churchill Crittenden	San Francisco, Cal	So.,	1859
James Crome	Albion, Ill	Fr.,	1871
Luther M. Cromer	Crossroads	Fr.,	1873
Martin L. Cromer	Middletown	Sel.,	1874
Joseph W. Cron	Bloomington	Fr.,	1858
John W. Crook	Springville	Pr.,	1853
Belle Crook	Springville	Pr.,	1874
John A. Crose	Cloverdale	Pr.,	1858
Samuel C. Crose	Cloverdale	Pr.,	1858
W. Scott Crosley	Macon, Ill.	Pr.,	1868
John M. Cross	Madison	Pr.,	1837
Amos W. Crozier	Wilmington	Fr.,	1859
Joel H. Crum	Pigeon Roost	Pr.,	1861
William D. Culbertson	Indianapolis	Pr.,	1875
Ananias Cullison	Bloomfield	So.,	1869
Sampson Cullison	Parke	Fr.,	1872
Timothy Culver	Jefferson	Pr.,	1863
George W. Cummins	Napoleon	Irr.,	1848
Kate Cunning	Bloomington	Pr.,	1876
Agnes Cunning	Bloomington	Pr.,	1878
Henry H. Cunningham	Martinsville	Pr.,	1856
Charles G. Cunningham	Terre Haute	Fr.,	1857

Frank Cunningham	Indianapolis So.,	1859
Clinton F. Cunningham	Bloomington Pr.,	1862
Andrew W. Cunningham	Hazelton Pr.,	1863
Thomas C. Cunningham	Burnsville Fr.,	1864
John I. Cuppy	Curryville Pr.,	1864
Robert S. Curry	Smithville Fr.,	1860
John C. Curry	Bloomington Pr.,	'1860
John J. Curry	Smithville Fr.,	1861
Flora A. Curry	Bloomington Pr.,	1880
Samuel Curtis	Ellettsville Pr.,	1856
John Curtis	Ellettsville Pr.,	1859
William Curtis	Ellettsville Pr.,	1859
Joshua B. Curtis	Bloomington Pr.,	1862
John T. Curtis	Bloomington Pr.,	1862
Nelson A. Curtis	Bloomington Sel.,	1864
Daniel E. Curtis	Winamac Pr.,	1867
Henry Cushman	Repton So.,	1860
Martin Cutsinger	Edinburg Pr.,	1876
Madison Dagger	Fountain County Jr.,	1835
Lewis M. Daily	Bluffton Fr.,	1861
William L. Dailey	Orange Pr.,	1882
Mary G. Daly	Bloomington Pr.,	1881
John Dalzell	Indianapolis Irr.,	1851
Milton S. Dame	Lafayette Pr.,	1857
Henry J. Darnell	Worthington Fr.,	1871
William Daugherty	Clinton, Miss Pr.,	1835
George Daugherty	Clinton, Miss Pr.,	1835
John Davenport	Indianapolis Pr.,	1846
William Davidson	Petersburg Pr.,	1853
Dorman N. Davidson	Indianapolis So.,	1859
Charles E. Davidson	Louisville, Ky So.,	1863
Henry C. Davis	Lexington, Ky So.,	1838
James W. Davis	Thorntown Pr.,	1845
William M. Davis	Bloomington Pr.,	1852
Isaac F. Davis	Anderson Pr.,	1854
Theodore P. Davis	Morristown Pr.,	1864
Thomas B. Davis	Memphis Pr.,	1866
Samuel E. Davis	Poseyville Pr.,	1868
John W. Davis	Terre Haute So.,	1870
Isaac M. Davis	Crawfordsville Fr.,	1873
Jasper M. Davis	Newburg Sel.,	1876

Richard M. Davis.................Elizabethtown ......Sel.,		1875
R. S. Davis.........................Charleston, Ill........Pr.,		1875
Edward E. Davis..................Newport................Pr.,		1876
Alva Eugene Davis ....Belleville ....Sel.,		1877
John W. Davis, Jr................Bloomington ....Pr.,		1878
John A. Davis.................... Solsberry ....Fr.,		1879
Fannie M. Davis ....Duncansville ....Pr.,		1879
Frederick Charles Davis........Auburn................So.,		1880
Minnie V. Davis ....Bloomington ....Fr.,		1880
Guy A. Davis......................Bloomington ....Pr.,		1882
F. Emma Davis ....Smithville. ....Pr.,		1882
Sherman L. Davis.................Bloomington ....Fr.,		1883
Florence G. Davis................Ellettsville ....Fr.,		1883
Alexander A. Davison..........Scipio....................Pr.,		1858
Andrew Day.......................Courtland.............Sel.,		1871
T. S. Dayhoff.....................Worthington........Pr.,		1879
Watson A. Dean..................Marshaltown, Ia.....Fr.,		1888
Daniel DeBlanc........... ....St.Martinsville,La., Pr.,		1878
William H. Deck................. Blountsville............So.,		1854
Frederick W. Decker............Evansville..............Pr.,		1880
Joseph A. Deadman ....Toddspoint, Ky......So.,		1869
Henry K. Deen...................Mauckport...........Pr.,		1860
Joseph M. Defries.................St. Joseph....... ....Jr.,		1848
Samuel DeHaven.................LaGrange, Ky........Jr.,		1878
John W. Deindorfer..............Jasper....................Pr.,		1865
George Delap......................Ellettsville ....Pr.,		1863
Charles H. Delph.................Louisville, Ky ....Pr.,		1858
Robert S. Demaree........ ......Lebanon ....Fr.,		1872
Daniel H. Demaree...............Bloomington........ So.,		1873
Charles S. Demaree...............Haney's Corner......Pr.,		1878
Ward W. Demaree..............Bloomington ,........Fr.,		1883
Thomas D. Demoss...............Pulaski.................Pr.,		1853
Lola Kate Demott.. ....Bloomington ....Fr.,		1880
William R. Demoss ....Monterey ....Fr.,		1853
John B. Denny ....Monroe................Sel.,	·	1851
Thomas L. Denny................Stanford ....Sel.,		1852
William Denny..................Monroe County......Sel.,		1852
Elias M. Denny...................Vincennes ....Pr.,		1866
Richard Denton ....Bloomington ....Pr.,		1841
John W. Denton.................Bloomington ....Pr.,		1865
Samuel F. Denton................Butlerville ....So.,		1870

Winfield S. Denton	Butlerville	Fr.,	1871
Clark Deputy	Paris	Sel.,	1865
Andrew Deshazo	Vincennes	Sel.,	1853
David A. Devin	Princeton	Fr.,	1858
C. B. Dewees	Fredericksburg	Fr.,	1879
David Dickenson	Steuben	Pr.,	1845
David Dickerson	Louisville, N. Y.	Fr.,	1846
Elbert R. Dickinson	Wolcotville	So.,	1880
Mary E. Dickson	Bloomington	Pr.,	1880
Margaretta Dickson	Bloomington	Pr.,	1882
Will. P. Dill	Morgantown	Sel.,	1878
Nellie Dillingham	Needmore	Pr.,	1877
Vannie Dillingham	Needmore	Pr.,	1878
Emma Dillingham	Needmore	Pr.,	1881
James S. Dillon	Bloomington	Fr.,	1871
Andrew J. Dillon	Maxinkuckee	Fr.,	1882
Mary Dillon	Bloomington	Fr.,	1883
Joseph S. Dinsmore	Bloomington	Fr.,	1857
Francis M. Dixon	Leesville	Pr.,	1851
Wiley Dixon	Leesville	Pr.,	1854
Josiah Doan	Monroe County	Sel.,	1852
Elias C. Dobkins	Hausertown	Fr.,	1868
David M. Dobson	Spencer	Pr.,	1858
Benjamin F. Dobson	Spencer	Pr.,	1858
Joseph L. Dobson	Spencer	Pr.,	1858
W. Sharp Dodd	Wheeling, Miss	Fr.,	1869
Harvey Dodd	Clear Creek	Pr.,	1879
Cranston Harvey Dodd	Clear Creek	Fr.,	1881
Clelland F. Dodds	Monroe County	Sel.,	1848
William F. Dodds	New Lebanon	Pr.,	1861
J. Kemper Dodds	Bloomington	Pr.,	1863
Ella B. Dodds	Bloomington	Pr.,	1877
James Andrew Dodds	Bloomington	Fr.,	1881
Morton C. Dodds	Bloomington	Pr.,	1881
William J. Dodds	Bloomington	Fr.,	1883
Simon P. Domer	Milford	Fr.,	1883
W. Harry Donaldson	Terre Haute	Fr.,	1864
Enoch E. Donaldson	Bloomington	Pr.,	1867
George T. Donelly	Columbus	Fr.,	1869
Samuel D. Dorsey	Fort Branch	Sel.,	1874
John W. Dorst	New Albany	Sel.,	1875

Frank Doster................Lafayette........ ......Pr.,		1868
William Dougherty.............Columbus..............Pr.,		1853
Adelbert B. Douglass............Seymour..... ....Pr.,		1868
William Douglass................Corydon...............Fr.,		1883
John A. Dowden................Harrisonburg, La...Pr.,		1850
John L. Dowden.....'...............Smithville........... Pr.,		1856
William H. Dowden.............Bloomington......... So.,		1864
Frank C. Dowden................Smithville..............Pr.,		1875
William T. Downs ....Woodville, Miss......Pr.,		1841
Franklin R. Drake ....Lancaster.............Fr.,		1868
James F. Drake ....Prairietown...........Fr.,		1883
Daniel Driscoll.....................Bedford..................Fr.,		1883
George W. Dubois ....Nashville..............Pr.,		1862
Hobart Dubois....................Oak Farm ....Pr.,		1875
J. A. G. Duckworth..............Martinsville...........Pr.,		1861
J. O. Dudozel ....St. Martinsville, La..Fr.,		1835
Washington Dudley...... ......Ripley........ ....Irr.,		1847
Samuel W. Duff....................Salem ....So.,		1870
Joseph M. Dufour.................Vevay ....Sen.,		1864
Robert L. Dulany............ ....York, Ill...............Jr.,		1839
Charles L. Duncan ....Bowling Green, Ky..Fr.,		1838
Lycurgus Duncan .... Bedford.... ....So.,		1855
Elizabeth Duncan................Russellville, Ky......Fr.,		1870
Isis Duncan ....Bedford..................Fr.,		1873
Robert C. Duncan ....Princeton..............Fr.,		1876
Marion Duncan....................Nashville................Pr.,		1877
Morton Duncan........ ....Bedford........ .... Pr.,		1880
Robert Duncan... ....Bedford.. ....Pr.,		1882
C. Moore Dunham ....Valley Farm ....Fr.,		1854
Williamson D. M. Dunn........Monroe County......So.,		1839
Benjamin Dunn.....'.............Bloomington ....Pr.,		1845
William Dunn ....Lawrenceburg........Fr.,		1846
John P. Dunn ....Indianapolis...........Pr.,		1856
Samuel G. Dunn ....Bloomington ....Pr.,		1867
S. Harrison Dunn................Spencer.................Jr.,		1869
Charles C. Dunn ....Spencer ....Fr.,		1870
Samuel F. Dunn...................Bloomington ....Irr.,		1871
William H. Dunn.................Aurora'.................Sel.,		1872
George G. Dunn..................Bloomington ....Fr.,		1873
Ella Dunn...........................Bloomington ....Sel.,		1873
Alexander Dunning.............Owen County.........Pr.,		1835

Paris C. Dunning, Jr	Bloomington	Pr.,	1860
James A. Dunning	Bloomington	Pr.,	1862
Rowland Dupuy	New Castle, Ky	So.,	1866
Charles S. Durand	Bloomington	Pr.,	1881
Conrad B. Durborow	Chicago, Ill	So.,	1881
Clarence E. Durborow	Williamsport	So.,	1880
William Durham	Prairietown	Sel.,	1850
Cass Durham	Seymour	Fr.,	1859
George W. Duzan		Pr.,	1837
James Duzan	Boone	Sel.,	1848
William S. Dye	Springville	Pr.,	1863
William Holton Dye	Indianapolis	Fr.,	1883
Grace Dysart	Bloomington	Pr.,	1882
Hughes East	Hobbieville	Pr.,	1858
Martin A. Eastman	Stanford	Pr.,	1876
Albert Eberhart	Shelbyville	Pr.,	1882
James C. Edgar	Santa Fe, N. M	Pr.,	1860
T. J. Edmondson	Monroe County	Irr.,	1841
Hiram L. Edmondson	Monroe County	Pr.,	1851
B. B. L. Edmonson	Jasper	Pr.,	1860
John Edmondson	Ellettsville	Pr.,	1879
Ebner D. Edson	Mt. Vernon		
Isaac Edwards	Leavenworth	Pr.,	1842
William Edwards	Spencer	Pr.,	1855
Frederick Edwards	Louisville, Ky	Pr.,	1857
Eli Edwards	Mitchell	Sel.,	1871
William Milan Edwards	Peru	Sel.,	1878
Emma Ehrie	Bloomington	Pr.,	1877
James W. Eller	Bloomington	Jr.,	1870
John G. Eller	Bloomington	Fr.,	1871
Henrietta Eller	Erie	Sel.,	1874
Leander J. Elliott	Largo	Irr.,	1846
John B. Elliott	New Harmony	Irr.,	1853
James B. Elliott	Vincennes	Pr.,	1856
Thomas C. Elliott	Bruceville	Sen.,	1857
Charles W. Ellis	Ditney Hill	Fr.,	1865
Mary E. Ellis	Noble, Ill	Irr.,	1871
William A. Ellis	Hardinburg	Sel.,	1871
Ralph Elston	Benton, Ill	Pr.,	1860
Henry W. Emerson	Lafayette	Sel.,	1874
William W. Emerson	Albion, Ill	Pr.,	1880

Fannie C. Emory	Bloomington	Pr.,	1880
Julia L. Emory	Bloomington	Pr.,	1882
Robert L. Engle	Butterville	Fr.,	1868
Milton Engler	Marietta	Pr.,	1859
James P. Ennis	Martinsville	Fr.,	1870
John P. Ensley	Auburn	Pr.,	1877
O. P. Ergenbright	Edinburgh	Fr.,	1867
Joshua Ernest	Turman's Creek	So.,	1863
David M. Erwin	Mount Vernon	Pr.,	1875
Minnie F. Erskine	Rockland, Me	Sel.,	1875
Oscar P. Erskine	Rockland, Me	So.,	1879
Melville Eshman	Terre Haute	Jr.,	1883
Nathaniel F. Ethel	Delaware County	So.,	1851
Frank D. Etter	Providence	Pr.,	1881
James M. Evans	Lawrence County	Fr.,	1846
Leighroy W. Evans	Warrick County	Irr.,	1847
Walter N. Evans	Sugar Creek	Irr.,	1848
William M. Evans	New Harmony	Fr.,	1847
John N. Evans	West Feliciana, La.	So.,	1850
Robert G. Evans	Rockport	Jr.,	1873
Jacob C. Evans	Lakeville	Pr.,	1874
William L. Evans	Bloomington	Pr.,	1879
Fannie Evans	Bloomington	Pr.,	1880
Mrs. B. W. Everman	Camden	Fr.,	1882
Dora Everman	Burlington	Pr.,	1882
Josephus B. Everts	Valparaiso	Irr.,	1845
Thomas J. Ewing	Vallonia	Pr.,	1876
Joseph W. Ewing	Sparta, Ill	Fr.,	1855
James N. Ewing	Wabash	Pr.,	1876
Anna Falkner	Bloomington	Pr.,	1882
James M. Fanning	Tallahatchie, Miss.	So.,	1838
Henry O. Faris	Monroe County	Pr.,	1851
James W. Faris	Bloomington	Pr.,	1855
William B. Faris	Bloomington	Pr.,	1855
Francis A. Faris	Bloomington	Pr.,	1859
Erwin J. Faris	Bloomington	Pr.,	1876
Eugene M. Faris	Bloomington	Fr.,	1881
A. V. Faris	Bloomington	Pr.,	1882
John A. Farmer	Monroe County	Pr.,	1842
John M. Farmer	Monroe County	Pr.,	1846
Joel A. Farmer	Bloomington	Pr.,	1860

William S. Farnham ....Madison ....Pr., 1846
Edwin Farquhar ....Logansport ....Fr., 1839
Dewitt C. Farrington............Valparaiso ....Se., 1855
Francis A. Farris ....Bloomington ....Pr., 1855
Joseph Fawcett.....................Columbus..............Pr., 1860
Irene Fee ....Bloomington ....Sel., 1871
Eva Fee................................Bloomington ....Pr., 1875
Owen R. Fegan ....Montgomery ....Fr., 1881
Charles D. Felkner ....Milford........ ....Pr., 1860
William J. Fell.....................Bloomington ....Pr., 1882
Ida Fellows ....Bloomington ....Pr., 1876
John Fellows.......................Bloomington ....Jr., 1882
Henrietta Fellows.................Bloomington ....Pr., 1882
George W. Fennel ....Georgetown, Ky.....So., 1855
John A. Ferguson ....Marion County......Irr., 1848
William T. Ferguson ....Bloomfield..... ....Fr., 1860
Hugh P. Ferguson ....Fairfield ....Fr., 1871
Charles S. Ferguson.............Charlestown ....Fr., 1871
L. O. Ferguson............. ....Buena Vista ....Pr., 1878
E. T. Ferguson......................Buena Vista ....Pr., 1878
Isaac M. Ferguson ....Center Point..........Pr., 1881
Joseph Ferguson...................Bedford.................Pr.. 1882
Frank Fetter ....Peru......................Jr., 1882
William H. Field..................Mitchell................Fr., 1877
Oscar Fife............................Plymouth..............So., 1875
Erastus M. Finley.................Bloomington ....Pr., 1867
Ephraim M. Fine ....Wallace ....Pr., 1868
Herman H. Finley................Xenia ....Pr., 1881
David Firebaugh..................Robinson, Ill ....Pr., 1866
Isaac L. Firebaugh...............Robinson, Ill ....So., 1870
Joseph Firebaugh.................Robinson, Ill ....Jr., 1873
Mary J. Firebaugh...............Robinson, Ill ....Sel., 1875
Joseph A. Fish.....................Boone County ....Pr., 1848
Leander E. Fish....... ....Bloomington ....So., 1870
James C. Fish......................Bloomington ....Fr., 1871
William S. Fish...................Bloomington ....So., 1871
Alenis J. Fishback................Kewana................Pr., 1851
William H. M. Fishback.......Independance.......So., 1855
John B. Fisher.....................Patoka..................Pr., 1856
Lincoln Fisher ....Rockville..............Pr., 1881
John R. Fitch......................Jackson County .....Pr., 1848

Frank O. Fitton	New Harmony......Fr.,	1879
David A. Fitzgerald	Indianapolis.........Pr.,	1851
Silvester Fitzgerald	Benton, Ill.........So.,	1869
George P. Fleischer	Lima...............So.,	1880
Allen T. Flemming	Crawford..........Pr.,	1844
G. L. Floyd	Shelby.............Pr.,	1845
E. Lewis Floyd	Shelby..............Fr.,	1846
Sallie A. Floyd	Smithville..........Fr.,	1873
Walter M. Floyd	St. Paul............Jr.,	1879
John Flynn	East Feliciana, La...Pr.,	1835
Eustace Foley	Springhill..........Fr.,	1881
Alonzo M. Forbes	Dover Hill.........Sel.,	1865
Louisa L. Forbes	Petersburg.........Sel.,	1872
Elizabeth Forbes	Petersburg.........Fr.,	1872
Lillie May Forbes	Bloomington.......Fr.,	1878
Lealdas S. Forbes	Bloomington.......Fr.,	1878
James Ford	Paris, Ky...........Pr.,	1838
Charles Ford	Oxford.............Fr.,	1857
J. Fletcher Ford	Oxford.............Sel.,	1855
Albert Ford	Oxford.............Pr.,	1865
Morris Ford	New Harmony......Sel.,	1865
Ewell Ford	Jeffersonville......So.,	1871
C. Gale Ford	Owenton...........Sel.,	1878
Ann B. Ford	New Harmony......Fr.,	1879
Orlando Foster	Monroe County......Pr.,	1838
William C. Foster	Bloomington.......Irr.,	1844
George Foster	Petersburg.........Sel.,	1845
Jethro Wood Foster	Indianapolis.......So.,	1846
James R. Foster	Randolph..........Irr.,	1846
James P. Foster	Bloomington.......Irr.,	1846
Robert H. Foster	Bloomington.......Irr.,	1851
Alexander Foster	Evansville.........So.,	1858
Charlotte Foster	Heltonville........Pr.,	1875
John T. Foster	Whitehall..........Pr.,	1878
S. O. Foster	Bloomington.......Pr.,	1878
John M. Foster	Knightstown.......So.,	1880
Henry G. Foster	Bellefontaine......So.,	1881
G. M. Foster	Heltonville........Pr.,	1881
Dow D. Foster	Whitehall..........Pr.,	1881
Samuel Foster	Villa Vista, La......Pr.,	1882
Addie Foster	Heltonville........Pr.,	1882

27—HISTORY.

Victor F. Foster	Bloomington	Fr.,	1882
Jesse Fountain	Heltonville	So.,	1882
Ella Fowler	Bloomington	Pr.,	1882
M. Fannie Fowls	Bloomington	Pr.,	1876
Calvin R. Fox	Lawrence County	Pr.,	1848
Mary E. Foxworthy	Terre Haute	S. Fr.,	1869
Ezra E. Frame	Solsberry	Pr..	1873
Lou M. Frame	Solsberry	Pr.,	1879
Dora Franklin	Spencer	So.,	1873
Mollie E. Franklin	Ellettsville	Pr.,	1881
Benjamin F. Franklin	Spencer	So.,	1882
James Fravel	Harrison County	Irr.,	1844
Edwin H. Frazer	Bridgeport	So.,	1877
Frederick Freed	Newburg	Pr.,	1866
Robert Freeland	Monroe County	Pr.,	1835
John Freeland	Bloomfield	Pr.,	1837
John F. Freeland	Bloomington	Fr.,	1865
William T. Freeland	Bloomfield	So..	1868
Henry P. Freeland	Bloomfield	Pr.,	1868
William E. French	Princeton	Irr.,	1846
Hayden T. French	Jeffersonville	So.,	1860
William M. French	King's Station	Sel.	1876
John B. French	Bloomington	Pr.,	1880
Harmon A. Friedley	Elizabeth	So.,	1875
William C. Fritts	Paducah, Ky	So.,	1864
John L. Fritts	Paducah, Ky	Fr.,	1864
Charles A. Fry	Utica	Fr.,	1869
Floyd J. Fry	Utica	Fr.,	1870
John H. Fulk	Hart's Mills	Pr.,	1858
Benjamin Fuller	Warrick County	Irr.,	1852
Joseph M. Fuller	Warrick County	Pr.,	1853
William W. Fuller	Booneville	So.,	1881
Robert Fullerton	Fayettville, Tenn.	Jr.,	1847
Alfred W. Fullerton	Bloomington	So.,	1870
Edward Fulton	Jordan's Grove, Ill.	Fr.,	1867
Joseph P. Funk	Elizabeth	Pr.,	1856
Major W. Funk	Milltown	Fr.,	1872
James R. Funk	Milltown	Sel.,	1872
Zachary T. Funk	Milltown	Sel.,	1874
Felix F. Gaar	Jefferson Co., Ky	Pr.,	1837
Simeon L. Gaar	Jefferson Co., Ky	Pr.,	1838

James T. Gabbert	Bloomington	Pr.,	1867
Anna L. Gabbert	Bloomington	Pr.,	1882
Marshall C. Gadberry	Yazoo, Miss	Fr.,	1847
William G. Gaffney	Washington	Pr.,	1852
Aden G. Gainey	Bloomfield	Fr.,	1873
William F. Gallemore	Jeffersonville	Fr.,	1870
Henry J. Gallemore	Paragon	Fr.,	1870
S. S. Gallemore	Paragon	Pr.,	1879
Charles Gallion	Brookville	Sel.,	1878
Wade B. Galloway	Bloomington	Pr.,	1882
James Gamble	Bloomington	Pr.,	1859
Henry C. Gamble	Bloomington	Fr.,	1868
Mollie W. Gardener	Paducah, Ky	Fr.,	1883
Thomas B. Garr	Louisville, Ky	Fr.,	1861
Press Garr	O'Bannon, Ky	Fr.,	1861
John A. Garrett	Carlisle	Irr.,	1847
Jennie Garriott	Little York	Fr.,	1872
John Wesley Garrison	Bloomington	Pr.,	1881
Elias N. Gaskins	Wayport	Pr.,	1867
Martha A. Gaskins	Bloomington	Pr.,	1882
John Henry Gay	Bloomington	Fr.,	1872
Bessie Gay	Bloomington	Sel.,	1873
C. Dora Gay	Bloomington	So.,	1875
A. B. Gayler	Danville	Pr.,	1835
John S. Geiger	Louisville, Ky	Jr.,	1838
Adam Geiger	Bloomington	Sel.,	1875
John B. Gent	Columbus	So.,	1870
William Benton Gentry	Mt. Tabor	Pr.,	1857
Tilghman H. Gentry	Stinesville	So.,	1866
Franklin A. Gentry	Little Point	Fr.,	1882
Lillie E. Gentry	Bloomington	Pr.,	1882
Bailey George	Holems, Miss,	Pr.,	1835
W. J. George	Scroggsfield, O.	Fr.,	1881
R. A. George	Scroggsfield, O.	Jr.,	1881
George B. Gerold	Yazoo, Miss	Irr.,	1852
Nannie Getty	Bloomington	Pr.,	1878
Lafayette Gibbs	Milltown	So.,	1869
John B. Gibson	Mitchell	Fr.,	1879
William C. Gibson	Loogootee	Pr.,	1864
Thomas Gibson	Loogootee	Fr.,	1869
George H. Gifford	Groves	So.,	1871

John R.Gifford	Orleans	So., 1871
Dennis C. Gilfillan	Centerpoint	Pr., 1880
Franklin Gill	Ashley's Mill	Pr., 1858
William B. Gillespie	Bloomington	Fr., 1861
Samuel Gillespie	Oxford	Pr., 1865
Isaac W. Gillespie	Bloomington	Pr., 1863
William B. Gilliott	Young's Creek	Fr., 1869
John B. Gilson	Mitchell	Jr., 1883
Sanford S. Givan	Moore's Hill	Se., 1864
Strawther Givens	Laharpe, Ill.	Pr., 1858
T. A. Gladden	Scottsburgh	Pr., 1881
Jeremiah Gladish	Petersburg	Pr., 1856
Earl K. Glass	Knightstown	Fr., 1883
Rufus R. Glick	Romney	Pr., 1855
Benjamin R. Glick	Lafayette	Fr., 1873
Wilson T. Goble	Knightstown	Fr., 1848
Albert B. Godden	East Enterprise	Pr., 1866
D. Charles Goepper	Louisville, Ky	Pr., 1876
Sydney H. Golson	Clay	Pr., 1844
Lyman T. Goodner	Nashville, Ill	Pr., 1865
Aaron D. Goodwin	Queensville	Fr., 1856
Friend C. Goodwin	Bloomington	Pr., 1856
Willis B. Goodwin	Utica	Fr., 1861
Jesse A. Goodwin	Bloomington	Pr., 1859
George W. Goodwin	Nioga, Ill	Fr. 1865
Thomas M. Gootee	Loogootee	So., 1861
Aaron Gordon	Bloomington	Pr., 1862
Emerson Gordon	New Albany	Fr., 1867
Richard L. Gorman	St. Paul, Minn	Fr., 1856
James Gorman	Owensville	So., 1869
George C. Gorman	Owensville	Fr., 1870
William B. Goss	Gosport	Fr., 1861
Noah J. Goshorn	Plainville	Fr., 1869
Morton L. Gould	Terre Haute	Jr., 1883
Lizzie B. Gourley	Bloomington	Pr., 1880
John L. Gow	Evansville	So., 1874
Thomas Grace	Terre Haute	So., 1880
James A. Graham	Jasper	Fr., 1844
James G. Graham	Bloomington	Pr., 1846
Christopher C. Graham	Jasper	Fr., 1847
Andrew E. Graham	Monroe County	Irr., 1847

Robert Graham............................Martinsville............Pr.,	1860
Edmund Graham ....Bloomington..........Pr.,	1861
Kate Graham..............................Richland..............Fr.,	1873
Mattie E. Graham ....Richland...............So.,	1881
Mary Etta Graham..................Rushville...............Fr.,	1880
Eli D. Grant.........................Wabash ....Pr.,	1845
Daniel B. Grant....................Wabash ....Pr.,	1848
William Grant......................Shelburn................Pr.,	1868
Charles Grant ....Shelburn................Pr.,	1868
Leonard Gray ....Bloomington..........Pr.,	1857
James Gray ....Curriesville............Pr.,	1858
James T. Gray.....................Newburg...............Pr.,	1859
John W. Gray ....Springfield.............Pr.,	1859
Charles W. Gray..................Pine Village...........Pr.,	1860
Samuel R. Gray...................Greencastle ....So.,	1862
Mary M. Gray......................Unionville..............Fr.,	1870
Bayard S. Gray ....Union City............Fr.,	1873
Truman W. Gray.................Gosport ....Pr.,	1876
Allen Gray............................Graysville..............Sel.,	1876
George D. Gray ....Columbia..............Fr.,	1883
Abner Green.......................Bloomington..........Pr.,	1838
James Green.......................Bloomington..........Pr.,	1841
James H. Green ....Owen County........Pr.,	1842
Sebastian Green ....Indianapolis..........Pr.,	1853
Milton Green ....Shelbyville............Fr.,	1857
Charles S. Green.................Logansport ....Pr.,	1858
Lewis A. Green....................Livonia..................Pr.,	1858
William O. Green ....Brownstown ....So.,	1869
Basil L. Green ....Jasper...................Irr.,	1871
Sina E. Green ....Bloomington ....Irr ,	1871
Thomas M. Green...................Ogden. ....So.,	1873
Joseph M. Greer..................Knoxville, Tenn......Fr ,	1864
James A Greer...................Knoxville, Tenn......Irr.,	1865
William A. Greeson..............Alto ....Fr.,	1874
Robert C. Greeves..............Bloomington ....So.,	1862
Virgil D. Gregg....................Springfield.............Irr.,	1871
James Gregory...................Lafayette...............Fr.,	1853
William T. Gregory...............Bloomington ....Pr.,	1867
Beverly Gregory..................Brooklyn................Jr.,	1873
Henry Gregory, Jr.................Salem...................Jr.,	1878
Henry V. Gregory...............Michigan City........Pr.,	1877

Walter Q. Gresham	Corydon	Pr.,	1852
William H. Griffey	Bloomington	Pr.,	1881
Ida Griffey	Bloomington	Pr.,	1882
William A. Griffing	Paris, Ky	Pr.,	1838
J. T. Griffith	Monroe County	Irr.,	1845
John M. Griffith	Colfax	So.,	1882
Lewis C. Griffith	Bloomington	Irr.,	1871
Charles M. Griggs	New Winchester	Irr.,	1871
Silas Grimes	Smithville	Pr.,	1857
Lewis A. Grimes	West Union	Fr.,	1859
William S. Grimes	Bluffton	So.,	1865
Albert L. Grimes	Spring Garden, Ill.	Fr.,	1870
James Grimsley	Monroe County	Pr.,	1851
Pola N. Groundt	Edinburgh	Pr.,	1880
David McKee Gunn	Shakopee, Minn	Pr.,	1866
Melvin S. Guthrie	Tunnelton	Fr.,	1871
Samuel Guy	Bloomington	Pr.,	1857
George K. Gwartney	Mauckport	Pr.,	1876
William F. Gwin	Cataract	Fr.,	1871
Frederick L. Gwin	Cataract	Fr.,	1871
William R. Hadden	Carlisle	Pr.,	1854
David A. Hadden	New Lebanon	Pr.,	1855
Henry C. Hagenbaugh	Clinton	Sel.,	1864
John Hagle	Kent's Station	Pr.,	1864
Thomas W. Hadkins	Greenough	Pr.,	1858
J. H. Haldeman	Lareville	Pr.,	1881
L. Hall	Bloomington	Pr.,	1839
George W. Hall	Woodland	Pr.,	1854
George A. Hall	Covington	So.,	1860
Lafe G. Hall	Raleigh	Fr.,	1868
John A. Hall	Louisville Ky	Pr.,	1868
Eva Hall	Stanford	Pr.,	1868
Martin M. Hall	Bloomington	Pr.,	1882
Edward Allen Hall	Kentland	Fr.,	1883
Joseph S. Hambleton	Danville	Pr.,	1848
Carlin Hamblin	Bowling Green	Pr.,	1850
Charles D. Hamill	Bloomington	Pr.,	1852
Robert J. Hamilton	Bloomington	Fr.,	1854
Samuel R. Hamilton	Fayetteville	Pr.,	1858
Martin D. Hamilton	Mooney	So.,	1869
Mary J. Hamilton	Bloomington	Sel.,	1871

Amanda Hamilton	Solsberry	Pr.,	1876
Ida M. Hamilton	Bloomington	Pr.,	1878
Alice Elizabeth Hamilton	Bloomington	Irr.,	1880
Harry Hamilton	Muncie	So.,	1880
Oliver A. Hammond	Petersburg	Pr.,	1857
Hamilton C. Hammond	Young's Creek	Pr.,	1867
David M. Hammond	Marengo	So.,	1869
Perry C. Hammond	Petersburg	Fr.,	1869
Thomas Hampton	Bowling Green, Ky.	Pr.,	1835
Jesse D. Hamrich	Bellville	Pr.,	1877
James H. Handy	Booneville	Irr.,	1851
Laura Handy	Bloomington	Pr.,	1876
Thomas Haney	Wolf Lake	Pr.,	1862
Moses K. Hanna	Bloomington	Pr.,	1877
Delmer Hanna	Bloomington	Pr.,	1878
Mattie L. Hansee	Ellenville, N. Y.	So.,	1881
William H. Hansford	Ellettsville	Fr.,	1870
Levi Hanson	Harrodsburg	Se.,	1859
George Harbinson	Lanesville	Fr.,	1861
Dixon T. Harbinson	Parkville	Fr.,	1861
Joseph C. Harbison	Bloomington	Pr.,	1862
Arthur F. Harbison	Portland Mills	Pr.,	1862
James Harbison	Lanesville	Sel.,	1865
Samuel M. Harbison	Bloomington	Fr.,	1870
Alexander M. Harbison	Portland Mills	Pr.,	1877
Josie O. Harbison	Bloomington	Pr.,	1878
Minnie Harbison	Bloomington	Fr.,	1879
Thomas P. Hardesty	Bloomington	Pr.,	1847
Charles H. Hardin	Columbia, Mo.	So.,	1839
Thomas Hardin	Glen's Valley	So.,	1868
William L. Hargrove	Oakland City	Fr.,	1869
John W. Hargrove	Patoka	Fr.,	1872
Frank M. Harned	Fairview, Ky	Sel.,	1877
Hiram Harrah	Whitehall	Fr.,	1870
James Harrell	Bloomfield	Fr.,	1870
Lucius Harris	Albion, Ill.	Pr.,	1857
Levinus Harris	Albion, Ill.	Se.,	1858
Joseph F. Harris	Bloomington	So.,	1863
Henry C. Harris	Oxford	Sel.,	1865
Bedford E. Harris	Albion, Ill.	Pr.,	1866
Albert G. Harris	Macon, Ill.	So.,	1868

Thomas S. Harris	Columbus	So.,	1870
Annie Harris	Albion, Ill	Fr.,	1879
Herbert H. Harris	Albion, Ill	Jr.,	1882
P. O. Harris	Ellettsville	Pr.,	1882
Edwin R. Harrison	Owensboro, Ky	So.,	1866
Belle Harrison	Ladoga	Fr.,	1873
Sanford H. Harrod	Lexington.	Pr.,	1853
Thomas H. Harrod	New Albany	Pr.,	1855
Columbus B. Harrod	Austin	Fr.,	1870
Ida Harrold	Bloomington	Pr.,	1882
Charles Andy Harryman	Mooresville	Sel.,	1878
Augustus W. Harshbarger	Gosport.	Pr.,	1863
G. C. Hart	Booneville	Irr.,	1850
Thomas Niles Hart	Cloverdale	Pr.,	1857
Hiram P. Hart	Rising Sun	Pr.,	1860
George W. Hart	Lee	Sel.,	1871
Edward James Hart	Vevay	Jr.,	1876
James Robert Hart	Pleasant.	Sel.,	1876
James M. Hartley	Osgood	Pr.,	1860
John N. Hartsock	Waynetown	Fr.,	1858
Della M. Harvey	Plainfield	Pr.,	1874
Catlin P. Haskett	Palestine, Ill	So.,	1876
Arthur D. Hastings	Trinity Springs	Pr.,	1854
W. Green Hastings	Bryantsville	Se.,	1857
Wesley Hatfield	Rono	Fr.,	1859
William I. Hatfield	Rono	Fr.,	1875
William H. Hathaway	Bloomington	Pr.,	1859
Benjamin F. Hauser	Columbus	Pr.,	1856
Jeremiah Hauser	Columbus	Fr.,	1857
Zack Hauser	Columbus	Fr.,	1857
Benjamin Franklin Havens	Rushville	Fr.,	1857
John Havron	Bedford	Irr.,	1855
Arthur J. Hawhe	Wickliffe	So.,	1860
William T. Hawkins	Putnamville	Pr.,	1837
J. W. Hawkins	Danville	Pr.,	1845
John W. Hawkins	Alton	Pr.,	1878
I. W. Hawkins	Brownville	Pr.,	1879
Nellie Hawkins	Brownville	Pr.,	1879
Edward W. Hawkins	Newport, Ky	So.,	1880
J. P. Hawks, Jr	Goshen	Fr.,	1878
George D. Hay	Vincennes	Pr.,	1885

Charles D. Hay	Charlestown	So.,	1859
Benjamin Hayden	Elizabethtown, Ky.	Fr.,	1865
Isaac R. Hays	Columbus	Pr.,	1861
John C. Hays	Reynold's Station	Pr.,	1864
Samuel C. Hays	Bloomington	Fr.,	1870
Harriet Hays	Gosport	Sel.,	1872
Oliver P. Hazard	Edinburg	Pr.,	1876
Mattie Hazard	Utica	Fr.,	1879
Jeremiah Hazelwood	Stanford	Pr.,	1852
Homer E. Hazen	Newburg	Pr.,	1856
Dyer B. Hazen	Newburg	Sel.,	1871
William R. Hazen	Sunman	Sel.,	1873
Thomas J. Headly	Bennington	Se.,	1866
James M. Headly	Bloomington	Pr.,	1867
Isaac W. Headley	Bloomington	Pr.,	1868
Charles E. Headley	Bloomington	Pr.,	1882
William Heath	Lafayette	Pr.,	1856
James M. Hedrick	Spencer	Fr.,	1861
David F. Hefron	Black Oak Ridge	Fr.,	1867
Laurence A. Hefron	Black Oak Ridge	Pr.,	1868
Eber W. Helburn	Newburg	Pr.,	1860
Levi M. Helburn	Newburg	Pr.,	1860
Orlando Helmar	Springville	Pr.,	1854
Arnold Helton	Bloomington	Pr.,	1851
Michael Helton	Heltonville	Jr.,	1851
Absalom Helton	Bloomington	Pr.,	1852
Isaac W. Helton	Bloomington	Pr.,	1862
I. Calvin Hemphill	Bloomington	Fr.,	1852
Daniel P. Henderlider	Woodville	Pr.,	1860
Benjamin Henderson	Indianapolis	So.,	1837
S. M. Henderson	Indianapolis	Pr.,	1838
William L. Henderson	N. Washington	Pr.,	1848
Ebenezer Henderson	Martinsville	Fr.,	1855
John A. Henderson	Vincennes	Pr.,	1859
Carey W. Henderson	Bloomington	Fr.,	1862
William W. Henderson	James' Switch	So.,	1869
George W. Henderson	Heltonville	Fr.,	1871
Jessie M. Henderson	Bloomington	Irr.,	1872
William P. Hendricks	Madison	So.,	1848
Paul Hendricks	Madison	Irr.,	1851
George W. Henley	Bloomington	Sr.,	1881

William C. Henry	Portland Mills........Pr.,	1875
Maud Henry	Bloomington ....So.,	1880
Charles Henshaw	Knightstown.........Fr.,	1882
Howard Hensley	Bloomington ....Sel.,	1865
Theodore Henson	Smithville.............Fr.,	1873
Lottie Henson	Smithville.............Pr.,	1875
N. A. Herring	Goshen ....Pr.,	1875
U. A. V. Hester	Charleston ....Jr.,	1837
William F. Hester	Bloomington ....So.,	1848
Kiah O. Hert	Owensburg............Pr.,	1879
Henry S. Hickman	Georgetown ....Pr.,	1854
William T. Hicks	Orangeville...........So.,	1872
William G. Higgenbotham	Clinton, La ....Pr.,	1835
William U. Higgins	Rush County........ Sel.,	1845
Thomas Hight	Bloomington.........So.,	1848
Thomas M. Hight	Bloomington.........Fr.,	1876
Harry Hight	Bloomington.........Pr.,	1882
Wallace Hight	Monroe County......Pr.,	1850
James M. Hill	Jennings County....Pr.,	1844
S. M. Hill	Jennings County....Sel.,	1845
Addison J. Hill	Bloomington.........Irr.,	1847
J. W. Hill	Rushville ....Pr.,	1850
William F. Hill	Bloomington ....Sel.,	1864
Johnson Hill	Pleasantville......... Fr.,	1867
William L. Hill	Brooksburg...........Sel.,	1871
Marion Hinchcliff	Fredonia, Ill ....Pr.,	1867
Otis Hinchley	Petaluma, Cal........Jr.,	1865
Thomas N. Hinde	Carmi, Ill ....So.,	1866
Mary A. Hinds	Bloomington ....Pr.,	1875
Alfred P. Hinds	Bloomington ....Pr.,	1877
Frank W. Hinsdale	Bedford ....Pr.,	1882
James Hisey	Corydon ....Pr.,	1854
William J. Hisey	Corydon ....Fr.,	1864
Francis Hitchcock	Terre Haute..........Fr.,	1865
Frederick Hitchcock	Princeton..............Fr.,	1865
John W. Hitchcock	Owensburg............Irr.,	1871
William Hite	Madison ....Pr.,	1837
L. Joel Hitt	Greensburg .... Pr.,	1877
Abraham Hoadley	Plainfield ....Fr.,	1867
M. M. C. Hobbs	Salem ....Jr.,	1852
William H. Hobbs	Owensville ....Pr.,	1867

Charles H. Hobbs...............	Carthage...............	Sel.,	1871
Walton Hobbs.....................	Carthage...............	Sel.,	1871
John W. Hobbs	Gasburg	Pr.,	1876
James N. Hodges	Martinsville...........	Pr.,	1867
John M. Hodges	Martinsville...........	Fr.,	1870
Benjamin F. Hodges	Martinsville...........	Pr.,	1876
Samuel W. Hogueland	Nashville	Pr.,	1867
James McG. C. Holden	Perryville, Mo........	Irr.,	1847
Henry P. Hole....................	Butlerville	Irr.,	1871
David Holland....................	Henry County........	Irr.,	1847
John Holland......................	Leesville...............	Pr.,	1874
William G. Holland.............	Bennington	So.,	1870
William H. Holland.............	Leesville.........	Fr.,	1882
J. R. Hollingsworth..............	Dublin..................	Pr.,	1879
Atha W. Holman..................	Utica.....................	Sel.,	1865
William C. Holmes...............	Indianapolis..........	Pr.,	1846
Squire W. Holmes................	Terre Haute...........	Fr.,	1863
Henry C. Holmes.................	New London	So.,	1875
Laura Holzapple..................	Bloomington	Pr.,	1879
N. H. Holson......................	Mansfield, O...........	Irr.,	1850
J. Thomas Holtzman............	Bloomington	Pr.,	1856
Samuel E. Holtzman.............	Bloomington	So.,	1859
Isaac A. Holtzman	Bloomington	Pr.,	1864
Henry A. Holtzman..............	Bloomington	Pr.,	1867
Jefferson P. Holtzman...........	Bloomington	Sel.,	1873
Mattie B. Holtzman..............	Bloomington	Pr.,	1881
Frederick Honneus	Clark County........	Irr.,	1846
George B. Hoopingarner.......	Butler	Fr.,	1875
Charles L. Hoover	New Albany..........	So.,	1844
Samuel A. Hoover.........	Lafayette...............	Jr.,	1855
Kate Hoover........	Bloomington	So.,	1881
Ada Hoover.........	Bloomington	Pr.,	1882
Joshua H. Hopewell.............	Owen County........	Irr.,	1846
John S. Hopkins...................	Evansville.............	So.,	1865
Robert P. Hopkins................	Evansville.............	Sel.,	1865
Charles S. Hopkins...............	Evansville.............	Pr.,	1881
Leander Hopper...................	Livonia.................	Pr.,	1857
John W. Horner...................	Lanesville.............	Pr.,	1879
Charles W. Horner	Lanesville......	Pr.,	1880
John Horton.......................	Yankeetown	Fr.,	1873
Melville M. Hoss.................	Bloomington	Sel.,	1875

Walter S. Hoss.....................Indianapolis...........Pr.,		1877
Joseph A. W. Hostetter.........Greenbush, Wis......Pr.,		1855
Kate Hostetter... ....Bedford................Fr.,		1873
Walter Hotchkiss.................Nashville..............Irr.,		1844
Jacob H. Hottell..................Corydon................Sel.,		1876
J. B. Hottell......................Corydon................Pr.,		1879
Hattie Houghton..................Loogootee.............So.,		1880
John S. Hougland............ .....Warrick County.....Irr.,		1852
T. W. Houston....................Jackson County .....Pr.,		1840
Jefferson P. Houston............Monroe County......Pr.,		1845
William J. Houston..............Ellettsville ....Sel.,		1857
Calvin H. Houston................Bloomington ....Pr.,		1860
James A. Houston................Bloomington ....Pr.,		1867
Gustavus C. Houston............Bedford................So.,		1870
Nathaniel Houston...............Ellettsville............Sel.,		1873
Richard W. Houston ....Ellettsville.............Pr.,		1875
Kate Houston.....................Bloomington ....Pr.,		1875
Fannie D. Houston...............Cornell.................Pr.,		1878
Ensley C. Houston...............Ellettsville.............Pr.,		1880
Mollie F. Hoveis..................Bryant's Creek ......Pr.,		1875
Frank M. Howard................Rockville......'......Fr.,		1862
Martin Howard.......... ....Jeffersonville.........Sel.,		1858
Joshua O. Howe ....Bloomington .... Pr.,		1838
Robert C. Howe ....Spencer ....Jr.,		1839
James M. Howe..................Bloomington ....Pr.,		1844
James H. Howe..................Monroe County......Pr.,		1850
Joseph M. Howe.................Bloomington ....Fr.,		1852
Ezra Howe........................Lebanon ....Pr.,		1854
Walter Howe.....................Bloomington ....So.,		1863
Joshua Howe, Jr ....Bloomington ....Pr.,		1867
Alfred E. Howe..................Bloomington ....Fr.,		1868
C. Carrie Howe..................Bloomington ....Sel.,		1875
Lucie Belle Howe................Bloomington ....Fr.,		1876
Ida M. Howe.....................Bloomington ....Pr.,		1877
Mrs. M. F. Howe................Bloomington ....Jr.,		1880
Minnie E. Howe ....Bloomington ....So.,		1881
Lillie Howe .... Bloomington ....So.,		1882
Alonzo M. Howes................Utica......... ....Sel.,		1865
Thomas P. Howland ....Indianapolis..........Pr.,		1875
Helen Z. Hubbard ....Springfield, Minn....Pr.,		1881
Andrew P. Huckleberry ....Charlestown ....Pr.,		1865

John A. Huddleson	Paoli ....Pr.,	1856
William Hudelson	Patoka ....So.,	1860
John M. Hudelson	Ogden ....Fr.,	1873
Mattie Hudelson	Bloomington ....Pr.,	1879
Lanville R. Hudelston	Paoli............Jr.,	1871
John B. Hudspeth	Boonville............Sel.,	1848
Silas Hudson	Paris ....Pr.,	1851
Henry H. Hudson	Knightsville............Pr.,	1878
William J. Huff	Troy............So.,	1870
Henderson M. Huff	Troy ....Irr.,	1871
W. K. Huff	Troy............Pr.,	1882
George W. Huffstetter	Polk Run............Pr.,	1854
David I. Huffstetter	Orleans ....Sen.,	1857
Levi Hughes	Bloomington ....So.,	1840
James Hughes	Bloomington ....So.,	1840
James L. Hughes	Bloomington ....Pr.,	1867
Robert Hughes	Okawville, Ill........Fr.,	1867
Florence Hughes	Bloomington ....Sel.,	1877
Levi A. Hughes	Bloomington ....Sel.,	1878
James D. Hughes	Bloomington ....Fr.,	1880
Julia R. Hughes	Bloomington ....Irr.,	1880
Frank H. Hughes	Bloomington ....Pr.,	1881
Walter H. Hull	Moore's Hill............So.,	1864
John O. Hulley	Ogden............Fr.,	1872
Heilin J. Humphrey	Vallonia............So.,	1870
Samuel G. Humphreys	Patoka............Fr.,	1872
James H. Humphreys	Linton............Fr.,	1874
James E. Humphries	Rockville............Sel.,	1875
James E. Humston	Bedford............Pr.,	1868
John Hunsucker	Vallonia............Pr.,	1855
John Hunt	Lawrenceburg........Sel.,	1835
W. L. Hunt	Corydon ....Pr.,	1850
Wesley S. Hunt	Jasper ....Pr.,	1867
Numa B. Hunt	Prosperity ....Pr.,	1868
D. Eckley Hunter	Philadelphia, Pa.....Fr.,	1855
William H. H. Hunter	Versailles ....Pr.,	1856
Hiram A. Hunter	Nashville, Tenn......Fr.,	1858
David Hunter	Bloomington ....Fr.,	1860
Lizzie E. Hunter	Bloomington ....Sel.,	1875
Darwin M. Hunter	Bloomington ....Pr.,	1878
John A. Hunter	Bloomington ....So.,	1880

Joseph H. Hunter............Bloomington.........Fr.,	1881
Cyrus R. Hunter..............Southport............Fr.,	1881
Frank T. Hunter................Bloomington........Pr.,	1882
James A. Hupp....................Hindostan............Pr.,	1880
Henry W. Hurlburt............Aurora............... Fr.,	1857
Lewis G. Hurlburt..............Aurora................ So.,	1863
Edward P. Hurlbut ....Mishawaka............Irr.,	1853
Ida A. Husted.....................Muncie..................So.,	1869
David H. Huston................Bloomfield............Fr.,	1867
David C. Hutchings.............Columbus...............Pr.,	1877
Nellie A. Hutchinson............New Albany...........So.,	1876
Isaac H. Hutchinson ....Evansville ....Pr.,	1858
Milton W. Hutto..................Kokomo ....So.,	1883
William E. Hyatt.................Utica......................Fr.,	1869
Robert Hyneman................ .....Monroe County......Pr..	1835
George Ingels, Jr..................Centre....................Pr.,	1875
Robert K. Ingle.....................Sandersville............Pr.,	1862
John K. Ingle........................Sandersville............Sel.,	1864
Heber Ingle........................ Evansville..............Fr.,	1865
Edward E. Ingles...................Scotland................Pr.,	1880
William S. Ingram.................Rockport ....So.,	1861
Orlando C. Irvin....................Warsaw ....Pr.,	1867
J. W. Irwin ....Elkhart..................Fr.,	1844
Lycurgus Irwin.......... ....Bedford.................Irr.,	1852
Ulysses W. Irwin .... Bedford.................Pr.,	1845
Walter J. Isanagle ....Chesterfield ....Pr.,	1880
J. A. Howard Isenhauer........ Bloomington..........Pr.,	1837
Calvin P. Isley.......................Edinburgh ....Pr.,	1879
Enoch M. Jackson ....Andersonville ....Irr.,	1848
Francis M. Jackson ....Rockville................Irr.,	1852
J. William M. Jackson ....Walnut Hills, O......Fr.,	1869
George Jackson ....Glendale......... ......Sel.,	1871
Lincoln N. Jackson...............Centreville ....Fr.,	1882
James H. Jackson ....Leesville................Pr.,	1882
William R. Jacob.. ....Louisville, Ky ....Irr.,	1846
Charles W. Jacobs ....Ditney Hill ....Sel.,	1864
Samuel W. Jacoby ....Plymouth..............Sel.,	1878
Hugh Jameson......................Rising Sun ....Pr.,	1854
Albion S. Jaquith..................Knight's Corner .....So.,	1870
James W. Jefferson ....Bloomington, Ill.....Se.,	1874
James D. Jeffries..................Bloomington ....Pr.,	1866

Carrie C. Jeffries.....:.............Bloomington ....Fr.,	1876
William G. Jenckes ....Terre Haute.......... Irr.,	1856
William A. Jenkins ....Leavenworth ....Pr.,	1861
Nathan S. Jenkins ....Leavenworth ....Sel.,	1864
Edward E. Jenkins................St. Paul................Pr.,	1876
Theodore S. Jennings.............Bloomington ....Sel.,	1872
Charles E. Jennings...............Bloomington ....Fr.,	1877
John R. Jerauld....................Patoka...................Fr.,	1857
Thomas H. Jerauld...............Patoka...................Sel.,	1857
Henry Jerauld......................Patoka........... ....So.,	1860
Theodore W. Jessup...;..........Friendswood .... Pr.,	1876
Charles L. Jewett.................Lexington..............Fr.,	1866
George A. John ....Logansport............So.,	1858
F. Henry Johanning..............Haubstadt...............Pr.,	1876
Thomas Johnson ....Petersburg.............Pr.,	1844
Edward C. Johnson ....Lawrence County...So.,	1848
Jarvis Johnson ....Lawrence County...Pr.,	1848
Samuel F. Johnson...............Boonville ....Irr.,	1852
Alonzo Johnson................... Clark....................Pr.,	1853
Elihu Johnson.....................Boonville .. ..Fr.,	1854
Robert Johnson... ....Boonville ....Pr.,	1855
Wesley Johnson ....Boonville ....Fr.,	1857
Levi S. Johnson ....Spencer..................Pr.,	1857
James A. Johnson...............Danville ....Sel.,	1858
Benjamin F. Johnson.............Hart's Mills............Pr.,	1859
Thomas J. S. Johnson...........Sellersburg.............Sel.,	1859
John T. Johnson...................Yankeetown ....So.,	1860
John Johnson .... Vincennes ....Fr.,	1860
James Johnson .... Williamsport ....Pr.,	1860
Henry B. Johnson ....Newburg ....Pr.,	1860
John F. Johnson ....Bloomington ....Pr.,	1860
Samuel M. Johnson ....Bloomington ....Pr.,	1860
David L. Johnson................Bloomington ....Pr.,	1860
William H. Johnson ....Freedom ....Pr.,	1861
Abner Johnson ....Freedom ....Pr.,	1861
Newton A. Johnson.............Stout's Grove, Ill....Fr.,	1862
Thomas J. Johnson ....New Harmony.......Pr.,	1864
Barnett L. Johnson...............Owensboro, Ky......Sel.,	1865
Maggie B. Johnson...............Bloomington ....Fr.,	1873
Washington Johnson............Owensville ....Sel.,	1873
William A. Johnson.............Edinburgh ....Sel.,	1873

James M. Johnson	Freedom	Pr.,	1879
James M. Johnson	Bloomington	Pr.,	1880
Charles E. Johnson	Evansville	So.,	1882
A. Johnston	Boonville	Pr.,	1845
Alexander Johnston	West Point, Iowa	...Jr.,	1850
Edward D. Johnston	Fair Play	Pr.,	1852
James N. Johnston	Brookville	Pr.,	1856
James M. Johnston	Leesville	Pr.,	1858
Pressley A. Johnston	Francisville	Sel.,	1865
James Johnston, Jr	New Albany	Fr.,	1871
Maggie Johnston	Bloomington	Pr.,	1855
John M. Jones	Bloomington	Pr.,	1837
Logan D. Jones	Columbus	Pr.,	1838
Daniel D. Jones	Franklin	Pr.,	1842
John D. Jones	New Harmony	Pr.,	1853
Aaron L. Jones	Valparaiso	Fr.,	1854
James I. Jones	Gentryville	Fr.,	1857
Robert M. Jones	Louisville, Ky	Pr.,	1857
Lucius B. Jones	Rising Sun	Fr.,	1858
William T. Jones	Louisville, Ky	Pr.,	1861
John N. Jones	Bloomfield	Pr.,	1863
Andrew W. Jones	Corydon	So.,	1864
Aquila Jones	Indianapolis	Pr.,	1867
Lewis H. Jones	Bloomfield	Irr.,	1871
Rita C. Jones	Newport	Sel.,	1875
Nellie C. Winfried Jones	Newport	Sel.,	1876
Moses A Jones	Raysville	Pr.,	1875
Lora Jones	Bloomington	Pr.,	1878
Ella Jones	Fort Branch	Pr.,	1880
Lewis Jordan	Corydon	Fr.,	1854
Charles H. Jordan	Corydon	Fr.,	1854
Alfred Jordan	Vincennes	Pr.,	1856
Henry Jordan	Corydon	Fr.,	1857
Amasa Joslin	Spencer	Pr.,	1853
Samuel Judah	Bloomington	Pr.,	1859
Winepark Judah	Bloomington	So.,	1862
Noble B. Judah	Vincennes	Fr.,	1870
George W. Julian	Logansport	So.,	1857
Nathan J. Julian	Logansport	Pr.,	1858
Charles A. Junkin	Bloomington	Fr.,	1873
Maurice Kahn	Sarraquemines, Fr.	Pr.,	1867

Lewis R. Kean	Louisville, Ky	So.,	1863
Taletha Keck	Loogootee	Pr.,	1879
Myra Keck	Kecksville	Pr.,	1879
John L. Keck	Bloomington	Fr.,	1882
Allie Keene	Versailles, Ky	Pr.,	1878
James Keigwin	Louisville, Ky	Irr.,	1850
Theodore Keigwin	Louisville, Ky	Irr.,	1852
William H. Keith	Rockford, Ill	Fr.,	1870
Edwin E. Kellam	Accomac, Va	Irr.,	1851
Isaac H. Kellar	Kokomo	Pr.,	1876
Lizzie Kellog	Valparaiso	Fr.,	1882
Mary Kelly	Bloomington	Fr.,	1872
James T. Kelsey	Bloomington	Pr.,	1859
J. F. Kelso	Dubois County	Irr.,	1841
Thomas M. Kelso	Morgan County	Fr.,	1848
II. A. Kelso	Morgan County	Pr.,	1850
Erasmus L. Kelso	Ireland	Fr.,	1879
Marcus A. Kendal	Richland	Sel.,	1875
Harvey Kendall	Mount Auburn	Pr.,	1876
Gertrude V. Kendall	Santa Rosa, Cal	Sel.,	1877
Alexander Kennedy	Boligee, Ala	So.,	1846
Joseph W. Kennedy	Carlisle	Pr.,	1855
W. M. Kennedy	Bloomington	Pr.,	1879
Addie Kennedy	Bloomington	Pr.,	1879
John W. Kenner	Graysville, Ill	Pr.,	1876
John M. Kenny	Louisville, Ky	Pr.,	1842
James O. Kenny	Bloomington	Pr.,	1875
Ada Kenny	Bloomington	Pr.,	1880
Jenny Kenny	Bloomington	Pr.,	1882
Alexander Kent	New Albany	Fr.,	1871
J. Edgar Kenton	Bloomington	Fr.,	1866
Stanton A. Kenton	Canton, O	Fr.,	1867
Leonidas Kern	Fayetteville	Fr.,	1858
Minnie Kern	Mattoon, Ill	Pr.,	1877
Frank A. Kerns	Wyoming, Ill	Fr.,	1880
William H. Kerr	Rogersville	Fr.,	1865
Henry Kerr	Bloomington	Pr.,	1882
John C. Kestor	Vigo County	Irr.,	1846
Henry T. Ketcham	Monroe County	Jr.,	1835
Absalom Ketcham	Monroe County	Irr.,	1868
William F. Ketcham	Monroe County	Pr.,	1855

28—HISTORY.

Frank W. Ketcham	Smithville	Pr.,	1857
Lewis Ketcham	Keck's Church	Fr.,	1855
Henry B. Ketcham	Paris, Ill	Pr.,	1865
James L. Ketcham	Bloomington	Sc.,	1874
Emma Ketcham	Bloomington	Sel.,	1878
Charles W. Keys	Solsberry	Pr.,	1867
L. S. Keyser	Elkhart	Fr.,	1878
William A. Kight	Poseyville	Fr.,	1869
Robert J. Killian	Martinsville	Pr.,	1862
John Killough	Bloomington	Pr.,	1841
Michael Kime	Marion County	Irr.,	1846
Rufus R. Kime	Union	Pr.,	1877
Thomas J. Kincaid	Paducah, Ky	Fr.,	1865
Owen Kincaid	Andersonville	S. Fr.,	1873
Willis King	Harrison County	Irr.,	1844
Jacob F. King	Otto	Pr.,	1866
Henry C. King	Otto	Pr.,	1866
William B. King	Hardensburg	Pr.,	1868
Helena Emma King	Bloomington	Pr.,	1880
William C. King	Nashville	So.,	1881
Nan King	Nashville	Pr.,	1881
James Kirby	Bloomington	Pr.,	1878
J. R. Kirby	Bloomington	Pr.,	1879
Francis B. Kirby	Bloomington	Pr.,	1882
Thomas Kinkman	Jacksonville	Pr.,	1848
William P. Kirkpatrick	Sellersburg	Pr.,	1878
Andrew J. Kiser	Peru	Pr.,	1847
James K. Kiser	West Point	Pr.,	1845
Albert B. Kitchell	Palestine, Ill	Pr.,	1837
Alfred Kitchell	Palestine, Ill	Pr.,	1838
Elijah W. Knapp	Queensville	Irr.,	1848
Gustave Knapp	Ferdinand	Pr.,	1878
James H. Knight	Bloomington	Sc.,	1862
Avery Knight	Belleville, Ill	Pr.,	1865
Elmer Knight	Bedford	Pr.,	1882
Isaac Koons	Utica	S. Fr.,	1859
John P. Kramer	Evansville	Pr.,	1859
Alice M. Kriner	Bloomington	Pr.,	1880
William Krogman	Tell City	Fr.,	1881
W. Butler Krumbhaar	Terre Haute	Fr.,	1852
Ira M. Krutz	Florence	Pr.,	1876

Henry Kurtz............................Princeton ....Fr.,		1868
Robert B. Kyle ....Louisville, Ky ....Pr.,		1863
P. B. Labertew ....Bloomington ....Fr.,		1889
Gabriel Labertew.................Bloomington ....Pr.,		1842
William A. Labertew..............Dover, Mo..............Pr.,		1860
Homer LaFaver...................Gosport ....Pr.,		1882
Charles E. Lake ....Stockwell.. ....Sel.,		1872
A. Lamar..............................Rockport ....Pr.,		1856
Will E. Lancaster..................Larwell.................Pr.,		1882
Amos Lane............................:..Aurora..................S. Fr.,		1859
William C. Lane...................Zionsville..............So.,		1860
Milton Lane........................Zionsville ....So.,		1860
Steven W. Lane....................Organ Spring.........Pr.,		1862
Samuel T. Langdon..............Vincennes..............Irr.,		1852
Lewis L. Lange....................Napoleon...............Pr.,		1858
Alexander C. Lanier .... Madison.................So.,		1839
J. W. Lanman.....................Grandview ....Pr.,		1882
William H. Larue.................Solsberry...............Pr.,		1878
J. M. Laselle.......................Madison.................So.,		1835
Charles B. Laselle.................Logansport............Fr.,		1839
James B. Lathrop................Greensburg............Fr.,		1845
Nettie Latimer.....................Bloomington ....Pr.,		1876
William B. Laughlin ....Rushville...............Sen.,		1859
Samuel B. Laughlin..............Evansville ....Sel.,		1865
R. L. Law............................Vincennes ....Pr.,		1839
William G. Law...................Solsberry...............Fr.,		1882
Elias D. Lawrence............ .....Louisville ....Fr.,		1846
Ovid Lawrence................, ...Terre Haute...........Fr.,		1881
J. W. Lawton.....................Elizabethtown, Ky..Pr.,		1854
Joseph Lawven....................Nashville...............Sel.,		1871
David A. Leech....................Franklin...............Sel.,		1875
Lemuel F. Leake............ ....Waveland..............Irr.,		1852
Oliver S. Leavenworth ....Leavenworth ....S. Fr.,		1857
Elias P. Leavenworth...........Leavenworth ....Fr.,		1863
Andrew J. Lee ....Putnam..................Pr.,		1846
Clement L. Lee...................Gosport ....Irr.,		1848
Jasper N. Lee......................Riley .. ..Pr.,		1863
Auguste Ledoux ....St. Martinsville, La.Pr.,		1855
William Leeper....................Marion County ......Pr.,		1846
John W. LeFevre......... ....Houston ....Fr.,		1875
Clara Belle Leffler. ....Bloomington ....Pr.,		1882

J. B. Leach........,.....................Edgar County........Pr.,	1860
S. M. Lemon....................Lawrence.............Pr.,	1845
Homer A. Lemon..............Harrodsburg..........Pr.,	1856
John Herschel Lemon...........Bloomington........So.,	1863
James Lemond....................Jasper County........Pr.,	1848
W. Matthew Lenon..............Camden.................Pr.,	1877
John Leonard....................Monroe County......Irr.,	1853
John F. Leonard..................Bloomington........Pr.,	1857
John H. Leonard.................Smithville........ .....Pr.,	1863
Silas M. Leonard..................Smithville..............Fr.,	1881
Homer Leonard...................Bloomington........Pr.,	1882
Frank A. Lesley ....Petersburg...........Pr.,	1863
James R. Lester......................Bloomfield ....Irr.,	1872
George B. Lewis...............Jennings County....Irr.,	1846
George H. Lewis................Lewisburg, W. Va..Sel.,	1865
Jesse Lewis......................Bellemore..............Pr.,	1879
Isaac P. Leyden.....................New Albany.........So.,	1863
T. Edward Leyden................New Albany.........So.,	1864
L. Likens............................Greenfield.............Pr.,	1850
Charles W. Lindley..............Harveysburg........So.,	1870
Sylvia J. Lindley................Eldora, Iowa.........Pr.,	1878
Walter C. Lindley..............Bloomington........Pr.,	1881
William H. Lindley..............Owen County.........Pr.,	1845
Henry C. Littlejohn..............Jasonville..............Pr.,	1876
Jefferson Litton...................Pinhook ....Pr.,	1854
William I. Littrel.................Warren.,...............Irr.,	1844
Anthony Livers...................Floyd County........Pr.,	1848
Frank E. Locke............. .....Newport..............Pr.,	1879
Frank T. Lockhart.............Vallonia..............Pr.,	1866
Armwell Lockwood..............Washington County Pr.,	1841
Edgar C. Loehr....................Noblesville............So.,	1869
John S. Logan....................Salem...............So.,	1862
Lilian Logan......................Bloomington........Fr.,	1883
Elisha Long......................Charlestown..........Fr.,	1845
Wm. C. Long........................Hartsville..............Fr.,	1851
John H. Long ....Hartsville..............So.,	1852
David F. Long.....................Hartsville..............So.,	1852
D. Horatio Long.................Brownstown ....Pr.,	1868
John S. Long......................Princeton.............Irr.,	1871
Hugh D. Long....................Angola...............Sel.,	1874
Jesse W. Longacre............. Goshen...............S. Fr.,	1870

Charles W. Loper	Oakdam	Pr.,	1857
Maggie E. Lorch	Troy	Pr.,	1870
Washington Lostetter	Milton, Ky	S. Fr.,	1872
Jeremiah C. Lotz	Portland	Pr.,	1847
Cyrus Loudon	Springville	Pr.,	1863
William R. Lough	Kewanna	Irr.,	1853
Lee Love	Mauckport	Fr.,	1868
George C. Lowe	Louisville, Ky	Pr.,	1845
Howard R. Lowder	Springville	So.,	1870
Lindley T. Lowder	Springville	Fr.,	1871
Allie Lowder	Springville	Pr.,	1881
Ananias W. Lowdermilk	Poland	Irr.,	1867
William W. Lowe	Burlington, Ia.	Irr.,	1846
Jefferson Lowe	Bloomington	Pr.,	1853
Lafayette Lowe	Monroe County	Pr.,	1848
William Lowe	Bloomington	Pr.,	1855
John R. Lowe	Harrodsburg	So.,	1877
Ettie Lowe	Harrodsburg	Pr.,	1877
A. A. Lowe	Cynthiana	Pr.,	1881
William Lowndes	Vincennes	Pr.,	1835
Thomas P. Lucas	Monroe County	Pr.,	1842
Desdemona Lucas	Bloomington	Sel.,	1878
Omar T. Ludlow	Lawrenceburg	So.,	1864
George Ludwig	Ladoga	S. Fr.,	1861
Frederick Luring	Haubstadt	Pr.,	1877
Henry Lutes	Houston	Pr.,	1853
Howard B. Lutes	Bloomington	Sel.,	1871
George M. Lutes	Bloomington	Sel.,	1871
Ira Lutes	Topeka, Kan	Pr.,	1874
Peter T. Luther	Bowling Green	Pr.,	1866
John Luzadder	Perryville	Pr.,	1878
Margaret Luzadder	Bloomington	Fr.,	1881
Grant Luzadder	Bloomington	Pr.,	1881
Lillie M. Luzadder	Bloomington	Pr.,	1882
James E. Lynn	Indianapolis	Pr.,	1880
Eveline Lyon	Bloomington	Pr.,	1881
James B. Mabury	Jeffersonville	So.,	1855
W. J. McBride	Elkhart	Pr.,	1842
William S. McBride	Goshen	Irr.,	1844
John McBride	Martin County	Pr.,	1848
James McBride	Bloomington	Pr.,	1855

J. McBroom	Fountain County	Sel.,	1845
Mattie McCabe	Bloomington	Pr.,	1880
Lizzie McCabe	Bloomington	Pr.,	1882
James McCall	Terre Haute	Pr.,	1837
William McCall	Terre Haute	Sen.,	1839
H. McCall	Terre Haute	Pr.,	1839
Henry McCalla	Monroe County	Irr.,	1851
William McCalla	Monroe County	Irr.,	1851
Samuel McCalla	Bloomington	Pr.,	1858
Joseph McCalley	Martinsville	S. Fr.,	1861
James McCann	Connersville	So.,	1854
Newton McCann	McCutchins	S. Pr.,	1866
William J. McCaughan	Monroe County	Pr.,	1848
Daniel McCaughan	Monroe County	Irr.,	1854
Agnes McCaughan	Bloomington	Pr.,	1875
Lizzie B. McCaughan	Bloomington	Pr.,	1875
James T. McCaw	Chester Dis'ct, S. C.	Pr.,	1853
Maggie McCaw	Bloomington	Pr.,	1882
Joseph H. McCleskey	Daviess County	Irr.,	1851
Rufus S. McClung	Rochester	Fr.,	1859
David McClure	Gosport	Irr.,	1844
Daniel W. McClure	Gosport	Sel.,	1845
William McClure	Mohawk Village	Pr.,	1882
Erastus McClure	Marion	S. Fr.,	1864
David W. McClurkin	Elkhorn, Ill	Pr.,	1860
John C. McClurkin	Princeton	Fr.,	1869
Ira McCluskey	Washington	Irr.,	1847
Findley McCollough	Bloomington	Pr.,	1839
Milton L. McCollough	Bloomington	Irr.,	1852
Charles J. McCollough	Cincinnati	Pr.,	1853
John O. McCollough	Bloomington	Irr.,	1853
M. Smith McCollough	Summitsville	Pr.,	1855
William H. McCollough	Bloomington	S. Fr.,	1857
William S. McCollough	Summitsville	Pr.,	1858
Henry McCollough	Bloomington	Pr.,	1867
W. W. McCollough	Rockport	Sel.,	1875
Martin L. McCollough	Haney's Corner, Ia.	Pr.,	1878
Stella McCollough	Bloomington	Pr.,	1879
James C. McConahy	Mitchell	S. Fr.,	1857
David E. McConaghy	Goshen	Fr.,	1877
John D. McConnell	Booneville	Fr.,	1845

Robert A. McConnell	Aurora	S. Fr., 1871
John McCord	Alfordsville	Pr., 1861
Arianna P. McCord	Bloomington	Sel., 1872
William H. McCord	Bloomington	So., 1880
Enos McCormack	Owensboro, Ky	Sel., 1865
Wilson I. McCormack	Wolcottville	So., 1883
William A. McCoy	Charleston	Pr., 1866
Lewis McCoy	Golconda	So., 1864
John H. McCoy	Bean Blossom	Pr., 1879
W. M. McCoy	Greensburg	Jr., 1880
Edward McCrea	Harrodsburg	Pr., 1854
John McCrea	Bloomington	Pr., 1861
E. McCrillis	Jasper County	Pr., 1845
S. B. McCrillis	Jasper County	Pr., 1845
Aaron McCrillis	Jasper County	Pr., 1857
Sylvanus F. McCrillis	Jasper County	Pr., 1857
James H. McCullough	Indianapolis	Sen., 1865
Samuel McCune	Bloomington	Pr., 1857
Edwin McCurdy	Princeton	So., 1877
Cornelius McDaniel	Owen County	Pr., 1845
Reuben E. McDaniel	Portland Mills	Fr., 1868
John W. McDaniel	Little York	Irr., 1871
Clark McDermont	Bloomington	Pr., 1861
Samuel H. McDill	Richland	So., 1882
David McDonald	Bloomington	Pr., 1837
Alfred McDonald	Bloomington	Pr., 1842
Malcolm A. McDonald	Indianapolis	So., 1868
Horace E. McDonald	Crothersville	So., 1881
William H. McDowel	Springville	Pr., 1863
Thomas J. McElrath	Warrenton, Miss	Sen., 1838
Theodore R. McFerson	Evansville	Sen., 1862
Pleasant C. McGannon	Vernon	Irr., 1856
Rufus McGee	Martinsville	Pr., 1861
Ben A. McGee	Bloomington	Sel., 1872
Monroe McGill	Cloverdale	Pr., 1857
Belle McGilvrey	Hollandsburg	Pr., 1881
John R. McGinnes	Putnam County	Pr., 1842
Archibald McGinnis	Bloomington	Pr., 1856
George G. McGinnis	Martinsburg	Pr., 1881
Charles C. McGinnis	Martinsburg	Pr., 1882
Nicholas H. McGuire	Loogootee	S. Fr., 1860

Luther M. McHenry	Carmi, Ill	Fr.,	1869
George M. McHenry	Carmi, Ill	So.,	1870
Martin B. McHenry	Sugar Branch	Pr.,	1875
Charles S. McHenry	Sugar Branch	Pr.,	1878
Alexander A. McHatton	Morea, Ill	Pr.,	1878
Edwin C. McIntire	Bryantsville	Fr.,	1868
William McKee	Wheeling, W. Va	Fr.,	1844
James T. McKee	Lawrenceburg	Pr.,	1860
William B. McKee	Bloomfield	Pr.,	1877
Emma P. McKee	Bloomfield	Pr.,	1877
John H. Mackey	Rochester	Pr.,	1861
James L. Mackey	Evansville	So.,	1880
Cyrus W. McKenzie	Waverly	Pr.,	1875
Lucy McKinlay	Bloomington	Pr.,	1881
A. M. McKinney	Livonia	Sel.,	1845
A. J. McKinney	Sullivan County	Sel.,	1845
Lawson E. McKinney	Martinsville	Pr.,	1861
Morton C. McKinney	Bloomington	Pr.,	1882
Elmer Grant McKinney	Bloomington	Pr.,	1881
Ethel G. McKinney	Bloomington	Pr.,	1882
George W. McKinstry	Hamburg, Ark	Jr.,	1874
Oliver P. McKissick	Cooperstown, Pa	S. Fr.,	1865
Rankin B. McKissick	Bloomington	Pr.,	1868
Aaron H. McKissick	Bloomington	Pr.,	1868
George W. McKnight	Bedford	Fr.,	1870
Inez C. McKnight	Bedford	Pr.,	1881
Hiram H. McLane	Bedford	Pr.,	1835
William McMahan	Harrison County	Pr.,	1842
John McMahan	Salem	Pr.,	1842
Dennis McMahan	Salem	Pr.,	1842
William H. McMakin	Vevay	Fr.,	1855
Robert McMaster	Princeton	Fr..	1861
Cora McMichael	Bloomington	Pr.,	1882
Gavin Riley McMillan	Xenia, Ohio	Jr.,	1845
Samuel H. McMillan	Xenia, Ohio	Jr.,	1858
William B. McMillan	Bloomington	So.,	1858
William B. McMillan	Sugar Grove	Fr.,	1873
John W. McMullen	Manchester	So.,	1870
William S. McMurtrie	Parke County	Sen.,	1838
James H. McMurtrie	Parke County	Jr.,	1848
Lucille M. McNay	Duncansville	Jr.,	1882

HISTORY OF INDIANA UNIVERSITY. 429

Gilbert McNutt..................Bloomington........Pr.,	1875
Finley McNutt....................Bloomington........Pr.,	1877
Irvin H. McPhetridge............Bloomington........Pr.,	1856
John McPheeters................Canton, Ill............Pr.,	1839
William H. McPheeters.........Canton, Ill............Pr.,	1846
Joseph G. McPheeters, Jr......Bloomington........So.,	1860
Charles H. McPheeters..........Bloomington........Pr.,	1862
Samuel McPheeters..............Turkey Cove, N. C..Pr.,	1868
Ida B. McPheeters................Santa Fé, Ill..........Pr.,	1874
Lulu McPheeters..................Santa Fé, Ill..........Pr.,	1879
Hugh R. McPherson.............Morgan................Pr.,	1844
Joseph W. McRae................Elizabeth..............Fr.,	1854
John A. McRae...................Springdale............Pr.,	1855
William McVey...................Danville................Pr.,	1845
Rufus Magee......................Indianapolis..........So.,	1865
James Maidlow...................Evansville..............Pr.,	1853
William S. Major..................Martinsville..........So.,	1856
John Malott........................Bedford................So.,	1870
Ida Manley.........................Bloomington......... Pr.,	1882
Albert N. Mann...................Mt. Vernon...........Pr.,	1874
James Manners...................Ladoga..................Pr.,	1848
John D. Mansfield................Leavenworth........Pr.,	1860
John S. Mansfield.................Leavenworth........So.,	1863
George A. Marcellus.............Nashville.............S. Fr.,	1872
Jacob C. Marchand..............Larwill..................Pr.,	1881
James Marlin.....................Bloomington........ Sel.,	1874
Hubbard A. L. Marshall........Bloomington........ Pr.,	1837
Randolph W. Marshall..........Bloomington........ Fr.,	1839
David Marshall....................Rush County........ Jr.,	1848
R. J. Taylor Marshall............ Warrenton, Va......Fr.,	1852
James H. Marshall...............New Albany..........So.,	1863
George D. Marshall..............Bardstown, Ky......Pr.,	1866
Sarah Marshall....................Martinsville..........Fr.,	1870
Andrew H. Marshall............Martinsville..........So.,	1872
J. Blaine Marshall................New Albany..........Jr.,	1860
Claudius B. H. Martin..........Livonia.................Fr.,	1846
E. S. Martin.......................Clermont County, O.Irr.,	1850
Robert L. Martin..................Wheeling, Miss......Irr.,	1851
Henry D. Martin.................New Philadelphia...Pr.,	1856
Benjamin F. Martin.............Leavenworth........Pr.,	1856
Nevius Lowrie Martin..........Neosho County, Ks. Sel.,	1877

Emma T. Martin............South Mound, Ks...Fr.,		1881
James W. Martindale............Cloverdale............S. Fr.,		1867
Elsberry Martindale............Cincinnati............Pr.,		1882
Mahalie E. Martindale............Buena Vista............Pr.,		1882
C. C. Mason............Rockport............Pr.,		1850
William T. Mason............Cannelton............Irr.,		1851
James L. Mason............Brownsville............Irr.,		1853
Ferdinand Mason............Grandview............Irr.,		1853
William T. Mason............Rockport............S. Fr.,		1865
Lycurgus C. Mason............Rockport............So.,		1866
George C. Mason............Somerville............Fr.,		1872
William C. Mason............Grandview............Fr.,		1882
John M. Mathony............Brown County............Pr.,		1851
Samuel Mathers............Monroe County............Fr.,		1868
J. C. Mathers............Monroe County............Fr.,		1835
William N. Mathers............Monroe County............Irr.,		1847
James E. Mathers............Bloomington............Fr.,		1868
Samuel M. Mathers............Bloomington............Fr.,		1868
Presley M. Mathers............Bloomington............Pr.,		1880
J. M. Mathes............Bloomington............Sel.,		1841
Jeremiah V. Mathes............Bloomington............Pr.,		1847
John C. Mathes............Morgan County............Irr.,		1847
J. C. Mathes............Bloomington............Pr.,		1850
Robert J. L. Matthews............New Albany............So.,		1854
James E. Matthews............Bloomington............Pr.,		1857
Lillie Matthews............Bloomington............Pr.,		1882
Samuel Mattox............Livonia............So.,		1857
T. Harvey Mauck............Princeton............Fr.,		1872
James W. Mavity............Titusville............Sen.,		1869
Joseph M. Maverty............Bloomington............Pr.,		1856
Joseph P. Maxey............Shoal Creek, Ill............So.,		1866
Edward N. Maxwell............Louisville, Ky............Fr.,		1840
David H. Maxwell, Jr............Bloomington............So.,		1845
Edward B. Maxwell............Bloomington............Pr.,		1847
Levi D. Maxwell............Brownstown............Sen.,		1862
T. Howard Maxwell............Bloomington............So.,		1866
Charles E. Maxwell............Bloomington............Pr.,		1868
Walter E. Maxwell............Bloomington............Sel.,		1875
Franklin Maxwell............Mitchell............Pr.,		1876
Mary E. Maxwell............Bloomington............Sel.,		1876
John F. May............Monroe County............Irr.,		1848

Charles May	Newbern	Pr.,	1851
Robert May	Newbern	Pr.,	1851
Jonathan M. May	Monroe	Irr.,	1852
James H. May	Michigan City	Pr.,	1860
Kitty May	Ellettsville	Pr.,	1878
Laura C. May	Ellettsville	Pr.,	1879
John L. May	Bloomington	So.,	1880
John Otto May	Bloomington	Pr.,	1881
Clara May	Clear Creek	Pr.,	1881
Christian P. Mayer	Palestine	S. Fr.,	1859
Levi P. Mayer	Palestine	So.,	1860
Herman B. Mayes	Lexington, Ky	Fr.,	1837
Robert B. Mayes	Lexington, Ky.	Fr.,	1837
Nettie Mayfield	Bloomington	Pr.,	1878
Louis Mayo	Albion, Ill.	Pr.,	1857
H. Mays	Lexington, Ky	Pr.,	1835
Annie E. Mays	St. Bernice, Iowa	Pr.,	1878
Charles A. Meacham	Rockville	Pr.,	1858
Claudius M. Meek	Monroe County	Pr.,	1845
William P. Meek	Bloomington	Pr.,	1851
Hanford E. Meeker	Salem Centre	Pr.,	1862
Tilghman W. Mefford	Bloomington	Pr.,	1881
Peter M. Mefford	Bloomington	Fr.,	1881
Edward Mefford	Bloomington	Pr.,	1882
John M. Meissner	Ludlow	S. Fr.,	1866
Chapman C. Menaugh	Salem	Pr.,	1862
Charles R. Menaugh	Delphi	So.,	1870
John Mendenhall	Napoleon	Irr.,	1846
Samuel G. Meredith	Hobbieville	S. Fr.,	1871
James B. Merriwether	Jefferson	Pr.,	1847
Orlando R. Merriwether	Jefferson	Pr.,	1847
Orlando Mershon	Bloomington	Pr.,	1835
Orrick Metcalf	Adams County, Mis.	Jr.,	1842
James W. Metcalf	Adams County, Mis.	Fr.,	1842
John A. Metzler	Laud	Sel.,	1877
Charles F. Meyer	North Vernon	S. Fr.,	1873
William M. Michener	Connersville	Fr.,	1876
Scott Michener	Connersville	Jr.,	1883
Morgan L. Miers	Greensburgh	Pr.,	1877
George D. S. Milam	Monroe County	Pr.,	1851
Enos M. Miles	Bowling Green	Irr.,	1847

T. M. Miles	Aurora	Pr.,	1850
Curtis C. Millen	Indianola	Pr.,	1879
S. F. Miller	Louisville, Ky	Pr.,	1838
Horace Miller	Louisville, Ky	Pr.,	1838
George W. Miller	Montgomery Co	Irr.,	1848
Griffey Miller	Kosciusko	Pr.,	1852
George Miller	Chester Dis., S. C	Fr.,	1854
Charles S. Miller	Russellville	Se.,	1857
William B. Miller	Bloomington	S. Fr.,	1857
Benjamin F. Miller	Jeffersonville	Fr.,	1860
James H. Miller	Smithville	S. Fr.,	1861
Daniel S. W. Miller	Old Point	Pr.,	1861
George B. Miller	Jeffersonville	S. Fr.,	1861
Charles Miller	Bloomington	S. Fr.,	1871
Belle V. Miller	Mahalasville	Pr.,	1878
John B. Miller	Glenwood	Jr.,	1883
Benjamin F. Miller	Connersville	So.,	1883
James Milligan	Monroe County	Pr.,	1845
Joseph Milliron	Lafayette	Pr.,	1865
James L. Millis	Paoli	S. Fr.,	1857
William A. Mills	Bridgeport	Fr.,	1870
James B. Milner	Sedalia	Jr.,	1880
Sylvanus Milner	Mt. Vernon	Pr.,	1851
William H. Minet	Bloomington	Pr.,	1857
Jennie Misener	Bloomington	Pr.,	1881
Emma Misener	Bloomington	Pr.,	1880
Giles B. Mitchell	Morgan County	Pr.,	1839
Joseph C. Mitchell	Monroe	Pr.,	1844
James C. Mitchell	Monroe County	Irr.,	1846
John K. Mitchell	Bloomington	Pr.,	1855
Thomas B. Mitchell	Martinsville	Pr.,	1855
James F. Mitchell	Hopewell	Pr.,	1856
James Mitchell	Martinsville	Pr.,	1857
John Mitchell	Martinsville	Pr.,	1858
Andrew Jackson Mitchell	Bloomington	Pr.,	1858
Albert S. Mitchell	Martinsville	Pr.,	1863
William C. Mitchell	Martinsville	So.,	1864
Henry E. Mitchell	State-Line City	Pr.,	1866
George K. Mitchell	Bloomington	Fr.,	1867
Edgar V. Mitchell	Martinsville	Fr.,	1870

James I. Mitchell	Beck's Mill	Pr.,	1876
Robert Bartlett Mitchell	Beck's Mill	Fr.,	1877
Walter J. Mitchell	Vernon	Fr.,	1881
R. Lee Mitchell	Bloomington	Pr.,	1882
J. Mix	Lafayette	Pr.,	1835
Alexander J. Moberley	Monroe County	Pr.,	1844
Edward Emmett Moberley	Gosport	Pr.,	1847
Kate Moberley	Bloomington	Pr.,	1878
Laura J. Moberley	Bloomington	Fr.,	1879
Welton M. Modisett	Terre Haute	Sr.,	1837
James A. Modisett	Terre Haute	Pr.,	1838
James E. Moffatt	Bloomington	So.,	1864
Walter E. Moffatt	Perrysville	Sel.,	1876
Joshua Moffitt	Independence	So.,	1850
Martha L. Moffitt	Bloomington	Fr.,	1868
Thomas Monahan	Bloomington	Pr.,	1875
Leander J. Monks	Winchester	Jr.,	1864
Alexander J. Montgomery	Princeton	Pr.,	1865
Francis M. Montgomery	Poseyville	S. Fr.,	1872
William Montgomery	London	So.,	1873
Mary E. Montgomery	Sacramento, Ill.	Fr.,	1873
Ettie M. Montgomery	Carmi, Ill	Sel.,	1875
J. Euphemia Montgomery	Carmi, Ill	Pr.,	1875
J. Knox Montgomery	Carmi, Ill	Fr.,	1881
Obra F. Montgomery	Rochester	So.,	1882
Jacob Mood	Stanford	Pr.,	1862
George R. Moon, Jr	Warsaw	So.,	1869
Thomas B. Mooney	Columbus	Fr.,	1873
John A. Moore	Indianapolis	Pr.,	1835
William M. Moore	Georgeton, Ill	Pr.,	1842
John T. S. Moore	Owen County	Pr.,	1844
Anthony W. Moore	Owen County	Pr.,	1844
Thomas Moore	Jackson	Irr.,	1844
David Moore	Bloomington	Pr.,	1844
George Green Moore	Carroll	Irr.,	1844
John Moore	Monroe County	Irr.,	1845
T. W. Moore	Jackson	Fr.,	1845
Rufus F. G. Moore	Owen County	Sel.,	1845
Robert Moore	Jackson	Fr.,	1845
Robert Moore	Monroe County	So.,	1847
John S. Moore	Bloomington	Pr.,	1848

Jackson L. Moore	Lawrence	Pr.,	1851
Gholson A. Moore	Spencer	So.,	1856
William J. Moore	Springville	Sel.,	1864
James K. P. Moore	Owensboro, Ky	S. Fr.,	1865
Edward J. Moore	Springville	Sel.,	1864
William M. Moore	Bloomington	Pr.,	1866
Samuel B. Moore	New Belleville	Pr.,	1866
William H. Moore	Nashville, Ill	So.,	1867
Juliet M. Moore	Owego, N. Y	Sel.,	1877
Lou Moore	Bloomington	Pr.,	1881
George Frank Moore	Bloomington	Sel.,	1882
John R. Moore	Bloomington	Pr.,	1882
James Morgan	Rockport	Pr.,	1835
James Morgan	Olathe, Kas	So.,	1860
Lewis T. Morgan	Franklin	Pr.,	1866
Eugene A. Morgan	Brownsville	Pr.,	1866
John W. Morgan	Columbus	Fr.,	1868
William Morgan	Trafalgar	S. Fr.,	1870
Thomas J. Morgan	Austin	Fr.,	1880
Fannie H. Morgan	Knightstown	So.,	1881
Calvin C. Morrical	Laporte	Pr.,	1857
Robert Morris	Washington Co	Pr.,	1841
Charles C. Morris	Colona	Fr.,	1873
W. Henry Morrison	Indianapolis	Irr.,	1847
Willard L. Morrison	Alpha	Pr.,	1880
Lora Morrison	Bloomington	Pr.,	1881
Lafayette Mortimer	Shelbyville	So.,	1856
T. L. Morton	Bloomington	Irr.,	1850
B. L. Morton	Lake County	Pr.,	1854
George J. Mosbaugh	Cicero	Pr.,	1861
Manville S. Moser	Georgetown	So.,	1869
Charles W. Moss	Clay County	Pr.,	1846
David Moss	Marion County	Pr.,	1846
Peter W. Moss	New Bavaria, O	Pr.,	1860
George W. Mounts	Columbus	Pr.,	1861
Hiram Moyer	Orleans	So.,	1842
Horace B. Mulky	Bloomington	Sel.,	1876
James W. Mullikin	Bloomington	Pr.,	1857
William Mullikin	Bloomington	Pr.,	1860
Olie Mullikin	Bloomington	Pr.,	1882
Metta Mullinix	Bloomington	Fr.,	1882

Elmer Mullinix	Bloomington......Fr.,	1882
O. E. Mullinix	Bloomington......Pr.,	1882
Julius Mulvey	Madison......Jr.,	1850
Thomas H. Mumford	New Harmony......Sel.,	1865
Alexander M. Murphy	Bloomington......So.,	1838
Julian Murphy	Pulaski......Pr.,	1857
Alexander D. Murphy	Sullivan......Fr.,	1860
Anderson R. Murray	Breckin'dge Co., Ky.Pr.,	1839
Charles T. Murray	Indianapolis......So.,	1867
Daniel Murray	Bloomington......Fr.,	1869
John S. Murray	Louisville, Ky......Fr.,	1879
Samuel A. Mutchmore	Philadelphia, Pa......Jr.,	1853
Charles Mutz	Edinburgh......So.,	1870
William J. Myers	Decatur......Fr.,	1859
Noah D. Myers	Wallace......Fr.,	1868
Columbus L. Myers	Wallace......Fr.,	1869
Lida Myers	Bloomington......Pr.,	1876
Moses H. Naber	Laketown......Sel.,	1871
J. C. Nall	Elizabethtown, Ky..Pr.,	1854
Samuel C. Neal	Benton, Ill......Fr.,	1868
Nathan Neeld	Monroe County......Pr.,	1858
James H. Neeld	Monroe County......Pr.,	1841
Alice M. Neely	Mocksville, N. C.....So.,	1879
Frank T. Neely	Hookerton, N. C.....Pr.,	1881
Arthur C. Neely	Hookerton, N. C.....Pr.,	1881
Francis L. Neff	Hendricks County...Fr.,	1852
James L. Neff	Winchester......So.,	1864
John E. Neff	Winchester......Fr.,	1864
John W. Negley	Indianapolis......Fr.,	1869
Simon Neidigh	Morgantown......Pr.,	1875
Lizzie Neidigh	Bean Blossom......Pr.,	1879
William Neill	Newark......Pr.,	1881
Martha E. Nellinger	Hobbieville......Pr.,	1874
Joseph W. Nelson	Jefferson County....Sel.,	1845
Thomas B. Nesbit	Monroe County......Irr.,	1848
William G. Nesbit	Carthage, Ill......Pr.,	1859
James P. Nesbit	Lebanon......Pr.,	1879
William F. Nevitt	Lawrenceburg......Pr.,	1846
James A. New	Greenfield......So.,	1871
Willard New	Vernon......Fr.,	1881
Joseph Newby	Bridgeport......Fr.,	1870

John Quincy Newlin	Carthage	Fr.,	1883
Jonathan W. Newman	Richmond	So.,	1859
Scott Newman	Louisville, Ky	Pr.,	1863
Dale O. Newton	Indianapolis	Fr.,	1873
John Newsom	Columbus	S. Fr.,	1856
Nathan Newsom	Azalia	So.,	1859
Williamson T. Newsom	Columbus	So.,	1865
G. Albert Newsom	Columbus	Pr.,	1877
J. R. Newson	Bartholomew	Irr.,	1850
John Q. A. Newson	Azalia	So.,	1857
Eli James Newton	Wabash	Sr.,	1868
William E. Niblack	Dubois	Fr.,	1840
Morton Nickols	Bloomington	Pr.,	1881
Thomas A. Nicholson	Jeffersonville	Fr.,	1861
Richard Nicholson	Bloomington	Pr.,	1882
Jacob Nickles	Winamac	Pr.,	1859
William Niel	Bloomington	Pr.,	1879
Charles T. Noble	Terre Haute	So.,	1862
Philip Nodurft	Williamsport	Pr.,	1857
Francis Noffsinger	Rockville	Pr.,	1852
R. W. N. Noland	Terre Haute	Pr.,	1840
Allen D. Norman	Louisville, Ky	Sel.,	1872
Alice Norman	Louisville, Ky	Fr.,	1872
Joseph S. Norman	Louisville, Ky	So.,	1872
G. M. Norman	Heltonville	Fr.,	1879
Morton Norman	Heltonville	Pr.,	1881
Nannie Norman	Bloomington	Pr.,	1882
Martin Norman	Bloomington	Pr.,	1882
Estelle Norman	Heltonville	Pr.,	1882
Elizabeth Norman	Bloomington	Pr.,	1882
Robert S. Northcott	Vevay	Fr.,	1882
Joseph R. Northcraft	Madison	So.,	1856
Thomas V. Norvell	Springville	Pr.,	1864
Marion Nuckalls	Bloomington	Pr.,	1868
Ella J. Nuckalls	Salem	Pr.,	1875
Augustus Nugent	Juliette	Pr.,	1857
John E. Nutt	Bloomington	Pr.,	1861
Omar Oakes	Valparaiso	So.,	1846
Ovid Oakes	Valparaiso	Fr.,	1848
Floyd G. Ogden	Utica	Pr.,	1861

J. S. Ogg	Solsberry Fr.,	1879
Albert W. Ogg	Solsberry Fr.,	1879
Frederick H. Ogle	Prairietown Fr.,	1880
Blanche E. Ogle	Prairietown Pr.,	1880
Jesse O'Hair	Paris, Illinois Fr.,	1866
Frank J. O'Haver	Sullivan Pr.,	1875
Charles A. Olcott	North Vernon Irr.,	1871
Thomas D. Olin	Omro, Wis Irr.,	1871
Andrew S. Oliphant	Union So.,	1870
Joseph Oliver	Louisville, Ky Pr.,	1838
Alcide Olivier	St. Martinsville, La.Pr.,	1875
Hugh O'Neal	Indianapolis Jr.,	1835
William H. O'Neal	Newberry Pr.,	1856
William S. Oppenheim	Bluffton So.,	1875
Calvin C. Orahood	Camden Pr.,	1877
Baynard R. Orchard	Bloomington Pr.,	1859
James R. Orchard	Bloomington So.,	1866
Isaac S. Orchard	Bloomington Pr.,	1866
Samuel J. Orchard	Bloomington Pr.,	1868
John B. O'Reilly	Yazoo, Miss Pr.,	1852
Jackson Orr	Elkhart Irr.,	1852
William Orr	Elkhart Irr.,	1852
Francis B. Orr	Mishawaka Irr.,	1853
Thomas B. Orr	Plymouth Jr.,	1875
Robert Elmwood Orr	Attica Sel.,	1877
Samuel C. Osborn	Carpentersville Jr.,	1862
James S. Otis	Butler Sel.,	1875
William S. Otwell	Bloomington S. Pr.,	1863
Francis Overman	Bryantsville Fr.,	1870
William D. Owen	Bloomington Irr.,	1865
William H. Owen	New Harmony S. Fr.,	1866
McHenry Owen	Medora Sel.,	1876
Lizzie Owen	Bloomington Pr.,	1879
Alexander Owens	Bloomington Sel.,	1845
William J. Owens	Monroe County Sel.,	1846
Samuel R. Owens	Springville Pr.,	1846
Robert N. Palmer	Bedford Jr.,	1870
Wallace C. Palmer	Elkhart	
Romanta J. Paquinette	Benton, Mo Irr.,	1847
D. Lizzie Parham	Bloomington Pr.,	1880

William Park	Blue Grass	Pr.,	1854
Arthur Parke	Oakdam	Pr.,	1856
Charles Parke	Oakdam	S. Fr.,	1861
Shelby Parke	Perryville	Pr.,	1878
Thomas Parker	Oxford	Pr.,	1846
Noah Parker	Tipton	Pr.,	1859
Basil J. Parker	Oxford	Sel.,	1865
Victor H. Parker	Carmi, Ill	S. Fr.,	1872
J. W. Parker	Grandview	Fr.,	1882
Della Parker	Grandview	Fr.,	1882
J. R. Parkinson	Monroe County	Fr.,	1845
Thomas S. Parks	Bloomington	So.,	1838
Elijah M. Parks	Bloomington	So.,	1842
Ambrose C. Parks	Lawrence County	Pr.,	1865
James M. Parks	Bloomington	Irr.,	1850
Milton H. Parks	Martinsville	So.,	1862
John A. Parks	Aurora	Fr.,	1871
James L. Parks	Coldwater, Miss	Pr.,	1877
William H. H. Parks	Bloomington	Pr.,	1880
Clarence M. Parks	Ellettsville	So.,	1883
Clara L. Parmenter	Loogootee	Sel.,	1871
Richard M. Parrish	Bloomington	Pr.,	1852
George W. Parrish	Cuba	Pr.,	1861
Amos W. Parrish	Falmouth	S. Fr.,	1871
Lewis C. Parrish	Cuba	Fr.,	1871
Frank Parsons	Portland, Ky	So.,	1869
M. Frank Pate	Dresden	So.,	1883
Daniel H. Patrick	Carmi, Ill	Pr.,	1877
Chambers Patterson	Rockville	Pr.,	1837
A. H. Patterson	Fountain County	Pr.,	1837
Ewing L. Patterson	Terre Haute	Jr.,	1881
Charles M. Patterson	Mt. Liberty	Pr.,	1881
George S. Pattie	Eureka	Fr.,	1869
J. Randolph Patton	Livonia	Pr.,	1862
Samuel A. Patton	Livonia	Pr.,	1863
Harry W. Patton	Vincennes	Pr.,	1874
Charles H. Pauley	Bloomington	Pr.,	1876
Egbert Paxton	Sullivan	Pr.,	1875
William Payne	Bloomfield	Pr.,	1844
Rollin A. Payne	Vernon	Irr.,	1851
Joseph S. Payne	Bloomington	Sel.,	1865

HISTORY OF INDIANA UNIVERSITY.   439

Agnes S. Payne...................Bloomington.........Pr.,	1876
Lillie C. Payne ....Bloomington.........Pr.,	1880
Florence B. Payne ....Bloomington.........Pr.,	1882
Charles N. Peake ....New Marion ....Pr.,	1878
William L. Pearson ....Springville............Irr.,	1848
Theodore A. Peck ....Bloomington.........Pr.,	1868
George Peckenpaugh.............Alton ....Sel.,	1878
Simeon Pedigo ....Hobbieville ....S. Fr.,	1871
Thomas A. Peden ....Spencer................Pr.,	1855
Joseph B. Pedrick ....Columbus.............Pr.}	1859
Harry D. Peet ....Jeffersonville.........S. Fr.,	1871
James A. Peirce ....Louisville, Ky........Pr.,	1852
Elijah T. Pence....................Stanford, Ky.........Pr.,	1866
Ames W. Pence ....Stanford, Ky ....Pr.,	1866
George W. Pence ....Stanford, Ky.........Fr.,	1866
George Pence........ ....Columbus...... .....So.,	1870
Charles Rollin Pence ....Peru.....................So.,	1877
S. S. Pendleton ....Vernon ....Pr.,	1850
William Pennington..............Mooresville............Fr.,	1859
Andrew Percifield. ....Nashville ....S. Fr.,	1872
Lulu Perdue......................:...Bloomington.........Pr.,	1879
Jehu W. Perkins...................Lebanon ....Fr.,	1857
Eugene L. Perham ....Indianapolis..........Pr.,	1842
Charles Hine Pering ....Livonia ....Pr.,	1851
Alfred Hine Pering.. ....Bloomington.........Pr.,	1852
Charles C. Pering ....Bloomington.........Fr.,	1862
Ezra Pering........................Bloomington.........So.,	1863
Francis Pering.....................Bloomington.........Sel.,	1875
Charles K. Pering................Clear Creek..........Pr.,	1875
Ella M. Pering.....................Clear Creek..........Pr.,	1875
Lucy Pering........................Bloomington.........Pr.,	1877
Ella Pering.........................Bloomington..........Pr.,	1878
Frances E. Pering................Bloomington.........Sel.,	1878
Clinton C. Pering ....Clear Creek..........Pr.,	1881
Herschel Peters ....Jeffersonville ....S. Fr.,	1865
Henry Peterson. ....Union Village . ...Pr.,	1867
Ebenezer H. Pettus..............Bloomington.........Fr.,	1870
Samuel Pfrimmer . ...Lanesville.............Pr.,	1879
Allie Pfrimmer . ...Lanesville. ....Pr.,	1879
Lizzie Pfrimmer ....Lanesville.............Pr.,	1879
Alfred W. Phillips ....Bloomington.........Pr.,	1858

Samuel H. Phillips	Louisville, Ky	Sel.,	1865
Joseph L. Phillips	Bowling Green, Ky.	So.,	1839
E. P. Phillips	Bloomington	Fr.,	1879
Joseph A. Phillips	Cincinnati	Fr.,	1879
Fannie J. Phillips	Bloomington	Pr.,	1879
Kate Phillips	Bloomington	Pr.,	1880
Eva J. Phillips	Ellettsville	Fr.,	1883
Charles W. Philputt	Bloomington	Jr.,	1888
Washington H. Phipps	Freedom	Fr.,	1864
Samson C. Phipps	Seabury	Fr.,	1881
Isaac W. Pickard	Sylvania	Fr.,	1882
Homer T. Pickel	Harrodsburg	Pr.,	1875
Samuel O. Pickens	Cuba	Sel.,	1865
W. A. Pickens	Spencer	Jr.,	1881
Henry Pitts	Knightstown	S. Fr.,	1871
William R. Pleak	Adams	Sel.,	1875
Elwood Pleas	Henry County	Irr.,	1853
William A. Poindexter	Stamp'g Gr'nd, Ky.	So.,	1863
Willy F. Poindexter	Keck's Church	Pr.,	1876
B. C. Polk	Lafayette	So.,	1835
William L. Polk	Greenwood	Sr.,	1866
Godfrey Pope	Louisville, Ky	Fr.,	1835
Wallace Pope	Louisville, Ky	Irr.,	1846
Edward J. Pope	Louisville, Ky	Fr.,	1858
Benjamin Pope	Shepherdstown, Ky.	Pr.,	1863
J. Worden Pope	Louisville, Ky	So.,	1864
Afred T. Pope	Corydon	Fr.,	1859
Hamilton Pope, Jr	Louisville, Ky	Irr.,	1866
H. D. Pope	Mitchell	Fr.,	1867
Isaac Newton Porch	Ladoga	Fr.,	1855
David F. Porter	Paoli	Pr.,	1848
Henry Potts	Knightstown	Fr.,	1872
James W. Powell	Boland, Illinois	Pr.,	1861
Henry L. Powell	New Castle	So.,	1866
Lafayette Powers	Fort Branch	Pr.,	1867
Nehemiah B. Powers	Muncie	Jr.,	1871
Joseph A. Pownal	Columbus	Fr.,	1848
Thomas A. Prather	Jeffersonville	So.,	1859
Isaac O. Prather	Jeffersonville	Pr.,	1861
Martin L. Prather	Jeffersonville	Sen.,	1862

Douglass B. Pressel	Bloomington	Pr.,	1867
George W. Pressley	Ogden	Fr.,	1852
James L. Pringle	Washington	Fr.,	1870
Lewis Prosser	Brown County	Irr.,	1848
George Prosser	Bean Blossom	Pr.,	1856
Isaac N. Prosser	Bean Blossom	S. Fr.,	1856
James F. Prosser	Bean Blossom	Pr.,	1878
James Prowe	Bloomington	Pr.,	1859
Samuel E. Puett	Rockville	Pr.,	1864
Sabin J. Puett	Gosport	Pr.,	1879
Francis Pruyn	Richmond	Pr.,	1837
Emery Raber	Wolcottville	Fr.,	1878
George W. Rahn	Savannah, Ga.	Sel.,	1842
Napoleon A. Rainbolt	Springville	Fr.,	1859
W. T. Rader	Monroe County	Pr.,	1850
George B. Rader	Monroe County	Pr.,	1851
Wesley Rader	Bloomington	S. Fr.,	1869
William A. Rafferty	Shelby	Pr.,	1846
Theodore N. Rafferty	Springville	Pr.,	1864
F. Bradley Rafferty	Fredericksburg	So.,	1875
John M. Ragan	Benton, Ill	So.,	1870
Algern Ragle	Loogootee	Fr.,	1882
Miles Ragsdale	Washington	Pr.,	1866
James M. Ragsdale	Washington	Pr.,	1856
Samuel B. Railsback	Argos	Pr.,	1874
Fannie M. Ralston	Manville	So.,	1883
Hannah M. Ramage	Bloomington	Pr.,	1878
Alfred A. Ramsey	Putnam County	Irr.,	1848
Robert B. Ranard	Whitehall	Pr.,	1859
Jacob M. Ranard	Whitehall	S. Fr.,	1859
John L. Rand	Hart's Mills	Pr.,	1859
Richard R. Randall	Bloomington	Pr.,	1880
George S. Randall	Greenbush	Pr.,	1882
Charles F. Randall	Aurora	Jr.,	1882
James W. Randall	Aurora	Jr.,	1883
Ruth Randolph	Bloomington	Pr.,	1879
Jackson Randolph	Bloomington	So.,	1883
James S. Rankin	Bedford	Pr.,	1838
John Rankin	Evansville	Pr.,	1851
Samuel C. Rankins	Spencer	Pr.,	1861
Samuel A. Rariden	Paoli	Pr.,	1837

Beverley Ratcliff	Washington	Fr.,	1841
Mattie Rawles	Bloomington	Fr.,	1880
Daniel A. Rawlings	Monroe County	Pr.,	1837
John Rawlings	Monroe County	Pr.,	1845
David B. Rawlings	Oxford	Fr.,	1875
James S. Rawlins	Bedford	Fr.,	1838
James M. Rawlins	Bedford	Irr.,	1841
James S. Rawlins	Bloomington	Pr.,	1861
Joseph F. Rawlins	Salt Lake City, U	Jr.,	1873
Leroy L. Rawlins	Bloomington	Pr.,	1880
William F. Rawlins	Maple Valley	So.,	1883
J. Ebersole Rawson	Bloomington	Pr.,	1858
George V. Rawson	Bloomington	Pr.,	1859
Joseph D. Ray	Monroe County	Fr.,	1841
James A. Read	Jeffersonville	Jr.,	1851
Henry K. Read	Muncie	Fr.,	1879
William Reader	Mauckport	So.,	1838
Henry Reader	Harrison County	Irr.,	1847
James Reader	Mauckport	Irr.,	1850
Charles H. Reader	Corydon	Pr.,	1867
George Ream	Columbia City	Pr.,	1867
Jenny Reavill	Morea, Ill	Pr.,	1876
James D. Reavill	Robinson, Ill	Sr.,	1881
David Allen Reavill	Flat Rock, Ill.	Pr.,	1881
Charles Mc. Reavill	Flat Rock, Ill.	Pr.,	1881
J. O. Reay	Louisville, Ky	Irr.,	1850
Thomas A. Record	New Harmony	Pr.,	1877
William R. Reddick	Nashville	Pr.,	1875
James I. Reed	Trinity Springs	S. Fr.,	1856
Isaac O. Reed	Bloomington	Pr.,	1868
John Reed	Bloomington	Pr.,	1875
Nettie E. Reed	Greensburg	Pr.,	1878
Mary Reed	Worthington	Pr.,	1879
Ira H. Rees	Bloomington	Pr.,	1853
George Reese	White County	Pr.,	1846
John D. Reese	Terre Haute	Pr.,	1881
James H. Reeves	Bloomington	Pr.,	1860
Joseph H. Reeves	Bloomington	Fr.,	1861
Albert Benton Reeves	Warrington	So.,	1883
George W. Register	New Lebanon	Pr.,	1866
William A. Reid	Bloomington	Pr.,	1861

Adelaide L. Reid............Salem ....Fr.,		1872
Anna B. Reid............Lyons ....Pr.,		1878
George G. Reily ....Mt. Pleasant.......So.,		1859
J. Reno ....Gosport............Pr.,		1850
Henry N. Reubelt............Bloomington ....Jr.,		1870
B. F. Reynolds ....Crawford County...Pr.,		1840
Chalmers Reynolds ....Fair Haven, O........Fr.,		1846
Benjamin Reynolds ....Bloomington.........Pr.,		1862
Jacob M. Rhode ....Rainsville............Pr.,		1855
Samuel A. Rhorer............Monroe County......Pr.,		1844
Milton M. Rhorer............Monroe County......Sel.,		1845
George H. Rhorer............Monroe County......Pr.,		1854
Melvin Rhorer ....Louisville, Ky........Pr.,		1857
Samuel Kentucky Rhorer......Louisville, Ky........Pr.,		1858
Daniel Rhorer ....Bloomington........Pr.,		1859
William H. Rhorer............Bloomington.........Sel.,		1865
Mary B. Rhorer............Bloomington.........Sel.,		1874
Eliza E. Ribble............Selma............Fr.,		1882
John W. Rice............Wickliffe............Irr.,		1844
J. Harrison Rice............Waveland............So.,		1846
John B. Rice............Bloomington.........Fr.,		1870
William G. Richards............Orleans.............Pr.,		1857
James Richardson............Rockport............Pr.,		1875
Allison G. Richardson............Mooresville........ Pr.,		1876
Brewer Richardson............Mooresville............Pr.,		1876
David R. Richeson ....Monroe County......Pr.,		1851
S. H. Ricks............Rome............Pr.,		1850
Hiram D. Riddile............Bluffton............ Sel.,		1856
William Riddle,............Louisville, Ky........S. Fr.,		1866
Elias D. Riddle............Louisville, Ky ....Pr.,		1866
Lannie A. Rider. ....Crothersville........Pr.,		1882
William Ridge............Crawford County...Pr.,		1835
Lizzie E. Ridge............Ellettsville ....Pr.,		1876
William L. Rieley............Orleans............Irr.,		1844
William R. Righter............Morristown............Pr.,		1866
W. S. Riley............Orleans.. .... Sel.,		1845
Th. J. Riley............ Jefferson County....Sel.,		1845
John E. Riley............Bloomington.........So.,		1879
Caleb A. Ritter............Valley Mills............Fr.,		1873
David A. Roach............Wallace............Fr.,		1869
Addison L. Roach, Jr............Indianapolis............Pr.,		1880

Lincoln Road	Peru.	Pr.,	1860
John M. Robb	Princeton	Sel.,	1865
William G. Roberts	Newburg	Fr.,	1846
Phelps S. Roberts	Yazoo, Miss	So.,	1852
Aurelius H. Roberts	Bruceville	Pr.,	1854
Marcellus P. Roberts	Bruceville	Pr.,	1856
Walker Roberts	Yelvington, Ky	Sel.,	1865
E. Adelia Roberts	West Gardiner	Fr.,	1869
Robert R. Roberts	Newburg	S. Fr.,	1873
Fenwick Robertson	Kingston	Irr.,	1851
Sylvester H. Robertson	Newburg	Pr.,	1852
William F. Robertson	Bloomington	Pr.,	1859
John W. Robertson	Bloomington	S. Fr.,	1867
Middleton C. Robertson	Deputy	Pr.,	1874
Charles T. Robertson	Bloomington	Pr.,	1866
James Robertson	Bloomington	Pr.,	1862
Samuel G. Robertson	Bloomington	Pr.,	1859
Milton S. Robertson	Bloomington	So.,	1864
James M. Robinson	Bloomington	Irr.,	1846
Thomas J. Robinson	Bloomington	Pr.,	1854
Henry A. Robinson	Lewisburg, W. Va	Fr.,	1856
Melville C. Robinson	Paris	Sen.;	1864
Milton S. Robinson	Bloomington	S. Fr.,	1861
William H. Robinson	Delphi	So.,	1870
John M. Robinson	Tipton	So.,	1870
Charles W. Robinson	North Vernon	Sel.,	1871
F. Ella Robinson	Bloomington	Pr.,	1875
James E. Robinson	Bloomington	Pr.,	1876
John N. Robinson	Hindostan	Pr.,	1876
William C. Robinson	Owensville	Jr.,	1881
Robert P. Robison	New Harmony	Pr.,	1844
Andrew Robison	Johnson	Irr.,	1852
Thomas Robison	Bloomington	Pr.,	1853
Andrew B. Rock	Fairhaven	Pr.,	1858
Emma C. Rock	Bloomington	Pr.,	1877
Andrew R. Roddy	Smithville	Pr.,	1859
Rufus Roddy	Smithville	So.,	1863
Samuel D. Roddy	Bloomington	Fr.,	1867
Andrew D. Roddy	Bloomington	Pr.,	1867
James L. Roddy	Bloomington	Pr.,	1867
Benjamin F. Rogers	Monroe County	Pr.,	1835

Franklin J. Rogers............Monroe County......Fr.,		1837
Lewis Rogers..................Monroe County......Pr.,		1838
Ephraim H. Rogers............Monroe County......Pr.,		1844
Dudley Rogers..................Monroe County......Pr.,		1846
Ephraim A. Rogers............Laporte.............Irr.,		1846
Isaac M. Rogers ....Bloomington.........Pr.,		1846
Benjamin F. Rogers............Laporte County.....Fr.,		1847
John W. Rogers ....Laporte.............Irr.,		1852
John D. Rogers................New Albany .... Pr.,		1855
David W. Rogers ....Bloomington .... Pr.,		1859
Benjamin F. Rogers............Bloomington.........Pr.,		1857
Samuel B. Rogers..............Bloomington.........Pr.,		1857
Franklin Rogers ....Bloomington.........Pr.,		1858
Napoleon B. Rogers............Bloomington.........Pr.,		1858
Francis M. Rogers ....Bloomington.........S. Fr.,		1861
David W. Rogers ....Bloomington.........Sel.,		1862
Thomas I. Rogers..............Bloomington.........Fr.,		1863
Thomas P. Rogers..............Bloomington.........So.,		1864
Dudley Rogers.................Bloomington.........Sel.,		1865
Walstein Q. Rogers............Loogootee...........S. Fr.,		1866
George W. Rogers..............Bloomington.........Sel.,		1867
Mary S. Rogers................Bloomington ....Fr.,		1868
Benjamin A. Rogers............Bloomington.........Fr.,		1869
Minnie M. Rogers..............Bloomington.........Pr.,		1876
Mattie I. Rogers ....Bloomington.........Sel.,		1878
William P. Rogers ....Bloomington.........So.,		1879
John S. Rogers................Bloomington.........Pr.,		1881
Joe M. Rogers.................Bloomington.........So.,		1882
Nannie Rogers.................Bloomington.........Pr.,		1882
Emma L. Rogers................Bloomington.........Pr.,		1882
Hugh Ronalds.................. Albion, Illinois......So.,		1878
Patrick Ronan.................Bloomington.........Pr.,		1867
John Ronan, Jr................Bloomington.........Pr.,		1868
Christian Y. Roop.............Lagrange............Sel.,		1873
Franklin S. Root..............Kent's Station......Pr.,		1864
William L. Root ....Vincennes...........Pr.,		1874
Ida W. Rose...................Bloomington.........Pr.,		1882
George W. Roseberry...........Hopewell............Pr.,		1856
N. P. Roseberry...............Bloomington.........Pr.,		1879
Morris Rosenthal..............Jefferson...........Pr.,		1867
Samuel Ross...................Whitestown..........S. Fr.,		1861

Bernard Ross...	Elizabeth	Pr.,	1867
George N. Rouse	Bloomington	Pr.,	1866
Richard H. Rousseau	Louisville, Ky.	Pr.,	1863
Wesley Rout	Lawrence County	Fr.,	1851
David Routson	Two Mile Prairie	Pr.,	1859
William O. Rowan	Winamac	S. Fr.	1870
Lewis S. Rowan	Winamac	So.,	1870
Henry P. Rowan	Winamac	So.,	1870
Marel Rowland	Bolivar, Miss	Pr.,	1867
Joseph P. Rowland	Charlestown	S. Fr.,	1859
David W. Rowland	Charlestown	Pr.,	1866
John S. Royer	Charlestown	S. Fr.,	1861
William E. Ruble	Edinburgh	Pr.,	1858
William Ruddick	Columbus	Irr.,	1841
Robert L. Ruddick	Columbus	So.,	1852
Dewitt C. Rugg	Decatur	Fr.,	1855
James T. Runcie	Fort Branch	Fr.,	1872
H. W. Runnells	Madison, Missouri	Sel.,	1842
James B. Runnion	Lafayette	Pr.,	1855
James A. Russel	Bloomington	Pr.,	1861
James R. Russel	New Albany	Pr.,	1866
Frederick Rust	Holland	Pr.,	1860
T. J. Ryan	Bloomington	Pr.,	1842
J. Howe Ryors	Bloomington	So.,	1868
Joseph J. Sadler	Bloomington	Pr.,	1846
Milton V. Sadler	Stanford	Pr.,	1859
Edward M. Salyards	Orleans	Pr.,	1866
T. Boys Sample	Lafayette	Pr.,	1856
James T. Sanders	Indianapolis	Pr.,	1837
Griffin P. Sanders	Indianapolis	Pr.,	1838
L. W. Sanders	Monroe County	Pr.,	1838
Emma E. Sanders	Plainfield	Pr.,	1875
Avis Sanders ..	Bloomington	So.,	1880
Nathan Sanford	Washington	Sel.,	1872
James M. Sankey	Terre Haute	Fr.,	1858
John M. Sappenfield	Parkville	Pr.,	1861
Eusebius M. Sappenfield	Parkville	Sel.,	1864
Henry Sargent	Buck Creek	Pr.,	1857
William Saunders	Greensburg	Fr.,	1845
James M. Scantlin	Evansville	Fr.,	1861
John C. Schafer	Lanesville	Fr.,	1864

Valentine Scharger	Blue Creek........Pr.,	1859
Francis Schell	Frederick, Md......Pr.,	1840
William W. Schermerhorn	...Delphi........So.,	1859
J. G. Schleuchter	Zurich, Ont., Can...Fr.,	1879
Charles S. Schofield	Indianapolis......Sel.,	1875
Jennie S. Schofield	Indianapolis......Sel.,	1875
James P. Scott	Burnettsville......Fr.,	1858
William H. Scott	Logansport......Pr.,	1862
William T. Scott	Mauckport......Fr.,	1866
Isaiah Scott	Greentown......Pr.,	1868
Truston K. Scott	Paoli......Pr.,	1868
H. A. Seall	Bloomington......Pr.,	1838
Linezey Seals	Salem......Sr.,	1840
Anna Seay	Washington......Pr.,	1876
James B. Sedwick	Ellettsville......Pr.,	1856
Christopher Seiger	Columbus......Pr.,	1868
George A. Seldemridge	Delphi......Pr.,	1881
Emma J. Semple	Bloomington......Pr.,	1881
Ida S. Semple	Bloomington......Pr.,	1882
John Serring	Madison......Pr.,	1835
Daniel H. Sessions	Madison, Miss......Sel.,	1842
George Setchell	Evansville......Pr.,	1859
Abner Severs	Monroe County......Sel.,	1845
James Seward	Bloomington......Pr.,	1841
Bryson Seward	Bloomington......Pr.,	1844
Wm. H. Seward	Bloomington......Sel.,	1875
Flora L. Seward	Bloomington......Pr.,	1879
William Frost Seward	Bloomington......Pr.,	1881
George Seward	Bloomington......Pr.,	1882
William Seward	Bloomington......Pr.,	1882
May Seward	Bloomington......Pr.,	1882
Lemuel B. Sexton	Green......Pr.,	1844
James H. Shadday	Moorefield......Sel.,	1872
Charles A. Shaffer	Bluffton......Irr.,	1853
James G. Shaffer	Kewanna......Pr.,	1860
Henry L. Shank	Rome......Irr.,	1871
Samuel R. Shannon	Carmi, Ill......Fr.,	1869
Josiah Shaw	Vermillion County. Pr.,	1837
Carpus N. Shaw	Bloomfield......Jr.,	1852
E. Sheble	Louisville, Ky......Pr.,	1835
Benjamin Sheeks	Mitchell......Jr.,	1864

Oliver Sheets	Madison	Pr.,	1835
William O. Sheets	Madison	Fr.,	1837
Phœbe C. Shelhorn	Adams	Pr.,	1882
Albert L. Shelton	Hall	Pr.,	1867
John A. Shepherd	Cumberland	Sel.,	1877
Jacob F. Sherfy	Bloomington	Pr.,	1860
George R. Sherman	Mauckport	Pr.,	1867
Walter N. Sherman	Bloomington	Fr.,	1872
Alexander Shields	Merom	Pr.,	1840
James W. Shields	Orleans	Pr.,	1846
James E. Shields	Rockport	Pr.,	1850
Lycurgus Shields	Rockport	Pr.,	1851
L. Harper Shields	Columbus	Fr.,	1856
T. Bruce Shields	Seymour	Jr.,	1863
William H. Shields	Seymour	Jr.,	1863
William H. Shields	Columbus	Pr.,	1867
Alfred M. Shields	Rochester	Pr.,	1874
A. J. Shields	Solsberry	Fr.,	1879
W. D. Shields	Eminence	Fr.,	1880
John W. Shields	Bloomington	Pr.,	1882
J. E. Shipman	Solsberry	So.,	1879
Milford B. Shipp	Edinburgh	Fr.,	1853
James A. Shirk	Brookville	Pr.,	1875
John Shirk	Brookville	Pr.,	1876
Elizabeth Shirk	Peru	Sel.,	1878
James M. Shirk	Whitcomb	Fr.,	1881
George M. Shirk	Brookville	Pr.,	1881
L. O'Brien Shirley	Orangeville	So.,	1869
Jasper N. Shirley	Lebanon	Fr.,	1877
John C. Shirts	Scotland	Pr.,	1880
A. S. Shively	Louisville, Ky	So.,	1850
John C. Shockley	Sugar Creek	Pr.,	1860
William Shoemaker	Winchester	Irr.,	1847
John W. Shoemaker	Laporte	Pr.,	1867
Frederick C. Shoemaker	Bloomington	Fr.,	1871
Bruce W. Shoemaker	Bluffton	Sel.,	1876
Charles M. Shook	Versailles	Sel.,	1845
Owens Short	Springville	Pr.,	1844
Doddrige Short	Springville	Irr.,	1844
Samuel W. Short	Springville	Pr.,	1846
Hansford Short	Lawrence	Pr.,	1846

Senteny Short	Monroe County	Irr., 1853
Hiram E. Short	Springville	Pr., 1864
Morris T. Short	Carthage	Jr., 1870
Emerson Short	Owensburg	So., 1870
Thales Short	Springville	So., 1873
B. Orrin Short	New Marion	Pr., 1877
John G. Shryer	Monroe	Pr., 1844
Oscar W. Shryer	Bloomfield	So., 1868
Joseph E. Shryer	Bloomfield	Irr., 1871
Lewis I. Shryer	Worthington	Pr., 1881
J. William Shuey	Elkhart	Pr., 1867
Oscar F. Shumway	Azalia	Fr., 1864
Jesse P. Siddall	Richmond	Pr., 1837
Robert A. Silliman	Carmi, Ill	Fr., 1873
Guy C. Silliman	Carmi, Ill	Fr., 1873
William A. Simler	Harrison	Irr., 1846
Denton Simpson	Lawrence	So., 1848
John R. Simpson	Paoli	Pr., 1854
Richard D. Simpson	Paoli	Irr., 1871
Orrin Simpson	Centre	Pr., 1874
Lawrence Simpson	Centre	Pr., 1875
Henry Sims	Martinsville	Pr., 1838
William M. Sims	Utica	Pr., 1852
Lafayette Sims	Corydon	Pr., 1867
James A. Sims	White Hall	Fr., 1872
Kate May Sims	Utica	Pr., 1879
John T. Sims	Columbus	Pr., 1880
Charles E. Sims	Utica	Fr., 1882
Benjamin F. Simmons	Benton, Miss	Pr., 1860
John W. St. Clair	Switz City	Pr., 1878
William S. Slagley	Organ Spring	Pr., 1875
John B. Slater	Glendale	Fr., 1871
John W. Sloan	Bloomington	Pr., 1867
Leroy C. Slocomb	Francisville	Pr., 1860
Eva Slocomb	Bloomington	Pr., 1882
James R. Sluss	Bloomington	Pr., 1853
Edward J. Sluss	Bloomington	So., 1862
Henry C. Sluss	Tuscola, Illinois	Fr., 1865
Thomas M. Sluss	Bloomington	Pr., 1867
James G. Sluss	Bloomington	Fr., 1870
Eva B. Sluss	Bloomington	Sen., 1874

Lizzie Sluss	Bloomington	So.,	1880
Addie May Sluss	Bloomington	Fr.,	1882
Clara Sluss	Bloomington	Pr.,	1882
William R. Small	Bloomington	Sen.,	1876
Charles S. Small	Bloomington	Pr.,	1879
Elizabeth D. Small	Bloomington	Jr.,	1881
J. Oliver M. Small	Bloomington	So.,	1883
John G. Smalley	Springfield	Fr.,	1881
William M. Smallwood	Harrodsburg	Sel.,	1864
Levi Smallwood	Harrodsburg	Fr.,	1871
Samuel Smallwood	Harrodsburg	Pr.,	1867
William C. Smith	Monroe County	Pr.,	1835
Thomas A. Smith	Louisville, Ky	Pr.,	1837
Thomas H. Smith	Louisville, Ky	Pr.,	1838
Townsend Smith	Bloomington	Sel.,	1845
Wilson Smith	Cambridge	Fr.,	1846
Robert A. Smith	Boonville	Irr.,	1848
W. H. Smith	Salem	Pr.,	1850
Thomas F. Smith	St. Louis, Missouri	Irr.,	1851
Daniel W. Smith	Lawrenceburg	Pr.,	1851
Rodney D. Smith	Stanford	Irr.,	1853
William C. Smith	Warrick County	Pr.,	1853
Reuben W. Smith	Wawpecong	Pr.,	1854
James M. Smith	Zionsville	So.,	1857
James W. Smith	Mahalasville	Pr.,	1859
Robert H. Smith	Stanford	Pr.,	1861
James W. Smith	Bloomington	Pr.,	1861
Dudley Frederick Smith	Stanford	Sr.,	1861
Calvin W. Smith	Versailles	So.,	1863
David F. Smith	Unionville	Sel.,	1864
Calvin B. Smith	Bowling Green, Ky.	Fr.,	1866
David F. Smith	Bryant's Creek	Pr.,	1867
George D. Smith	Cynthiana	Fr.,	1868
Samuel T. W. Smith	Bloomington	Pr.,	1868
William Smith	Bryant's Creek	Fr.,	1869
Benjamin J. Smith	Bloomington	Irr.,	1871
I. Brown Smith	College Corner, O.	Sen.,	1874
James Polk Smith	Kokomo	Fr.,	1876
John F. Smith	Perrysville	Sel.,	1876
Jesse F. Smith	Perrysville	Sel.,	1876
George W. Smith	Kokomo	Pr.,	1877

Joseph Smith	Bloomington	Pr.,	1877
Alvin E. Smith	Bloomington	Pr.,	1877
Ally Smith	Bloomington	Pr.,	1878
Fielding Henry Smith	Kokomo	So.,	1883
Elmer Smith	Bloomington	Pr.,	1882
George W. Smith	Harrodsburg	Pr.,	1880
Winona E. Smith	Rose Creek	Pr.,	1881
Nelson T. Smith	Pierceton	Fr.,	1881
Rosa Smith	San Diego, Cal	So.,	1882
Charles Smith	Gosport	So.,	1882
Charles E. Smith	Clear Creek	Pr.,	1882
William M. Smith	Bloomington	So.,	1882
Lon Smith	Bloomington	Pr.,	1882
William C. Smydth	Monroe County	So.,	1838
Abraham F. Snapp	Vincennes	Pr.,	1851
Charles P. Snapp	Indianapolis	Pr.,	1858
Daniel S. Snapp	Edinburgh	So.,	1864
John M. Snoddy	Stylesville	Fr.,	1857
Luther Snodgrass	Monroe County	Irr.,	1853
Anna Belle Snodgrass	Bloomington	Fr.,	1873
Jennie Snodgrass	Bloomington	Pr.,	1879
H. Snyder	Bloomington	Pr.,	1850
John P. Sonner	Harrison	Irr.,	1848
Horace F. Soliday	Indianapolis	Pr.,	1880
Pleasant N. Spain	Patoka	Pr.,	1859
James W. Spain	Patoka	Fr.,	1859
Thomas W. Sparks	Sanford	Fr.,	1873
Philip Speed	Louisville, Ky	Jr.,	1838
J. Smith Speed	Louisville, Ky	Irr.,	1841
Henry P. Speed	Louisville, Ky	Fr.,	1863
Albert Speer	Nebraska	Pr.,	1868
John W. Spencer	Bloomington	Pr.,	1844
Calvin Spencer	Caddo Parish, La	So.,	1845
Robert Spencer	Parke County	Pr.,	1848
Barton W. Spencer	Bloomington	Pr.,	1854
Alexander Spencer	Portland Mills	Pr.,	1860
Obiel Spencer	Ladoga	Fr.,	1861
Barton P. Spencer	Bloomington	Sel.,	1865
Alexander Spencer	Bloomington	Pr.,	1867
Tilghman R. Spencer	Portland Mills	Pr.,	1875
Alexander T. Spencer	Portland Mills	Pr.,	1880

William Spencer	Parkeville	Pr.,	1880
Ollie E. Spencer	Parkeville	Pr.,	1880
Mollie R. Spencer	Portland Mills	Pr.,	1880
Newton R. Spencer	Portland Mills	Pr.,	1881
Philip Augustine Spink	Washington	So.,	1864
Charles H. Spinning	Warren	Irr.,	1846
Thomas J. Spitler	Rensselaer	Pr.,	1855
Adam V. Spivey	Orange	Pr.,	1881
Martin V. Spivey	Orange	Pr.,	1882
James Spooner	Harrison	Fr.,	1848
William Spooner	Harrison	Irr.,	1848
Frederick O. Spooner	Point Commerce	Irr.,	1853
Lizzie T. Sprowle	Bloomington	Sel.,	1873
Edward L. Stacy	Prather	So..	1881
James Stafford	Aurora	Fr.,	1871
J. M. Stallard	Bloomington	Sel.,	1842
James Stallings	Union County, O.	Fr.,	1846
William Standiford	Greencastle	So.,	1844
Isaac H. Stanley	Fairfield, Ill	Fr.,	1872
Oliver W. Stanton	Laporte	Jr.,	1848
Isaac Starbuck	Bridgeport	Sel.,	1871
Oliver P. Stark	Lewis	Fr.,	1867
Mollie Stark	Gosport	Pr.,	1879
Ida M. Starr	Heltonville	Pr.,	1881
Nathaniel Steele	Madison	Fr.,	1857
Edgar C. Steele	Gosport	Sel.,	1877
Francis N. Stephenson	Gosport	Pr.,	1867
Milburn Stepp	Indianapolis	Pr.,	1845
Paris Stepp	Trenton, Missouri	Fr.,	1870
John Stevens	Morgan	Pr.,	1851
William A. Stevens	Terre Haute	Pr.,	1863
Warder W. Stevens	Corydon	Fr.,	1865
Jacob Stevenson	Washington	Pr.,	1856
John H. Stevenson	Concordia, Ky	Pr.,	1858
James Stevenson	Rockport	Sel.,	1865
Charles B. Stevenson	Logansport	Sel.,	1873
Abraham B. Stevenson	Alvarado	Sel.,	1874
William Stewart	Indianapolis	Sen.,	1844
Alfred Stewart	Albion, Ill	Pr.,	1857
John G. Stewart	Richland	Sel.,	1874
Alice Stewart	Worthington	Fr.,	1879

Hettie Stimpson ....Keokuk, Ia............Pr.,		1877
William Stipp ....Indianapolis ....Pr.,		1844
Alice Stipp........................Bloomington ....Pr.,		1881
M. G. Stirman ....Owensboro, Ky......Jr.,		1879
Frederick V. Stirman............Owensboro, Ky......Fr.,		1881
Joseph S. Stirman ....Owensboro, Ky......Fr.,		1881
James L. Stites...................Milan....................Pr,		1853
Henry Stockinger, Jr ....Ballstown..............Fr.,		1864
Strother M. Stockolager........Mauckport............Pr.,		1863
Andrew Jackson Stockton.....Lafayette..............Pr.,		1858
Howe Stockwell ....Bloomington ....Sel.,		1865
William C. Stogdell..............Thorntown............Fr.,		1857
John Stone .... Indianapolis...........Pr.,		1841
William Stone ....Monroe County......Pr.,		1842
Caleb Stone ....Monroe County......Sel.,		1846
Mattie Stone ....Bloomington ....Sel.,		1873
William P. Stone ....Camden, Ark ....Pr.,		1876
Robert Stoops....................Putnamville...........Pr.,		1855
Robert S. Storey.................Bloomington ....Pr.,		1880
Lincoln S. Storey................Bloomington ....Pr.,		1880
Gilbert R. Stormont.............Princeton..............So.,		1869
J. Lewis Story.................... Smith Mill ....Fr.,		1869
William Stout ....Bloomington ....Pr.,		1842
John W. Stout....................Azalia ....Fr.,		1869
James Strack.....................Patriot..................Pr.,		1881
Francis P. Strader...............Madison................Irr.,		1852
J. G. Strain ....Laporte.................Pr.,		1838
Eugene J. Strain ....Ireland................ Sel.,		1874
James S. Strickland.............Owensville ....Pr.,		1867
James G. Strong................Lebanon ....Fr.,		1858
William P. Stropes ....Bloomfield ....Pr.,		1851
Olwin T. Struble.................Taylorsville ....So.,		1857
Jonathan Stuart..................Philipstown, Ill......Fr.,		1858
George M. Stuart................Philipstown, Ill......Fr.,		1858
Joshua Stubbs ....Indianapolis..........Irr.,		1848
Robert Stunkard.................Terre Haute....*......Fr.,		1880
Thomas Stunkard...............Terre Haute..........Fr.,		1880
Lewis T. Sturgis ....Fort Wayne..........Pr.,		1865
David S. Summers..............Wallace ....Fr.,		1870
William D. Summers ....Eminence ....Fr.,		1882
Henry Surber.....................Gosport ....Pr.,		1866

30—HISTORY.

John A. Sutherland	Bloomington ....Pr.,	1865
Joseph W. Sutherland	Bloomington ....Pr.,	1867
Frederick Sutter	Bloomington ....So.,	1862
Harley H. Sutton	Aurora ....Sel.,	1873
Fannie Swain	Pendleton ....So.,	1883
Elbert M. Swan	Rockport ....So.,	1871
Charles A. Swartz.	Utica ....Pr.,	1879
James W. Swayzee	Marion ....So.,	1871
Van Swearingen	Monroe ....Pr.,	1842
James W. Swearingen	Bloomington ....Pr.,	1860
James A. Sweeney	Bucyrus, O ....Pr.,	1858
Jesse A. Swem	Providence ....Pr.,	1881
William L. Swindler	Laconia, Ky ....Pr.,	1857
David Tadlock	Leavenworth ....Pr.,	1835
William H. Talbott	Orleans ....Fr.,	1873
William F. Talbott	Orleans ....Fr.,	1874
Josephus Tam	Logansport ....Pr.,	1857
M. G. W. C. Tanner	Jackson County .....So.,	1850
Thomas B. Tanner	Brownstown ....Pr.,	1857
John F. C. Tanner	Brownstown ....Pr.,	1857
William Tarkington	Howard ....Pr.,	1851
William W. Tarkington	Bloomington ....Pr.,	1866
Eliza Tarkington	Bloomington ....Sel.,	1871
Cornelia E. Tarkington	Bloomington ....Sel.,	1871
James J. Tate	Monroe County ....Pr.,	1845
Henry F. Tate	Indianapolis ....Pr.,	1865
David J. Tate	Johnstown, Ill. ......Pr.,	1877
Emma Tate	Carmi, Ill ....Pr.,	1882
Cicero H. Tatman	Rensselaer ....Fr.,	1860
Benedict Burgess Taylor	Madison ....Fr.,	1838
Richard Taylor	Jefferson Co., Ky ...Fr.,	1839
J. W. Taylor	Frankfort ....Fr.,	1845
John W. Taylor	Waveland ....So.,	1846
Marshall B. Taylor	Lafayette ....Pr.,	1853
Robert Taylor	Indianapolis ....Pr.,	1856
William J Taylor	Smithville, ...Pr.,	1858
John L. Taylor	Booneville ....So.,	1873
Simon Taylor	Booneville ....Sel.,	1874
John Taylor	Oakdale ....Pr.,	1877
James T. Terhune	Lagrange ....Fr.,	1865
William D. Terhune	Linton ....Pr.,	1881

James D. Test	Centerville	So.,	1845
George Teter	Noblesville	So.,	1868
Newton Teter	Noblesville	So.,	1869
Horace M. Tibbetts	Alhambra, Illinois	Pr.,	1876
David W. Tilford	Edinburgh	Pr.,	1862
Simeon Tilghman	Newburg	Fr.,	1864
Lizzie Tilley	Harrodsburg	Pr.,	1881
Jennie Tilley	Bloomington	Pr.,	1882
H. Carroll Timmonds	Lamar, Mo	Fr.,	1872
Jonathan Tinkey	Warsaw	Pr.,	1867
Lizzie Title	Bloomington	Pr.,	1882
Isaac N. Thacker	Defiance, O	Fr.,	1867
Anna Thicksten	Bloomington	Pr.,	1882
Barak G. Thomas	Lexington, Ky	Fr.,	1842
Henry C. Thomas	Louisville, Ky	Pr.,	1863
John L. Thomas	New Bellville	Pr.,	1866
William C. Thomas	Louisville, Ky	So.,	1867
Antipas Thomas	Leesburg	Pr.,	1867
James W. Thomas	Muncie	Pr.,	1868
Alonzo S. Thomas	Union City	Sel.,	1873
Francis H. Thompson	St. Mary's, La	Irr.,	1847
Ayres Thompson	Russellville, Ky	Pr.,	1865
John M. Thompson	Tampico	Pr.,	1865
Roy A. Thompson	Solsberry	Pr.,	1867
George W. Thompson	Elizabeth, Ky	Pr.,	1867
Julius H. Thompson	Albion, Ill	Pr.,	1867
Leroy A. Thompson	Solsberry	Pr.,	1868
George W. Thompson	Elizabeth, Iowa	Pr.,	1868
Lafayette Thompson	Benton	Fr.,	1870
Amy Thompson	Albion, Ill	Sel.,	1874
Robert T. Thompson	Solsberry	Pr.,	1876
J. Taliaferro Thompson	Newport Ky	Sel.,	1877
Benjamin F. Thompson	Larwell	Pr.,	1880
Fannie S. Thompson	Newport, Ky	So.,	1881
Francis M. Thomson	New Marion	Pr.,	1878
Otho S. Thornberry	Thorntown	Fr.,	1883
Felix Thornton	Bloomington	Fr.,	1868
James J. Thornton	Logansport	Pr.,	1837
George A. Throop	Bloomington	Jr.,	1839
Andrew Todd	Randolph Co., Ill	Pr.,	1835
Elhanan P. Todd	Madison	Irr.,	1851

Robert C. Todd	New Harmony......Pr.,	1857
Fannie Todd	Bloomington.........Pr.,	1881
Samuel C. Tomlinson	Indianapolis...........Pr.,	1865
Arnold Tompkins	Paris, Ill...............So.,	1869
P. F. Torrence	Solsberry...............So.,	1881
George Torrence	Solsberry...............Pr.,	1882
John S. Torrens	Elkhorn, Ill...........Pr.,	1860
Henry P. Tourner	Bloomington.........Sel.,	1872
Ella E. Tourner	Bloomington.........Pr.,	1880
Frank F. Tourner	Bloomington.........Pr.,	1880
Charles Tourner	Bloomington.........Pr.,	1882
N. T. Tower	Aurora.................Sel.,	1845
John S. Townsend	Putnamville..........Pr.,	1838
Edward M. Tracewell	Corydon...............Pr.,	1867
Sarah Trainer	Heltonville............Pr.,	1876
Joel B. Traylor	Jasper...................Irr.,	1877
William Trent	Cuba......................Sel.,	1876
D. H. Trimble	Shelby County.......Sr.,	1847
Ernest H. Tripp	North Vernon........Fr.,	1873
Franklin Trotter	Danville................Pr.,	1835
Welford H. Trotter	Valley City............Fr.,	1867
Lewis Trumbull	Larwill.................Pr.,	1881
Samuel Tucker	Bloomington.........Pr.,	1882
Virgil E. Tucker	New Philadelphia...Fr.,	1883
Seth W. Tuley	New Albany..........Fr.,	1859
Ella L. Tuley	Bloomington.........Fr.,	1879
John N. Turner	Grant County........Irr.,	1846
Austin Turner	Bloomington.........Pr.,	1863
Eugene Turner	Bloomington.........Pr.,	1863
Thomas E. Turner	Northern Depot......So.,	1864
Charles C. Turner	Bloomington.........Pr.,	1868
Cyrus C. Turner	Washington...........Sel.,	1873
Clara M. Turner	Bloomington.........Sel.,	1873
Walter Turner	Bloomington.........Pr.,	1874
Anna Turner	Bloomington.........So.,	1879
Leander J. S. Turney	Fairfield, Ill...........Fr.,	1844
William Turpin	Tipton...................Pr.,	1859
Charles D. Tyler	Newark, N. J.........So.,	1865
John Van Buskirk	Gosport.................So.,	1880
Thomas Van Buskirk	Gosport.................So.,	1881
Lawrence Van Buskirk	Bloomington.........Pr.,	1882

Hart Vance....................New Albany..........Jr.,		1871
Peter Vandenbark..............Knightstown.........Irr.,		1847
I. Newton Vanmeter............Florida...............Fr.,		1870
George W. Vannoy..............Bloomington.........Pr.,		1865
Lizzie C. Van Nuys..............Bloomington.........Sel.,		1875
Jacob Van Schoik...............Hope....................Pr.,		1852
Jacob Van Skike.................Bartholomew Co.....Sel.,		1853
Peter Van Slyke..................Greene County......Pr.,		1842
Henry Van Slyke................Bloomfield............Pr.,		1868
J. M. Vantrees....................Washington..........Irr.,		1850
D. Edgar Van Valkenburg.....Plymouth..............Pr.,		1858
Waldo Van Zandt...............Bloomington.........Pr.,		1878
Jerome G. Vickers...............Indianapolis..........Pr.,		1858
Thomas B. Vigus................Logansport............Pr.,		1837
John Vinnedge....................Wayne County......Pr.,		1845
David W. Voiles.................Salem..................Fr.,		1854
Harvey B. Voris.................Pleasant...............Jr.,		1879
William Daily Voss..............Bloomington.........Pr.,		1859
John C. Voss......................Bloomington.........Pr.,		1868
Edward M. Voss.................Bloomington.........Pr.,		1881
John Q. Voyles...................Salem..................Fr.,		1872
Harvey Voyles....................Salem..................Fr.,		1872
Thomas A. Wade................Epsom..................Fr.,		1869
John H. Wade....................Bloomington ....So.,		1870
William W. Waggener..........Bloomington.........Pr.,		1857
Austin S. Waggener.............Bloomington.........Fr.,		1858
Thomas H. Waggener..........Bloomington.........Fr.,		1858
Abram Wagner....................Vernon..................Fr.,		1864
Chapin Wagner...................Vernon..................Fr.,		1882
William Frank Wakefield......Beech Fork, Ky.....Fr.,		1866
Lawrence E. Wakefield.........St. Joseph.............Pr.,		1880
Edgar L. Wakeman..............Chicago, Ill...........Fr.,		1869
John B. Waldron................Bloomington.........Pr.,		1874
Mollie Waldron...................Bloomington.........Pr.,		1882
George L. Walker................Amesville..............Pr.,		1853
Isaac W. Walker..................Bloomington.........Pr.,		1856
William H. Walker...............Evansville.............So.,		1859
Jesse W. Walker..................Evansville.............So.,		1859
William G. Walker..............Bloomington .... Pr.,		1860
Irwin S. Walker..................Aurora..................Pr.,		1861
Christopher R. Walker.........Bloomington.........Pr.,		1863

James D. Walker...	Bloomington	Pr., 1867
Charles S. Walling	Knightstown	Fr., 1883
Flora Wallingford	Bloomington	Pr., 1882
William A. Wallingford	Bloomington	Jr., 1882
John L. Walters	Lancaster	So., 1869
John Walton	Eugene	Pr., 1848
Frank Wantland	Springville	Pr., 1868
David L. Ward	Monroe County	Pr., 1858
Granville B. Ward	Bloomington	Pr., 1861
William R. Ward	Benton, Ill	Fr., 1868
Laura Ward	Winchester	Sel., 1878
Jacob E. Warner	Washington	Pr., 1862
Avery W. Warner	Edinburgh	Pr., 1879
Robert E. Warren	St. Louis, Missouri	Pr., 1847
Johnson Warwick	Centre	Pr., 1875
Byron Washburn	Columbus	Pr., 1844
Mollie Waters	Poseyville	Pr., 1879
George G. Watkins	Newark	Pr., 1882
William G. Watson	Harrison	Irr., 1852
Louisa Watts	Bloomington	Sel., 1871
John Watts	Santa Fè, N. M	Pr., 1878
Robert J. Watts	Nashville	Pr., 1879
Harry C. Weatherby	Bloomington	Pr., 1880
John R. Weathers	Marengo	So., 1870
George C. Weaver	Poseyville	Pr., 1866
Thomas M. Weaver	Poseyville	Fr., 1870
Anna A. Webb	Bedford	Fr., 1881
James A. Weed	Bloomington	Pr., 1859
Otis W. Weisel	Salem Centre	Pr., 1862
Andrew B. Weir	New Albany	Fr., 1859
Corwin O. Weir	Bloomington	Sel., 1871
Walter L. Weir	Bloomington	Fr., 1871
James C. Weir	New Philadelphia	Pr., 1876
William P. Welborn	Owensville	So., 1856
James F. Welborn	Owensville	So., 1856
Joseph B. Welborn	Owensville	So., 1869
Thomas Welch	Simpsonville, Ky.	Pr., 1838
George W. Welch	Bloomington	Pr., 1858
John W. Welch	Kansas, Ill	Fr., 1859
Samuel T. Wells	Jackson County	Irr., 1844
William F. Wells	Jackson County	Irr., 1848

HISTORY OF INDIANA UNIVERSITY. 459

James C. Wells................Jackson County.....Jr.,		1850
Kitty Wells...................Clear Spring.........Pr.,		1877
Sallie Wells...................Clear Spring.........Pr.,		1877
Felix G. Welman...............Valeene................So.,		1860
Augustus L. Welsh.............Dexter.................Pr.,		1878
James E. Wesner...............Washington...........Fr.,		1861
Jacob E. Wesner...............Washington...........Fr.,		1863
John A. Wesner................Washington.......... Pr.,		1863
Charles St. J. West............Indianapolis..........Pr.,		1848
William W. West...............Fort Branch..........Sel.,		1873
John A. West..................Fort Branch..........Fr.,		1874
J. F. West....................Brookville...........Sel.,		1876
John C. Wharton..............Tuscola...............Pr.,		1867
Alfred Wheeler................Bristol................So.,		1848
Charles Wheeler..............Evansville............Irr.,		1850
Sherman G. Wheeler..........Plymouth.............Pr.,		1858
Samuel Whinery...............Butlerville............Fr.,		1868
John H. Whipple...............Winamac.............Sel.,		1864
John Whisenand...............Monroe County......Pr.,		1853
Cynthia Whisenand............Bloomington.........Pr.,		1881
David H. Whitaker............Chatsworth, Ill......Pr.,		1865
J. S. Whitaker.................Alaska................So.,		1881
J. Maunsell White.............Louisville, Ky........Pr.,		1840
Paul White....................Laporte County......Sel.,		1845
John White...................New Orleans, La.....Pr.,		1847
L. Burpe White................Cincinnati............Fr.,		1880
Abraham Whitesell............Bloomington.........Pr.,		1866
Philip Whiting................Carmi, Ill.............Pr.,		1882
Charles A. Whitsell............Ellettsville............Fr.,		1870
John S. Whitten..............Leavenworth.........Irr.,		1863
James V. Whitten.............Washington..........Fr.,		1871
Jesse C. Wier.................Bloomington.........Pr.,		1879
Charles W. Wickersham.......Winamac.............So.,		1870
Edward C. Wedekamper.......Louisville, Ky........Sel.,		1865
Robert A. D. Wilbanks........Mt. Vernon, Ill......So.,		1865
C. E. Wilcox..................Utica.................Pr.,		1878
John R. Wilcox...............Evansville............Pr.,		1853
Frank M. Wiles...............Spencer..............So.,		1877
William V. Wiley..............Edgarton, O.........So.,		1881
James B. Willhite.............Owensboro, Ky......Fr.,		1865
Charles T. Wilkerson..........Scipio................Pr.,		1858

James Wilkins	Washington	Pr.,	1855
Brannick Wilkinson	Warrick	Irr.,	1852
F. M. Williams	Indianapolis	Fr.,	1845
Jesse J. Williams	Franklin	Sel.,	1845
Newton H. Williams	Jacksonville	Irr.,	1847
Thomas M. Williams	Bloomington	Pr.,	1847
Augustus M. Williams	Madison County	Pr.,	1847
Elkanah Williams	Bedford	Sr.,	1847
John E. Williams	New Albany	Pr.,	1856
John L. Williams	Brownsville	Pr.,	1856
Abraham Williams	Bedford	So.,	1858
John F. Williams	Leesville	Sr.,	1861
Daniel B. Williams	Bedford	Pr.,	1864
George Williams	Terre Haute	Pr.,	1866
Leroy Williams	Cynthiana	Fr.,	1867
John A. Williams	Lancaster	Fr.,	1868
William R. Williams	Lancaster	So.,	1869
John R. Williams	Terre Haute	Fr.,	1869
Samuel D. Williams	Edinburgh	Fr.,	1870
Green B. Williams	Cynthiana	Fr.,	1873
Elisha D. Williams	Salem	So.,	1874
John M. Williams	Fort Branch	Fr.,	1876
Lawrence Williams	Bloomington	Pr.,	1876
Charles Williams	Edinburgh	Pr.,	1876
Richard C. Williams	Edinburgh	Pr.,	1877
Fannie Williams	Bloomington	Pr.,	1878
Alice Williams	Bloomington	Pr.,	1878
Julia Williams	Bloomington	Pr.,	1880
James R. Williams	Dupont	Jr.,	1881
Elmer B. Williams	Grayville, Ill.	Fr.,	1882
Samuel R. Williamson	Elkhorn, Ill.	Pr.,	1860
Mamie Williamson	Bloomington	Fr.,	1878
Lizzie B. Williamson	Bloomington	Fr.,	1881
Benjamin Willis	Bloomington	Fr.,	1835
Flournoy Willis	Bloomington	So.,	1835
Nathaniel Wilson	Vermillion County	Jr.,	1838
Abner A. Wilson	Monroe County	Pr.,	1844
Tancred R. Wilson	Madison	Fr.,	1848
William W. Wilson	Morgan County	Pr.,	1845
Henry D. Wilson	Noblesville	Jr.,	1853
George W. Wilson	Noblesville	Pr.,	1852

William W. Wilson	Leesville	Pr., 1852
William N. Wilson	Ellettsville	Pr., 1855
William M. Wilson	Ellettsville	Pr., 1857
John C. Wilson	Sullivan	Fr., 1858
Josiah M. Wilson	Sullivan	Pr., 1858
William B. Wilson	Ellettsville	Pr., 1859
David H. Wilson	Sullivan	So., 1863
James B. Wilson	Sullivan	Pr., 1863
George W. Wilson	Aurora	Fr., 1864
William C. Wilson	Paris	Pr., 1864
Walter W. Wilson	Brandenburgh, Ky.	Pr., 1867
Alonzo K. Wilson	Tipton	Pr., 1868
Amos L. Wilson	Granville	Fr., 1869
William O. Wilson	Bloomington	Sel., 1873
Samuel A. Wilson	Franklin	Fr., 1872
Charles M. Wilson	Waldron	Sel., 1876
J. M. Wilson	Scotland	Pr., 1878
Robert J. Wilson	Troy	Pr., 1879
Amanda Wilson	Bloomington	Pr., 1879
Ada L. Wilson	Bloomington	Pr., 1879
Davison Wilson	Greensburg	Jr., 1880
James R. Wilson	Boonville	So., 1883
Millard F. Wimar	Burnettsville	Fr., 1872
Mary Winans	Muncie	So., 1883
Joseph Windsor	Angola	Pr., 1845
Robert B. Winlock	Russellville	Pr., 1866
Joseph Winsor	Cooperstown, N. Y.	Fr., 1846
William J. Wirt	Bloomington	Pr., 1864
George D. Wise, Jr	Accomack, Va.	Jr., 1851
Andrew F. Wise	Decatur	So., 1857
Luther D. Wishard	Knightstown	Fr., 1871
Jacob Wisner	Newberry	Pr., 1858
F. L. Wolfe	Mauckport	Pr., 1850
Benjamin S. Wolfe	Bloomington	Fr., 1859
Clater C. Wolfe	Bloomington	Pr., 1861
Leonidas O. P. Wolfe	Mauckport	Pr., 1862
William R. Wolfe	Morristown	Fr., 1866
James H. Wolfe	Corydon	Fr., 1870
Luke Wood	Crawford County	Pr., 1844
William D. Wood	Spartansburg	Irr., 1847
Emsley Wood	Bloomington	Pr., 1860

Name	Location	Class	Year
John C. Wood	Bloomington	Pr.,	1862
Elisha B. Wood	Ridgeville	Pr.,	1867
Austin E. Wood	Bloomington	Pr.,	1868
Paris E. Wood	Bloomington	Pr.,	1868
John E. Wood	Marengo	So.,	1870
James B. Wood	Bloomington	Fr.,	1870
Julia R. Woodall	Bloomington	Pr.,	1881
Matthew W. Woodburn	Monroe County	Jr.,	1851
Walter E. Woodburn	Bloomington	So.,	1866
T. Wylie Woodburn	Bloomington	Pr.,	1867
William N. Woodbury	Nineveh	Fr.,	1856
Herschel Wooden	Greensburg	Sel.,	1875
William N. Woodruff	Nineveh	Pr.,	1855
John T. Woodruff	Lima	Pr.,	1860
David Woods	Rutledge, Tenn	Pr.,	1837
Emsley H. Woods	Ellettsville	Fr.,	1861
Wilbur Woods	Knightstown	So.,	1883
Harrison Woodsmall	Gosport	So.,	1861
Thaddeus Woodward	Harrodsburg	Fr.,	1868
Mary S. Woodward	Stanford	Sel.,	1873
Belle Woodward	Logansport	Pr.,	1875
Mary J. Woodward	Harrodsburg	Pr.,	1879
John J. Woodward	Buena Vista	Pr.,	1879
Lena A. Woodward	Harrodsburg	Pr.,	1882
Eric Woolery	Linton	Fr.,	1869
Ella M. Woolie	Bloomington	Pr.,	1879
Peter R. Wordsworth	Raglesville	Pr.,	1876
James Craig Worley	Bloomington	Pr.,	1856
Francis E. Worley	Ellettsville	Pr.,	1857
A. May Worrall	Bloomington	Fr.,	1878
Samuel A. Wray	Greenfield	Fr.,	1870
Anson Wright	Terre Haute	Sr.,	1835
Lester Wright	Terre Haute	Sr.,	1839
Henry Wright	Washington Co	Pr.,	1841
Solomon Wright	Vevay	Sel.,	1845
Napoleon B. Wright	Madison	Pr.,	1856
William Wylie	Bloomington	Sr.,	1835
Jonathan D. Wylie	Monroe County	Fr.,	1847
J. Dixon Wylie	Monroe County	Irr.,	1848
Samuel W. Wylie	Sparta, Ill	Irr.,	1853
John H. Wylie	Bloomington	Fr.,	1867

Theophilus A. Wylie, Jr........	Bloomington.........Fr.,	1871
Agnes Wylie..........................	Bloomington.........Fr.,	1873
Margaret Wylie....................	Philadelphia, Pa.....Sel.,	1877
Sallie Wylie...........................	Bloomington.........Pr.,	1879
L. J. Wylie............................	Bloomington.........Fr.,	1882
Emma J. Wylie.....................	Bloomington.........Pr.,	1880
Henry R. Wysor...................	Muncie..................Pr.,	1877
Leander Yarito.....................	Troy......................Sel.,	1871
Alexander Yates...................	Hinds County, Miss.So.,	1848
Luke D. H. Yates.................	Hinds County, Miss.Irr.,	1848
Robert G. Yates	Hinds County, Miss.Irr.,	1848
Henry A. Yeager..................	Fort Branch..........Jr.,	1870
James B. Yearns...................	Greensburg............Irr.,	1844
Andrew E. York...................	Bloomington.........Pr.,	1877
Rena M. York......................	Bloomington.........Pr.,	1879
Henry Young.......................	Bloomington.........Pr.,	1867
Thomas S. Young.................	Vincennes.............Fr.,	1871
Jacob Brown Young	Newark..................So.,	1877
Belle L. Young.....................	Bloomington.........Pr.,	1878
Emma Young.......................	Natchez, Miss........Pr.,	1879
Tully Young.........................	Bloomington.........Pr.,	1880
Martin Young.......................	Bloomington.........Pr.,	1881
Edward C. Zaring................	Princeton..............Pr.,	1879
W. L. Zaring........................	Princeton..............Pr.,	1879
Winfield S. Zena..................	Centre Point..........Fr.,	1873

A LIST OF THE BOARD OF TRUSTEES, FROM 1820 TO 1890, PRECEDED BY A SKETCH OF DR. DAVID H. MAXWELL, FIRST PRESIDENT OF THE BOARD.

With regard to the foundation of Indiana University in its present locality, its survival during its infancy while a seminary and its successful opposition to many adverse influences during his lifetime, there is no one to whom more credit is due than to David H. Maxwell as a legislator and as a trustee. For these reasons he is worthy of more than a passing notice.

Dr. Maxwell was born near Lancaster, Garrard County, Ky., September 17, 1786. His parents were from Virginia and his grandparents from County Londonderry, in the north of Ireland. They were Scotch-Irish Presbyterians, and emigrated at a very early date to the colony of Virginia. Dr. Maxwell's early training was under that rigid discipline characteristic of the Scotch-Irish, a discipline from which he did not depart when training his own family. His early education was at home, and such as the neighboring schools afforded. When about eighteen years old, in order to avail himself of better advantages, he went to school in Danville, Ky., where he became well versed in mathematics, as they were taught in that day, and was an excellent, well-read English, though not classical, scholar. He studied medicine with Dr. Ephraim McDowell, a distinguished physician and surgeon of Danville. Having completed his professional studies, he married Miss Mary E. Dunn, of Danville, in 1809. Soon after this he moved to Jefferson County, Ind., where Hanover now stands. Here he practiced medicine till 1812. In this year he joined a volunteer company of rangers under Captain Williamson Dunn, and served for about a year in keeping back the Indians from their incursions on the white settlements. Soon after this he moved to Madison and practiced medicine there. While there he was elected a delegate to the first constitutional convention, held at Corydon in 1816. In this year President Madison designated Perry Township in Monroe County, as the additional township to which Indiana was entitled for educational purposes on becoming a State. From this time Dr. Maxwell's attention was directed to Monroe County, and having bought a lot at the first sale in Bloomington in 1818, he, with his family moved to this place, arriving here May 10, 1819.

Dr. Maxwell appreciated more than most of the early settlers the advantages of an education higher than that of the country schools, and also anticipated the educational possibilities at Bloomington. He chose this place as his home, and ever since, to the end of his life, in his character as a private citizen, as a representative and senator, as an excellent writer, as a man of sound judgment, and for many years as President of the Board of Trustees, he was indefatigable in his labors for the interest of the University.

Dr. Maxwell, presuming somewhat, perhaps, upon his acquaintance with many of the old members of the constitutional convention, of which he himself had been a member, went to Corydon to use his influence as a lobbyist, and to procure, if possible, the location of the State Seminary at Bloomington. The result was favorable, and on the 20th day of January, 1820, an act was passed establishing the Seminary at this point on the Seminary township. Dr. Maxwell was then appointed one of its Trustees, and soon after the organization was elected President of the Board. This position he continued to hold with but little intermission, till the establishment of Indiana College, January 24, 1828. He was President of the College Board from 1828 to 1840, with the exception of one year. During this year, 1838, he was a member of the Legislature, a representative from Monroe County. In 1840 the Board consisted of twenty-two members, too large for the dispatch of business, and on the passage of the act February 15, 1841, chartering the University, the number of the members of the Board was cut down to nine. Of this Board Dr. Maxwell was chosen President, which office he held continuously till his resignation in 1851.

During the Seminary period of the Institution it may, in truth, be said that Doctor Maxwell was not only the presiding officer, but also its executive officer and corresponding secretary.

The erection of the new building was in a great measure under his supervision. By him all accounts and orders for money were allowed. Besides all this there were other minor duties which took up much of his time. Not the least among these was a large correspondence with prominent men in different parts of the state, to interest them in behalf of the new Institution of learning. Many of these subsequently were members of the Board. He worked not only among a disaffected element at home, to popularize the Institution, but sought favorable consideration from the Legislature. To this end he asked his constituents to send him to the Legislature, and was elected a representative in the House for four consecutive years, namely, the years 1821, 1822, 1823 and 1824. In one of these years he was chosen speaker. During this time many important matters touching the interest of the seminary came up, more especially as to its prospective financial capability.

In the years 1825–26 he was elected as senator from the district composed of the counties of Monroe, Owen and Greene, and was still ever watchful as to the legislation affecting the seminary. It was during his senatorial term, in 1826, that the question as to what disposition should be made of the seminary land in Gibson and Monroe counties came up. It was *the* question of the canvass for that year before the people of Monroe County, for they were personally interested. Much of the desirable and very excellent land in Perry township had been leased for a term of years, according to the law, and of course the lease-holders, men of little means generally, were anxious to hold on, while others of more means were anxious to be owners in fee simple. The Doctor advocated the idea of actual sale to *bona fide* settlers. His opponent, Craven P. Hester, was in favor of leasing for ninety-nine years, as had been the policy of Ohio with her seminary townships. The Doctor was elected, and the policy which he had advocated before the people was that adopted by the Legislature, with reference to seminary townships both in Monroe and Gibson counties. While it may be true that the lands were put upon the market too soon, and at too low a valuation, yet as compared with the result in Ohio it was a success. Other instances might be given of Dr. Maxwell's prudence and management. During nearly all the time of his connection with the board he was its president. He was liberal and judicious in his views and zealous and fearless in his advocacy of what he regarded as the best interests of the University. In 1851 he resigned, and with full faith and trust in the religion of his fathers, he died, May 24, 1854.

THE TRUSTEES OF INDIANA UNIVERSITY FROM ITS ORIGIN AS A SEMINARY, AS A COLLEGE, AND AS A UNIVERSITY.

The Legislature of the State of Indiana, January 20, 1820, appointed the following named persons as Trustees of Indiana Seminary:

1820, Charles Dewey.   1820, John M. Jenkins.
1820, Jonathan Lindley. 1820, Jonathan Nichols.
1820, David H. Maxwell. 1820, William Lowe.
          1820, John Ketcham.

By an act approved January 24, 1828, the College was established, and the following named persons appointed trustees:

†1828......*Edward Borland..........Monroe Co................1829
1828........Samuel Dodds..............Monroe Co................1829
1828........Leroy Mayfield............Monroe Co................1840
1828........Jonathan Nichols..........Monroe Co.........Died 1838
1828........James Blair................Monroe Co................1840
1828-1836.David H. Maxwell........Monroe Co.........1838–1851
1828........William Bannister........Monroe Co................1834
1828........William Lowe. ....Monroe Co................1829
1828........George H. Dunn...........Dearborn Co...............1835
1828........Christopher Harrison ...Washington Co.........1828
1828........Seth M. Leavenworth ...Crawford Co..............1840

NOTE.—When there are four dates the first and third indicate the first term of service, and the second and fourth, the second term.
*The above named Trustees of the College, from Ed. Borland to W. Hendricks, inclusive, with the exception of Messrs. Dunn and Harrison, met in Bloomington May 5, 1828, in the Seminary building, and organized the Board, at which meeting Dr. David H. Maxwell was chosen President. In 1829 Thomas H. Blake, of Marion County, was elected to fill the place of Edward Borland, resigned. Mr. Blake served till 1840. Governor Hendricks was chosen in place of Christopher Harrison, who never met with the Board.
† The dates preceding the names of the members and officers of the Board indicate the beginning of their service, and the dates following, the termination.

1828	John Law	Knox Co	1845
1828	Williamson Dunn	Montgomery Co	1831
1828	Ovid Butler	Shelby Co	1831
1828	Bethuel F. Morris	Marion Co	1835
1829	Thomas H. Blake	Marion Co	1840
1829	Ratliff Boone	Warrick Co	1831
1829	Gov. Wm. Hendricks*	Jefferson Co	1840
1830	Rev. John Strange		1831
1834	Rev. Allen Wiley	Switzerland Co	1840
1834	William C. Foster	Monroe Co	1838
1835	Joshua O. Howe	Monroe Co	1840
1835	William B. Laughlin	Rush Co	1836
1835	Dennis Pennington	Harrison Co	1837
1836	James M. Farrington	Vigo Co	1838
1836	Nathaniel West	Marion Co	1843
1836	Rev. William Turner	Monroe Co	1840
1836	Chester G. Ballard	Monroe Co	1839

In the act to establish a University, approved February 15, 1838, the following persons were appointed trustees:

1838.........His excellency, Gov. David Wallace, *ex-officio*, Vice-President, and his successors in office forever.

1838	Gov. Wm. Hendricks	Jefferson Co	1840
1838	Seth M. Leavenworth	Crawford Co	1840
1838	David D. Mitchell	Harrison Co	1840
1838	James M. Farrington	Vigo Co	1838
1838	John Law	Knox Co	1845
1838	Rev. Allen Wiley	Montgomery Co	1840
1838	Nathaniel West	Marion Co	1842
1838	Isaac Blackford	Marion Co	1840
1838	Jesse L. Holman	Dearborn Co	1839
1838	Jonathan Nichols	Monroe Co	Died 1838
1838	Paris C. Dunning	Monroe Co	1839
1838	James Blair	Monroe Co	1840
1838	Chester G. Ballard	Monroe Co	1839
1838	Joshua O. Howe	Monroe Co	1840

We do not find this list where it ought to be, viz., in the Laws and Resolutions Concerning Indiana University, but in the Record Book of the University, which escaped destruction in the fire of '83.

1838	Richard W. Thompson	Lawrence Co	1841
1838	Samuel R. Hoshour	Wayne Co	1841

HISTORY OF INDIANA UNIVERSITY. 469

1838.........George W. Ewing.........Cass Co......................1839
1838.........Hiram A. Hunter.........Gibson Co...................1838
1838.........Tilghman A. Howard...Parke Co..................1841
1838 ....Craven P. Hester.........Monroe Co..................1840
1838.........Col. Thomas H. Blake...Vigo Co 1840

By an act of the Legislature, approved February 15, 1861, the board of trustees was reduced to the number of nine.

1841.........Miles C. Eggleston.........Jefferson Co..............1849
1841..........William T. S. Cornet....Ripley Co..................1850
1838–1849..Robert Dale Owen........Posey Co............1846–1851
1841.........Nathaniel West........... Marion Co 1843
1828.........John Law....................Knox Co 1845
1828.........David H. Maxwell........Monroe Co 1851
1841.........Elisha M. Huntington*..Vigo Co 1841
1841.........Lot Bloomfield .... Wayne Co 1842
1841.........James Scott................Clark Co....................1850
1841–1853..Joseph S. Jenckes..........Vigo Co 1851–1854
1842.........Pinckney James...........Ohio Co 1846
1843.........James Morrison ....Marion Co..................1850
1846.........John W. Davis ....Sullivan Co 1848
1846,'50,'73.John I. Morrison†........Henry Co.........1849,'55,'78
1846.........Albert S. White...........Tippecanoe Co 1851
1850.........John R. Porter............Vermillion Co........:....1851
1850........ Michael G. Bright........Jefferson Co..............1851
1851.........William M. Dunn... ......Jefferson Co..............1854
1851.........Jacob Helwig......,.......DeKalb Co..................1852
1851.........Rev. John Benoit.........Allen Co....................1852
1851.........George Evans..............Henry Co......... 1856
1851.........Michael Malott............Lawrence Co..............1854
1851–1856..Rev. P. J. R. Murphy...Martin Co 1854–1857
1851.........Thomas M. Adams.......Brown Co..................1854
1851.........Johnson McCollough....Monroe Co.................1887
1851–1862..Nathaniel Browning.....Monroe Co.........1854–1870
1851.........Joseph G. McPheeters...Monroe Co..................1854
1852–1857..Rev. Wm. M. Daily. ..Monroe Co.........1853–1858
1853 ....Cyrus L. Dunham.........Jackson Co.................1854
1854.........Col. Jas. R. M. Bryant...Warren Co.................1859

---
*Mr. Huntington, having been appointed Commissioner of the Land Office, resigned, never having met with the board, and Joseph S. Jenckes, Sr., of Vigo, was appointed in his stead.

†John I. Morrison was appointed during his first term of service from Washington County (1846-55), and second term (1873-78) from Henry County.

31—HISTORY.

1854	Joel B. McFarland	Tippecanoe Co	1856
1854–1859	Ransom W. Akin	Monroe Co	1856–1860
1854	William M. French	Clark Co	1858
1855–1861	William K. Edwards	Vigo Co	1856–1878
1855	David McDonald	Marion Co	1856
1856	Samuel C. Wilson	Montgomery Co	1860
1856	John L. Robinson	Rush Co	1859
1856	James Hughes	Monroe Co	1860
1857–1878	*Addison L. Roache	Marion Co	1859–1882
1858	John B. Winstanley	Floyd Co	1865
1858	David Garland Rose	Laporte Co	1860
1858	John S. Tarkington	Marion Co	1862
1858	James Sweetser	Grant Co	1861
1858	John O'Boyle	Vigo Co	1859
1859	Bayless W. Hanna	Vanderburgh Co	1862
1860	David Sheeks	Monroe Co	1862
1860	James D. Maxwell	Monroe Co	†—
1860	James S. Ferris	Henry Co	1861
1860	L. Humphrey	St. Joseph Co	1861
1861	David Dayton	St. Joseph Co	1864
1861	George A. Irvin	Allen Co	1865
1862	Newton F. Malott	Lawrence Co	1867
1862	William A. Hannaman	Marion Co	1873
1866–1875	Isaac Jenkinson	Wayne Co	1869†
1866	Bascom E. Rhoads	Vermillion Co	1873
1866	R. M. Chapman	Knox Co	1868
1867	Wash'gton C. De Pauw	Floyd Co	1874
1868	Hiram W. Cloud	Vanderburgh Co	1874
1869	Rev. John S. Irwin	Allen Co	1875
1870	Milton McPhetridge	Monroe Co	1879
1873	John R. Elder	Marion Co	1874
1874	John Love	Marion Co	1877
1874	E. W. H. Ellis	Elkhart Co	1877
1874	A. Patton	Knox Co.	1879
1877	‡David D. Banta	Johnson Co	†1889
1878	Godlove S. Orth	Tippecanoe Co	1882
1878	Rev. James R. Stone	Allen Co	1882

---

* A. L. Roache, first term from Parke County; second, from Marion.

† The —— indicates that the trustee is still (1889) in office.

‡ Judge Banta having been elected Professor of Law in the University in June, 1889, his place on the board was vacated.

1879.........Robert W. Miers..........Monroe Co...............†——
1879.........Robert B. Richardson....Vanderburgh Co....... ——
1882.........Rev. Herbert L. Stetson..Cass Co...... 1885
1882......... James H. Smart ....Marion Co 1883
1882.........Robert S. Robertson.......Allen Co. .... ——
1883.........James L. Mitchell.........Marion Co .... ——
1885.........Julius W. Youche.........Lake Co...... .... ——
1890.........Isaac Leyden..............Floyd Co................. ——

OFFICERS OF THE BOARD OF TRUSTEES FROM 1828 TO 1885.

PRESIDENTS OF THE BOARD OF TRUSTEES.

David H. Maxwell, M. D., first President of the Seminary Board, and also of the board of Indiana College; elected at its first meeting in 1828; continued till 1837, when Jonathan Nichols was chosen, who died in 1838. In 1839 Paris C. Dunning was chosen President of the University Board. In 1840 a new board was appointed by the Legislature; David H. Maxwell made president, which office he held till 1851.

1852.........Jos. G. McPheeters, M. D..President.. 1853
1853.........Hon. John I. Morrison.....In office 1855
1856.........Hon. Wm. K. Edwards....In office 1857
1857.........Hon. James Hughes.......In office 1858
1858.........Hon. Samuel C. Willson..In office 1861
1862.........Jas. D. Maxwell, M. D.....In office 1865
1866 ....William A. Hannaman....In office 1874
1875.........Hon. John I. Morrison....In office 1878
1879.........Addison L. Roach..........In office 1881
1882.........Judge David D. Banta.....In office 1889
1889.........Isaac Jenkinson ....——

THE SECRETARIES OF THE BOARD.

1828.........Prindiwell M. Dorsey....Secretary ....,
1835.........Lewis Bollman ....Secretary ....
1837.........Craven P. Hester ....Secretary ....
1838.........James D. Maxwell........Secretary 1855
1856.........Michael W. Helton.......Secretary 1857
1857.........Robert C. Foster..........Secretary 1880
1880.........William Wesley Spangler ....,.....——

TREASURERS OF THE BOARD.

1828..........James Borland..
1835..........John Borland................Treasurer..................1838
1838..........William Alexander........Treasurer..................1841
1841..........Joseph M. Howe..........Treasurer..................1854
1855..........William C. Tarkington..Treasurer..................1861
1861..........Ransom W. Akin..........Treasurer 1862
1862..........Milton Hight................Treasurer..................1867
1867..........Joseph M. Howe..........Treasurer..................1880
1880..........Alfred R. Howe............Treasurer..................1886
1886..........Walter E. Woodburn...

www.ingramcontent.com/pod-product-compliance
Lightning Source LLC
Chambersburg PA
CBHW051849300426
44117CB00006B/326